**De
Coı
Cor
Architecture**

Published in 2012 by
Laurence King Publishing Ltd
361–373 City Road
London
EC1V 1LR
e-mail: enquiries@laurenceking.com
www.laurenceking.com

A catalogue record for this book is
available from the British Library

ISBN: 978 1 78067 009 6

Designed by Hamish Muir
Illustrations by Advanced Illustrations
Limited
Picture Research by Sophia Gibb

Printed in the UK

Laurence King Publishing is
committed to ethical and sustainable
production. We are proud participants
in The Book Chain Project ®
bookchainproject.com

Detail in Contemporary Concrete Architecture

David Phillips and Megumi Yamashita

Laurence King Publishing

Contents

Concrete, despite its image as a modern material, was invented by the Romans. Its use in structures such as the Pantheon in Rome allowed for the first time the formation of large spans. Despite concrete's manifold qualities its early use was limited, and, like many other technologies, after the fall of the Roman Empire it was nearly forgotten. Over the next thousand years the use of concrete declined to almost nothing and extant examples of concrete as a construction material from this period are infrequent.

In 1756 the process of making cement, the key material for making concrete, was essentially reinvented. This was the work of the pioneering British engineer John Smeaton, who conducted experiments with hydraulic lime and a combination of pebbles and powdered brick as aggregate. Through the nineteenth century concrete continued to be developed as a structural construction material.

The French architect Auguste Perret was a key figure in the adoption of concrete as a key construction material by the modern movement. Starting in the early twentieth century he, along with his brother Gustave, pioneered many of the techniques that characterize contemporary concrete construction. This leading role was obscured in the post-war period, the beautiful St. Joseph's Church at Le Havre and the reconstruction of his city being overshadowed by the dramatic work of his former employee Corbusier.

The influence of Corbusier allowed concrete to become the pre-eminent 'modern' material. The use of concrete as a raw unfinished material was a central theme of much of Perret's post-war work; and the influence can still be seen clearly in contemporary projects.

Modern concrete differs from the material used by the Romans in a couple of important ways. The Roman material was formed as a dry mix that was layered up in the wall or other structure it was a part of. Its strength was almost entirely in compression and it did not make use of any additional internal strengthening. In contrast, contemporary concrete is placed into formwork in a fluid state. This allows the concrete to be formed into complex shapes. Modern concrete also makes extensive use of internal steel reinforcement, giving the finished concrete strength in tension in addition to compressive strength.

Today concrete is the most used man-made material in the world. At every scale and in every area of building design concrete fulfils diverse functions. We have buildings where concrete is almost the only material used, others where it performs a traditional structural role and yet others where it forms a delicate skin.

The projects in this book bring together, from around the world, a range of approaches to building with concrete. In these projects we can see concrete used in many varied ways: concrete as structure, concrete as enclosure and concrete as decoration. There are large public buildings and tiny structures that are no more than huts. In each case concrete's unique properties have been utilized differently. Because concrete is both fluid and rigid there are two stages to the design of many details. We can think of these as the detail of construction and the detail of use. Architectural details explain to us how materials come together. It is in these junctions that we can observe and then understand the nature of the structure. Many of the details are very simple, essentially because concrete as a construction material is a very simple material.

Concrete's ability to record as an impression the form of an element that is now absent allows it to become a transitional material – recalling the past in the present. We can see concrete being used in this way in the raw simplicity of AFF's forest hut (p76). At first sight it mimics the simple wooden structure that it replaces. It has the quality of a Dada found object, having the unrefined appearance of something that has just occurred. We then discover that it contains in its form a history, a reflection of the past.

Concrete gives the architect the opportunity to shape the structural elements of buildings into complex shapes. De-La-Hoz's twin towers (p170) have a dramatic lattice-like typographic structural skin that proclaims a message across the landscape. Likewise in Caruso St John's Nottingham Contemporary art gallery (p22), a historic narrative is etched into the building's surface as a record of the local lace industry. The patterned surface in scalloped panels appears like a curtain just about to shimmer in the wind. Concrete's image as a hard material is challenged by many of the projects in this book. The delicate eau-de-nil patina that wraps the skin of Pezo von Ellrichshausen's FOSC House (p120) confers on it the quality of a ripe fruit.

Just as softness can be found in concrete so too can hardness. Souto de Moura's gallery for the display of the painter Paula Rego's work (p62) also uses a coloured surface, but here the effect is of a tough mineral density. The red pyramid roofs are evocative of objects fashioned from the earth. At the Mostyn Gallery (p30) the crystalline-faceted cavern that Ellis Williams has designed as the central axis has a majestic power that both complements the original gallery spaces and establishes a new language for the building's circulation. Here the board-marked concrete gives an impression of a fissure carved and impressed into the solid.

Since the 1950s Japanese architecture has developed a distinct language of geometric forms and simple spaces; concrete has become the principal construction material in this country that is so challenged by nature. Perhaps best represented by the work of Tadao Ando, the origins of this architecture are to be found in the influence of Corbusier and Louis Kahn. Today a new generation of architects are reinterpreting these themes and forms. EASTERN Design Office's MON House (p88) is an example of this. A subtle addition to the Kyoto streetscape, this live/work building interacts with its users and the environment to create a contemporary place for a traditional craft. Pure orthogonal forms are here pieced by a series of round openings.

The quality of concrete as a protective material is evident in a number of the projects. In Tanzania SPASM's powerful and serene office building (p178) combines the vernacular form of a giant sheltering roof with the structural properties of concrete, to provide a defended and environmentally responsive space in which to work. Here robust details and simple planning generate a modern architecture without redress to complex technologies. In a very different context concrete also provides a strong and secure envelope for storage. At the collection of the Bern Historiches Museum (p42) the architects have utilized the concrete walls like a metaphorical protective cloak that surrounds the precious objects stored within. Enclosing a small square the building composes a new urban environment that advocates potential interactions.

Often seen as a material close to stone, cast concrete easily communicates in its appearance and performance a relationship with rock formations. In PleskowRael's highway walls project (p166) concrete is placed in giant fractured planes, becoming a petrified illustration of California's lively geology.

Concrete's potential continues to be the propagator of great architecture. The projects selected for this book show that concrete remains a material full of latent possibility and surprise.

David Phillips
Megumi Yamashita

Notes

US and Metric Measurements
Dimensions have been provided by the architects in metric and converted to US measurements except in the case of projects in the USA, which have been converted to metric.

Terminology
An attempt has been made to standardize terminology to aid understanding across readerships, for example 'wood' is generally referred to as 'timber' and 'aluminum' as 'aluminium'. However materials or processes that are peculiar to a country, region or architectural practice that have no direct correspondence are presented in the original.

Floor Plans
Throughout the book, the following convention of hierarchy has been used – ground floor, first floor, second floor, and so on. In certain contexts, terms such as basement level or upper level have been used for clarity.

Scale
All floor plans, sections and elevations are presented at conventional architectural metric scales, typically 1:50, 1:100 or 1:200 as appropriate. An accurate graphic scale is included on the second page near the floor plans of every project to aid in the understanding of scale. Details are also presented at conventional architectural scales, typically 1:1, 1:5 and 1:10.

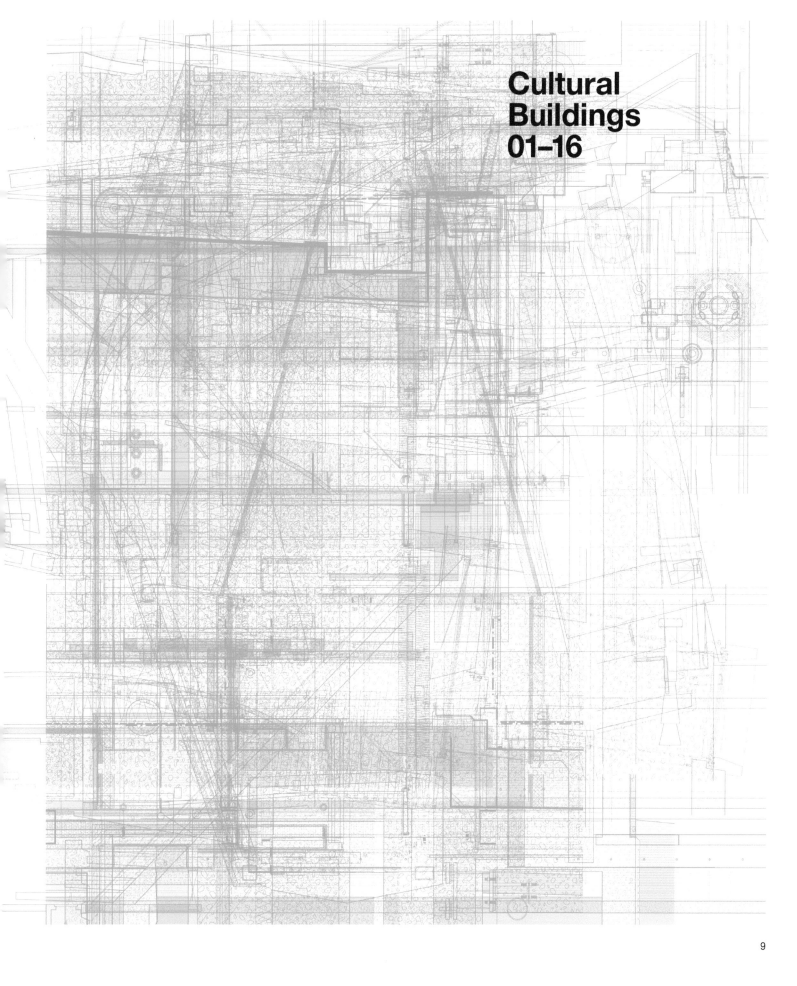

Cultural Buildings 01–16

01
BNKR Arquitectura
Esteban Suárez (Founding Partner)
and Sebastián Suárez (Partner)

Sunset Chapel
Acapulco, Guerrero, Mexico

Client
Private client

Project Team
Esteban Suárez, Sebastián Suárez,
Mario Gottfried, Javier González,
Roberto Ampudia, Mario Gottfried,
Rodrigo Gil, Roberto Ampudia, Javier
González, Óscar Flores, David
Sánchez, Diego Eumir, Guillermo
Bastian, Adrian Aguilar

Structural Engineer
Juan Felipe Heredia and José Ignacio
Báez

Main Contractor
Fermín Espinosa / Factor Eficiencia

Perched on top of a mountain near to
Acapulco, this funeral chapel has the
appearance of a giant boulder. The
brief was very simple. Three things
were required: the building must make
the best of the site's grand sea views;
the sun should set behind the altar;
and there must be provision for crypts
around the chapel. However, there
was a problem achieving the first two
demands. Large trees around the site
and a massive boulder to the west
obscured the view. There was no
budget for overcoming these
obstacles. The solution was to raise
the chapel up by more than five
metres (16 feet). To reduce the impact
on the beautiful site, the building's
overall footprint was reduced to nearly
half that of the main floor.

You enter via a triangular cut. To
reach the place of worship you climb a
stair that hugs the internal walls, and
then, in a single turn through the dark,
you rise through the floor into the light.
The chapel itself is like a cage; the
concrete columns that form the walls
mimic the trees around the site. The
seating is banked in the manner of a
lecture theatre; in the western wall a
simple metal cross waits for the sun to
go down. Sunset Chapel is a place to
celebrate life.

1 Sitting on top of a
mountain, the chapel
has a mysterious
sense of wonder.
2 The chapel's respect
for the environment
around it is evident in
every element. It seeks
to be a part of the
place, not just in
the place.
3 The dark of the
stairway conditions
the visitor for entry
to the chapel.
4 The complex
geometry of the chapel
and the vertical
columns of the walls
create a theatre of
shadows.
5 The pews for the
congregation are
stepped up towards
the east like a natural
hillside – a place to
think and listen.

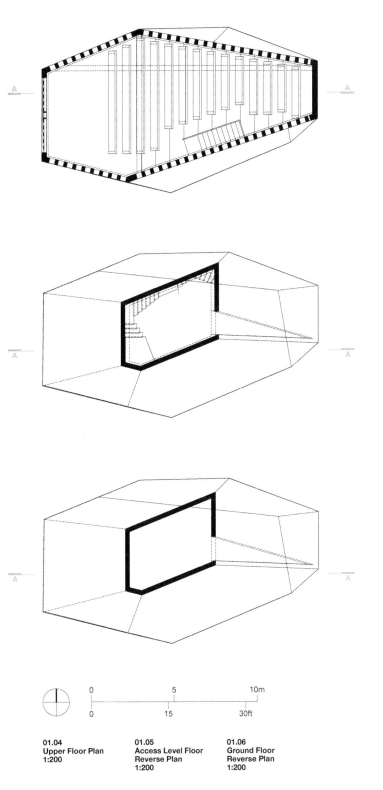

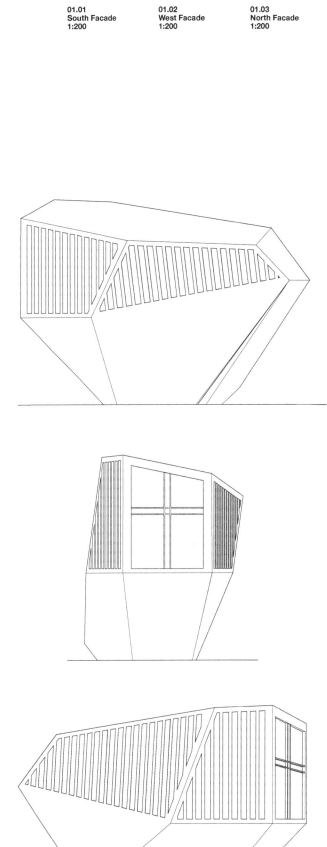

01.01
South Facade
1:200

01.02
West Facade
1:200

01.03
North Facade
1:200

0   5   10m
0   15   30ft

01.04
Upper Floor Plan
1:200

01.05
Access Level Floor
Reverse Plan
1:200

01.06
Ground Floor
Reverse Plan
1:200

11

01.07
Detail Section A–A
1:50
　1 Concrete
　2 Pews
　3 Stair
　4 Drain
　5 Metal cross

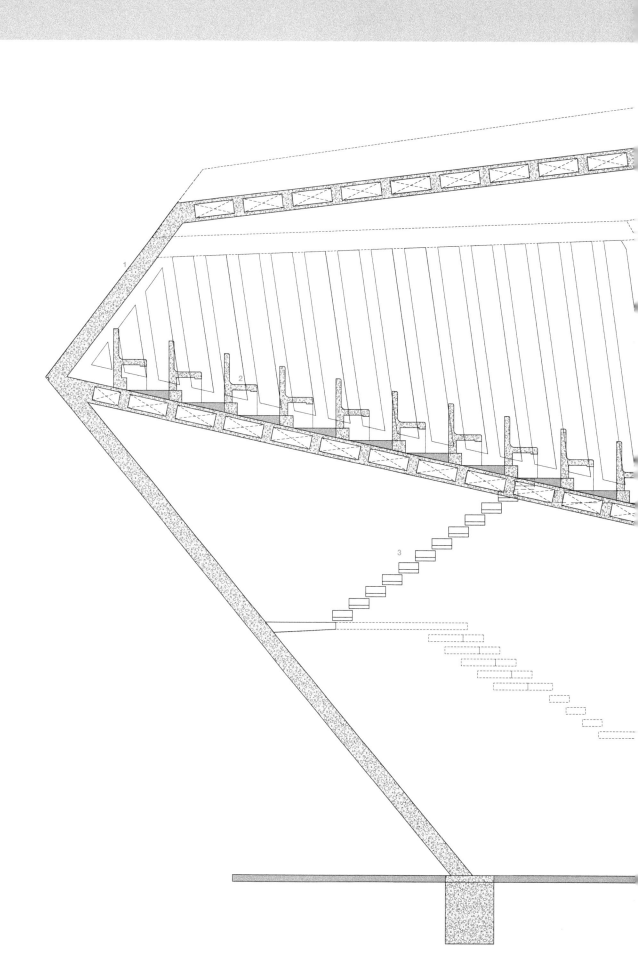

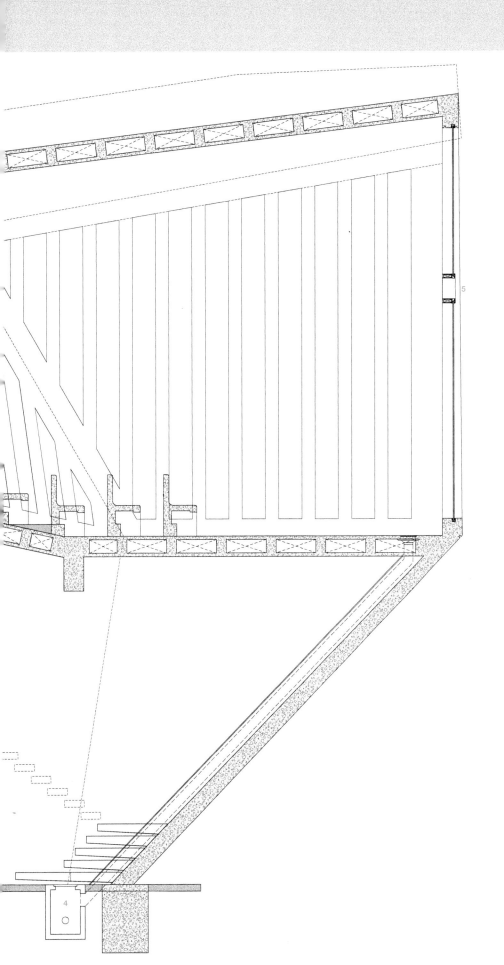

Acropolis Museum
Athens, Greece

Client
Organization for the Construction of
the New Acropolis Museum (OANMA)

Project Team
Bernard Tschumi, Joel Rutten, Adam
Dayem, Jane Kim, Aristotelis
Dimitrakopoulos, Eva Sopeoglou, Kim
Starr, Anne Save de Beaurecueil, Joel
Aviles, Valentin Bontjes van Beek,
Jonathan Chace, Allis Chee, Thomas
Goodwill, Robert Holton, Liz Kim,
Daniel Holguin, Michaela Metcalfe,
Justin Moore, Georgia Papadavid, Kriti
Siderakis, Véronique Descharrères,
Cristina DeVizzi, Kate Linker

Structural Engineer
ADK and Arup, New York

Main Contractor
Aktor

The Acropolis Museum is situated
adjacent to the Acropolis on top of an
archeological excavation. More than
100 carefully positioned concrete
columns support its lowest level.

The building is conceived as a base,
a middle zone and a top. As you move
upwards through the building you also
move through time, passing from
prehistory through to the late Roman
period. At the top of the building there
is a glass gallery, over seven metres
(23 feet) high, which is rotated 23
degrees from the lower floors to allow
a direct view of the Acropolis. From
here the sculptures taken from the
Parthenon can be viewed, while also
seeing the temple itself beyond. Below
are the main galleries, a multimedia
space, a bar and a restaurant.

The museum rejects monumentality;
instead it focuses the visitor's
attention on the extraordinary works
of art that it contains. An air of
transparency pervades the whole – at
each level views to the layer above
and the layer below can be seen. The
use of light is a constant theme. As
most of the works are sculptural there
is extensive use made of filtered
natural light in all the gallery spaces.
This is permitted to penetrate the
building from the upper glazed areas
down to the archaeology below.

1 The giant entrance canopy supported on three columns draws visitors into the museum.
2 From the upper gallery you can look across towards the Acropolis and see the location from which the statues on display have come.
3 The museum is raised up on concrete columns. The archaeological remains beneath are revealed through large holes cut into the floor plates.
4 In the upper gallery fragments of the Parthenon frieze are displayed so they can be viewed in the correct relationship with each other.
5 Rhythmic columns recall the classical ordered spaces of the Parthenon. Natural light is filtered through all of the building.
6 In the main gallery the sculptures are arranged to allow an impression of both intimacy and monumentality.

02.01
Second Floor
1:2000
1 Public terrace
2 Shop
3 Restaurant
4 Balcony lounge
5 Void
6 VIP area

02.02
Third Floor
1:2000
1 Parthenon Gallery

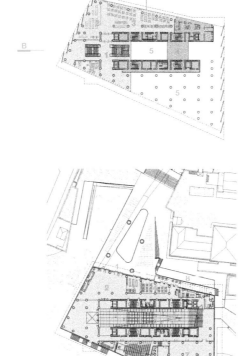

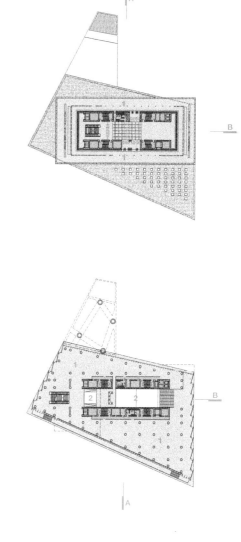

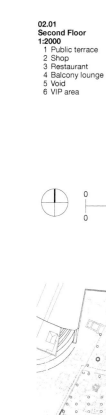

02.03
Basement
1:2000
1 Excavations
2 Offices
3 Deliveries

02.04
Ground Floor
1:2000
1 Entrance
2 Lobby
3 Shop
4 Cafe
5 Glass ramp
6 Auditorium
7 Temporary
 exhibition space
8 Void

02.05
First Floor
1:2000
1 Gallery
2 Void

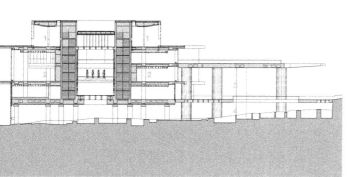

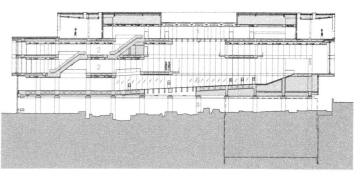

02.06
Section A–A
1:1000
1 Parthenon Gallery
2 Gallery
3 Entrance
4 Excavations

02.07
Section B–B
1:1000
1 Parthenon Gallery
2 Gallery
3 Glass ramp
4 Excavations

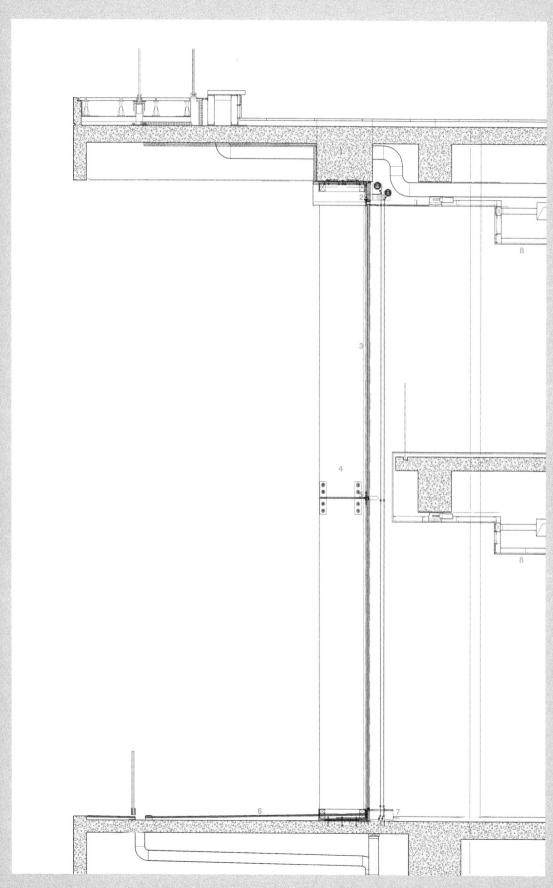

02.08
Gallery Facade
Section
1:50
1 Concrete
2 Steel glazing
channel
3 Glazing
4 Glass fin
5 Steel fixing
6 Marble floor
7 Stainless-steel fin
bracket
8 Suspended ceiling

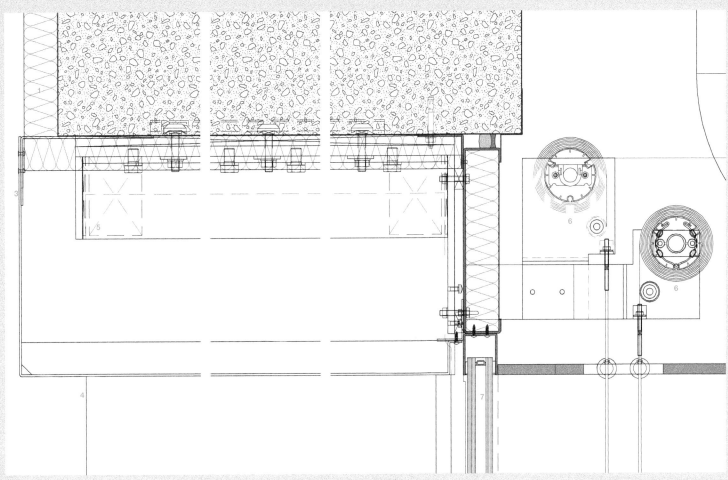

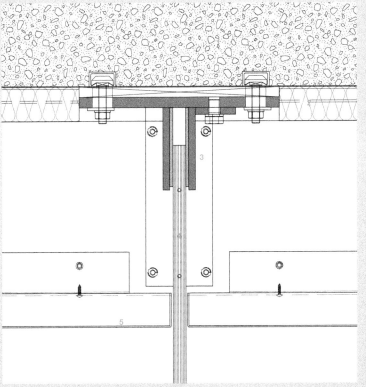

02.09
Lintel Section
1:5
1 Insulation
2 Concrete beam
3 Aluminium cladding
4 Glass fin
5 Mild steel bracket
6 Sunscreen system
7 Glazing

02.10
Glazing Fixing
Section
1:5
1 Concrete
2 Insulation
3 Steel fixing
4 Glazing
5 Aluminium cladding

C.F. Møller Architects

Darwin Centre
London, UK

Client
The Natural History Museum

Project Team
C.F. Møller Architects (Architect and
Landscape Architect)

Structural Engineer
Arup

Mechanical and Electrical Engineer
Fulcrum Consulting

Main Contractor
BAM Construct UK

This extension to the Natural History
Museum makes a dramatic contrast
to the original terracotta construction
of 1881. The basic form is a giant
eight-storey-high concrete cocoon
placed within a glass box.

The new building has been
designed to provide a home for the
museum's unique collection of 17
million insect and three million plant
specimens, and to provide a working
area for taxonomic research. Visitors
are able to take self-guided tours in
and around the cocoon; this allows
them to observe scientists at work in
the research facility and to see the
extent of the collections.

The cocoon is constructed of 300
to 425 mm (11 ⅕ to 16 ¾ inch) thick
sprayed-concrete walls, with a curved
geometric form. The surface finish is
ivory-coloured polished plaster, giving
the resemblance to a silk cocoon;
across the surface there is a series of
expansion joints, which wrap around
the form like silk threads. The thermal
mass of the reinforced concrete shell
aids the thermal stability, which in turn
reduces the risk of pest infestations
and minimizes energy usage.

The atrium space is dramatic, tall
and filled with daylight, and creates a
link that completes the western side
of the Natural History Museum and
clarifies the circulation patterns within
the building. Because of the close
proximity of the glass envelope to the
concrete storage area, it is not possible
see the form in its entirety from any
one place, adding to the impression
of monumentality and tension.

1 The intricate
detail of Waterhouse's
terracotta facades
contrast with the
glazed skin of the
Darwin Centre. The
form of the cocoon can
partially be seen.

2 When inside the
surrounding space,
it is difficult to get a
sense of the cocoon's
size, as it cannot be
seen in its entirety.
The incised lines of
the expansion joints

describe the surface.
3 Laboratory spaces
have large windows
overlooking the
cocoon. The public
can look in and see
what is happening as
they visit the museum.

4 Within the cocoon,
the exhibition areas
explain how the
collection is preserved
and used for research.

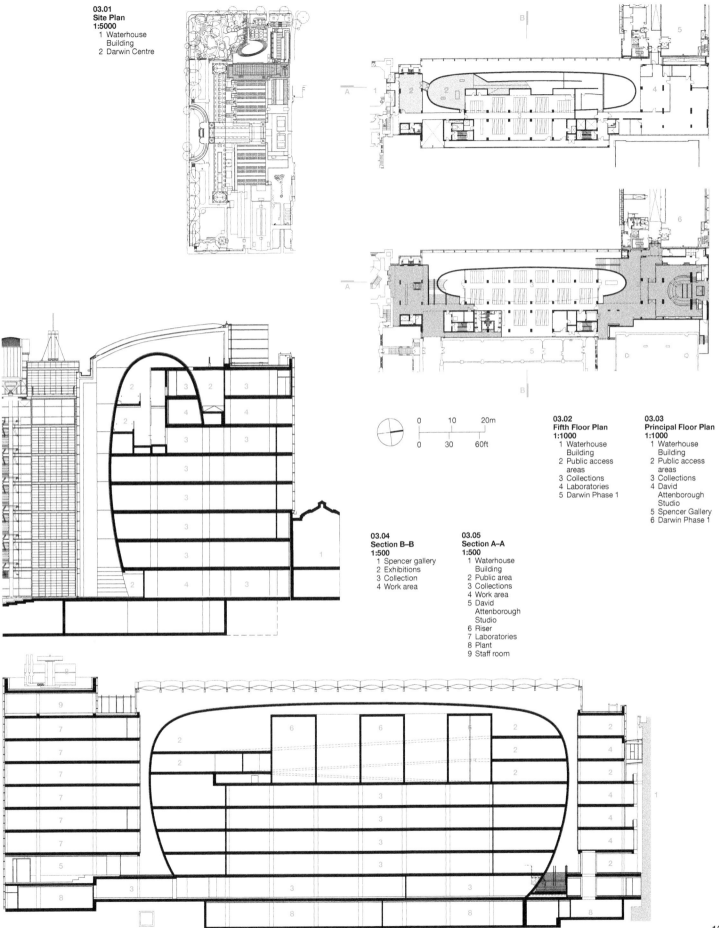

03.01
Site Plan
1:5000
1 Waterhouse
  Building
2 Darwin Centre

03.02
Fifth Floor Plan
1:1000
1 Waterhouse
  Building
2 Public access
  areas
3 Collections
4 Laboratories
5 Darwin Phase 1

03.03
Principal Floor Plan
1:1000
1 Waterhouse
  Building
2 Public access
  areas
3 Collections
4 David
  Attenborough
  Studio
5 Spencer Gallery
6 Darwin Phase 1

03.04
Section B–B
1:500
1 Spencer gallery
2 Exhibitions
3 Collection
4 Work area

03.05
Section A–A
1:500
1 Waterhouse
  Building
2 Public area
3 Collections
4 Work area
5 David
  Attenborough
  Studio
6 Riser
7 Laboratories
8 Plant
9 Staff room

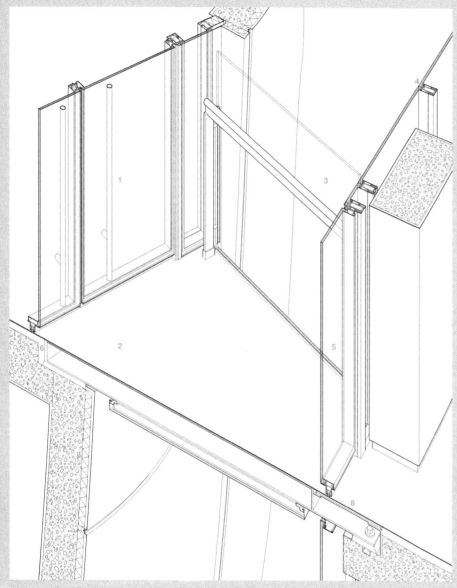

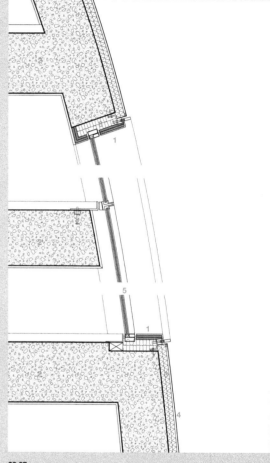

03.06
Construction Detail
Not to Scale
 1 Cocoon doors
 2 Bridge deck
 3 Balustrade
 4 Atrium: glazed
screen
 5 Lobby doors
 6 Cocoon floor
 7 Cocoon wall
 8 Lobby floor

03.07
Double Curved
Glazed Apertures
Detail
1:20
 1 Recessed fixings
bolted to concrete
shell concealed by
plaster reveals
 2 Concrete
 3 Insulation
 4 Polished plaster
 5 Double curved
glazed panels
laminated and
chemically toughened
separately by hand

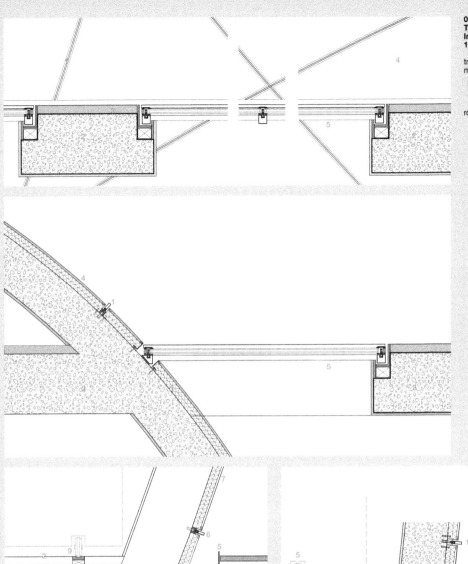

03.08
Typical Cocoon
Internal Roof Detail 1
1:20
 1 Control joint bead
trim, double curvature,
mechanically fixed
 2 Concrete
 3 Insulation
 4 Polished plaster
 5 Double-glazed
rooflight

03.09
Typical Cocoon
Internal Roof Detail 2
1:20
 1 Control joint bead
trim, double curvature,
mechanically fixed
 2 Concrete
 3 Insulation
 4 Polished plaster
 5 Double-glazed
rooflight

03.10
Detail
1:20
 1 Reinforced
concrete structural
slab
 2 Floor build-up:
50 mm (2 inch) screed,
160 mm (6 3/10 inch)
lightweight reinforced
concrete
 3 Glazed lightning
trench
 4 Atrium floor:
Portland stone 30 mm
(1 1/5 inch) Whitbed
limestone honed finish.
Base: reinforced
screed separating
membrane, sand

cement reinforced
semi-dry bedding
 5 Stainless-steel
edge trim
 6 Plaster bead / trim
profile Flexi curve
series divided into
areas of 25 metre²
maximum (83 foot²).
Maximum length 5
metre (16 foot 4 4/5
inch), mechanically
fixed
 7 Cocoon: Insulated
render, polished
plaster finish (superfine
marble and lime
stuccolustro) on a
substrate of reinforced
gypsum plaster.

Insulation: 50 mm
(2 inch) expanded
polystyrene board
 8 Insulation to
basement
 9 Compactor rail
recessed within depth
of screed
 10 Cementitious board

03.11
Cocoon Wall Detail,
Collections Area
1:20
 1 Control joint bead
trim
 2 Concrete
 3 Insulation
 4 Polished plaster
 5 Compactor rail
recessed within depth
of screed

03.12
Fixing Detail
1:5
 1 Control joint bead
trim, double curvature,
mechanically fixed
 2 Concrete
 3 Insulation
 4 Polished plaster

Nottingham Contemporary
Nottingham, UK

Client
Nottingham City Council Project

Project Team
Adam Caruso, Tim Collett, Christiane
Felber, Adam Gielniak, Ah-Ra Kim
Bernd Schmutz, Peter St John,
Stephanie Webs, Frank Wössner

Structural Engineer
Arup

Main Contractor
ROK/SOL Construction

Nottingham's new gallery of
contemporary art is located in a part
of the city called the Lace Market.
The building is arranged on a difficult
steeply sloping site that backs onto a
sandstone cliff; previously it was a
railway cutting. The openings are
edged with warm gold anodized
aluminium frames.

The gallery takes its inspiration from
the industrial architectural heritage of
Nottingham. The building offers a wide
range of interiors, of various sizes and
proportions. In contrast to the usual
white box these spaces are
reminiscent of the found spaces of a
factory or warehouse. The upper level
is top lit, then descending through the
gallery the spaces become more
enclosed as if they were caves within
the sandstone cliff.

The cast pattern that is used on the
scalloped panels that form the exterior
walls originated from an example of
Nottingham lace. The lace was first
scanned, then the scale and contrast
of the two dimensional image was
altered. From this modified image a
3D file was create. This was used to
control a milling machine that
produced, 14 metre-long (40 inch)
positive forms. The four latex moulds
made from the forms cast all of the
pre-cast elements on the building.

The vertical roof parts are clad in
sheets of the gold anodized aluminium
that is used elsewhere. These have a
gently billowing profile that serves to
stiffen the very thin material.

1 A large canopy
marks the point of
entry into the gallery.
This is at the upper
level of the building.
From the exterior the
public can see,
through the glazed
entrance, deep within
the building to the
artworks that the
building contains.
2 The fine lace pattern
that is cast into the
concrete characterizes
the exterior of the
gallery. The concave
fluted walls give the
building a strong
vertical emphasis.
3 The strong
relationship between
the gallery and the
surrounding buildings
is established through
a careful interrelation
of scale and rhythm.
4 Interior circulation
spaces use the same
raw material language.

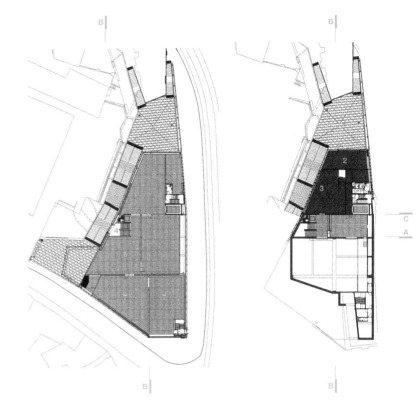

04.01
Sub-basement
1:500
 1 Loading bay
 2 Workshops
 3 Lift
 4 Services
 5 Stair

04.02
Basement
1:500
 1 Lower yard
 2 Cafe
 3 Bar
 4 Family changing
   place
 5 Lobby
 6 WC
 7 Performance
   space /gallery

04.03
Ground Floor
1:500
 1 Lower yard
 2 Gallery
 3 Education
 4 Stair
 5 Upper yard
 6 Reception / shop
 7 Galleries

04.04
Mezzanine
1:500
 1 Lower yard
 2 Archive / meeting
   area
 3 Office
 4 WC
 5 Lobby
 6 Education

0   5   10m

0   15   30ft

04.05
Section A–A
1:500
 1 Plant room
 2 Gallery
 3 Education
 4 WC
 5 Lobby
 6 Stair

04.06
Section B-B
1:500
 1 Gallery
 2 Archive
 3 Education
 4 Cafe
 5 Lobby
 6 Performance
   space / gallery
 7 Services

04.07
Section C–C
1:500
 1 Reception / shop
 2 Gallery
 3 Performance
   space / gallery
 4 Services

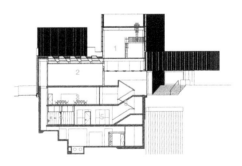

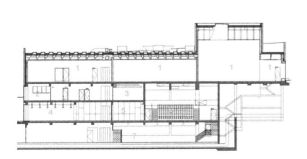

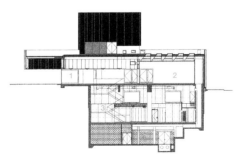

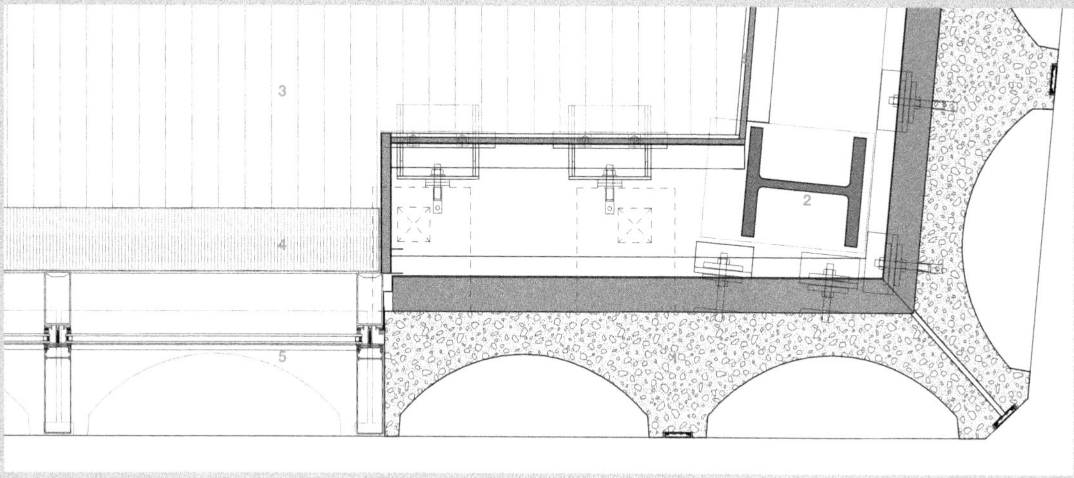

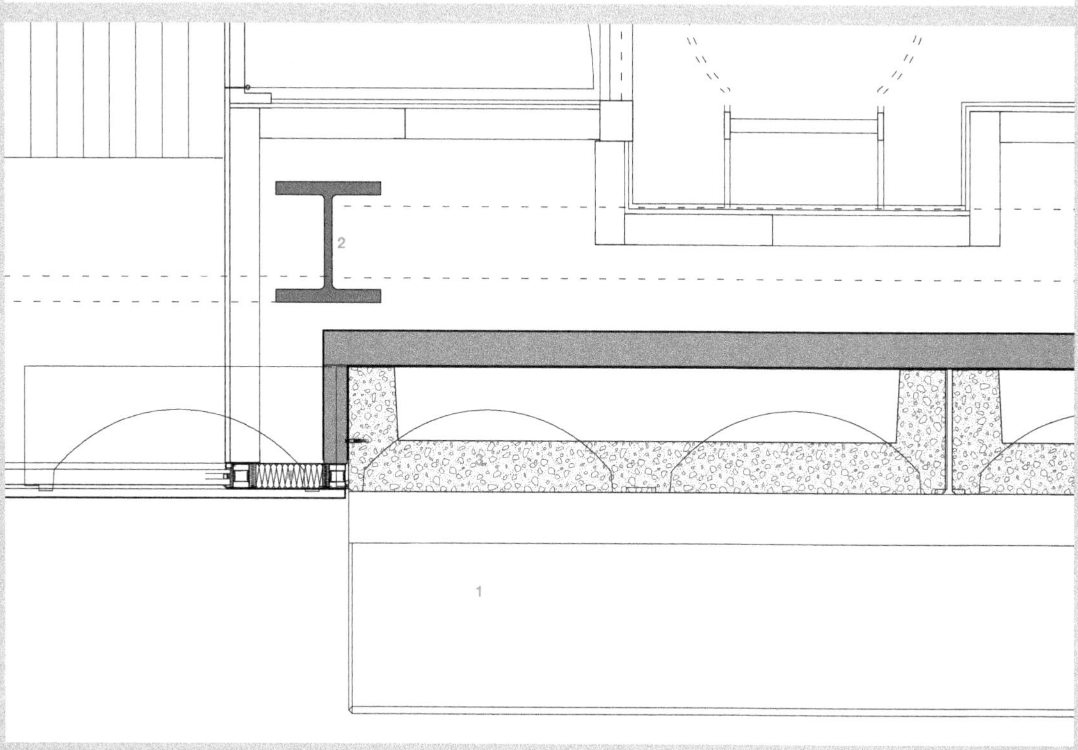

04.10
Detail Section
1:20
  1 Green precast panel
  2 Restraint for precast panel
  3 Insulation
  4 Composite slab on metal decking
  5 Primary steel structural beam
  6 Insulation
  7 Stainless steel precast panel fixing
  8 Golden anodized aluminium coping
  9 Double-glazed unit
  10 Black polished precast bench
  11 Reinforced concrete infill slab

04.11
Detail Section
1:20
  1 25 mm (1 inch) sedum blanket on 50 mm (2 inches) compost
  2 155 mm (6 inches) insulation
  3 Composite slab on metal decking
  4 Stainless steel precast panel fixing
  5 Primary steel structural beam
  6 Insulation
  7 Restraint for precast panel
  8 Powder-coated aluminium frame
  9 240 mm (9 $1/2$ inches) aluminium mullion
  10 Double-glazed curtain wall
  11 450 mm (17 $3/4$ inches) concrete
  12 Insulation
  13 Black polished precast

04.08
Detail Plan
1:20
  1 Precast concrete panel
  2 Steel column
  3 Wood floor
  4 Grill
  5 Double-glazed curtain wall
  6 Restraint for precast concrete panels

04.09
Detail Plan
1:20
  1 Black polished precast concrete bench
  2 Steel column
  3 Precast concrete panel
  4 insulated golden anodized aluminium frame

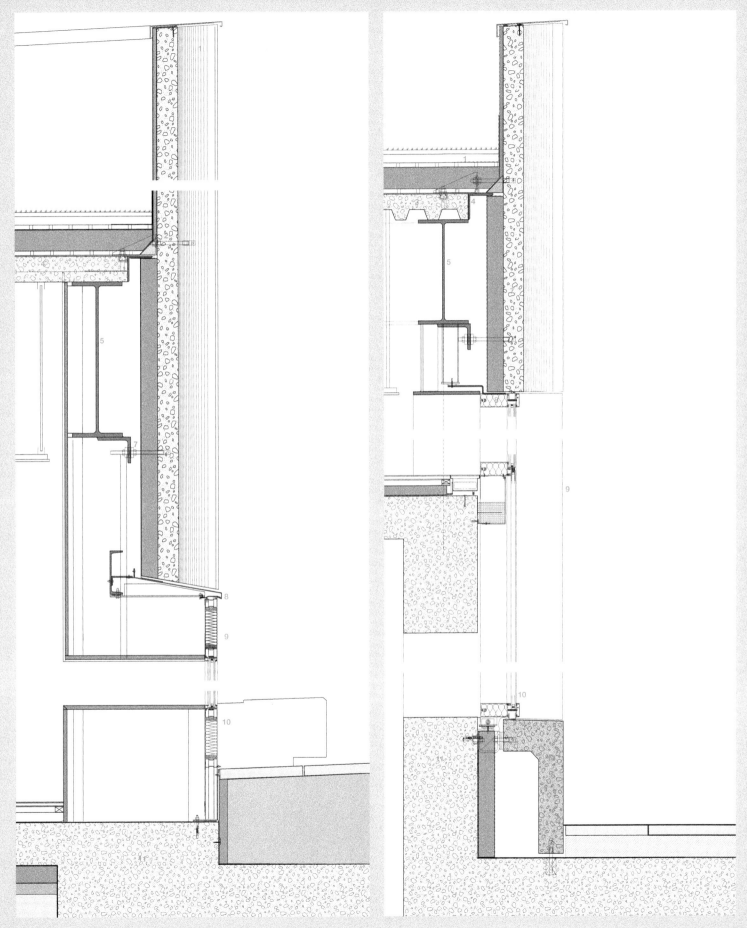

David Chipperfield Architects

The Hepworth Wakefield
West Yorkshire, UK

Client
Wakefield Council

Project Team
David Chipperfield Architects

Structural Engineer
Ramboll UK Limited

Main Contractor
Laing O'Rourke Northern Limited

This new structure provided for the relocation and expansion of Wakefield's existing art gallery. The site is on the banks of the River Calder. The gallery houses works by renowned artist Barbara Hepworth, who was born in Wakefield, and also exhibits the existing collection, which contains works by major British and European artists.

To fulfill the architects' desire to provide many different types of space, each with its own atmosphere, the building is formed from ten trapezoidal blocks of different sizes. These blocks are arranged in a seemingly random way, and have the character and density of a miniature city. In part they are a response to the scale and roof lines of the surrounding small-scale industrial buildings. With water on three sides and visibility from all directions, the building has no formal front or back elevation. Where the gallery meets the river, the water laps and swirls around the walls.

All of the galleries are placed on the upper floor with the service areas located below. The exhibition spaces are sized according to the scale of the works. On the lower level there are a performance space, an area for educational workshops, public facilities and the administration and back-of-house areas. The building is constructed from in-situ cast concrete, which is pigmented a dark grey. The windows are set flush to the surface, giving the building's exterior a taut, membrane-like quality.

1 The gallery has the appearance of a collection of solid boxes that have accumulated at the turn in the river. This gives the impression of a natural development of related forms, each a reflection of the other.
2 A footbridge brings visitors across the river to the gallery entrance.
3 Each gallery is proportioned to the works displayed in it. The quality of light is controlled to generate different atmospheres.

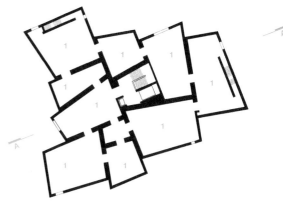

05.01
Ground Floor Plan
1:1000
1 Main entrance
2 Lobby
3 Cafe
4 Kitchen
5 Shop
6 Learning rooms
7 Picnic area
8 WCs
9 Multi-purpose room
10 Office
11 Archive / study area
12 Staff room
13 Display production
14 Picture hanging
15 Loading bay
16 Store

05.02
First Floor Plan
1:1000
1 Gallery

05.03
Section A–A
1:500
1 Gallery
2 Lobby
3 Stair
4 Display production
5 Picture hanging

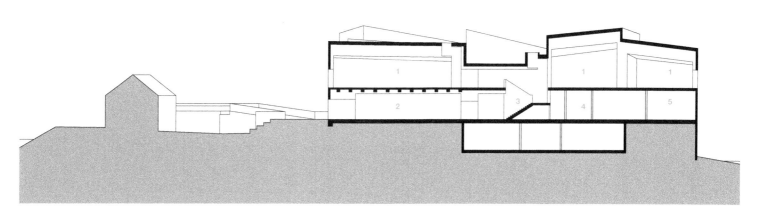

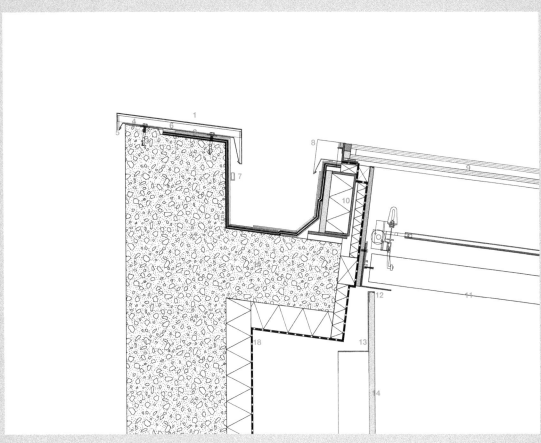

05.04
Wall Skylight Detail
1:10
1 1.5 mm ($^1/_{10}$ inch) zinc capping with butt joints and UDS soakers
2 Straps at 400 mm (15 $^3/_4$ inch) centres
3 Galvanized steel fixings
4 18 mm ($^7/_{10}$ inch) WBP plywood,
5 Insect screen
6 Sealant
7 Lightning conductor
8 Powder-coated pressed aluminium flashing
9 Rooflights
10 180 x 75 mm (7 $^1/_{10}$ x 3 inch) PFC upright
11 Internal sunscreening
12 Stop bead
13 Galvanized steel angle support to wall lining
14 18 mm ($^7/_{10}$ inch) Fermacell wall lining
15 Hydrogard protection sheet, brush rolled into final coat with 75 mm (3 inch) laps. Hydrotech structural waterproofing system: two coats of monolithic membrane 6125 incorporating Flex Flash F polyester reinforcement fabric or Flex Flash UN uncured neoprene rubber enforcement between both layers
16 Eaves beam, insulation local to prevent cold bridging
17 In-situ concrete
18 Vapour-control layer

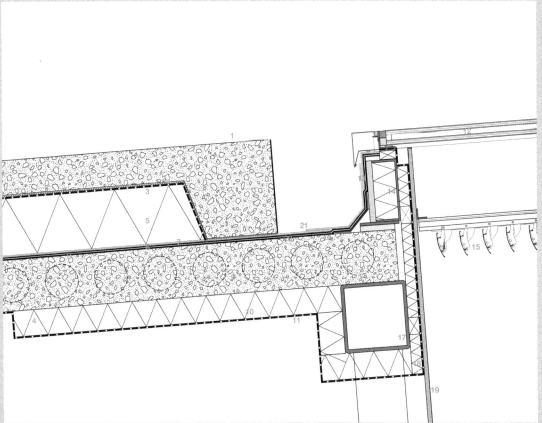

05.05
Roof Skylight Detail
1:10
1 In-situ concrete
2 Hydrodrain 200
3 MK separating layer
4 1 metre (39 $^2/_5$ inch) insulation local to prevent cold bridging
5 EPS insulation
6 Hydrotech structural waterproofing system
7 2 coats of monolithic membrane 6125 incorporating Flex Flash F polyester reinforcement fabric between both layers
8 Flex Flash UN uncured neoprene rubber enforcement fully encapsulated in monolithic membrane 6125
9 Precast planks to contractors' detail
10 c.1 metre long (c.39 $^2/_5$ inch) insulation, local to prevent cold bridging
11 Vapour-control layer
12 Rooflights
13 Powder-coated pressed aluminium flashing
14 Channel upright to structural engineers' detail
15 Internal sunscreening
16 Flex Flash UN uncured neoprene rubber enforcement fully encapsulated in monolithic membrane 6125
17 Truss to structural engineer's detail
18 Insulation
19 12.5 mm ($^1/_2$ inch) plasterboard
20 Hydrogard protection sheet, brush rolled into final coat with 75 mm (3 inch) laps
21 Gutter dressed with Hydrogard 30

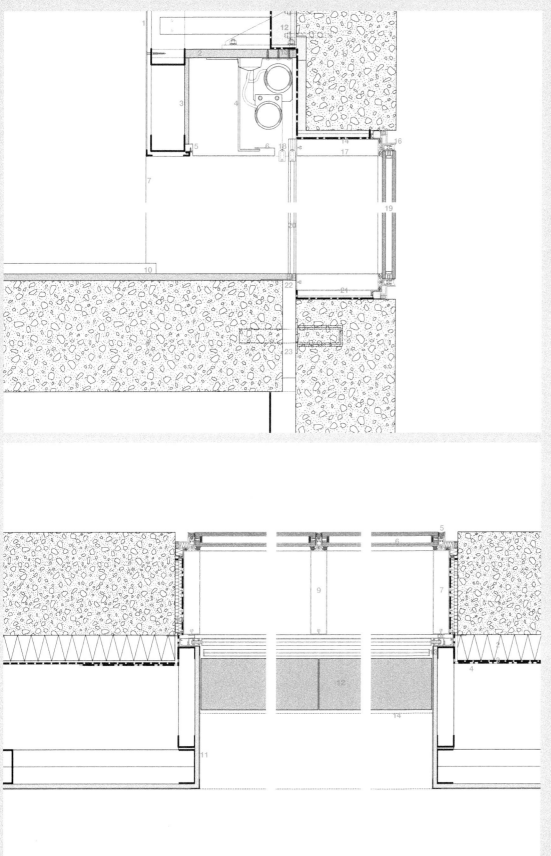

05.06
Window Detail
1:10
1 Fermacell wall
lining
2 25 mm (1 inch)
WPB ply soffit board
fixed to underside of
steel brackets and
between studs
3 12 mm (1/2 inch)
WBP ply fixed to studs
4 Removable support
bracket
5 Continuous
hardwood timber
batten
6 Pressed aluminium
cover plate, finish PPC
RAL 9016
7 Elevation line of
window reveal
8 20 x 95 x 3 mm (4/5
x 3 4/5 x 1/10 inch)
aluminium angle
9 Concrete slab
10 Polished screed
11 In-situ concrete
12 Insulation
13 Vapour-control
layer
14 DPC

15 Silicone joint
16 3 mm (1/10 inch)
thick aluminium lining,
powder coated to
non-standard RAL
colour
17 50 x 250 mm (2 x 9
4/5 inch) transom
18 Solar shading /
black-out blind
19 Fixed glazing
20 Sidetrack of
black-out blind
21 50 x 250 mm (2 x 9
4/5 inch) transom
22 Floor movement
joint
23 40 mm (1 3/5 inch)
insulation

05.07
Roof Detail
1:10
1 In-situ concrete
2 Vapour-control
layer
3 DPC
4 3 mm (1/10 inch)
thick powder-coated
aluminium profile
5 Silicon joint
6 Fixed glazing
7 50 x 250 mm (2 x 9
4/5 inch) mullion
8 10 x 20 mm (2/5 x
4/5 inch) extruded
aluminium channel
recessed 15 mm (3/5
inch) behind dim-out
guide
9 50 x 250 mm (2 x 9
4/5 inch) mullion
10 20 x 200 mm (4/5 x
7 9/10 inch) insulation
above head
11 Fermacell wall
lining
12 Pressed aluminium
access panel PPC RAL
9016, 30 per cent
gloss
13 Sidetrack of
black-out blind
14 10 mm (2/5 inch)
recess for fixings

29

Mostyn Gallery
Llandudno, North Wales, UK

Client
Mostyn Gallery Trust

Project Team
Dominic Williams, Mark Anstey

Structural Engineer
Buro Happold, Manchester

Main Contractor
R.L. Davies & Son Ltd

The redevelopment and expansion of the Mostyn Gallery in Llandudno, North Wales have provided new exhibition and circulation spaces, which enhance the visitor experience whilst retaining the spirit and atmosphere of the original building.

Before design of the new development commenced, the characteristics of the existing galleries were carefully analyzed. It was concluded that these were their natural light and elegant proportions. The new galleries seek to replicate these conditions, while also allowing for the display of all forms of contemporary work.

Insertion of a bold atrium space through the building accommodates movement between the entrance, the galleries and the social spaces. This space, which the architects have named the 'tube', is a pure faceted sculptural volume bisected by a bridge. Coming into this geological space after entering via the Victorian entrance is an exhilarating experience. Constructed from board-formed, in-situ concrete, the large slab surfaces reveal on examination a textural detail that describes their production. Above, large south-facing roof lights allow light to flood down through the interior. The subtle control of illumination is a theme that occurs throughout this project. In the galleries, north light is channelled into the spaces to provide daylight without glare or excess shadows.

The floors through the galleries are oak boards reminiscent of the board-marked concrete in the 'tube'. The original gallery's spire has been re-clad in gold-anodized aluminum, creating an external symbol of the richness within.

1 The rear of the gallery is clad in gold-anodized aluminum. Carefully composed facades integrate the new galleries into their Victorian context.

2 The new 'tube' atrium links all the parts of the gallery. A dramatic canyon of board-marked concrete, spanned by a faceted bridge, this space establishes an exuberant atmosphere of expectation.

3 The original gallery facade has been restored. Above the entrance, the enhanced spire announces the gallery's presence in the town.

4 The gallery shop leads off from the 'tube'. Here, the control of light, space and materials creates a delicate atmosphere.

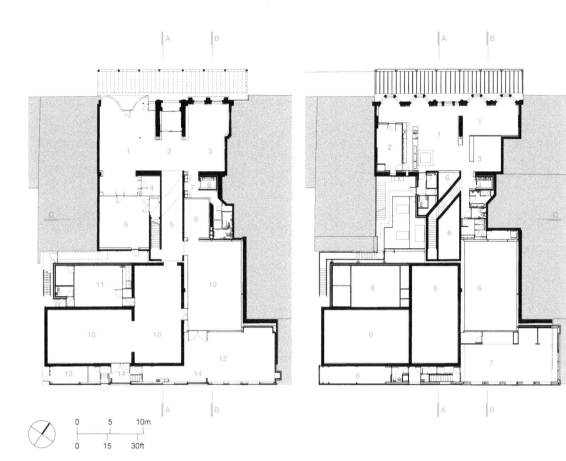

06.01
Ground Floor Plan
1:500
1 Shop
2 Lobby
3 Gallery
4 Shop office
5 Tube
6 Lift
7 Lockers
8 Meeting room
9 Gallery
10 Gallery
11 Education
12 Workshop
13 Plant
14 Loading bay

06.02
First Floor Plan
1:500
1 Cafe
2 Kitchen
3 Gallery
4 Lift
5 WC
6 Void
7 Gallery office
8 Plant

0 5 10m
0 15 30ft

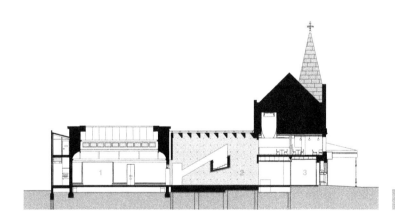

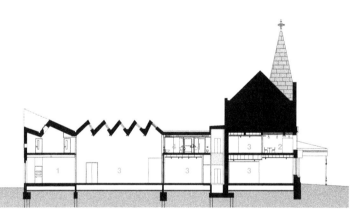

06.03
Section A–A
1:500
1 Gallery
2 Tube
3 Foyer/shop
4 Cafe

06.04
Section B–B
1:500
1 Workshop
2 Cafe
3 Gallery
4 WC

06.05
Section C–C
1:200
1 Gallery
2 WC
3 Tube
4 Meeting room

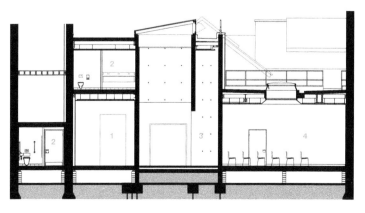

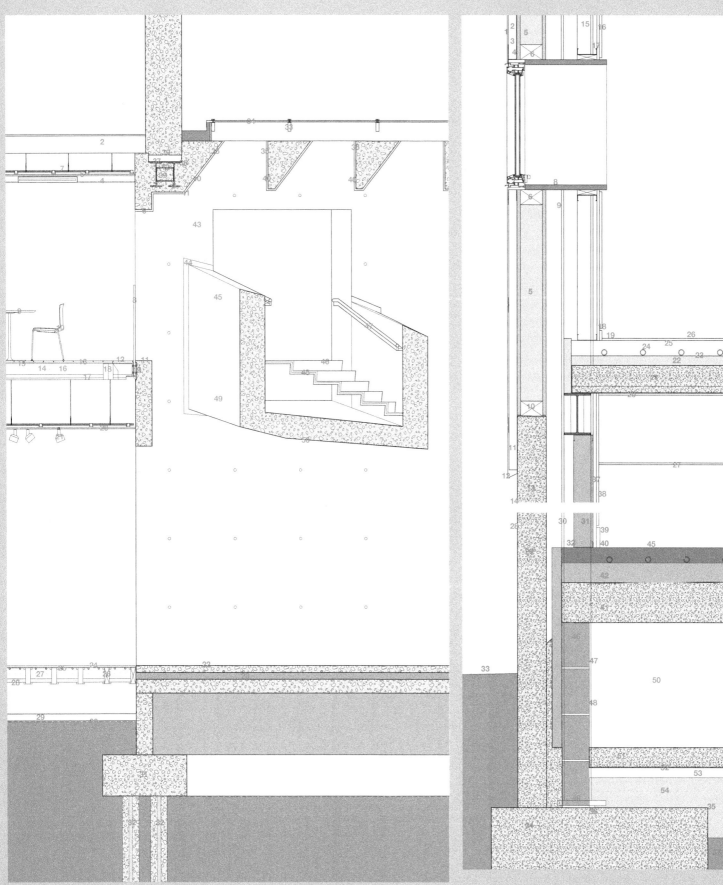

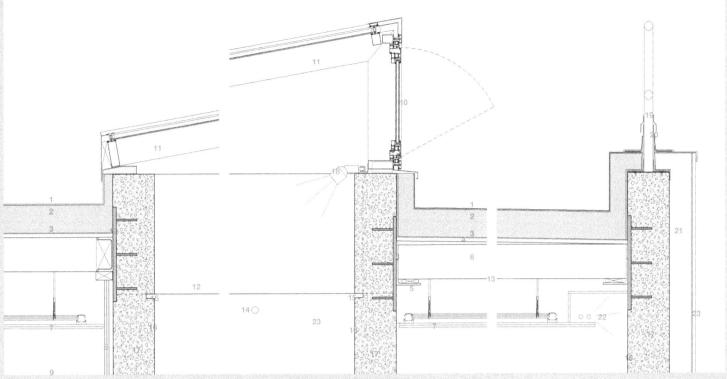

06.06
'Tube' Section
1:50

1 Original masonry wall of 1901 building
2 Existing second floor timber joists
3 Two 356 x 171 x 51 mm (14 x 6 $^{7}/_{10}$ x 2 inch) UB perforated with 25 mm (1 inch) holes to allow rebar threading
4 12.5 mm ($^{1}/_{2}$ inch) plasterboard secondary ceiling
5 Double boarded primary ceiling on acoustic MF suspension system with 100 mm (3 $^{9}/_{10}$ inch) insulation
6 Timber-board-marked in-situ concrete aperture
7 Whitegoods recessed linear lamp fitting with opaque diffuser
8 20 mm ($^{4}/_{5}$ inch) toughened glass balustrade
9 Arper Dizzie table
10 Arper Catifa 53 bi-colour chair
11 In-situ concrete beam flush with cafe floor
12 Removable timber boards
13 21 mm ($^{4}/_{5}$ inch) oak engineered boards
14 Rehau underfloor heating tubes with aluminium diffusion plates
15 Regupol acoustic matting strips
16 160 mm (6 $^{3}/_{10}$ inch) Rockwool insulation
17 50 mm (2 inch) rigid insulation on timber battens
18 230 x 75 mm (9 $^{1}/_{10}$ x 3 inch) timber trimming joists
19 Steel fixing plate cast into concrete
20 Double boarded ceiling on MF suspension system

21 Erco lighting to Oriel 5 with recessed track
22 In-situ concrete hand-burnished floor
23 Rehau underfloor heating tubes
24 21 mm ($^{4}/_{5}$ inch) oak engineered boards
25 Rehau underfloor heating tubes with aluminium diffusion plates
26 230 x 75 mm (9 $^{1}/_{10}$ x 3 inch) timber joists
27 160 mm (6 $^{3}/_{10}$ inch) rockwool insulation
28 50 mm (2 inch) rigid insulation on timber battens
29 100 mm (3 $^{9}/_{10}$ inch) concrete capping layer
30 3 mm ($^{1}/_{10}$ inch) contamination capping sheet
31 In-situ concrete ground beams
32 Branlow self-drill micro piles to 16 metre (52 foot 6 inch) depth
33 Powder-coated aluminium section
34 Double-glazed unit
35 Timber-board-marked in-situ concrete blades
36 Insulated pre-formed aluminium drainage channel with Bauder single-ply membrane
37 Continuous packing around sacrificial Abbey Pinford propping
38 500 x 400 x 10 mm (19 $^{4}/_{5}$ x 15 $^{7}/_{10}$ x $^{2}/_{5}$ inch) plate at 800 mm (31 $^{1}/_{2}$ inch) centres
39 203 x 203 x 46 mm (8 x 8 x 1 $^{4}/_{5}$ inch) UB at 1000 mm (39 $^{4}/_{10}$ inch) centres
40 Shadow gap
41 Timber-board-marked in-situ concrete beam encasing steelwork
42 100 mm (3 $^{9}/_{10}$ inch) diameter holes to

allow concrete flow around steelwork
43 100 mm (3 $^{9}/_{10}$ inch) timber board marked in-situ concrete wall
44 Shadow gap around bridge
45 In-situ concrete bridge
46 21 mm ($^{4}/_{5}$ inch) oak engineered board tread and riser
47 Oak handrail
48 18 mm ($^{7}/_{10}$ inch) plywood on timber carcassing
49 100 mm (3 $^{9}/_{10}$ inch) vertical timber-board-marked in-situ concrete face
50 Timber-board-marked folded soffit of concrete bridge, cast in-situ

06.07
Rear Wall Section
1:20

1 Gold-anodized aluminium panels fixed to top hats with gold-anodized rivets
2 45 mm (1 $^{4}/_{5}$ inch) aluminium top hat sections arranged vertically
3 45 mm (1 $^{4}/_{5}$ inch) air gap
4 Bonded waterproof membrane
5 150 mm (5 $^{9}/_{10}$ inch) SIP panels
6 Timber trimmer to reveal
7 Gold-anodized aluminium window frames
8 25 mm (1 inch) MDF liner to reveal
9 Primary steel frame
10 Timber sole plate bolted down through concrete
11 Waterproofing membrane sealed over concrete wall
12 Drip profile
13 175 mm (6 $^{9}/_{10}$ inch) in-situ black concrete wall
14 150 mm (5 $^{9}/_{10}$ inch) wide vertical sand-blasted timber-board marking
15 MF system
16 12.5 mm ($^{1}/_{2}$ inch) plasterboard skimmed and painted
17 12 mm ($^{1}/_{2}$ inch) plywood
18 Shadow gap
19 Painted MDF skirting
20 35 mm (1 $^{2}/_{5}$ inch) profiled metal deck
21 140 mm (5 $^{1}/_{2}$ inch) in-situ concrete floor slab
22 50 mm (2 inch) rigid insulation
23 Separation layer
24 Rehau underfloor heating tubes
25 75 mm (3 inch) sand and cement screed

26 Carpet tiles
27 Primary steel structure
28 150 mm (5 $^{9}/_{10}$ inch) wide vertical timber-board marking
29 175 mm (6 $^{9}/_{10}$ inch) in-situ black concrete wall
30 Primary steel frame
31 100 mm (3 $^{9}/_{10}$ inch) foil-backed rigid insulation
32 100 mm (3 $^{9}/_{10}$ inch) jumbo stud
33 Garage Street
34 In-situ concrete ground beam
35 16 mm ($^{6}/_{10}$ inch) bored steel piles
36 Concrete grout encasement
37 15 mm ($^{3}/_{5}$ inch) Megadeco boards
38 12 mm ($^{1}/_{2}$ inch) plywood
39 Shadow gap
40 MDF skirting
41 Concrete beam and block flooring
42 100 mm (3 $^{9}/_{10}$ inch) rigid insulation
43 Rehau underfloor heating tubes
44 75 mm (3 inch) sand and cement screed
45 Floor paint
46 Concrete blocks
47 Membrane dressed up the wall
48 Primary steel column
49 Steel base plate fixed to ground beam
50 Accessible void
51 100 mm (3 $^{9}/_{10}$ inch) oversite concrete capping layer
52 3 mm ($^{1}/_{10}$ inch) sealed contamination membrane
53 50 mm (2 inch) sand blinding
54 300 mm (11 $^{4}/_{5}$ inch) hardcore
55 Ground contaminated with hydrocarbons

06.08
'Tube' Section
1:20

1 Bauder single-ply membrane
2 160 mm (6 $^{3}/_{10}$ inch) rigid insulation
3 Bauder base layer membrane
4 25 mm (1 inch) WBP deck laid to falls
5 Steel support for timber joists welded to cast-in fixing plates
6 200 x 75 mm (7 $^{9}/_{10}$ x 3 inch) timber joists
7 Suspended MF plasterboard ceiling
8 Two layers 12.5 mm ($^{1}/_{2}$ inch) MR plasterboard
9 Female WC
10 Tube rooflight opening vents electrically operated with wind / rain sensors and manual override
11 150 x 50 mm (5 $^{9}/_{10}$ x 2 inch) PPC aluminium box sections
12 Timber-board-marked, in-situ concrete blade
13 Steel fixing plate tied into reinforcement and cast into walls
14 Tie bolt holes back filled and colour-matched to leave 25 mm (1 inch) circular recess
15 25 mm (1 inch) shadow gap
16 Timber-board-marked concrete finish
17 250 mm (9 $^{4}/_{5}$ inch) cast-in-situ concrete wall
18 Continuous recessed lighting track with lamps fitted between blades
19 Galvanized metal guarding, mechanically fixed to top of concrete
20 Bauder membrane apron around each post with galvanized aluminium cowel over

21 140 mm (5 $^{1}/_{2}$ inch) rigid insulation
22 Recessed lighting strip
23 Through colour render

**Masdar Institute
Masdar, Abu Dhabi, United Arab
Emirates**

Client
Mubadala Development Company

Project Team
David Nelson, Gerard Evenden, Ross
Palmer, Austin Relton, Barrie Cheng,
Joern Herrmann, Ho Ling Cheung,
Jeffrey Morgan, Sidonie Immler,
Alison Potter

Structural Engineer
Adams Kara Taylor

Services Engineer
PHA Consult

Main Contractor
Al Ahmadiah–Hip Hing Joint Venture

This building is an initial part of the
new city of Masdar situated near to
Abu Dhabi, and embodies the
sustainable principles of the Masdar
City Masterplan. The campus, of
which it forms part, is being built in
four phases and on completion will
provide living and working space for
between 600 and 800 postgraduate
students. This building is a test bed
for many sustainable technologies
that, if proven effective, will be used
in later phases of the development of
the city. These include wind towers,
chilled beams and photovoltaic
panels. The entire campus will be
carbon neutral and produce all its
own energy requirements.

The elements are carefully
positioned so as to provide shade
and reduce cooling loads, while
colonnades at podium level exploit
the benefits of exposed thermal
mass. The facades of the four-storey
residential blocks are made from
glass-reinforced concrete, which has
a strong red colour from the use of
local sand. The windows are protected
from direct light by projecting oriels
that are pierced with a traditional
latticed pattern. Elsewhere, walls
make extensive use of a concrete that
includes ground-granulated blast-
furnace slag as aggregate. This, along
with a high level of insulation, further
enhances the environmental
credentials of the project. Green
landscaping and water features, which
provide evaporative heat reduction,
also assist in cooling public spaces.

1 The building,
designed as a dense
megastructure, is
energy self-sufficient.
Over 5000 square
metres (53,000 square
feet) of roof-mounted
photovoltaic
installations provide
power and protection
from the sun.
2 Internal courtyards
between the buildings
are shaded from the
sun. Lattice patterns
are cast by the
surrounding screens.
3 The concrete is
tinted a distinctive red
colour through the use
of local sand. Water
features in the open
spaces help to cool the
environment.
4 The projecting oriel
windows in the
residential buildings
utilize a wave form and
are protected by a
contemporary
reinterpretation of the
mashrabiya, a
traditional feature of
local buildings.

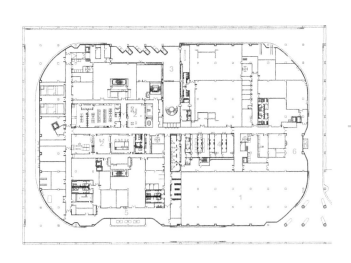

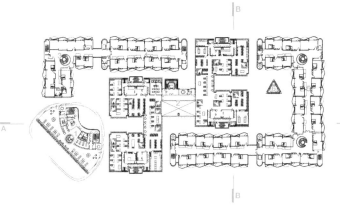

07.01	07.02
Basement Plan	**First Floor Plan**
1:2000	1:2000
1 Basement to adjacent plot	1 Knowledge centre
2 Laboratory high bays	2 Laboratory
3 PRT station	3 Family residential block
4 Clean room	4 Female residential block
5 Lab loading bay	5 Male residential block
6 Residential loading bay	6 PDEC wind tower

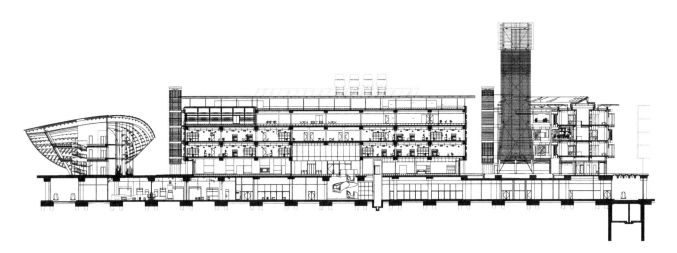

07.03
Long section A-A
1:1000

07.04
Section B–B
1:1000

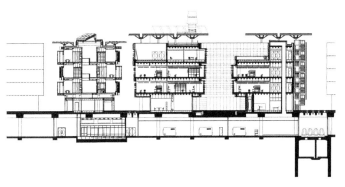

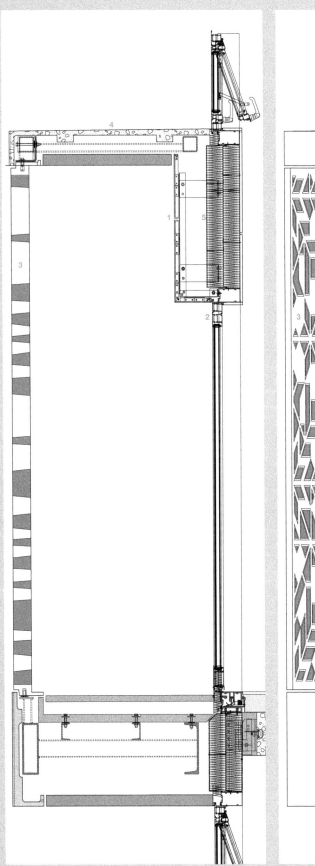

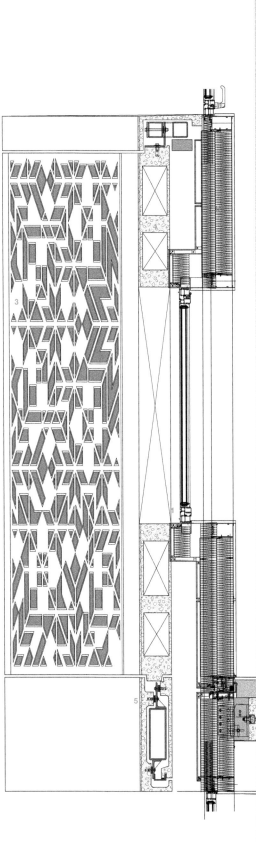

07.05
Window Section
1:20
1 90 per cent recycled aluminium panel on support frame
2 Prefabricated unitized highly insulated aluminium-frame facade, weather and airtight
3 Patterned glass-reinforced-concrete screen designed by Jean-Marc Castera
4 Concrete
5 Insulation

07.06
Window Section
1:20
1 90 per cent recycled aluminium panel on support frame
2 Prefabricated unitized highly insulated aluminium-frame facade, weather and airtight
3 Patterned glass-reinforced-concrete screen designed by Jean-Marc Castera
4 Glass-reinforced-concrete panel on metal frame suspended from primary structure
5 Concrete
6 Insulation

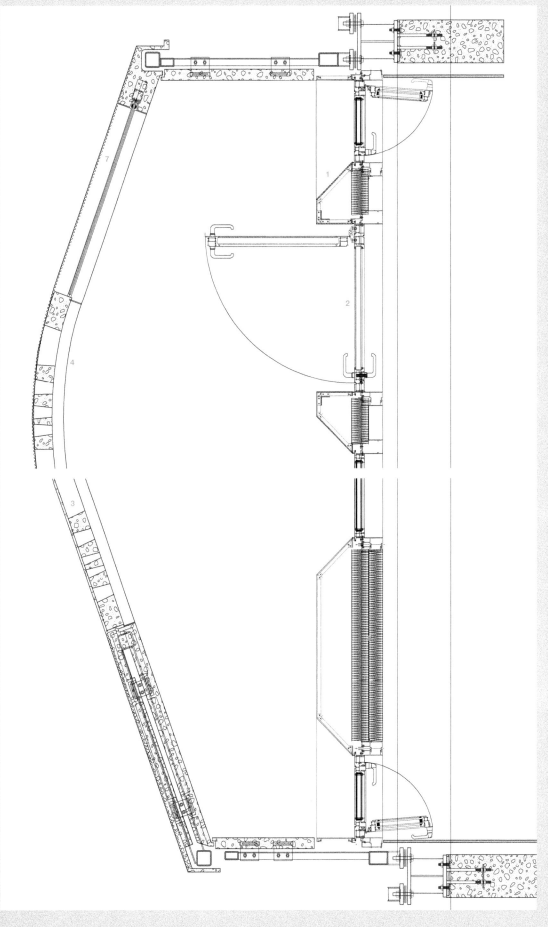

07.07
Oriel Window Plan
1:20
1 90 per cent
recycled aluminium
panel on support
frame
2 Prefabricated
unitized highly
insulated aluminium
frame facade,
weather- and airtight
3 Patterned
glass-reinforced-
concrete screen
designed by
Jean-Marc Castera
4 Glass-reinforced-
concrete panel on
metal frame
suspended from
primary structure
5 Concrete
6 Insulation
7 Glass balustrade

Frontier Project
Rancho Cucamonga, California,
USA

Client
Cucamonga Valley Water District

Project Team
Pasqual Gutierrez, Laurie McCoy,
Raymond Pan, Dexter Galang, Daniel
Sandoval, Eddy Santosa

Structural Engineer
R.M. Byrd & Associates

Main Contractor
Turner Construction Company

The Frontier Project Foundation in
Rancho Cucamonga, California, is a
1300-square-metre (14,000-square-
foot) demonstration building that
showcases environmentally friendly
design technologies. It seeks to show
to both developers and public that
these technologies are economical,
efficient and appropriate. This
ambitious structure uses the latest in
sustainable technology, systems and
products. These include photovoltaic
panels, a green-roof system, a cool
tower and a solar chimney.

The positioning and form of the
building was the result of extensive
study of local environmental
conditions. The project also shows
how sustainable technologies can be
incorporated into domestic spaces,
with a demonstration kitchen and
living room. Internally the building
uses reclaimed redwood from a
local winery.

The walls are constructed using
Insulated Concrete Forms (ICFs).
These are hollow expanded
polystyrene bricks that interlock when
stacked in place. Concrete is then
poured into this permanent formwork,
creating a solid, fully insulated
structure. Engineered webs made
from recycled industrial polypropylene
plastic then connect the ICF surfaces,
making the concrete walls stronger.
The benefits of this method of
construction include better energy
efficiency, excellent air quality and a
reduction in construction waste. The
Frontier Project received a Leadership
in Energy and Environmental Design
(LEED) Platinum Certification from the
US Green Building Council.

1 The Frontier Project's entrance facade shows off many of the alternative technologies that it utilizes. The building's relation to the path of the sun dictated the orientation and details of the plan.
2 At night the building's layered composition is enhanced by careful lighting design.
3 The roof provides a terrace area to relax. Parts of the roof use green-roof technology to insulate and to increase the sustainability of the structure.
4 Wrapped around the courtyard, the atrium exhibition space is walled on one side by a canted glazed wall.

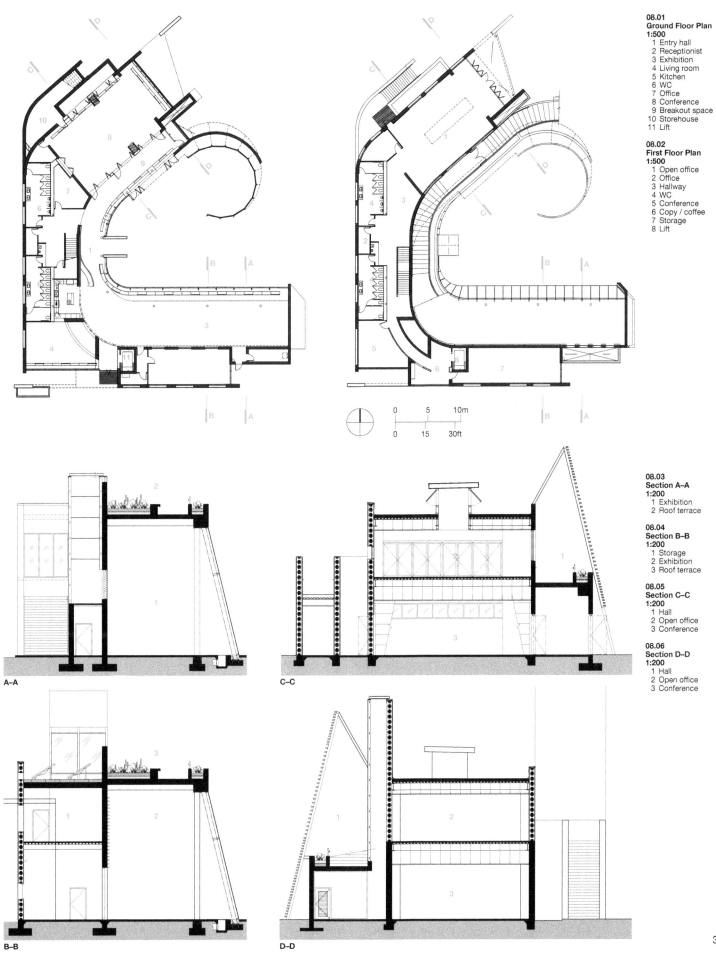

08.01
Ground Floor Plan
1:500
1 Entry hall
2 Receptionist
3 Exhibition
4 Living room
5 Kitchen
6 WC
7 Office
8 Conference
9 Breakout space
10 Storehouse
11 Lift

08.02
First Floor Plan
1:500
1 Open office
2 Office
3 Hallway
4 WC
5 Conference
6 Copy / coffee
7 Storage
8 Lift

0   5   10m
0   15   30ft

A–A

C–C

08.03
Section A–A
1:200
1 Exhibition
2 Roof terrace

08.04
Section B–B
1:200
1 Storage
2 Exhibition
3 Roof terrace

08.05
Section C–C
1:200
1 Hall
2 Open office
3 Conference

08.06
Section D–D
1:200
1 Hall
2 Open office
3 Conference

B–B

D–D

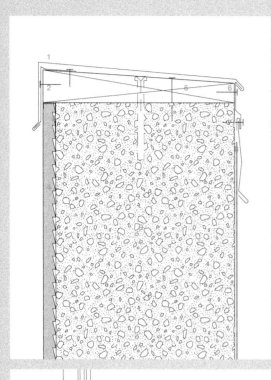

08.07
Parapet Detail
1:10
　1 Coping
　2 GI Clip
　3 Plaster stop
　4 Exterior plaster over paper-backed lath
　5 Pressure wood nailer
　6 Waterproof membrane and vertical overlap each side under flashing
　7 Counter flashing
　8 Flashing membrane
　9 Concrete

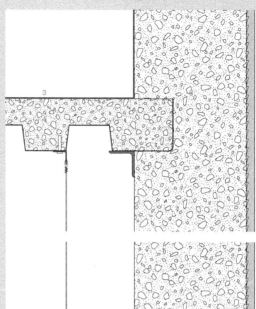

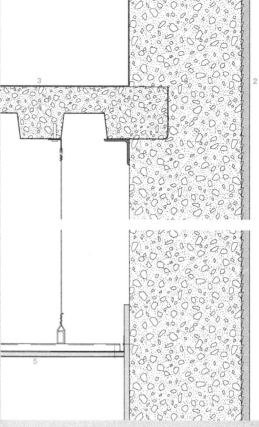

08.09
Structural Beam to ICF Connection Detail
1:10
　1 Roofing turned up back side of parapet wall
　2 Exterior stucco
　3 Base flashing
　4 Concrete deck
　5 Suspended ceiling
　6 Concrete

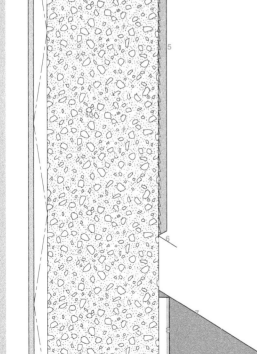

08.08
Sill Detail
1:10
　1 Glazing
　2 Aluminium sill
　3 Sealant
　4 Corner bead
　5 Stucco
　6 Continuous weep screed
　7 Finished grade
　8 Below grade waterproofing over top of footing
　9 Wood shim
10 Concrete

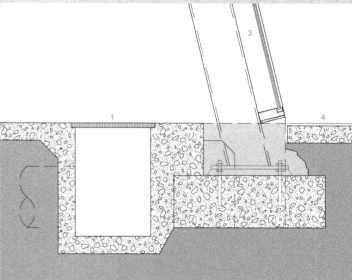

08.10
Footing Sloped Curtain Wall Detail
1:10
　1 Floor vent
　2 Concrete slab
　3 Curtain-wall system
　4 Exterior deck

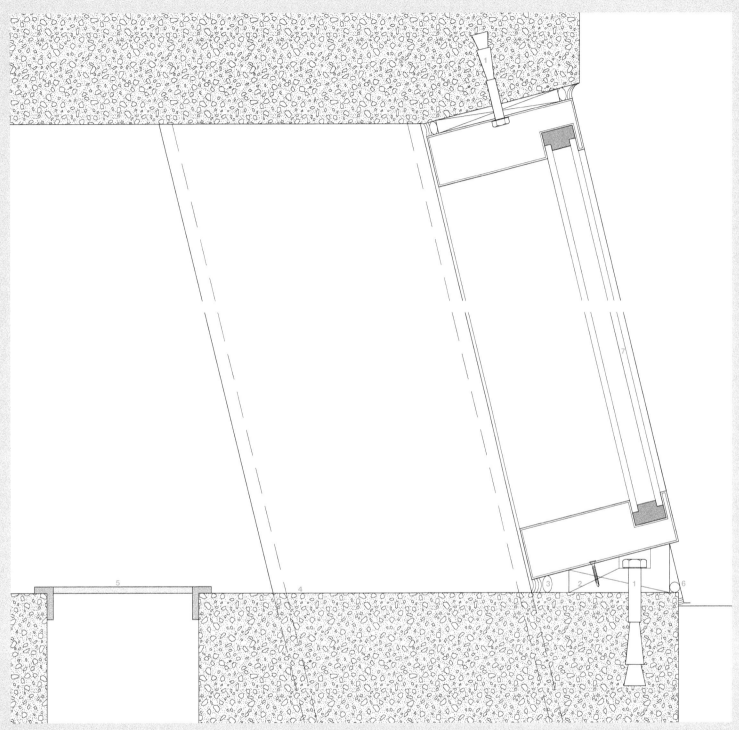

08.11
Sloped Curtain Wall
Glazing Sill Detail
1:10
  1 Countersunk
anchor
  2 Shaped block to
match glazing angle
  3 Continuous backer
rod and caulking
  4 Finished floor
  5 Floor register
  6 Flashing
  7 Curtain-wall system
  8 Concrete

**Extension to the
Historisches Museum
Bern, Switzerland**

Client
Historisches Museum Bern BHM

Project Team
Daniele Di Giacinto, Pat Tanner,
Roman Lehmann, Claude Marbach,
Lars Mischkulnig, Regina Wüger,
Roman Tschachtli, Lukas Gerber,
Lukas Thalmann, Uli Gradenegger,
Andreas Sager, Claudia Gabathuler,
Eva Kiese, Kai Bögli, Katharina
Handke, Marc Doberstein, Monika
Hausammann, Martina Scholze,
Nicole Schneider, Yannick Roschi

Structural Engineer
Tschopp Ingenieure, CH-Bern

This project is an extension to the
Historisches Museum Bern, which
was built by André Lambert in 1894 in
a style that evokes Swiss architecture
of the fifteenth and sixteenth
centuries. It is composed of two
distinct elements. The first is a
1000-square-metre (10,765-square-
foot) temporary exhibition hall located
beneath a new civic square; the
second is a monolithic six-storey
block along the southern side of the
site, which houses the Bern city
archives, offices and a library. The
exhibition space under the square is a
double-height 'black box' space
suitable for a range of different visiting
exhibitions. Below the exhibition
space are two levels for the storage of
artifacts in secure, climate-controlled
conditions. This close relationship of
storage and exhibition space
facilitates the easy care and display of
collections.

The second element has two very
different faces. Towards the civic
square the building presents a
transparent orthogonal modernist
curtain wall. The activities within the
building are clearly visible. In contrast
the south facade rises up as a folded
cliff of cast concrete, punctured by
small, seemingly random openings
and indentations. This concrete skin
wraps around the building, embracing
and sheltering its contents. Behind the
south wall, in a vertical slot, a
triple-height staircase connects the
floorplates. Outside, a sweep of broad
steps rises up to the square in front of
the glazed north facade.

1 The steps at the
side of the south block
provide a place to sit
and observe the city.
The modelled surfaces
of the concrete echo
the carved stone of
adjacent historic
buildings.
2 The small recessed
block impressions in
the concrete imitate
the stone construction
of the original
museum.
3 Through reflections
and shadows the
building establishes
direct relationships
with its context.
4 The triple-height
stair that connects the
floors of the vertical
block is illuminated by
small punched
openings.

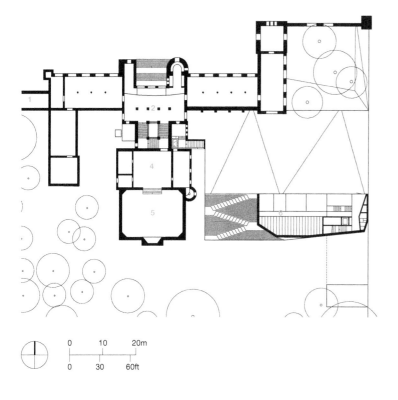

09.01
Entrance Level Plan
1:1000
1 Bistro Steinhalle
  restaurant
2 Entrance hall,
  Historic Museum
3 Lift
4 Little Mosersaal
5 Large Mosersaal
6 Office and city
  archive

09.02
Plans of Levels
1, 2 and 3
1:500
1 Library and
  conference / meeting
  space
2 Offices

0   10   20m

0   30   60ft

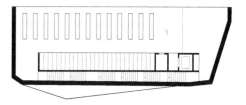

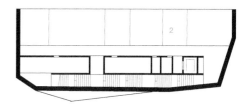

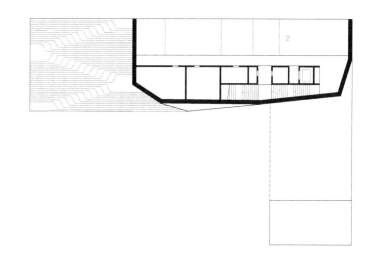

09.03
Section
1:1000
1 Library, and
  conference space
2 Office
3 Office and city
  archive
4 Preparation
5 Depot / storage
6 Main square
7 Half-pace
8 Services

09.04
Section
1:1000
1 Exhibition hall
2 Depot / storage
3 Main square

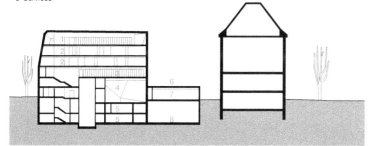

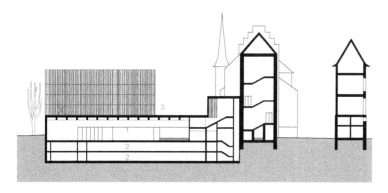

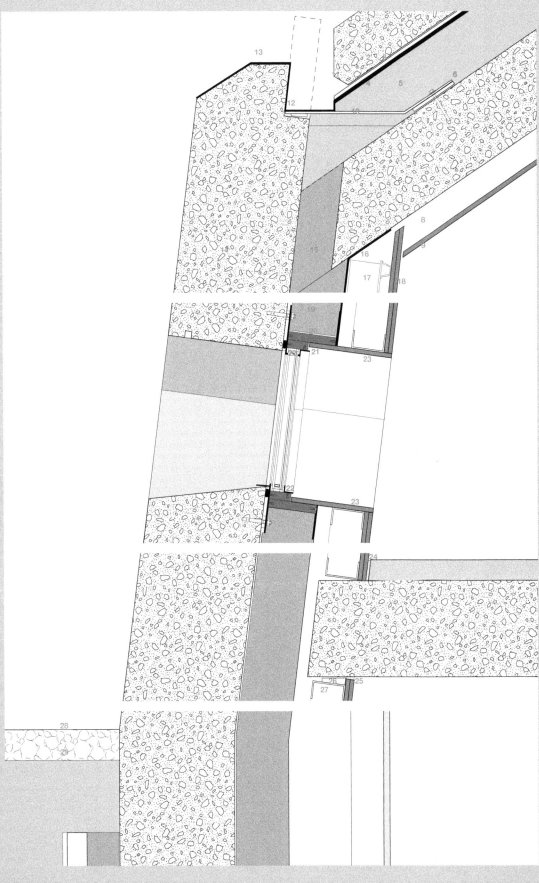

09.05
Wall and Gutter
Vertical Section
1:10
1 160 mm (6 $^{3}/_{10}$ inch)
concrete, pigmented
2 20 mm ($^{4}/_{5}$ inch)
drainage, air layer
3 10 mm ($^{2}/_{5}$ inch)
vulcanized rubber
4 Bituminous sealing
two-ply
5 160 mm (6 $^{3}/_{10}$ inch)
Foamglas insulation
6 Primary coat
7 240 mm (9 $^{2}/_{5}$ inch)
concrete
8 Substructure
9 Plasterboard
10 Substructure: metal
sheet
11 Drainage
12 Gutter
13 Plastics coating
wall mounting
14 350 mm (13 $^{4}/_{5}$
inch) concrete,
pigmented
15 160 mm (6 $^{3}/_{10}$ inch)
insulation polystyrene
16 Water barrier
17 75 mm (6 inch)
substructure
18 2 x 12.5 mm ($^{1}/_{10}$ x
$^{5}/_{10}$ inch) plasterboard
window
19 Water barrier at
architrave
20 Water barrier,
tensed up three sided
21 Decoration for glass
22 Aluminium L-profile
23 Plasterboard
24 Gap
25 Putty gap
26 Cotter
27 C-profile terrain
28 Coating
29 500 mm (19 $^{7}/_{10}$
inch) gravel

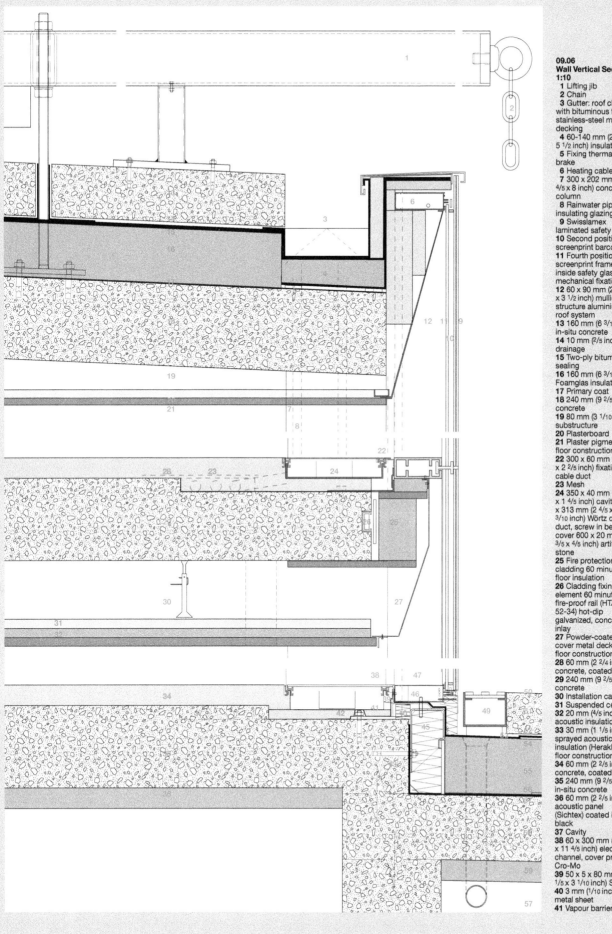

09.06
Wall Vertical Section
1:10
1 Lifting jib
2 Chain
3 Gutter: roof cladder with bituminous finish, stainless-steel metal decking
4 60-140 mm (2 2/5-5 1/2 inch) insulation
5 Fixing thermal brake
6 Heating cable
7 300 x 202 mm (11 4/5 x 8 inch) concrete column
8 Rainwater pipe insulating glazing
9 Swisslamex laminated safety glass
10 Second position screenprint barcode
11 Fourth position screenprint frame inside safety glass mechanical fixation
12 60 x 90 mm (2 2/5 x 3 1/2 inch) mullion structure aluminium roof system
13 160 mm (6 3/10 inch) in-situ concrete
14 10 mm (2/5 inch) drainage
15 Two-ply bituminous sealing
16 160 mm (6 3/10 inch) Foamglas insulation
17 Primary coat
18 240 mm (9 2/5 inch) concrete
19 80 mm (3 1/10 inch) substructure
20 Plasterboard
21 Plaster pigmented floor construction
22 300 x 60 mm (11 4/5 x 2 2/5 inch) fixation cable duct
23 Mesh
24 350 x 40 mm (13 4/5 x 1 4/5 inch) cavity, 72 x 313 mm (2 4/5 x 12 3/10 inch) Wörtz cable duct, screw in bed cover 600 x 20 mm (23 3/5 x 4/5 inch) artificial stone
25 Fire protection cladding 60 minute, floor insulation
26 Cladding fixing element 60 minute fire-proof rail (HTA 52-34) hot-dip galvanized, concrete inlay
27 Powder-coated cover metal deck floor construction
28 60 mm (2 2/4 inch) concrete, coated
29 240 mm (9 2/5 inch) concrete
30 Installation cavity
31 Suspended ceiling
32 20 mm (4/5 inch) acoustic insulation
33 30 mm (1 1/5 inch) sprayed acoustic insulation (Heraklith) floor construction
34 60 mm (2 2/5 inch) concrete, coated
35 240 mm (9 2/5 inch) in-situ concrete
36 60 mm (2 2/5 inch) acoustic panel (Sichtex) coated in black
37 Cavity
38 60 x 300 mm (2 2/5 x 11 4/5 inch) electro channel, cover profile Cro-Mo
39 50 x 5 x 80 mm (2 x 1/5 x 3 1/10 inch) St-FLA
40 3 mm (1/10 inch) metal sheet
41 Vapour barrier

42 80 x 8 x 180 mm (3 1/10 x 3/10 x 7 1/10 inch) St-FLA
43 14 x 30 mm (3/5 x 1 1/5 inch) elongated hole vertical
44 4 mm (5/32 inch) metal sheet with Spickel
45 10 x 60 mm (2/5 x 2 2/5 inch) CNS bolt, 12 x 40 mm (1/2 x 1 3/5 inch)elongated hole horizontal
46 12 x 30 mm (1/2 x 1 1/5 inch) elongated hole horizontal
47 Aluminium profile (EBL RAL)
48 15 mm (3/5 inch) substructure, slideable
49 Water gutter, guard on insulation , removable grid
50 Construction suspension-lifting jib roof base with counter-sunk screw and ring bolt
51 120 mm (4 7/10 inch) concrete pigmented
52 Mat
53 10 mm (2/5 inch) drainage
54 Two-ply water barrier
55 160 mm (6 3/10 inch) Foamglas T4 insulation to lay on hot asphalt
56 Bituminous sealing one-ply (temporary seal)
57 Prime coat
58 190 mm (7 1/2 inch) concrete, down grade 2 per cent
59 60 mm (2 2/5 inch) acoustic panel (Sichtex) coated in black

**Volcano Interpretation Center
Capelinhos, Faial Island, Azores,
Portugal**

Client
Azores Regional Government,
Regional Secretariat for the
Environment and the Sea

Project Team
Sara Moncaixa Potes, Manuel Baião

Structural Engineer
Mário Veloso

Main Contractors
Consórcio Mota-Engil, S.A. /
Somague-Ediçor, S.A. /
Marques, S.A.

During the volcanic eruption of
1957–8, the landscape of the island
of Faial in the Azores was reshaped.
Lava buried the lighthouse that stood
on the tip of the island. In addition,
our understanding of underwater
volcanoes was transformed.

Within the barren landscape
formed by this volcanic action, an
interpretation centre has been
constructed, which explains both the
events that altered the landscape and
the history of the lighthouse. The area
around has been restored and the
lighthouse preserved in its ruined
state. Visitors approach the site along
a path. On the final approach there is
a choice of surfaces on which to walk
– either spaced flagstones or basalt
cobblestones.

The building is set into the original
ground. As you pass through the
exhibitions, you experience the history
of the place in three stages: before,
during and after the eruption. Each
stage is presented in isolation,
allowing it to be contemplated on its
own. The journey begins in a large,
circular foyer, 25 metres (82 feet) in
diameter. This space is constructed
from reinforced concrete, without any
finishing to the surface. A single
central column flares outwards
towards the rim of the drum and
supports the giant roof. Progressing to
the final, glazed space you learn about
the power of the earth before
emerging to see the beauty of its
destructive force.

1 The view across the
roof of the circular hall
towards the ruined
lighthouse.
2 The path to the
exhibition centre takes
a sharp turn before
entering the earth.
3 The new building
emerges from the dark
soil as if it had been
discovered rather than
built. Here a giant
telescope reaches up
to the stars.
4 Within the
windowless drum,
the impression of the
earth's power is
emphasized by the
dramatic curved forms.

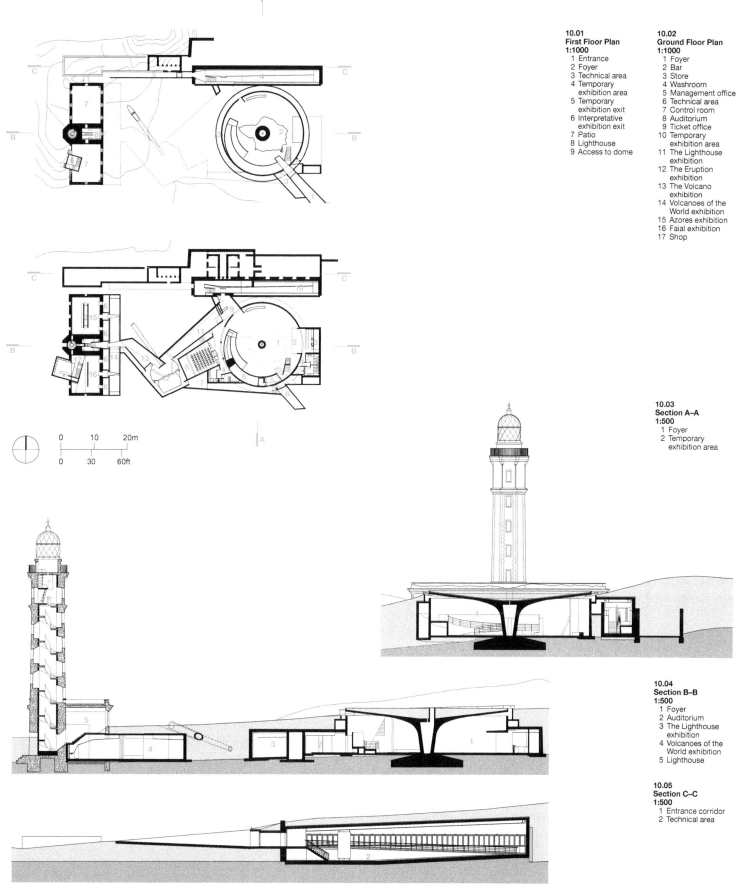

10.01
First Floor Plan
1:1000
1 Entrance
2 Foyer
3 Technical area
4 Temporary
  exhibition area
5 Temporary
  exhibition exit
6 Interpretative
  exhibition exit
7 Patio
8 Lighthouse
9 Access to dome

10.02
Ground Floor Plan
1:1000
1 Foyer
2 Bar
3 Store
4 Washroom
5 Management office
6 Technical area
7 Control room
8 Auditorium
9 Ticket office
10 Temporary
   exhibition area
11 The Lighthouse
   exhibition
12 The Eruption
   exhibition
13 The Volcano
   exhibition
14 Volcanoes of the
   World exhibition
15 Azores exhibition
16 Faial exhibition
17 Shop

10.03
Section A–A
1:500
1 Foyer
2 Temporary
  exhibition area

10.04
Section B–B
1:500
1 Foyer
2 Auditorium
3 The Lighthouse
  exhibition
4 Volcanoes of the
  World exhibition
5 Lighthouse

10.05
Section C–C
1:500
1 Entrance corridor
2 Technical area

47

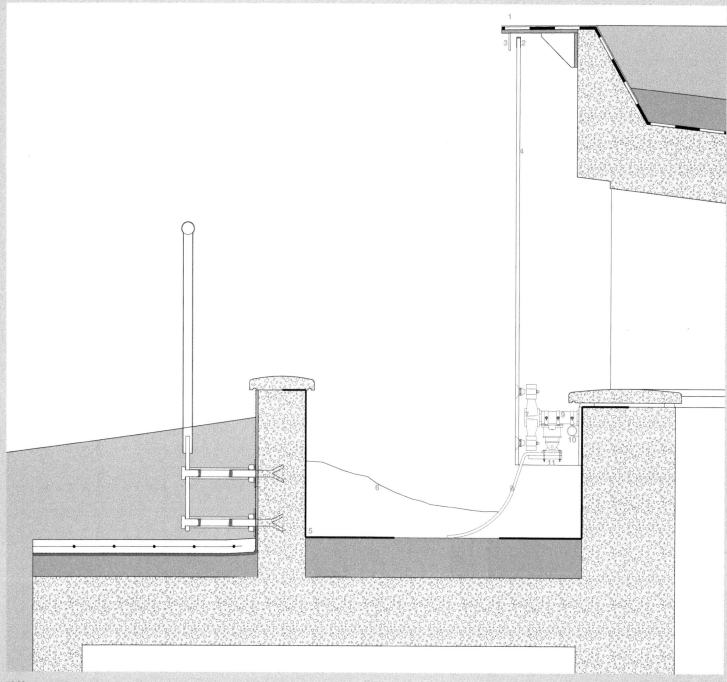

10.06
Roof Detail Section
1:20
 1 Stainless-steel
casing
 2 2 mm ($^1/_{12}$ inch)
thick shot sheet metal
 3 PVC screen
 4 10 mm ($^2/_5$ inch)
thick laminated glass
 5 3 coats of paint,
rubber and glass-fibre
mesh
 6 Ash deposit
 7 Claw part
 8 Neoprene screen
 9 Stainless-steel
clamp
10 Steel tube
11 Magnetic notifier

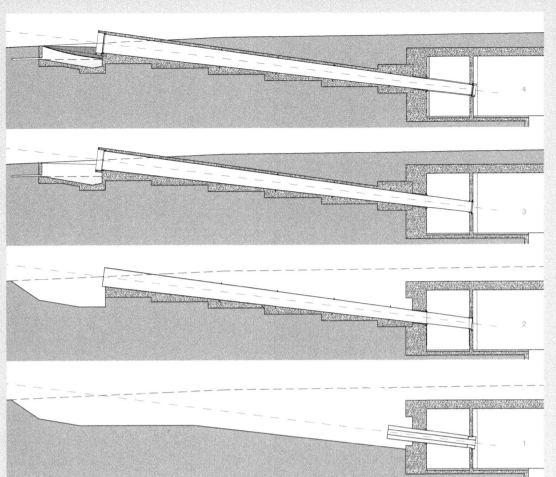

10.07
Telescope
Construction
Sequence
1:200
1 Building the walls
2 Building the tube
3 Cementing the tube
4 Finishing

10.08
Telescope Details
1:20
1 Stainless steel
2 Concrete
3 Glass

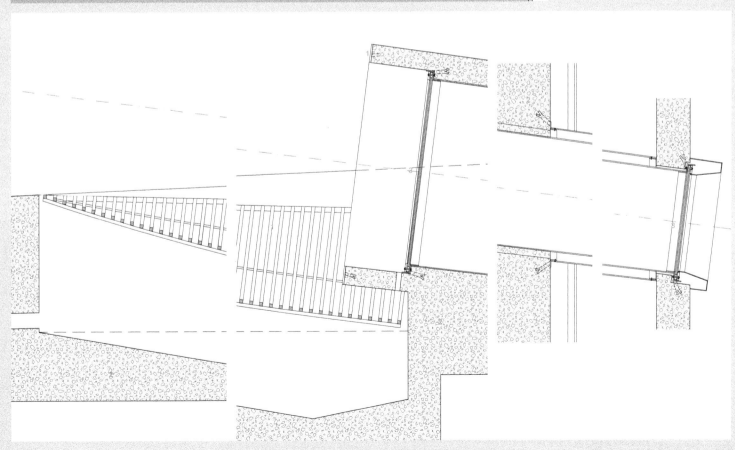

**An Gaeláras Irish Language
and Cultural Centre
Derry, Northern Ireland**

Client
Cultúrlann Uí Chanáin

Project Team
John Tuomey, Sheila O'Donnell,
Willie Carey, Anne-Louise Duignan

Structural Engineer
Albert Fry Associates

Main Contractor
JPM Contracts Ltd

Constructed on a narrow, constrained site among terraced housing in the Northern Irish city of Derry, this cultural centre is an open building that welcomes visitors in to explore its interior. At the threshold between the interior and the exterior, a terrazzo pavement pushes into the building, drawing visitors into the glass-roofed courtyard around which the building is wrapped. Through this courtyard and the use of large windows, natural light is brought into the building at every opportunity.

The facade is a careful composition of folded walls that integrate the building into its context. A rhythmic pattern of windows, framing different views of the urban landscape, allows the building's functions to be expressed on the street.

The complex fractured geometries of the plan create a rich interior that reflects the pattern of the city. The faceted central courtyard, which rises through the four floors of the building, is walled with board-marked concrete. This concrete vocabulary continues out onto the street facade, further integrating the interior with the street. The dimensions of these boards are the same as the coursing of the brickwork found in the surrounding houses. The centre also provides a shop, cafe, performance space, backstage facilities, start-up offices, teaching spaces and offices.

1 The folded entrance wall continues the scale and rhythm of the street. Views from the street into the interior court invite the public to enter.

2 Shadows on the board-marked concrete surface further enhance the sequential articulation of the facade between wall and window.

3 The language of concrete and red-painted steel continues within. The courtyard walls are perforated by galleries from which the activities below can be observed.

4 The vertical volume of the courtyard, with its theatrical layered pattern of openings and stairs, suggests and reflects the scale of the surrounding city.

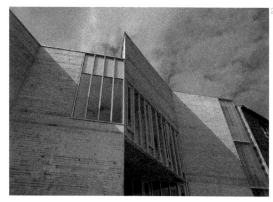

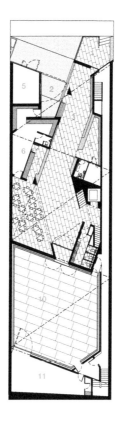
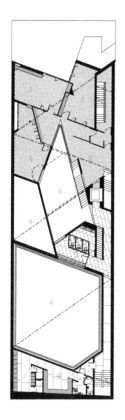
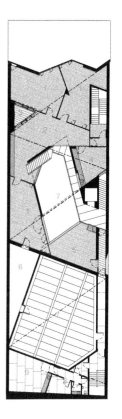
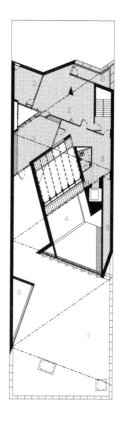

11.01
Ground Floor Plan
1:500
1 Entrance terrace
2 Entrance
3 Shop
4 Reception
5 Substation
6 Kitchen
7 Servery
8 Cafe
9 Courtyard
10 Performance
    space
11 Backstage

11.02
First Floor Plan
1:500
1 Office
2 Lobby
3 Projection room
4 Void
5 WC
6 Make-up room
7 Changing room

11.03
Second Floor Plan
1:500
1 Teaching room
2 Lobby
3 External courtyard
4 Staff room
5 Art and craft room
6 Plant room
7 Void
8 Dimming room
9 Green room

11.04
Third Floor Plan
1:500
1 Boardroom
2 Office
3 Lobby
4 Void
5 Store
6 Plant room
7 Roof
8 External terrace

11.05
Street Elevation
1:200

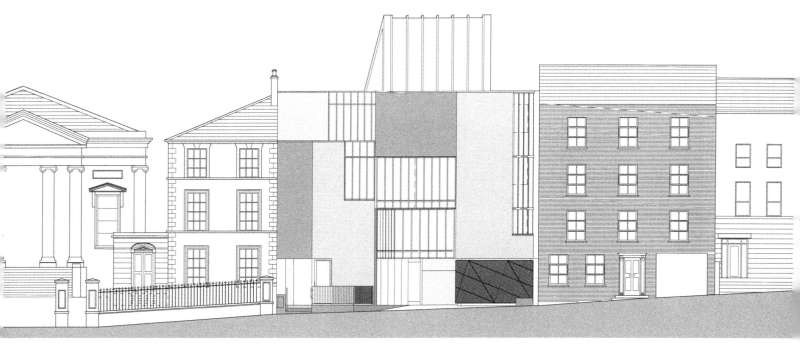

11.06
Wall Elevation 1
1:100
1 Lightly sand-blasted fair-faced concrete soffit
2 Housing for light fitting cast in
3 Timber ceiling
4 High quality board-marked concrete wall

11.07
Wall Elevation 2
1:100
1 Lightly sand-blasted fair-faced concrete soffit
2 High quality board-marked concrete wall, 50 x 70 x 135 mm (2 x 2 2/5 x 5 3/10 inch) recess for lift call button.
3 High quality board-marked concrete wall, 50 x 70 x 135 mm (2 x 2 2/5 x 5 3/10 inch) recess for lift call button

4 Housing for light-fitting conduit cast in high quality board-marked concrete wall, 50 x 70 x 100 mm (2 x 2 2/5 x 3 9/10 inch) recess for lift call button

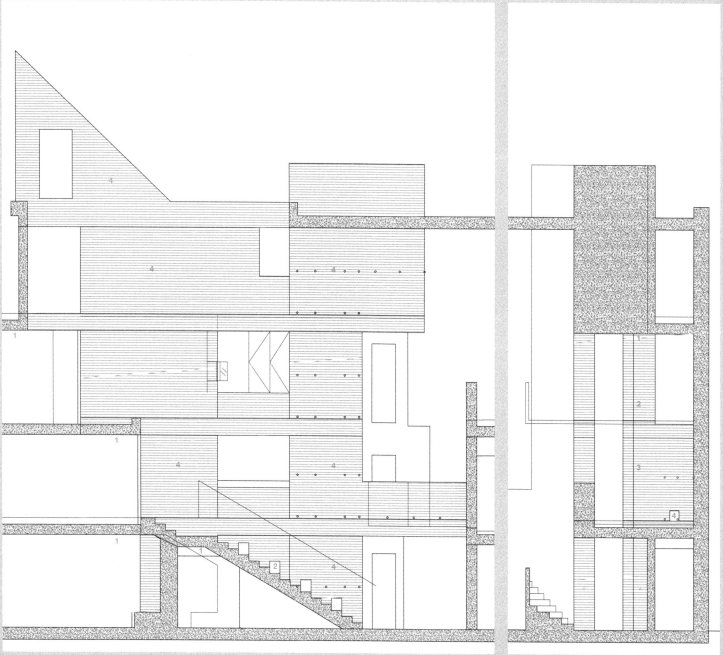

11.08
Stair Section
1:50
  1 45 mm (1 $^{4/5}$ inch) tubular steel handrails on steel brackets fixed to uprights 45 mm (1 $^{4/5}$ inch) from steel plate guard
  2 350 x 20 mm (13 $^{4/5}$ x $^{4/5}$ inch) steel stringers as structural support to stair
  3 High quality board-marked concrete wall
  4 75 x 19 mm (3 x $^{3/4}$ inch) tongued and grooved character oak floorboards with sawn and brushed surface

11.09
Wall Elevation 3
1:100
  1 Lightly sand-blasted fair-faced concrete soffit
  2 High quality board-marked concrete wall to coloured finish
  3 Housing for cast-in light fitting

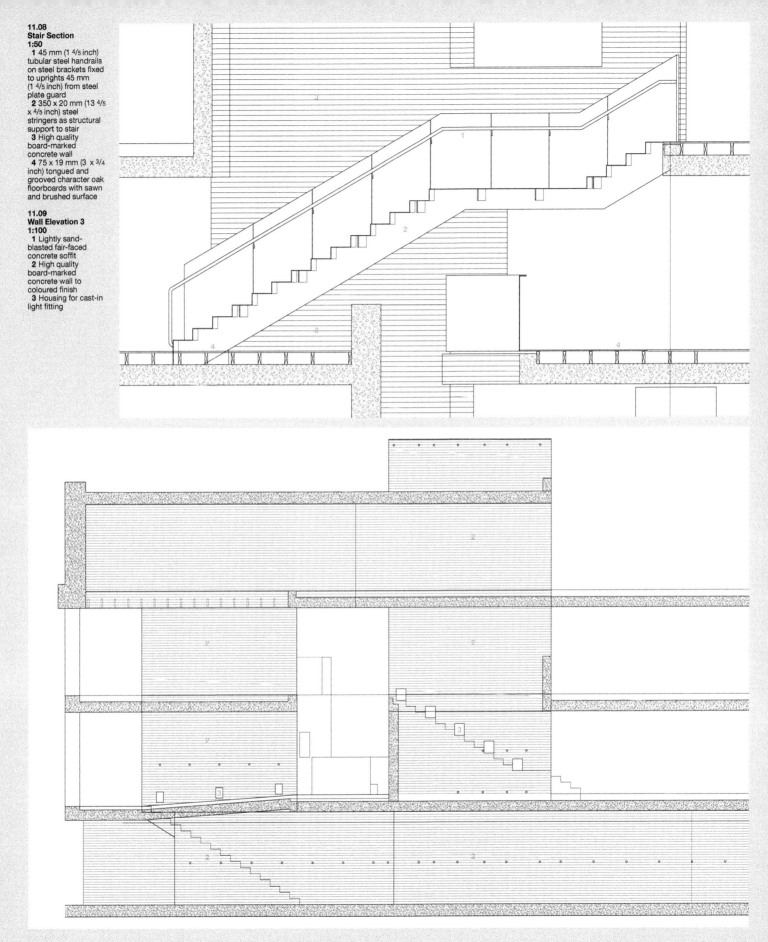

Museum of Polish Aviation
Kraków, Poland

Client
Muzeum Lotnictwa Polskiego

Design Author
Pysall Ruge Architekten with
Bartlomiej Kisielewski

Project Team
Justus Pysall, Peter Ruge, Bartlomiej
Kisielewski, Katarzyna Ratajczak,
Mateusz Rataj, Alicja Kepka-Guerrero

Structural Engineer
Arup International

Main Contractor
Probadex

Located in Kraków, the Museum of
Polish Aviation is one the most
significant collections of historic
aircraft in the world. The museum's
new visitor centre is built on the same
basic 60-metre-square (196-foot-
square) plan as the three existing
hangers; it also adopts the same
12-metre (39-foot) height. Starting
from this form, the new structure was
devised by cutting three wedges into
the cube and then bending the cuts
down to form walls. This creates a
building with three wings. The building
is entered near the centre; from here
the functions of the three spaces are
clearly understood. One wing contains
a 3D cinema and an education space,
another contains the cafe, library and
ticket desk, and the final space is for
the display of the aircraft.

The three wings are formed from a
concrete skin that appears to have
been folded like a giant paper plane.
The open ends of the wings are
glazed, giving views across the
museum grounds. In places the walls
are penetrated by small round
windows. The building pays close
attention to environmental issues. It is
naturally ventilated, and both inside
and outside the materials are left in a
simple, self-finished state, reducing
future maintenance costs.

1 The building sits
lightly on the site in a
manner reminiscent of
the planes within. The
curved lower section
of each wall visually
separates the weight
of the structure from
the ground.
2 From each angle the
building presents a
radically different
silhouette.
3 The thickness of the
walls is expressed by
the circular windows
punched into the
surface.
4 The scale of the
building complements
the exhibits within. The
large glazed areas
allow views of the
open airfield around.
5 The round cinema
volume inside the
main foyer.

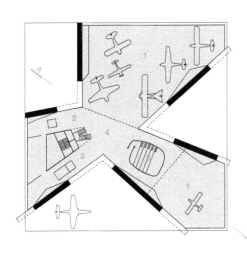
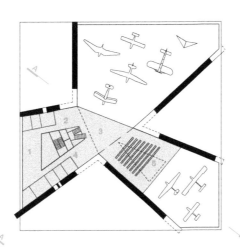
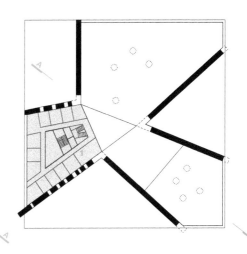

12.01
Ground Floor Plan
1:1000
1 Education display
2 Bookshop
3 Tickets
4 Foyer
5 Cinema

12.02
First Floor Plan
1:1000
1 Library
2 Cafe
3 Foyer
4 Computer area
5 Lecture theatre

12.03
Second Floor Plan
1:1000
1 Offices

12.04
South Elevation
1:500

12.05
East Elevation
1:500

12.06
Section A–A
1:500
1 Exhibition hall
2 Foyer
3 Cinema
4 Exhibition hall
5 Lecture theatre

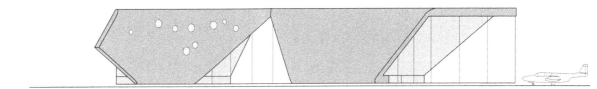

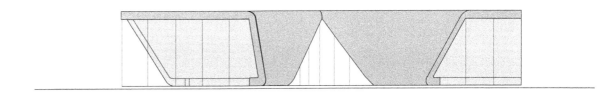

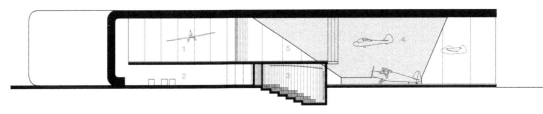

12.07
Sectional Detail of the External Concrete Wall, Exhibition Wing (Ground Floor)
1:20
1 Fair-faced concrete, anthracite pigmented
2 Heating duct
3 Steel grid cover
4 100 mm (3 9/10 inch) reinforced industrial floor, anthracite pigmented, in the exhibition wings, concrete core tempering
5 80 mm (5/16 inch) thermal insulation
6 EPDM sealing
7 280 mm (11 inch) reinforced concrete ceiling

12.08
Sectional Detail of the External Concrete Wall and Glass Facade Connection, Exhibition Wing
1:20
1 400 mm (15 3/4 inch) fair-faced concrete, polished interior wall surface
2 120 mm (4 25/32 inch) thermal insulation
3 1000 mm (39 9/24 inch) substructure in the air space, galvanized steel construction, back-ventilated
4 150 mm (5 9/10 inch) fair-faced concrete, polished exterior wall surface, substructure trapezoidal sheet metal
5 Fair-faced concrete reveal
6 Ceiling-high glazing, laminated glass with PVB foil
7 Facade profile, aluminium, anodized C0

12.09
Sectional Detail of the External Concrete Wall and Roof Connection, Exhibition Wing
1:20
1 400 mm (15 3/4 inch) fair-faced concrete, polished interior wall surface
2 120 mm (4 25/32 inch) thermal insulation
3 1000 mm (39 9/24 inch) substructure in the air space, galvanized steel construction, back-ventilated
4 150 mm (5 9/10 inch) fair-faced concrete, polished exterior wall surface, substructure trapezoidal sheet metal
5 10 mm (2/5 inch) aluminium sheet, anodized C0
6 Pivoting window in offices
7 Roof drainage
8 280 mm (11 inch) fair-faced concrete ceiling
9 Air space with steel frame structure and installations
10 Trapezoidal sheet metal
11 140 mm (1/2 inch) thermal insulation
12 EPDM sealing
13 50 mm (1 31/32 inch) concrete slabs
14 Domed rooflight, triple acrylic glass, diameter: 1500 mm (59 inch)
15 10 mm (2/5 inch) aluminium sheet

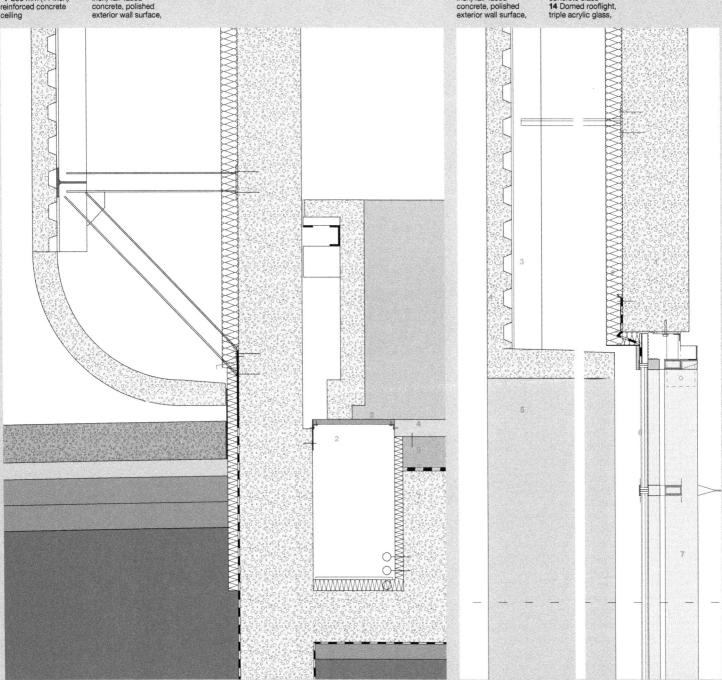

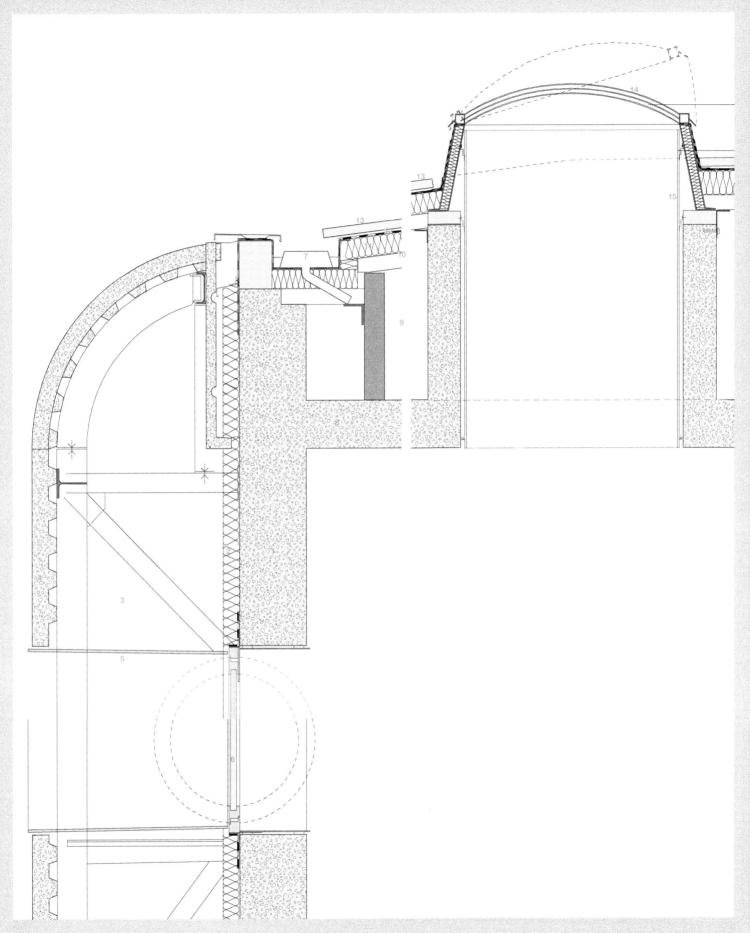

Teshima Art Museum
Teshima, Kagawa, Japan

Client
Naoshima Fukutake Art Museum

Project Team
Ryue Nishizawa, Yusuke Oshi

Structural Engineer
Sasaki Structural Consultants

Main Contractor
Kajima Corporation

Teshima Art Museum stands on a hill overlooking the Inland Sea on the small island of Teshima. The project is a collaborative work between architect Ryue Nishizawa and artist Rei Naito, and is dedicated to housing a single installation, *Matrix*, by the latter. The building's form is inspired by the shape of a drop of water, creating a powerful architectural space that is in harmony with the undulating landscape around it.

The concrete shell is four and a half metres (14 feet 9 inches) high at its apex, and covers a total floor area of 2334 square metres (25,122 square feet) without any columns. The building was cast onto formwork made from a mound of earth. Steel reinforcing rods were carefully positioned after the surfaces had been lined with plaster, then the expansive dry concrete was poured over the top. After the concrete had dried, the earth beneath was removed.

There are two oval-shaped openings in the shell, which allow wind, sound and light to enter the space. On the concrete floor, tiny pinholes are installed from which water 'beads' appear periodically. The droplets slide down the subtly sloped water-repellent floor. Some droplets remain separate; others join together and form bigger drops.

1 The form is a continuation of the landscape, but the pure white surface gives it the magical quality of a field of snow.
2 The route to the entrance is a winding path through trees. The narrow entrance tunnel suggests nothing of the interior.
3 Within the space, the spots of light cast by the oculi edge across the floor as the sun moves across the sky.
4 The scale of the interior is hard to judge without the presence of visitors. As all the surfaces are white, the edges are also difficult to discern.
5 The sky is framed in the oculi, captured as part of the structure.

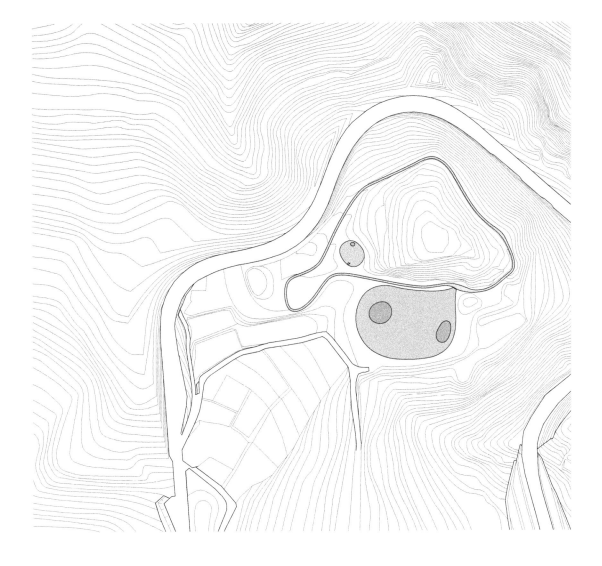

13.02
Plan
1:500
  1 Entrance
  2 Oculus

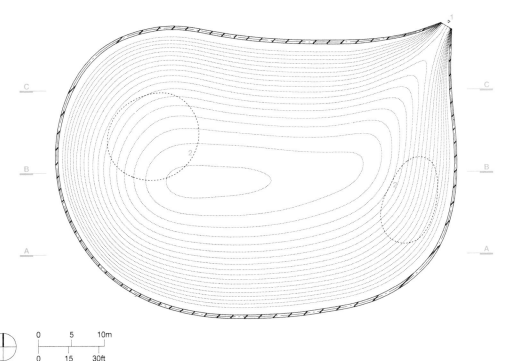

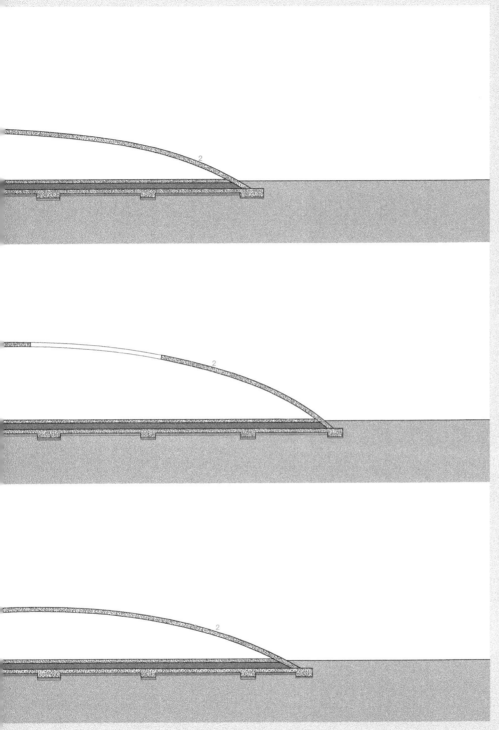

13.03
Section A–A
Section B–B
Section C–C
1:200
1 Concrete
2 Plaster skin

Casa das Histórias Paula Rego
Cascais Portugal

Client
Cascais City Hall

Structural Engineers
AFAconsult

Electrical Engineers
Raul Serafim & Associados

Mechanical Engineers
Paulo Queirós de Faria

This distinctive red building is a museum dedicated to the Portuguese painter Paula Rego. Located in Cascais along the coast from Lisbon, the project was conceived as a part of the city's tourism strategy that seeks to establish a contemporary architectural heritage. The museum is located within an old wood that is surrounded by a wall. Naturally the site contained many beautiful mature trees, and the desire of the architect to preserve as many of them as possible has determined the plan, volume, height and position of the buildings.

The two pyramid-shaped towers, which create a negative shape in the sky between them, are emblemic of the divergent relationship between architecture and nature. This idea of contrast has also inspired the exterior material, a red-coloured concrete that looks almost like terracotta. The walls have been cast against shuttering formed from narrow timber planks, and it is the impressions of these planks that provide the rough and irregular character of the building's surface. This surface is further enhanced by the complementary shadows cast by surrounding trees.

The museum houses a collection of more than one hundred works by Rego. There is also a temporary exhibition space, a two hundred seat auditorium, a library, a shop and a cafe, which opens directly on to the garden.

1 The carefully placed gallery is surrounded by mature trees, their dark trunks silhouetted against the light red walls and roofs.
2 The hard geometry of the building is softened by the rough textured board marking from the formwork. A window cut into the south west corner connects the interior to the exterior.
3 The enclosed internal courtyard that is situated between the gallery spaces.
4 One of the main gallery spaces for the display of the permanent collection.

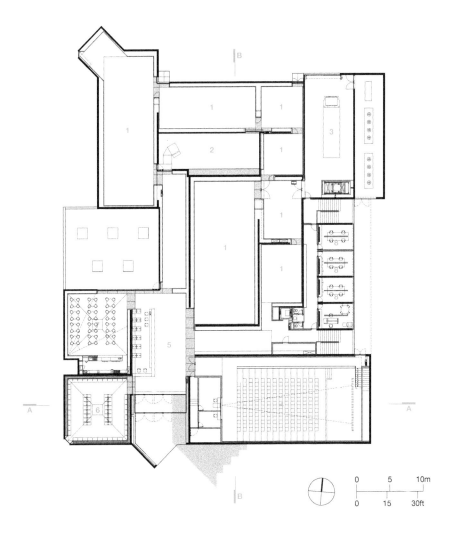

14.01
Ground Floor Plan
1:500
  1 Gallery
  2 Courtyard
  3 Loading bay
  4 Lecture theatre
  5 Entrance
  6 Library
  7 Cafe
  8 Office

0   5   10m
0   15   30ft

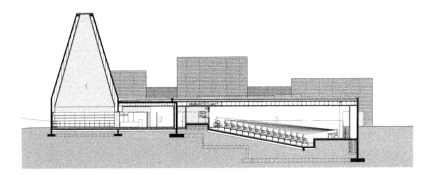

14.02
Section A-A
1:500
  1 Library
  2 Entrance
  3 Lecture theatre

14.03
Section B-B
1:500
  1 Gallery
  2 Lecture theatre
  3 Courtyard

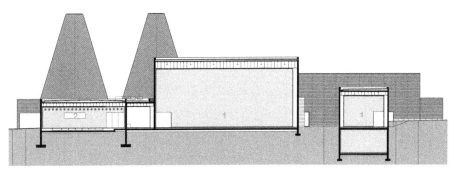

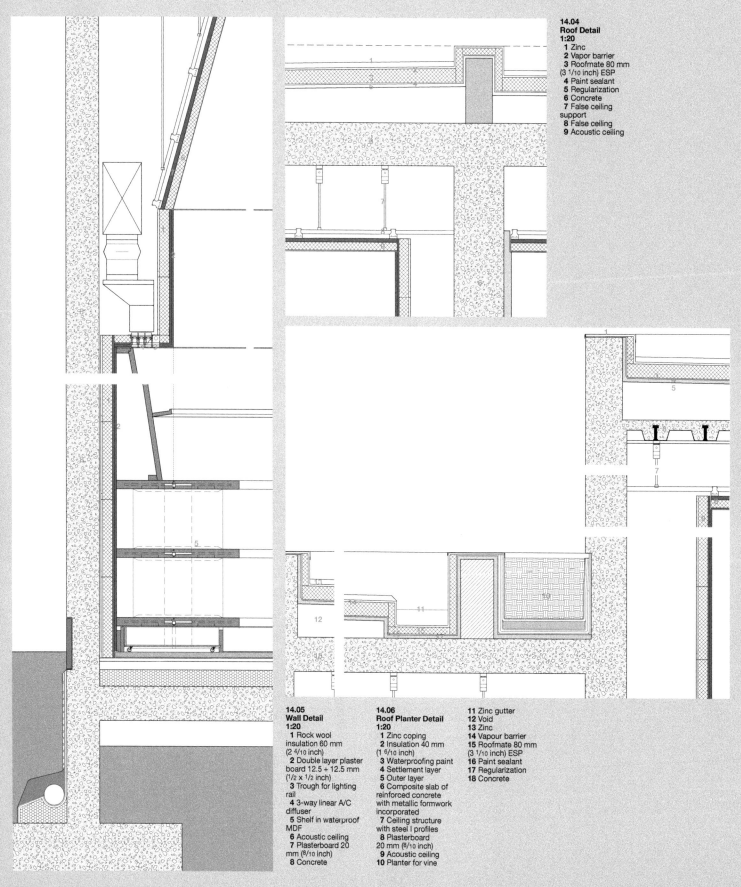

14.04
Roof Detail
1:20
1 Zinc
2 Vapor barrier
3 Roofmate 80 mm
(3 1/10 inch) ESP
4 Paint sealant
5 Regularization
6 Concrete
7 False ceiling
support
8 False ceiling
9 Acoustic ceiling

14.05
Wall Detail
1:20
1 Rock wool
insulation 60 mm
(2 4/10 inch)
2 Double layer plaster
board 12.5 + 12.5 mm
(1/2 x 1/2 inch)
3 Trough for lighting
rail
4 3-way linear A/C
diffuser
5 Shelf in waterproof
MDF
6 Acoustic ceiling
7 Plasterboard 20
mm (8/10 inch)
8 Concrete

14.06
Roof Planter Detail
1:20
1 Zinc coping
2 Insulation 40 mm
(1 6/10 inch)
3 Waterproofing paint
4 Settlement layer
5 Outer layer
6 Composite slab of
reinforced concrete
with metallic formwork
incorporated
7 Ceiling structure
with steel I profiles
8 Plasterboard
20 mm (8/10 inch)
9 Acoustic ceiling
10 Planter for vine

11 Zinc gutter
12 Void
13 Zinc
14 Vapour barrier
15 Roofmate 80 mm
(3 1/10 inch) ESP
16 Paint sealant
17 Regularization
18 Concrete

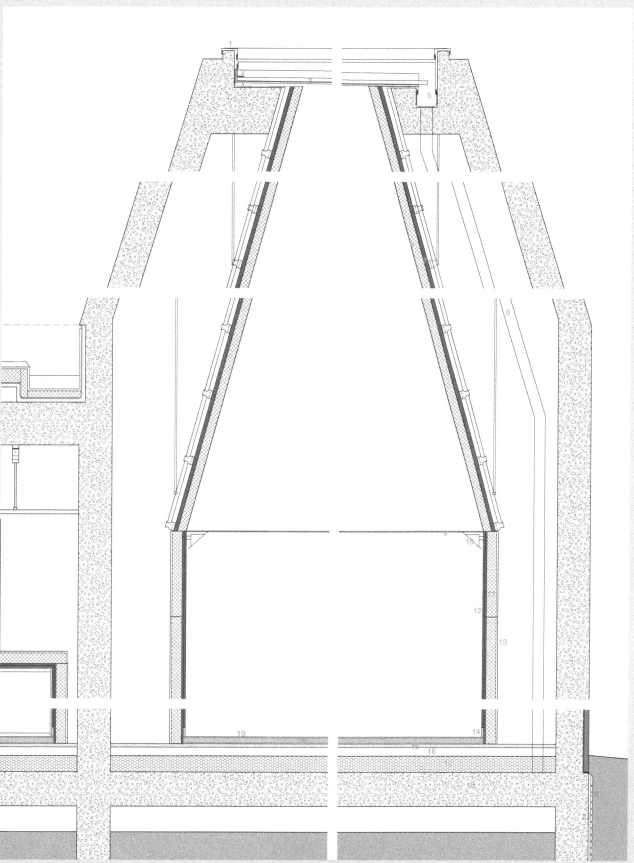

1 Zinc coping
2 Stainless steel bracket 40 x 40 mm (1 $^4/_{10}$ x 1 $^4/_{10}$ inch) ESP
3 HS glass 6 + 6 + 6 + 3 mm ($^2/_{10}$ + $^2/_{10}$ + $^2/_{10}$ + $^1/_{10}$ inch)
4 Stainless steel profile T with 80 x 80 mm (3 $^1/_{10}$ x 3 $^1/_{10}$ inch)
5 Zinc gutter
6 Acoustic ceiling
7 Plasterboard 20 mm ($^8/_{10}$ inch)
8 Drain pipe
9 ESP 5 mm ($^2/_{10}$ inch) vane
10 Lighting
11 Rock wool insulation 60 mm (2 $^4/_{10}$ inch)
12 Double-layer plasterboard 12.5 + 12.5 mm ($^1/_2$ x $^1/_2$ inch)
13 Galvanized steel profiles for attaching drywall
14 White marble skirting board
15 Bedding mortar
16 Screed
17 Filling in lightweight concrete
18 Concrete
19 Vane 5 mm ($^2/_{10}$ inch)
20 Marble
21 Mortar
22 Drainage panel

Grand Rapids Art Museum
Grand Rapids, Michigan, USA

Client
Grand Rapids Art Museum

Project Team
Kulapat Yantrasast (Partner), Yo-ichiro Hakomori (Partner), Aaron Loewenson (Project Architect), Megan Lin, Jenny Wu

Structural Engineer
Dewhurst Macfarlane and Partners

Main Contractor
Rockford / Pepper Construction

The new Grand Rapids Art Museum occupies a single city block in the centre of Grand Rapids. Its iconic role as a symbol of the city and of civic pride is tempered by the humanistic engagement with art that it affords its visitors.

A large canopy projects out, offering shelter while also capturing views of the city. The entrance facade extends in three sections into the park beyond, seeking to attract and capture visitors into a welcoming embrace. These projecting sections house a museum cafe and other areas with which the public can engage without necessarily visiting the museum's galleries.

Behind the glass and translucent screens of the facade, the galleries are housed in a three-level tower. At the top of this tower are skylights, which allow filtered natural light to penetrate down into the galleries. At night these skylights become likw beacons, expressing the museum's cultural activities across the city.

The Grand Rapids Art Museum has as one of its central design philosophies the conservation of energy. Natural light has therefore been used wherever possible throughout the structure. This and other energy conservation strategies have lead to the building obtaining LEED (Leadership in Energy and Environmental Design) certification.

1 At the museum entrance, a massive canopy protrudes into the city. Above, the brightly illuminated tower proclaims the cultural intentions of the building across the night sky.
2 At the side, the monumental scale of the museum is broken down to address the urban grain of the surrounding streets.
3 Around the building, social spaces have been designed to encourage interaction and multiple uses.
4 The galleries focus on providing flexible space to display artworks. In all areas extensive use is made of natural light.

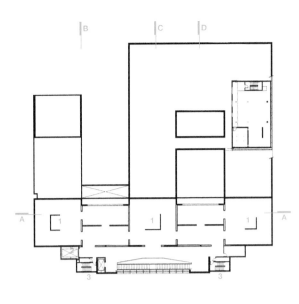

15.01
Second Floor Plan
1:1000
  1 Gallery
  2 Lift
  3 Stair

15.02
First Floor Plan
1:1000
  1 Gallery
  2 Library

15.03
Ground Floor Plan
1:1000
  1 Lobby
  2 Auditorium
  3 Gallery
  4 Museum shop
  5 Cafe
  6 Dining court
  7 Offices
  8 Sculpture court
  9 Reflecting pool

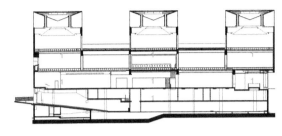

15.04
Lantern Section A–A
1:1000
  1 Gallery
  2 Auditorium

15.05
Reflecting Pool
Section B-B
1:1000
  1 Gallery

15.06
Lobby Section C-C
1:1000
  1 Gallery
  2 Lobby

15.07
Canopy Section D-D
1:1000
  1 Gallery
  2 Lobby
  3 Sculpture court

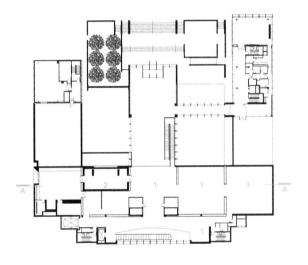

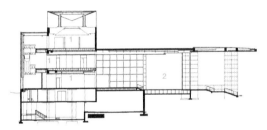

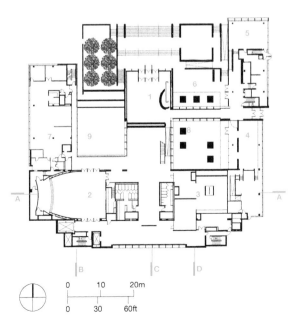

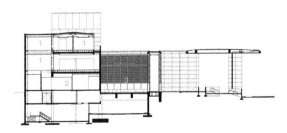

0 10 20m
0 30 60ft

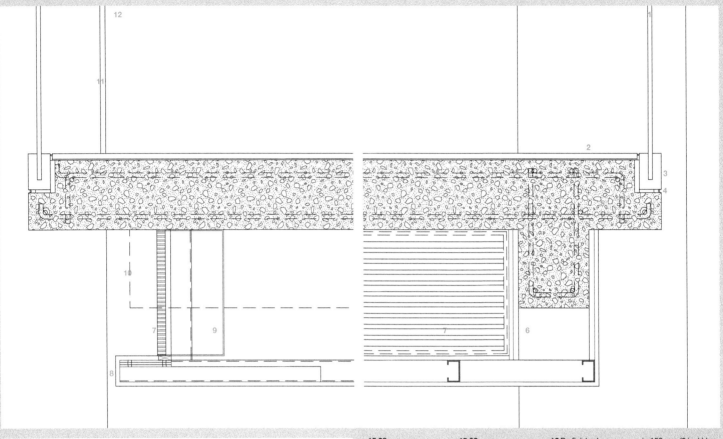

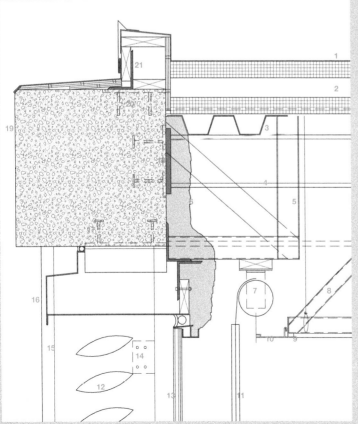

15.08
Balcony Detail
1:10
1 13 mm (1/2 inch) tempered glass guard rail
2 10 mm (3/8 inch) wood flooring directly adhered to 203 mm (8 inch) concrete structural floor slab
3 1010 mm (40 inch) wide aluminium guard rail shoe. Clear anodized aluminium brake. Metal cover sheet over
4 Sealant
5 Reinforced concrete slab and beam
6 Return gypsum board c.178 mm (c.7 inch) in at side returns at concrete beam
7 Mechanical grille and frame
8 Firr-out beam with 16 mm (5/8 inch) gypsum board over to align with face of gypsum-board wall finish beyond finish
9 Mechanical duct behind grille
10 Outline of cast-in-place concrete beam at south end of balcony, to align with masonry wall.
11 13 mm (1/2 inch) gap for glass and cap rail
12 Face of wall beyond

15.09
Concrete Roof /
Curtain Wall Detail
1:20
1 Single-ply membrane over insulation
2 Two layers of 64 mm (2 1/2 inch) polyisocyanurate, with tapered expanded polystyrene insulations sandwiched between layers
3 76 mm (3 inch) steel roof deck
4 Steel roof beams at column locations with steel plates at ends
5 Framing at 406 mm (16 inch) on centre, bracing at 1220 mm (48 inch) on centre
6 51 mm (2 inch) 2# density polyurethane spray foam, with 25 mm (1 inch) cover coat over for exposed application
7 Motorized sunshade
8 Suspended glass-fibre reinforced-concrete panel ceiling system. Brace suspension system to structure above
9 Permanent shade pocket edge moulding secured to edge of suspension system
10 127 mm (5 inch) removable closure cover strip
11 152 mm (6 inch) wide prefinished aluminium enclosure over sunshade ends at vertical mullion locations

12 Prefinished aluminium sun shades
13 33 mm (1 5/16 inch) insulated glass in prefinished aluminium curtain wall system
14 Outline of connector between steel tube column and curtain wall mullion
15 406 x 102 x 2840 mm (16 x 4 x 112 inch) steel tube columns secured at bottom of concrete beam above with steel L angles: 102 x 102 x 8080 mm (4 x 4 x 318 inch), one each side of column. L-angles welded to weld plate and to side wall of column
16 3 mm (1/8 inch) prefinished formed aluminium fascia panel. Closure at curtain wall
17 Embedded steel weld plate cast into bottom of concrete beams at centreline of tube column locations
18 Steel plate embedded in back side of concrete fascia beam. Plates located at centreline of roof beams
19 Concrete fascia beam
20 254 mm (10 inch) square embedded steel weld plates at 1200 mm (48 inch) maximum on centre
21 Continuous steel L: 152 x 102 x 8 mm (6 x 4 x 5/16 inch). Welded to weld plates in beam. Holes provided

in 152 mm (6 inch) leg at 813 mm (32 inch) on centre for 6 mm (1/4 inch) diameter bolts used for blocking attachment

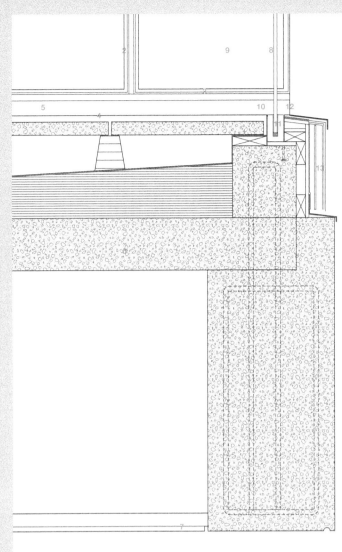

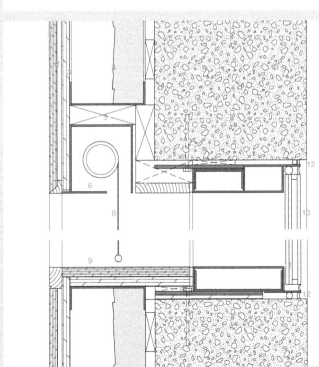

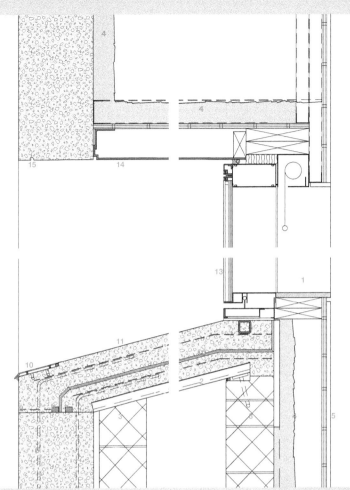

**15.10
Exterior Concrete Guard Rail Detail
1:20**

1 Roof flashing membrane over blocking and extended up aluminium shoe moulding. Concrete pavers on protective pad over flashing
2 Butt glazed aluminium curtain wall mullion
3 Base assembly components of prefinished aluminium curtain wall system
4 610 mm square x 51 mm thick (24 inch square x 2 inch thick) concrete pavers on pedestal system
5 83 x 241 mm (3 1/4 x 9 1/2 inch) recess in top of concrete wall along column
6 Reinforced concrete slab and beams
7 Suspended glass fibre reinforced concrete soffit panel
8 13 mm (1/2 inch) tempered glass guard rail system
9 25 mm (1 inch) insulated spandrel glass in corner panel
10 Prefinished aluminium flashing strip on 'terrace' side of rail system
11 105 x 64 mm (4 1/8 x 2 1/2 inch) aluminium shoe moulding screwed down at 305 mm (12 inch) on centre to 114 x 16 mm (4 1/2 x 5/8 inch) galvanized steel plate anchor

plate into concrete sill beam with 13 x 105 mm (1/2 x 4 1/8 inch) headed stud at 305 mm (12 inch) on centre
12 Ends of flashing fitted into top inside grooves in vertical legs of alum. shoe moulding
13 Prefinished alum. composite panel system. Prefinished alum. sills above and below, with back frames, trims, etc.

**15.11
Concrete Punched Opening Detail
1:10**

1 10 mm (5/8 inch) white oak timber veneer
2 10 mm (5/8 inch) fire-treated plywood backer
3 152 x 508 mm (6 x 20 inch) galvanized steel studs at 406 mm (16 inch) on centre. Stud framing secured to 19 mm (3/4 inch) furring system
4 64 x 51mm (2 1/2 x 2 inch) two-component spray foam polyurethane insulation applied to exterior concrete wall
5 38 mm (1 1/2 inch) treated, non-combustible wood blocking, secured to concrete wall and to bottom track of 152 mm (6 inch) stud system
6 Recessed enclosure box for sun shade unit
7 White oak trims,

head and jamb
8 6 mm (1/4 inch) reveal created between materials
9 White oak veneer and hardwood trim
10 Reinforced concrete exterior wall
11 Prefinished aluminium sections and mounting
12 Continuous backer rod and sealant
13 33 mm (1 5/16 inch) insulated glass panel in prefinished alum. curtain-wall system

**15.12
Window Head and Sill Detail
1:20**

1 19 mm (3/4 inch) ACX plywood window sill with plastic laminate top surface and back edge
2 38 x 762 mm (1 1/2 x 30 inch) galvanized floor deck
3 203 mm (8 inch) masonry block walls
4 64 mm (2 1/2 inch) spray foam insulation
5 16 mm (5/8 inch) gypsum board over 16 mm (5/8 inch) non-combustible plywood on 92 mm (3 5/8 inch) steel studs at 406 mm (16 inch) on centre
6 Reinforced concrete exterior wall
7 Bentonite water plug strip
8 Layered drainage course strips over back of weep strip
9 Weep strip (CVS010

by Masonry Tech. Inc.)
10 Stainless-steel drip sill
11 105 mm (4 1/8 inch) concrete sill
12 Fluid-applied (or single sheet) waterproofing system with watercourse drainage layer over
13 41 mm (1 5/8 inch) insulated glass in curtain wall framing with four-sided butt glazing
14 Glass fibre reinforced concrete panel soffit
15 Continuous drip reveal

MUMUTH – Haus für Musik und Musiktheater, Graz, Austria

Client
University of Music and Performing Arts Graz (KUG)

Structural Engineers
Arup, Cecil Balmond, Volker Schmid, Charles Walker, Francis Archer

Ben van Berkel, the architect of this concert hall constructed for the University of Music and Performing Arts Graz, has said that it was his desire to make a building that was as much about music as possible. His original concept – of a building in the form of a spring that expresses the forces and tensions of music – remains in the finished structure.

Within the free-flowing space of the foyer is a giant spiralling constructive element that connects the entrance to the auditorium and music rooms above. Around this structure all the other elements revolve. Light from the skylights above is filtered through dark wood lamellae to further accentuate the drama of the forms. The seemingly liquid spiral is a massive concrete construction. A technical *tour de force*, it required very high precision in its construction. To achieve the finishes desired, self-compacting concrete was pumped up from below into the formwork instead of being poured from above, as is the usual method.

The foyer leads to a multipurpose auditorium, which can seat up to 6500 people. This space can adapt its form and acoustics for many different types of performance, from solo instruments or dance to a full orchestra.

Throughout the building a repetitive pattern is applied in a variety of ways to the facades. This creates both a rhythmic flowing movement that echoes the structures found in music and a varied acoustic surface. The outer layer of the facade is a gossamer mesh of steel.

1 The translucent bowed mesh facade creates a barrier between the street and the interior that is both fragile and resilient.
2 The ribbon-like internal forms that wrap around the performance space are expressions of musical movement.
3 The spiral stair that connects the second and third floors: the rich red and the reflective steel evoke the spectacle and atmosphere of performance.
4 The carefully designed lighting and glazing details suggest movement in every surface. The moiré effect of the outer mesh further enhances the spacial fluidity.

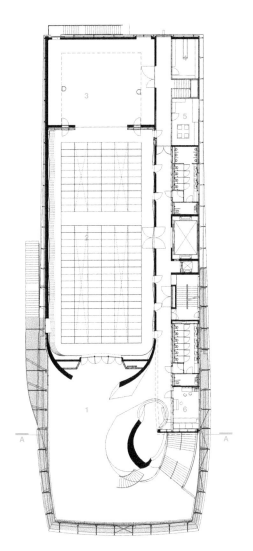

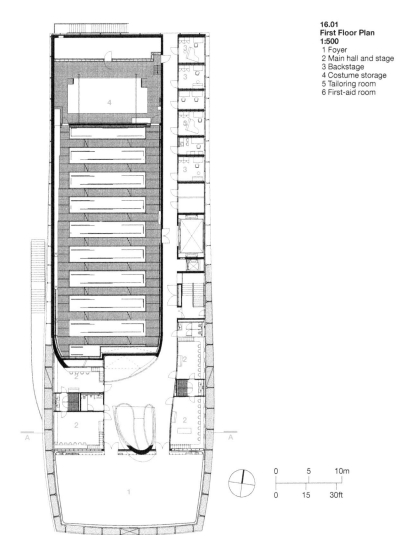

16.01
First Floor Plan
1:500
1 Foyer
2 Main hall and stage
3 Backstage
4 Costume storage
5 Tailoring room
6 First-aid room

16.02
Second Floor Plan
1:500
1 Rehearsal room for
  theatre
2 Dressing room
3 Dressing room
4 Professors' rooms
5 Backstage gallery
6 Fly gallery

0   5   10m
0   15   30ft

16.03
Section A–A
1:200
1 Foyer
2 Dressing room
3 Stair

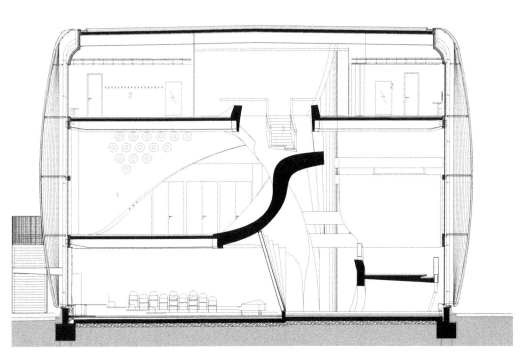

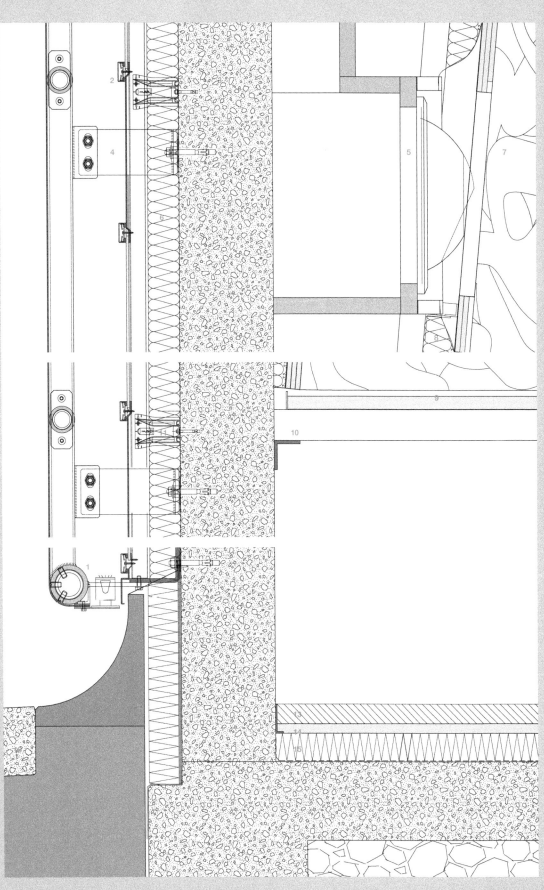

16.04
Sectional Wall Detail
1:10
1 121 mm (4 3/4 inch)
diameter inserted
round galvanized rod
suspended by eye
bolts at top, middle
and base fixations
2 Ventilated facade
panel consisting of
powder-coated metal
plate and 100 mm (3/8
inch) mineral wool
3 Concrete wall
4 Steel structure
fixing mesh facade to
the concrete wall
5 Ventilation system,
34 swivel jet nozzles
6 100 mm (3/8 inch)
vertical facade
insulation
7 Acoustical wall
composed of 1 x 2
metre (36 1/4 x 78 3/4
inch) concave and
convex acoustical
panels bent in one
direction with an arch
rise of 11 mm (7/16
inch) each. 3 concave
panels added to 3
convex panels result in
a c.6 metre (c.236
inch) waved wall with
200 mm (7 7/8 inch)
deepness (amplitude).
One panel is built out
of three bonded layers;
each 16 mm (5/8 inch)
flame resistant MDF
8 Mineral rock wool
fixed, disjoined by a
non-combustible
acoustic mat
9 Movable platform,
stage floor of three
wooden layers, with
topping of Oregon pine
10 Subconstruction of
stage floor
11 Facade fixture
12 Precast concrete
segment bedded in
concrete
13 60 mm (2 13/36 inch)
screed, resin-coated
PE foil
14 30 mm (1 3/16 inch)
TDPS 35 / 30 mm (1
3/8 / 1 3/16 inch) impact
sound insulation
15 80 mm (3 3/20 inch)
foam insulation,
moisture barrier
16 In-situ concrete
finished by brush
stroke

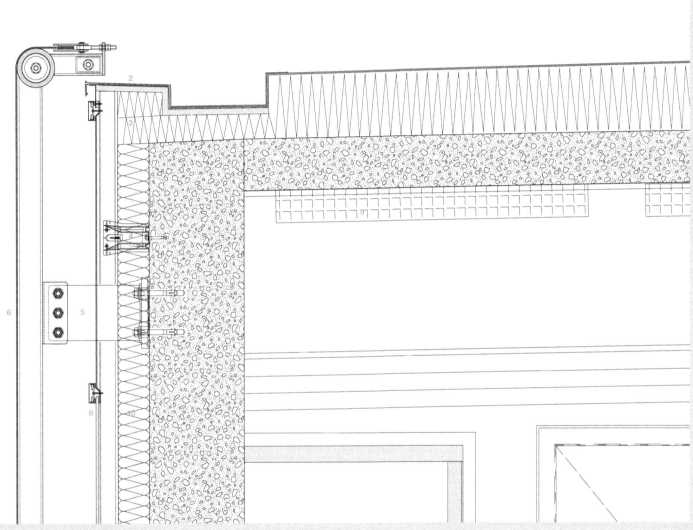

16.05
Sectional Wall Roof Detail
1:10

1 121 mm (4 ³/4 inch) diameter inserted round galvanized rod, suspended by eye bolts at top, middle and base fixations
2 Roof parapet with hidden rain drain
3 Horizontal roof insulation with slope
4 Facade fixture
5 Steel structure fixing mesh facade to the concrete wall

6 Mesh facade, stainless steel net type OMEGA 1520 with roles / screws hidden in cover strip
7 Concrete wall
8 Ventilated facade panel consisting of powder-coated metal plate and 100 mm (³/8 inch) mineral wool
9 Acoustical broadband compact absorber laid out along the edges of the hall
10 Vertical facade insulation

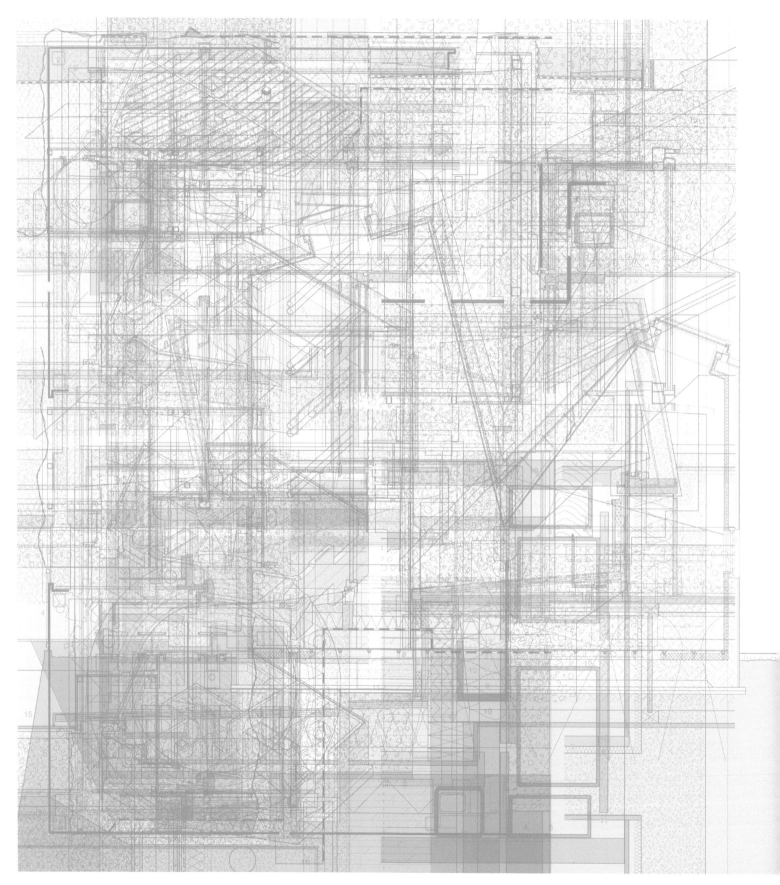

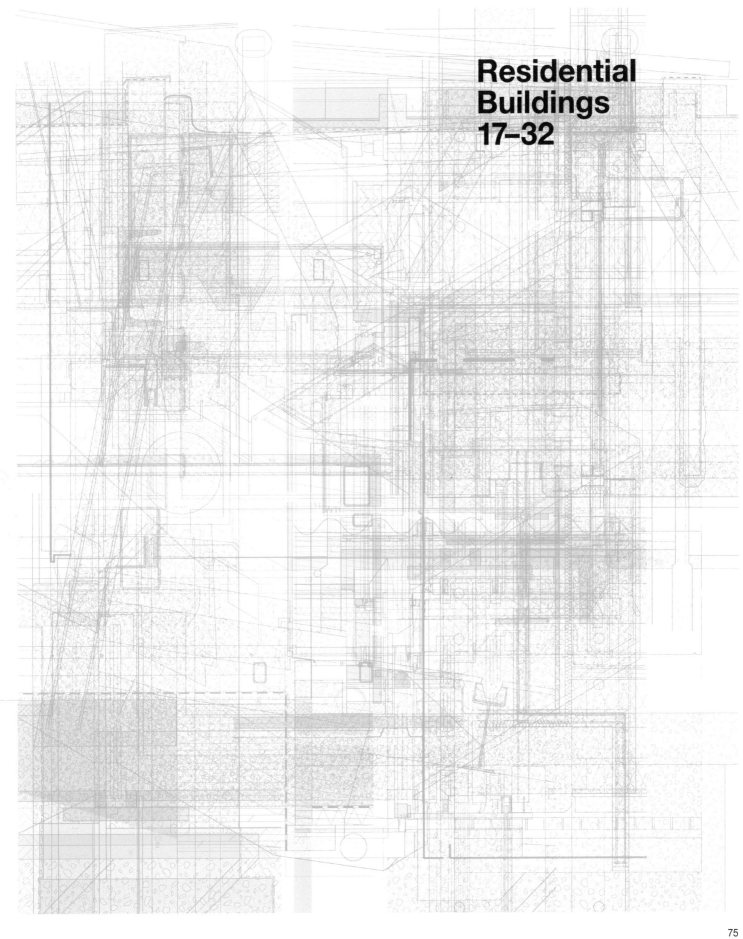

Residential
Buildings
17–32

Fichtelberg Mountain Hut
Saxony, Germany

Client
Private client

Architects
AFF Architeckten (Martin Fröhlich,
Sven Fröhlich)

Project Team
Sven Fröhlich (lead architect and
construction management), Ulrike Dix,
Torsten Lockl, Thomas Weisheit

Structural Engineer
Ingenieurbüro BauArt, Peter Klaus

This utilitarian mountain refuge is high up on Fichtelberg, a mountain in Saxony, replacing an earlier hut that stood on the site. The architects say that it grew out of a desire to return to a more basic way of life, to make a connection with the elemental forces that used to shape our lives but now do not. Protruding from the mountain like a boulder, this is a building that gives the appearance of having been pulled out of the ground.

The interior is a raw shelter. There are no comforts here – only the essentials for sheltering in the mountains are provided. The walls and ceilings are formed from concrete, presented without any further finish. Within the building, the new walls have been cast against the walls of the previous structure. They display the indentations and patterns of the timber structures they have replaced like an impression left by a boot in the snow. This record of the past as an ephemeral mould is evocative in this place of temporary residence. The floorboards are made of locally felled spruce, and other fittings are recycled.

The simple spaces, with their basic domestic forms, suggest a special type of habitation. This shelter, built in the harsh environment of the mountain, recalls the old typology of the hut in a vibrant new form. It teaches us what it means to build and live in a simple way.

1 The stark white front facade of the hut emerges from the ground as if it were a part of nature. Framed against the forest, it is both severe and welcoming.
2 The interiors of the two sleeping areas are raw, and the folded geometry of the rock-like roofs is reflected on the ceiling.
3 The dining area, furnished with recycled chairs and a table fabricated from reclaimed wood, provides a space for those staying at the hut to socialize. The walls bear impressions of the original hut.
4 At the rear of the hut, a line of windows gives views to the garden and to the forest beyond.

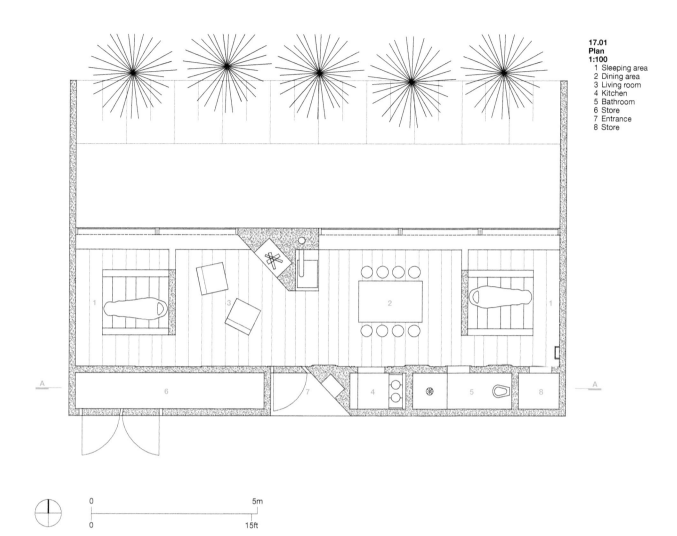

17.01
Plan
1:100
1 Sleeping area
2 Dining area
3 Living room
4 Kitchen
5 Bathroom
6 Store
7 Entrance
8 Store

0   5m

0   15ft

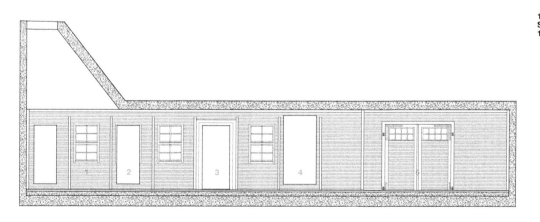

17.02
Section A–A
1:100
1 Store
2 Bathroom
3 Kitchen
4 Entrance
5 Store

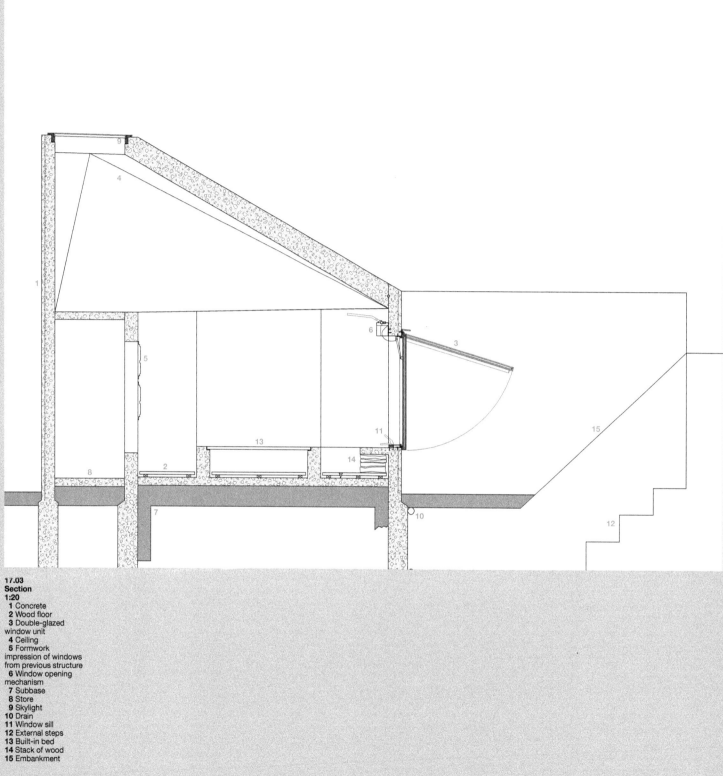

17.03
Section
1:20
 1 Concrete
 2 Wood floor
 3 Double-glazed
window unit
 4 Ceiling
 5 Formwork
impression of windows
from previous structure
 6 Window opening
mechanism
 7 Subbase
 8 Store
 9 Skylight
10 Drain
11 Window sill
12 External steps
13 Built-in bed
14 Stack of wood
15 Embankment

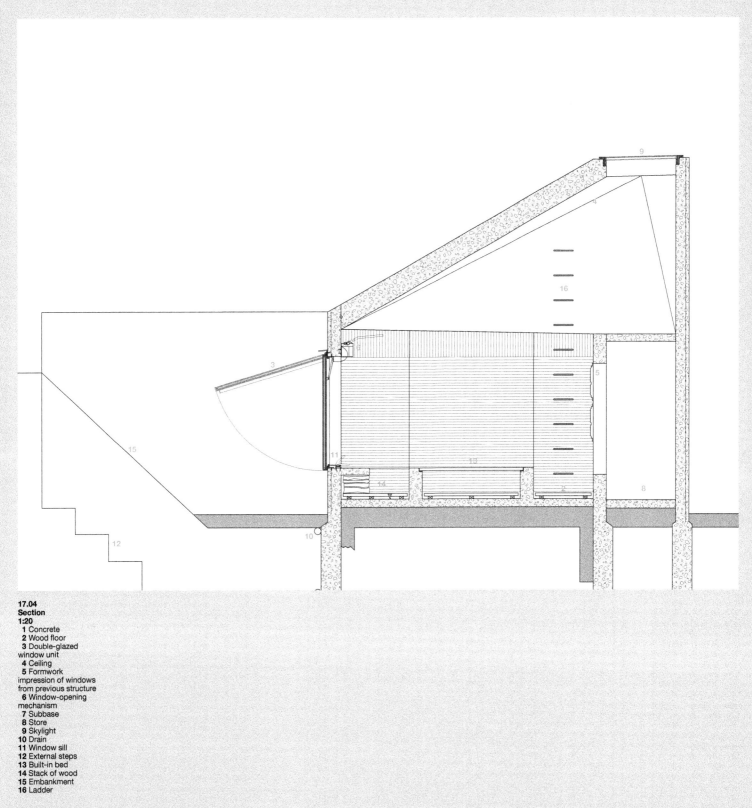

17.04
Section
1:20
1 Concrete
2 Wood floor
3 Double-glazed
window unit
4 Ceiling
5 Formwork
impression of windows
from previous structure
6 Window-opening
mechanism
7 Subbase
8 Store
9 Skylight
10 Drain
11 Window sill
12 External steps
13 Built-in bed
14 Stack of wood
15 Embankment
16 Ladder

Casa de Hormigón
Mar Azul, Buenos Aires, Argentina

Client
María Victoria Besonías, Guillermo de Almeida

Project Team
María Victoria Besonías, Guillermo de Almeida, Luciano Kruk

Structural Engineer
Luciano Kruk

Positioned on a densely wooded, sloping site near to the sea, this single-storey house was designed to make a minimal impact on the environment. The small budget and the desire to build a structure that required little subsequent maintenance also informed the plans.

The form of the building is an elongated box, the rear wall of which is folded into a prismatic groove. Rooted on a small plateau, the land slopes away under the house, giving it the appearance of a rock formation. One corner of the box is buried into the hill, and the opposite one projects out above the ground.

The external and internal walls carry strong horizontal board marks that suggest geological strata. Principally used as summer house, its solid concrete construction ensures a stable internal environment. The roof has a deep covering of pine needles, which is constantly replenished by the surrounding trees.

Across the front of the house a rhythmic pattern of short walls, set at right angles to the facade, mimics the trunks of the surrounding trees. Behind these walls, the glass reflects both the real forest and these concrete reproductions. A small terrace constructed from finished wood boards connects the forest with the house through its scale and material.

1 The house is located in a dense wooded landscape; it echoes the random cadence of the tree trunks with its pattern of vertical concrete walls.
2 A linear glass wall runs the length of the house behind the concrete mullions.
3 Emerging from the site, and in close proximity to mature trees, the concrete walls give an impression of solidity and permanence.
4 The interior walls have the same rough board-marked finish as the exterior. Simple timber furniture echoes both the formwork and the trees that surround the house.
5 The folded wall suggests an object extruded from the ground by the forces of nature.

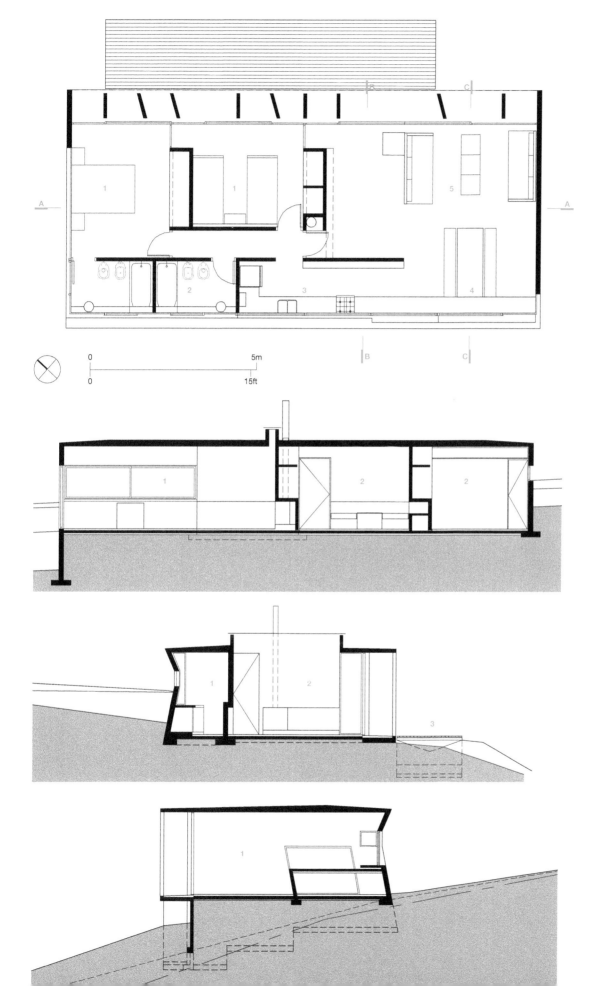

18.01
Plan
1:100
  1 Bedroom
  2 Bathroom
  3 Kitchen
  4 Dining area
  5 Living area

18.02
Section A–A
1:100
  1 Kitchen
  2 Bedroom

18.03
Section B–B
1:100
  1 Kitchen
  2 Dining area
  3 Terrace

18.04
Section C–C
1:100
  1 Living area

0   5m
0   15ft

81

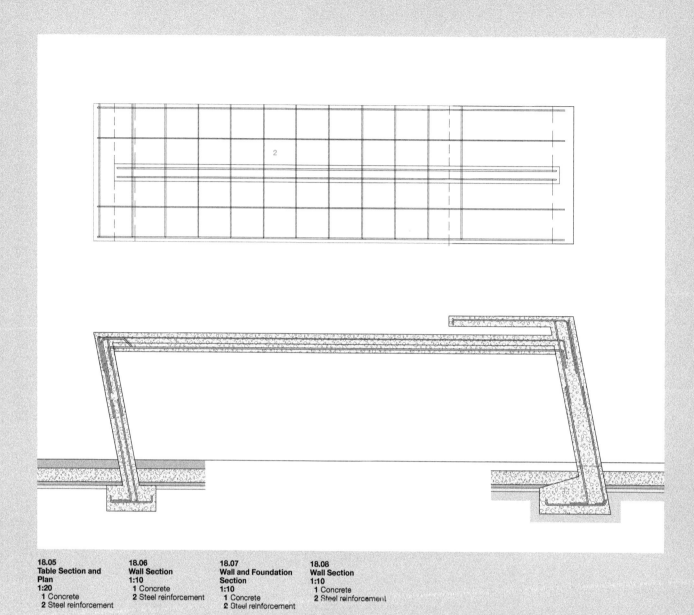

18.05
Table Section and Plan
1:20
  1 Concrete
  2 Steel reinforcement

18.06
Wall Section
1:10
  1 Concrete
  2 Steel reinforcement

18.07
Wall and Foundation Section
1:10
  1 Concrete
  2 Steel reinforcement

18.08
Wall Section
1:10
  1 Concrete
  2 Steel reinforcement

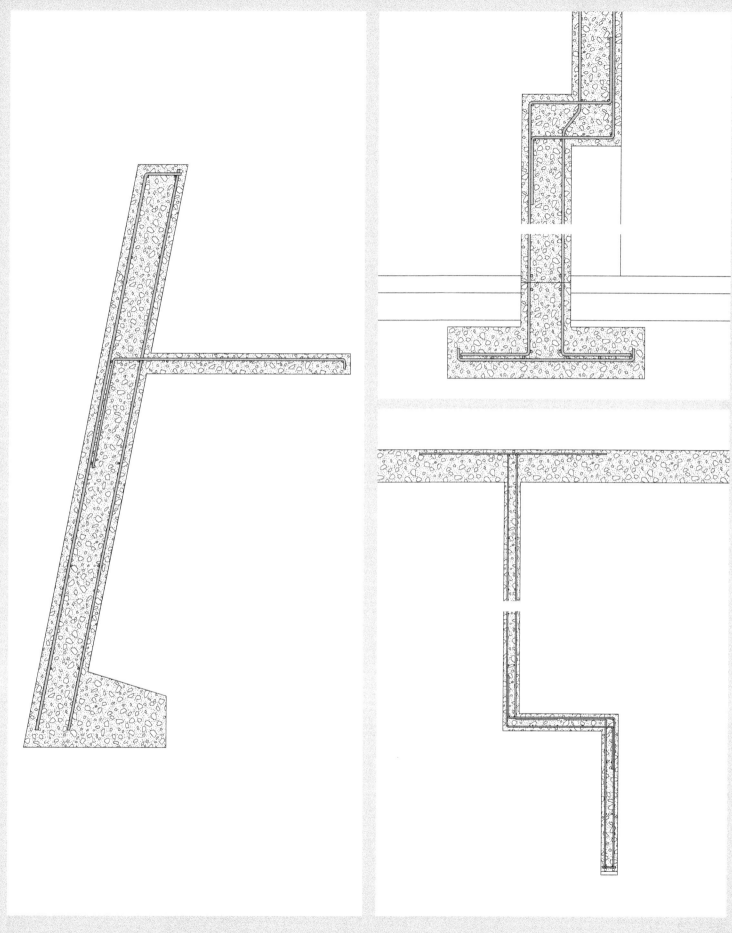

102 Dwellings in Carabanchel
Madrid, Spain

Client
EMVS (Empresa Municipal de la
Vivienda y Suelo de Madrid)

Project Team
Ignacio Borrego, Néstor Montenegro
and Lina Toro (Dosmasuno
Arquitectos)

Structural Engineer
José Luis de Míguel

Consulting Engineers
GRUPO JG

Main Contractor
BEGAR

This project has been built using
industrialized technology similar to
that used in automobile production. It
introduces an important innovation
into the construction process by
fabricating the formwork from
aluminium. This makes the individual
formwork parts much lighter and
enables workers to safely manipulate
them without additional cranes.

This Project for 102 apartments in
Carabanchel consists of 52 one-
bedroom dwellings, 35 two-bedroom
dwellings and 15 three-bedroom
dwellings. Each apartment is based
on a single concrete cast unit. Using
the precision aluminium formwork
over and over again, the common
one-bedroom type of apartment can
be constructed very rapidly. The unit is
cast to include all the facades, the
dividing walls, partitions and even
wardrobes. It also incorporates
thermal insulation and all the services.

The one-bedroom unit can be
extended with the addition of light
steel cantilevered bedroom parts to
make the two- and three-bed
apartments. The building uses two
types of walls throughout; external
walls that are 240 mm (9 1/2 inches
thick made up of 100 mm (4 inches) of
concrete either side of an insulation
core, and 100 mm (4 inch) solid
internal walls. All of these walls are
structural. The building is constructed
sequentially from the first unit to the
last, each unit built off the previous.
The system allows for the construction
of a single unit in one day.

1 The apartments are
arranged in two blocks
set at right angles.
Cantilevered additional
accommodation units
are applied to the
basic unit.
2 The extra bedroom
spaces push out from
the building to create a
highly articulated
cuboid surface.
3 Connecting
walkways link the
apartments to the
service cores. The
bright monochrome
palette applied to all
the surfaces ensures
that the structure's
sharp forms are
emphasized in the
strong sunlight.
4 Light is modulated
on the south east
facade through the use
of metallic screens.

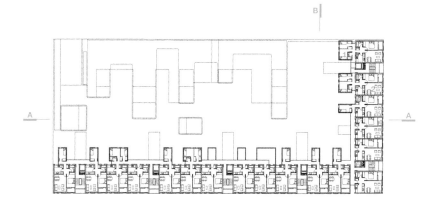

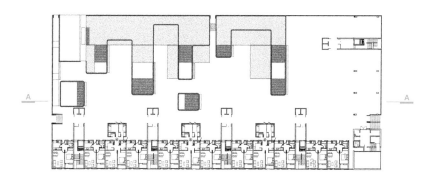

0.01
2nd Floor Plan
1:1000
  1 Bedroom
  2 Living room
  3 Bathroom
  4 Balcony
  5 Stair
  6 Lift

0.02
Ground Floor Plan
1:1000
  1 Bedroom
  2 Living room
  3 Bathroom
  4 Stair
  5 Lift

0.03
Basement Floor Plan
1:1000
  1 Store
  2 Parking
  3 Stair
  4 Lift

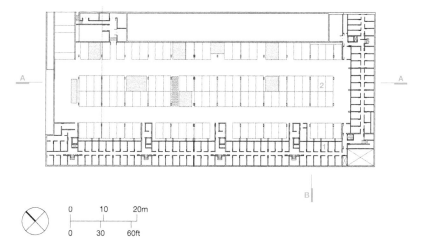

0.04
Section B–B
1:500

0.05
Section A–A
1:500

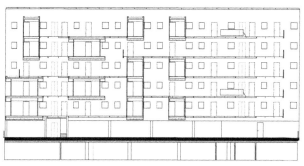

85

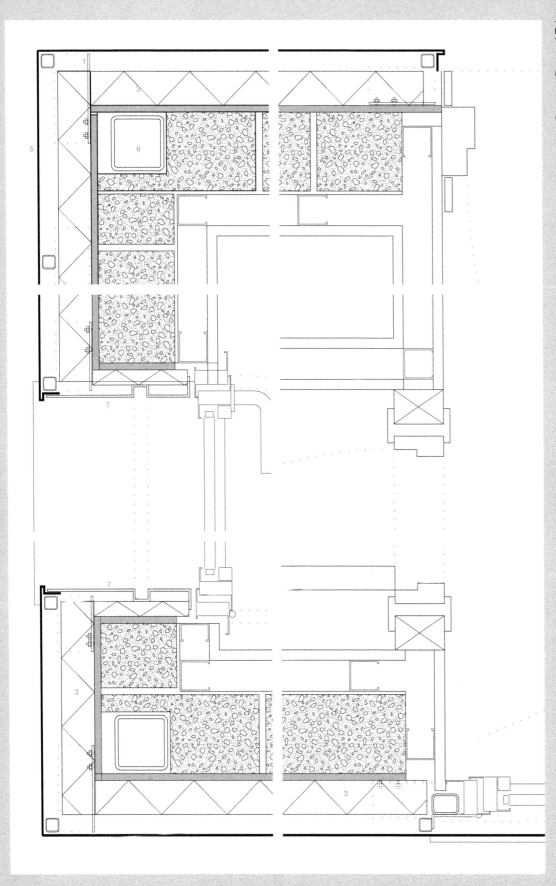

19.06
Modular Room Plan
1:5
 1 Galvanized steel
 2 Concrete block
 3 Glass wool
insulation
 4 Plasterboard
 5 Aluminium sheet
 6 Steel structure
 7 Lacquered
aluminium jamb

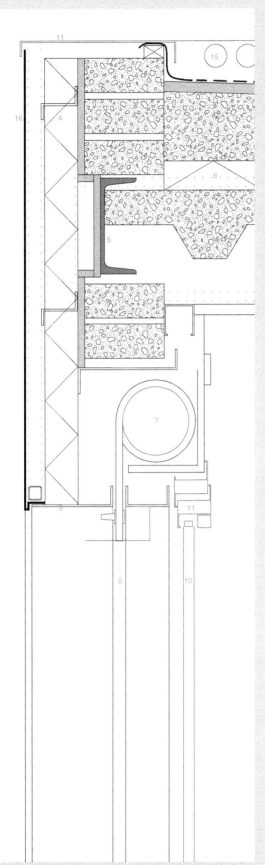

19.07
Detail Lintel Section
1:5
  1 Galvanized steel
  2 Concrete block
  3 Plasterboard
  4 Glass wool
insulation
  5 Steel UPN 160
channel
  6 Extruded
polystyrene 400 mm
(1 ft 3 $^7/_{10}$ inch)
  7 Blind
  8 Blind channel
  9 Folded sheet metal
lintel
10 Double glazing
4 / 6 / 3 + 3 mm ($^2/_{10}$ /
$^3/_{10}$ / $^1/_{10}$ + $^1/_{10}$ inch)
11 Aluminium coping
12 Window frame
lacquered aluminium
with thermal break
13 Concrete and
forged steel decking
14 Concrete
15 Macael marble
crushed gravel
16 Aluminium sheet

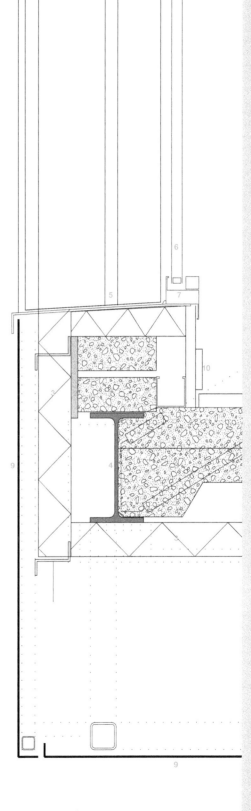

19.08
Detail Sill Section
1:5
  1 Concrete block
  2 Plasterboard
  3 Glass wool
insulation
  4 Steel IPE 160 beam
  5 Blind channel
  6 Double glazing
4 / 6 / 3 + 3 mm ($^2/_{10}$ /
$^3/_{10}$ / $^1/_{10}$ + $^1/_{10}$ inch)
  7 Window frame
lacquered aluminium
with thermal break
  8 Concrete and
forged steel decking
  9 Aluminium sheet
10 Painted skirting
board

MON Factory/House
Kyoto, Japan

Client
Morita MON factory

Project Team
EASTERN Design Office

Structural Engineer
HOJO Structure Research Institute

Main Contractor
Kotobuki Kensetsu

Situated in the Gojo area of Kyoto, this building is both a home and a workshop. It is occupied by a traditional Japanese business that applies family crests (mon) onto clothing. The design of these crests, which are usually round in form, was the inspiration behind the 26 circular openings that pierce the structure's walls.

The site is typical of Kyoto – long, thin and facing directly onto a narrow busy street. With the exception of the entrance to the shop area, the building is raised up three metres (ten feet) along its entire length, and the area underneath is let out for parking. The upper element is composed of three interior parts separated by two exterior courts. The first part is the workshop, the next is the living space and the last is a sleeping area. This rhythm establishes patterns of solid and void, light and dark, work and living, connection and separation. The circular openings project beams of light into the circulation spaces deep within the interior. As garments arrive to be marked, and completed work is collected, the building casts its patterns onto users.

The front façade is formed from two overlapping walls that mimic the method and direction in which a Kimono is crossed. As you enter you slip between walls into the warm embrace of the building.

1 The concrete skin is marked with a cross pattern formed of circular openings. These refer to the round family badges that the occupants apply onto clothing.
2 Along the long side of the building there is an access road. The building is raised to provide shaded parking space beneath.
3 From within, the round windows frame views of the world outside the quiet contemplative interior.
4 Domestic spaces look out over an internal courtyard, which acts as a filter between work and home.

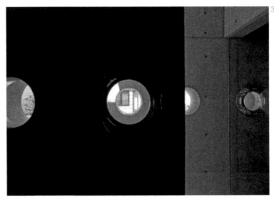

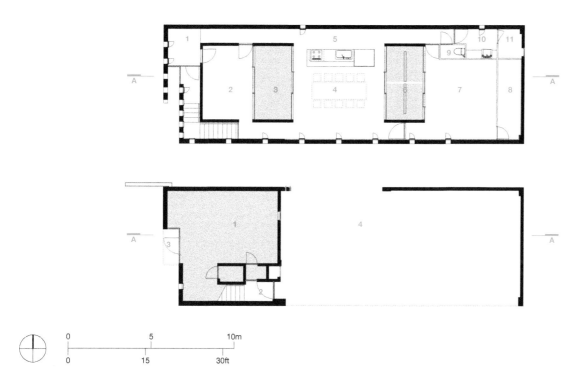

20.01
First Floor Plan
1:200
1 Hall
2 Workroom
3 Terrace
4 Living area
5 Kitchen
6 Terrace
7 Bedroom
8 Closet
9 WC
10 Dressing room
11 Bathroom

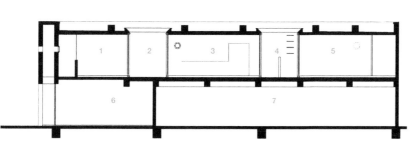

20.02
Ground Floor Plan
1:200
1 Shop
2 House entrance
3 Shop entrance
4 Parking

0   5   10m

0   15   30ft

20.03
Section A–A
1:200
1 Workroom
2 Terrace
3 Kitchen
4 Terrace
5 Bedroom
6 Shop
7 Parking

20.04
Axonometric
Not to Scale

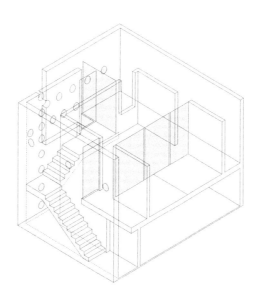

89

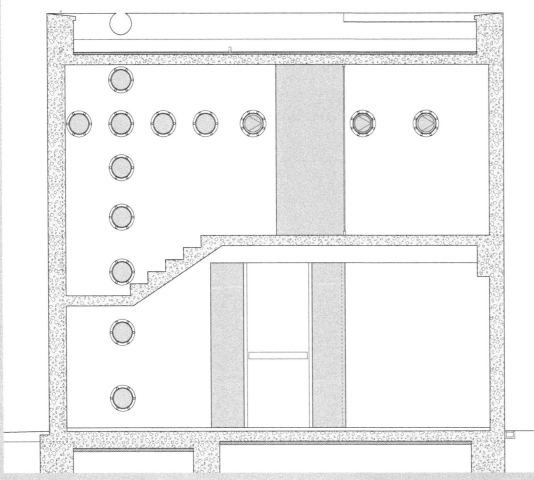

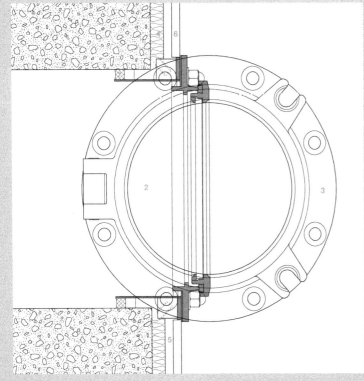

20.05
Section Detail
1:50
1 Coping
2 Concrete
3 Waterproof
membrane / insulation
4 Insulation

20.06
Window Detail
1:5
1 Concrete
2 Glass
3 Aluminium window
frame
4 Insulation
5 Void
6 Plasterboard
7 Mastic

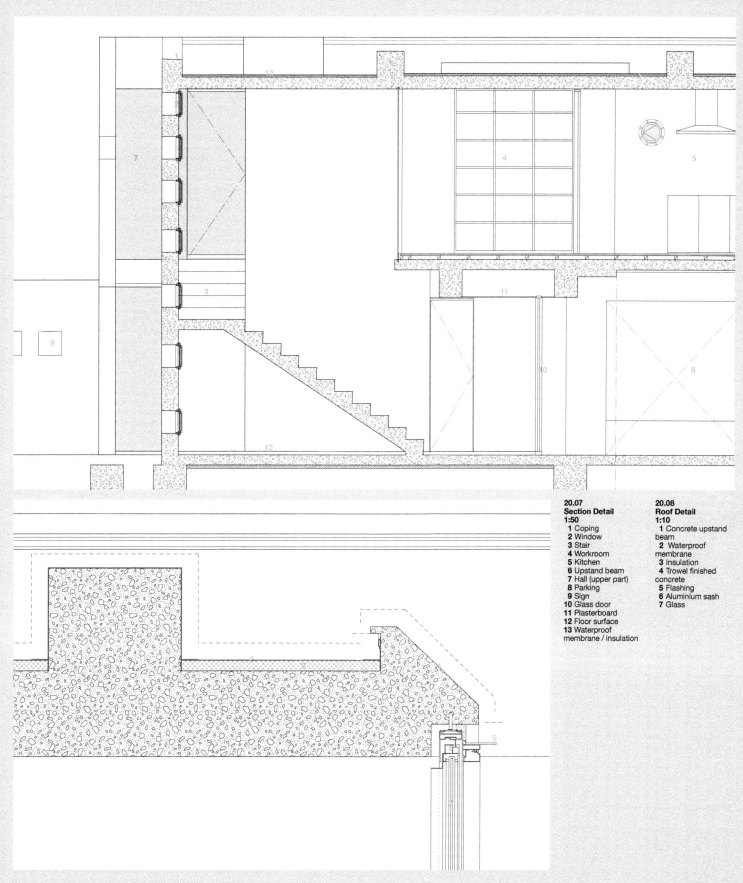

20.07
Section Detail
1:50
1 Coping
2 Window
3 Stair
4 Workroom
5 Kitchen
6 Upstand beam
7 Hall (upper part)
8 Parking
9 Sign
10 Glass door
11 Plasterboard
12 Floor surface
13 Waterproof
membrane / insulation

20.08
Roof Detail
1:10
1 Concrete upstand
beam
2 Waterproof
membrane
3 Insulation
4 Trowel finished
concrete
5 Flashing
6 Aluminium sash
7 Glass

**Ensamble Studio &
Antón García-Abril**

**The Truffle
Costa de Morte, Spain**

Client
Private client

Project Team
Ensamble Studio (Ricardo Sanz,
Javier Cuesta)

Structural Engineer
Ensamble Studio

Main Contractor
Materia Inorgánica

When we first see this building it appears not to be man-made; rather we might think that it is a piece of nature. In some ways this is true, because nature played a large part in the making of this space.

The construction of this project is a story that is both poetic and pragmatic. It commenced with digging a hole. As the earth was removed, it was built up around the hole to make a wall. This earth wall was retained by temporary formwork, and once the wall was the required height the interior was filled with a smaller volume of hay bales. Concrete was then poured between and over the straw and the earth. When the concrete had set the earth was removed to expose a large monolithic stone, a reflection of the earth that formed it.

The architects then made some cuts into this stone to reveal the interior form. The pressure of the concrete had compressed the straw, producing ribbed walls. Removing the hay from the interior was the job of a calf called Paulina. Over a year, she ate her way through all 50 cubic metres (1765 cubic feet) of hay, emerging as an adult cow weighing 300 kilograms (660 pounds).

Overlooking the sea, this tiny building is a place for contemplation. It speaks quietly of natural forces and the passage of time.

1 One sliced end of the 'rock' is fitted with a steel window. This acts like a screen between two worlds: the static straw-cast interior and the dynamic sea beyond.
2 The cave-like interior displays the precise impression of the straw that had formed the void.
3 At the rear, another sharp slice cuts through the rough form to make a smooth surface. Into this facade an enigmatic dark steel door is set.
4 In the niche by the front window is a bed that affords incredible views of the sea.

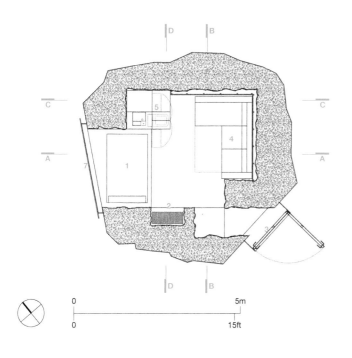

21.01
Plan
1:100
  1 Bed
  2 Bookshelf
  3 Door
  4 Seating
  5 Washing / WC
  6 Concrete
  7 Window

0   5m
0   15ft

21.02
Section A–A
1:100
  1 Concrete
  2 Interior
  3 Window

21.03
Section B–B
1:100
  1 Concrete
  2 Interior

21.04
Section C–C
1:100
  1 Concrete
  2 Interior
  3 Skylight

21.05
Section D–D
1:100
  1 Concrete
  2 Interior

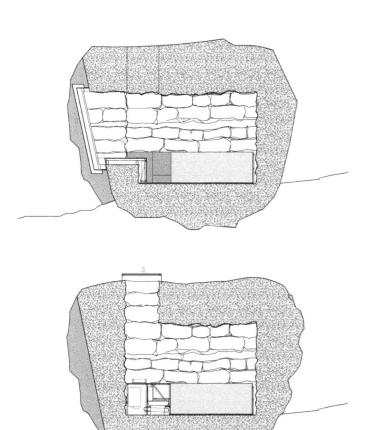

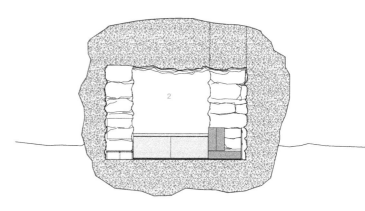

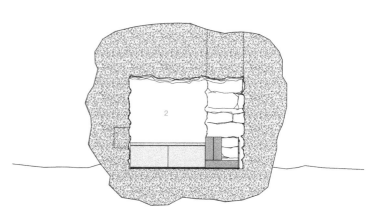

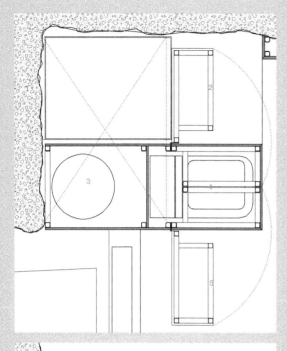

21.06
Bathroom Plan
1:20
1 Concrete
2 Door
3 Basin
4 WC
5 Door

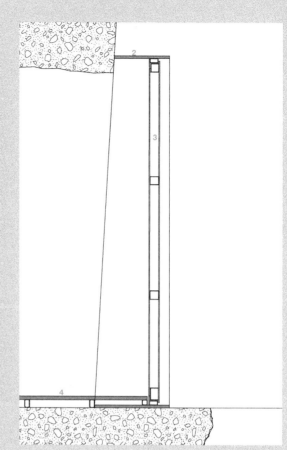

21.09
Door Section
1:20
1 Concrete
2 Door frame
3 Steel door
4 Wood floor

21.07
Bathroom Section
1:20
1 Concrete
2 Basin
3 Water heater
4 Cabinet
5 WC

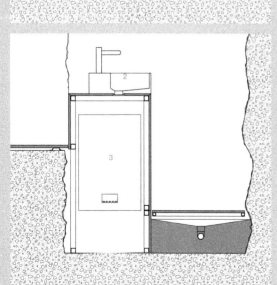

31.08
Bathroom Section
1:20
1 Concrete
2 Basin
3 Water heater

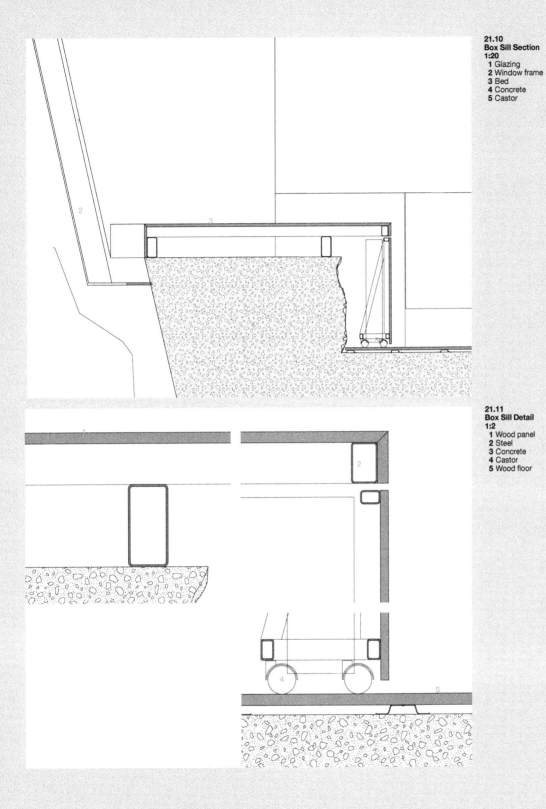

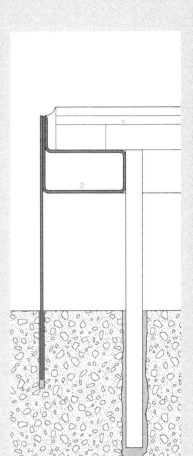

21.10
Box Sill Section
1:20
  1 Glazing
  2 Window frame
  3 Bed
  4 Concrete
  5 Castor

21.11
Box Sill Detail
1:2
  1 Wood panel
  2 Steel
  3 Concrete
  4 Castor
  5 Wood floor

21.12
Skylight Detail
1:2
  1 Concrete
  2 Steel tubing
  3 Glazing

Villa Lokaator
Paldiski, Estonia

Client
Private client

Project Team
Indrek Peil, Siiri Vallner

Structural Engineer
Maari Idnurm, Juhan Idnurm EEB

Located near to the coast, this house has the vigilant, defensive quality of a gun emplacement. Using elements of a redundant army barracks at its core, this small residence deliberately evokes the harsh, functional ascetic of military facilities. A nearby Soviet-era nuclear submarine training base provided additional inspiration.

On top of the original structure's 650 mm (25 ½ inch) thick calcium silicate brick walls, and facing out to the sea, the architects have placed two cantilevered concrete pavilions. Each of these is accessed via its own stair. At the side of the house at ground level is a third projection, which provides a motorcycle garage. Towards the sea, the facade is almost entirely glazed and opens onto a broad terrace; on the street side the angled slit windows present a closed, defensive facade.

Light filters down into the open-plan living space from the southeast-facing dormer windows. This indirect sunlight reflected off the concrete walls gives the interior a luminous glow. The house maintains a pleasant internal environment whilst remaining very energy efficient. The massive external concrete walls ensure an effective thermal mass, while a geothermal pump provides underfloor heating in the cast concrete floors.

1 The two upper parts of the house look out towards the sea like giant eyes. Below, a large terrace extends out into the garden.
2 The entrance front presents a series of vertical louvre walls that closes the interior to the street.
3 An open-plan living area is organized around two light steel stairs, which access upper sleeping areas.
4 There has been no attempt to disguise the rough texture of the walls that remain from the original structure.
5 From the sleeping areas, there are views of the sea through large windows.

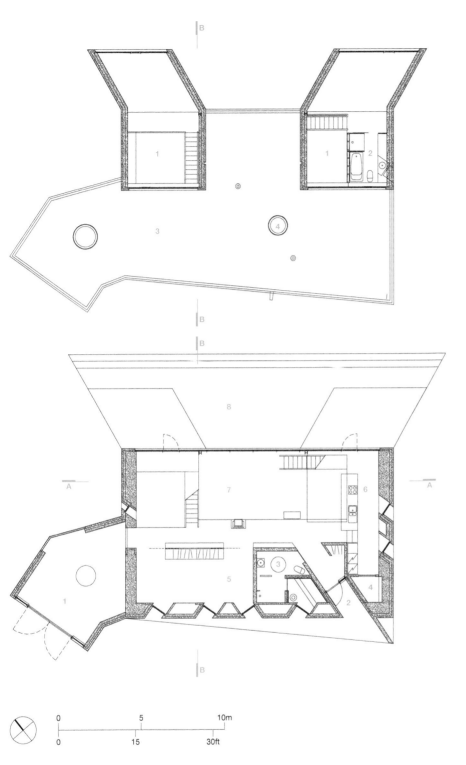

22.01
Mezzanine Plan
1:200
1 Bedroom
2 Bathroom
3 Flat roof
4 Skylight

22.02
Ground Floor Plan
1:200
1 Garage
2 Entrance
3 Bathroom / sauna
4 Services
5 Bedroom
6 Kitchen
7 Living area
8 Terrace

22.03
Section A–A
1:200
1 Bedroom
2 Living area
3 Kitchen

22.04
Section B–B
1:200
1 Bedroom
2 Bedroom
3 Living area

0   5   10m
0   15   30ft

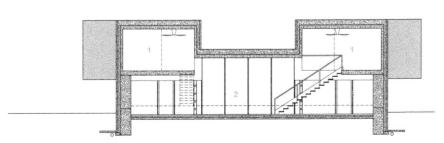

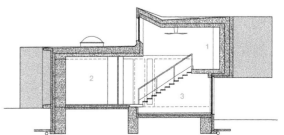

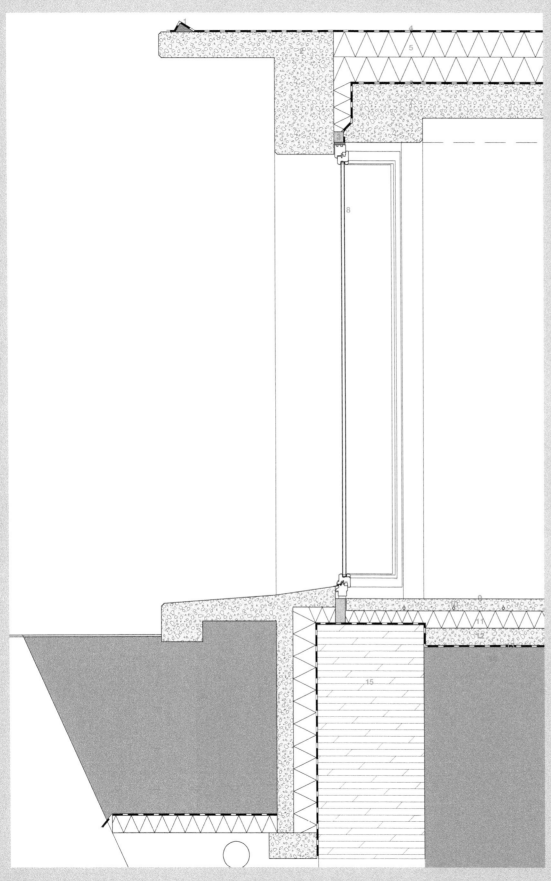

22.05
**Vertical Section of
Small Window
1:20**
1 Parapet cap steel
sheet
2 In-situ concrete
3 60 x 60 mm (2 $\frac{1}{3}$ x
2 $\frac{1}{3}$ inch) treated
timber
4 Two layers of
bituminous roof
membrane
5 200 mm (8 inch)
and 300 mm (11 $\frac{4}{5}$
inch) insulation
6 Vapour barrier
7 200 mm (7 $\frac{7}{8}$ inch)
concrete slab
8 Double-glazed
window
9 70 mm (2 $\frac{3}{4}$ inch)
concrete floor with
mineral surface
hardener
10 Underfloor
geothermal heating
system
11 100 mm (4 inch)
insulation
12 100 mm (4 inch)
concrete slab
13 Waterproofing
14 Sand
15 Existing limestone
foundation

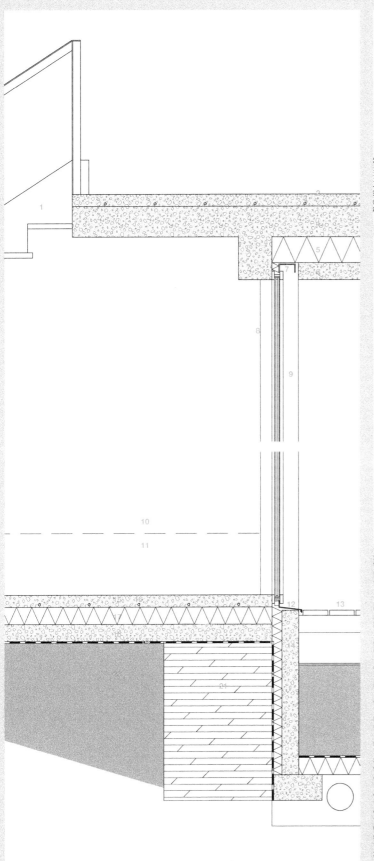

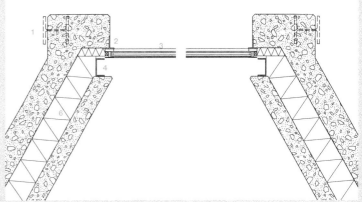

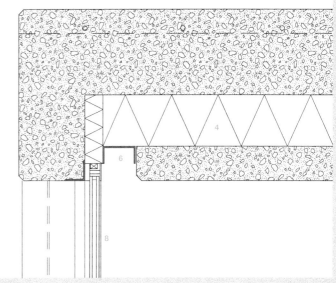

22.06
Vertical Section of
Big Window
1:20
  1 Stair to mezzanine
  2 70 mm (2 4/5 inch)
concrete floor with
mineral surface
hardener
  3 Underfloor
geothermal heating
system
  4 180 mm (7 1/10 inch)
concrete slab
  5 150 mm (5 9/10 inch)
insulation
  6 100 mm (4 inch)
concrete slab
  7 100 x 50 x 3.5 mm
(4 x 2 x 1/10 inch)
U-shaped steel section
  8 I-post with rusted
surface
  9 Glass facade:
Schüco FW50+
window with double
glazing
10 Above dashed line:
existing brick wall
11 Below dashed line:
existing limestone wall
12 Exterior window sill:
0.8 mm (1/32 inch)
stainless-steel sheet
13 30 x 150 mm (1 1/5
x 5 9/10 inch) larch

board
14 Existing limestone
foundation
15 70 mm (2 4/5 inch)
concrete floor with
mineral surface
hardener
16 Underfloor
geothermal heating
system
17 100 mm (4 inch)
insulation
18 100 mm (4 inch)
concrete slab
19 Waterproofing
20 Sand
21 Existing limestone
foundation

22.07
Horizontal Section of
Cantilever
1:20
  1 150 x 150 mm (5
9/10 x 5 9/10 inch)
I-shaped steel
  2 50 x 70 x 4.5 mm (2
x 2 4/5 x 3/16 inch)
T-shaped steel profile
  3 Glass facade:
Schüco FW50+
window with double
glazing
  4 100 x 30 x 3.5 mm
(4 x 1 1/5 x 1/10 inch)
U-shaped steel

  5 100 mm (4 inch)
concrete
  6 150 mm (5 9/10 inch)
insulation
  7 150 mm (5 9/10 inch)
concrete

22.08
Vertical Section of
Cantilever
1:10
  1 70 mm (2 4/5 inch)
concrete floor with
mineral surface
hardener
  2 Underfloor
geothermal heating
system
  3 180 mm (7 1/10 inch)
concrete slab
  4 150 mm (5 9/10 inch)
insulation
  5 100 mm (4 inch)
concrete slab
  6 100 x 50 x 3.5 mm
(4 x 2 x 1/10 inch)
U-shaped steel section
  7 60 x 60 mm (2 2/5 x
2 2/5 inch) steel angle
bar
  8 Glass facade:
Schüco FW50+
window with double
glazing

Alam Family Residence
Jakarta, Indonesia

Client
Alam Family

Project Team
Elsye Alam

Structural Engineer
Arsitek dan Rekan Sehati

Main Contractor
Arsitek dan Rekan Sehati

A rhythmic pattern of slots perforates the concrete screen that forms the front of this house. This filter serves a number of functions. It shades the interior, allows privacy and provides security for occupants. In addition, it projects an ever-varying arrangement of light into the house while also animating the building's exterior with evidence of the activities inside.

The house is arranged in an E-shaped plan. Two courts between three wedge-shaped wings bring air and light deep into the interior. Around these courts, extensive vertical glazing, along with skylights, makes artificial lighting unnecessary except at night. The pure white palette used on the walls and floors further develops the sense of a house built from light and reflections as much as from solid materials.

The open plan-interior is designed to encourage family interaction and a shared family lifestyle. The wall that encloses the house and the ability to open up the glazed walls allow exterior spaces to be used as living areas. At the top of the house there is a multi-level roofscape, providing expansive views and a number of recreational spaces – parts of these are covered by grass. Amid the interior's bright, milky coolness, a dramatic red prayer area is the symbolic heart of the house.

1 The front facade of the house is pierced by a diagonal pattern of slots. This transitional screen filters the interior and exterior light and creates an active elevation.
2 In the stairwell, the white surfaces reflect light through the house. Glimpses of the exterior are evident through the screen.
3 The roofed inner courtyard blends seamlessly with the internal spaces around it. The relationships between the spaces suggest a pattern of habitation rooted in communication and sharing.

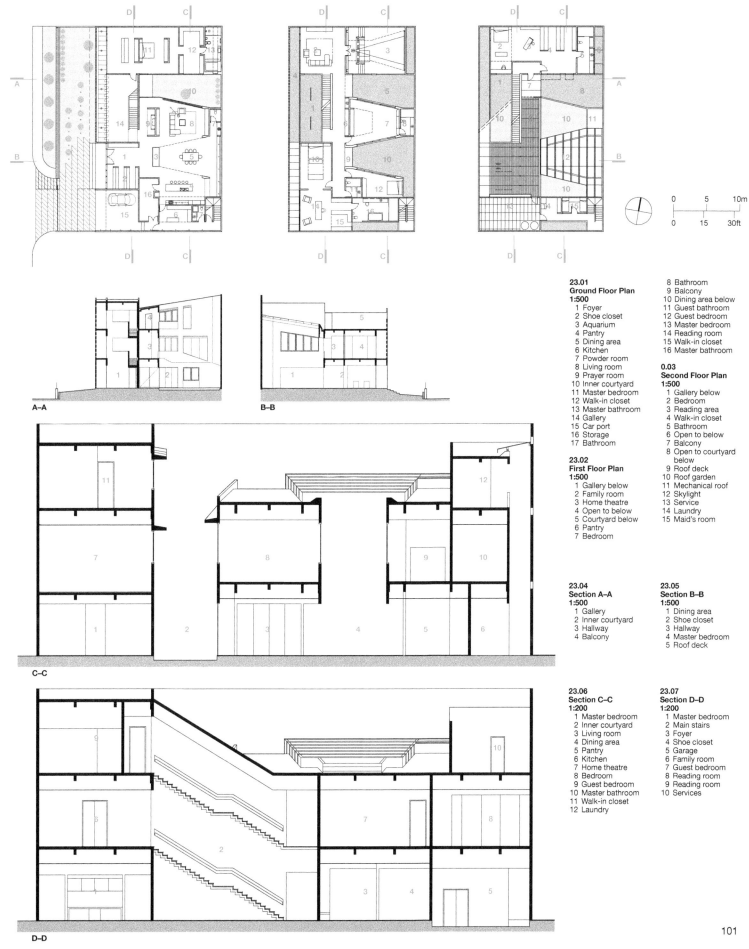

23.01
Ground Floor Plan
1:500
1 Foyer
2 Shoe closet
3 Aquarium
4 Pantry
5 Dining area
6 Kitchen
7 Powder room
8 Living room
9 Prayer room
10 Inner courtyard
11 Master bedroom
12 Walk-in closet
13 Master bathroom
14 Gallery
15 Car port
16 Storage
17 Bathroom

23.02
First Floor Plan
1:500
1 Gallery below
2 Family room
3 Home theatre
4 Open to below
5 Courtyard below
6 Pantry
7 Bedroom

8 Bathroom
9 Balcony
10 Dining area below
11 Guest bathroom
12 Guest bedroom
13 Master bedroom
14 Reading room
15 Walk-in closet
16 Master bathroom

0.03
Second Floor Plan
1:500
1 Gallery below
2 Bedroom
3 Reading area
4 Walk-in closet
5 Bathroom
6 Open to below
7 Balcony
8 Open to courtyard below
9 Roof deck
10 Roof garden
11 Mechanical roof
12 Skylight
13 Service
14 Laundry
15 Maid's room

23.04
Section A–A
1:500
1 Gallery
2 Inner courtyard
3 Hallway
4 Balcony

23.05
Section B–B
1:500
1 Dining area
2 Shoe closet
3 Hallway
4 Master bedroom
5 Roof deck

23.06
Section C–C
1:200
1 Master bedroom
2 Inner courtyard
3 Living room
4 Dining area
5 Pantry
6 Kitchen
7 Home theatre
8 Bedroom
9 Guest bedroom
10 Master bathroom
11 Walk-in closet
12 Laundry

23.07
Section D–D
1:200
1 Master bedroom
2 Main stairs
3 Foyer
4 Shoe closet
5 Garage
6 Family room
7 Guest bedroom
8 Reading room
9 Reading room
10 Services

A–A

B–B

C–C

D–D

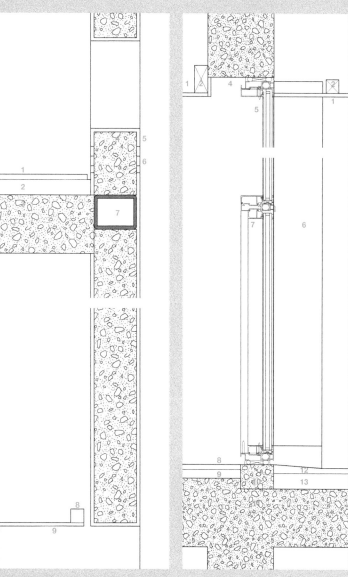

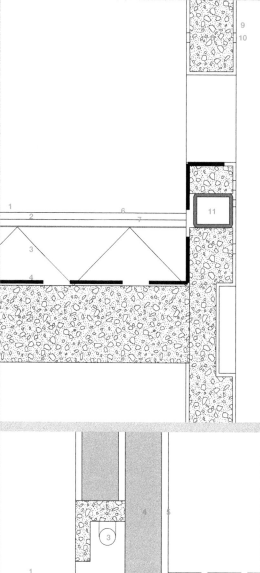

23.10
Roof Section
1:10
  1 26 mm (1 inch)
composite wood
decking
  2 42 mm (1 7/10 inch)
composite wood joists
with bailast in gaps
  3 170 mm (6 7/10 inch)
rigid EPS insulation
  4 Hot-melt rubberized
bitumen sheet
  5 225 mm (8 9/10 inch)
reinforced concrete
slab
  6 20 mm (4/5 inch)
honed natural stone
  7 20 mm (4/5 inch)
bed of mortar
  8 Lightweight
concrete block
  9 Coarse mortar base
and plaster finish
  10 20 mm (4/5 inch)
reveal
  11 Tube steel

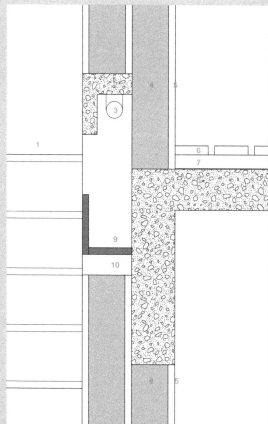

23.11
Stairs Section
1:10
  1 Stairs beyond
  2 Reinforced
concrete bottom
  3 Fluorescent light
pocket
  4 Brick
  5 Coarse mortar base
and plaster finish
  6 26 mm (1 inch)
composite wood
decking
  7 42 mm (1 7/10 inch)
composite wood joists
with ballast in gaps
  8 Reinforced
concrete slab
  9 Solid wood handrail
  10 Reinforced
concrete top

23.08
Second Floor Terrace
Ceiling Section
1:10
  1 15 mm (3/5 inch)
terrazzo
  2 45 mm (1 4/5 inch)
bed of mortar with
cushion of sand
  3 Reinforced
concrete slab
  4 Lightweight
concrete block
  5 Coarse mortar base
and plaster finish
  6 20 mm (4/5 inch)
reveal
  7 Tube steel
  8 Wood block
  9 Suspended
gypsum-board ceiling

23.09
Second Floor Terrace
Section
1:10
  1 Suspended
gypsum-board ceiling
  2 Wood block
  3 Concrete beam
  4 Curtain pocket
  5 Fixed glazing
  6 Vertical structural
glass fin
  7 Operable window
with anodized
aluminium frame
  8 15 mm (3/5 inch)
parquet
  9 40 mm (1 3/5 inch)
screed
  10 Concrete curb
topping
  11 Reinforced
concrete slab
  12 15 mm (3/5 inch)
terrazzo
  13 45 mm (1 4/5 inch)
bed of mortar with
cushion of sand

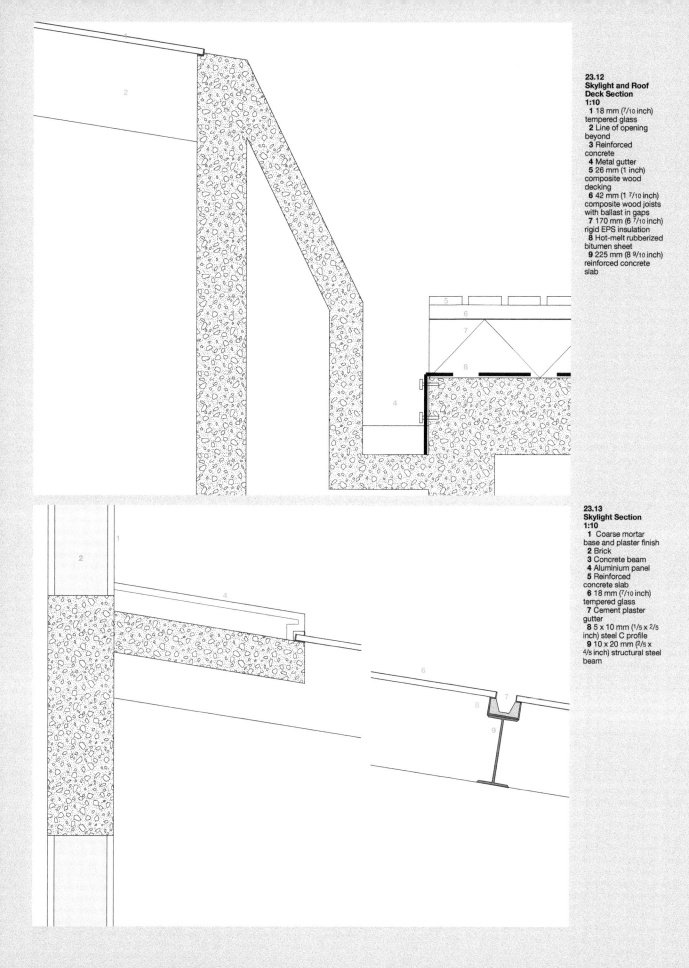

23.12
Skylight and Roof Deck Section
1:10
 1 18 mm ($^7/_{10}$ inch) tempered glass
 2 Line of opening beyond
 3 Reinforced concrete
 4 Metal gutter
 5 26 mm (1 inch) composite wood decking
 6 42 mm (1 $^7/_{10}$ inch) composite wood joists with ballast in gaps
 7 170 mm (6 $^7/_{10}$ inch) rigid EPS insulation
 8 Hot-melt rubberized bitumen sheet
 9 225 mm (8 $^9/_{10}$ inch) reinforced concrete slab

23.13
Skylight Section
1:10
 1 Coarse mortar base and plaster finish
 2 Brick
 3 Concrete beam
 4 Aluminium panel
 5 Reinforced concrete slab
 6 18 mm ($^7/_{10}$ inch) tempered glass
 7 Cement plaster gutter
 8 5 x 10 mm ($^1/_5$ x $^2/_5$ inch) steel C profile
 9 10 x 20 mm ($^2/_5$ x $^4/_5$ inch) structural steel beam

House Equanimity
Northampton, Pennsylvania, USA

Client
Private client

Project Team
Joseph Balsamo, Sierra Krause,
Patrick Ruggiero

Structural Engineer
E.D. Pons Associates

Main Contractor
Joseph N. Biondo

This house in Northampton, Pennsylvania – the birthplace of American Portland cement – is constructed of concrete in homage to the history of the region. The area has many industrial ruins that tell the story of the industry. The working aesthetic of this past is reflected in the strong functionality of House Equanimity.

Like the surrounding relics, this structure is rooted in its landscape. It rejects the scale and forms of the nearby housing, choosing instead to take many of its references from the topography and nature of the area. The concrete base slab, which is deliberately crude in its finish, emerges from the sloping ground as if it were a natural feature or part of a pre-existing ruin. It is a permanent feature of great substance. On and around this platform are arranged carefully detailed boxes, clad in fibrous cement panels, which contain the domestic spaces. The materiality of the surfaces suggests that they will accommodate future patinas. They invite your touch, and each material meets another in a satisfying manner that speaks of care and understanding. The double-height living space opens onto a generous terrace. From within the views are controlled and carefully framed.

1 Constructed on an elegant, balanced platform that appears to slide out from the ground, the house is responsive to the landscape, giving an impression that the two could have been formed at the same time.
2 Large parts of the facade fall away to open the structure to the surrounding garden.
3 The open court at each end of the main living area provides undercover seating.
4 The double-height living area is framed with a carefully animated arrangement of overlapping wood, concrete and plaster panels. Visible through the large panes of glass, the surrounding trees imbue the space with the gentle spirit of nature.

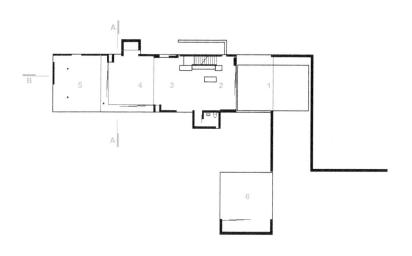

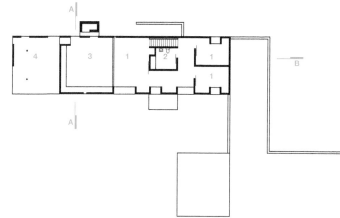

24.01
Ground Floor Plan
1:500
1 Courtyard
2 Kitchen
3 Dining area
4 Living area
5 Deck
6 Car port

24.02
First Floor Plan
1:500
1 Bedroom
2 Bathroom
3 Open to below
4 Deck

24.03
Section A–A
1:200
1 Living area
2 Basement

24.04
Section B–B
1:200
1 Courtyard
2 Kitchen
3 Dining area
4 Living area
5 Deck
6 Bedroom
7 Bathroom
8 Basement

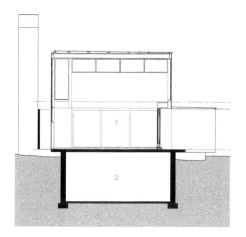

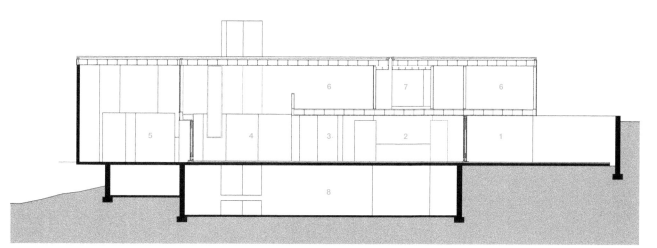

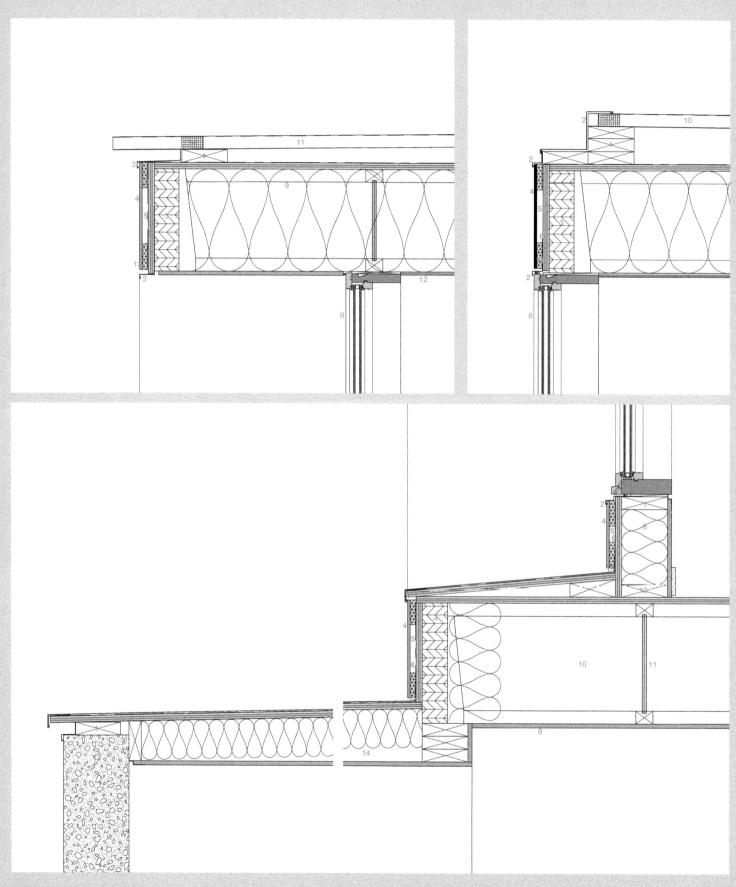

24.05
Deep Eaves Section
1:10
  1 Wood blocking
  2 Lead-coated
copper flashing
  3 Engineered timber
beam
  4 11 mm (7/16 inch)
cement board
  5 19 mm (3/4 inch)
wood firring and air
space
  6 Air and vapour
barrier
  7 16 mm (5/8 inch)
plywood
  8 Wood fixed window
  9 305 mm (12 inch)
TJI roof joist
10 Waterproof
membrane
11 22 mm (7/8 inch)
corrugated metal roof
12 10 mm (3/8 inch)
veneer plywood
(stained)
13 Insect fabric
14 Neoprene flute infill

24.06
Typical Eaves Section
1:10
  1 Wood blocking
  2 Lead-coated
copper flashing
  3 Engineered timber
beam
  4 11 mm (7/16 inch)
cement board
  5 19 mm (3/4 inch)
wood firring and air
space
  6 Air and vapour
barrier
  7 16 mm (5/8 inch)
plywood
  8 Wood fixed window
  9 Waterproof
membrane
10 22 mm (7/8 inch)
corrugated metal roof
11 Insect fabric
12 Neoprene flute infill

24.07
**Low Roof and
Deep Sill Section**
1:10
  1 Wood blocking
  2 Lead-coated
copper flashing
  3 Engineered timber
beam
  4 11 mm (7/16 inch)
cement board
  5 19 mm (3/4 inch)
wood firring and air
space
  6 Air and vapour
barrier
  7 16mm (5/8 inch)
plywood
  8 Thermal Batt
insulation
  9 16 mm (5/8 inch)
10 356 mm (14 inch)
TJI floor joist
11 305 mm (12 inch)
TJI roof joist
12 51 x 152 mm (2 x 6
inch) wood stud
framing
13 Exposed reinforced
concrete wall
14 Wood roof joist
15 Insect fabric

24.08
**Sliding Glass Wall
Section**
1:10
  1 Wood sliding-glass
system
  2 Wood blocking
  3 Lead-coated
copper flashing
  4 203 mm (8 inch)
reinforced structural
concrete
  5 51 mm (2 inch)
sealed concrete
topping
  6 51 mm (2 inch) rigid
insulation
  7 Engineered timber
beam
  8 11 mm (7/16 inch)
cement board
  9 19 mm (3/4 inch)
wood firring and air
space
10 Air and vapour
barrier
11 16 mm (5/8 inch)
plywood
12 Thermal Batt
insulation
13 16 mm (5/8 inch)
gypsum wall board
14 Wood-fixed window
15 356 mm (14 inch)
TJI floor joist
16 Insect fabric

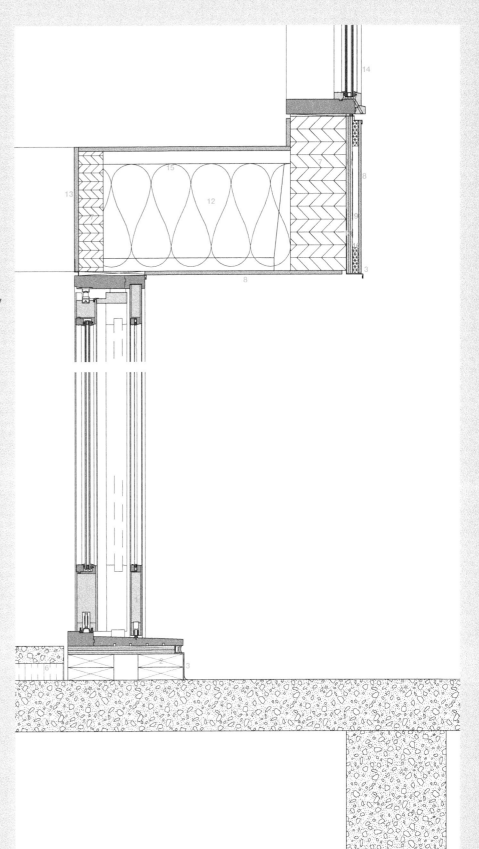

Rainy / Sunny House
Tokyo, Japan

Client
Private client

Project Team
Masahiro Harada, Mao Harada

Structural Engineer
Jun Sato

Main Contractor
Sun Walk Construction

The concept behind this project was to build a house that appeared to be part of the terrain, to have been in place for a long time, and to have many years still ahead of it. Built in a dense residential area of Tokyo, the structure is positioned diagonally on its rectangular site, creating triangular open spaces on either side. To the north at the front there is a parking space; on the south side there is a secluded courtyard garden.

Concrete has been chosen to realize this 'terrain', but the architects wanted to increase the durability of the material as the climate in Japan has been becoming almost subtropical in recent years. They came up with the idea of casting the exterior walls against a staggered board shuttering, which creates a weatherboard surface. This allows the walls to quickly shed water.

The boards used were larchwood ply, as the architects wanted a strong wood-grain pattern on the finished concrete. This ridged surface gives the house an ever-changing appearance. On clear days, the sun casts strong shadows on the uneven surface. On cloudy days, the concrete absorbs the humidity and turns the ridges into dark horizontal cracks, while on rainy days necklaces of water droplets form across the walls.

In contrast to the hard exterior, the floors, walls and ceiling inside are covered with wooden parquet blocks arranged in a herringbone pattern. This gives the house a hand-crafted domestic warmth.

1 The street facade shows the strongly ridged textural quality of the walls. The building's general form recalls vernacular structures but does not copy directly.

2 The wood interiors have a rich quality that suggests warmth and comfort. Using the same parquet blocks on floors, walls and ceilings creates a luxurious, enveloping environment.

3 The fully glazed wall to the living area allows natural light to enter the house, illuminating both the upper and lower floors.

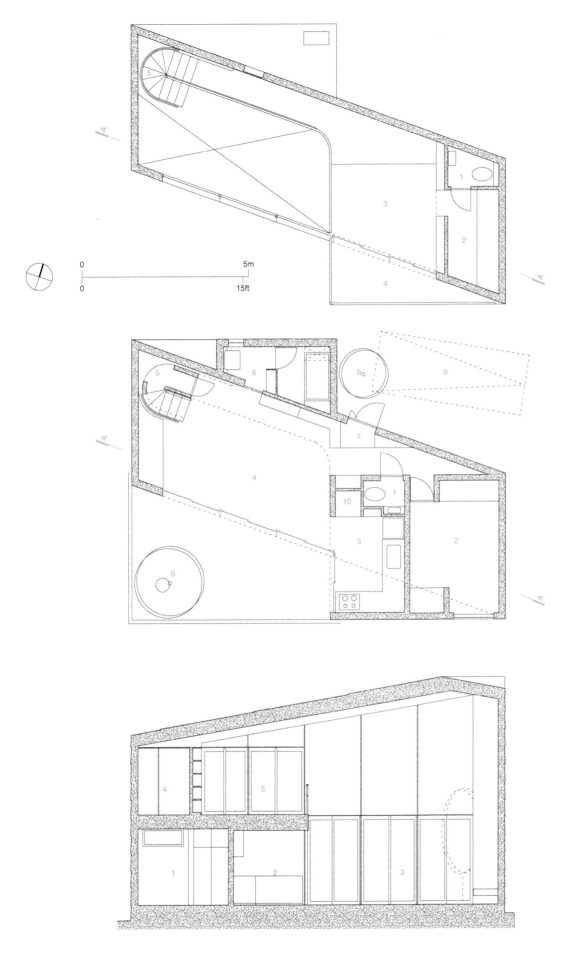

25.01
First Floor Plan
1:100
  1 WC
  2 Wardrobe
  3 Study
  4 Terrace
  5 Stair

25.02
Ground Floor Plan
1:100
  1 WC
  2 Bedroom
  3 Kitchen
  4 Living area
  5 Store
  6 Bathroom
  7 Entrance
  8 Tree
  9 Car-parking space
  10 Cupboard

25.03
Section A–A
1:100
  1 Bedroom
  2 Kitchen
  3 Living area
  4 Wardrobe
  5 Study

0   5m

0   15ft

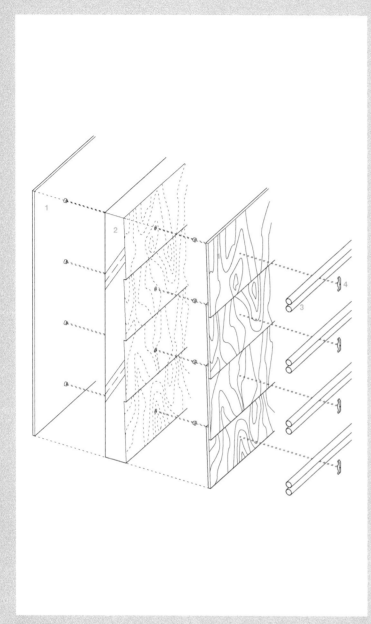

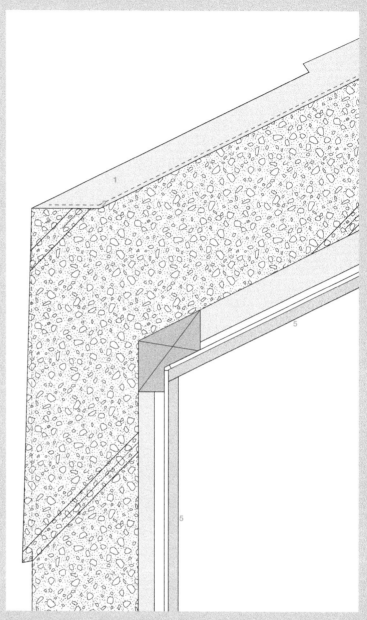

25.04
Formwork
Construction
Not to Scale
 1 Larchwood ply
 2 Concrete
 3 Strengthening bars
 4 Tie rod ends

25.05
Wall Section Detail
1:5
 1 Trowelled mortar
 2 Waterproofing
membrane coating
 3 Trowelled concrete
 4 Larchwood
moulded concrete
 5 Herringbone with
Osmo finish

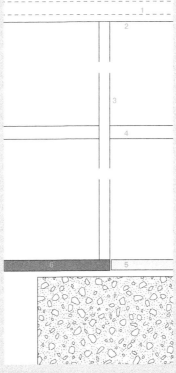

25.06
Study: Catwalk
Section Detail 1
1:5
  1 16 mm (3/5 inch)
steel plate, adiabatic
paint
  2 Herringbone with
Osmo finish

3 75 x 75 x 6 mm (3 x
3 x 1/5 x inch) steel
angle
4 Luan-wood
moulded concrete

25.07
Study: Catwalk
Section Detail 2
1:5
  1 40 x 55 mm (1 3/5 x
2 1/5 inch) oak with
Osmo finish
  2 32 x 19 mm (1 3/10
x 7/10 inch) steel flat
bar

3 32 x 16 mm (1 3/10
x 7/10 inch) steel flat
bar
4 Rounding steel
5 16 mm (3/5 inch)
steel plate, adiabatic
paint
6 Lauan-wood
moulded concrete

25.08
Study: Catwalk
Section Detail 3
1:5
  1 40 x 55 mm (1 3/5 x
2 1/5 inch oak with
Osmo finish
  2 32 x 19 mm (1 3/10
x 7/10 inch) steel flat
bar

3 32 x 16 mm (1 3/10
x 7/10 inch) steel flat
bar
4 Rounding steel
5 Herringbone with
Osmo finish
6 16 mm (3/5 inch)
steel plate, adiabatic
paint
7 Lauan-wood
moulded concrete

25.09
Study: Catwalk
Section Detail 4
1:5
  1 40 x 55 mm (1 3/5 x
2 1/5 inch oak with
Osmo finish
  2 32 x 19 mm (1 3/10
x 7/10 inch) steel flat
bar

3 32 x 16 mm (1 3/10
x 7/10 inch) steel flat
bar
4 Rounding steel
5 Herringbone with
Osmo finish
6 Lauan-wood
moulded concrete

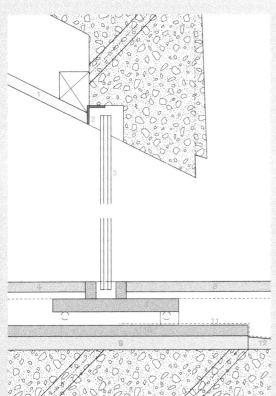

25.10
Fixed Window
Section Detail
1:5
  1 Herringbone with
Osmo finish
  2 27 x 27 x 3 mm (1 x
1 x 1/10 inch)
aluminium angle
  3 5 mm (1/5 inch) float
glass
  4 Herringbone with
Osmo finish
  5 25 x 16 mm (1 x
7/10 inch) steel flat bar
  6 25 x 16 mm (1 x
7/10 inch) steel flat bar
  7 190 x 19 mm (7 1/2
x 7/10 inch) steel flat
bar
  8 Australian cypress
herringbone
  9 Mortar
10 400 x 100 x 16 mm
(15 3/4 x 3 15/16 x 3/5
inch) steel flat bar
11 FRP waterproofing
12 Mortar

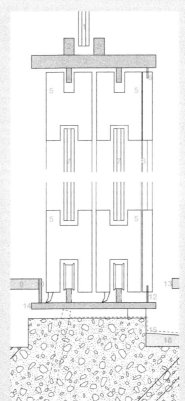

25.11
Sliding Door Detail
1:5
  1 5 mm (1/5 inch) float
glass
  2 25 x 16 mm (1 x
7/10 inch) steel flat bar
  3 190 x 19 mm (7 1/2
x 7/10 inch)steel flat bar
  4 21 x 8 mm (4/5 x
3/10 inch) steel flat bar
  5 2.3 mm (1/10 inch)
steel plate
  6 15 x 2 mm (3/5 x 1/5
inch) stainless-steel
flat bar
  7 5 mm (1/5 inch) float
glass
  8 Window screen
  9 Herringbone with
Osmo finish
10 35 x 4 mm (1 2/5 x
1/5 inch) stainless-steel
flat bar
11 Australian cypress
herringbone
12 21 x 8 mm (4/5 x
3/10 inch) stainless-
steel flat bar
13 190 x 9 mm (7 1/2 x
2/5 inch) stainless steel
flat bar
14 24 x 2 mm (9/10 x
1/10 inch) stainless-
steel flat bar
15 FRP waterproofing
16 Mortar

House F
Rameldange, Luxembourg

Client
Mr and Mrs F.

Project Team
Paul Bretz, Petra Schmitt

Structural Engineer
InCA, Ingénieurs Conseils Associés
S.à.r.l.

Main Contractor
Socimmo Construction S.A.

Built on a narrow, sloping site, this family house in a village on the outskirts of Luxembourg is organized around three immense walls that emerge from the hillside. Other than these concrete walls, all other divisions of space are made with light plasterboard or glazing. The flexible open-plan living areas are arranged over a number of half levels and double-height spaces. This allows the patterns of possible habitation to be both open and closed.

At the rear of the house a large terrace with a pool serves as a summer open-air living room. From the glazed front facade, set behind open balconies, there are views across the valley. The strong, linear, orthogonal forms of the building establish a dialogue of contrasts with the natural forms of the landscape.

Through the use of high levels of insulation, with double-skinned concrete walls and triple-glazed windows, the house achieves a very good rating for energy use. The concrete spine walls further aid this through their high thermal mass.

The solidity of the polished concrete is contrasted with the fragile and ductile qualities of the light that penetrates and permeates the domestic spaces of this house.

1 The street elevation showing the garage entrance – the main entrance is on the left. Large recessed balconies are located on the upper floors.
2 The rear terrace looking towards the kitchen. Cantilevered above is one of the bedroom suites.
3 A view of the pool from the exterior stair. A second access to the garden is located on the right side. The dining area is situated behind glazing at the end of the pool area.
4 The terrace with pool looking towards the garden. The stair leads to the garden and upper terrace.
5 The main living area looking towards the fire place, which acts as a partition dividing the living room and the dining room beyond. The opening on the right leads to the kitchen.

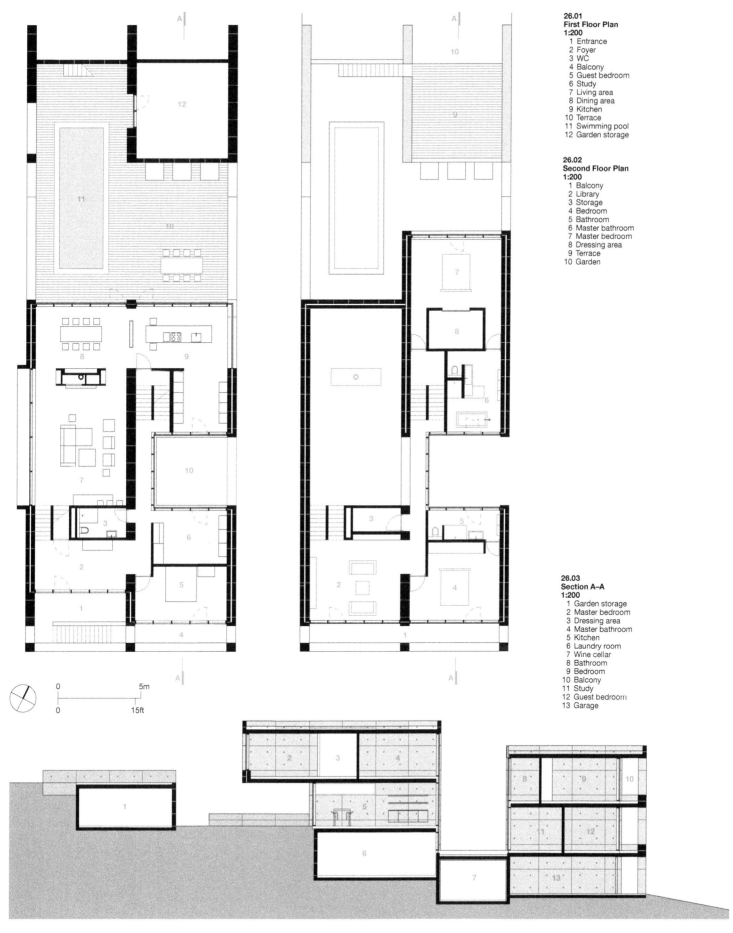

26.01
First Floor Plan
1:200
1 Entrance
2 Foyer
3 WC
4 Balcony
5 Guest bedroom
6 Study
7 Living area
8 Dining area
9 Kitchen
10 Terrace
11 Swimming pool
12 Garden storage

26.02
Second Floor Plan
1:200
1 Balcony
2 Library
3 Storage
4 Bedroom
5 Bathroom
6 Master bathroom
7 Master bedroom
8 Dressing area
9 Terrace
10 Garden

26.03
Section A–A
1:200
1 Garden storage
2 Master bedroom
3 Dressing area
4 Master bathroom
5 Kitchen
6 Laundry room
7 Wine cellar
8 Bathroom
9 Bedroom
10 Balcony
11 Study
12 Guest bedroom
13 Garage

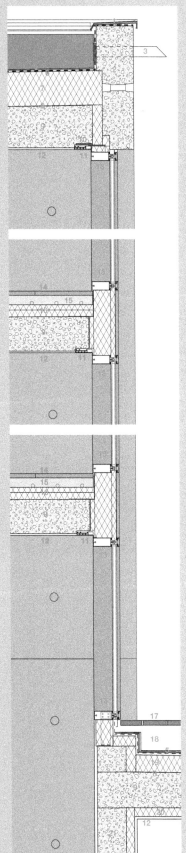

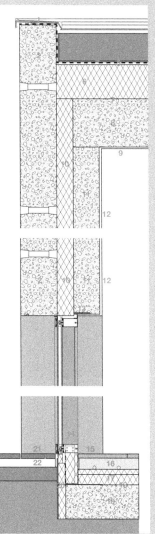

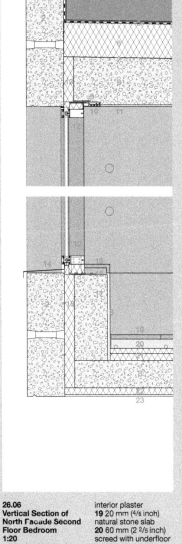

26.04
Vertical Section of Courtyard Southside 1:20
 1 Alwitra MAK parapet capping
 2 Fair-faced concrete wall
 3 Emergency overflow
 4 Slag
 5 Building protection mats
 6 Waterproofing
 7 200 mm (7 9/10 inch) thermal insulation
 8 Vapour barrier
 9 200 mm (7 9/10 inch) concrete slab
10 100 x 100 x 8 mm (3 9/10 x 3 9/10 x 3/10 inch) welding plate
11 Curtain rail
12 10 mm (2/5 inch) interior plaster
13 Schüco FW50+ facade system
14 20 mm (4/5 inch) natural stone
15 60 mm (2 2/5 inch) screed with underfloor heating
16 70 mm (2 4/5 inch) thermal / impact sound insulation
17 28 mm (1 1/10 inch) IPE wood deck
18 140 mm (5 1/2 inch) wooden beam
19 100 mm (3 9/10 inch) Foamglas insulation
20 50 mm (2 inch) interior insulation
21 Concrete wall

26.05
Vertical Section of North Facade First Floor Dining Room 1:20
 1 Alwitra MAK parapet capping
 2 Fair-faced concrete wall
 3 Slag
 4 Building protection mats
 5 Waterproofing
 6 200 mm (7 9/10 inch) thermal insulation
 7 Vapour barrier
 8 200 mm (7 9/10 inch) concrete slab
 9 15 mm (4/5 inch) interior plaster
10 100 mm (3 9/10 inch) core insulation
11 160 mm (6 3/10 inch) concrete wall
12 15 mm (3/5 inch) interior plaster
13 100 x 100 x 8 mm (3 9/10 x 3 9/10 x 3/10 inch) welding plate
14 Schüco FW50+ facade system
15 20 mm (4/5 inch) natural stone slab
16 60 mm (2 2/5 inch) screed with underfloor heating
17 70 mm (2 4/5 inch) thermal / impact sound insulation
18 Vapour barrier
19 200 mm (7 9/10 inch) concrete floor slab
20 40 mm (1 3/5 inch) perimeter insulation
21 28 mm (1 1/10 inch) IPE wood deck
22 40 mm (1 3/5 inch) IPE substructure)
23 80 mm (3 1/10 inch) lava stone

26.06
Vertical Section of North Facade Second Floor Bedroom 1:20
 1 Alwitra MAK parapet capping
 2 225 mm (8 9/10 inch) fair-faced concrete wall
 3 Slag
 4 Building protection mats
 5 Waterproofing
 6 200 mm (7 9/10 inch) thermal insulation
 7 Vapour barrier
 8 200 mm (7 9/10 inch) concrete slab
 9 100 x 100 x 8 mm (3 9/10 x 3 9/10 x 3/10 inch) welding plate
10 Curtain rail
11 10 mm (2/5 inch) interior plaster
12 Schüco FW50+ facade system
13 60 mm (2 2/5 inch) core insulation
14 Window sill exterior: sheet metal aluminium
15 Window sill interior: natural stone
16 Mortar
17 200 mm (7 9/10 inch) concrete wall
18 15 mm (3/5 inch) interior plaster
19 20 mm (4/5 inch) natural stone slab
20 60 mm (2 2/5 inch) screed with underfloor heating
21 70 mm (2 4/5 inch) thermal / impact sound insulation
22 40 mm (1 3/5 inch) insulation
23 10 mm (2/5 inch) exterior plaster

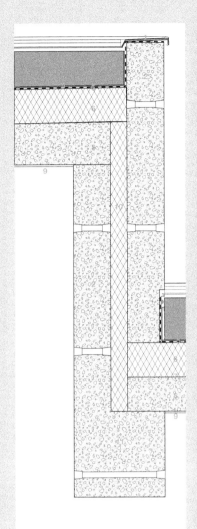

26.07
Vertical Section of Roof Connection Fair-faced Concrete Wall
1:20
1 Alwitra MAK parapet capping
2 225 mm (8 9/10 inch) fair-faced concrete wall
3 Slag
4 Building protection mats
5 Waterproofing
6 200 mm (7 9/10 inch) thermal insulation
7 Vapour barrier
8 200 mm (7 9/10 inch) concrete slab
9 15 mm (3/5 inch) interior plaster
10 100 mm (3 9/10 inch) core insulation
11 550 mm (9 7/10 inch) fair-faced concrete wall

26.08
Vertical Section of South Facade
1:20
1 Alwitra MAK parapet capping
2 225 mm (8 9/10 inch) fair-faced concrete wall
3 Slag
4 Building protection mats
5 Waterproofing
6 200 mm (7 9/10 inch) thermal insulation
7 Vapour barrier
8 190 mm (7 1/2 inch) concrete slab
9 20 mm (4/5 inch) interior plaster
10 Lighting
11 Venetian blinds
12 110 mm (4 3/10 inch) insulation
13 100 x 100 x 8 mm (3 9/10 x 3 9/10 x 3/10 inch) welding plate
14 Curtain rail
15 10 mm (2/5 inch) interior plaster
16 Schüco FW50+ facade system
17 20 mm (4/5 inch) natural stone slab
18 60 mm (2 2/5 inch) screed with underfloor heating
19 70 mm (2 4/5 inch) thermal / impact sound insulation
20 200 mm (7 9/10 inch) concrete slab
21 Tension cord for Venetian blinds
22 30 mm (1 1/5 inch) natural stone
23 100 mm (3 9/10 inch) screed
24 Drainage mat
25 Waterproofing
26 500 x 720 mm (19 7/10 x 28 3/10 inch) concrete parapet
27 160 mm (6 3/10 inch) concrete slab
28 60 mm (2 2/5 inch) insulation
29 40 mm (1 3/5 inch) insulation
30 Door rail
31 Sliding glass door with expanded metal cladding
32 Steel angle
33 60 mm (2 2/5 inch) screed with surface sealing
34 20 mm (4/5 inch) insulation
35 Waterproofing
36 150 mm (5 9/10 inch) concrete floor slab
37 Trench drain
38 100 x 70 mm (3 9/10 x 2 8/10 inch) natural stone paving
39 50 mm (2 inch) mortar bed
40 200 mm (7 9/10 inch) concrete floor slab

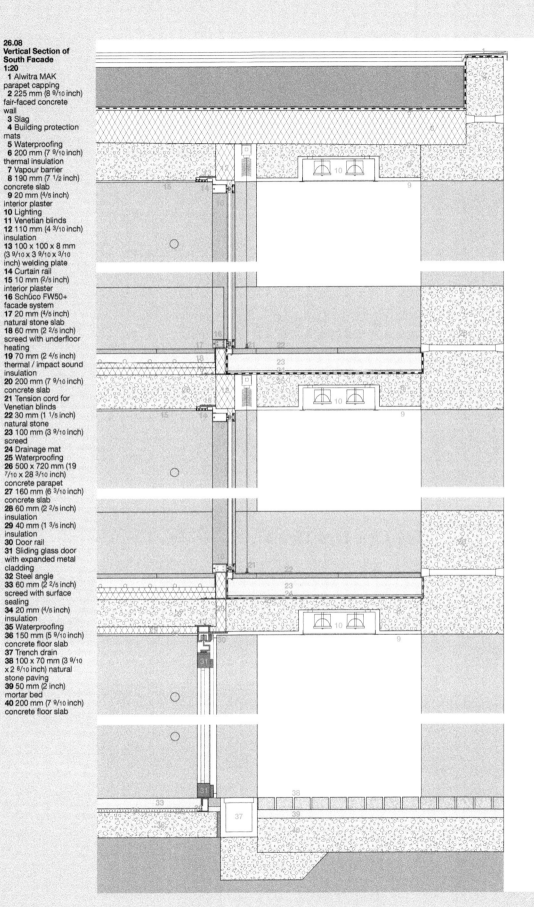

Springwater
Seaforth, Sydney, Australia

Client
Private client

Project Team
Peter Stutchbury, James Stockwell

Structural Engineer
Professor Max Irvine

Main Contractor
Watpow Constructions Pty Ltd

This house is positioned on a wooded, west-facing site on the coast of Sydney Harbour. Despite its solid materiality, it is a delicate structure that acts primarily as an absence enclosure. Designed to interact with the natural conditions of the area, the house does not impose itself as closed space; rather it is developed as a series of simple framed areas open to the landscape. The architects conceived the house as a 'reliable camp' – a place where you can rest amongst nature.

In plan, the building reaches out like fingers across the site towards the sea. Within its concrete frame, the building has a simple skin that can be adjusted to control the environment. The house does not seek to dominate its surroundings, but to exist in balance with them. Ceiling heights are carefully shifted according to their relationship with the adjacent landscape. The platforms that extend out from the house offer multiple possible areas for occupation. Throughout, the materials of the house are presented in their raw state. Galvanized steel frames are bolted directly to the structure, while polished timber is set in contrast against cast-in-situ concrete.

This is a house in which nature is always present. The transition between the interior and the exterior is fragile; it is a place of both permanent and transitory atmospheres.

1 The living areas of the house extend out across the layered platforms, an arrangement that subtly melds the interior and exterior. The basic materials remain in their raw state.
2 The main stair slices through the house within a canyon-like cut that recalls the local topography.
3 On the upper level, beneath the deep eaves, a pool runs alongside the house, its infinity edge merging into the landscape.
4 Transparency and permeability allow the house to be integrated with its surroundings. Each space is visually connected to those that surround it.

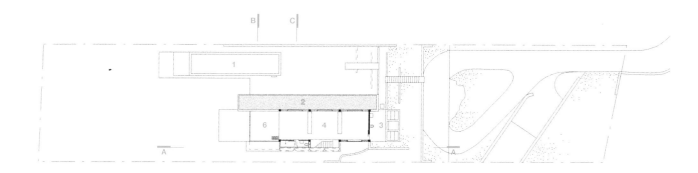

27.01
Upper Floor Plan
1:500
1 Roof
2 Lap pool
3 Outdoor bathroom
4 Bedroom
5 En-suite bathroom
6 Concrete deck

27.02
Middle Floor Plan
1:500
1 Concrete deck
2 Living area
3 Dining area
4 Kitchen
5 Laundry
6 Pantry
7 Plant room
8 Service
9 Courtyard
10 Void to gallery
11 Timber deck
  below

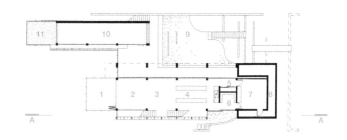

27.03
Lower Floor Plan
1:500
1 Timber deck
2 Gallery
3 Wardrobe
4 En-suite bathroom
5 Services
6 Outdoor kitchen
7 Paved terrace
8 Recreation room
9 Water feature

0   5   10m
0   15   30ft

27.04
Section A–A
1:200
1 Bathroom
2 Stair
3 Concrete deck

27.05
Section B–B
1:200
1 Pool
2 Bedroom
3 Bathroom
4 Dining area

27.06
Section C–C
1:200
1 Pool
2 Bedroom
3 Stair
4 Living area
5 Study / recreation
  room
6 Terrace
7 Gallery

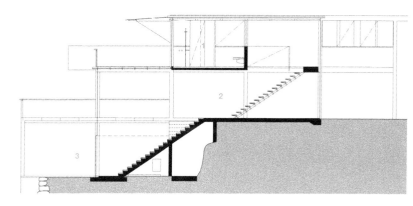

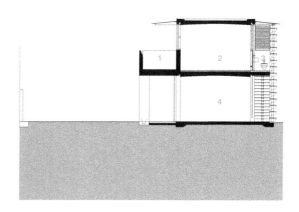

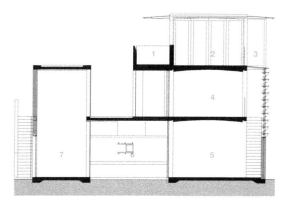

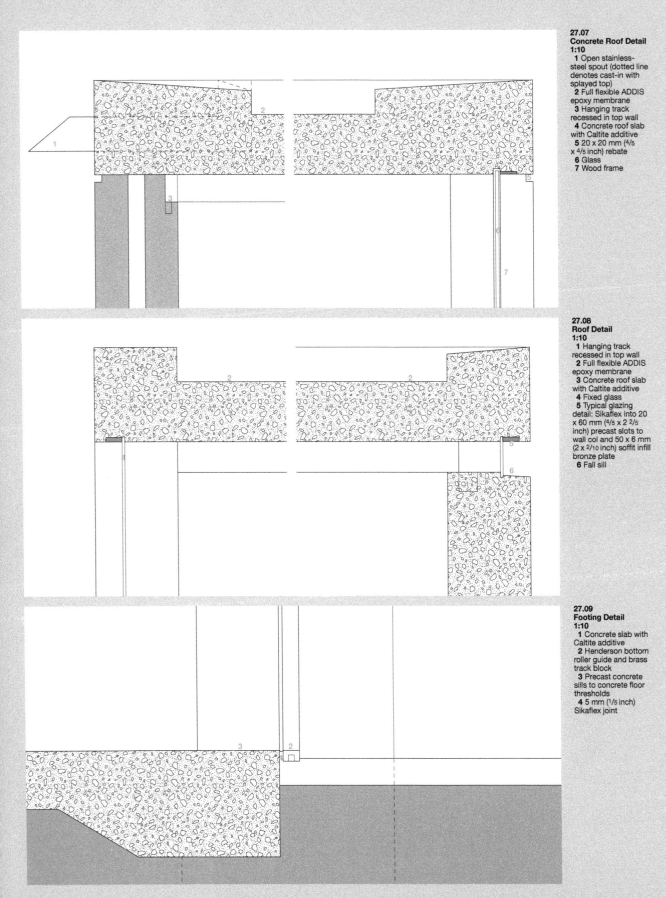

27.07
Concrete Roof Detail
1:10
1 Open stainless-steel spout (dotted line denotes cast-in with splayed top)
2 Full flexible ADDIS epoxy membrane
3 Hanging track recessed in top wall
4 Concrete roof slab with Caltite additive
5 20 x 20 mm (⁴/5 x ⁴/5 inch) rebate
6 Glass
7 Wood frame

27.08
Roof Detail
1:10
1 Hanging track recessed in top wall
2 Full flexible ADDIS epoxy membrane
3 Concrete roof slab with Caltite additive
4 Fixed glass
5 Typical glazing detail: Sikaflex into 20 x 60 mm (⁴/5 x 2 ²/5 inch) precast slots to wall col and 50 x 6 mm (2 x ²/10 inch) soffit infill bronze plate
6 Fall sill

27.09
Footing Detail
1:10
1 Concrete slab with Caltite additive
2 Henderson bottom roller guide and brass track block
3 Precast concrete sills to concrete floor thresholds
4 5 mm (¹/5 inch) Sikaflex joint

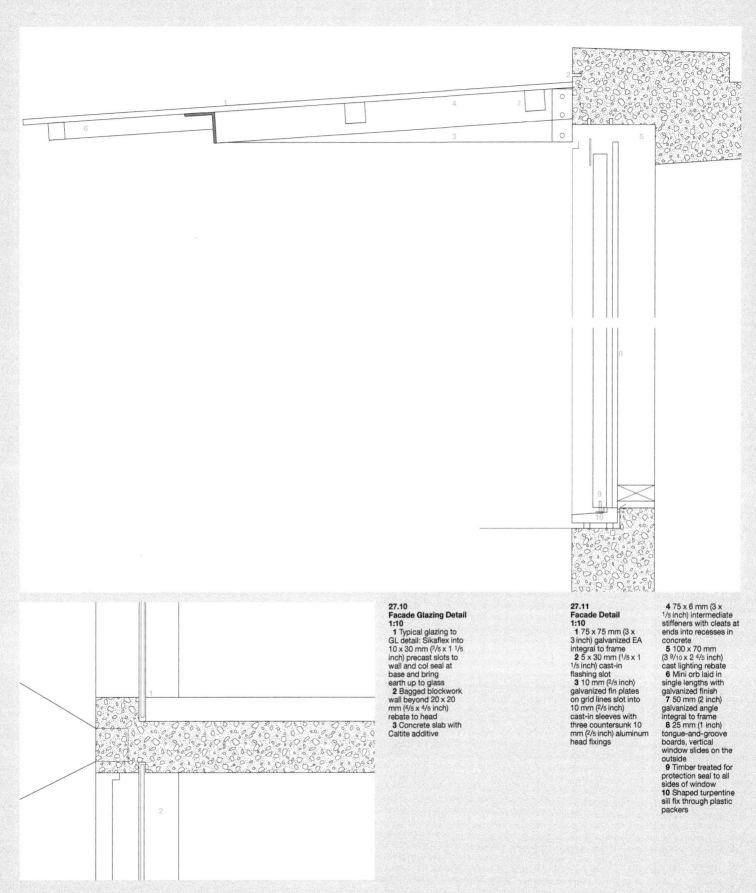

27.10
Facade Glazing Detail
1:10
  1 Typical glazing to
GL detail: Sikaflex into
10 x 30 mm (^{2}/5 x 1 ^{1}/5
inch) precast slots to
wall and col seal at
base and bring
earth up to glass
  2 Bagged blockwork
wall beyond 20 x 20
mm (^{4}/5 x ^{4}/5 inch)
rebate to head
  3 Concrete slab with
Caltite additive

27.11
Facade Detail
1:10
  1 75 x 75 mm (3 x
3 inch) galvanized EA
integral to frame
  2 5 x 30 mm (^{1}/5 x 1
^{1}/5 inch) cast-in
flashing slot
  3 10 mm (^{2}/5 inch)
galvanized fin plates
on grid lines slot into
10 mm (^{2}/5 inch)
cast-in sleeves with
three countersunk 10
mm (^{2}/5 inch) aluminum
head fixings

  4 75 x 6 mm (3 x
^{1}/5 inch) intermediate
stiffeners with cleats at
ends into recesses in
concrete
  5 100 x 70 mm
(3 ^{9}/10 x 2 ^{4}/5 inch)
cast lighting rebate
  6 Mini orb laid in
single lengths with
galvanized finish
  7 50 mm (2 inch)
galvanized angle
integral to frame
  8 25 mm (1 inch)
tongue-and-groove
boards, vertical
window slides on the
outside
  9 Timber treated for
protection seal to all
sides of window
  10 Shaped turpentine
sill fix through plastic
packers

FOSC House
San Pedro, Chile

Client
Claudio and Simonetta Rossi

Project Team
Mauricio Pezo, Sofia von
Ellrichshausen

Structural Engineer
German Aguilera

Main Contractor
Ricardo Ballesta

A six-sided crystalline tower, this compact, three-storey concrete house is positioned on a hilltop in San Pedro, Chile. Built on the highest part of the site, it dominates the landscape and offers an expansive view. The house is buried into the hill and entered on its middle level, which provides the living areas; the bedrooms are on the upper floor and the lower floor. The five bedrooms, three bathrooms, living room and studio are arranged in a tight plan, which circles around a central vertical void containing a simple folded-steel stair. Internal walls are constructed from wood and suggest future flexibility for the internal arrangements.

The external walls are constructed as two independent cast-in-place walls – an inner structural one and an outer protective skin. Both of the walls were cast at the same time in wood formwork, with an insulation layer between them. The exterior concrete skin is coloured green using a water-repellent copper oxide wash. Windows are set flush with the outer skin and positioned in the walls according to both the arrangement of the rooms and the best views of the surrounding landscape.

The inspiration for the copper oxide stain on the exterior walls came from the clients' observation of staining on the pedestals of monuments in the local square.

1 The entrance facade rises up out of the landscape like an emerald jewel. The entrance cuts into the sharply formed wall, drawing you deep into the building.
2 The surfaces of the walls record the history of their construction. The green pigment and the layered strata depict two different sorts of time.
3 Large windows open up the interior to the landscape.
4 Internal walls are made from the same boards as those used to form the walls.
5 Simple wooden furniture is built in, providing storage and sleeping areas within the compact plan.

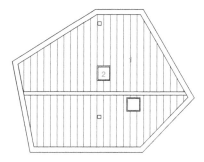

28.01
Roof Plan
1:200
 1 Roof
 2 Skylight

28.02
Upper Floor Plan
1:200
 1 Bedroom
 2 Bathroom
 3 Stair
 4 Study

28.03
Middle Floor Plan
1:200
 1 Kitchen
 2 Living area
 3 Dining area
 4 Entrance hall
 5 Stair
 6 Utility room

28.04
Lower Floor Plan
1:200
 1 Living area
 2 Bedroom
 3 Bathroom
 4 Stair

28.05
Section A-A
1:200
 1 Living area
 2 Bedroom
 3 Living area
 4 Bedroom

28.06
Section B-B
1:200
 1 Bedroom
 2 Stair
 3 Kitchen
 4 Utility
 5 Bathroom

28.07
Section C-C
1:200
 1 Living area
 2 Stair
 3 Living area
 4 Kitchen
 5 Bedroom

28.08
Section D-D
1:200
 1 Living area
 2 Bathroom
 3 Living area
 4 Kitchen
 5 Bedroom
 6 Bathroom

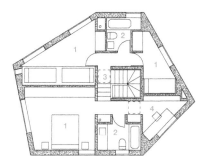

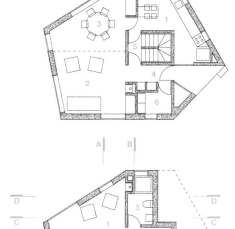

0   5m

0   15ft

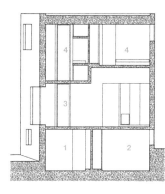

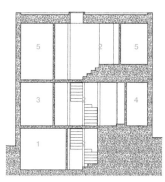

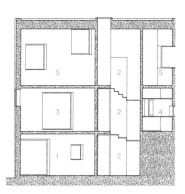

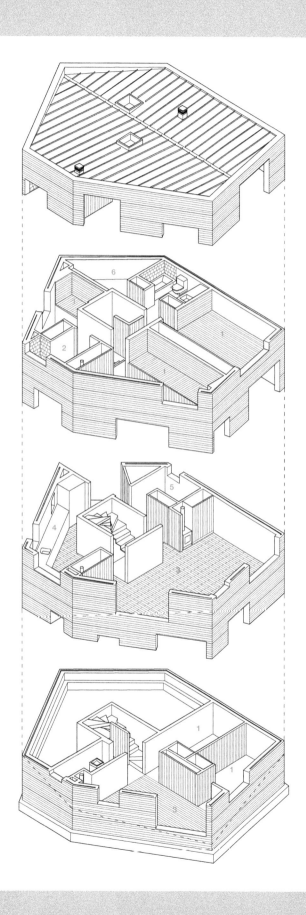

28.09
Exploded
Axonometric
Not to Scale
1 Bedroom
2 Bathroom
3 Living area
4 Kitchen
5 Utility room
6 Study

28.10
Axonometric
Not to Scale

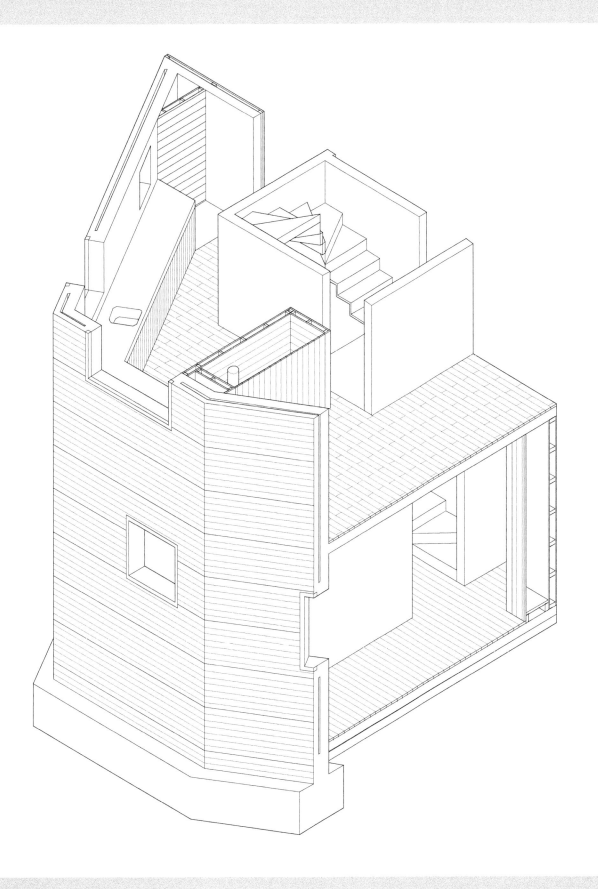

Toro Canyon Residence
Santa Barbara, USA

Client
John Mike and Marcia Cohen

Project Team
John Mike Cohen, Robin Donaldson,
Greg Griffin, Sheida Owrang, Karl
Hamilton

Structural Engineer
Taylor & Syfan Consulting

Main Contractor
Paul Franz Construction

Set among oak and eucalyptus trees
in the Toro Canyon near Santa
Barbara, this house has the rawness
of nature in its materiality and form.
The sharp grey concrete walls set
against the yellow soil give the
building the character of a Donald
Judd sculpture. The site is positioned
along the canyon axis, and there are
dramatic views of the ocean and
islands in the distance.

Approached along a tree-lined
drive, the house at first gives the
appearance of being composed of
three parallel wedge-shaped cast-
concrete volumes. These are a carport
and service volume to the north; a
public living volume to the south west;
and a sleeping volume to the south
east. The carport intersects with the
living volume and is offset to reveal a
glass entry pavilion that separates the
two other volumes. This transparent
part also divides the public and
private spaces. Throughout, the
hardness of the concrete is contrasted
with mahogany doors and windows
and eucalyptus ceilings.

Beneath the upper volumes, there is
a lower level containing guest rooms
and an exercise space.

1 The house slides out
like a rock formation
from the desert, its
three sliced wedge
forms pierced with
deep openings.
2 In the canyon void
between the wings, a
glass-roofed entrance
hall defines the
transition between the
public and private
areas of the house.
3 A terrace flows
around and between
the volumes, and floats
over the pool.
4 The interior living
area opens up towards
the framed landscape.
Above, a pale wood
ceiling reduces the
weight of the large
enclosing walls.
Throughout, the
boundaries between
interior and exterior are
carefully shifted
through the plane of
the concrete skin.

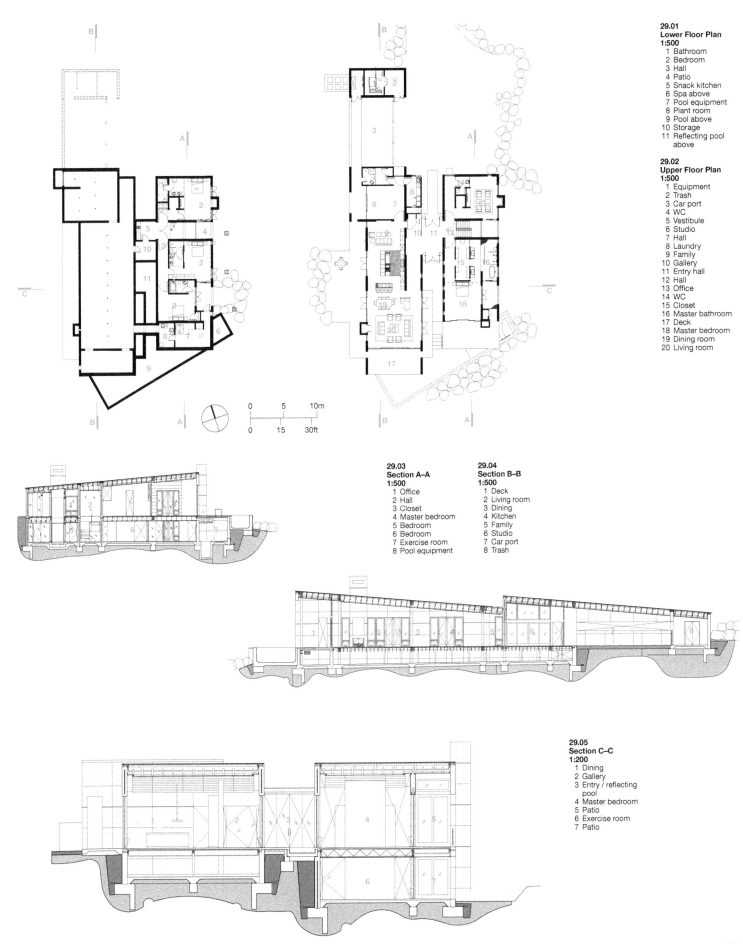

29.01
Lower Floor Plan
1:500
1 Bathroom
2 Bedroom
3 Hall
4 Patio
5 Snack kitchen
6 Spa above
7 Pool equipment
8 Plant room
9 Pool above
10 Storage
11 Reflecting pool
above

29.02
Upper Floor Plan
1:500
1 Equipment
2 Trash
3 Car port
4 WC
5 Vestibule
6 Studio
7 Hall
8 Laundry
9 Family
10 Gallery
11 Entry hall
12 Hall
13 Office
14 WC
15 Closet
16 Master bathroom
17 Deck
18 Master bedroom
19 Dining room
20 Living room

0 5 10m
0 15 30ft

29.03
Section A–A
1:500
1 Office
2 Hall
3 Closet
4 Master bedroom
5 Bedroom
6 Bedroom
7 Exercise room
8 Pool equipment

29.04
Section B–B
1:500
1 Deck
2 Living room
3 Dining
4 Kitchen
5 Family
6 Studio
7 Car port
8 Trash

29.05
Section C–C
1:200
1 Dining
2 Gallery
3 Entry / reflecting
pool
4 Master bedroom
5 Patio
6 Exercise room
7 Patio

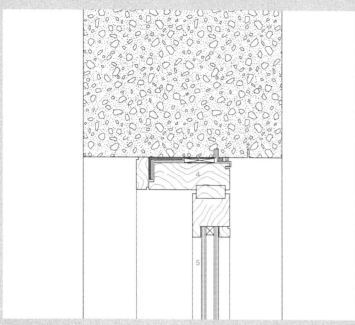

29.06
Door Head Detail
1:5
 1 Concrete
 2 Drip
 3 Waterproof
membrane
 4 Wood door frame
 5 Double glazing

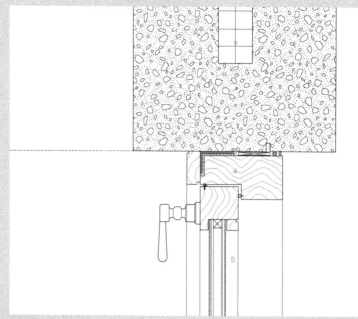

29.07
Jamb at Casement to
Concrete Wall Detail
1:5
 1 Concrete
 2 Insulation
 3 Waterproof
membrane
 4 Wood door frame
 5 Double glazing

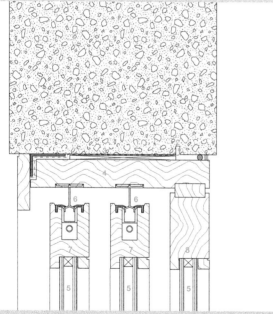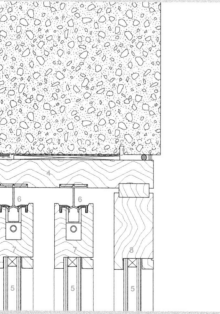

29.08
Head at Sliding Door
to Concrete Wall
1:5
 1 Concrete
 2 Drip
 3 Waterproof
membrane
 4 Wood door frame

 5 Double glazing
 6 Door runner
 7 Sliding door frame
 8 Fixed door frame

29.09
Sill at Swing Door to
Concrete Floor Detail
1:5
 1 Concrete
 2 Insulation
 3 Plywood substrate
 4 Stainless-steel L
section
 5 Swing door

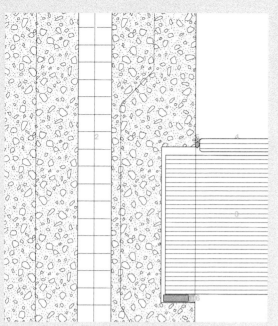

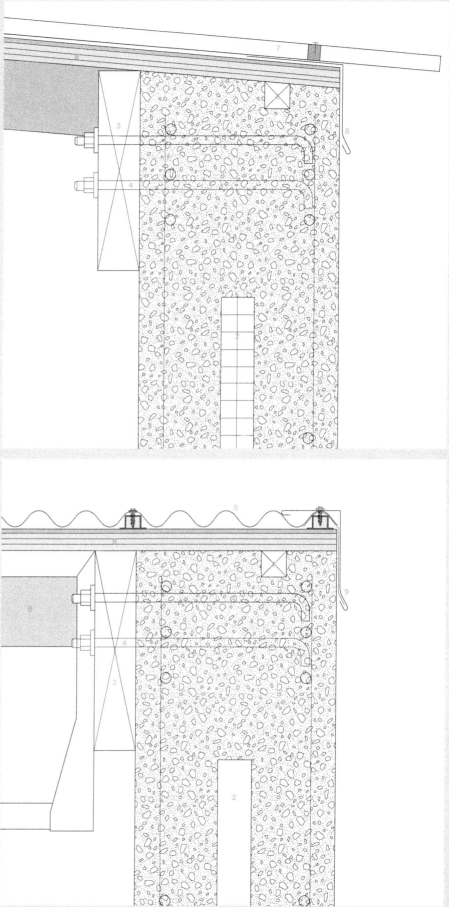

29.10
Glass Entry Beam to Concrete Wall Detail
1:5
1 Concrete
2 Insulation
3 38 x 203 mm (1 1/2 x 8 inch) tempered laminated glass beam
4 10 mm on 10 mm (3/8 on 3/8 inch) tempered laminated glass
5 Silicone
6 (3/8 inch) neoprene

29.11
Roof Eaves at Down Slope Detail
1:5
1 Concrete
2 Insulation
3 Wood beam
4 Steel fixing
5 Wood nailer
6 Plywood sheathing
7 Corrugated metal roofing
8 Stainless-steel flashing

29.12
Roof Rake Detail
1:5
1 Concrete
2 insulation
3 Wood beam
4 Steel fixing
5 Corrugated metal roofing
6 Plywood sheathing
7 Wood nailer
8 Roof rafter
9 Stainless-steel flashing

Colour Concrete House
Yokohama, Japan

Client
Private client

Project Team
Makoto Takei, Chie Nabeshima

Structural Engineer
Akira Suzuki

Main Contractor
Matsumoto Corporation

As is typical in Japanese cities, the site for this house is very small and very narrow at only 46 square metres (495 square feet). It also faces onto a busy main road in Yokohama. The clients wanted to replace an existing two-storey house with a taller structure that better suited its surroundings. The new building is designed for a family of five individuals across three generations.

Although the site is not big, it is located in a commercial area where buildings can be as high as 31 metres (102 feet). The architects decided to set the house one-and-a-half metres (59 inches) back from the road, but otherwise make the most of the available height and width. The result is a five-storey house in which each floor is allocated to a member of the family. Reinforced concrete was chosen for the construction. To make the facade appear softer and smoother, a light green pigment was added. This colour hides the joints between individual pours of concrete.

Great care has been given to the positioning of the windows. As other buildings closely surround the house, the windows were cut out from the corners of each alternate floor. This arrangement maximizes the structure's openness and ensures a unique character in a busy urban location.

1 The tall structure, with its sinuous, rhythmic facade, is a dominant presence on the city street. The corner openings alternate between open and closed around the building.
2 Glass is used for the internal walls. In contrast to the monolithic exterior, the interior appears fragile and delicate.
3 From the kitchen and dining area, broad views of the street and city can be seen through the large corner windows.
4 Rising above the roofs of surrounding buildings, the combined study and bedroom on the third floor has a small private balcony.

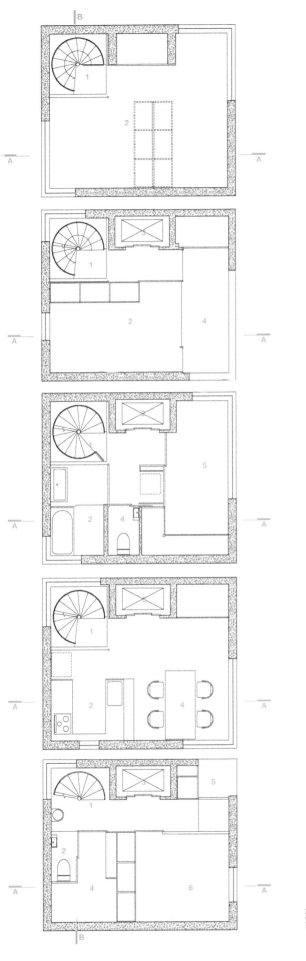

30.01
Fourth Floor Plan
1:100
1 Stair
2 Study / bedroom

30.02
Third Floor Plan
1:100
1 Stair
2 Study / bedroom
3 Lift
4 Balcony

30.03
Second Floor Plan
1:100
1 Stair
2 Bathroom
3 Lift
4 WC
5 Bedroom

30.04
First Floor Plan
1:100
1 Stair
2 Kitchen
3 Lift
4 Dining room

30.05
Ground Floor Plan
1:100
1 Stair
2 WC
3 Lift
4 Closet
5 Entrance
6 Living room

0   5m

0   15ft

30.06
Section A–A
1:100
1 Study / bedroom
2 Study / bedroom
with balcony
3 Bathroom
4 WC
5 Bedroom
6 Kitchen
7 Dining area
8 Closet
9 Room

30.07
Section B–B
1:100
1 Study / bedroom
2 Study / bedroom
3 Bathroom
4 Kitchen
5 Closet
6 Stair

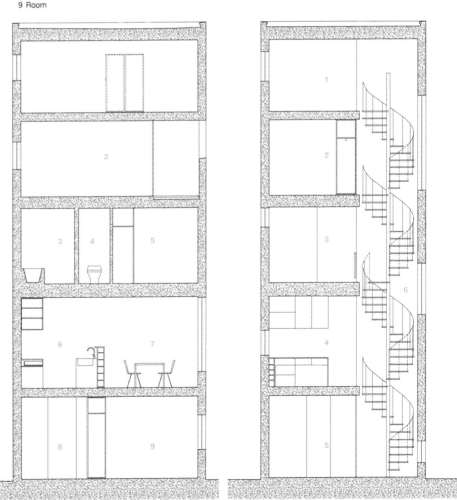

129

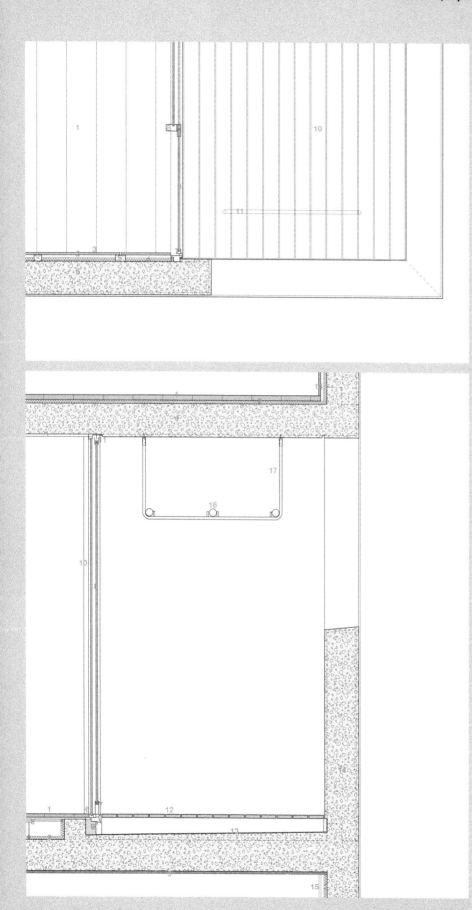

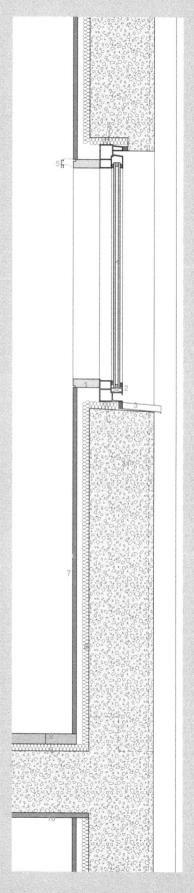

30.08
Balcony Plan
1:20
 1 18 mm (7/10 inch) solid wood flooring (rocky pine), 180 mm (7 1/10 inch) wide, 12 mm (1/2 inch) wood boards, 20 mm (4/5 inch) spray urethane foam insulation
 2 12.5 mm (1/2 inch) plasterboard
 3 Pitted cheesecloth acrylic emulsion paint finish
 4 20 mm (4/5 inch) urethane foam insulation
 5 Movable shelf support
 6 195 mm (7 7/10 inch) exposed coloured concrete
 7 Steel window frame
 8 Steel window support
 9 Double glazing
 10 19 mm (7/10 inch) ulin-wood deck, with 6 mm (1/5 inch) shadow gap boarding
 11 20 mm (4/5 inch) diameter laundry pipe, FB bending

30.09
Balcony Section
1:20
 1 18 mm (7/10 inch) solid wood flooring (rocky pine), 180 mm (7 1/10 inch) wide
 2 20 mm (4/5 inch) urethane foam insulation
 3 12 mm (1/2 inch) wood boards
 4 195 mm (7 7/10 inch) exposed coloured concrete
 5 15 mm (3/5 inch) placing insulation
 6 Flat rail
 7 Steel window frame
 8 Double glazing
 9 Mortar
 10 Steel window support
 11 Caulking
 12 19 mm (7/10 inch) ulin wood deck, 96 mm (3 8/10 inch) wide, with 6 mm (1/5 inch) shadow gap boarding
 13 Waterproof rising
 14 195 mm (7 7/10 inch) exposed coloured concrete
 15 12.5 mm (1/2 inch) plasterboard
 16 20 mm (4/5 inch) diameter laundry pipe
 17 FB bending

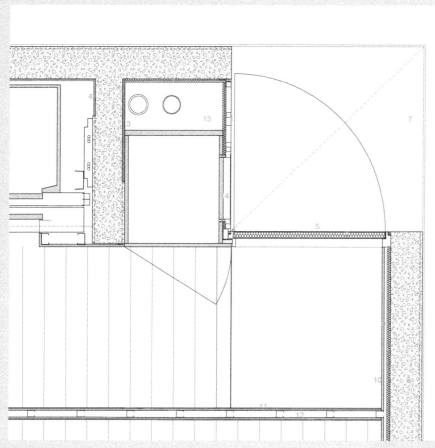

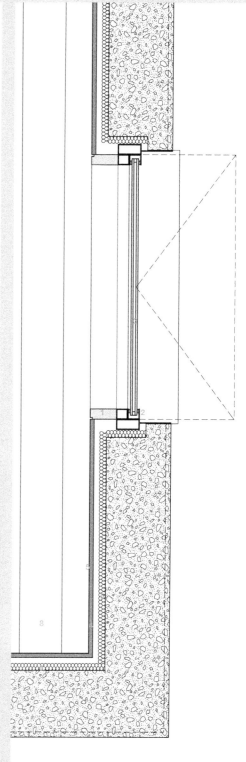

30.10
Window Section
1:10
  1 Wood window
frame (western
hemlock)
  2 Steel window frame
  3 1.5 mm (1/10 inch)
steel plate
  4 Double glazing
  5 Curtain flat rail
  6 12.5 mm (1/2 inch)
plasterboard
  7 Pitted cheesecloth
acrylic emulsion paint
finishing
  8 20 mm (4/5 inch)
urethane foam
insulation
  9 18 mm (7/10 inch)
solid wood flooring
(rocky pine), 130 mm
(5 1/2 inch) wide
10 15 mm (3/5 inch)
placing insulation
11 195 mm (7 7/10 inch)
exposed coloured
concrete

30.11
Wall Plan
1:20
  1 30 mm (1 1/5 inch)
flash panel insulator,
lined side
  2 20 mm (4/5 inch)
urethane foam
insulation
  3 15 mm (3/5 inch)
placing insulation
  4 15 mm (3/5 inch)
urethane foam
insulation
  5 Steel flash door
  6 Glass wool fill-up
  7 100 mm (3 9/10 inch)
trowelled exposed
concrete
  8 195 mm (7 7/10 inch)
exposed coloured
concrete
  9 12.5 mm (1/2 inch)
plasterboard
10 Pitted cheesecloth
acrylic emulsion paint
finishing
11 5 mm (1/5 inch) and
10 mm (2/5 inch)
plasterboard
12 45 x 40 mm (1 4/5
x 1 3/5 inch) metal
support for
plasterboard
13 Technical
compartment
14 Mailbox

30.12
Wall Plan
1:10
  1 Wood window
frame (western
hemlock)
  2 Steel window frame
  3 Double glazing
  4 12.5 mm (1/2 inch)
plasterboard
  5 Pitted cheesecloth
acrylic emulsion
paint finishing
  6 20 mm (4/5 inch)
urethane foam
insulation
  7 195 mm (7 7/10 inch)
exposed coloured
concrete
  8 18 mm (7/10 inch)
solid wood flooring
(rocky pine), 130 mm
(5 1/2 inch) wide,
12 mm (1/2 inch) wood
boards, 20 mm (4/5
inch) urethane foam
insulation

House in Kohoku
Yokohama, Japan

Client
Private client

Project Team
Koichi Suzuno, Shinya Kamuro

Structural Engineer
MID Architectural Structure Laboratory

Main Contractor
Yamasho

The clients for this project wanted to demolish their existing two-storied house as their children had left home, and to replace it with a smaller house that would be filled with natural light. This was problematic as houses already surrounded the L-shaped site, with a particularly tall house on the south side. The only solution that could fulfill the brief while also dealing with the potential problem of being overlooked was to bring light in from the top.

The house is therefore composed of four funnel-like roofs that are each glazed on the top. These roof lights are positioned to bring the maximum light into the house while avoiding the gaze of the neighbours. The materials used are standard – as is common in Japan, the roofs and the walls are made only of 150 mm (5 9/10 inch) thick reinforced concrete.

The entire upper part was cast as a single pour, hence there are no joints and in turn no weaknesses. There are no columns inside the house – the external form is an exact reflection of the internal form. The single-storey interior has been softly divided into four areas according to the shape of the roofs. In the area with the highest ceiling, a mezzanine floor has been added as an office space. The exterior of the building is left in exposed concrete, while the interior is painted white to reflect the light and to make the shadows more visible. Space has been maximized by constructing much of the furniture from MDF – this has been left in its raw condition to reflect the spirit of the building.

1 The house opens directly onto the garden. Its pyramid roofs are angled to bring in light at different seasons and times of day.
2 The white-painted interior catches both light and shadow, communicating the passing of time and the prevailing external conditions.
3 Amongst its suburban neighbours, the house has an air of permanence and of a natural connection with its environment.
4 The scale and materiality of the interior suggest a place well suited to a calm and cosy domestic life.

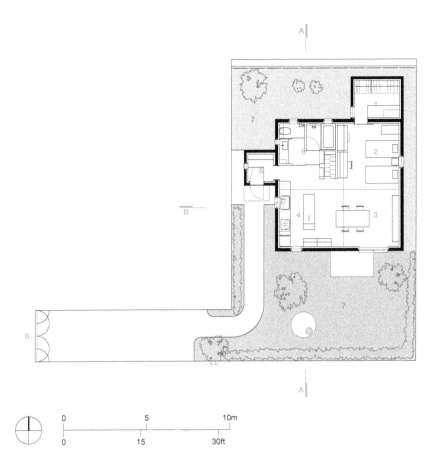

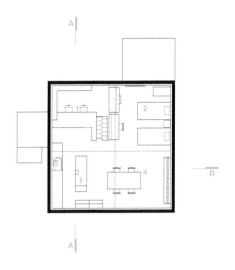

31.01
Ground Floor Plan
1:200
1 Dressing room
2 Bedroom space
3 Living and dining space
4 Kitchen
5 Entrance lobby
6 Bathroom
7 Garden
8 Entrance from street

31.02
First Floor Plan
1:200
1 Studio / office
2 Bedroom space
3 Kitchen
4 Living space

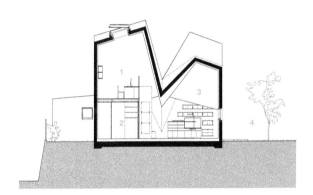

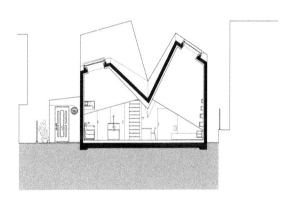

31.03
Section A–A
1:200
1 Studio / office
2 Bathroom
3 Living and dining space
4 Garden

31.04
Section B–B
1:200
1 Front door
2 Kitchen
3 Living and dining space

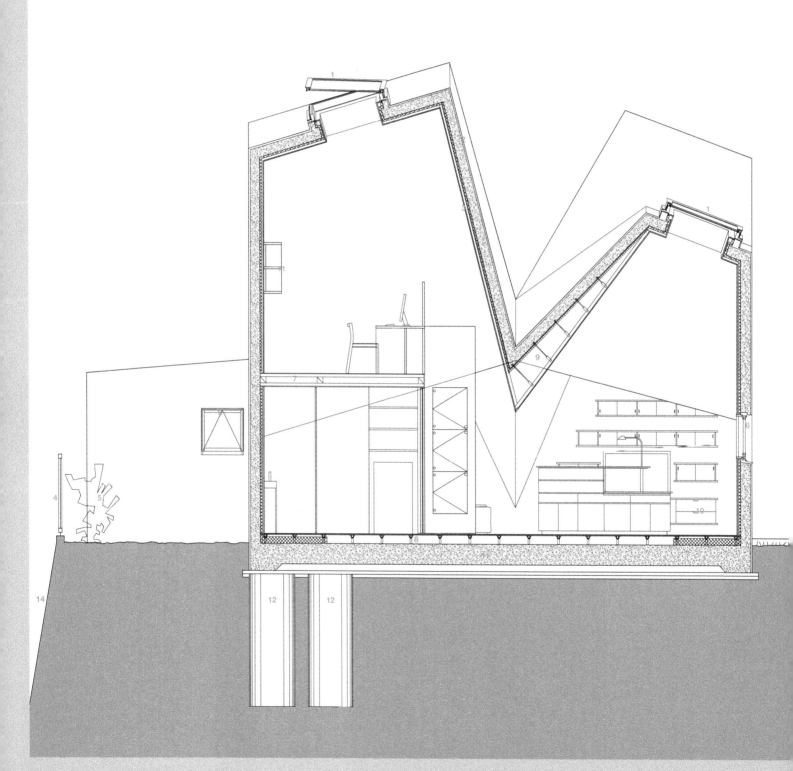

31.05
Detail Section
1:50
  1 Aluminium tilt sash
skylight
  2 Exposed watertight
concrete roof with
water-repellent-paint
finish
  3 Emulsion on 12.5
mm ($^1/_2$ inch)
plasterboard wall with
30 mm (1 $^1/_5$ inch)
urethane insulation
spray finish
  4 1200 mm (47 $^1/_5$
inch) high fence
  5 Planting: climbing
rose
  6 Aluminium tilt sash
  7 12 mm ($^1/_2$ inch)
MDF floor with white
wax finish, urethane
clear paint
  8 12 mm ($^1/_2$ inch)
MDF floor with white
wax finish, urethane
clear paint, and electric
floor-heating panel
below
  9 Hanging stirrup bolt
to suspended ceiling
10 MDF island table
with white wax finish,
urethane clear paint
and 10 mm ($^2/_5$ inch)
artificial marble top
11 300 mm (11 $^4/_5$
inch) raft foundation
12 Deep pile
foundations
13 Terrace of
interlocking blocks
14 Existing retaining
wall

Merricks House
Mornington Peninsula, Victoria,
Australia

Client
Joseph Gersh

Project Team
Roger Wood, Randal Marsh, David
Goss, Matthew Borg

Structural Engineer
John Gardner & Associates

Main Contractor
DC Construction

Approached along a long winding
drive through an established vineyard,
Merricks House overlooks the
Mornington Peninsula. The brief was
to build a large, flexible family home of
a high quality and with a sense of
solidity, constructed from materials
that would age well and require
minimal upkeep. Through the centre of
the house, a pair of curved walls
constructed from rammed earth – a
material that is essentially a primitive
form of concrete – form the spine of
the building. Large south-facing
windows provide views across the
landscape to the ocean. The structural
engineer was involved early in the
design process to ensure the
seamless integration of services,
openings and frameless glazing.

There are six bedrooms to
accommodate the large family, with a
range of spaces that can be enjoyed
in differing weather conditions. Mainly
used as a holiday and weekend
residence, the bedrooms are
positioned in three wings, accessed
through discreet openings in the
central corridor. This layout allows
autonomy between visitors and also
ensures that the house does not
appear empty when it is not fully
occupied.

A basement cellar provides storage
for wine, including that produced on
the property's vineyard. The building
makes particular use of mass to store
energy and modulate the environment.
Materials with low embodied energy
ratings have been used throughout. All
of the spaces are cross-ventilated,
and each building volume can be
heated and cooled independently. As
the house is not connected to mains
water, all rainwater is harvested for
use, while sewage is treated on site.

1 The entrance is
between the two
parallel arcs of the
spine walls. The house
appears comfortable
and established in its
raw coastal
environment.
2 A dark pool across
the centre of the house
reflects the sky and
cools the environment.
The strong shadows
define and accentuate
the forms.
3 Main living spaces
flow from one to
another without the
constraint of doors.
Views of the
surrounding landscape
are always present.
4 The curved corridors
provide space to
display the owners'
art collection.
5 As the central
corridor passes
through the house,
the ceiling compresses
the space in a gentle
swelling arc.

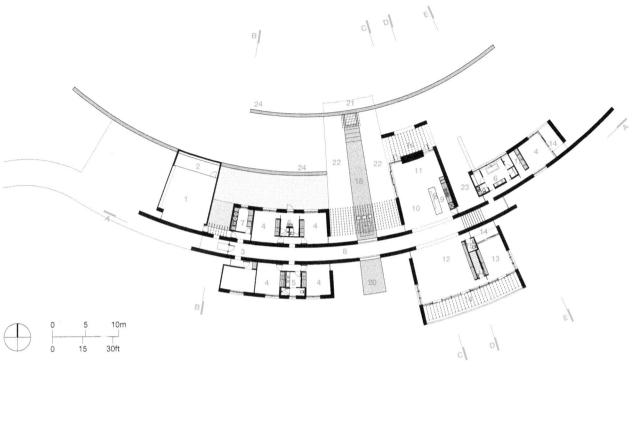

32.01
Plan
1:500
1 Garage
2 Store
3 Entry
4 Bedroom
5 Bathroom
6 En suite
7 Laundry
8 Corridor
9 Kitchen
10 Dining area
11 Lounge
12 Living area
13 Study
14 Terrace
15 Powder room
16 Basement stair
17 Robe
18 Pool
19 Spa
20 Pond
21 Pool equipment
22 Pool terrace
23 Courtyard
24 Garden wall

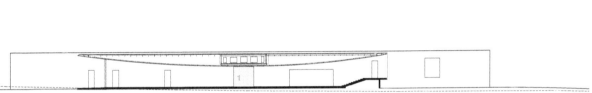

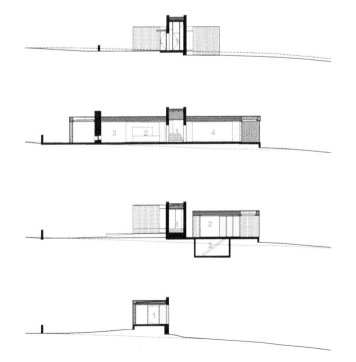

32.02
Section A–A
1:500
1 Corridor

32.03
Section B–B
1:500
1 Corridor

32.04
Section C–C
1:500
1 Corridor
2 Kitchen
3 Lounge
4 Living area

32.05
Section D–D
1:500
1 Corridor
2 Study
3 Wine cellar

32.06
Section E–E
1:500
1 Corridor

32.07
Entry Door Window Plan
1:10
1 Solid timber door
2 Full-height timber frame
3 Selected glazing
4 Recessed glazing channel
5 Rammed-earth wall

32.08
Window Plan
1:10
1 Rammed-earth wall
2 Recessed glazing channel
3 Edge of slab
4 Line of ceiling over
5 Angle below
6 Selected glazing
7 13 mm (1/2 inch) plasterboard
8 Recessed glazing channel
9 Shiplap cladding

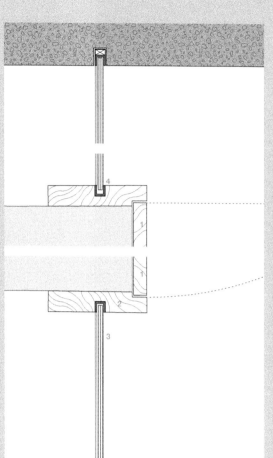

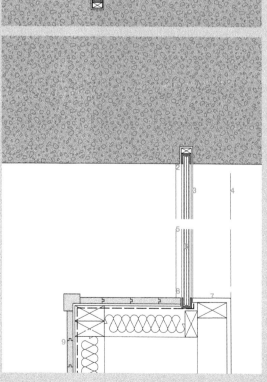

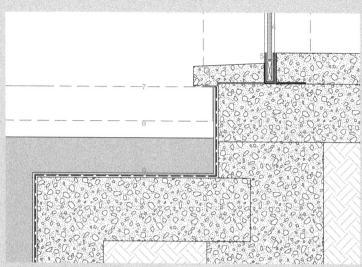

32.09
Window Section at Pool Edge
1:10
1 Rammed-earth wall
2 Structural slab
3 Concrete screed
4 Selected glazing
5 Recessed glazing channel
6 Concrete window ledge / sill
7 Pool terrace
8 Pool waterline
9 Selected pool tiles

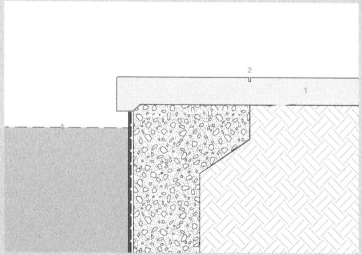

32.10
Pool Edge Section
1:10
1 Paving slab
2 Sawcut to slab
3 Concrete pool shell
4 Pool waterline

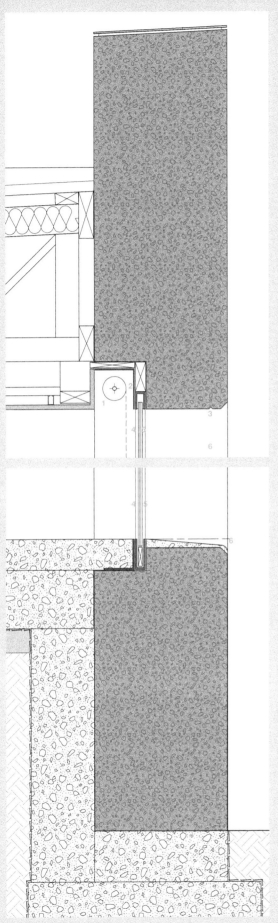

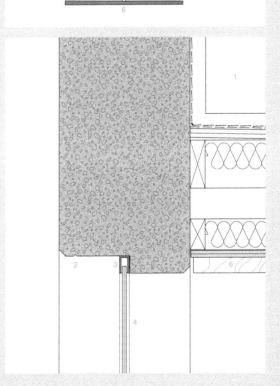

32.11
Recessed Blind
Section
1:10
 1 Recessed blind
 2 Folded aluminium sheet conceal fixed to reveal
 3 Drip groove
 4 Recessed side glazing channel
 5 Selected glazing
 6 Rammed-earth wall

32.12
Window Sill Section
1:10
 1 Rammed-earth wall
 2 Structural slab
 3 Concrete screed
 4 Selected glazing
 5 Recessed glazing channel screed to window sill
 6 Finished floor level
 7 Concrete blockwork

32.13
Lintel Section
1:10
 1 Timber battened ceiling
 2 Hopleys truss roof structure.
 3 13 mm (1/2 inch) plasterboard suspended ceiling with shadow gap to earth wall junction
 4 Rammed earth
 5 Concrete beam
 6 Steel plate to underside of lintel

32.14
Window Head Section
1:10
 1 A/C equipment
 2 Drip groove
 3 Glazing channel
 4 Selected glazing
 5 Rammed-earth wall
 6 Timber ceiling

139

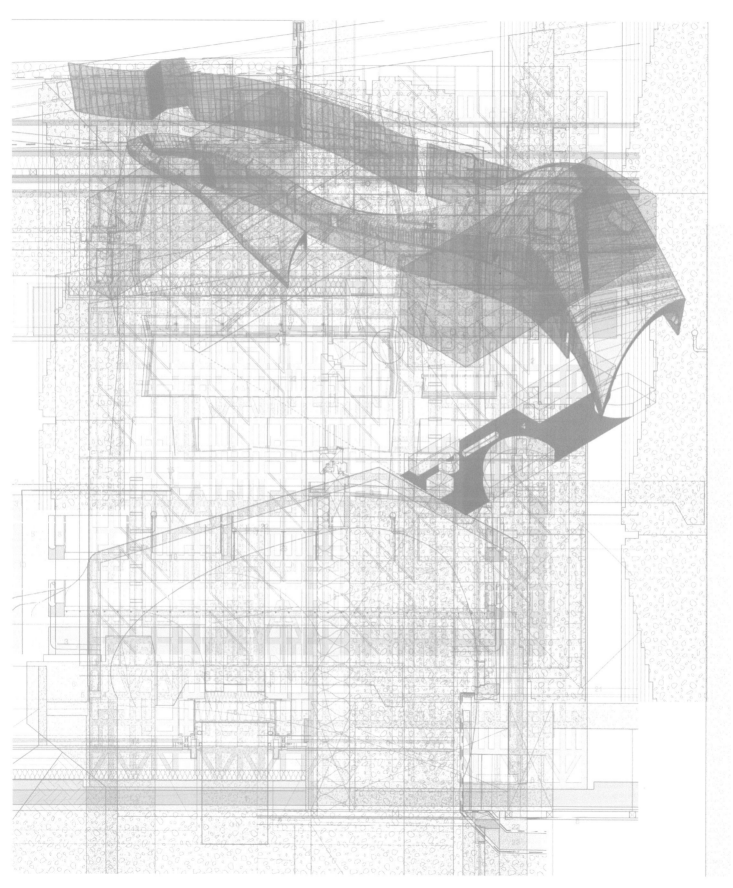

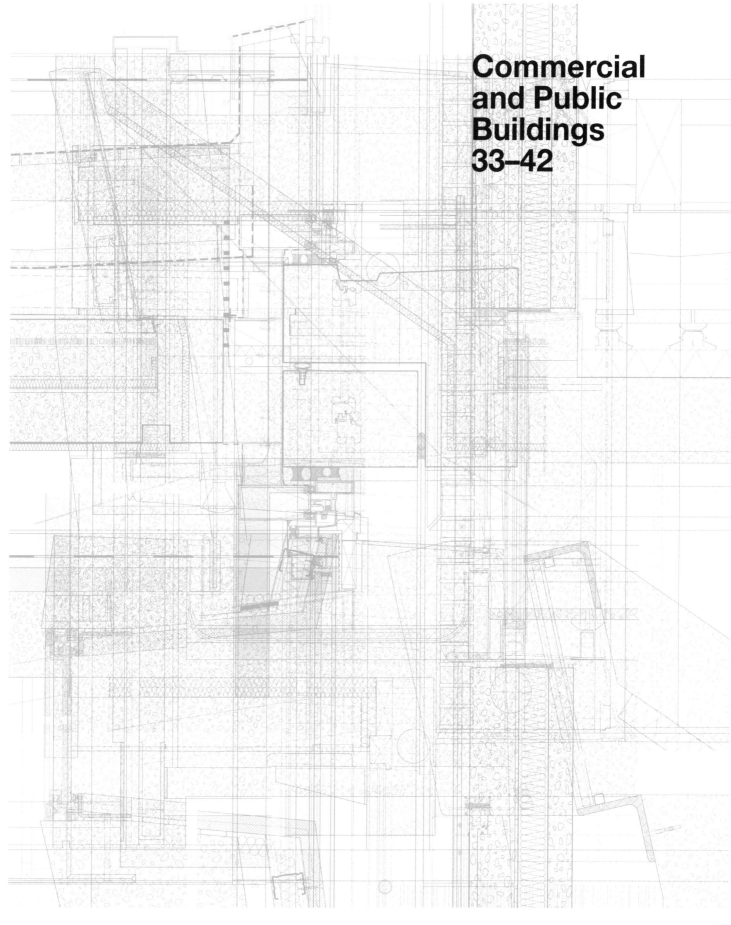

Commercial and Public Buildings
33–42

**Vodafone Building
Porto, Portugal**

Client
Vodafone

Project Team
José António Barbosa and Pedro
Lopes Guimarães
Ana Campante, Ana Carvalho, Ana
Mota, Daniela Teixeira, Eunice Lopes,
Filipe Secca, Henrique Dias, Hugo
Abreu, Nuno Felgar, José Marques,
Miguel Pimenta, Pablo Rebelo, Paula
Fonseca, Paulo Lima, Raul Andrade,
Sara Caruso

Structural Engineer
Afaconsult / Carlos Quinaz

Main Contractor
Teixeira Duarte

This building for the mobile telephone
company Vodafone adopts a dynamic
form that communicates linear, flowing
movement to its facades. The effect of
a surface in motion is obtained in part
through the qualities concrete has as
a plastic material. The ability of
concrete to be both structure and
surface allows the building to place
the majority of its support in its skin,
augmented by two stairways and
three central columns. This
arrangement allows maximum
flexibility in the internal plan.

The fractured geometry of the main
facade faces out onto a busy avenue.
The alignment is a response to the
adjacent buildings to the east and
west. The shell structure on the north
and south elevations is constructed of
white self-compacting concrete. This
concrete was cast entirely in-situ
using marine plywood formwork. The
outer window frames are stainless
steel and aluminium, while the interior
frames are stainless steel and wood.

The building has eight floors; five
are above ground and three below.
On the ground floor, in addition to the
auditorium, office and cafeteria, there
is a large retail store. The four upper
floors contain open-plan offices; on
the third floor and the roof there are
open terraces. Two of the three
basement floors are for car parking
while the other is occupied by
technical areas and training rooms.
At the rear, there is a south-facing
courtyard garden that can be
accessed via the auditorium and
cafeteria; here a few mature trees
have been preserved.

1 The folded concrete facade wraps the building like an origami model. Between the bands of linear wall, diamond-shaped windows expose the open interior.

2 The rear of the building has the same language of articulated forms. At ground level sculpted lights illuminate the basement.

3 Within the building the walls are bright white; both artificial and natural light are manipulated to create dramatic effects.

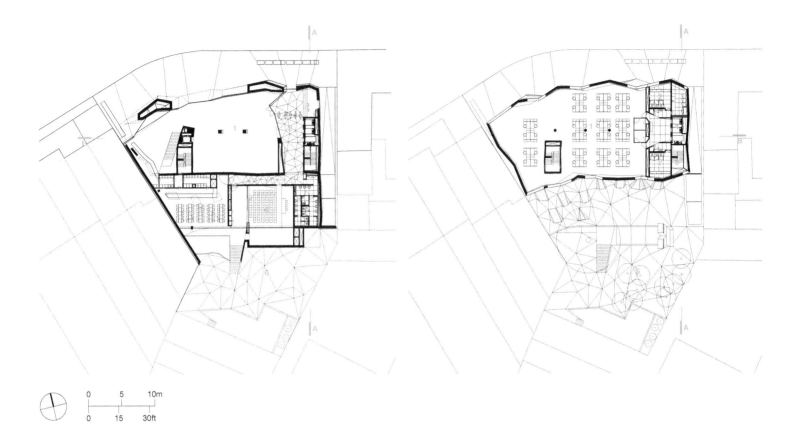

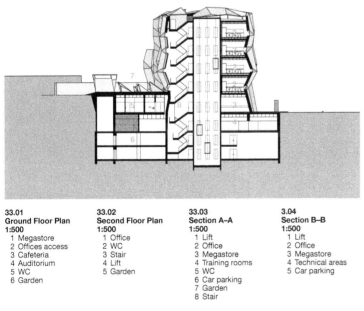

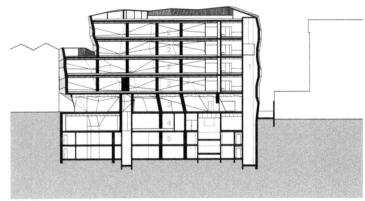

33.01
Ground Floor Plan
1:500
1 Megastore
2 Offices access
3 Cafeteria
4 Auditorium
5 WC
6 Garden

33.02
Second Floor Plan
1:500
1 Office
2 WC
3 Stair
4 Lift
5 Garden

33.03
Section A–A
1:500
1 Lift
2 Office
3 Megastore
4 Training rooms
5 WC
6 Car parking
7 Garden
8 Stair

3.04
Section B–B
1:500
1 Lift
2 Office
3 Megastore
4 Technical areas
5 Car parking

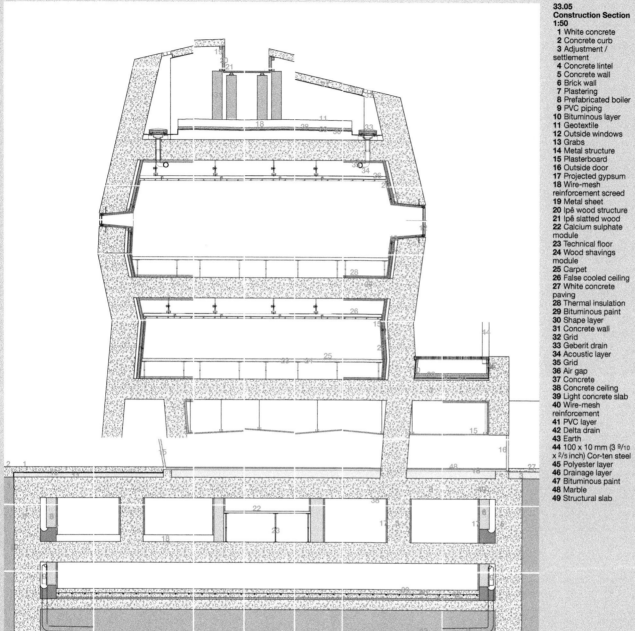

33.05
Construction Section
1:50
 1 White concrete
 2 Concrete curb
 3 Adjustment / settlement
 4 Concrete lintel
 5 Concrete wall
 6 Brick wall
 7 Plastering
 8 Prefabricated boiler
 9 PVC piping
10 Bituminous layer
11 Geotextile
12 Outside windows
13 Grabs
14 Metal structure
15 Plasterboard
16 Outside door
17 Projected gypsum
18 Wire-mesh reinforcement screed
19 Metal sheet
20 Ipê wood structure
21 Ipê slatted wood
22 Calcium sulphate module
23 Technical floor
24 Wood shavings module
25 Carpet
26 False cooled ceiling
27 White concrete paving
28 Thermal insulation
29 Bituminous paint
30 Shape layer
31 Concrete wall
32 Grid
33 Geberit drain
34 Acoustic layer
35 Grid
36 Air gap
37 Concrete
38 Concrete ceiling
39 Light concrete slab
40 Wire-mesh reinforcement
41 PVC layer
42 Delta drain
43 Earth
44 100 x 10 mm (3 $^{9}/_{10}$ x $^{2}/_{5}$ inch) Cor-ten steel
45 Polyester layer
46 Drainage layer
47 Bituminous paint
48 Marble
49 Structural slab

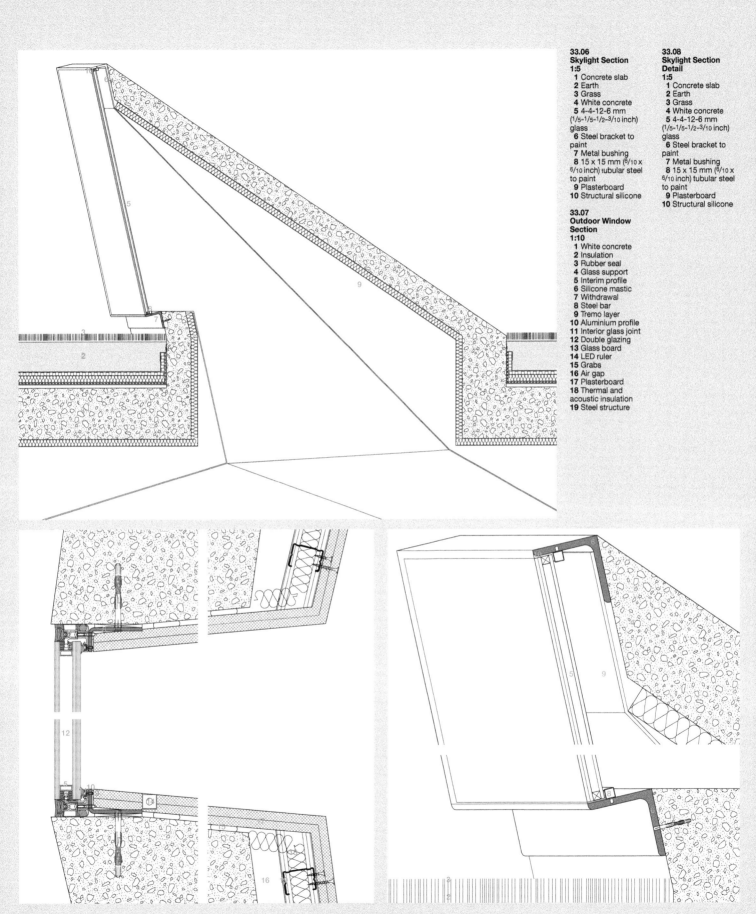

33.06
Skylight Section
1:5
 1 Concrete slab
 2 Earth
 3 Grass
 4 White concrete
 5 4-4-12-6 mm
($^1/_5$-$^1/_5$-$^1/_2$-$^3/_{10}$ inch)
glass
 6 Steel bracket to
paint
 7 Metal bushing
 8 15 x 15 mm ($^6/_{10}$ x
$^6/_{10}$ inch) tubular steel
to paint
 9 Plasterboard
 10 Structural silicone

33.07
Outdoor Window
Section
1:10
 1 White concrete
 2 Insulation
 3 Rubber seal
 4 Glass support
 5 Interim profile
 6 Silicone mastic
 7 Withdrawal
 8 Steel bar
 9 Tremo layer
 10 Aluminium profile
 11 Interior glass joint
 12 Double glazing
 13 Glass board
 14 LED ruler
 15 Grabs
 16 Air gap
 17 Plasterboard
 18 Thermal and
acoustic insulation
 19 Steel structure

33.08
Skylight Section
Detail
1:5
 1 Concrete slab
 2 Earth
 3 Grass
 4 White concrete
 5 4-4-12-6 mm
($^1/_5$-$^1/_5$-$^1/_2$-$^3/_{10}$ inch)
glass
 6 Steel bracket to
paint
 7 Metal bushing
 8 15 x 15 mm ($^6/_{10}$ x
$^6/_{10}$ inch) tubular steel
to paint
 9 Plasterboard
 10 Structural silicone

34

Becker Architekten

Hydroelectric Power Station Kempten, Germany

Client
Allgäuer Überlandwerk GmbH (AÜW), Kempten

Project Team
Michael Becker, Bernhard Kast, Franz G. Schroeck

Structural Engineers
RMD Consult, Konstruktionsgruppe Bauen

Main Contractor
Xaver Lutzenberger Co.

Many influences provided the inspiration for this power station's appearance, each of them carefully melded into a single, dynamic structure. Essentially a reinforced-concrete tunnel 100 metres (328 feet) long by 23 metres (75 feet) wide, its sculpted form, inspired by the motion of the river and local rock formations, twists and flows in homage to the forces it seeks to utilize.

Providing power for 3000 homes, it replaces a previous power station from the 1950s. The form of its external shell creates a harmonious dialogue between a group of adjacent nineteenth-century industrial buildings, the hills beyond and the river itself. This skin, mounted on sliding bearings to compensate for movement, is constructed from pale spray-coated concrete; the 'soft' surface and the exposed, fine-gravel aggregate within exude a soft luminosity. In contrast, the interior is constructed from raw board-marked concrete reinforced with lateral ribs – this more basic language is well suited to the generation process.

Water is channelled into a holding basin, then downwards through the turbines, and finally back into the River Iller. Conserving the river's ecology and contributing to the local area were important to the evolution of the design. The power station incorporates a fish ladder to aid migration, a cycle path, and measures to minimize noise. At night it is dramatically lit.

1 The fluid forms of the power station's structure recall the action of water erosion on river rocks.
2 The historic buildings adjacent to the facility provide a contrasting orthogonal backdrop to the organic water tunnel.
3 The surface of the upper parts has a rough grit texture that catches the light.
4 Within the tunnel the walls are strengthened with ribs. The effect is reminiscent of a cathedral.
5 The board-marked lower areas are supported by rhythmic cast arches.

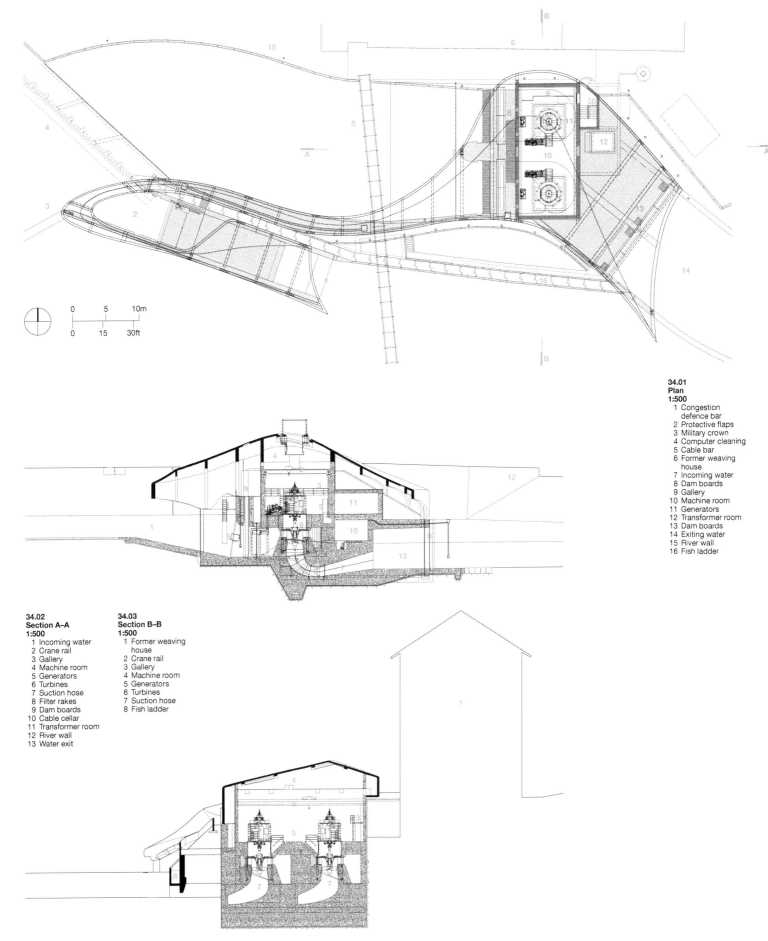

34.01
Plan
1:500
1 Congestion
 defence bar
2 Protective flaps
3 Military crown
4 Computer cleaning
5 Cable bar
6 Former weaving
 house
7 Incoming water
8 Dam boards
9 Gallery
10 Machine room
11 Generators
12 Transformer room
13 Dam boards
14 Exiting water
15 River wall
16 Fish ladder

34.02
Section A–A
1:500
1 Incoming water
2 Crane rail
3 Gallery
4 Machine room
5 Generators
6 Turbines
7 Suction hose
8 Filter rakes
9 Dam boards
10 Cable cellar
11 Transformer room
12 River wall
13 Water exit

34.03
Section B–B
1:500
1 Former weaving
 house
2 Crane rail
3 Gallery
4 Machine room
5 Generators
6 Turbines
7 Suction hose
8 Fish ladder

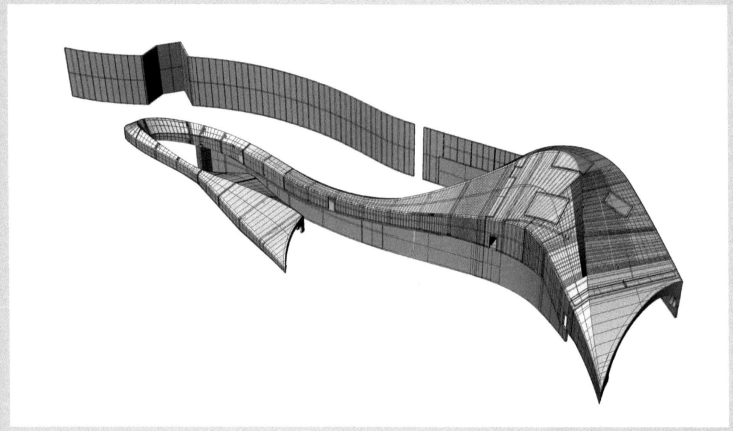

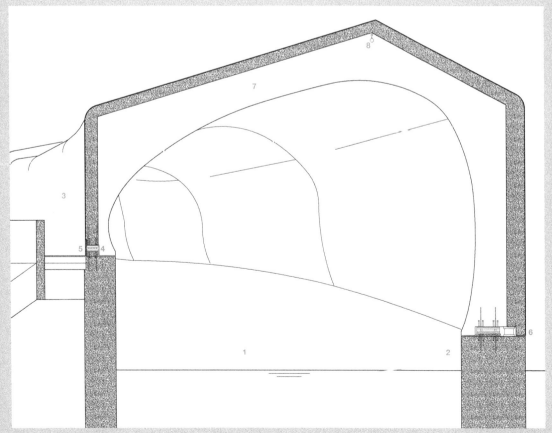

34.04
CAD Model
Not to Scale

34.05
Section
1:200
  1 Right water inlet
  2 Incoming spur
  3 Maintenance
  4 Bearings
  5 Cover
  6 Hydraulic press
  7 Ribs
  8 Ridge lighting

34.06
Vertical Section of Ridge Detail
1:10
  1 8 mm (³/10 inch) diameter lightning protection V2A roof ridge
  2 8 mm (³/10 inch) lightning protection V2A stainless steel
  3 Two-part polyurethane spray, BASF Co. or comparable with gravel scattered on surface
  4 Thread rod
  5 40 mm (1 ³/5 inch) galvanized steel tube
  6 Galvanized pipe clip
  7 50 mm (2 inch) gap along roof ridge
  8 Suspension via thread rod
  9 Galvanized pipe clip around luminaire
  10 90 mm (3 ¹/2 inch) Zumtobel Tubilux

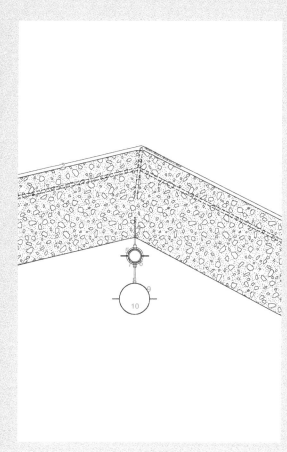

34.07
Vertical Section of Gap Building Element Number 5: Roof Ridge and Roof Point
1:10
  1 Two-part polyurethane spray, BASF Co. or comparable with gravel scattered on surface
  2 10 mm (²/5 inch) stainless-steel panel
  3 5 mm (¹/5 inch) stainless-steel panel
  4 150 x 5 mm (5 ⁹/10 x ¹/5 inch) stainless-steel panel
  5 150 x 25 mm (5 ⁹/10 x 1 inch) stainless-steel plate; 4 pieces
  6 100 x 16 mm (3 ⁹/10 x 16 mm (³/5 inch) core dowel, Pfeifer Co.
  7 Lightweight concrete LC 30/33

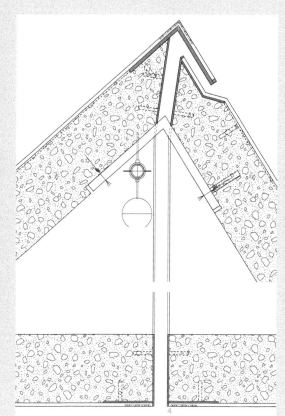

34.09
Vertical Section of Steel Shelf Locking / Rail 1
1:10
  1 Two-part polyurethane spray, BASF Co. or comparable with gravel scattered on surface
  2 200 x 200 mm (7 ⁹/10 x 7 ⁹/10 inch) steel shelf with 16 mm (³/5 inch) blind hole

34.10
Vertical Section of Steel Shelf for Removable Units
1:10
  1 Pfeiffer Co. 42 x 4.5 mm (1 ¹³/20 x ¹/6 inch) flat bar tie rod for generators; 30 x 3.5 mm (1 ²/10 x ¹/10 inch) flat bar tie rod for transformer
  2 100 mm (3 ⁹/10 inch) inner insulation, Foamglas Co.
  3 Two part polyurethane-spray, BASF Co. or comparable with gravel scattered on surface

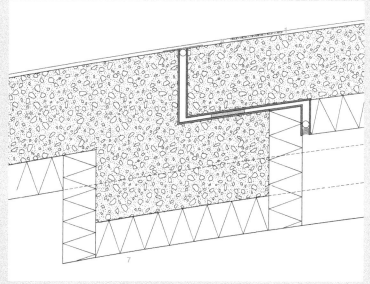

34.08
Section of Lip Turbine / Transformer Detail
1:10
  1 Two-part polyurethane spray, BASF Co. or comparable with gravel scattered on surface
  2 10 x 100 mm (4/10 x 3 ⁹/10 inch) ESZ bearing
  3 5 mm (¹/5 inch) stainless-steel frame
  4 Elastic dividing strip
  5 Round cord
  6 Concrete C30/37
  7 Inner insulation, Foamglas Co.

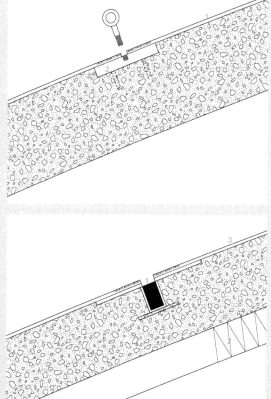

149

Mint Hotel Tower of London
City of London, UK

Client
Mint Hotel Group

Project Team
Bennets Associates (Architects);
Gleeds (Project Manager); Jones Lang
LaSalle (Cost Consultant); Bennetts
Associates / Woods Bagot (Interior
Design); AECOM (Acoustic Consultant
& M&E Engineer); DP9 (Town Planning
Consultant); In Your Stride (Accessibility
Consultant); Frost Landscape
Construction (Living Wall Contractor)

Structural Engineer
Buro Happold

Main Contractor
Laing O'Rourke

Located on a tight urban site near
Tower Bridge in the City of London,
this hotel has been carefully inserted
into the medieval street pattern. The
hotel replaces a 1960s' building that
failed to connect to the dense
contextual fabric. The new
development seeks to address this by
building out to the original street line
and by populating the ground level
with a variety of public uses.

Although this is very much a city
building, nature has been brought
deep into the hotel. The courtyard
incorporates the largest green wall in
Europe, rising up from the ground
floor to the eleventh-floor terrace. This
space provides welcome calm in the
turbulent city.

There are 583 bedrooms in the
hotel, along with meeting rooms,
conference facilities, three bars and
an award-winning restaurant. The
main bulk of the building is scaled to
adjacent buildings. At the roof level,
the SkyLounge is treated as a discrete
lighter element that hovers above the
adjacent roofs, allowing spectacular
views over London's skyline.

Throughout the project, a clear,
strong and disciplined material
language lends the hotel a powerful
image. This is particularly evident in
the powerful concrete columns and
beams of the entrance canopy.

1 The confined island site does not allow the entire building to be viewed from any point. The scale and metre of the building is measured to its surroundings.
2 The materials used reflect those found in buildings adjacent to the site.
3 The green wall brings a welcome natural element to the intense urban environment.
4 Giant concrete columns and deep beams support the hotel over the entrance area.
5 The glazed roof with its delicate lattice covers the bar area and allows views of the courtyard and green wall above.

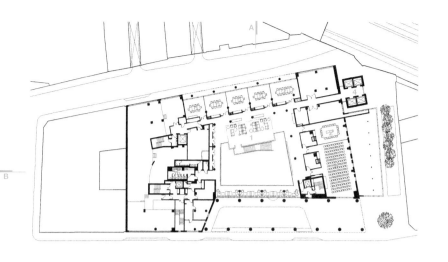

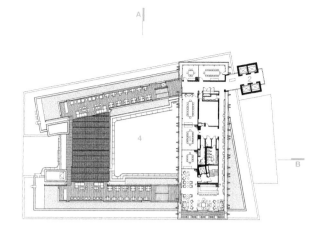

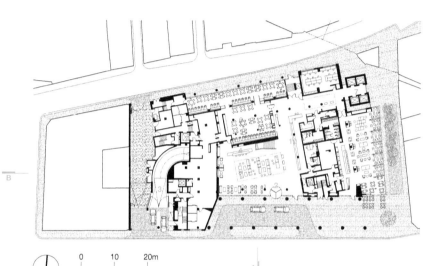

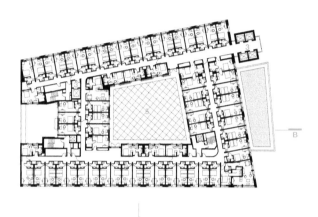

```
      0    10    20m
      0    30    60ft
```

35.01
First Floor Plan
1:1000
1 Break-out space
2 Meeting room
3 Conference space
4 Lift
5 WC

35.02
Ground Floor Plan
1:1000
1 Car drop area
2 Entrance
3 Car park entrance
4 Bar
5 Foyer
6 Restaurant
7 Lift
8 Lounge bar
9 WC
10 Reception desk

35.03
SkyLounge Floor
Plan
1:1000
1 SkyLounge
2 Lift
3 Bar
4 Courtyard
5 Terrace
6 WC

35.04
Typical Floor Plan 2–8
1:1000
1 Bedroom
2 Bathroom
3 Lift
4 Stair
5 Courtyard

35.05
Section A–A
1:1000
1 SkyLounge
2 Bedroom
3 Break-out space
4 Car drop area
5 Restaurant
6 Car park
7 Reception / foyer

35.06
Section B–B
1:1000
1 SkyLounge
2 Bedroom
3 Lounge bar
4 Reception / foyer
5 Car park

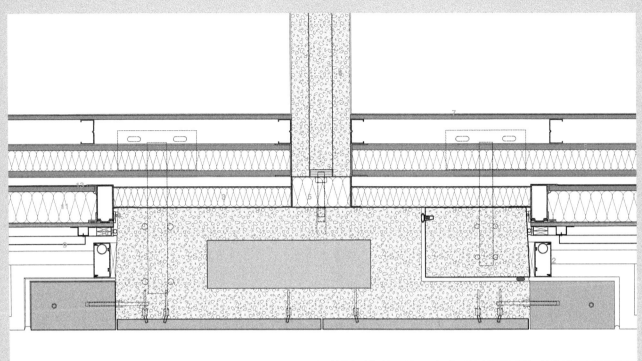

35.07
Horizontal Section
Wall Detail
1:20

1 Natural stone (Jura, cross cut, bed 11), panels bonded / pinned to prefabricated cladding panel. Thickness: 40 mm (1 3/5 inch) to 140 mm (5 1/2 inch)
2 Vertical silver-anodized facade drainage channel with removable cover panel

fixed behind stone panels
3 60 mm (2 2/5 inch) Kooltherm thermal insulation boards with vapour barrier, bonded to back of prefabricated cladding panel. All joints foil taped
4 Backing rod and mastic seal
5 90 mm (3 1/2 inch) thick firestop / acoustic insulation at slab level, contained

by 3 mm (1/10 inch) galvanized steel angle top and bottom
6 180 mm (7 1/10 inch) prefabricated structural concrete twin-wall system between rooms with nominal 3 mm (1/10 inch) spray-plaster finish on both sides
7 12.5 mm (1/2 inch) plasterboard internal lining fixed to proprietary framing behind

8 89 mm (3 1/2 inch) thick prefabricated Panablock walls comprising rigid insulation with 18 mm (7/10 inch) moisture-resistant MDF bonded both sides, fixed to structural frame on three sides with proprietary channel system
9 VM zinc clip-on panels on 25 mm (1 inch) carrier system fixed to 12 mm (1/2

inch) marine ply. Edges of ply full sealed with EPDM with Tyvec vapour barrier over
10 50 x 12 mm (2 x 1/2 inch) marine ply battens fixed to backboard overlapped with EPDM and fully sealed around edges
11 100 mm (3 9/10 inch) Rocksilk RainScreen slab insulation fitted between ply and Sound Bloc

12 15 mm (3/5 inch) Gyproc Sound Bloc board, fully silicone sealed
13 Powerlon Vapour Barrier

35.08
Horizontal Section
Wall / Window Detail
1:20

1 18 mm (7/10 inch) pre-finished MDF window board fixed to softwood battens behind
2 12.5 mm (1/2 inch) plasterboard lining forming internal window head / jambs to fixed proprietary framing behind
3 Coloured precast concrete spandrel as part of prefabricated cladding panel with formed gutter to top side and compression seals between prefabricated frames
4 PPC black aluminium bar with mastic seal on both sides
5 Prefabricated Kawneer AA100 fully sealed system with integral opening vent, full-height low-emissivity double SSG glazing unit comprising 9.5 mm (2/5 inch) laminated inner and 3 mm (1/5 inch) heat-soaked outer with black warm edge spacers
6 60 mm (2 2/5 inch)

thick Kooltherm thermal insulation boards with vapour barrier, bonded to back of prefabricated cladding panel. All joints foil taped
7 Cavity closer and sound barrier
8 3 mm (1/10 inch) full-height galvanized steel angle
9 180 mm (7 1/10 inch) prefabricated structural concrete twin-wall system between rooms with nominal 3 mm (1/10 inch) spray-plaster finish on both sides
10 Coloured precast concrete vertical fin as part of prefabricated cladding panel

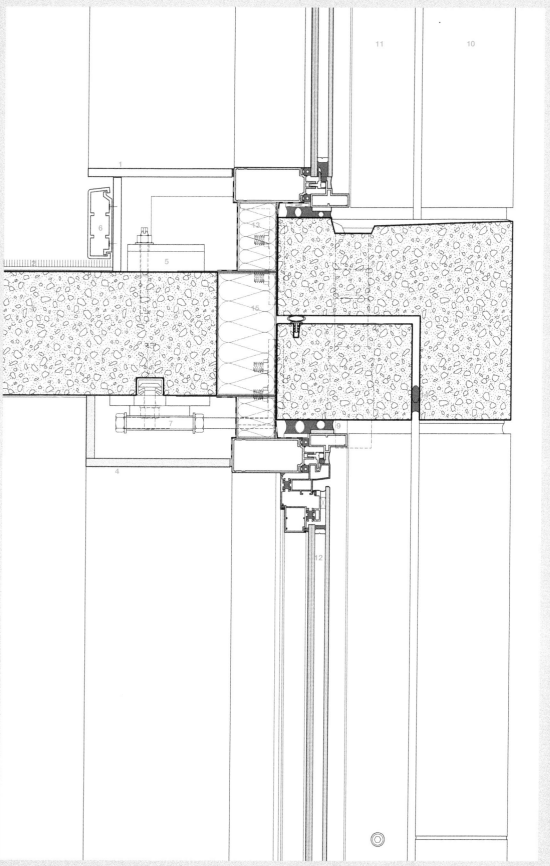

35.09
Vertical Wall / Floor
Section Detail
1:5

1 18 mm (^{7}/$_{10}$ inch) pre-finished MDF window board fixed to softwood battens behind

2 Floor finish: carpet on top of acoustic underlay and latex leveller

3 180 mm (7 ^{1}/$_{10}$ inch) concrete floor slab (50 mm [2 inch] prefabricated slab with 130 mm [5 ^{1}/$_{10}$ inch] structural topping), 3 mm (^{1}/$_{10}$ inch) nominal spray plaster to ceiling

4 12.5 mm (^{1}/$_{2}$ inch) plasterboard lining forming internal window head / jambs to fixed proprietary framing behind

5 Prefabricated cladding panel structural support. Fixing resin anchored to concrete slab

6 100 mm (3 ^{9}/$_{10}$ inch) high extruded conduit skirting

7 Prefabricated cladding panel structural restraint fixed to cast-in Halfen channel

8 Coloured precast concrete spandrel as part of prefabricated cladding panel with formed gutter to top side and compression seals between prefabricated frames

9 PPC black aluminium bar with mastic seal on both sides

10 Natural stone (Jura, cross cut, bed 11), panels bonded / pinned to prefabricated cladding panel. Thickness: 40 mm (1 ^{3}/$_{5}$ inch) to 140 mm (5 ^{1}/$_{2}$ inch)

11 Vertical silver-anodized facade drainage channel with removable cover panel fixed behind stone panels

12 Prefabricated Kawneer AA100 fully sealed system with integral opening vent, full-height low-emissivity double SSG glazing unit comprising 9.5 mm (^{2}/$_{5}$ inch) laminated inner and 6 mm (^{1}/$_{5}$ inch) heat-soaked outer with black warm-edge spacers

13 60 mm (2 ^{2}/$_{5}$ inch) thick Kooltherm thermal insulation boards with vapour barrier, bonded to back of prefabricated cladding panel. All joints foil taped

14 Compressive joint / mastic seal

15 90 mm (3 ^{1}/$_{2}$ inch) thick firestop / acoustic insulation at slab level, contained by 3 mm (^{1}/$_{10}$ inch) galvanized steel angle top and bottom

Crematorium Heimolen
Sint-Niklaas, Belgium

Client
Intercommunale Westlede
Sint-Niklaas, Belgium

Project Team
Kees Kaan, Vincent Panhuysen,
Hannes Ochmann, Luuk Stoltenborg,
Yaron Tam, Hagar Zur

Structural Engineer
Pieters Bouwtechniek

Main Contractor
Roegiers

The brief for this project called for a reception building and crematorium to be located within an existing cemetery. The two parts of the programme are separated into two discrete structures for environmental and practical reasons. A common language links the two buildings, as it was considered important to the bereaved families for the ceremony to have at least a symbolic connection with the cremation. The reception building is situated in the southwest of the cemetery, with the smaller crematorium in the northeast. Between the two is a small lake.

The horizontal and linear reception building has a large overhanging roof (100 x 40 metres, 328 x 131 feet) that extends beyond the walls to form a generous canopy. Beneath this shelter mourners can gather and funeral corteges can arrive. The invisible structural support for the canopy gives it a quality of easy elegance.

Within is an austere anteroom that looks out across the lake. From here mourners can move to one of the two chapels, simple non-religious spaces in which the services take place. In the main space, which can hold up to 280 people, the mourners are invited to contemplate a wall of marble. There are no windows; light enters via a row of large circular roof lights.

The crematorium is a nine metre (29 ½ foot) high block; its walls are formed from square, cream-coloured concrete panels. These have a coffer pattern of reducing recessed squares, in the centre of which many have small glass windows of various sizes. The steel furnaces inside are accessible to the public and are presented as a dignified mechanism for the process of cremation.

1 At the front of the reception building a large sheltered area is sliced into the corner. It provides a space for families and friends to gather before and after ceremonies.

2 The facade of the crematorium block is composed of a grid of 306 square concrete panels. They are either solid, or have glass centres of three different sizes.

3 The cast concrete panels are recessed in steps. As the sun moves across their surface, shadows enhance the monumental quality of the structure.

4 Within the reception building, cast concrete benches provide a place for rest and reflection. Illumination is provided by top lights.

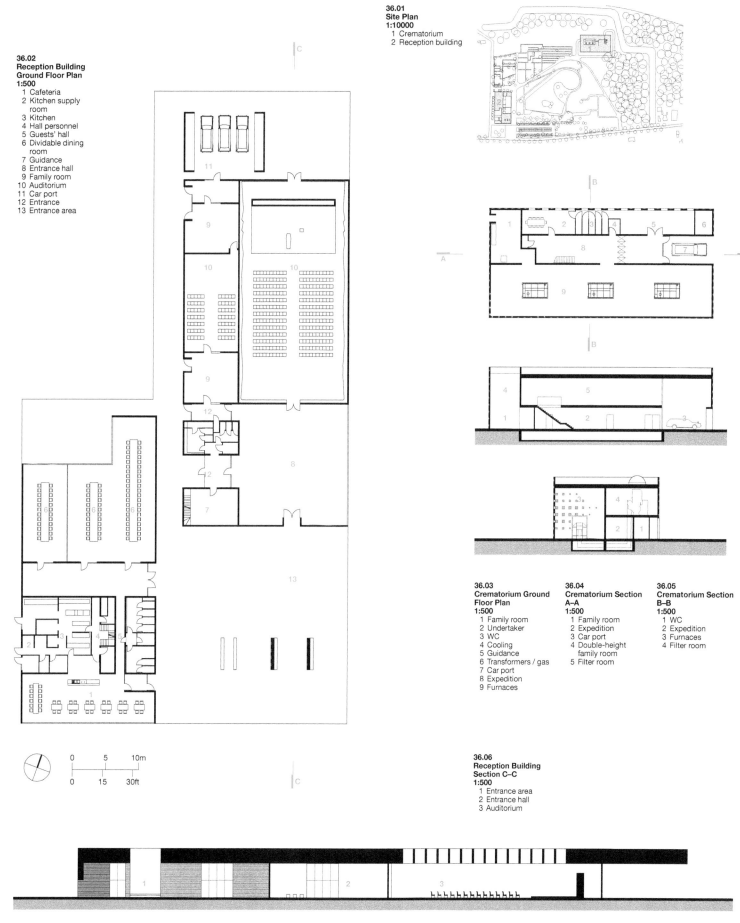

36.01
Site Plan
1:10000
1 Crematorium
2 Reception building

36.02
Reception Building
Ground Floor Plan
1:500
1 Cafeteria
2 Kitchen supply
   room
3 Kitchen
4 Hall personnel
5 Guests' hall
6 Dividable dining
   room
7 Guidance
8 Entrance hall
9 Family room
10 Auditorium
11 Car port
12 Entrance
13 Entrance area

36.03
Crematorium Ground
Floor Plan
1:500
1 Family room
2 Undertaker
3 WC
4 Cooling
5 Guidance
6 Transformers / gas
7 Car port
8 Expedition
9 Furnaces

36.04
Crematorium Section
A–A
1:500
1 Family room
2 Expedition
3 Car port
4 Double-height
   family room
5 Filter room

36.05
Crematorium Section
B–B
1:500
1 WC
2 Expedition
3 Furnaces
4 Filter room

36.06
Reception Building
Section C–C
1:500
1 Entrance area
2 Entrance hall
3 Auditorium

0   5   10m
0   15   30ft

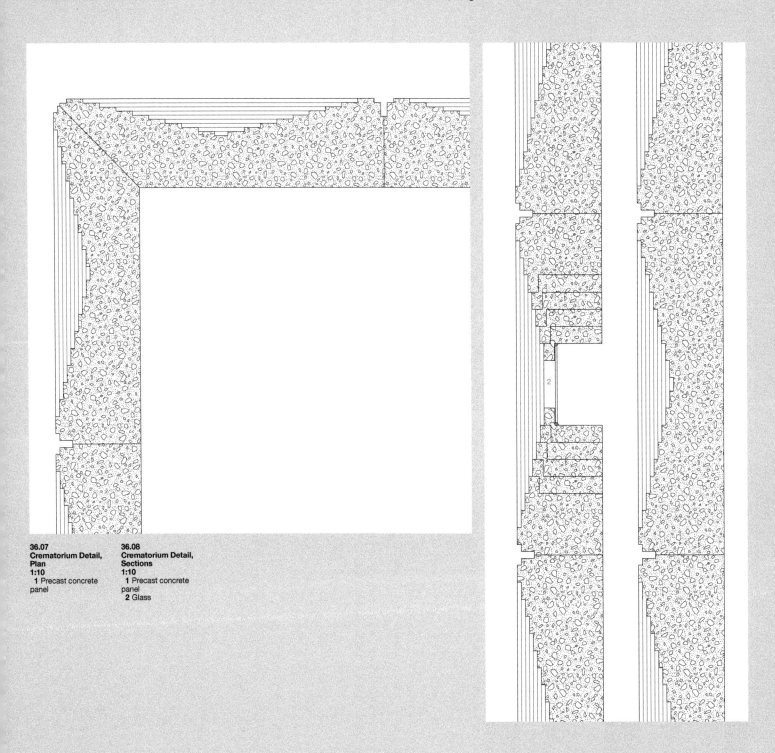

36.07
Crematorium Detail,
Plan
1:10
 1 Precast concrete
panel

36.08
Crematorium Detail,
Sections
1:10
 1 Precast concrete
panel
 2 Glass

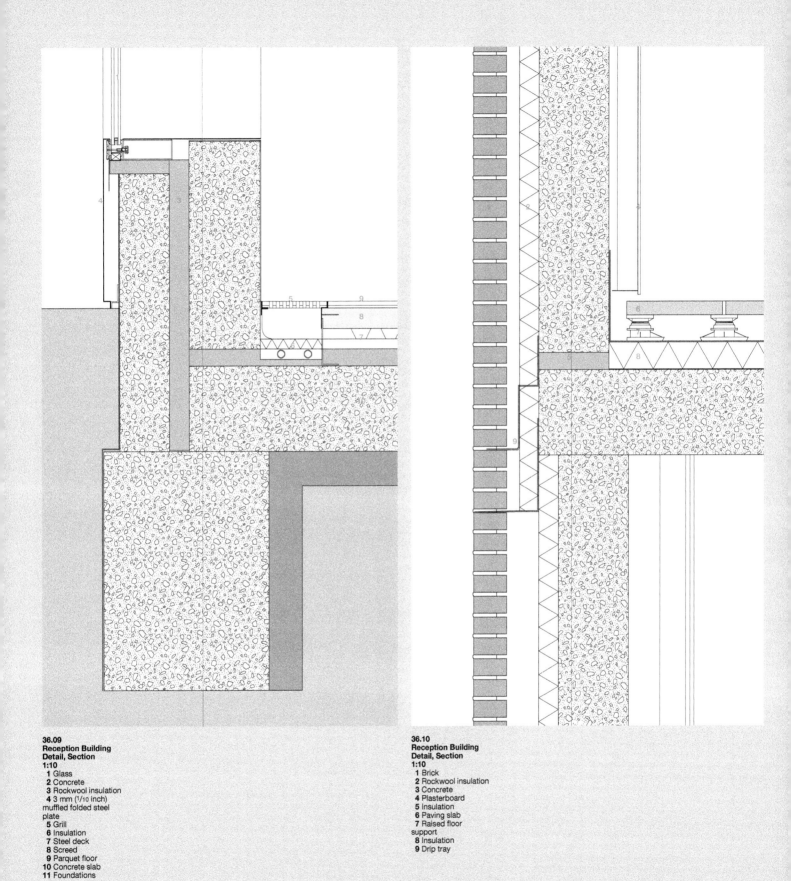

36.09
Reception Building
Detail, Section
1:10
  1 Glass
  2 Concrete
  3 Rockwool insulation
  4 3 mm (1/10 inch)
muffled folded steel
plate
  5 Grill
  6 Insulation
  7 Steel deck
  8 Screed
  9 Parquet floor
10 Concrete slab
11 Foundations

36.10
Reception Building
Detail, Section
1:10
  1 Brick
  2 Rockwool insulation
  3 Concrete
  4 Plasterboard
  5 Insulation
  6 Paving slab
  7 Raised floor
support
  8 Insulation
  9 Drip tray

**Hämeenlinna Provincial Archive
Hämeenlinna, Finland**

Client
Senate Properties

Project Team
Mikko Heikkinen and Markku
Komonen, Markku Puumala

Structural Engineer
Contria Oy

Main Contractor
Peab Oy

Despite its remote location 100 kilometres (60 miles) north of Helsinki, the city of Hämeenlinna has a rich history and a large archive of documents that record events dating back to the sixteenth century.

A building that contains the collective history of a place and its people can never be just a store. It must also be a place that holds significance for the city. The striking design seeks to make the archive itself the focus of the architectural composition. The building contains three parts: the treasury where the documents are stored; offices and workshops for staff; and an area for the public to come and view the contents of the archive.

The lower storey is a transparent box containing, in island-like areas, study rooms, an auditorium, a library, a cafeteria and an exhibition space. Above is an enclosed three-storey concrete box. Its surface is covered inside and out with typographic patterns designed by the artist Aimo Katajamäki. The letters used are taken from documents in the collection. This heavy treasure chest floats effortlessly, in defiance of its obvious weight. The offices and workshops at the rear are covered with brown aluminum plates. Between the two parts there is a top-lit canyon.

1 The graphic facade hangs above the glass lower storey like a curtain. The letters give glimpses of the treasures within.
2 The solidity of the archive block and of the brown service block behind give a civic quality to the building, appropriate to its function.
3 The letters form a pattern across the surface that recall the importance of words in defining the meaning of things.
4 The cladding of the rear block is linear, giving the surface the appearance of wood marquetry.
5 The graphic images are also present on the interior of the archive.

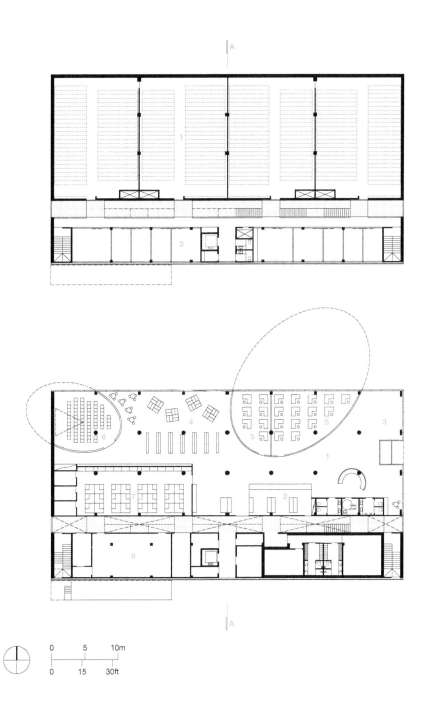

37.01
Upper Floor Plan
1:500
1 Archive
2 Offices

37.02
Ground Floor Plan
1:500
1 Lobby
2 Information desk
3 Exhibition space
4 Library
5 Desks for
  researchers
6 Lecture hall
7 Microfilms
8 Workshops

0   5   10m

0   15   30ft

37.03
Section A–A
1:500
1 Archive
2 Office
3 Library

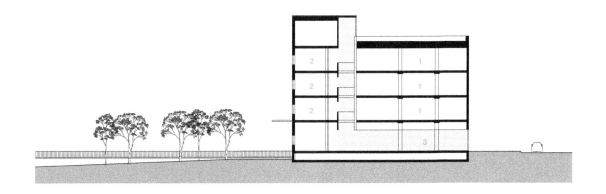

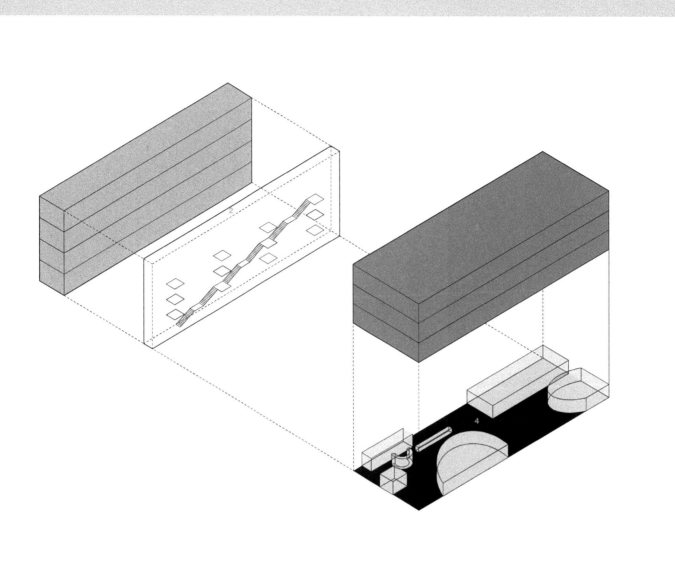

37.04
Concept Diagram
Not to Scale
1 Offices
2 Void
3 Archive
4 Public spaces

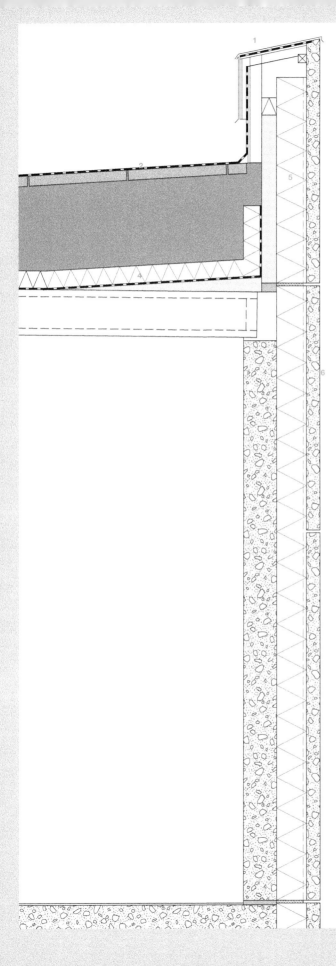

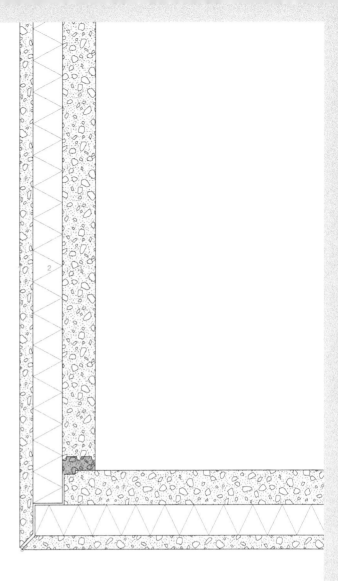

37.05
Vertical Wall Section
1:20
 1 Plastic-covered
sheet metal
 2 Bitumen roofing felt
 3 Expanded-clay
aggregate insulation
 4 Expanded
polystyrene insulation
 5 180 mm (7 1/10 inch)
insulation
 6 90 mm (3 1/2 inch)
concrete outer shell
 7 200 mm (7 9/10 inch)
load-bearing inner
concrete shell)

37.06
Horizontal Wall
Section
1:20
 1 90 mm (3 1/2 inch)
concrete outer shell
 2 180 mm (3 1/2 inch)
insulation
 3 200 mm (7 9/10 inch)
load-bearing inner
concrete shell
 4 In-situ concrete
 5 Corner element

38
Hohensinn Architektur

Hotel am Domplatz
Linz, Austria

Client
Stiftung St. Severin, Linz

Project Management
Erich Ganster (Hotel), Helmut Lanz
(Houses 36 and 38), Karlheinz Boiger
(Design)

Project Team
Pair Dicke, Thomas Klietmann, Ognjen
Persoglio, Klemens Mitheis, Mario
Mayrl, Franz Jelisitz

Structural Engineer
Peter Pawel, Praher & Schuster ZT
GmbH

Main Contractor
Hohensinn Architektur

Since the completion of the neo-Gothic cathedral in Linz in 1924, the surrounding area had never been developed as intended. It had been proposed to remove the buildings around the cathedral to create a park setting. This did not happen and the area was left unresolved.

A new plan for the square has resulted in the construction of a hotel and the revitalization of two existing Baroque buildings on the southwest side. The square has been reconceived as space of possibilities; the paving pattern is laid so as not to allow any directional influence to emerge. Beneath is a large underground car park.

The two historic houses have been restored to their original condition and now contain long-stay apartments and a restaurant. The clear intention of the new hotel is to be a confident element in the composition of the Domplatz, and this is evident in its rigorous orthogonal concrete frame. The large openings give the structure a transparency that contrasts with the solidity of its context.

The hotel is composed of two perforated concrete blocks folded, with a simple cranked articulation, around a long funnel-like atrium. The internal room circulation is accessed from the top-lit atrium, negating the need for internal corridors. Guest rooms are bright and spacious, with full-height glass walls that give views of the cathedral and immediate surroundings.

1 The hotel is sited parallel to the cathedral, establishing a new boundary for the urban space around. Beneath the paving is a large car park.
2 The facade facing the cathedral has a staggered rhythm of syncopated openings. The glazing reflects intricate Gothic detail.
3 The rooms are bright and generous; the glazed walls of the bathrooms increase the penetration of light into the space. Outside the cathedral is a constant presence.
4 A bright atrium rises through the building, linking the reception to the rooms. The building's circulation is arranged around this dramatic space.

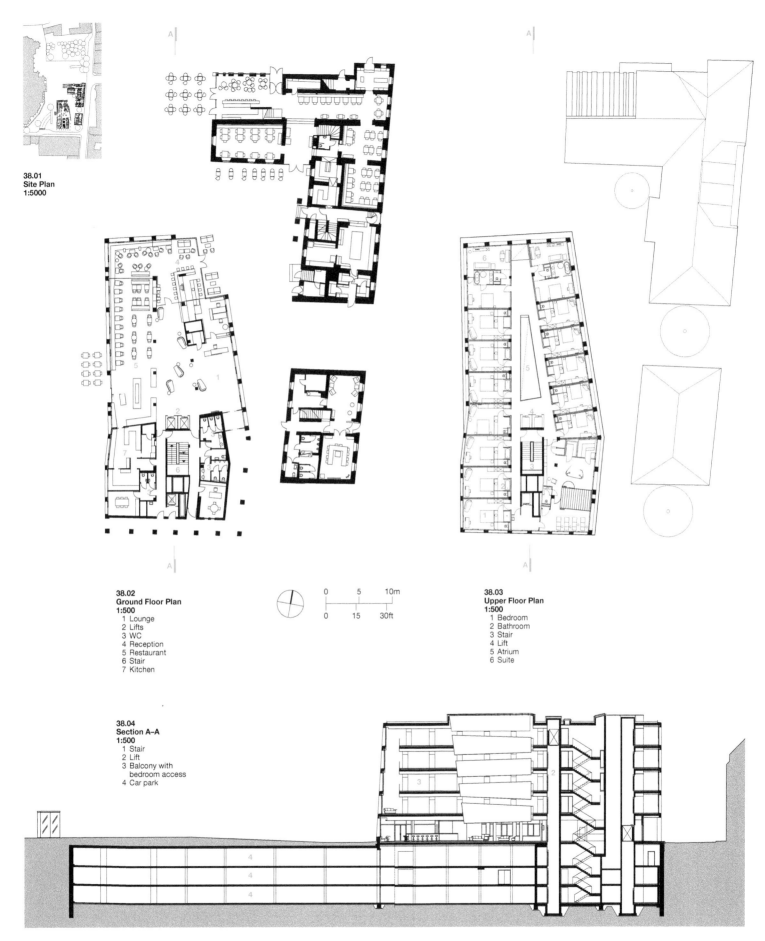

38.01
Site Plan
1:5000

38.02
Ground Floor Plan
1:500
1 Lounge
2 Lifts
3 WC
4 Reception
5 Restaurant
6 Stair
7 Kitchen

0 5 10m
0 15 30ft

38.03
Upper Floor Plan
1:500
1 Bedroom
2 Bathroom
3 Stair
4 Lift
5 Atrium
6 Suite

38.04
Section A–A
1:500
1 Stair
2 Lift
3 Balcony with
  bedroom access
4 Car park

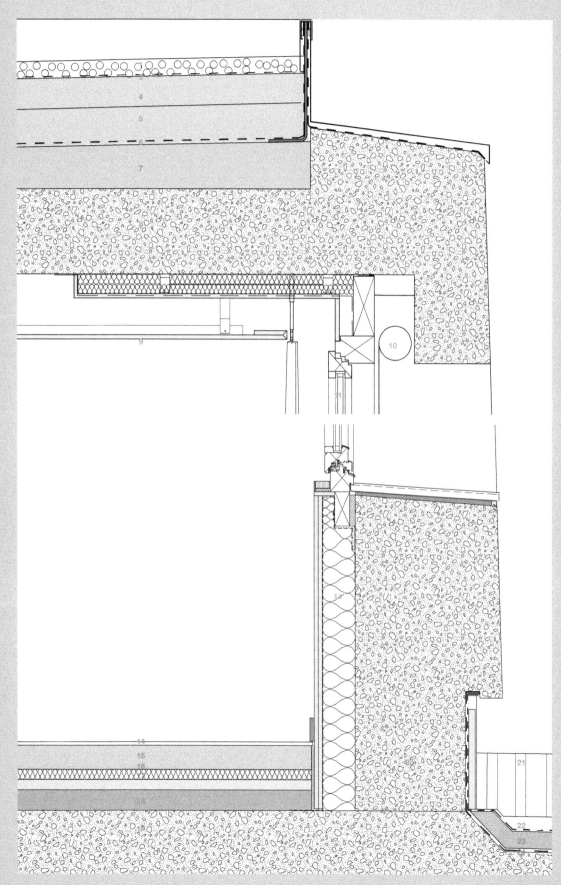

38.05
Attic Section
1:10

Roof Construction
 1 5 mm (¹/₅ inch) gravel
 2 0.5 mm (¹/₁₀ inch) protective fleece
 3 0.2 mm (¹/₅₀ inch) PVC insulation
 4 On average 8 mm (³/₁₀ inch) EPS insulation
 5 12 mm (¹/₂ inch) EPS W25 insulation
 6 0.01 mm (¹/₁₀₀ inch) vapour barrier
 7 25 mm (1 inch) STB blanket
 8 Concrete slab
 9 180.5 mm (7 ³/₁₀ inch) suspended ceiling with skim coating
 10 Blind
 11 Glass
 12 Window frame
 13 Insulation

Floor 00
 14 10 mm (²/₅ inch) wood parquet floor
 15 70 mm (2 ⁴/₅ inch) heating screed
 16 Foil
 17 30 mm (1 ¹/₅ inch) TDPS
 18 70 mm (2 ⁴/₅ inch) packing
 19 250 mm (9 ⁴/₅ inch) concrete slab
 20 Concrete slab

Square Construction
 21 420 x 420 x 140 mm (16 ¹/₂ x 16 ¹/₂ x 5 ¹/₂ inch) concrete paving
 22 40 mm (1 ³/₅ inch) gravel bed
 23 200 mm (7 ⁹/₁₀ inch) Mech. support 0 / 32
 24 200 – 300 mm (7 ⁹/₁₀ – 11 ⁴/₅ inch) Case Frost

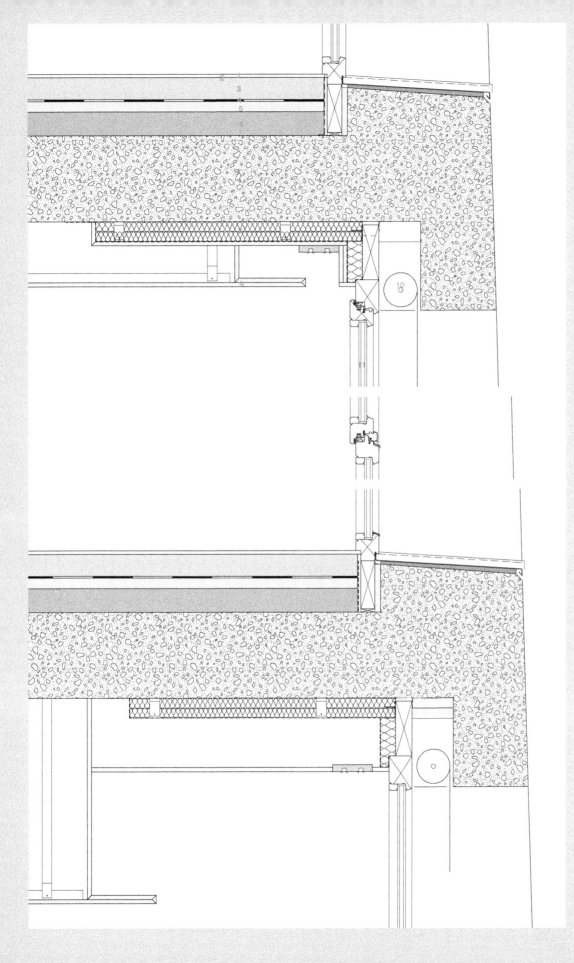

 1 Wood parquet floor
 2 Sealing
 3 70 mm (2 4/5 inch)
heated screed
 4 Foil
 5 30 mm (1 1/5 inch)
TDPS
 6 Packing
 7 250 mm (9 4/5 inch)
concrete slab
 8 Insulation
 9 Suspended ceiling
10 Blind
11 Glass

Santa Monica Boulevard Transit Parkway Wall
Los Angeles, USA

Client
City of Los Angeles

Project Team
Tony Pleskow, David Kim

Structural Engineer
Bureau of Engineering, City of
Los Angeles

Main Contractor
Excel Paving Corporation

Seeking to redefine a busy urban area characterized by its transport infrastructure, this project was designed to accommodate the changes in level between two sections of highway and their surroundings. The retaining wall structure is composed of six independent freestanding concrete walls of different heights that are placed along a very narrow footprint. These six walls slide past each other in a shifting configuration of layered planes. Between the planes are ramps and stairs that connect the levels.

Formed from dark sand-coloured concrete, the stratified walls make reference to the active seismology of the area. Along the length of the assembly, the walls form an arched cliff, resembling a giant slice of the earth that has been forced up by geological forces. The plane of each wall is patterned with relief panels of tilted planes, which appear like the stratified layers of a rock face. The edges of the panels catch the sunlight, casting shadows along their margins. At night, spotlights and the headlights of passing vehicles illuminate and animate the walls. Earth mounds, combined with confident planting, soften the edges. This engineering structure both surprises and delights, achieving a successful piece of urban placemaking.

1 Seen from above, the road makes a brutal slice through the area. The new retaining walls seek to reconnect two neighbourhoods that the infrastructure has separated.
2 Layered plates, like the scales of a giant snake, create a fractured pattern of shadows across the surfaces of the retaining walls.
3 Between the walls, broad stairways connect the levels.
4 The upper parts of the walls feature horizontal observation slots.
5 The intense Californian sunshine describes every edge with sharp shadows.

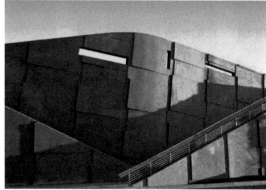

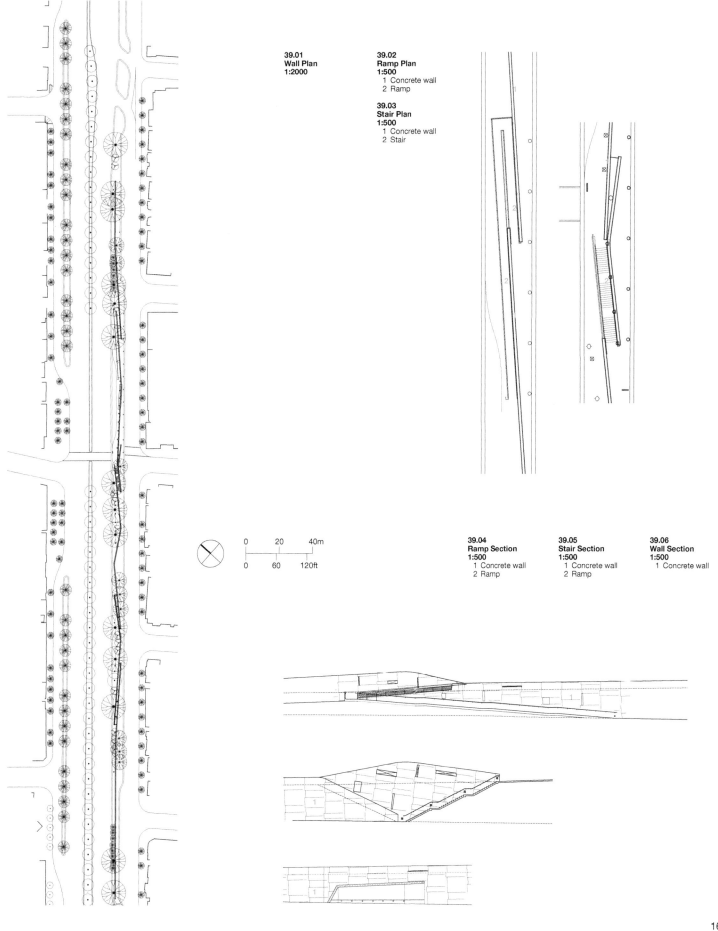

39.01
Wall Plan
1:2000

39.02
Ramp Plan
1:500
  1 Concrete wall
  2 Ramp

39.03
Stair Plan
1:500
  1 Concrete wall
  2 Stair

39.04
Ramp Section
1:500
  1 Concrete wall
  2 Ramp

39.05
Stair Section
1:500
  1 Concrete wall
  2 Ramp

39.06
Wall Section
1:500
  1 Concrete wall

0   20   40m
0   60   120ft

39.07
Ramp Section
1:20
 1 Pedestrian light
pole
 2 Concrete guard rail
 3 38 mm (1 1/2 inch)
steel pipe handrail
 4 Concrete expansion
joint
 5 Concrete ramp
 6 Concrete wall
 7 Ramped earth
 8 Void

39.08
Bus Stop Section
1:20
 1 Concrete wall
 2 Concrete expansion
joint
 3 Light fitting
 4 Steel bench
support
 5 Concrete bench
 6 Drain

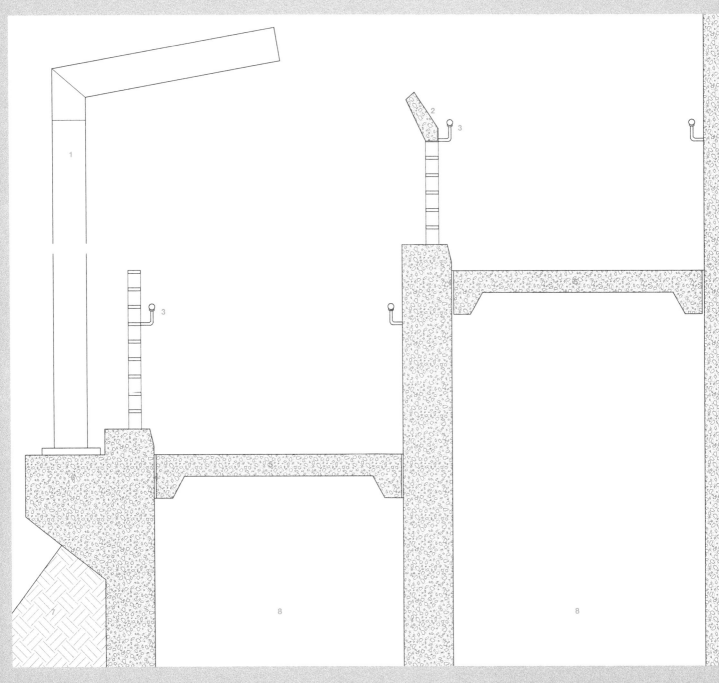

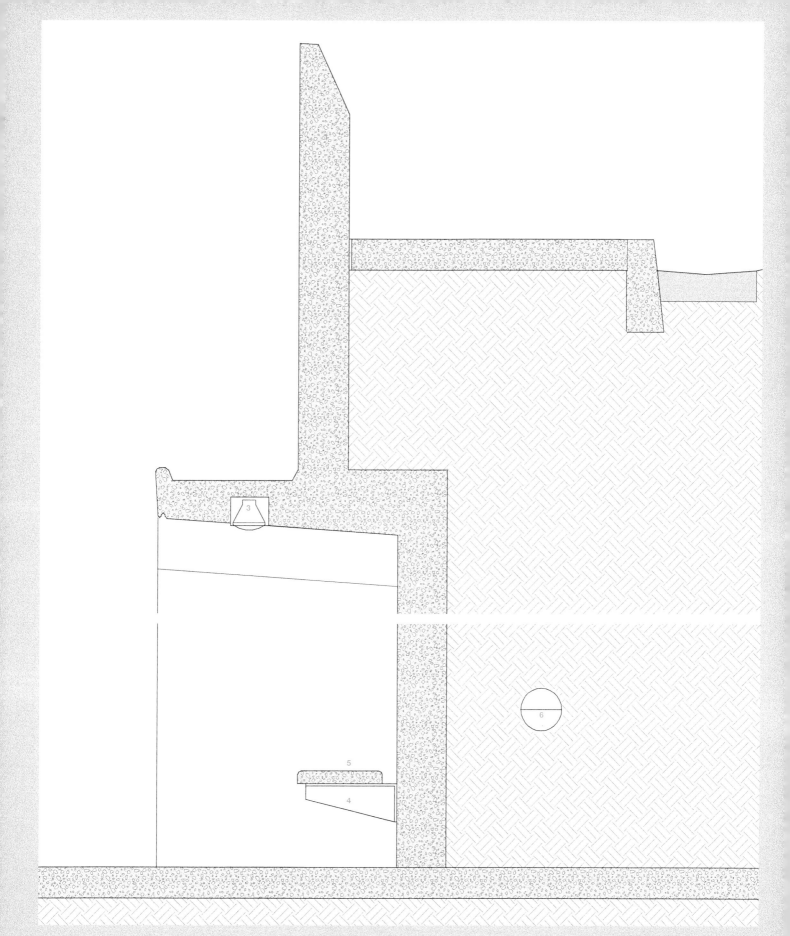

Torres de Hércules
Los Barrios, Cádiz, Spain

Client
Valcruz

Architect
Rafael de La-Hoz Castanys

Project Team
Jesús Román, Peter Germann,
Markus Lassan, Alex Cafcalas, Ulrik
Weinert, Iván Ucrós, Ángel Rolán,
Margarita Sánchez, Nicolas André,
Ivonne de Souza, Paola Merani

Quantity Surveyor
Rafael Vegas

Structural Engineer
Inepro S.L. and NB 35

Electrical Engineer
IG Ingeniería y Gestión and Úrculo
Ingenerios

Main Contractor
Construcciones Sánchez
Domínguez-Sando

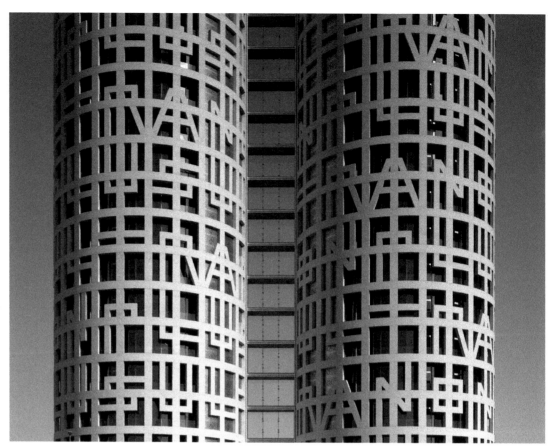

These two slender white office towers,
linked by a glazed block, rise from a
shallow pool at their base to a height
of 126 metres (413 feet). Dominating
the surrounding landscape, they are
the tallest structures in Andalusia.

The structural outer screen of each
tower is a pierced white concrete wall
400 mm (15 ¾ inch) thick. In addition
to providing the main support for the
floor slabs in combination with the
service core, the wall also act as a
solar screen and provides thermal
mass. Each storey was cast in-situ
using a self-climbing, curved
formwork panel system. The pure
white concrete finish was achieved
after many tests to obtain the desired
colour and texture. A naturally
ventilated glazing wall is placed inside
this exterior wall.

In homage to the original Pillars of
Hercules that, according to legend,
stood nearby, giant filigree letterforms
around the towers spell out the Latin
motto 'Non Plus Ultra'. This has a
double meaning: either 'nothing
beyond' or 'perfection'. The letters
were cast in special formwork made
from expanded polystyrene. This
fast-track construction method
allowed lower floors to be finished
while construction continued above.
Each of the twenty floors has a gross
area of 900 square metres (9,687
square feet).

1 Cast in a ring around
each storey of the
concrete facade is the
motto 'Non Plus Ultra'.
2 The two slender
towers are linked by
delicate glazed bridges
on each storey.

3 Looking across one
of the glazed linking
bridges, the landscape
spreads out on either
side. The absence of
handrails or glazing
bars accentuates the
impression of

openness and light.
4 At the top of each
tower is an open roof
terrace, surrounded by
the continuation of the
tower's structural
screen wall.

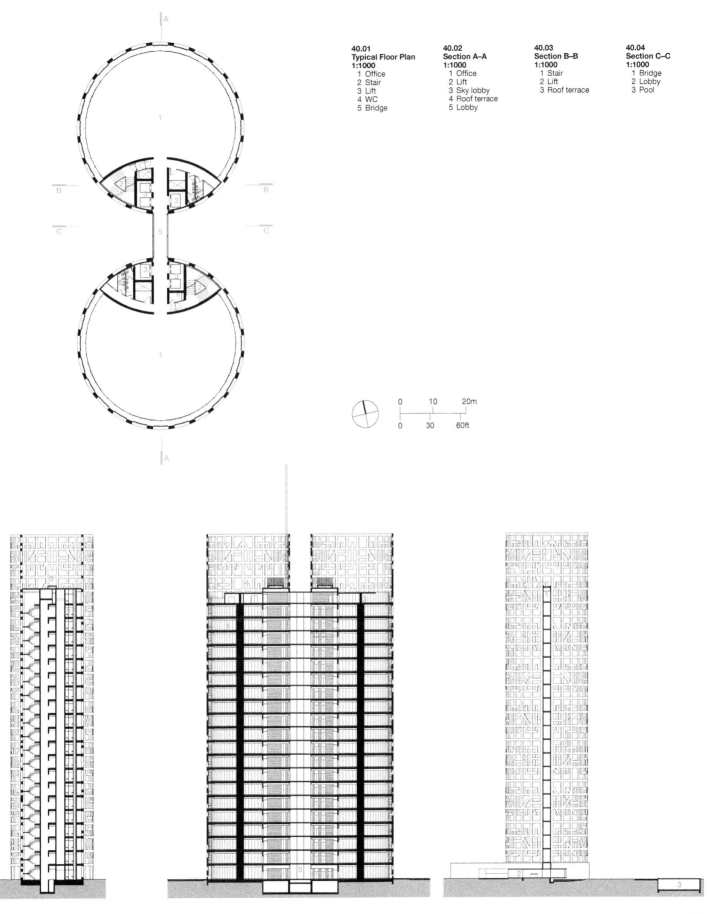

40.01
Typical Floor Plan
1:1000
1 Office
2 Stair
3 Lift
4 WC
5 Bridge

40.02
Section A–A
1:1000
1 Office
2 Lift
3 Sky lobby
4 Roof terrace
5 Lobby

40.03
Section B–B
1:1000
1 Stair
2 Lift
3 Roof terrace

40.04
Section C–C
1:1000
1 Bridge
2 Lobby
3 Pool

0   10   20m

0   30   60ft

40.05
Concrete Facade
Layout
1:500

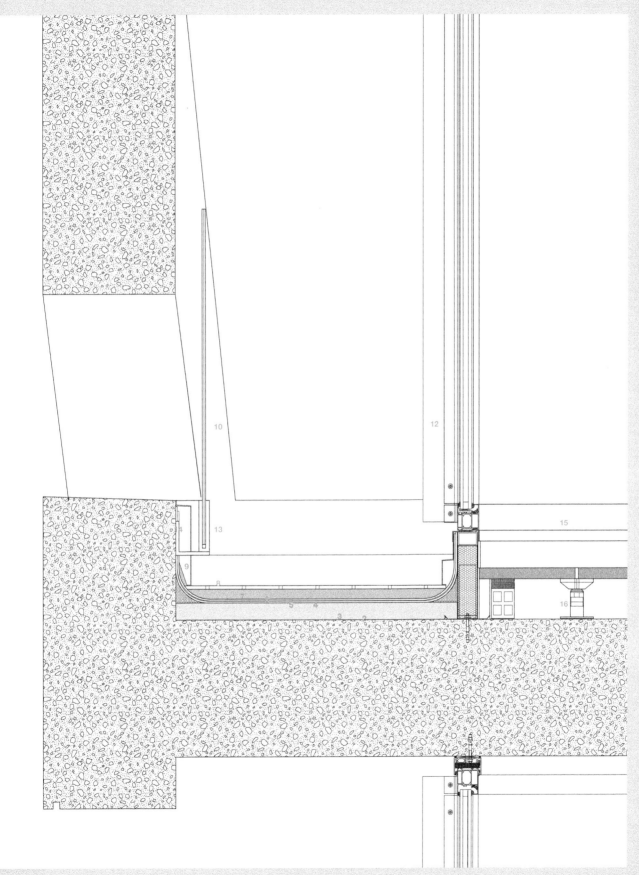

40.06
Wall Detail
1:10
1 Concrete slab
2 Slope of cellular concrete (slope = one per cent)
3 20 mm (³/₄ inch) cement mortar bed
4 Bituminous primer
5 Double asphalt layer
6 Geotextile
7 Fixing material
8 Paving
9 Plinth of stainless-steel plate
10 Extra-clear 10 mm (²/₅ inch) laminated glass railing, height 1100 mm (43 ³/₁₀ inch)
11 400 mm (15 ³/₄ inch) white concrete beam
12 Stainless platen stiffener
13 U-profile galvanized steel to hold glass railing
14 L-profile painted galvanized steel
15 Raised floor
16 Floor support

Bodleian Book Storage Facility
South Marston, Swindon, UK

Client
Bodleian Library

Project Team
Richard McCarthy (Project Director);
Kelly Foster (Project Architect);
Stephanie Kom (Architect)

Structural Engineer
Peter Brett Associates

Main Contractor
Mace

This building has been built to solve the problems caused by an ever-increasing collection of books. The Bodleian Library is one of the largest in the world by number of books, and its collections are currently expanding at the rate of 5000 books every week.

A very simple utilitarian building has here been made special through the use of high quality materials and attention to detail. The 11,700 square metre (126,000 square foot) facility provides a long-term solution for the storage in optimum conditions of up to eight million volumes on 246 kilometres (153 miles) of shelving. The facility has been designed to have a life of 100 years. The modular design will also allow the building to be extended in the future.

Internally the building is divided into four sealed sections. Each of these 12 metre (39 foot) high sections is independently fire rated and isolated from the other three. Their walls are constructed from prefabricated insulated concrete sandwich panels. These panels give the building a high thermal mass, which in turn helps to regulate temperature and humidity.

Alongside the east facade of the archive areas, a single-storey area provides offices, storage, data and IT support and staff spaces. The exterior is clad in the same insulated concrete panels as the storage chamber. The surface of these panels features a cast-in graphic pattern representing the millions of books within. A wall of timber cladding marks the entrance facade.

1 The wooden entrance facade has the appearance of pages in a book, pressed between the concrete covers.
2 The concrete-insulated sandwich panels are set into a galvanized steel frame.
3 The incised graphic pattern that covers the service facade is intended to represent the many volumes within.
4 The unrestricted open spaces of the interior provide a working environment ideally suited to the preservation of the collection.

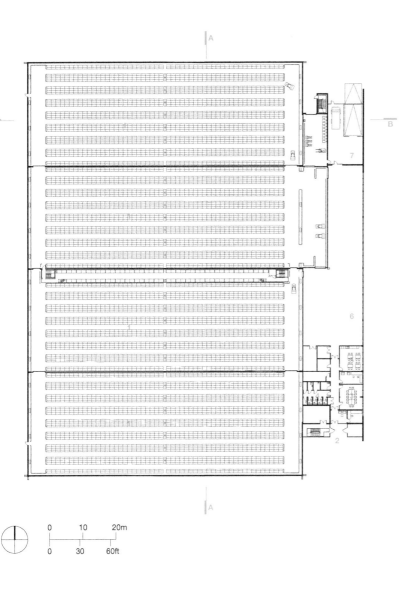

41.01
Ground Floor
1:1000
1 Book storage
2 Entrance
3 Meeting room
4 WC
5 Office
6 Book sorting
7 Loading bay

0　10　20m
0　30　60ft

41.02
Section A–A
1:1000
1 Book storage

41.03
Section B–B
1:500
1 Book storage
2 Book sorting
3 Loading bay

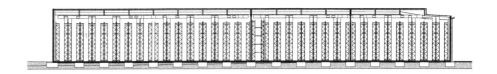

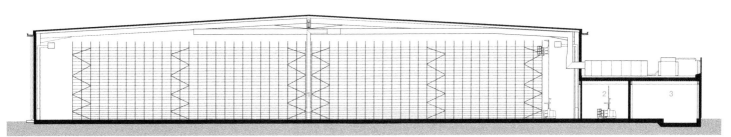

175

41.04
Facade Pattern
1:50
Surface pattern is a
repeating panel of
dimensions 3025 mm
(119 in) high x 1480 mm
(58 in) wide. Setout
point is the base
centreline of each
panel with a 250 mm
(9 3/4) horizontal space
between the centre
joint and pattern and
also between pattern
repeats. Recess is a
20 mm wide x 20 mm
deep (3/4 x 3/4 in) alcove.

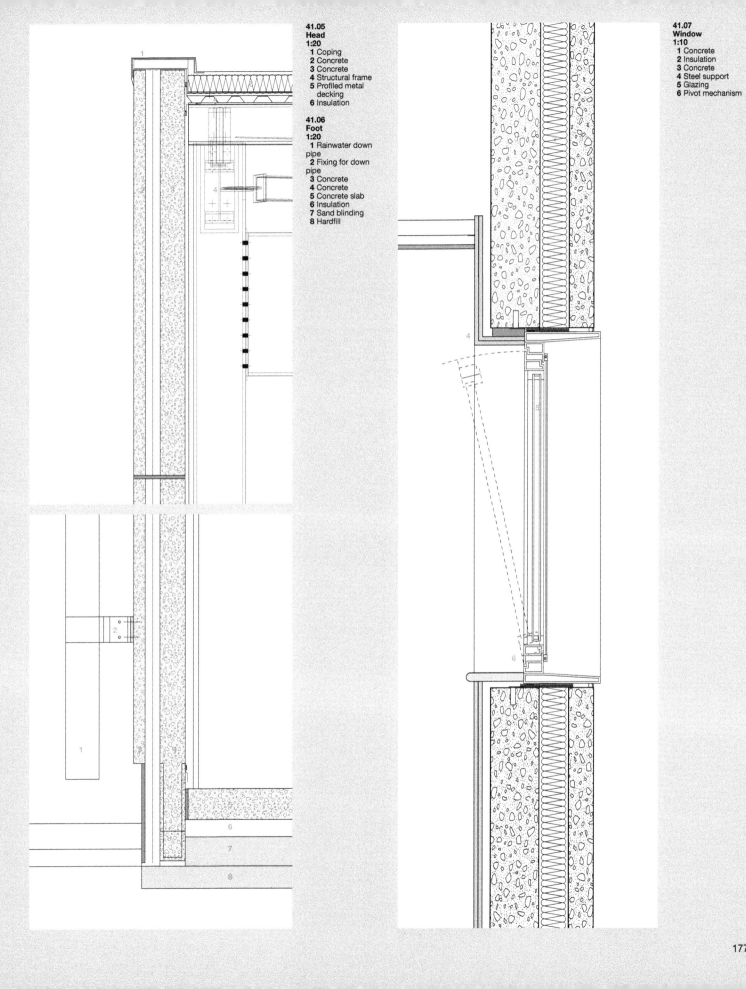

41.05
Head
1:20
1 Coping
2 Concrete
3 Concrete
4 Structural frame
5 Profiled metal decking
6 Insulation

41.06
Foot
1:20
1 Rainwater down pipe
2 Fixing for down pipe
3 Concrete
4 Concrete
5 Concrete slab
6 Insulation
7 Sand blinding
8 Hardfill

41.07
Window
1:10
1 Concrete
2 Insulation
3 Concrete
4 Steel support
5 Glazing
6 Pivot mechanism

177

Aon Insurance Headquarters
Dar es Salaam, Tanzania

Client
AON Corp.

Project Team
Sangeeta Merchant, Maithali Joshi,
Sanjay Parab, Sanjeev Panjabi

Structural Engineer
Pendharkar Associates Ltd

Main Contractor
Holtan (East Africa) Ltd

This building, designed as the headquarters of an insurance company, is located on the coast of Tanzania in East Africa. It is surrounded by a rich and fragrant landscape of acacias, frangipanis and areca palms. Protection of the company archives necessitated the construction of three shutter-formed concrete cabinets. These structures form the main enclosure, and views of the garden are framed between them.

Under deep eaves the upper storey is entirely glazed and encircles the structure, detaching the solid podium from the roof. Distant views across the surrounding trees connect the building to the landscape. The modulated light is reflected into the interior working spaces. Through the openings at this level, fresh cool breezes penetrate the building and reduce the energy loads. Outside the meeting rooms are shallow pools of water that provide delicate reflections and gentle sounds.

The roof that overhangs the building all around is a shallow pyramid that is preserved at its edge as a blade-like free-floating plane. A contemporary interpretation of indigenous thatch roofs, it shelters the building from the heavy tropical rains that are common in the area.

This is a building that affords its occupants an acute awareness of the changing environment around it, creating a wonderful place in which to work.

1 The entrance facade is marked with a simple punched opening. The seemingly independent roof floats above, its sharp edge outlined against the sky.

2 The thick external walls have a defensive fortress-like quality, and create a calm oasis within. Tall vertical slot openings allow glimpses of the interior.

3 A water pool in the courtyard helps to provide a cool environment. The spaces are defined by floor-to-ceiling glazing sheltered beneath a deep soffit.

4 The roof is supported on elegant steel columns allowing the glass wall below to wrap the around the building.

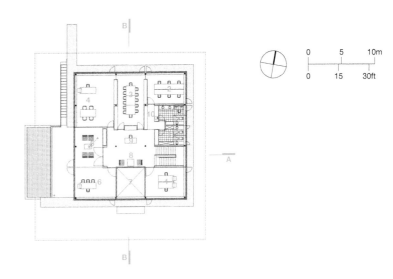

42.01
Ground Floor Plan
1:500
1 Main entrance
2 Waiting area
3 Double-height space
4 Reception desk
5 Meeting room

6 Large archive
7 Executive area
8 WC
9 Kitchen area
10 Staff area
11 Body of water
12 AC plant
13 Store

42.02
First Floor Plan
1:500
1 Finance manager's office
2 Finance department
3 Boardroom

4 Managing director's office
5 Entertainment lounge
6 General manager's office
7 Double-height space
8 Waiting area

9 Personal assistant
10 Kitchen area
11 WC

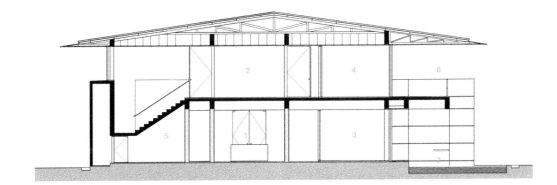

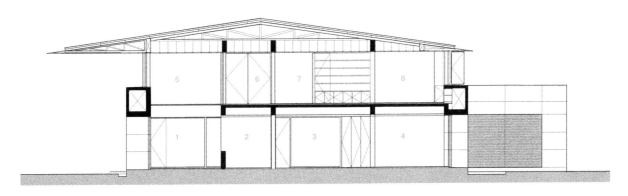

43.03
Section A–A
1:200
1 Reception foyer
2 Waiting area
3 Meeting area
4 Entertainment lounge
5 Store
6 Terrace
7 Body of water

44.04
Section B–B
1:200
1 Double-height reception foyer
2 Reception
3 Staff area
4 Large archive
5 General managers's office behind
6 Waiting area
7 Personal assistant
8 Boardroom

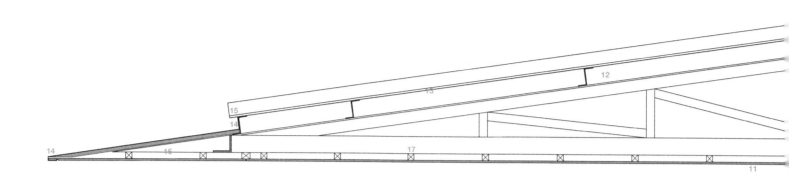

42.05
Wall and Glazing Section
1:20

1 Mild steel L-angle fixed onto the reinforced concrete peripheral beam. The wooden frames for the glazing system will be fixed on the underside

2 150 mm x 50 mm (5 $^{9}/_{10}$ x 2 inch) top timber frame fixed to the soffit of mild steel L-angle with a GI or equivalent flashing

3 48 mm x 150 mm (1 $^{9}/_{10}$ x 5 $^{9}/_{10}$ inch) vertical and top timber frames (Afzelia / Mkongo wood), to hold 12 mm ($^{1}/_{2}$ inch) fixed glass

4 Vertical and horizontal timber stiles of size 60 mm x 100 mm (2 $^{4}/_{10}$ x 3 $^{9}/_{10}$ inch) to the doors. Double rebated. Finish in clear epoxy polish. To have a 10 mm thick flat strip beading on the inside to hold the glass panel

5 Clear laminated glass panel 10 mm ($^{4}/_{10}$ inch) thick for the doors / window shutters, held within a 60 mm thick timber frame on all sides

6 150 mm x 35 mm (5 $^{9}/_{10}$ x 1 $^{4}/_{10}$ inch) timber frame at the bottom of the glazing fixed onto the bottom rough ground

7 Rough ground with a GI flashing for the bottom frame 23 mm thick x 135 mm ($^{9}/_{10}$ x 5 $^{3}/_{10}$ inch). To be fixed onto the fair-faced concrete sill. Finished in waterproof, termite- and borer resistant paint

8 Tongue-and-groove wooden boards 12 mm ($^{1}/_{2}$ inch) thick (Afzelia / Mkongo) finished in clear epoxy matt polish

9 48 mm x 48 mm (1 $^{9}/_{10}$ x 1 $^{9}/_{10}$ inch) timber square member fixed on the edge of the reinforced concrete sill finished in clear epoxy matt polish

10 Fair-faced concrete windowsill with a slope to the outside

11 Nutec fibre cement sheet 12 mm ($^{1}/_{2}$ inch) thick suspended ceiling to the undersoffit of the first floor terrace (external)

12 Insulation under the metal corrugated sheet roof

13 Corrugated iron metal sheet laid and fixed on Z-purlins spaced at 1200 mm (3 ft 11 $^{2}/_{10}$ inch) c/c with ridge and hip capping. SAFLOK-dark green colour sheets

14 100 mm x 100 mm (4 x 4 inch) waterproof membrane flashing / aluminium flashing

15 Mild steel metal L-angle finished in anti-rust hammered oil paint

16 20 mm ($^{8}/_{10}$ inch) thick, 600 mm (1 ft 11 $^{6}/_{10}$ inch) wide superior grade marine plywood sheet fixed onto the underside of roof edge of eaves

17 Seasoned hardwood brandering, finished in waterproof paint, treated for termite / borer

18 Fair-faced concrete wall

19 Clear glass

20 White wear-and-wash paint

21 Polyurethane clear varnish (matt)

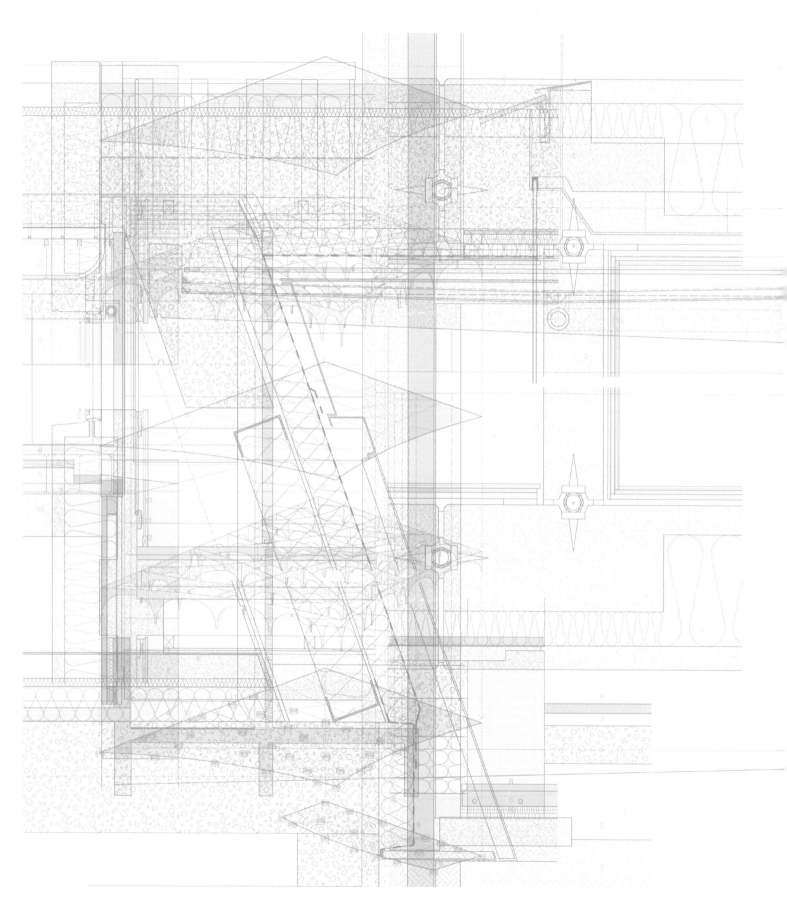

182

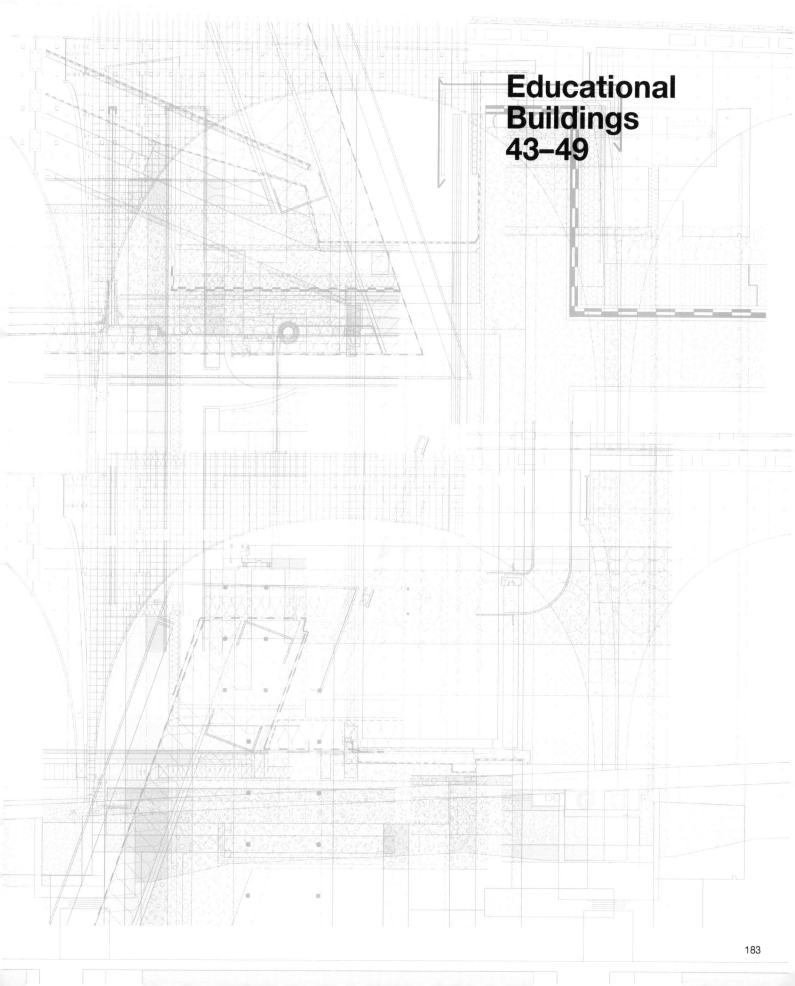

Educational
Buildings
43–49

**Schulheim Rossfeld Renovation
and Extension
Bern, Switzerland**

Client
Stiftung Rossfeld, Schulungs und
Wohnheime, Bern

Project Team
Bernhard Aebi / Pascal Vincent

Structural Engineer
Weber & Broenimann AG, Bern

This renovation and extension of a
boarding school for disabled children
near Bern, Switzerland, has involved a
careful restoration of the original
1960s building's clarity of form along
with the addition of a new pavilion.
The aim of the project was to increase
the amount of space available for
teaching and to make this space more
flexible. The building is E shaped, and
small classrooms are arranged along
a spine corridor with service spaces
in the three wings. Throughout the
building a simple austere palette of
materials has been utilized.

The building makes clever use of
its basement areas, which are flanked
by open-stepped terraces that allow
light deep within. The lower walls
are constructed from multiple thin
columns of fair-faced concrete.
Concrete fins in front of the floor-to-
ceiling windows allow variable light
conditions and modulate the
transparency of the building.

The position of the new building
emphasizes the axial alignment of the
complex and additionally creates an
architectural tension with the bell
tower of the adjacent church.

1 The rhythmic vertical
concrete fins that
line the building's
perimeter shade the
floor-to-ceiling glazing
behind.
2 There is a clear
relationship between
the column pattern
and the trees that
surround the site.
3 A broad corridor
runs along the spine of
the building.
4 Interior circulation
spaces made excellent
use of natural light and
bright reflective
surfaces.
5 The classrooms have
floor-to-ceiling glazing,
allowing views out
across the grounds.

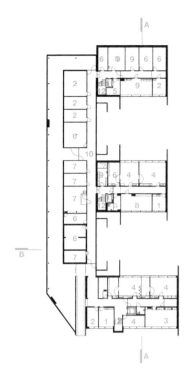

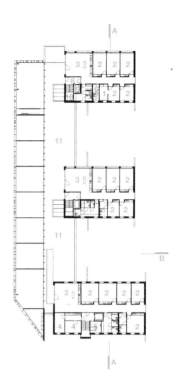

43.01	43.02	43.03	43.04	43.05
Basement	**Ground Floor**	**First Floor**	**Section A–A**	**Section B–B**
1:1000	**1:1000**	**1:1000**	**1:500**	**1:500**
1 Office	1 Office	1 Office	1 Office	1 Classroom
2 Room	2 Room	2 Room	2 Room	2 Office
3 Kitchen	3 Kitchen	3 Kitchen / living	3 Kitchen / Living	3 Technical room
4 Therapy room	4 Therapy room	room	room	4 Corridor
5 Cleaning room	5 Classroom	4 Logopedics	4 Therapy room	
6 Storage	6 Storage	5 Therapeutic bath	5 Storage	
7 Technical room	7 Multipurpose	6 Shower	6 Corridor	
8 Workshop	Room	7 WC		
9 WC	8 Entrance	8 Corridor		
10 Corridor	9 WC	9 Lift		
11 Lift	10 Corridor	10 Stair		
12 Stair	11 Lift	11 Terrace		
	12 Stair			

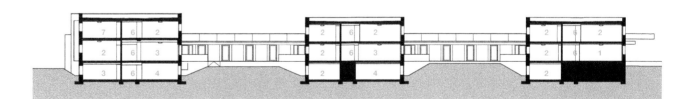

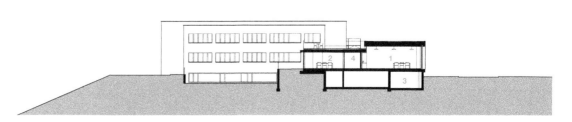

185

**43.06
Porch Connecting
Wing
1:20**
1 Lino 5 mm (2 inch)
2 Underlay 70 mm
(27 1/2 inch)
3 Concrete 200 mm
(7 9/10 inch)
4 Insulation 100 mm
(3 9/10 inch)
5 Oiled Siberian larch
115 x 26 mm (451/5 x
101/5 inches)
6 Battens
7 Protective foil 1.3
mm (1/2 inch)
8 Plastic foil 1.8 mm
(7/10 inch)
9 PUR insulation
(aluminium-laminated)
100 mm (39 3/10 inch)
10 Vapour barrier 3.5
mm (1 2/5 inch)
11 Concrete between
180-240 mm (70 4/5
- 87 3/10 inches) 1%
slope + 20 mm (7 9/10
inch) deflection
12 Acoustic plaster
perforated ceiling
13 Drainage pipe 90
mm (35 2/5 inch) + 40
mm (15 4/5 inch)
insulation 0.5% slope

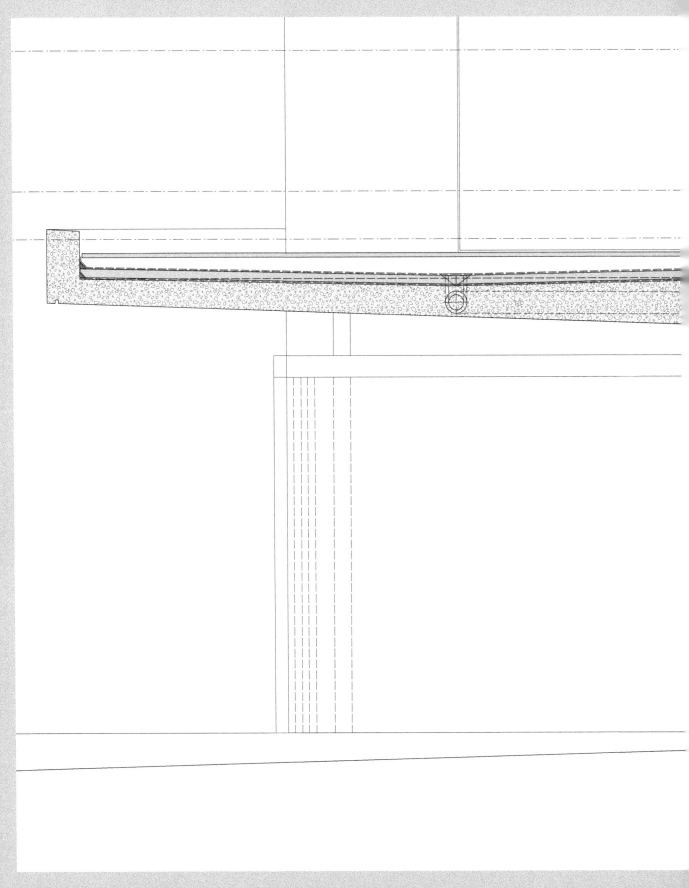

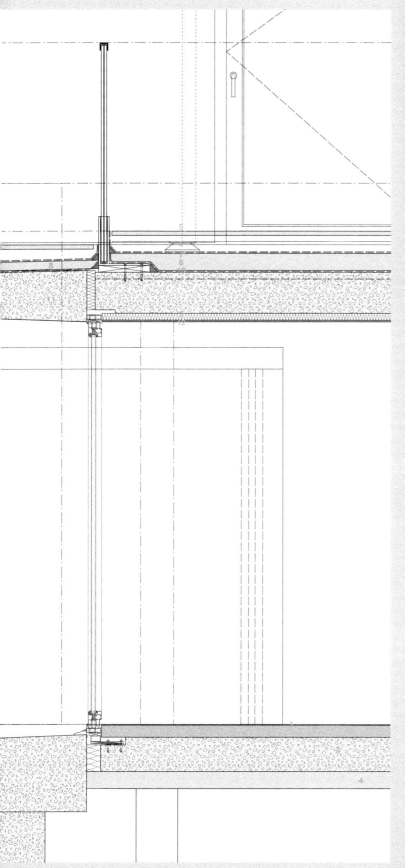

43.07
Concrete Detail
Section
1:20
  1 Concrete slats
400 x 100 mm (39
$^{3}/_{10}$ x 157$^{1}/_{2}$ inches)
  2 Concrete
  3 Insulation
  4 Extensive green
roof
  5 Protective layer
  6 Insulation
  7 Window
  8 Awning / sunscreen
  9 Convector
10 Insulation

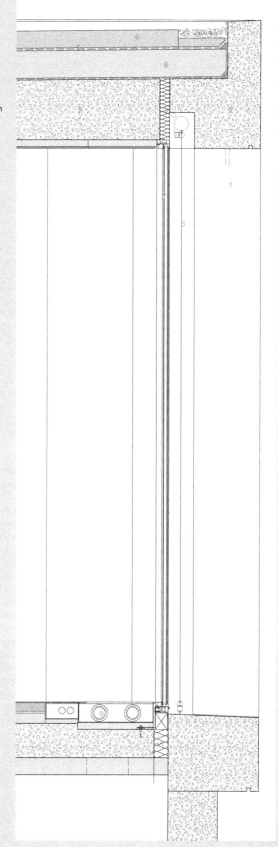

Four Boxes Gallery
Skive, Denmark

Client
Krabbesholm Højskole

Project Team
Yoshiharu Tsukamoto, Momoyo
Kaijima, Takahiko Kurabayashi (Atelier
Bow-Wow), Naho Maki, Kazuaki
Horikake (University of Tsukuba
Kaijima Lab.)

Structural Engineer
Fritz Nielsen & J. Juul Christensen A/S

Main Contractor
Dan-Element A/S

This gallery is located in northern
Denmark, on a former farm property
that has been converted into an art
school. It's directly adjacent to a port
area, which is characterized by its
silos and warehouse buildings. On the
campus, there is a diverse collection
of buildings both traditional and
modernist, and in addition there are
some art pavilions. In contrast with the
existing structures, the gallery is built
entirely of pre-cast concrete panels.
This gives it a primitive, raw
appearance that reflects the nearby
industrial buildings.

The concrete panels, which are of
different heights, enclose a three-
storey volume placed between two
equally sized exterior grass
courtyards. The front courtyard leads
into the large ground-floor exhibition
space; this space is lit by diffused light
from clerestory windows located
along the lateral walls. All of the
interior surfaces have been kept clear,
without openings or interruptions,
allowing for easy display, light control
and spatial flexibility.

Above the gallery there are two
additional spaces, one is a second
gallery and the other is a workshop.
These spaces are stacked on top of
the main gallery and are reached by a
side staircase. The courtyards can
also be used as additional exhibition
areas. The building's users are mainly
students engaging in all forms of
artistic experimentation and creation,
so the finishes have been designed to
accommodate such activities. The
school's alumni funded the building,
and the wider local community also
uses it as a social space.

1 From the road the
gallery presents an
austere private facade.
The windows at the
upper levels provide
clear illumination
throughout the gallery.

2 The entrance to the
courtyard is via a
cut-away corner, the
end wall also has a
large 'window' that
frames the view

3 The building's
composition of walls
and openings
references the features
of vernacular
architecture at different
scales.

4 The interior of the
gallery has been made
as simple as possible.
The proportional
relationship between
the interior and exterior
spaces is clearly
evident.

5 Simple details and a
limited material palette
produce exemplary
exhibition spaces.

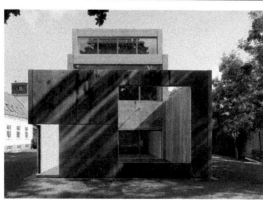

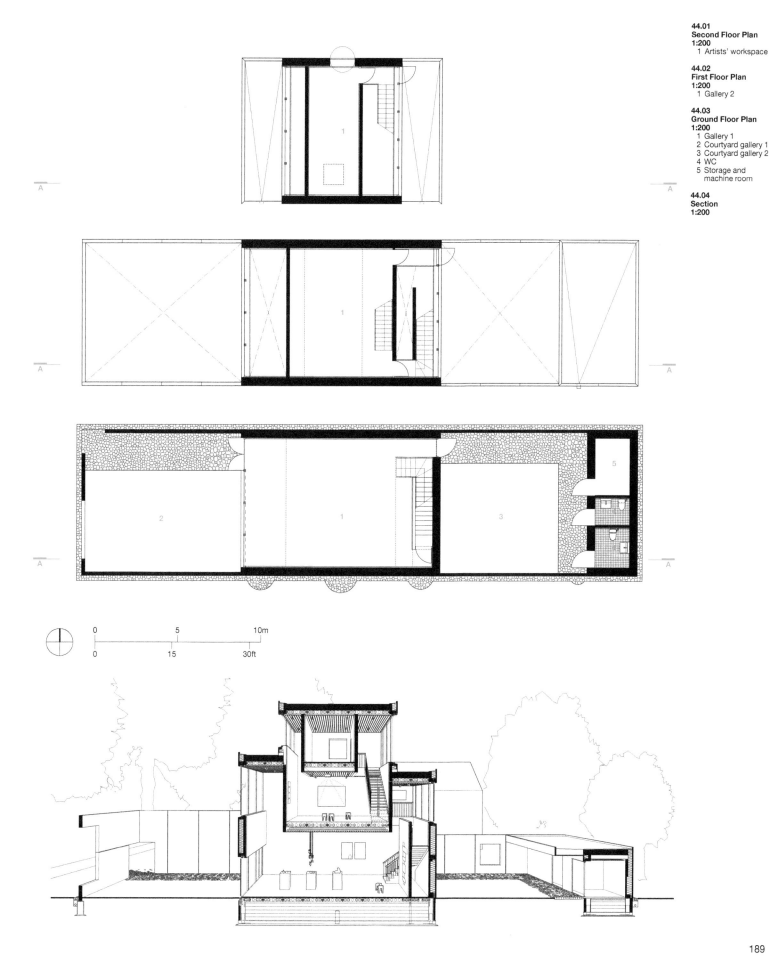

44.01
Second Floor Plan
1:200
   1 Artists' workspace

44.02
First Floor Plan
1:200
   1 Gallery 2

44.03
Ground Floor Plan
1:200
   1 Gallery 1
   2 Courtyard gallery 1
   3 Courtyard gallery 2
   4 WC
   5 Storage and
       machine room

44.04
Section
1:200

0   5   10m

0   15   30ft

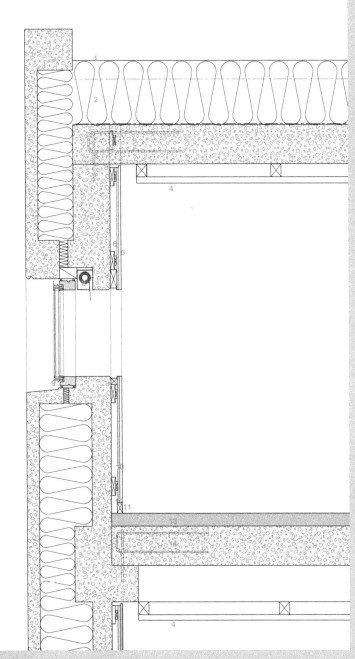

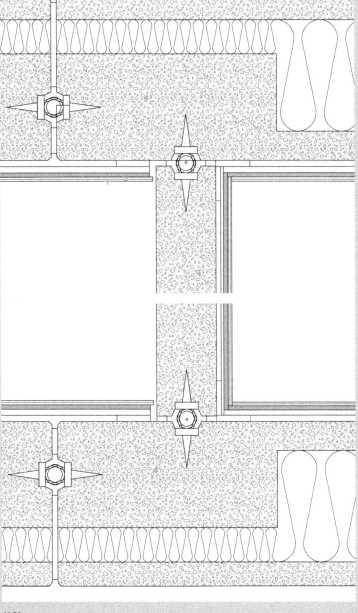

44.05
Section Detail
1:20
 1 Double-layered felt roofing
 2 Insulation 250–350 mm (9 8/10–13 8/10 inch) with slope 1:40
 3 Precast concrete 215 mm (8 1/2 inch)
 4 Wood louvres 34 × 98 mm (1 3/10 x 3 9/10 inch) at 133 mm (5 1/4 inch), paint finish RAL9003 signal white
 5 Plasterboard 13 mm (1/2 inch), paint finish RAL9003 signal white
 6 Plywood 15 mm (3/5 inch), firring strips 22 mm (7/8 inch)
 7 Concrete sandwich panel 480 mm (1 ft

6 9/10 inch)
 8 Roll curtain
 9 Aluminium and wood sash
 10 Plasterboard 13 mm (1/2 inch), paint finish RAL9003 signal white
 11 Aluminium plate 1 mm (1/24 inch), paint finish RAL9003 signal white
 12 MDF 28 mm (1 1/10 inch)
 13 Polish-finish concrete 70 mm (2 3/4 inch)
 14 Precast concrete panel 215 mm (8 1/2 inch)

44.06
Plan Detail
1:10
 1 Plasterboard 12.5 mm (1/2 inch), paint finish RAL9003 signal white
 2 Plywood 12.5 mm (1/2 inch), firring strips 22 mm (7/8 inch)
 3 Precast concrete panel 180 mm (7 inch)
 4 Concrete sandwich panel 480 mm (1 ft 6 9/10 inch)

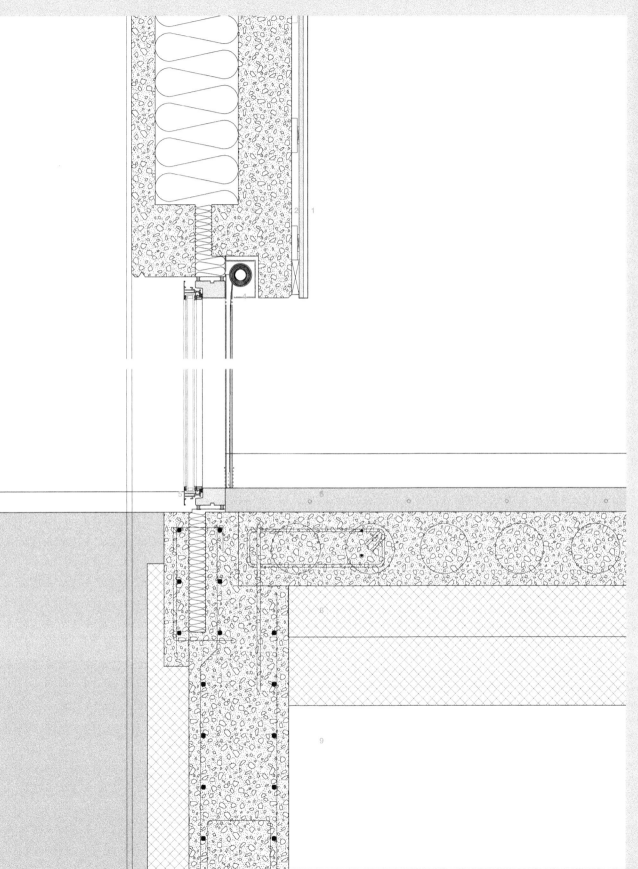

1 Plasterboard 13 mm
(1/2 inch), paint finish
RAL9003 signal white
2 Plywood 15 mm
(3/5 inch), firring strips
22 mm (7/8 inch)
3 Concrete sandwich
panel 480 mm (1 ft 6
9/10 inch)
4 Roll curtain
5 Aluminium and
wood sash
6 Polish-finish
concrete 70 mm (2 3/4
inch)
7 Precast concrete
panel 150 mm (5 9/10
inch)
8 Insulation 350 mm
(1 ft 1 4/5 inch)
9 Pebbles 150 mm
(5 9/10 inch)

Music House for Instrumental Practise and Choral Rehearsal, Benedictine Einsiedeln Abbey

Client
Benedictine Einsiedeln Abbey

Structural Engineer
Conzett, Bronzini, Gartmann

Main Contractor
Butti Bauunternehmung AG Pfäffikon

The music house forms part of the small educational campus of the Benedictine Einsiedeln Abbey. The abbey was originally founded in 934 and made up from buildings from many periods: notably it has some magnificent baroque structures. Music is central to the educational philosophy here and the central location of the music house is indicative of this.

Built on the site of the previous music building from the 1930s, the new larger structure anticipates a possible future extension of the schoolrooms in the eastern wing. On the ground floor a large hall is designed to be a hub for the school, a place for exhibitions, meetings and chance encounters. This space, which is glazed with sliding doors on both sides, opens onto the student courtyard, an area that in the winter becomes a skating rink.

A top-lit stair gives access to the upper floor. Bridging over the hall below, there are ten practise rooms and beyond this a space for performance and rehearsal. A large window in the north wall of this space opens out on the landscape. A pale muted material language of white concrete combined with larch windows subtly rhymes with and echoes the baroque surroundings.

1 The new music school is positioned in front of the baroque buildings of the abbey, its simple orthogonal form both in harmony and in contrast with the existing structures.

2 The rehearsal space is illuminated by a large glazed opening in the north wall of the building.
3 The top-lit half landing of the internal stair provides a quiet

space for students to prepare for their performances.
4 At night the transparency of the central section of the building reveals the activities within.

5 The rehearsal space, with its high angled ceiling, is designed to provide an excellent acoustic performance.

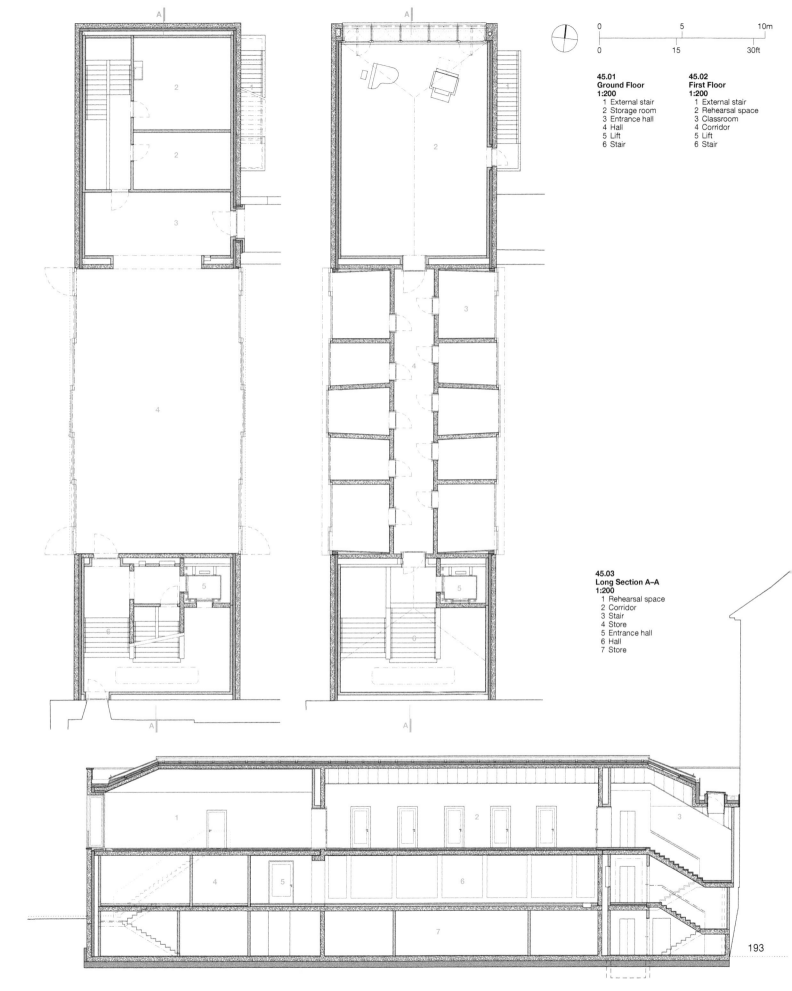

45.01
Ground Floor
1:200
1 External stair
2 Storage room
3 Entrance hall
4 Hall
5 Lift
6 Stair

45.02
First Floor
1:200
1 External stair
2 Rehearsal space
3 Classroom
4 Corridor
5 Lift
6 Stair

45.03
Long Section A–A
1:200
1 Rehearsal space
2 Corridor
3 Stair
4 Store
5 Entrance hall
6 Hall
7 Store

193

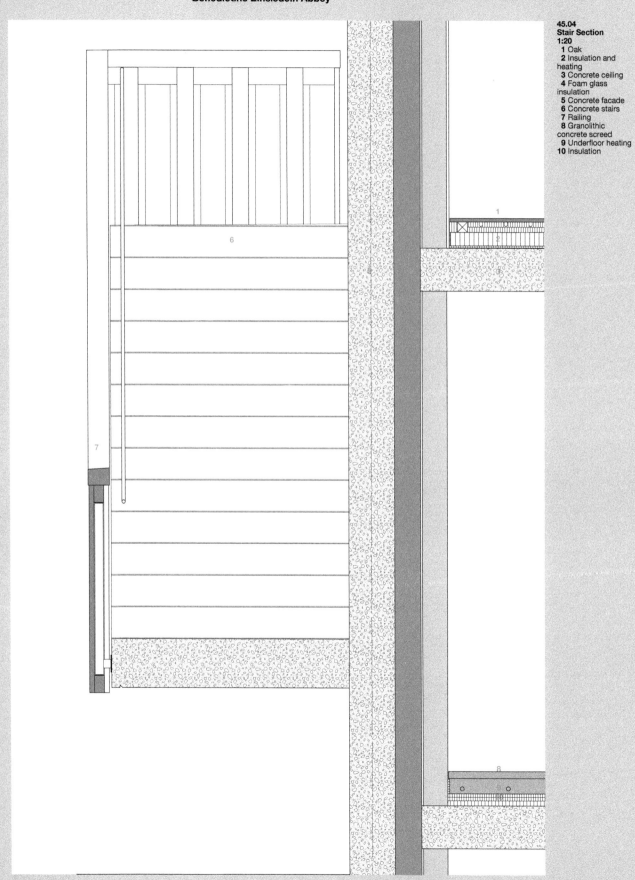

45.04
Stair Section
1:20
1 Oak
2 Insulation and heating
3 Concrete ceiling
4 Foam glass insulation
5 Concrete facade
6 Concrete stairs
7 Railing
8 Granolithic concrete screed
9 Underfloor heating
10 Insulation

Music House for Instrumental Practise and Choral Rehearsal, Benedictine Einsiedeln Abbey   Einsiedeln, Switzerland

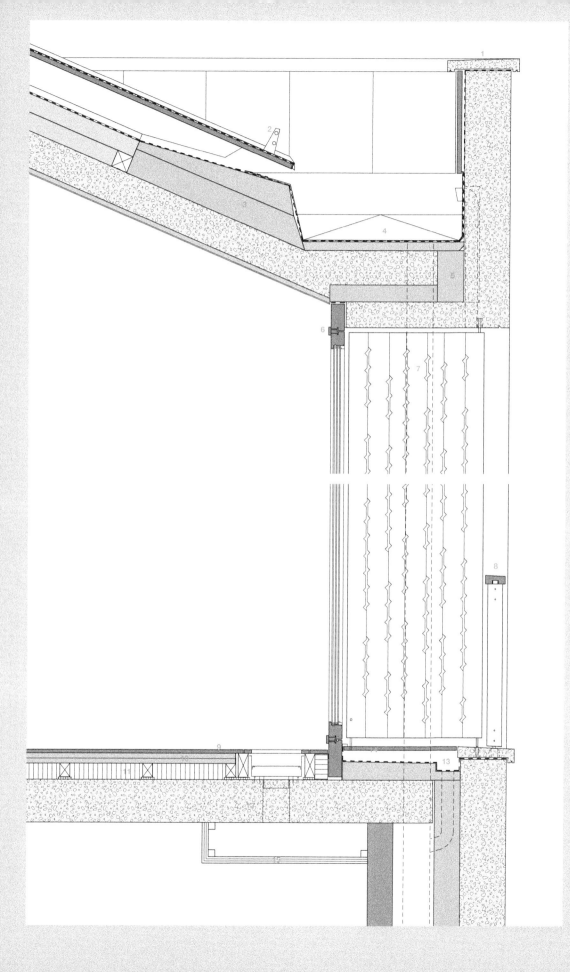

45.05
Roof / Gutter / Wall
Section
1:20
1 Precast concrete element
2 Copper
3 Foam glass
4 Rainwater gutter
5 Foam glass insulation
6 Window
7 Shutters
8 Railing
9 Oak floor
10 Heating
11 Insulation
12 Concrete ceiling
13 Drainage
14 Wooden grid
15 Air supply

Indian Institute of Management
Ahmedabad, Gujarat, India

Client
Indian Institute of Management

Project Team
Principal Designers: Bimal Patel,
Jayant Gunjaria, Gajanan Upadhyay
Core Design Team: Brijesh Bhatha,
Niki Shah, Samarth Maradia
Project Managers: Viplav Shah, Amar
Thakkar, Mahendra Patel

Structural Engineer
VMS Engineering and Design Services
Pvt. Ltd.

Built alongside the seminal campus of
the Indian Institute of Management,
Ahmedabad (IIMA) by Louis Khan, the
new campus is adjacent to the old
campus but separated by a busy road.
The development of this new 39-acre
site provides a range of new teaching
and residential facilities.

There is no direct visual link
between the two parts; however, the
new part is directly connected to the
old by a wide passageway under the
road. This passage houses an
exhibition about Khan's work at IIMA.
Emerging into the new campus we
find it to be both familiar but also
different. Rather than copy the distinct
'brick' forms of Kahn's campus, the
architects have made a subtle
translation of the forms and motifs
into new materials. The principal new
material is crisp white concrete. As in
Khan's campus there is a central axis
from which the teaching areas and
accommodation have been arranged.
All of Khan's language of circular
openings, steps and chamfered
corners can be found in the new
campus. This referencing has been
achieved with a clear sense of respect
for the original campus.

The teaching spaces are designed
to address the needs of the education
programme at IIMA. Around the
campus the architecture provides
many opportunities for students and
lecturers to engage with one another.

In several locations there are giant
steel screens based on plant motifs.
These graphic elements create a new
super scale within the complex that
succinctly expresses the monumental
yet human character of the buildings.

1 The strong
sculptural forms of the
new buildings are
evolutions of forms
found in the original
campus. The
architecture uses the
strong sunlight and
shadows to animate
the spaces.
2 The campus is
composed of
interlinked open space
and shady cloisters.
The residential blocks
are positioned near to
the teaching spaces.
3 Open stretches of
water provide a
cooling element in the
landscape. The plant
forms in the pools are
referenced in the steel
panels that fill the
openings in the
concrete frame.

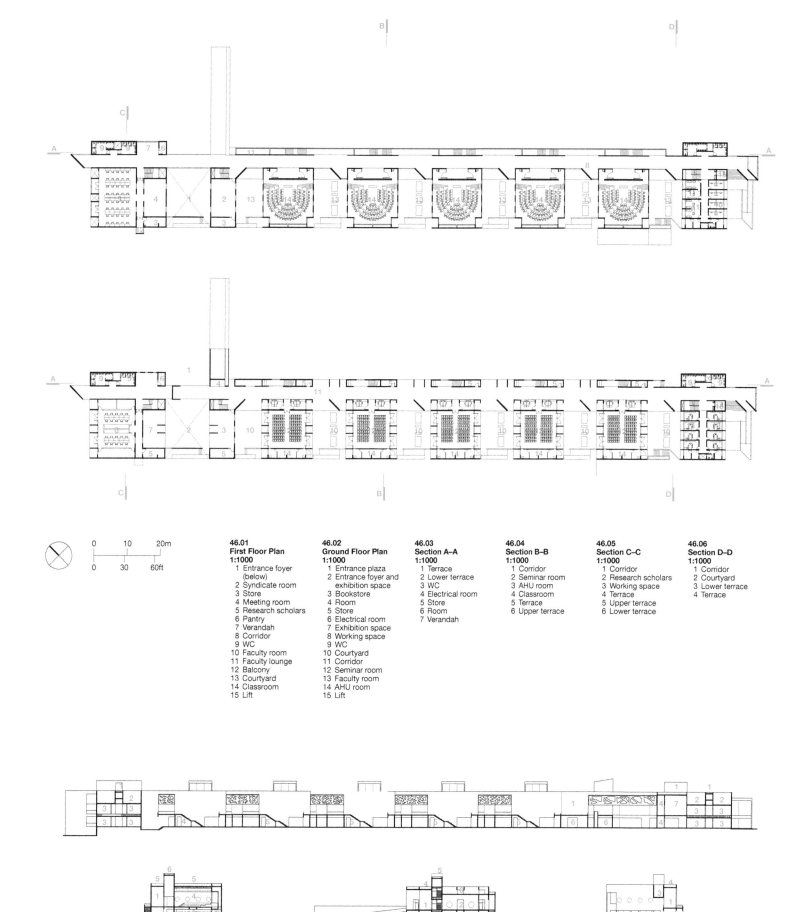

46.01
First Floor Plan
1:1000
1 Entrance foyer
   (below)
2 Syndicate room
3 Store
4 Meeting room
5 Research scholars
6 Pantry
7 Verandah
8 Corridor
9 WC
10 Faculty room
11 Faculty lounge
12 Balcony
13 Courtyard
14 Classroom
15 Lift

46.02
Ground Floor Plan
1:1000
1 Entrance plaza
2 Entrance foyer and
   exhibition space
3 Bookstore
4 Room
5 Store
6 Electrical room
7 Exhibition space
8 Working space
9 WC
10 Courtyard
11 Corridor
12 Seminar room
13 Faculty room
14 AHU room
15 Lift

46.03
Section A–A
1:1000
1 Terrace
2 Lower terrace
3 WC
4 Electrical room
5 Store
6 Room
7 Verandah

46.04
Section B–B
1:1000
1 Corridor
2 Seminar room
3 AHU room
4 Classroom
5 Terrace
6 Upper terrace

46.05
Section C–C
1:1000
1 Corridor
2 Research scholars
3 Working space
4 Terrace
5 Upper terrace
6 Lower terrace

46.06
Section D–D
1:1000
1 Corridor
2 Courtyard
3 Lower terrace
4 Terrace

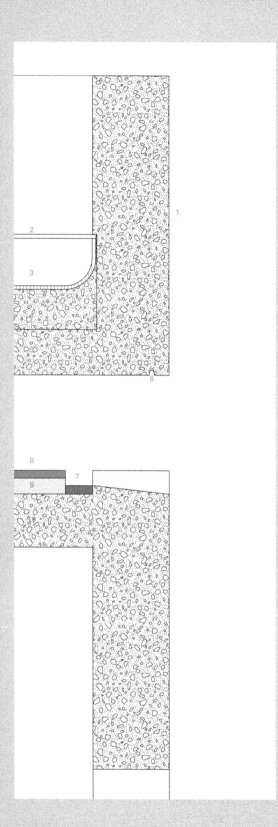

46.07
**Sectional Detail
Through Corridor
and Courtyard 1**
1:10
 1 Exposed reinforced
cement concrete
surface
 2 Groove 10 x 10 mm
($^3/_{10}$ x $^3/_{10}$ inch)
 3 China mosaic
flooring laid in slope
1:100
 4 Average 115 mm
(4 $^1/_2$ inch) thick brick
bat concrete with
waterproofing
 5 Exposed reinforced
concrete slab
 6 Drip mould
 7 Rainwater drain of
40 mm (1 $^1/_2$ inch)
depth with rainwater
channel in the floor
corridor
 8 Polished cement
flooring
 9 Screed
10 Reinforced
concrete slab

46.08
**Sectional Detail
Through Corridor
and Courtyard 2**
1:10
 1 Polished cement
flooring
 2 Screed
 3 Reinforced
concrete slab
 4 Plain cement
concrete ratio 1:4:8
 5 Rubble soling
 6 Compact sand
filling
 7 Natural ground
 8 Courtyard flooring

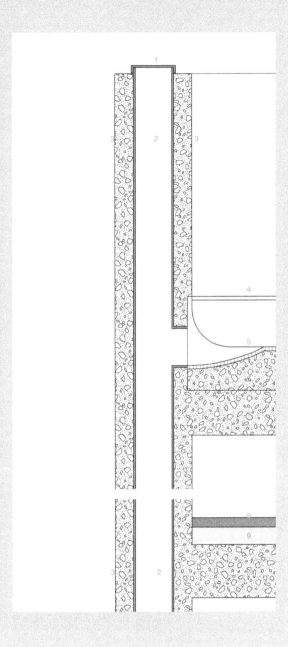

46.09
Sectional Detail
Showing Concealed
Rainwater Pipe From
Terrace 1
1:10
1 Openable polyvinyl
chloride grilled cover
for the rainwater pipe
2 Concealed
rainwater pipe 110 mm
(4 $^3/_{10}$ inch) diameter
3 Exposed reinforced
cement concrete
surface
4 Groove 10 x 10 mm
($^3/_{10}$ x $^3/_{10}$ inch)
5 China mosaic
flooring laid in slope
1:100
6 Average 115 mm
(4 $^1/_2$ inch) thick brick
bat concrete with
water proofing
7 Exposed reinforced
concrete slab
8 Polished stone
flooring
9 Screed
10 Reinforced cement
concrete slab of grade
M20, with 8 mm ($^3/_{10}$
inch) diameter TOR
steel reinforcement at
200 mm (7 $^9/_{10}$ inch)
centre

46.10
Sectional Detail
Showing Concealed
Rainwater Pipe From
Terrace 2
1:10
1 Concealed
rainwater pipe 110 mm
(4 $^3/_{10}$ inch) diameter
2 Exposed reinforced
cement concrete
surface
3 Polished stone
flooring
4 Screed
5 Reinforced cement
concrete slab of grade
M20, with 8 mm ($^3/_{10}$
inch) diameter TOR
steel reinforcement at
200 mm (7 $^9/_{10}$ inch)
center
6 Plain cement
concrete of ratio 1:4:8
7 Rubble soling
8 Compacted sand
filling
9 Natural ground
10 Rough stone finish
for plinth protection

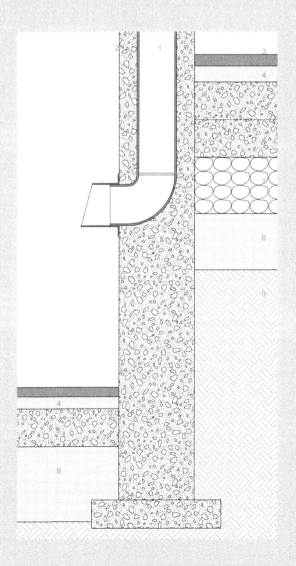

Tama Art University Library
Hachioji, Tokyo, Japan

Client
Tama Art University

Project Team
Toyo Ito, Takeo Higashi, Hideyuki
Nakayama, Yoshitaka Ihara

Associate Architect
Kajima Design

Structural Engineer
Sasaki Structural Consultants

Main Contractor
Kajima Corporation

This new library is located on the
campus of an art university in the
suburbs of Tokyo. Driven by the idea
of a cave, the building is formed from
a series of gently curved intersecting
walls placed at different angles in a
loose grid. Giant arches piece these
walls. The continuously curved and
arched walls articulate the space into
square and triangle areas.

The construction is of in-situ
concrete formed around flanged steel
plate cores that are augmented with
steel reinforcing rods positioned on
either side. In effect this is a steel
building with a concrete skin. The
concrete was cast into wooden
shuttering that was precisely made in
a factory. This allowed the walls to be
as thin as 200 mm (7 9/10 inch). The
arches spans vary from 1.8 to 16
metres (6 to 52 ½ ft). The external
concrete walls on the north and
west sides of the building are curved,
as is the glass that is fitted flush
within them.

The ground floor of the building has
a sloping floor that blends with the
external landscape; it is designed to
be like a promenade, a place where
students can walk through the
building from one side to the other. It
can also serve as a gallery or lecture
space. The main library space is on
the first floor; here 100,000 books are
on display, while another 100,000
books are stored behind the glass
walls. 60,000 additional books are
stored in the basement. The whole
building sits on 24 rubber buffers and
27 sliding bearings, which allow the
building to move up to 500 mm (19 ½
inches) horizontally in an earthquake.

1 The library's open
arched form creates a
lively rhythm. Planting
around the building
and the continuation of
the ground contours
into the building
establish a sense of
permanence and
solidity.
2 The arches are
expanded and
contracted across the
facade. With the glass
pushed flush to the
concrete surface the
building has a tight
skin.
3 On the side of the
building that faces to
the main road the wall
is cut flat to the
campus boundary.
4 The ground floor
entrance undercroft is
an important new
social space for the
university. Soft
spherical seats invite
students to sit and
talk.
5 The ground floor
contains sinuous
display cases for the
display of graphic
materials.

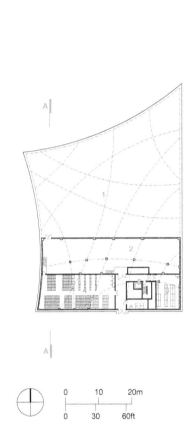

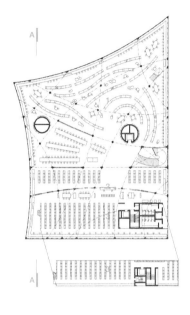

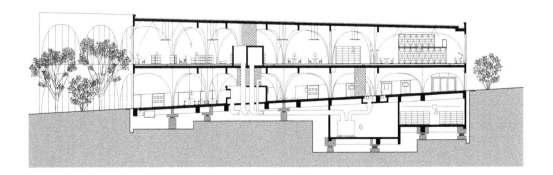

0 10 20m
0 30 60ft

47.01
Basement Plan
1:1000
1 Seismic isolation
  pit
2 Machine room
3 Valuable book
  stack
4 Compact
5 Lift

47.02
Ground Floor Plan
1:1000
1 Arcade gallery
2 Cafe
3 North entrance
4 South entrance
5 New arrival
  magazines
6 Lounge
7 Locker
8 Information desk
9 Office
10 WC
11 Lift
12 Stair
13 Multimedia

47.03
First Floor and
Mezzanine Plan
1:1000
1 Open stack and
  reading
2 Information desk
3 Closed stacks

47.04
Section A–A
1:500
1 Open stack and
  reading
2 Text
3 Closed stacks
4 Cafe
5 Arcade gallery
6 Machine room
7 Seismic isolation
  pad
8 Valuable book
  stack

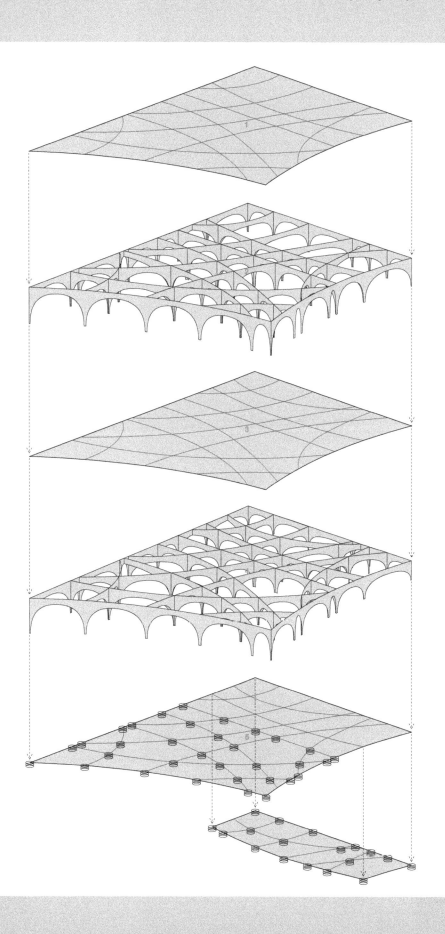

47.05
Axonometric
Not to Scale
1 Roof slab
2 Arch steel and concrete frame
3 Slab
4 Arch steel and concrete frame
5 Slab

47.06
Detail Section
1:50
1 Asphalt prepared roofing
2 Insulation 25 mm (1 inch)
3 Concrete panel 45 mm (1 8/10 inch)
4 Drainage slope 1:40
5 Flange (column) : FB 28 x 65 mm (1 1/10 x 2 6/10 inch)
6 Steel plate 9 x 167 x 320 mm (4/10 x 6 6/10 inch x 1 ft)
7 High tension bolt
8 Flange (beam) FB 22 x 65 mm (9/10 x 2 6/10 inch)
9 Web (bottom of column)
10 Reinforcement
11 Air conditioning outlet
12 Carpet tile 500 x 500 mm (1 ft 7 7/10 x 1 ft 7 7/10 inch) 10 mm (4/10 inch) thick
13 Raised access floor
14 Insulation 20 mm (8/10 inch)
15 Void slab 300 mm (11 8/10 inch)
16 Ceiling exposed concrete
17 Hydrophobizing agent finish
18 Exposed concrete
19 Hydrophobizing agent finish
20 Hole 50 mm (2 inch) @ 300 x @ 450 mm (11 8/10 x @ 1 ft 5 7/10 inch) separator pitch
21 Web (beam)
22 Flange (beam) FB 22 x 65 (9/10 x 2 6/10 inch)
23 Hole 150 mm (5 9/10 inch) (concrete connection)
24 Web (column)
25 Flange (column) FB 28 x 6 mm (1 1/10 x 2/10 inch)
26 Wire fabric hanger
27 Wire fabric on both sides D6 @ 100 x 100 mm (3 9/10 x 3 9/10 inch)
28 Web at bottom of column PL-40
29 Reinforcement D6 @100 x 100 mm (3 9/10 x 3 9/10 inch)
30 Base plate 36 x 460 x 460 mm (1 4/10 x 1 ft 6 1/10 x 1 ft 6 1/10 inch)
31 Anchor bolt 4-M36
32 Float glass 15 mm (6 2/10 inch)
33 Anti-scratching film
34 Exposed concrete 100 mm (3 9/10 inch)
35 Toughening agent finish
36 Seismic isolator
37 Steel mullion

Children's Toy Library
Bonneuil sur Marne, France

Client
Bonneuil sur Marne Local Authority

Project Team
LAN Architecture

Structural Engineer
Cabinet MTC

This children's toy library in Bonneuil sur Marne is located within a large 1960s social housing complex. It provides valuable social space for both local children and their parents. Created on a very small budget (the original brief was for an internal refit), the project carefully reuses and interprets an existing structure.

The original building has been completely wrapped by a new skin formed from board-marked concrete. Within these green-tinted walls the architects have conjured a place of security where children can play, as well as a social area for adults.

The precise folding of a new origami membrane around the existing structure has made a protective shell for the building's new functions to inhabit. This strategy of covering the building has provided spaces that are generous and surprising. At ground level there is a double-height atrium space and on the upper level an open decked play area that is accessed from the toy library. Externally the elevations provide little suggestion of scale; the structure is neither monumental nor is it insignificant. The architects have used a strong language of form and materiality to create a subtle interplay between the secluded safety of the interior and the strong monolithic exterior. This confident building suggests respect and commands attention.

1 The severe articulated facade that the building presents to the street gives few hints about the interior. The concrete wall surface has a fine texture like the bark of the surrounding trees.
2 The windows are set flush with the walls, which creates a tight sinuous skin. An ambiguous atmosphere of both lightness and heaviness pervades the project.
3 The upper roof terrace is covered by a wooden deck. When the doors are folded back the interior and exterior become one.
4 Use of strong colour and large windows gives the play area a welcoming atmosphere.

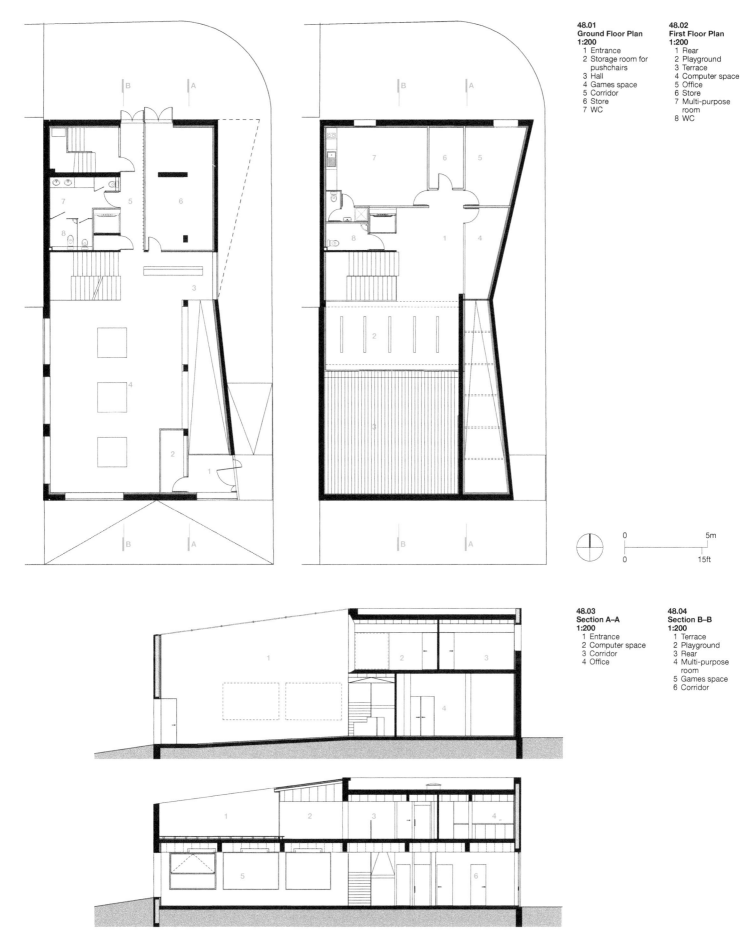

48.01
Ground Floor Plan
1:200
1 Entrance
2 Storage room for pushchairs
3 Hall
4 Games space
5 Corridor
6 Store
7 WC

48.02
First Floor Plan
1:200
1 Rear
2 Playground
3 Terrace
4 Computer space
5 Office
6 Store
7 Multi-purpose room
8 WC

48.03
Section A–A
1:200
1 Entrance
2 Computer space
3 Corridor
4 Office

48.04
Section B–B
1:200
1 Terrace
2 Playground
3 Rear
4 Multi-purpose room
5 Games space
6 Corridor

0   5m
0   15ft

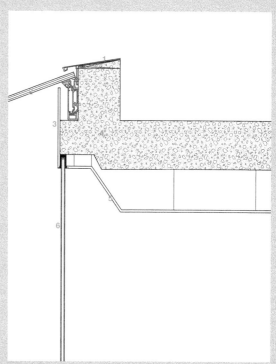

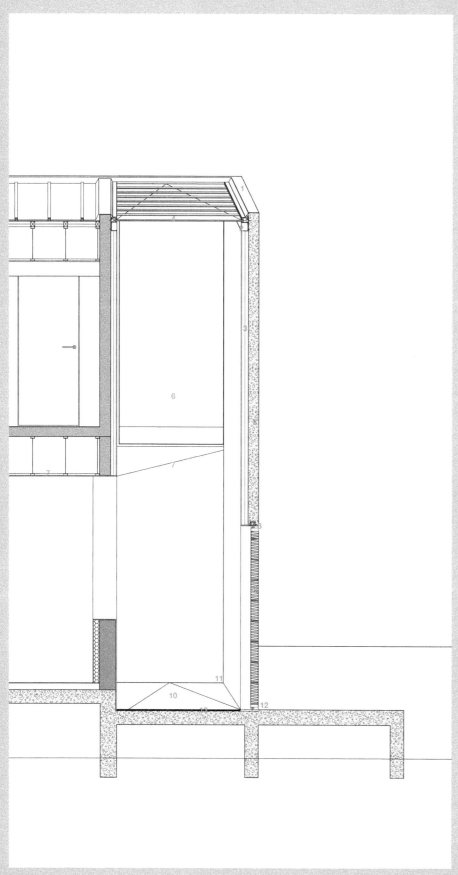

48.05
Entrance Ramp
Detail
1:50
 1 Zinc coping
 2 Aluminium frame
 3 Thermal and
acoustic insulation:
13 mm (1/2 inch)
plasterboard and rock
wool
 4 Interior and exterior
laminated glass
 5 Reinforced tinted
freestanding concrete
wall
 6 Fixed plate glass
 7 False ceiling
 8 Decentred and
embedded high pintle
 9 Steel door: folded
sheet joined on brace
crossbeams with
interior insulation
10 Ramp
11 Door frame
cladding in lacquered
aluminium
12 Gate hinge with
brake
13 Carpet

48.06
Roof Detail
1:20
 1 Zinc coping
 2 Glazing
 3 Steel plate
 4 Concrete
 5 False ceiling
 6 Glazing

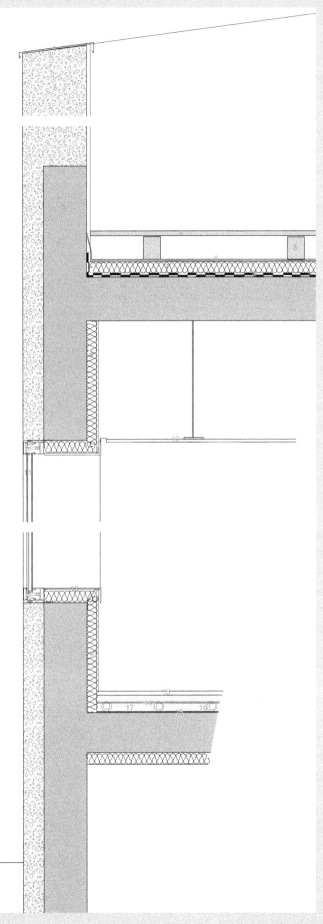

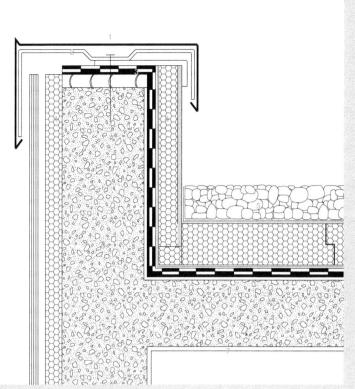

48.07
Wall and Floor
Section Detail
1:20
  1 Zinc coping
  2 Self-compacting
reinforced dyed
concrete structure
  3 Existing masonry
  4 Wood deck
  5 Battens
  6 Waterproof film
  7 Insulation
  8 Sealing membrane
  9 Insulation
10 Suspended ceiling
11 Two sheets
laminated glass 4 mm
(^{2}/10 inch) with 16 mm
(^{6}/10 inch) gap
12 Aluminium sheet
covering the perimeter
of the bay frame
13 Insulation
14 Waterproof film
15 Vapour barrier
16 Underfloor heating
17 Floating Screed
18 PVC Floor covering

48.08
Roof Detail
1:10
  1 Zinc coping
  2 Steel profile
  3 Sealing membrane
  4 Insulation
  5 Gravel
  6 Concrete
  7 Plaster

Evelyn Grace Academy
London, England

Client
School trust: Ark Education
Government: DCSF

Project Team
Zaha Hadid, Patrick Schumacher
Lars Teichmann, Matthew Hardcastle

Structural Engineer
Arup

Main Contractor
Mace Plus

Winner of the Royal Institute of British Architects Stirling Prize in 2011, this secondary school – set in a diverse area in South London – is the first major building by Zaha Hadid in England. Sponsored by a charitable organization set up by hedge-fund financiers, the school is designed to provide a good education and give a sense of pride to the pupils from a deprived area.

The zigzag-shaped building is squeezed onto a very tight urban site within a residential area. The strong sculptural forms of the exterior stand out against adjacent rows of Victorian houses. The main structure is built from in-situ concrete, with cladding of steel and glass.

As the academy is administratively structured into four small schools, the building is loosely divided into four sections. These are augmented with common spaces and facilities, such as an art and technology block, music and drama studios, sports facilities and a canteen. There are large balcony spaces where students from different 'schools' can meet up and relax, and the big windows of each classroom give an impression of openness.

To make the most of the limited space while also creating a dramatic effect, a 100 metre athletics track runs under the bridge that connects the two blocks where the main entrance is located. This also emphasizes the school's focus on sport, one of its core subject areas.

1 Pupils have many different types of space available for recreation and socializing. The spectacular angled facades that wrap around the building are fractured by slanted fissures.
2 Sharp graphic forms fabricated from steel are a signature of Hadid's architecture; they animate the glazed elevations.
3 The running track communicates the ambition of the school to place sport at the centre of its activities.
4 The generously proportioned interior spaces with dramatic lighting are atypical of those found in traditional school buildings.

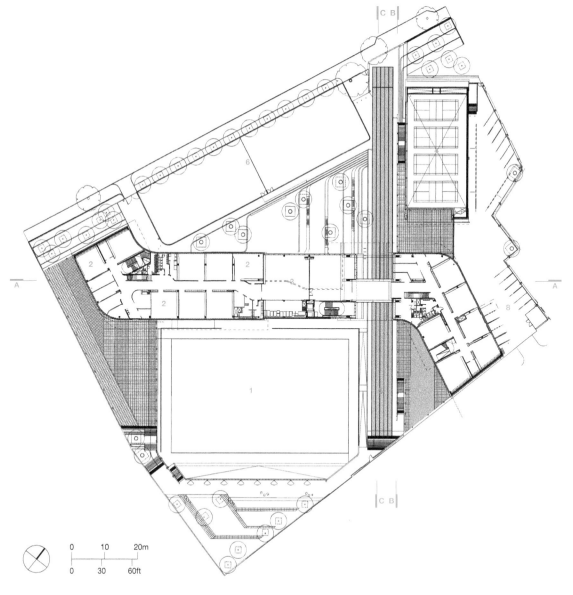

49.01
First Floor Plan
1:1000
1 All-weather pitch
2 Classroom
3 Common hall
4 Sports hall
5 100 metre sprint track
6 Multi-use games area
7 Staff room
8 Service area / parking on ground floor

0   10   20m
0   30   60ft

49.02
Longitudinal Section
A–A
1:1000

49.03
Section Through Bridge Link Showing Sports Block Elevation at Ground Level
B–B
1:1000

49.04
Short Section Through Building Showing Art Block Elevation at Ground Level
C–C
1:1000

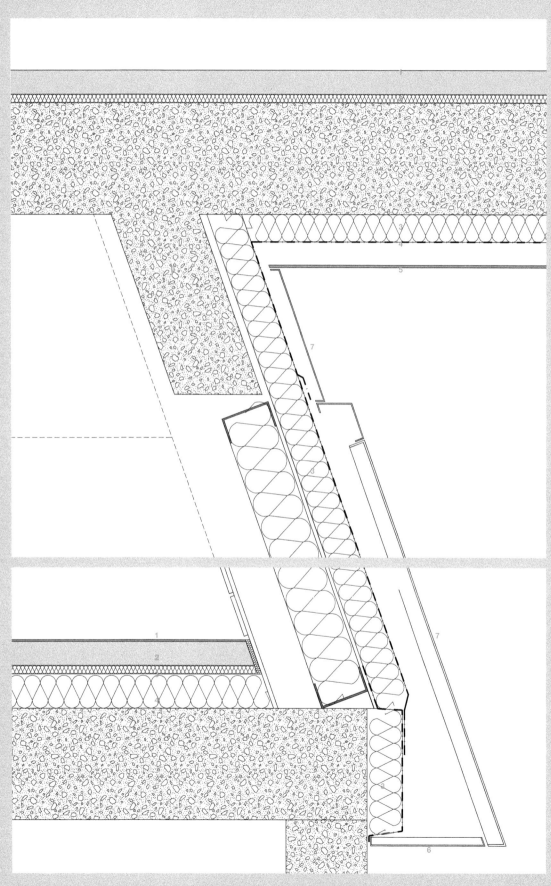

49.05
**Section End Inclined
Wall 3rd Floor
Shadow Band**
1:10
 1 Screed topped and
floor finish
 2 Insulation
 3 Insulation
 4 Breather membrane
 5 Cementitious soffit
panels
 6 Reinforced
concrete downstand
beam
 7 Aluminium
rainscreen 'shadow
band'

49.06
**Section End Inclined
Wall 1st Floor Soffit**
1:10
 1 Screed topped and
floor finish
 2 Insulation
 3 Insulation
 4 Membrane
 5 Reinforced
concrete
 6 Pressed aluminium
panels
 7 Aluminium
rainscreen panels on
metal framing

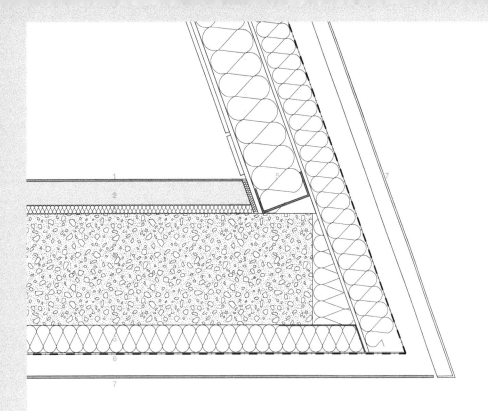

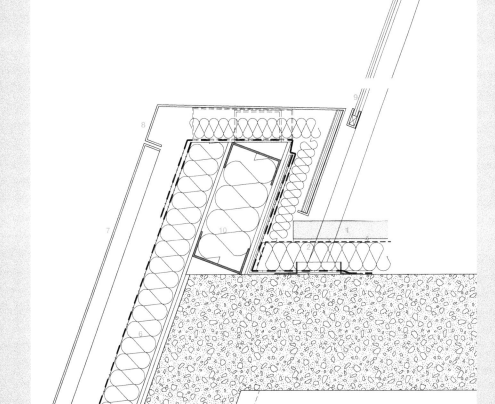

49.07
**Section End Inclined
Wall 3rd Floor
Shadow Band**
1:10
1 Screed topped and
floor finish
2 Insulation
3 Insulation
4 Reinforced
concrete
5 Insulation
6 Breather membrane
7 Cementitious soffit
panels
8 Aluminium
rainscreen panels on
metal framing

49.08
**Section 3rd Floor
Terrace Balustrade
at Ends**
1:10
1 Screed topped and
floor finish
2 Insulation
3 Pitch pocket
4 Membrane
5 Reinforced
concrete
6 Pressed aluminium
panels
7 PPC aluminium
rainscreen planks on
metal framing
8 PPC aluminium
coping with insulation
9 Guarding

211

Directory of Details

Walls

01.07 BNKR Arquitectura	**21.07** Ensamble Studio & Antón García-Abril	**42.06** SPASM Design Architects
03.06 C F Møller Architects	**21.08** Ensamble Studio & Antón García-Abril	**43.06** Aebi and Vincent
03.07 C F Møller Architects	**21.09** Ensamble Studio & Antón García-Abril	**43.07** Aebi and Vincent
03.11 C F Møller Architects	**22.05** Head Architektid	**44.05** Atelier Bow-Wow
03.12 C F Møller Architects	**23.08** id-ea Architects	**44.06** Atelier Bow-Wow
04.08 Caruso St John	**24.05** Joseph N. Biondo	**44.07** Atelier Bow-Wow
04.09 Caruso St John	**25.04** Mount Fuji Architects Studio	**45.04** Diener & Diener
04.10 Caruso St John	**25.05** Mount Fuji Architects Studio	**45.05** Diener & Diener
04.11 Caruso St John	**25.06** Mount Fuji Architects Studio	**46.07** HCP
05.06 David Chipperfield	**25.07** Mount Fuji Architects Studio	**46.09** HCP
05.07 David Chipperfield	**25.08** Mount Fuji Architects Studio	**46.10** HCP
06.06 Ellis Williams Architects	**25.09** Mount Fuji Architects Studio	**47.05** Toyo Ito & Associates
06.07 Ellis Williams Architects	**26.04** Paul Bretz Architectes	**47.06** Toyo Ito & Associates
08.07 HMC Architects	**26.07** Paul Bretz Architectes	**48.05** LAN
08.08 HMC Architects	**26.08** Paul Bretz Architectes	**48.07** LAN
08.09 HMC Architects	**28.09** Pezo von Ellrichshausen	**49.05** Zaha Hadid Architects
09.05 :mlzd	**28.10** Pezo von Ellrichshausen	**49.06** Zaha Hadid Architects
10.07 Nuno Ribeiro Lopes	**29.10** Shubin + Donaldson Architects	**49.07** Zaha Hadid Architects
10.08 Nuno Ribeiro Lopes	**30.09** TNA	**49.08** Zaha Hadid Architects
11.05 O'Donnell + Tuomey	**30.10** TNA	
11.06 O'Donnell + Tuomey	**30.11** TNA	
11.07 O'Donnell + Tuomey	**31.05** Torafu Architects	
11.08 O'Donnell + Tuomey	**32.11** Wood / Marsh	
11.09 O'Donnell + Tuomey	**33.05** Barbossa & Guimarães	
12.07 Pysall Ruge Architekten	**33.06** Barbossa & Guimarães	
12.08 Pysall Ruge Architekten	**33.07** Barbossa & Guimarães	
12.09 Pysall Ruge Architekten	**34.05** Becker Architekten	
13.03 Ryue Nishizawa	**35.07** Bennetts Associates	
14.05 Eduardo Souto de Moura	**35.08** Bennetts Associates	
14.07 Eduardo Souto de Moura	**36.07** Claus en Kaan Architecten	
15.11 wHY Architecture	**36.08** Claus en Kaan Architecten	
15.12 wHY Architecture	**36.09** Claus en Kaan Architecten	
16.04 UN Studio	**36.10** Claus en Kaan Architecten	
17.03 AFF Architekten	**38.06** Hohensinn Architektur	
17.04 AFF Architekten	**39.07** PleskowRael Architecture	
18.06 BAKarquitectos	**39.08** PleskowRael Architecture	
18.07 BAKarquitectos	**39.09** PleskowRael Architecture	
18.08 BAKarquitectos	**40.05** Rafael de La-Hoz Arquitectos	
19.06 Dosmasuno Arquitectos	**40.06** Rafael de La-Hoz Arquitectos	
19.07 Dosmasuno Arquitectos	**41.04** Scott Brownrigg	
19.08 Dosmasuno Arquitectos	**41.05** Scott Brownrigg	
20.05 EASTERN Design Office	**41.06** Scott Brownrigg	
20.07 EASTERN Design Office		
21.06 Ensamble Studio & Antón García-Abril		

Floors

Stairs

Screen

Table

Pool

Lintels

Glazing junctions

Directory of Architects

Australia

Peter Stutchbury Architecture
5/364 Barrenjoey Road
Newport, NSW 2106
info@peterstutchbury.com.au
T +61 2 9979 5030
F +61 2 9979 5367
www.peterstutchbury.com.au

Wood / Marsh Architecture
30 Beaconsfield Parade
Port Melbourne, Victoria 3207
wm@woodmarsh.com.au
T +61 3 9676 2600
F +61 3 9676 2811
www.woodmarsh.com.au

Austria

Hohensinn Architektur
Grieskai 80 A-8020 Graz
office@hohensinn-architektur.at
T +43 316 811188
F +43 316 811188 11
www.hohensinn-architektur.at

Chile

Pezo von Ellrichshausen Architects
Nonguen 776, Concepcion, Chile
info@pezo.cl
T +56 41 2210281
www.pezo.cl

Denmark

C.F. Møller Architects
Europaplads 2, 11
8000 Aarhus C
cfmoller@cfmoller.com
T +45 8730 5300
www.cfmoller.com

Estonia

Head Architektid
Kopli 25-605, 10412 Tallinn
indrek@peilmail.ee
T +372 6414070
F +372 6414070

Finland

Heikkinen-Komonen Architects
Kristianinkatu 11-13
00170 Helsinki
ark@heikkinen-komonen.fi
T +358 9 75102111
F +358 9 75102166
www.heikkinen-komonen.fi

France

LAN
25 Rue d'Hauteville
75010 Paris
info@lan-paris.com
T +33 1 43 70 00 60
F +33 1 43 70 01 21
www.lan-paris.com

Germany

AFF Architekten
Wedekindstraße 24
10243 Berlin
berlin@aff-architekten.com
T +49 30 275 92 92 0
F +49 30 275 92 92 22
www.aff-architekten.com

Becker Architekten
Beethovenstraße 7
D 87435 Kempten, Allgaeu
kontakt@becker-architekten.net
T +49 831 51220 00
F +49 831 51220 01
www.becker-architekten.net

Pysall Ruge Architekten
Zossener Straße 56-58
D-10961 Berlin
info@pysall.net
T +49 30 69 81 08 0
F +49 30 69 81 08 11
www.pysall.net

India

HCP Design and Project Management
Paritosh, Usmanpura
Ahmadabad 380 013
hcpahd@hcp.co.in
T +91 79 27550875
F + 91 79 27552924
www.hcp.co.in

SPASM Design Architects
310 Raheja Plaza, Shah Industrial Estate
New Andheri Link Road, Andheri West
Mumbai 400053
spasm@spasmindia.com
T +91 22 26735862
F +91 22 26733287
www.spasmindia.com

Ireland

O'Donnell + Tuomey
20A Camden Row
Dublin 8
info@odonnell-tuomey.ie
T +353 1 475 2500
F +353 1 475 1479
www.odonnell-tuomey.ie

Japan

Atelier Bow-Wow
8-79 Suga-cho Shinjuku-ku
Tokyo 160-0018
info@bow-wow.jp
T +81 3 3226 5336
F +81 3 3226 5366
www.bow-wow.jp

EASTERN Design Office
12-202 Sumizome-cho Fukakusa
Fushimi-ku
Kyoto 612-0052
eastern@sweet.ocn.ne.jp
T +81 75 642 9644
F +81 75 642 9644
www.eastern.e-arc.jp

Mount Fuji Architects Studio
Akasaka Heights 501, 9-5-26 Akasaka
Minato-ku, Tokyo 107-0052
fuji-s@rmail.plala.or.jp
T +81 3 3475 1800
F +81 3 3475 0180
www14.plala.or.jp/mfas

Ryue Nishizawa
1-5-27 Tatsumi Koto-ku
Tokyo 135-0053
office@ryuenishizawa.com
T +81 3 5534 0117
F +81 3 5534 1757
www.ryuenishizawa.com

TNA
3-16-3-3F Taishido Setagaya-ku
Tokyo 154-0004
mail@tna-arch.com
T +81 3 3795 1901
F +81 3 3795 1902
www.tna-arch.com

Torafu Architects
1-9-2-2F Koyama Shinagawa-ku
Tokyo 142-0062
torafu@torafu.com
T +81 3 5498 7156
F +81 3 5498 6156
www.torafu.com

Toyo Ito & Associates Architects
Fujiya Bldg.1-19-4 Shibuya
Shibuya-ku
Tokyo150-0002
T +81 3 3409 5822
F +81 3 3409 5969
www.toyo-ito.co.jp

Luxembourg

Paul Bretz Architectes
6 Rue Adolphe
L-1116
info@paulbretz.com
T +352 451861
F +352 451862
www.paulbretz.com

Mexico

BNKR Arquitectura
World Trade Center Mexico
Montecito 38 8th Floor Office 1
03810 Mexico City
info@bunkerarquitectura.com
T +52 55 9000 3988
www.bunkerarquitectura.com

The Netherlands

Claus en Kaan Architecten
Boompjes 55
3011 XB Rotterdam
info@ckr.nl
T +31 10 2060000
F +31 10 2060001
info@ckr.nl
www.clausenkaan.com

UN Studio
PO Box 75381
1070 AJ Amsterdam
The Netherlands
T +31 (0)20 570 20 40
F +31 (0)20 570 20 41
info@unstudio.com
www.unstudio.com

Portugal

Barbosa & Guimarães Arquitectos
Rua Brito Capelo n.1023
4450-077 Matosinhos
mail@barbosa-guimaraes.com
T +351 229 363 022
www.barbosa-guimaraes.com

Nuno Ribeiro Lopes
Rua Circular Norte n°1
Parque Industrial e
Tecnológico de Évora
7005-841 Évora
nrl.arquitectos@gmail.com
T: +351 266 744 473
F: +351 266 757 609
www.nurilo.com

Eduardo Souto de Moura
Rua Do Aleixo N° 53, 1°A
4150-043 Porto
geral@soutomoura.pt
T +351 22 6187547
F +351 22 6108092

Spain

Dosmasuno Arquitectos
Maudes 22, 2a
28003 Madrid
estudio@dosmasunoarquitectos.com
T +34 91 533 96 36
F +34 91 533 96 36
www.dosmasunoarquitectos.com

Rafael De La-Hoz Arquitectos
Paseo de la Castellana 82 2° A
28046 Madrid
estudio@rafaeldelahoz.com
T +34 91 745 35 00
F +34 91 561 78 03
www.rafaeldelahoz.com

Ensamble Studio
C/Mazarredo 10
28005 Madrid
administracion@ensamble.info
T +34 915 410 848
www.ensamble.info

Switzerland

Aebi & Vincent Architekten
Monbijoustrasse 61
CH-3007 Bern
info@aebi-vincent.ch
T +41 31 321 10 10
F +41 31 321 10 11
www.aebi-vincent.ch

Diener & Diener
Henric Petri-Strasse 22
CH-4010 Basel
buero.basel@dienerdiener.ch
T +41 61 270 41 41
F +41 61 270 41 00
www.dienerdiener.ch

:mlzd Architekten
Mattenstrasse 81
CH-2503 Biel/Bienne
office@mlzd.ch
T +41 32 323 04 72
F +41 32 325 51 22
www.mlzd.ch

UK

Bennetts Associates
1 Rawstorne Place
London EC1V 7NL
mail@bennettsassociates.com
T +44 20 7520 3300
F +44 20 7520 3333
www.bennettsassociates.com

Caruso St John
1 Coate Street
London E2 9AG
info@carusostjohn.com
T +44 20 7613 3161
F +44 20 7729 6188
www.carusostjohn.com

David Chipperfield Architects
11 York Road
London SE1 7NX
info@davidchipperfield.co.uk
T +44 20 7620 4800
F +44 20 7620 4801
www.davidchipperfield.com

Ellis Williams Architects
151 Rosebery Avenue
London EC1R 4AB
info@ewa.co.uk
T +44 20 7841 7200
F +44 20 7833 3850
www.ewa.co.uk

Foster + Partners
Riverside
22 Hester Road
London SW11 4AN
info@fosterandpartners.com
T +44 20 7738 0455
F +44 20 7738 1107
www.fosterandpartners.com

Scott Brownrigg
77 Endell Street
London WC2H 9DZ
enquiries@scottbrownrigg.com
T +44 20 7240 7766
F +44 20 7240 2454
www.scottbrownrigg.com

Zaha Hadid Architects
10 Bowling Green Lane
London EC1R 0BQ
T +44 20 7253 5147
F +44 20 7251 8322
www.zaha-hadid.com

USA

Bernard Tschumi Architects
227 West 17th Street Second Floor
New York, NY 10011
nyc@tschumi.com
T +1 212 807 6340
F +1 212 242 3693
www.tschumi.com

HMC Architects
633 W 5th Street Third Floor
Los Angeles, CA 90071-2005
losangeles@hmcarchitects.com
T +1 213 542 8300
F +1 213 542 8301
www.hmcarchitects.com

id-ea
612 S. Flower Street #1104
Los Angeles, CA 90017
elsyealam@id-ea.com
T +1 213 4001318
www.id-ea.com

Joseph N. Biondo
1750 Spillman Drive Suite 200
Bethlehem Pennsylvania 18015
jacmbiondo@verizon.net
T +1 610-865-2621
F +1 610-865-3236
www.josephnbiondo.com

PleskowRael Architecture
13432 Beach Avenue
Marina del Rey, CA 90292
rael@pleskowrael.com
T +1 310 577 9300
F +1 310 577 9302
www.pleskowrael.com

Shubin + Donaldson Architects
403 E Montecito Street #2A
Santa Barbara, CA 93101
info@sandarc.com
T +1 805 966 2802
F +1 805 966 3002
www.shubinanddonaldson.com

wHY Architecture
9520 Jefferson Blvd. Studio C
Culver City, CA 90232
work@why-architecture.com
T +1 310 839 5106
F +1 310 839 5107
www.why-architecture.com

Index and Further Information

Picture Credits

All architectural drawings are supplied courtesy of the respective architects and remain the © copyright of the architects, unless otherwise specified. These drawings are for private use and not for third party reproduction.

Photographic credits:
In all cases every effort has been made to credit the copyright holders, but should there be any omissions or errors, the publisher will insert the appropriate acknowledgment in any subsequent editions of the book.

10 © Esteban Suárez
14 © Christian Richters / VIEW
18 © Torben Eskerod
22 © Edmund Sumner / VIEW
26 © Iwan Baan
30 © Helene Binet
34 © Nigel Young
38 © Ryan Beck
42 © Alexander Gempeler
46 © Manuel Ribeiro **1, 3, 4**
46 © Sara Moncaixa Potes **2**
50 © Dennis Gilbert / VIEW
54 © Jakub Pierzchala **1**
54 © Jakub Pierzchala & © Marcin Przybylko **2**
54 © Jens Willebrand **3, 4, 5**
58 © Iwan Baan
62 © Paul Raftery / VIEW
66 Steve Hall / Hedrich Blessing **1, 2, 3**
66 Courtesy wHY Architecture **4**
70 © Christian Richters / VIEW
76 © Hans-Christian Schink **1, 3**
76 © Sven Fröhlich **2, 4**
80 © Daniela McAdden
84 © Miguel de Guzman **1, 2, 3**
84 © Alberto Nevado **4**
88 © Koichi Torimura
92 © Roland Halbe / ARTUR / VIEW
96 © Paul Riddle / VIEW
100 © Fernando Gomulya [www.tectography.net]
104 © Steve Wolfe
108 © Ryota Atarashi
112 © Lukas Roth
116 © Michael Nicholson
120 © Cristobal Palma Photography
124 © Ciro Coelho / www.cirocoelho.com
128 © Daici Ano / FWD Inc.
132 © Daici Ano / FWD Inc.
136 © Jean-Luc Laloux **1, 3, 4 & 5**
136 David Goss **2**
142 © Fernando Guerra / VIEW
146 © Brigida Gonzàlez
150 © Edmund Sumner / VIEW
154 © Christian Richters / VIEW **1, 2**
154 © Kim Zwarts **3, 4**
158 © Jussi Tiainen
162 © Paul Ott Photografiert
166 Images courtesy PleskowRael Architecture
170 © Roland Halbe / ARTUR / VIEW
174 © David Barbour
178 Images courtesy of Mr Muzu Suleimanji & Mr Rob Scheltens
184 Aebi & Vincent Architekten, Thomas Telley / Adrian Scheidegger
188 © Anders Sune Berg
192 © Christian Richters / VIEW
196 © Dinesh Mehta
200 Ishiguro Photographic Institute **1, 2, 3, 4**
200 Courtesy of Tama Art University / photo Eii Ina **5**
204 © Jean-Marie Monthiers
208 © Hufton & Crow / VIEW

Acknowledgments

Thanks above all to the architects who submitted material for this book. Special thanks to Hamish Muir, the designer of this book, and to Sophia Gibb for researching the pictures. Sincere thanks to Philip Cooper and Gaynor Sermon at Laurence King Publishing and to Justin Fletcher for editing the drawings, to Vic Brand for his technical expertise and to Vimbai Shire for her patient research. Thanks to Aoi for all the valuable advice.

The Architecture of EMPAC

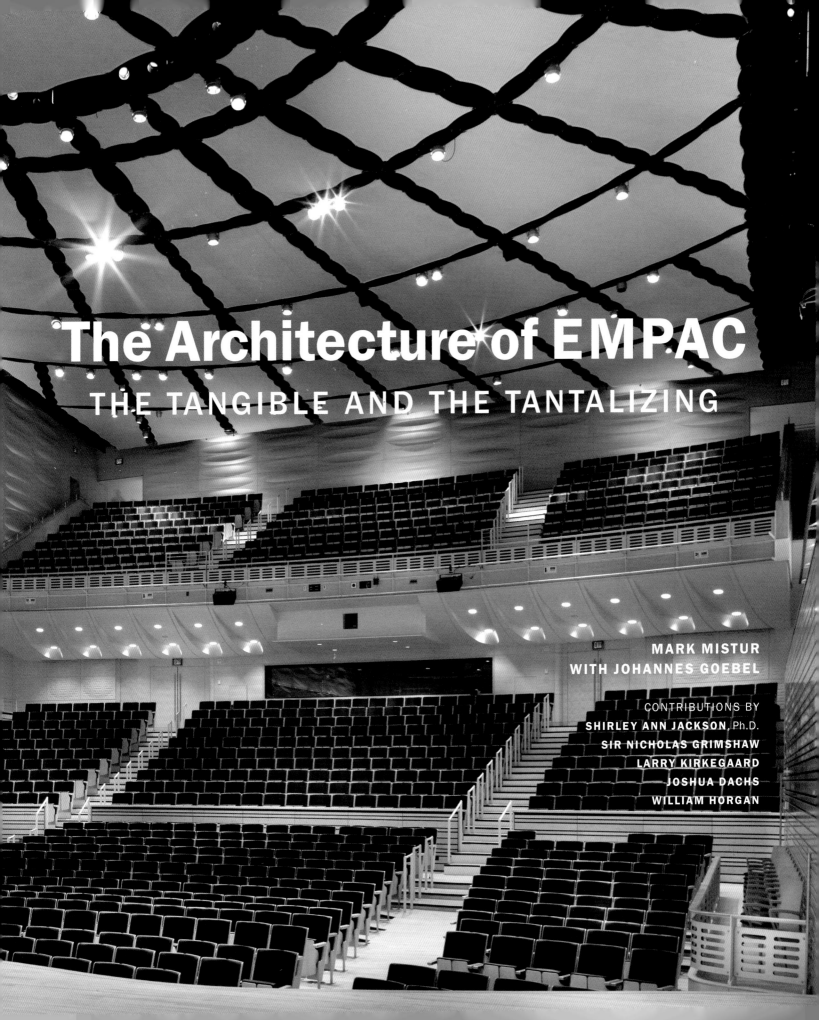

The Architecture of EMPAC
THE TANGIBLE AND THE TANTALIZING

MARK MISTUR
WITH JOHANNES GOEBEL

CONTRIBUTIONS BY
SHIRLEY ANN JACKSON, Ph.D.
SIR NICHOLAS GRIMSHAW
LARRY KIRKEGAARD
JOSHUA DACHS
WILLIAM HORGAN

CONTENTS

ACKNOWLEDGEMENTS

On a project of this size and scope, there are many individuals — literally thousands — to thank for their contributions. I am grateful for each person's good work. They all brought their talents, energy and imaginations to this historic endeavor, and I am proud to be associated with them.

EMPAC started at our leadership retreat early in my tenure, with all the deans and all the vice presidents of Rensselaer present. It was there that EMPAC was conceived and the "leap" was made. I thank them for their support and courage in helping us to realize the vision of EMPAC over the years since then.

A project this ambitious can be daunting. We would not have been able to move forward without the support and encouragement of our Board of Trustees. Under the leadership of Samuel F. Heffner Jr., Class of '56, the members' commitment continued over years and saw us through many challenges and struggles. It is impossible to believe that we would have achieved so much without their dedication.

I would like to acknowledge the leadership of the individuals and major enterprises involved in the design and creation of EMPAC:

First, Sir Nicholas Grimshaw, chairman of Grimshaw Architects. The firm was selected after an international design competition. The distinction of the Grimshaw design was in seeing the building as an ensemble of performance and research spaces, defined by technology, which seemed exactly appropriate to house the range of performances and to stimulate the new knowledge that Rensselaer will bring to the intersection of the arts with science and technology.

EMPAC's director, Johannes Goebel, brought his experiences and a deep understanding of working in the interfaces between disciplines. In particular, he advocated for a perspective that kept this enormous project firmly anchored in human scale.

On a project like this, there are many key leaders and consultants involved as well, among them:

> Cynthia McIntyre, former Chief of Staff and Assistant Secretary of the Institute, Rensselaer Polytechnic Institute, now Senior Vice President, Council on Competitiveness
> Alan Balfour, Professor and Dean of the School of Architecture, Rensselaer Polytechnic Institute, now Professor and Dean of the College of Architecture, Georgia Institute of Technology
> Turner Construction Company, construction manager
> Davis Brody Bond, LLP, the architect of record
> Buro Happold, consulting engineers
> Fisher Dachs Associates, theater design, project manager
> Kirkegaard Associates, acoustic design
> Architectural Woodwork Industries, manufacturer of wood products
> Saratoga Associates, landscape design
> Adirondack Studios, design-build on variable acoustics and fabric ceiling

North curtain wall looking westward into the sunset.

Many in the Rensselaer community contributed to EMPAC along the way, from the fine work of the architectural acoustics group in the School of Architecture, in the acoustical modeling of the canopy in the Concert Hall, to Professors Thomas Zimmie and Ricardo Dobry of the Department of Civil Engineering, who consulted with regard to water intrusion and earthquake mitigation, respectively, to all the faculty that used examples of the design and construction challenges of the site as a "living laboratory" for Rensselaer students.

EMPAC began as an idea that became a vision, and the vision is now a reality. We can make all the plans in the world, but to make them real requires that others believe in our vision. We are most grateful for the financial support of those who have helped us to deliver the dream—our benefactors.

I extend my deepest thanks to those whose generosity is the heart of this dream:

> The late David Goodman, Class of 1939, who believed in the promise before
>   we even drew the blueprints;
> Amy and David Jaffe, Class of 1964, true patrons of the arts;
> Susan and Gary DiCamillo, Class of 1973; and
> Judith and Thomas Iovino, Class of 1973, donors and volunteers who have given
>   so much time and effort to support our *Renaissance at Rensselaer* campaign.

I would also like to acknowledge two other major benefactors of the performing arts at Rensselaer: Gail and Jeffrey Kodosky, Class of 1970, who have been generous supporters of the classical music program at Rensselaer for many years.

Of course, our greatest benefactor is Curtis R. Priem, Class of 1982, along with his wife, Veronica. Curtis Priem's magnificent support will be acknowledged by our forever associating his name with this vision that has become real.

The EMPAC vision will synthesize the arts, science and technology in a way that is clearly Rensselaer—so that each builds upon and draws from the others to create what we *know* will be important for the world.

—Shirley Ann Jackson, Ph.D.

PREFACE: *COMMON GROUND*
SHIRLEY ANN JACKSON, Ph.D.

The Experimental Media and Performing Arts Center (EMPAC) offers space for researchers, performers, artists and engineers to push the limits of their disciplines—together.

It is typically unusual—but becoming less so—to bring together such a diverse group under one roof. We do this in recognition of new possibilities and a very old notion: As humans, we are neither left- nor right-brained. We are whole.

We need approaches that incorporate new tools and new ways of thinking that reach across the spectrum of science, technology, and the arts, and at their nexus. We need people who can think and act and work across the boundaries.

What science and technology bring to the issues our society faces is a creativity undergirded by an exacting, logical, quantitative perspective. These disciplines, in looking into hidden corners, are seeking clear answers derived by reliable and repeatable processes, energized by sometimes sudden insight.

What the arts bring is less tangible, because artistic inspiration defies quantification. The pathways of the human mind remain in great measure uncharted. Yet, there is research being done in neuroscience that attempts to explain insight—that moment when an artist or a scientist or an engineer says, "Aha! I get it!"[1]

Such moments are not merely a function of the right side of the brain, or the left side. Rather, they involve an intricate dance across the cerebral cortex. Although an insight seems to come from "nowhere," the brain carefully prepares itself for such a breakthrough.

First, the parts of the brain involved with executive control activate, and the brain starts "computing"—looking for answers in all the relevant places. When it "finds" the answer, gamma rhythm, the brain's highest electrical frequency, spikes. It is thought that this results from neurons binding with one another across the cortex, drawing themselves together into a new network, which is then able to enter the conscious mind. In brief, insight requires the brain to make a set of distant and unprecedented connections. This is a suitable metaphor for what we are trying to achieve with EMPAC, which is inspired by the desire to synthesize ideas across disciplines.

Our students understand this; they know they use their *whole* brains. Many of them come in the door desiring to join their music, their poetry and their visual arts with science and technology. EMPAC responds to these needs of Rensselaer students, who want to have creative outlets, places where they can perform, experience and produce art, and to discover, design and uncover.

EMPAC was built to serve them, but it is also part of a grander mission at Rensselaer: the development of leaders.

People with wider interests confidently bring together other talented people. They have vision and can see connections across a broad cultural and intellectual milieu. As leaders, they develop the ability to listen to those with different views, to evaluate with their heads and hearts, to express their ideas persuasively, and to respond with both good sense and empathy.

We critically need such people, but the development of intellectually curious, broadly educated and respectful leaders shifts in and out of fashion. When there is an emphasis on return on investment and measurable results, a culture leans more toward specialization. So we at Rensselaer have set out to change culture *through* culture. The Experimental Media and Performing Arts Center — meaning both the program we established and the building that houses it — provides a space, a justification and an agenda for a holistic perspective, bringing together science, technology and the arts. Certainly, we intend to change the culture of Rensselaer itself. But we also hope that EMPAC will change public discourse and ultimately transform views on how multiple communities, indeed the world, will approach the most challenging problems and the most promising opportunities of our times.

EMPAC is *a point of origin* for creativity in culture and the arts, and for creativity in research. The creativity that is embedded in the arts gives us our own sense of who we are and how we relate to other people in our pure appreciation of beauty. If we really intend to live out our mantra of "Why not change the world?" in the graduates we produce, we must stimulate them to explore their own creative roots, while learning from others' cultural underpinnings. This will help them to tease out and nurture their own creativity.

For most of our students, creativity will be expressed in scientific and technological ways. EMPAC is *a point of intersection* for technology and the arts, and for artists and scientists. Even if one has a very defined problem — an engineering or architectural design problem — there are flights of fancy, of thought, that must come into play, because, by definition, what one is trying to resolve does not have an answer. So one has to be able to take creative leaps, while building and utilizing analytical tools. The arts add an extra dimension.

Finally, EMPAC is *a gathering point*, because it is a platform that brings all of this together.

The story of EMPAC that you will read in these pages will tell you about a ship in a bottle and the inspiration of moonscapes. The pictures will show you striking views, unexpected turns, and many beauties of engineering that are now hidden within the infrastructure. The text will detail unprecedented capabilities and resources made available for research, for art, and for both — *together*.

But there is a part of the story that cannot yet be told. By intent, EMPAC is geared toward doing the unplanned, the unexpected and the previously impossible.

So this building — EMPAC — combines a set of needs and strengths in one place. It creates a platform for the future — as presentation space, electronic arts space, research space and creative space. Both the building and the program drive toward the leading edge of technology and art, bringing together people from all over our community, and from all over the world, to ask questions and to become a wellspring of creativity, discovery and innovation for the 21st century.

What makes EMPAC a one-of-a-kind facility?

EMPAC is a unique blend of the basic platform itself — its multiple venues.

EMPAC is at once, a world-class cultural platform and a major research resource.

EMPAC allows for different forms of communication, of movement and of experience.

EMPAC supports creation, investigation, innovation, production and performance.

EMPAC sits at Rensselaer, which enables it to be conjoined both to a set of activities that involves the arts and to a challenging program of scientific discovery and technological innovation.

EMPAC provides resources for

- theatrical performances
- rehearsal space for dance, complete with changing rooms
- the varied needs of artists-in-residence and researchers, along with the students they will involve in their projects
- high-end research spaces for visualizing animation, simulation, acoustics, haptics, lighting studies, design, and multi-modal communication and calculation

But a list like this misses the heart of EMPAC. The building gets attention, not just because it cannot be ignored, but because it entices, it invites and it lures. Stand in the lobby. People ask questions. They express opinions. They share ideas. Of course, these conversations go beyond the lobby, reaching out into the world, provoking thought and inspiring innovation. Even people who have never been to Troy, N.Y., are intrigued, delighted and occasionally scandalized.

The presence of EMPAC alone provides encouragement and inspiration. This is what makes it a natural catalyst for change. While EMPAC is a powerful instrument for science and technology, for the visualization of scientific problems, it is also an artistic venue, designed for the senses. It is a bridge between the quantifiable—the photons, the sound waves and the data bytes that are the "stuff" of science and technology—and the unquantifiable—the beauty, the paradox and the mystery—that brings a sense of the divine that the arts inspire in us.

For those who are innovative, EMPAC stands as a reminder of the importance of pushing the limits. Technically, the venues are designed to stake out new territory in how we can reach and use the senses. It allows the use of virtual worlds, while one works at human scale. At EMPAC, one can be surrounded by sound and be within the display in a way that mimics or expands on nature. One can use one's natural sense of oneself—in physical space—to fit within the art or the experiment. And one can share one's experience, not by having someone look over his or her shoulder, but by sitting or walking or dancing through the installation with others.

The new tools for research and expression touch the senses and invite us in. EMPAC, though a world-class performing arts center, is not solely a presentation space, and it is not limited to traditional electronic media. It includes photonics and haptics. It attracts artists, scientists and engineers on their own terms. They want to explore its capabilities, so they end up riding elevators together, walking down the same hallways and, perhaps, finding themselves in the same rooms, rubbing shoulders.

The program of EMPAC and proximity of its spaces invite curiosity, questions and interest. What begins as what a developmental psychologist might term "parallel play" leads to understanding, mutuality of interest and collaboration. We already have seen that there are instances when a scientist or engineer comes to understand that the artist may be the very person who can help illustrate or explore a technical concept. Conversely, artists, attracted by the light, noise, movement or peculiar instruments of the scientist or engineer, can recognize new forms of expression.

Such interactions motivate talented, creative people of all types to build bridges. They find ways to translate their ideas, to share interests and to develop a common language that allows deeper, more complex collaborations. Along the way, these very different communities begin to challenge and inspire each other, and new ideas explode.

We talk a lot about teamwork for the 21st century—people working together in multidisciplinary groups. Performance productions inherently involve teams and various disciplines: planning and management skills, working to deadlines, understanding audience responses or preferences—in effect, customer relationship management. As well, research is inherently collaborative. So EMPAC becomes a learning space for the very things that we want to reinforce in our students.

Sometimes scientists and engineers are left out of key conversations of our society because people do not expect them to think or act in nuanced ways. Artists sometimes are left out because they are not expected to think in purely quantitative or business-like ways. Scientists and artists, working together, can contribute more effectively to public discourse and appropriately influence important decisions. Science and technology are the concern of all our citizens, because they affect us all. Our society therefore needs scientists and engineers who are able to speak out, guide the public and establish policy—in short, serve as leaders. If Rensselaer's graduates are to live up to this role, they must be not only technically brilliant, but also articulate, broad-minded and humane.

I am confident that EMPAC will help our students grow into such leaders—while here and beyond—as they do important work. The challenges and possibilities they encounter here will help inspire them throughout their lives.

Rensselaer, from its inception, has been a transformational university. Stephen van Rensselaer, our founding benefactor, and Amos Eaton, the first Head of School, set out in 1824 to create an institution like none that had ever been attempted before.

"Serving the common purposes of life," as Rensselaer's founders put it, now relates to how the arts can help to advance science. Scientific advances in the understanding of human thought and perception, as well as human biology and physical principles can all be interpreted through the creative arts, and can be illustrated in compelling ways.

While interdisciplinarity has long been a hallmark of research at Rensselaer, the Digital Age has enhanced our capacity for reaching across disciplinary boundaries, as well as geographic and cultural boundaries, and those that separate institutions and sectors. The multiple venues for research at EMPAC—joined under one roof, linked to one of the world's most powerful supercomputers and deliberately placed on the campus of the oldest private technological university in the country—will provide rich opportunities for crossing even more boundaries.

Before it even opened, EMPAC proclaimed this to the world. In January 2008, we invited Jennifer Tipton, the acclaimed stage-lighting designer, to create an installation for the exterior of EMPAC. We asked her to create a way to announce this new enterprise to the world. In her years as a lighting designer, she had done work for dance, theater and opera, but she had never done anything like EMPAC before, and we had no instructions for her. She let her imagination play, creating a light sculpture of mysteriously shifting forms and colors that slowly changed in unexpected ways. For several weeks, the display became the talk of the town.

We at Rensselaer seek individuals who, like Ms. Tipton, have the ability to transcend traditional boundaries, who are willing to take risks in the name of creativity and inquiry, who will persist in spite of obstacles, and who can synthesize disparate ideas and approaches. The world of today—and tomorrow—will demand no less of creative thinkers.

EMPAC is the ultimate platform for people to be engaged, and to be interactive, in combined virtual and physical environments, and, in this way, to use its features to probe the natural world and to create new things. Just as Rensselaer led the way in making the technological advances that shaped the 19th and 20th centuries, it is reshaping itself to address the challenges of our time, in an age where the complexity of the challenge demands complexity of approach. We have built new platforms that join many perspectives—across a broad intellectual front—to create and to discover the new and the important. What we have created in EMPAC exists nowhere else in the world, and I am confident that the work that will arise from it will certainly change the world.

Every time we change the world, we change ourselves. All of us who dreamed of, struggled with, pushed for and came together to realize EMPAC know this. This book provides a glimpse of those experiences. The rest will be written over the years to come, in how EMPAC changes individuals, our communities and our culture. The full meaning of EMPAC is still emerging.

1. John Lehrer, Annals of Science, "The Eureka Hunt," *The New Yorker*, July 28, 2008.

INTRODUCTION

Design is more than skin deep. To many, especially in North America, this was a radical statement in 2001. The Curtis R. Priem Experimental Media and Performing Arts Center (EMPAC) challenged, and still challenges, the status quo. It became an ambitious architectural project among a growing number in North America, emerging from a decades-long conservative approach to building design. It is a testament to an architect and team of engineers and consultants who—given the challenge of a daring client—committed themselves to both aesthetic and technical excellence.

But before there was a building, there was an agenda: to transform a historic and accomplished polytechnic institution into a more intellectually diverse, tier-one research university. Leadership means venturing into new areas where there is the promise of significant contributions. In the case of EMPAC, this meant serious consideration and discussion of the frontier where the arts and media meet science and engineering. Bringing these together—not just in a building, but in conversations, activities, opportunities and debates—meant developing policies, providing guidance, exploring funding, attracting talent and facilitating collaboration. This was also understood early on and integrated into the planning for this endeavor.

EMPAC and the story of its journey are testaments to a Board confident in its President and her vision. They approved Dr. Shirley Ann Jackson's radical plan to transform the University by creating a nexus between art, engineering and science, and they stood behind her through many threats, challenges and might-have-been compromises. This story is about a founding Director, Johannes Goebel, who gave to the vision the unique and specific character of research venues that engage both the physical and the digital at the scale of human embodiment and perception. He provided Dr. Jackson's vision with the flesh, blood and organs of programmed venues and the supporting nerves and bones of infrastructure.

This story is also about the many critical participants on the design team, from cost consultants to theater consultants to acousticians, constructors, engineers, architects and the owner's representatives, who collaborated on what is, perhaps, the most complex form of building, a performing arts center—one that is also a research center.

However, the story is just unfolding. Generations of artists, scientists, engineers and innovators of all stripes will write the succeeding chapters with their performances, inventions, discoveries and initiatives that reach far beyond the walls of a building in Troy, NY. And lest we forget, none of the work has substance without the audiences, students, faculty, colleagues and community members who will be transformed by experiences within the Experimental Media and Performing Arts Center. This book is not just a record of a daring achievement. It is an invitation to participate, to seize the opportunity to excite the senses, to understand the world, to expand our knowledge of nature and to explore the limits of technology and humanity.

View from campus looking west over Troy.

Part I: The Agenda

The Agenda

"When you step into an intersection of fields, disciplines or cultures, you can combine existing concepts into a large number of extraordinary new ideas."
— Frans Johansson, *The Medici Effect*

By the 1990s, the idea of a "Renaissance man" seemed quaint. Educated people knew of and largely accepted C.P. Snow's powerful and compelling 1959 lecture, "The Two Cultures," which posited separate worlds of science and humanities and led to much hand-wringing about the social consequences.

In 2000, Rensselaer's new president, Dr. Shirley Ann Jackson, an accomplished physicist with a love of art and classical piano music, knew that the wall between the cultures had never been higher. Besides observing a general pattern of misunderstanding between the two cultures, she had experienced politicians and policymakers with an aversion to technology, and engineers who struggled to communicate the insights and joys of their profession to lay people. Even the mechanisms for funding between the two cultures differed (and still do, creating a continuing challenge for EMPAC).

And yet, Dr. Jackson knew that the space between disciplines, the space that was so fecund for Leonardo da Vinci and Thomas Jefferson and Alexander Borodin, was where we would find the answers for the most pressing problems of the 21st century. Evidence for success at the borders of science was plentiful. The names of relatively new hybrid disciplines: biochemistry, chemical engineering, social biology, etc., spoke to the possibilities. But reaching across the two cultures, to discover what hybrids might be viable, was a courageous act. On the other hand, the need for such a space in between was as obvious as the crisis in health care, new opportunities made possible by sophisticated simulation and the challenges of educating the next generation of innovators.

The realization of a President's bold vision, a Board's steadfast support, a Director's programmatic definition and a design team's commitment to performance-based design, EMPAC is first an agenda. It is tasked with engaging the arts and sciences in a single enterprise, dedicated to not merely extending the use of electronic arts, media and performance, but to the expansion of science, our understanding of the world and the exploration of perception. It was conceived to incubate cross-disciplinary approaches to research. It is dedicated to provoking discovery that is best catalyzed by sometimes awkward combinations between the research cultures of the artist, scientist and engineer. It is programmed to encourage unfamiliar exposures through unanticipated collisions between disciplines, with the expectation that seemingly "unnatural" juxtapositions of people, experiences and ideas will lead to productive engagements of the world we seek to know; and that these will mature into collaborations that yield valuable integrations between artists and scientists.

The exact outcomes of this vision cannot be predicted. The confident, informed assumption of those who have set this enterprise in motion is that it is the right thing to do and that it will yield discoveries that will prove to be significant. Keeping with Rensselaer's record of pioneering educational leadership, EMPAC demonstrates its daring to invest in a new research paradigm based on the principle that many of the important

View of skylit space between the south block and hull — looking west.

discoveries and insights of the 21st century will be borne out of trans-disciplinary settings —research environments that cross traditional boundaries and are not compartmentalized into disciplines, subdisciplines and/or isolated problem sets.

But this is not all. EMPAC is staged as a series of platforms for the tuning and expansion of human perception, the broadening of interdisciplinary awareness, the development of critical aptitudes within the university community, and revealing possibility in areas of research that will lead to significant discovery.

EMPAC goes beyond its research charge, commitment to experimentation and dedication to the production of new art, ideas and technologies. It is a performing arts center, prepared to bring together the larger campus and regional communities to experience performances that will challenge their perspectives. EMPAC will develop and present fresh new work that will expand awareness of and exposure to progressive art, culture and work, especially as they relate to the desegregation of virtual and physical worlds, to produce "augmented realities"[1] and the expansion of perception and possibility.

EMPAC demonstrates Rensselaer's commitment to broadening culture on campus, and in the region. At the same time it reveals a bias toward thinking not merely about canonized norms concerning cultural venues or acculturating a community, but about the importance of awakening, inculcating and exercising a broader spectrum of thought and possibility. EMPAC is intended to exercise and expand the boundaries of perception. It is concerned with creating an ever more grounded and ever more progressive academic culture that is ready to move beyond traditional boundaries and seeks to more fully engage, expand and stretch knowledge and understanding together with all the human senses and sensibilities.

EMPAC is an investment in research dealing with matters of space, perception and media, exploring how the physical world is mediated with on-demand tetherless communication and global-positioning capacities, how perceived reality is augmented with real-time datasets and novel visualization techniques, and how both the digital and virtual increasingly contribute to discovery and everyday life. In realizing this platform, Rensselaer has demonstrated its dedication to the belief that design matters. EMPAC is an agenda; it has a program and is supported, if not enlivened, by an architecture of environments that leverage inter-scalar possibilities (e.g., between the microscopic or the galactic and human scale in 3-D visualizations), create unanticipated intersections (e.g., between artists and scientific researchers), and are shaped by acoustic and other performance criteria. In all of its somewhat awkward, pregnant presence, EMPAC promises the birth of discoveries and the maturation of a culture: new ideas, novel approaches, enriched lives and expanded depth of perception among her scientists, engineers and artists.

1. Technology that combines real-world (physical) experience and computer-generated (virtual) images and data in real time and space.

Architecture Matters

In his speech regarding the rebuilding of Parliament, Prime Minister Winston Churchill warned, "If you change the shape of Parliament, you change the shape of England."[1] His argument for "the oblong," with its narrow aisle and shortage of seats as a progenitor of face-to-face debate and urgency, revealed a constructivist thought: architecture matters. He made the case for choosing an architectural approach based on its performance and in anticipation of its bias and consequence to the very fabric of a nation. In fact, he contrasted the shape of Parliament with the U.S. Congress' semicircular form, with but one fulcrum and speaker at a time, a hall where, in contrast to the "conversation" of parliament, utmost binary hierarchical order (the speaker and everyone else) is maintained.

Churchill was arguing that design has consequences, and that decisions should be made deliberately in the interest of larger visions and objectives. This is in line with what a social scientist would recognize as Actor Network Theory. ANT establishes that both the animate and the inanimate are actors in the shaping of reality, perception, cultures and societies. Neither the animate (person, program, process) nor the inanimate (product, building, space) is neutral—both having cause and effect in the lives and perceptions of individuals, and in the development of communities, institutions and societies.

The extent to which an owner or architect believes that cause can be designed into a building to render particular effects on the activities and imagination within (a version of ANT) influences the program and approach to an architectural project.

In the case of EMPAC, the proposition that "architecture matters" was clearly affirmed when Rensselaer's president, Dr. Shirley Ann Jackson, created the vision for the program and, on the advice of Architecture Dean Alan Balfour, determined to engage an invited international competition. The task was to identify and select the architect who best recognized the agenda and was ready to work together with the President and Rensselaer in creating something wholly new and supremely enabling. From the start, it was anticipated that EMPAC's formal, spatial and material construct would matter to its performance and the way it would be occupied, employed and experienced—according to those patterns of use and experience that the building uniquely creates, affects and/or limits. Use possibilities and patterns set by the architecture would affect the programmatic (research), experiential and social (interdisciplinary) possibilities, as well as the perceptions of the people and communities within. It was to be designed to enhance the propensity for certain positive consequences; for specific and yet unknown types of performances; for the imagination of artists, scientists and thinkers; and for the development of interdisciplinary interactions and communities that do not yet exist.

EMPAC's program and design add dimension to Rensselaer's campus, creating a means to enhance the University and fulfill its promises to catalyze the world of ideas and possibilities through its own programs. EMPAC is a change agent, imagined and deployed not merely to accommodate the practical needs of the Institute, or passively allow for "the experimental" to occur, but to affect the University and its constituents, and to have consequence in the larger world of its professors, researchers, students, artists, and scientists in residence.

Consider the vision of President Jackson, who set an ambition so seemingly radical as that embraced by EMPAC for a school known primarily for engineering and science. Think about the implications of EMPAC's demand for excellence and intention to provide leadership in higher education, advanced research and relevance to a future dependent upon interdisciplinary, integrated work and understanding, where vision and imagination are crossbred with expertise and knowledge. If these can be realized, then the building and its architecture, not merely the programs it houses, must also matter.

It is on this foundation that EMPAC was conceived, that its architects were selected, and that its forms and spaces were designed — with the intention that the architecture must not limit but encourage collaboration, multidisciplinary experimentation and discovery. To that purpose, its design should foster intersections within and between communities and disciplines that should be at the heart of not just Rensselaer, but any school aspiring to the ideal of a university.

1. "A Sense of Crowd and Urgency," *Winston S. Churchill: His Complete Speeches 1897–1963*, Vol. VII, 1943–1949, edited by Robert Rhodes James. Chelsea House Publishers in association with R.R. Bowker Co., New York and London.

The Emergence of a New American Context

Lead, follow or get out of the way. The burgeoning valuation of architecture and design in society and culture, and among premier institutions is driven by an expanding awareness of the value of design, the environmental mandate and those new tools that enable the construction and performance of ever more complex buildings.

With the selection of Grimshaw, Rensselaer has chosen to lead. EMPAC contributes to raising the bar for design integration and imagination. In addition to those North American building sectors that have traditionally valued architectural design—museums, cultural institutions, boutique hotels—the (re)emergence of design as having currency in corporate and mainstream building sectors is growing increasingly evident. Celebrity architects, design magazines, popular media, upscale department stores, celebrated product design and "Mac culture" are each evidence of design playing a greater role in more mainstream cultural sectors and consciousness.

Corporations (Disney, Apple, Genzyme, etc.), institutions (MIT, Cornell, Harvard, etc.), government agencies (NY MTA, San Francisco Federal Building, etc.), and even private housing developers are reaching out to celebrity design architects (e.g., Morphosis, Nouvel, Herzog & de Meuron, Gehry) for a variety of reasons—some better than others.

Design matters and is increasingly acknowledged in mainstream corporate and institutional sectors, just as it is in culture and everyday life. The concept has become so pervasive that Target's success is substantially tied to image and design equated with quality through a careful branding based on designer product lines (Philippe Starck, Michael Graves). Even Kmart's Martha Stewart and Jaclyn Smith lines speak to design relevance. Its currency is increasingly tied to value, moving away from the bottom line, lowest-cost, corporate pragmatism of previous decades.

Architecture is not immune to the trends of its times. Representing one of the largest, most visible and longest-lasting investments an institution or corporation makes, the design factor has become an increasingly higher priority, whether for representational branding value or in search for something more significant. Evidence of this shift is the increasing influence of European design and the growing number of international design architects and building engineering firms winning commissions and establishing practices in the U.S. Rensselaer's invited competition identified U.K. firm Nicholas Grimshaw and Partners, which at that time had designed only one project in North America from its London base. Not only did Rensselaer step beyond North American shores to identify the architect best matched to the ambitious task, it insisted that Grimshaw establish a New York office. By 2009, Grimshaw's New York office had more than 70 employees, doing major projects in Miami, Iowa, New York and Mexico City.

Though the basis for the selection of an architect is often superficial—initiated for purposes related more to ego than to substance, driven by peer or market expectations, or originating from an attempt to represent oneself or organization with a certain standard of excellence in order to attract a particular audience—design value is a part of the new context. From the Nike phenomenon to Apple's resurgence to the auto industry's battling for position based on design and performance (no longer options and amenities), the expansion of a more sophisticated design culture is seen at every scale, from products to fashion to buildings. A more resilient design approach is emerging, one that is "post-aesthetic,"[1] informed by the integration of performance and form, and interested in the environment, the program brief and the human experience. Beyond the skin and subjective aesthetics of "styling," ways of measuring the previously immeasurable — workplace performance, well-being and environmental consequences, for example — are increasingly recognized and factored in. Lower employee absenteeism, greater worker productivity, increased employee satisfaction, improved perception, more productive idea generation (IDEO), enhanced teamwork, improved environmental performance, and so forth have real value that is being recognized in the design and making of the built world.

At Rensselaer, EMPAC is a new kind of building, transparent, welcoming and turned inside out to greet all. It invites us to see and be seen — to linger and to appreciate, or even be confronted by matters unfamiliar. Little surprise then that this astonishing structure, EMPAC, has become a primary venue not just for the arts or research, but also as a gateway to the University, to project the new Rensselaer to prospective students and faculty. It provides a stage for its highest-profile public events: prospective student and faculty visits, convocations, colloquia and lectures. EMPAC is seen as the locus for convening town meetings and as a portal to the larger intellectual community through events held within and broadcast beyond the Rensselaer campus.

THE ENVIRONMENT MATTERS

The environment and sustainability matter, and this, too, has informed the progressive agenda and design of EMPAC. The easy large corporate targets of the manufacturing and auto industries are not the only environmental culprits in the degradation of nature. In the U.S., buildings contribute more significantly than does transportation to energy consumption, greenhouse gas production and landfills. With remarkable speed, the environmental agenda has become mainstream, adopted across virtually every sector of the economy.

It has drawn many responses by builders, from token greenwashing at one extreme to substantive environmental approaches that override aesthetics, human comfort or program at the other. At EMPAC, environmental performance is just one important and integrated design driver among many, whether expressed in the pressing of the structure into the ground, the design of the building-integrated heated curtain wall system, the integration of displacement ventilation or the selection of sustainable wood products for the hull. These, together with many other initiatives, contribute to the building's high environmental performance and give both impetus and permission for a new spirit of design. In best practice, the complex task of reducing consumption, improving a building's energy profile and providing better environmental performance is becoming a part of a new ethic that demands thoughtful innovation and relies on the engagement of new computational tools.

NEW TOOLS

The growing availability of powerful, relatively user-friendly computational tools and technologies has culminated in the ideal scenario for a new design context. Together with a heightened valuation of design and the environmental mandate, new tools make possible the emergence of an architecture invested in more integrated and progressive agendas, expressed in complex geometries and building systems. As never before, digital tools enable the integrated simulation, analysis and factoring of dynamic, complex performance criteria (e.g., climate, solar, wind, fluid dynamics, acoustic performance) with material properties and complex geometry. Geometric control of the hull and Concert Hall alone, for the many design consultants who had to coordinate their work with one another and the trades that had to construct them, would not have been feasible just a decade or two earlier. Structural modeling tools and indeterminate analysis techniques made it possible to design EMPAC's several independent structures within a single enclosure, considering stringent seismic considerations. Computational fluid dynamic (CFD) analysis of air movement and space conditioning around the hull resulted in the innovative design of a silent, high-performance, comfort-enhancing and energy-efficient heated curtain wall.

Furthermore, information technology provided tools that afforded a larger, geographically diverse team with an integrated, virtual collaboration space to facilitate a more interactive design conversation and construction process. The three-dimensional digital model was key, as was the capacity to exchange drawings across platforms within shared databases to expedite shop drawing approvals and coordinate between owners, designers and constructors.

Beyond the former approach to building design, which relied heavily on the layering of discrete systems by independent consultants, the whole building model enables integrated design according to multiple criteria. It brings various design and construction intelligences together. The mediated conversation afforded by new tools is in itself a realization of EMPAC's agenda. It enables more significant engagement by the many participants — the owner and the acoustician; the theater consultant; and the mechanical, environmental, structural and acoustic consultants — with the architects. Information technology provides the construction manager and the various constructors with efficient means to control and create forms that would have previously been 1) virtually impossible to describe and dimension, and 2) extraordinarily complex to build. EMPAC's director, Johannes Goebel, knew that it would require a diverse team of designers and experts from many disciplines and later reflected, "If the program accomplishes what the design process did in integrating multiple intelligences in a manner that affected the way each discipline worked, … it will be measured a success."

The shape of EMPAC's Concert Hall hull, its multi-layered cladding, steel frame, rear and side concrete sheer walls, the circulation space between, as well as its thermal and acoustic performance, and the mere fitting of the mechanicals without conflict would not have been possible without an integrated 3-D model. Those tools and techniques enabled an escape from the Cartesian, substituting virtual geometry for dimensional control.

This emerging performance-based design context is not merely about sculptural aesthetics, isolated from and exercised independently of other criteria. In its best practice, design is informed by factors that it must engage, and it leverages them to best use in a complex optimization schema that requires multiple intelligences. Without neglecting the aesthetic, performance design integrates consideration of the functions and the operations of a building: its social performance, functional performance, environmental performance, energy performance, acoustic performance and visual performance are integral to form-finding (form emerges from analysis) and design resolution at every scale.

1. Post-aesthetic is neither anti-aesthetic nor even dismissive or unconcerned with aesthetics. However, it is not concerned with appearance or composition as the a priori approach to design, nor does it address it as the beginning point, the process driver, or the ultimate measure. Aesthetics are one factor among many.

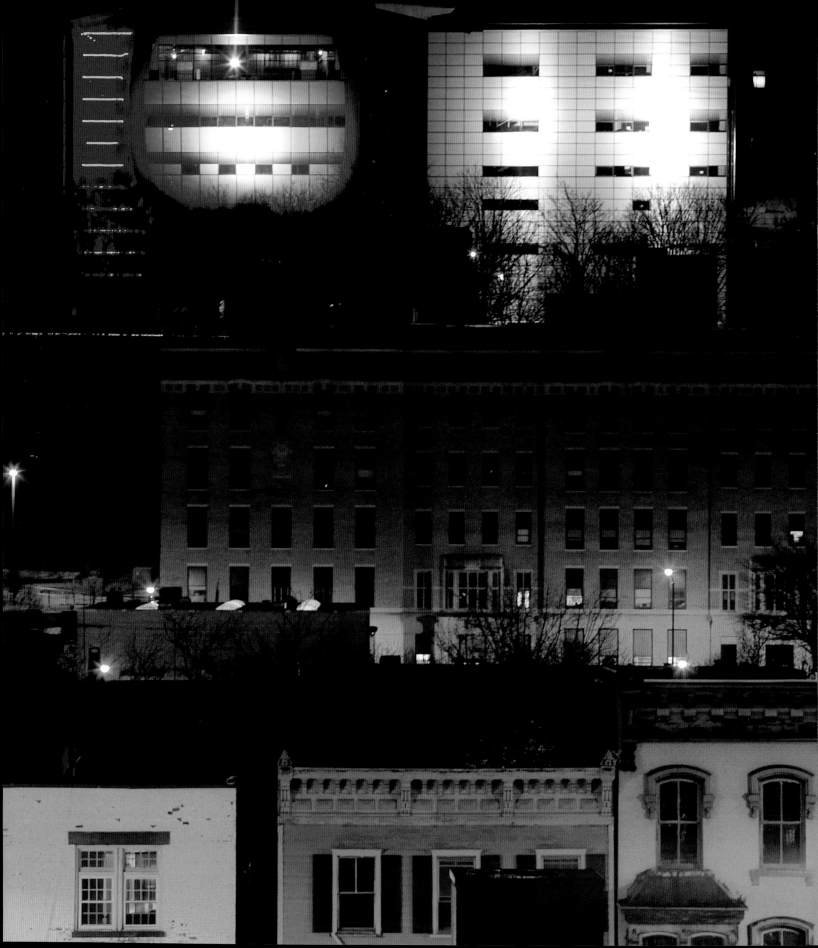

A Tradition of Excellence

S.V. Rensselaer III / B.F. Greene / S.A. Jackson

"Performing arts" is typically used to describe those arts expressed by live acts of the artist(s) received by a passive audience. Sometimes performances are to please cultured tastes and sensibilities. At other times they are intended to provoke or challenge. There can be many objectives to the art of "the play," "the concert" or "the performance," each privileged with the possibility of being a bit outside reality — or perhaps closer to it.

In the art of performance, rarely does history reveal efforts designed to entangle "the brain's left side,"[1] at least explicitly. Since this is the side that Rensselaer Polytechnic Institute is generally assigned in the imaginations of most Americans, a closer examination of the history of engineering and engineering education is in order. The history of Rensselaer's presidents reveals an unexpected tale: from the very beginning their views of engineering have reached past abstract calculation to include performance and right-brain values.

Founded in 1824 by American statesman, general and landowner Steven Van Rensselaer III and educator Amos Eaton "for the purpose of instructing persons, who may choose to apply themselves, in the application of science to the common purposes of life,"[2] the Rensselaer School was, as "the first non-military scientific school of engineering in the entire English Speaking world,"[3] a visionary and pioneering undertaking. These two men, before there was any other school of engineering in the U.S., recognized the value of research and, as far as they were able, developed "a love of it in their students."[4]

But the revolution wasn't finished. The School was significantly transformed in the 1850s by Institute Director Benjamin Franklin Greene. After completing the first systematic study of European schools of higher learning, Greene recommended the model of the French L'École Polytechnique in Paris. He had concluded that Rensselaer should assert that its mission — much like that of L'École Polytechnique after the French Revolution and new-found societal freedom and structure — was to prepare students for the creation of a new world. Rensselaer should similarly be dedicated to the education of students who would "contribute to the advancement of the great business of life-productive industry."[5]

But a new era for industry has been commenced during the present century. Science has cast its illuminating rays on every process of Industrial Art. The discoveries and improvements which have so frequently flashed into view, have indeed, attested, in a manner the most striking, the mutual advantage to Science and Art — to theory and practice — of a better mutual acquaintance. That there has been a large gain to both, as well of mutual enlightenment as of mutual rectification, is no longer, among intelligent and candid observers, a disputed question. And, in respect to Art, there is no point better established than that practical processes, by becoming more rational have become more certain, and thereby more economical.[6]

Greene's expanded mission was to bring science to industrial problems by breaking the artificial barrier between science, empiricist thinking, experimentation and hands-on

Jennifer Tipton's light installation of the building *Light above the Hudson* seen from downtown Troy

know-how. Combining engineering shop culture (applied) with first principles, scientific analysis and prediction (theoretical) became Rensselaer's strength, and its legacy. Straining not merely to make a better style of architecture, building or bridge, but reimagining the type itself—from the arch to the suspension structure, from bearing walls to the "iron cage" (and eventually steel-frame) structures and attached curtain-wall building enclosures—in lieu of bearing wall structures—Rensselaer and its alumni led in the paradigm shift that was critical to the Industrial Revolution because of expansive ways of thinking outside established canon. It linked the possibilities of science to the art of making.

In recognition of this emphasis, the School was renamed Rensselaer Polytechnic Institute in 1861. It was a polytechnic school, thereafter building specialized disciplines on the twin curricula of scientific and engineering studies, and this combined approach, with general studies and theoretical courses, gave generations of students an advantage in the Industrial Revolution.

> … besides the extensive system of disciplinary exercises for muscular and sensuous culture, if it be remembered that the various theoretical and technical courses, in addition to the large amount of positive knowledge which they are designed to convey to the student, are adapted to secure a discipline of the intellectual powers of a high order of excellence—it may be seen how a judicious combination of these two parallel but intimately connected systems of culture might conduce to the exaltation of the intelligence and executive power of the student and future practical man, up to the utmost perfection of development, of which merely secular education would appear to be capable.[7]

From this progressive tradition came the likes of Roebling (Brooklyn Bridge), Ferris (Ferris wheel) and many contributions to the "Chicago School,"[8] bridges and infrastructure of the Americas—"applying [as Van Rensselaer and Eaton had first framed it] science to the problems of everyday life."

> The evident pedagogical dimension introduced by Greene's (sic) in the education of architects and engineers is to be considered as the continuation of the Enlightenment tradition which saw pedagogical culture as part of raising general and individual welfare of all citizens.[9]
>
> —Ulrich Pfammatter

But the problems of everyday life just aren't what they used to be. Rensselaer graduates had contributed much to America's infrastructure and industry. Palmer C. Ricketts (Rensselaer president, 1901–1934) said, "Surely this school, for its primacy in almost everything found to be of value in methods of instruction in the scientific schools of this country today, must justly be recognized as the pioneer in schools of engineering and technology, and *even of architecture* [emphasis added]."[10] Its students, faculty and alumni have developed new knowledge, approaches to industry and expanded possibility. But as

View from the north of hovering wing-like roof over the EMPAC lobby.

knowledge advanced and the objectives of education at Rensselaer broadened, academic disciplines deepened, and divided into subdisciplines.

At the turn of the century, Rensselaer still offered only science and civil engineering. Then president Palmer Ricketts looked back to the Eaton/Greene agenda, and forward into the 20th century, and concluded that transformational shifts were necessary. He, like Greene, urged a broadening of the curriculum, with new disciplines and the addition of classical studies beyond French or German taught in service of engineering and scientific needs. "[The need for classical studies alongside technical] was particularly evident in Rensselaer's beginnings under Amos Eaton, and Greene, too, stressed the dichotomy between the classical and the technical lines of educational development, despite his efforts to equate and even to reconcile them."[11]

By 1957, the pressure for specialization and segmentation of disciplines had grown to the point where, though Rensselaer had added Schools of Humanities and Social Sciences to those of Architecture, Engineering and Science, it found it necessary to restructure. As with most universities (academies), Rensselaer's organizational structure was branched and had become hierarchical, consisting of several schools running in parallel under the Institute's administration, each with its own dean; departments, each with its own chair; and faculty, each with particular research areas. Little structure existed to create conversation laterally between the branches. Furthermore, the scientific method of *isolating and solving the problem*, though credited with countless discoveries in the sciences and industry, may also be complicit in the restraint of ideas that might have occurred in broader, more complex intersections of thought and research.

The segmentation that accompanied broadening the agenda to many disciplines did not satisfy the need to reach across. Perhaps even more pertinent to the EMPAC story is the development of the first science and technologies studies department in the Humanities and Social Sciences School at Rensselaer—dedicated to the principle that there is no better place for critical theory regarding the changes brought on to society by technological advance than in the belly of the beast. And to follow, many efforts to bridge the disciplines have occurred in educational and research-based initiatives at Rensselaer over the past several decades.

But Dr. Shirley Ann Jackson took an even bolder step with the EMPAC agenda—to suggest, in effect, that science can be stimulated by art and vice versa—that they can be mutual catalysts of each other in a journey to discovery, accomplishment and the fullest realization of a 21st-century university. So, in the tradition of S.V. Rensselaer, Eaton, Greene and Ricketts, Jackson's presidency is transformative. EMPAC is a bold vision linked to Rensselaer's pioneering tradition founded on the principle that differences complement and catalyze in ways that may not be predictable. It is a bold step for a technological university. Jackson envisioned and invested significantly in an experimental performing arts center to broaden the culture, deepen the inquiry and strengthen the research on the belief that at this intersection lay untapped possibility.

EMPAC will give artists access to an unparalleled set of facilities, and a great opportunity for reciprocal exchange with an extraordinary body of research scientists and engineers. The results, we hope, will be exciting and revelatory: for students and faculty, for audiences throughout our region and for the international arts community. Our goal is therefore to enable artists, engineers and scientists to meet in such a way that they respectfully challenge and change one another, while building on the distinct characters of their disciplines. I think this is the basis for true interdisciplinary work and will result in collaborations that cross otherwise untouched boundaries. At EMPAC, our facilities will be made in such a way that they offer artists and their audiences the opportunity, as well as the challenge, of using the full capability of their technology. We will give artists the chance to produce light out of darkness, and sound out of silence.

— Dr. Shirley Ann Jackson

1. Lateralization theories are by some discounted, but provide a useful distinction in support of the argument for understanding the whole brain and how both sides complement and combine. The left side is generally considered the rational, quantitative and logical side; the right side home to the creative and intuitive.

2. Steven Van Rensselaer, to the Rev. D. Blatchford, Lansingburgh, Rensselaer Founding Document, Nov. 5, 1824.

3. G.S. Emerson, *Engineering Education: A Social History*. New York, 1973, 144-46.

4. Palmer C. Ricketts, *History of Rensselaer Polytechnic Institute 1824-1934.* John Wiley & Sons: NY, 3rd Edition, 1934.

5. Benjamin Franklin Greene, *The Rensselaer Polytechnic Institute. Its Reorganization in 1849-50; Its Conditions at the Present Time; Its Plans and Hopes for the Future.* D.H. Jones & Co., Troy, NY, 1855. Report later published by Palmer Ricketts under the title *The Idea of a True Polytechnic,* an original chapter of which bears this title.

6. *Ibid.*

7. *Ibid.*

8. Movement in architecture and engineering at the turn of the century that departed from standard construction techniques to employ the steel frame and curtain (hung) wall construction, elevators and large glass panels.

9. Ulrich Pfammatter, *The Making of the Modern Architect and Engineer*. Birkhauser, 2000, 274.

10. Palmer Ricketts, *History of Rensselaer Polytechnic Institute 1824-1934.*

11. Samuel Rezneck, *Education for a Technological Society: A Sesquicentennial History of Rensselaer Polytechnic Institute. Troy, New York:* Rensselaer Polytechnic Institute: 1968 From chapter 15 "Academic Growth and Educational Diversification of Rensselaer" p. 281.

The Possible Dream

From Dr. Shirley Ann Jackson's initial vision through to the programming, team selection and design execution, the EMPAC designers understood their task to be informed by performance criteria. Goals were in place for the agenda, program, acoustics, scale, experience and environmental performance, and these goals were serious and ambitious. Additionally, there was an overarching and generative programmatic agenda. EMPAC should inspire and provoke. It should be neither limiting in its tight control of exactly how the facility should be used, nor neutral.

With an interest in catalyzing institutional and disciplinary change, the team understood that performance-based design could not merely be derived from certain forces or influences, or inspired by them, but that it must be inspirational and effective at accomplishing ends that would not have otherwise occurred. Not interfering with the functionality was not enough: the facility needed to catalyze possibility. The EMPAC team gave diligence to the careful design of spaces for specific tasks, while opening possibilities to reconfigure the way venues are used in order to stimulate the imagination, discovery and development of things that would not otherwise be possible.

> "When I examine myself and my methods of thought, I come to the conclusion that the gift of fantasy has meant more to me than my talent for absorbing positive knowledge." — Albert Einstein

A VISION REFINED

Other than Rensselaer's 18th president, Dr. Jackson, there is perhaps on the EMPAC project no person more driven, more demanding or more committed to excellence than Founding Director Johannes Goebel, who was brought on board in time for the competition presentations. His position and staffing budget were in place not merely to vet applications to fill a performance schedule, or even to frame and run an artist-in-residence program, but to engage in the conceptualizing, programming, realizing and guarding of that concept through the design and construction phase.

Goebel's charge is understood to be one that begins not merely with predetermined performance types, but with what EMPAC can do to enable the experiment and to attract not only the established, but also the aspiring and most thoughtful performing artists interested in the research agenda. Goebel can be credited with giving definition to the overarching vision of the President, playing a key role in the programming, design, realization and leadership of EMPAC.

Goebel's first experience with EMPAC was as a consultant to the President's team prior to and during the architectural competition phase. He advised in the early programming. Later, pursuant to the first of several world tours dedicated to learning about architecture, acoustic concert halls and projects having similar ambitions, Goebel was hired away from his position at the Center for Arts and Media (ZKM) in Karlsruhe, Germany, to become EMPAC's director. At ZKM, he had been involved in establishing the program, working with architect Rem Koolhaas, the design team and acousticians to

Joshua Bell performing in the Concert Hall

program and design a new facility. When this was not realized in a new facility, however, his task was to translate that program into a new vision that involved the installation of the ZKM program into an abandoned munitions factory.

Though his directorship was limited to the Institute of Music and Acoustics at ZKM, Goebel assumed the programming leadership for all the various program components (including the visual arts, performing arts and research). He developed an intimate understanding of the necessary diagrammatic relationships, overlaps, intersections, isolations and performance criteria necessary to create an enabling arts research facility building.

> Look at EMPAC as an instrument, as an instrument for artistic production
> and scientific and engineering research and application. … I think there is no
> place in the world that has these kinds of venues, this kind of infrastructure
> under one roof. So you will find individual spaces of EMPAC in other places
> of the world, but you do not find them as part of a university or institute. You
> don't find the technical infrastructure, the acoustical and the performance side
> integrated under one roof.
>
> — Johannes Goebel

In close alignment with the vision of intersecting artists and scientists in a research enterprise, Goebel is preoccupied with the relationship between the theoretical and the practical. Art, he says, "has to do with the tangible — happening between people, transmitted through material and media in a social context." EMPAC's umbrella agenda, not the bits and pieces and how they add up, is realized through seeing, hearing and moving in space. The building has been programmed to optimize for human perception.

Goebel held that programmed performance spaces should create the equivalent of a painter's blank canvas. They needed to create "quietness for the ears," and in the case of the studios, "darkness for the eyes." Anything less would produce an undesirable interference and impinge on the full spectrum of perception that should here be explored. In every space, Goebel called for 1) differentiation, 2) refinement and 3) the potential for high resolution. He argued that EMPAC can assist in expanding the spectrum of human aural perception by removing the acculturated restrictors of brains that have learned to unconsciously "tune out" the pervasive noise all around us — and consequently dull awareness and perception.

High acoustic isolation standards were a must. Goebel's favorite example for the design team was the requirement that a thunderous DJ party could happen in the Goodman Theater/Studio 1 just meters away from a simultaneous chamber music group in Studio 2 — without interference. Equally important to Goebel was the possibility for researchers to both listen to and measure perceptible and imperceptible sounds in one space, while activities were occurring elsewhere. He asserted throughout the process that the spaces had to be optimized for both the aural and the visual. This challenge was particularly effective in cross-linking the architect and acoustician in important and innovative ways, for the development of a new fabric ceiling material, the Concert Hall geometry and surface panels, and the studio diffusing panels. The charge was not merely to acoustically tune the space, but to understand and incorporate it visually, while at the same time accommodating all the visual requirements of time-based arts and performances.

The human dimension, hearkening back to Goebel's interest in linking the theoretical to practical, tangible experience, influenced the understanding of the spaces as full scale, human perception laboratories, ready to accept a vast range of performance types, installations and experiments — from avant-garde mixed media to developing new airport security remote scanning technologies. But at the same time, it led to the exploration of the possibilities of new media at human scale, not in a computer or on a 2-D screen, but in a social context in space and time. In one of his most titillating contributions, Goebel's tuned ear and vivid imagination led him to call for the studios to achieve the acoustic equivalent of "a clearing in the forest," and with this challenge he captured the imagination and harvested the creativity of the architectural designers, acousticians, material fabricators and many others. It has already caused many to listen a little closer, and perceive a little more.

The core ambition of technology has always been to extend the capacities of the human body. We have invented tools that move us faster than our legs can carry us, that transport what is larger and heavier than we can carry on our backs, that let us reach beyond what our hands can grasp. But we cannot escape our senses; they determine how we evaluate technology that does what we could not do unaided. Just as we must convert what technology delivers to what our eyes can see and our ears can hear, EMPAC recognizes that the physical dimensions of our bodies mean that we need a certain volume of space to move in.

Goebel has been key in not just establishing a program, but in assembling a team, realizing a design and overseeing its physical manifestation. EMPAC is an agenda, and he began to refine that agenda shortly after arriving and assembling a team of curators. Well before opening the facility, Goebel identified and EMPAC sponsored an ambitious number of provocative and inspiring performance events in, on and around the construction site, as well as in various campus venues. These events were designed to inform the community by showing what performance and installation-based art can do, and to build awareness of the EMPAC agenda and its potential impact on the University. The events, like none other the campus had ever seen, attracted and informed students, faculty and the larger regional community and built anticipation about what was coming.

Deconstructing "EMPAC": What's in a Name?

What's in a name can be revealing. For the Curtis R. Priem Experimental Media and Performing Arts Center, the reasons for its name are closely tied to the vision and history of its development, as well as to its future. For a polytechnic research institution to invest substantially in a performing arts center is a radical and, on the face of it, a curious undertaking. Words are significant, both individually and in the way they are assembled — something Rensselaer took very seriously in its naming. Failure of the reader, building user, artist, scientist or audience member to pause long enough to think about the name/idea might just result in failure to get it at all. EMPAC is not just another performing arts center where artists are booked, show up, perform and leave.

The first proposal was for an *electronic* media and performing arts center, but Dr. Shirley Ann Jackson had a larger view for the project, one that would engage both the arts and sciences around research. This name change was a critical decision that redirected the initiative and pushed it in a far more ambitious direction, one that steps outside normative boundaries of technological or liberal (classic) university studies. By deconstructing the name, we are able to illuminate the choices that helped shape EMPAC. A fundamental understanding of what these terms mean is what drove the agenda.

Experimental assumed the marquee position in the name, establishing research as the primary objective of EMPAC. While Rensselaer intended to strengthen its position and contributions in multiple research areas (artistic, technological and scientific) through EMPAC, from the beginning, the University had a more important agenda. It would create an extraordinary facility dedicated to a new kind of research across unfamiliar disciplinary boundaries. It was to be *Experimental*.

The etymology of the word *experimental* "relates to, or is based on [the word] experience."[1] And so it is that EMPAC incubates and creates knowledge through experience. It is a place built expressly for "trying things," in particular, to try things at the fertile interface of diverse intelligences. In a world that is increasingly realizing the interconnectivity of the whole and the limitations of isolating disciplines, this is no small matter. While hybrid disciplines, and interdisciplinary and multidisciplinary work increasingly appear, EMPAC moves that conceit to a higher order, creating intersections of fields and people (artists and scientists) normally considered at great intellectual odds, and then moving them toward a *transdisciplinary* condition. This notion builds on the pioneering heritage of Amos Eaton's and B.F. Greene's beliefs in 1) the importance of research, the laboratory and the experiment; 2) a broader education of the technical student; and 3) their then radical proposition to join scientific (theoretical) and engineering (applied) intelligences.

Media, "a medium of cultivation, conveyance or expression,"[2] is a complex term, at once having the possibility of referring to the environment for developing (cultivating) something (e.g., the petri dish of an experiment); the method of transmitting (conveying) something (e.g., an idea) from one state, place or person to another; and/or the means of communicating (expressing) the message.

The pairing of *Experimental* and *Media* provides substantial direction to the kind of research that will be the focus of the EMPAC enterprise, where new technologies will be provoked by imagination and where the imagination will be provoked by technological

Composer Hans Tutschku working in a suspended sound dome of 32 loudspeakers in the Goodman Theater/Studio 1

possibilities, perhaps yet unimagined by its inventor. Gunpowder was first invented as a skin salve, the Internet was developed for military communications between remote sites in case of a nuclear event, and the Web for communication between high-energy physicists at the European Center for Nuclear Research. Who would have predicted their impact in the transformation of world cultures and economies?

Author William Gibson said, "The street finds its own uses."[3]

Performing (or performance) is a term understood quite differently by the artist as an act in public, and the scientist as something that can be measured, analyzed, evaluated and quantified—both legitimate interpretations (uses) that are embraced by the project's mission. For the artist, the performance itself may be experimental and require technological innovation if not invention, but it may also surprise and provoke (perform) at another level entirely—to reveal that which is not seen or heard, to stimulate thought and to catalyze possibility. For the scientist, how something performs and the lessons and knowledge that can be derived may be primary. However, as transdisciplinary work emerges at EMPAC, the line between *the* performance and *its* performance may at times become inextricable.

The phrase *Performing Arts Center* is well known and exists in its own right. Performing arts centers usually include several performance venues for local and/or regional community activities. They are planned for the performance of artistic works before audiences of various sizes. What then is the distinction of an *Experimental Media* Performing Arts Center? While EMPAC is well equipped for and intended to host performances of known works and established orchestras, theater troupes and so forth, it is particularly dedicated to research and "the new"—that is, "trying things." It is equipped to both develop and to perform new work, to explore and push boundaries of media and performance.

Performing arts are those arts that involve active, live, public performance. Performances may occur in any one of the venues or, employing mediated technologies, may occur in and between the physically isolated venues, and/or remote real and/or cybersites. This is what's exceptional: As the only facility with full-scale venue spaces dedicated to the dissolution and recombination of realities between physical and virtually mediated realms, EMPAC's performing arts serve a specific, experimental research agenda.

1. Webster's Ninth New Collegiate Dictionary, Merriam-Webster, 1989.
2. *Ibid.*
3. "Burning Chrome," *Omni Magazine*, July 1982.

Residency of Workspace Unlimited in the panoramic screen in the Goodman Theater/ Studio 1

Performance Design

Even in some of the more progressive circles of 21st architectural design and theory, performance-based design is narrowly understood as the most efficient response to environmental forces in the design of a building that seeks to minimize its carbon footprint, energy use and environmental impact. Though these are important factors in architectural design, "creating a constructive climate for the recognition of new technology and civilized collaboration"[1] and challenging standard performance specification norms (e.g., acoustic), for example, are not always equally considered.

Not so at EMPAC. A broader understanding of performance design acknowledged from the start that buildings are more than providers of shelter: they are programmatic, social and, in EMPAC's case, institutional constructs that affect the persons and programs within and around them. The program charged its designers with resolving the south campus, creating a "living room" for the University, projecting its bold agenda to the region and catalyzing a place of interdisciplinary collaboration, while meeting high standards of acoustic performance, energy efficiency and sustainability. The center was purposed with promoting interdisciplinary research collaboration and raising awareness of the scholarly and artistic work of others, all the while linking Rensselaer to broader and more diverse global scholarly and experimental communities. It was to project a new Rensselaer to the world.

In designing for the broad spectrum of performance criteria at EMPAC, the builders responded to both internal programmatic desires (discrete venues with discrete purposes) and external forces and phenomena (e.g., location, climate, views). These boundaries informed the specifics of its creation, from its placement on the hill to its massing, expressed geometries, to its mix of warm and cool materials to where EMPAC would be opaque or transparent. Ultimately, these many influences underpinned the design and assembly of the formal, material construct and resulted in spaces and enclosures that enable, express and are specific to EMPAC's larger programmatic intent. They inform the realization of its formal and spatial design, whether in the hull design, the glass lobby and north curtain wall, the interstitial spaces or venues nested in the south block of the building.

EMPAC is the manifestation of an idea and desire to develop a productive intersection between the ambitious and diverse disciplines of, on the one hand, media-based art and performance, and, on the other hand, science and engineering. Furthermore, EMPAC is designed to do this within an existing historic, well-reputed and highly productive engineering and scientific research community. Even as it endeavors to create new intersections and catalyze possibilities yet unforeseen, it is not doing so in a "green field."

Because of this, EMPAC can be thought of as an institutional and disciplinary graft—at the scales of the building, campus, city and global network—seeking to stimulate awareness of new possibilities that lie at the fringes and intersections of surprisingly different disciplines, and not only in the deep wells of scientific inquiry and applications. Within, the design sets up diagonal views and a larger (urban) awareness of its various components and activities. Selective transparencies from the upper campus (north and east) and city (north and west) make EMPAC an inviting structure. The building does this by revealing the waiting form of the hull, clear and accessible interior passages and

The Concert Hall prepared for a concert with Deerhunter and Boredoms.

"EMPAC will inspire experimentation, cross-disciplinary inquiry and advanced research ... as a nexus of technological and artistic innovation, and optimized performance space. As we all know, scientific and technological advances have profound and wide-ranging impact on all citizens. Society therefore needs scientists and engineers who are not only technically brilliant, but also articulate and broad-minded. EMPAC will provide a facility and a program for exploring these synergies between technology and the performing arts — for our students, our faculty and a variety of artists-in-residence."

— Dr. Shirley Ann Jackson

the exhibition of occasional gathering masses associated with event activity. Its programmatic and technical infrastructure provide for global reach into and collaboration with progressive intellectual communities engaged in artistic, scientific and technological initiatives. Edward Shanken, in a 40-year retrospective analysis of collaborative research and interdisciplinary scholarship, begins with artist Robert Rauschenberg's and engineer Billy Klüver's 1967 initiative and manifesto, *Experiments in Art and Technology* (E.A.T.), and continues in part by recognizing that "the development by artists of one-point perspective, anatomy, photography and virtual reality attest to the deeply intermingled histories of art, science and technology." [2]

Today, more than ever, much of what is important and exciting in science and technology lies in interdisciplinary areas. ... EMPAC will help us to maximize Rensselaer's interdisciplinary potential, providing a platform where research and technology can interact with artistic creation and reflection.

As Johannes Goebel points out, EMPAC is designed to "give artists access to an unparalleled set of facilities, and a great opportunity for reciprocal exchange with an extraordinary body of research scientists and engineers. The results, we hope, will be exciting and revelatory: for students and faculty, for audiences throughout our region and for the international arts community."

"The goal," continues Goebel, "is therefore to enable artists, engineers and scientists to meet in such a way that they respectfully challenge and change one another while building on the distinct characters of their disciplines". This is the basis for true interdisciplinary work and will result in collaborations that cross otherwise untouched boundaries. At EMPAC, he forecasts, "our facilities will be made in such a way that they offer artists and their audiences the opportunity, as well as the challenge, of using the full capability of their technology. We will give artists the chance to produce light out of darkness, and sound out of silence."

The ultimate and most meaningful performance of the building will be measured by the successes of the programs, people and research it organizes, allows, enables and stimulates.

EMPAC is more than a series of performance venues; it is a crossroad, an intersection, a laboratory and a living room perched proudly on the hill between Rensselaer, that historic American polytechnic, and Troy, that equally historic post-industrial city at the head of the Hudson's navigable waters—a crossroad of 19th-century canal, railroad and river transportation and prior home to steel and textile industries.

EMPAC was imagined by a president who advocates the dynamics of culture and research. Dr. Shirley Ann Jackson exercised leadership in the creation of this new educational and research paradigm that looks toward the future and has a bias toward the practical. The EMPAC agenda is conceived and constructed not merely as an extension of Rensselaer's industrial heritage, success and legacy as a polytechnic, or merely as an extension of possibility afforded by the knowledge economy, but as an extension of its history of transformative pedagogic innovations. EMPAC is an investment in the premise that Rensselaer's ability to lead in the development of next-generation ideas and knowledge resides at the nexus of diverse disciplines and intelligences—and that this will be one of the most important engines of innovation, progress and prosperity in the 21st century. EMPAC is an experimental laboratory designed to incubate ideas and projects that will spawn new discoveries, insights and inventions not conceived in isolated tanks, but in hybridized collaborations and endeavors between unfamiliar bedfellows.

Performance design, which guided so much of EMPAC's creation, is informed by both internal and external forces—whether environmental, structural, social, cultural or programmatic. The performances of the individual spaces are critical to achieving excellence. However, it is important to consider EMPAC at a higher level than its individual spaces, to see it as a whole with the larger ambition: supporting experimentation (innovation, discovery, creativity) and research, creating a crossroads and intersection between disciplines and people, and establishing a social mixer and the living room of the campus. The program calls for both a social and an institutional performance. The design responds by setting up a series of interlinked interstitial spaces: café, lobby, outdoor terrace, exposed circulation routes along the south block and open stairways between levels. It creates an intersection between ordinarily sequestered and isolated students and faculty, researchers and artists in view of and from the campus and valley. Its hovering hull, often illuminated in the evening to announce events to the University and city of Troy, is both a symbol of EMPAC's progressive vision and an invitation for all to enter. And its two flights of grand stairs, ascending 80 vertical feet from Eighth Street to campus, make the linkage between them real.

Four unique performance venues are housed within EMPAC's twin masses. The relatively conventional, largely opaque south block contains the two experimental studios and fly-towered theater. Within the transparent, glazed north block hovers the wood-clad

hull, containing a 1,200-seat acoustic concert hall. The use of generous, towering, transparent void spaces between the formal building masses provides visual and physical access between the various program components. These spaces serve to move people throughout the building and operate as social mixers in a variety of enlarged exhibition areas, café and lobby/lounge spaces. The space between the forms is generous and filled with natural light to aid in influencing the mixing of artists, scientists, faculty, students and the public, while simultaneously, and ironically, assisting in acoustically isolating each venue from the other.

It is through the formal device of constructing multiple unique and separated forms, suited for the various performance venues, that the architectural strategy assists in achieving the highest acoustic isolation standards between each of the performance venues. With rigorous insistence, the sound specifications were held extraordinarily high for a university performing arts center. They survived cost pressures and value engineering, ensuring forever the possibility of simultaneous performances and use of the venues without cross-acoustic interference. This enables the ongoing development of multiple artist-in-residence projects, research experiments, and sound and event performances.

The brief, or broader, programmatic charge provided the "high level" directive for the facility that was worked out in the building program and design. The program spaces, their sizes, shapes, occupations, equipping and infrastructure are what enable the performance, and they too are performance-driven. Each venue was designed for a limited range of performance functions: lectures, town meetings, and acoustic and amplified performances in the Concert Hall; lectures, and classic and experimental theatrical performances in the Theater; classic chamber and experimental, media-based performances in each of the studios. Each venue had to meet highly specific and rigorous design parameters for the anticipated performance types, yet a critical part of the performance requirements for each space was flexibility. Even though the spaces conform to strict acoustic and performance requirements, artists and researchers should be able to imagine unconventional ways to use the spaces.

Flexibility and excellence, if not carefully considered, easily become self-canceling agendas. On the one hand, flexibility is often achieved by compromising specific programmatic and ideal performance criteria of specific venue requirements for the sake of accommodating multiple uses. Excellence, on the other hand, seeks to meet the highest and most specific demands of a single, predictable, well-understood task (orchestral concert, theater, speech, chamber music, acoustic music, multimedia, etc.), often contradicting or shackling the possibility for alternative, non-conventional explorations and venues.

The designers solved the problem by optimizing for excellence within each of several unique venues and then adding flexible variants within. No single venue was expected to provide the ultimate desired range of all performance types. That was the task of the entire facility, made up of unique and diverse venues, each with its own standard of excellence and limited range of flexibility. But within each venue, specific flexibilities that did not threaten the fidelity of its primary purpose were created—including the potential to adjust the boundaries between audience and performer, to perform acoustic or amplified music, to reconfigure the space with dropped panels, or to introduce audio and video media.

For a performing arts center especially, programmatic requirements affect its formal, spatial and material design. The delineation of back of house (for performers and support mechanisms) and front of house (for the public) spaces, queuing to different seating levels, and emergency exiting schemes are challenge enough, but meeting all the requirements for sightlines, acoustic excellence and flexibility also had to be worked out. For the performance spaces, these criteria and their propensity to affect the form and its surfaces are particularly acute. Not only did the volume, shape and configuration of the rooms have to follow well-understood conventions in order for all to see, hear and perform well, they had to create unique opportunities and memorable experiences. The designers determined early on that the response should be integrated and evident, in the wall surfaces and in the ceilings. EMPAC's four venues were each designed for a unique range of performance types and had to meet specific acoustic criteria (quantitative) and aural definitions (qualities).

This page and opposite:
Random Dance Residency in Studio 2

The challenge of acoustically isolating the major spaces for simultaneous use was significant in itself, requiring independent structural systems, gaps between the venues, heavy mass construction and extensive isolation details to prevent sound vibration from traveling between venues along mechanical, electrical and plumbing elements.

Creating an acoustic (non-amplified) concert hall for an audience of 1,200 with excellent sightlines and sound at every seat is no small order. It has been considered both an art and a science for centuries to 1) establish the optimal reverberation time, 2) prevent flutter and standing wave reflections between parallel surfaces and, perhaps most difficult, 3) establish the right amount of acoustic "liveness" in relation to the diffusion of sound. The Concert Hall needed to maintain the sound energy without becoming *muddy* on the one hand or too *dry* on the other — to use the acoustician's shop language.

And if that were not difficult enough, computational tools to model the intricacies of sound diffusion resulting from specific surface geometries and material properties at the boundaries of the room did not exist; the seats needed to be as much as 20 percent larger than they were in the 19th century (requiring a larger hall); and contemporary construction and aesthetics no longer rely heavily on ornate surfaces, which historically served to assist with diffusion. The requirement to add a level of flexibility that permitted, not only acoustic concerts, but also the spoken word and amplified performance that would typically overpower an acoustic hall, made the challenge even more significant, since compromise was not an option. These challenges were met in a variety of ways through close collaboration between acoustician, theater designer, architect and client, and are recorded in detail later in the book. At EMPAC, the "auralization" (visualization for the ear) of the spaces was linked to their visual character. It wasn't good enough to have quality sound; the means to that experience needed to please the eye as well.

> Underlying the development of the infrastructure with the architects and consultants of EMPAC is to provide spaces where the environment is optimized and determined by the quality and resolution of our senses. Technology is certainly integrated into it, but technology has, for instance in the visual world, not at all reached the resolution of our eyes, not at all — it's just 2-D, limited color space. But we are building spaces that can accommodate any event for our eyes, which will maybe eventually reach the resolution that can match our eyes — which we have already reached on the audio side for our ears.
>
> — Johannes Goebel

The association of the visual and the aural, linked to the perception agenda, played a key role throughout the design process and is credited with getting the best work from the design team. The geometric shaping of the Concert Hall, its fabric-ceiling innovation, rippled wood and dimpled cast stone wall panels, and the adjustable "moon surface" acoustic panels of the studios are each a testament to close collaboration between numerous disciplines dealing with the functional (Fisher Dachs), the visual (Grimshaw) and the acoustic (Kirkegaard).

The hovering form of the Concert Hall and hull performs technically within, to isolate the sound, create acoustic locks and sculpt the sound of the performances it anticipates. But it is also an expression of something else. It announces itself in dramatic relation to the building and its larger landscape — it creates an expectation and desire. The Theater and two black box studios are nested within the south block and do not perform figurally in the space. They find their unique acoustic and visual signatures within. The intimate, steeply raked seating of the Theater, with its double-stacked side galleries, red wall surfaces, infinite black ceiling and suppressed stage threshold, dissolves the division between actor and audience. The bright, active and pixilated white panel surface surround and maple floors of Studio 2 provide for both intimate and highly precise performances and interactive installations, while the Goodman Theater/Studio 1, the seemingly infinite black box, provides the artist or researcher with an architecturally unencumbered space that allows multiple configurations and experiments in performance and research. They are each finely tuned instruments designed to meet their own unique programmatic requirements and manifest themselves as unique responses.

The space between, itself a gap assisting in the isolation of sound interference, was opportunistically expanded to accommodate building circulation and program spaces (café, lobby, exhibition), and to catalyze the social agenda linked to the campus and landscape. The café in particular is tucked intimately under the hull and proves a place for sheltered yet open discourse, exposed to the circulation of the building to stimulate chance encounter between the scientist, artist and engineer.

The broader (and better) definition of performance-based design relates to programmatic and social performances, as well as to environmental and acoustic performances. Extremely high client expectations stimulated collaboration between accomplished professionals across multiple disciplines and became the catalyst for many innovations in the design and making of EMPAC. Human perception was a focus. Goebel's charge and William Horgan's[3] enthusiasm to make the invisible evident (in the acoustic treatments, for instance) inspired numerous custom solutions that are key to both the appearance and performance of the building. The need to isolate the four venues led to extravagant means of structurally separating them, but it also provided impetus to exploit the interstitial spaces to serve as the circulation and lifeblood of the project, while exposing it to the campus and city. Restraint is no enemy of talented designers.

1. Excerpt from the manifesto *Experiments in Art and Technology (E.A.T.) Statement of Purpose*, 1967.
2. Edward A. Shanken, *"Artists in Industry and the Academy: Collaborative Research, Interdisciplinary Scholarship and the Interpretation of Hybrid Forms."* Leonardo, MIT Press, October 2005, v. 38, No. 5.
3. Grimshaw Architects' designer responsible for the day-to-day work of the second schematic design through construction administration phases of the project under Sir Nicholas Grimshaw and Andrew Whalley, Vincent Chang and Mark Husser.

EMPAC: Scales, Senses and the Creation of Meaning

Johannes Goebel

This essay offers one perspective on EMPAC. My work with the architects and engineers was to ensure that the building and its infrastructure would enable "experimental media and performing arts" in all its facets. At the same time, I was to define, initialize and ramp up the program, staff and operational requirements that would realize the vision of EMPAC. The following text reflects some of my personal thoughts, which guided me during the collaborative effort to make this extraordinary project happen. EMPAC hopefully incorporates, and is sure to evoke, many more perspectives than were consciously pursued up to now. The intention with EMPAC was to create an environment that was uniquely defined while remaining open to yet unimagined realms. Such intention can only be reached when personal thoughts and criteria are both as equally important and defining as they are unimportant and receding.

FROM ELECTRONIC TO EXPERIMENTAL

In the beginning, EMPAC stood for *Electronic* Media and Performing Arts Center. This was a quite straightforward name at the end of the 20th century. Arts using electricity and electronics had been around for more than 100 years. In 1981, Rensselaer's Department of the Arts added electronic media to its program, and this is considered the first integrated electronic arts program within a research university in the United States. The combination of electronic media with performing arts in a large center was a clear testament to the radical change performing arts had experienced through electronics all the way to the development of new media, from video or music synthesis, and to the full integration of computer technology in interactive art, immersive environments and the construction of virtual reality.

The acronym soon changed to stand for *Experimental* Media and Performing Arts Center. This indicated an opening in two directions. On the one hand, the scientific understanding of "experiment" was introduced as part of the mission of EMPAC. On the other hand, the tradition of experimental art became part of the program. "Tradition of experimental art" may sound like a contradiction, but experimental art can be seen as having evolved and been put into practice in parallel with the electrification of media.

Scientific experiments may be defined as establishing and verifying causal relationships, supporting a hypothesis up to the point when another experiment falsifies the hypothesis, or generally as aiming for a non-ambiguous communication.

Art is not defined by "right" or "wrong," and quickly gets terribly boring when it sets out to verify literal or causal relationships. Experiments in the artistic domain stand even further opposed to scientific experiments. They are not about repetition of the known or agreed upon, but about a change of production, perception, experience and interpretation of the world.

The performing arts traditionally comprise music, dance and theater. These art forms are moving in time, in contrast to the fine arts that traditionally produce static works, like a painting or a sculpture. With the advent of electricity, new media were discovered; sound and moving images could be recorded or synthetically generated, and computers became instruments and artistic tools. New visual worlds, new forms of moving through space and of making our senses feel and interact were created. We may call all these arts that move and change perceivably on a vector of time, "time-based arts."

These time-based arts meet science and engineering through common tools that both may use, such as computer technology, image projections or robotics. The Experimental Media and Performing Arts Center provides a platform where all these different approaches, agendas, motivations and goals can communicate with one another through and with the media that yield themselves to shape new experiences and new tools, new directions and new interpretations. And at the center of this, we as humans stand to create and communicate; to explore, discuss and develop; to construct and to experience.

MEDIA AND PERFORMING ARTS

There is beauty in how words can change their meaning yet still retain some of the old meanings over centuries; when such old meanings of a word surface, they may yield new thoughts and perspectives.

A medium carries and channels between two worlds. A medium may carry messages from the world of the dead to the world of the living; or from eternal beings to us mortals; or it may serve to look into the future. Indeed, such a medium mediates a message by passing from one world to the other.

At some point in time, medium started to be used for naming scientific and technical relations. The medium that was seen as carrying electromagnetic waves was called ether, where *aether* was a name for an ancient Greek concept of what filled the space above the earth; and today we call one medium carrying digital information Ethernet. Air carries sounds and voices and smells; light moves through and around materials and to our eyes; warmth and touch meet our skin—our senses are the optimized interfaces to specific media, which mediate that which is outside of us to our insides. A medium allows us to communicate with others, through images, written words, sounds, smells or touch. There is no way between my thinking and feeling to your sensing and interpreting, and to your heart, except through the media that move between the interfaces that connect my "inside" and your "inside."

Artists have always used media; there is no art without media (just as there is no art without audience). Indeed, art is always a mediation. Art is about using and shaping media, be it paint on a canvas, marble in a sculpture, sounds of music or words, written text, movements in dance or creating an algorithmically defined visual environment. One could say that art has always been media art.

"The media," as a term, came about in the first half of the 20th century, when mass media such as radio, and later television, together with newspapers and magazines, created a new force in communication. Indeed, the media always incorporated three aspects: the technology; that which was communicated; and the goal that was pursued by using the specific media with a specific content. The media was associated with political power and with mass distribution, with establishing a fourth power next to the legislative, judicial and executive powers.

Parallel to this political use of the media, media also became a label for technology that uses electricity to produce, store and reproduce something we can perceive, see, hear or feel. If we talk about media today, we mean images distributed and created by electricity or light; sounds that can be generated and distributed through wires; and words and texts and plans and drawings —all of which can be converted from and to electricity and light and which can be stored on media—yet another use of the term, as for instance in "digital storage media." We cannot see, feel or hear these media unless the stored or generated formats get converted back to that which can meet our senses— through loudspeakers, video projectors and monitors, and computer-controlled systems that "speak to our senses."

Performing arts always take place as a social gathering. Performing arts implies that a performance with a beginning and an end brings an audience together to jointly experience an event during which performers and audience share the same space and time. This does not mean that only the performers are active and that the audience is merely sitting and watching; over the past century, performing arts have expanded in many different directions, and even "beginning" and "end" are no longer clear-cut. And performing arts have been complemented by performance art, which has come out of the visual arts and moved to the performing, time-based arts.

By merging media, technological research, computer technology, time-based arts, artistic creation, production and performance under one roof, EMPAC creates new potential for all areas involved. The interface of all these areas lies in our human senses, which we use to communicate, to create and to make sense. EMPAC is focused on our senses, without which media are senseless, and without which we cannot create meaning. EMPAC has been designed with the "human scale" as common ground for experimental media and performing arts, for research and production, for arts, science and technology.

TO HUMAN SCALE

EMPAC is designed and built to the human scale. EMPAC accommodates technology, but EMPAC is not built to the scale of technology, even though it is filled with perhaps more technology than any other performing arts center. And even though it has venues like no other research center.

Designing and building for technology is easy; designing and building to the human scale is very complicated. It would seem that it is easy to build for us humans, since that is what buildings were meant for in the first place. But politics, economics and technology have created such intertwined sets of criteria for buildings that basic human requirements are often not accommodated. We accept the creation of buildings without daylight, without high-quality artificial light, a pleasant level of humidity, or a quietness that allows our ears to rest and to hear the soft sounds our ears can perceive.

With EMPAC, a center for experimental media and performing arts has been designed and built to the scale that allows the expression and experience with our bodies and minds, through our senses. It is defined by the physical requirement of our senses and designed to our human scale.

Media carry to our senses that which is to be perceived, and the arts have always shaped media for our exchange, experience and communication. Building a center that is to connect media, time-based arts, research and engineering can only be rooted in the common factor of all of these—which indeed *is* the human scale.

Technology changes quickly, but the fundamental ways our senses enable us to communicate have probably changed very little over the past centuries and millennia. Our minds and our interpretations of the world do change with changes in science and technology, since the media through which we communicate are changing. Our understanding of our senses changes with science and technology as well, but the senses are still the interfaces through which all that is observed to be understood reaches our mind and imagination.

Our senses cannot be simply separated as functional units from our way of "making sense." It is hard to delineate perception and meaning in the path from the mechanical stimulation of a sense through the biochemical processes in our nerves all the way to the unknown process of how memory works (memory being a salient part in the creation of meaning). Making sense indeed starts right away when something meets one of our senses. The processing of the signals that meet our senses begins at once—within the sense organs, not just when the converted signals reach the brain. We can train our perception to a very high degree to become more and more refined in what we see, hear, feel, taste or smell. How such training and sharpening of our senses actually can change any or all stages from the sense organ to the brain to the creation of meaning is probably little understood. At any rate, it seems highly likely that such heightening of a sensitivity can also influence the physical properties involved in perception, not only the mental space. One can say that our perception and our senses can be tuned by our intentionality, and that our senses and perception tune our intentionality.

The interdependency and reciprocal change of sense, perception and meaning is the foundation of our growing up, our acculturation, our learning and our adaptation to our world and adoption of it. Art explicitly shapes matter and time for an aesthetic experience that cannot be subsumed under semantics or logic (which does not mean that semantics and logic cannot be part of art). Art is the strongest proponent of this unbelievably complex interplay between what we might declare to be the physical world and the world of "inner experience," of sense, sensitivity and sensibility.

In shaping the physical world in the arts, we have always applied new tools and technology as they arose. This is true from the very beginning, once we went beyond what we could produce just with our bodies by singing, clapping, dancing, acting or telling stories. We built drums and flutes, painted on walls and marked our faces. With the change of tools and technology, art changed, as well as our perceptions and what we considered "meaningful."

With science we learned to discover, describe and define the physical parameters of our senses, and we explored how meaning might be created. By applying quantitative methods, the threshold and bandwidth of each sense could be established. In parallel, technology resulted in high levels of sensory pollution, which meant that the bandwidths of our senses could not be addressed to their fullest as the levels of sound, light and smell around us rose to levels that were out of control for the individual. In our society, we hardly have places in our neighborhoods where we can gather with others that are not under the influence of unwanted light and sound. And yet, at the same time, technology offers us the opportunities to create new, refined impressions for our senses, which can actually span, more and more, the full bandwidths of our senses.

If we want to use media or create art that allows us to address our full human potential and at the same time use what technology has to offer, the spaces need to support the full bandwidths of our senses, as much as architecture and engineering allow us. Spaces should be large enough for us to move through: to walk and jump and run and dance. Spaces for social communication and interaction have to be large enough to accommodate groups of people. Spaces should be quiet enough to support the softest sounds we can hear, and they should support all the options we have to create and use light. We should be able to speak and sing without amplification, or to use technology to make a whisper as loud as a wind.

The technical goal of developing media technology has been to come closer and closer to meeting the bandwidths and resolution of our senses. The arts use, in an eclectic way, whatever technology makes accessible. Once a technology is available, one can be sure that some artist will use it right away for artistic creation. And artistic use may move technology in a direction that was not foreseen by the inventors of that technology.

With technology, we create instruments, tools and machines that are stronger than our muscles, sharper than our eyes, more sensitive than our skin, or faster and more accurate than our hands. Technology also enables us to make visible what our eyes cannot see unaided, manipulate that which our hands cannot touch, and shape and model what only our minds could imagine. In all this, technology changes the scale at which we can think, imagine and create.

By writing on papyrus or clay tablets, we took thinking and remembering out of time and communication out of simultaneity. We went beyond the lifespan of an individual by accumulating the lifetime of thousands of people to build monuments aimed at bringing immortality to just a few. Libraries accumulate beyond the individual memory and mind, and today, digital storage is being fed by millions of people and untold automated technology with incomprehensible amounts of information.

We change social time by taking individual time to write, compose, paint, sculpt and perform. We then ask and enable others to spend their time on what we created. The time of creation usually takes longer than the time to experience the creation. And with media technology, we are able to separate the producer from the spectator, to build tools to duplicate, distribute and recreate media for individual, asynchronous experiences.

The scales of time and of size were externalized, disembodied and extended beyond what our own senses are able to perceive directly. But each scale we create with the help of technology (such as spectroscopes or telescopes or microscopes) that is also incommensurate to our own human scale needs to be made to fit exactly our scale of perception, to our size and to the conditions of our senses.

We have to listen and read and watch in "real time," in the time of human scale. The shadows of X-rays have to be transposed to visible light, and text stored in digital form has to be brought to a physical appearance of letters on paper or on a computer screen that our eyes can see. And the split-second finish of a car race gets captured and frozen in time so we can determine who won.

Despite our wide-ranging individual heights, we have a certain sense of volume and distance regarding being outdoors or indoors. Most certainly, a 7-foot-high ceiling feels different to me, as a very tall person, than to someone two-thirds my height. But we have a definite measure within us that allows us to have "a feeling" for sizes around us—for how tall a tree in the distance might be or how fast a bird might be flying in relationship to us walking. The media we use to capture and communicate—like the aforementioned clay tablets or sheets of papyrus, or vellum, books or computer screens—were always adapted to be within reach of our hands, adapted to the fine movements our hands could make when creating graphic representations, and to the range of differentiation our eyes might detect over that close distance.

But there is also the other range of size—that of landscapes, murals, panoramic paintings and movie screens; the range beyond the reach of our hands but within the reach of our eyes and ears. Technologies like painting, photography, film or video allow us to scale those things, large and small, to "fit the frame." And as we zoom in and zoom out on a computer screen, we have to re-establish a frame of reference so we can judge the original size. Looking through a microscope or a telescope requires us to constantly make ourselves aware of a frame of

reference, since in those images we move outside the consistent frame of our normal view. And once we enter the worlds of totally synthetic environments (virtual worlds), we may lose our "innate" frame of reference and may have to adapt to continuously changing scales.

One may assume that technology increasingly allows us to move to "virtual worlds," worlds that are created with technology and that we can "inhabit" more and more independently of our actual physical environment (rather than inhabit as we do, our own world). It may be that this was a thought that came out of the limitations of technology in the last decades of the 20th century. Being limited to small screens or goggles that allow us to peek into such virtual spaces while sitting on a chair, listening through headphones to acoustical spaces we are not in, or moving in a "cave" of generated projections with three other persons—all these advances in technology have not yet mastered the "human scale" at its fullest.

EMPAC provides spaces with a certain volume and height

we feel lost or uncomfortable, and we create subgroups. And there are many other conditions that determine the human scale. Our senses are the measure for our "being in the world." They are best at certain speeds, sizes, distances, quantities and qualities.

EMPAC is dimensioned to accommodate what performing and media arts always knew would be good audience sizes for gatherings that would not need electricity to reach the audience —like one, two or five; 10, 20, 80 or 150; 200, 400 or maybe even up to 1,200—depending on the project or program. And if we are to explore while walking around or by sitting still to take in the experience, these groupings allow communication and sharing at a "comprehensible scale." And in such spaces, most certainly media technology can align with the human scale.

EMPAC, with its technical infrastructure, offers a platform for creation and communication that can be bound to simultaneous and social interaction. With EMPAC, it is proposed that everything has to be brought to human scale in order for us to

"...the senses are still the interfaces through which all that is observed

that may be commensurable with us as individuals or as groups. By being able to project images and sounds in spaces where we do not have to zoom in or out, but where we can move closer and farther away, our sense for volume and space can get engaged in a more direct way. We can establish a scale directly through our physical experience and perception.

Part of the human-scale conceit includes our characteristics as social beings. We have not only the scale of our senses, but also the scale of our human communication and interaction commensurate with our senses. We like to stand around in groups of three, four, five, 10 or 15 to look at things, to walk around to get a better view, to move closer or farther away from what we see or hear, to extend our arms and point with our fingers and say, "Look over there, did you see that?" "Did you hear the dog barking? I think it's behind the neighbor's house." "Let's go over there and look at the details."

And we naturally mingle in larger groups, sharing events such as a concert or a show, allowing it to reach our senses, and then for us to talk together about it. If the crowd is too large,

perceive, to share and to create meaning.

The center is a bold statement in a time when technology suggests that there are no boundaries to what we probe, be it the tiniest tiny or farthest far, way beyond our senses. EMPAC can be seen as a symbol in a time when individually distributed and accessed information seems to make getting together and sharing space obsolete.

THE SENSES:
PORTALS FOR THE CREATION OF MEANING
There is a common link between all those scales we can communicate through and about: our senses as interfaces for sharing a flow between "internal" and "external." There is most probably not a clearly definable boundary between internal and external. For this discussion, let us assume that the portals for experience and communication between "me" and "you" and the "rest of the world" are our senses and what we can produce with and for them—seeing; hearing; moving in space; using our voice and hands; smelling, tasting and talking or writing about it; making

films; building houses; developing mathematical proofs; touching and feeling; programming computers; making music; preaching; and going places.

There may be more senses available to us as interfaces between inside and outside than we might be able to define or agree on. But we can agree for sure that communication between me and you uses the portals of the senses that are part of our body at the boundary between "in me" and "outside of me" and "to you."

We can lose a sense organ as we can any other part of our body. And even though all our senses may still be working, we can reach a space where others call us senseless and crazy, which is when we cannot communicate anymore with others on a common basis. But as long as we have common ground with others, this ground is shaped by the portals of our senses.

And that which we communicate is also shaped by our senses. I cannot speak pictures; I cannot sing with my leg. And what I perceive from the outside and what I give to the outside is

or as force-feedback in a joystick. Or as a direct result of where we applied computer technology: a building collapses because of wrong calculations; the cattle grow too fast because a computer dispensed the wrong amount of hormones; or we are happy to see a great computer-generated movie.

To see if what we collected as data of incredibly small, fast or distant events actually makes sense, we again have to use technology to make visible what we cannot see, to make audible what we cannot hear and to make touchable what our bodies cannot feel or move. And in order to gain a handle on massive amounts of data, visualizing the data in charts, graphs or interactively controllable representations may yield a more sense-bound level of access than poring over long lists of values.

This is the central issue of our changed relationship with that which is around us and that which we cannot see or feel, but which we believe "makes sense." We have to transpose all events we want to evaluate and interpret into the realm of our senses. Only then can we find out if they make sense. Only then

to be understood reaches our mind and imagination."

deeply shaped by the condition of my senses. A sense is not a mere apparatus receiving external impulses and relaying that information in a neutral way to the brain. Our senses are highly refined and complex interpreters of what is around us and what reaches us. Indeed, they start the interpretation before anything is relayed to the brain. The property of our senses as physical interfaces between "outside" and "inside" shape our view of reality as much as we shape the physical reality around us based on what reaches us through these very senses.

Technology has always had at its core that we make things that extend beyond the scale of our senses — smaller than we can see, faster than we can move, larger than we can reach, heavier than we can carry, without catching breath, without getting tired. Most advances in science in the past century have come from that which is beyond the capabilities of our senses to perceive.

That a computer works as intended can only be evaluated when we can see, feel or perceive the result with our senses: as a printout in text and numbers; as a graph or picture; as a sound;

can we interpret the information and assign it meaning.

This mapping process for data (when in its raw form, it is smaller, larger or more massive than our senses can perceive) is where experimental media and time-based arts on the one side, and science and engineering on the other can learn from and benefit from each other. Arts have always dealt with the construction, mediation and mapping of complex experiences. Time-based artists are experts in moving through time and space, understanding the material and media that is used, as well as the experience that is to be evoked. Art differs from science and engineering in that art is not focused on unambiguous, formal and correct communications. And this has not changed, even though art is using more of the technical tools, based on "formal logic," that engineers make available.

EMPAC is built for our senses as the portals to communication and meaning. Media technology offers new ways to shape media perceived by our senses, minds and hearts, and new ways to direct our interest and the interpretation of what is around us and what is within us.

The three ways we communicate with others and with our environment helped lay the foundation for the specifications and design of EMPAC. The building and its technical infrastructure are centered on seeing, hearing and moving in space. We shape the media of light, sound and the space around us in ever different ways, and they are the most fundamental to how we as social beings connect.

Many have asked why EMPAC's design focuses on just these three areas of expression and perception and does not integrate the other senses like smell, taste and touch to the same degree. An answer may come from different perspectives: looking at which senses are used for what kind of communication; how the different senses are linked to different levels of reactions; how individualized an area of sensorial communication might be; or how it allows communication within larger groups—all the way to the differences between cultures in which interactions are acceptable or not.

sounds, doing things with our hands and using our body (from facial expression to jumping)—enable us to communicate simultaneously with just one other individual or with a small group, all the way up to very large audiences. They enable us to continuously and consciously shape communication; the expression and interaction they control are influencing understanding and misunderstanding in the most direct way. The other senses are by no means less determinate in our communication and in our creation of meaning, but how we use and apply them and how we create sensory experiences for them works predominantly on different scales and levels than do seeing, hearing and moving in space.

The sense of touch is bounded by the extension of our body; in an interpersonal setting, it is limited to the few people we can touch or who can touch us at any point in time. Touching things is limited by our coordination of what we do (driving a nail into the wall or adjusting an electronic microscope, for example) and by our awareness of what touches us (like a hard chair or a soft

"We have all our individually deeply rooted 'vocabulary' of smells and tastes,

Seeing and hearing are traditionally defined as two of our senses. In contrast, "moving in space" is not a proper name of a sense; it stands in here for the relationship of our body to the space around us. It subsumes the sense of balance and acceleration of our body (kinesthesia); the sensing of the relative position of our body parts—such as arms, feet or back—in space (proprioception); and the ability to localize ourselves and what surrounds us in the space around us (including auditory and visual cues).

Seeing, hearing, touching, smelling, the sense for balance and acceleration, and the orientation of our body in space are the senses that are part of our nature. Different environments shape them and us differently; different cultures emphasize or do not allow certain ways of touching; one culture deodorizes certain strong smells and finds others attractive; one culture prefers hot spices, another only those that leave our body cool.

Seeing, hearing, and moving in space, as well as their active counterparts—such as creating shapes and colors, creating

cushion). Haptics, as the study of touch, explores senses in direct contact, literally "in touch," with our bodies. Such research does not need, per se, special architecture.

One aspect of how much a sense may be expanded by cultural activities in a group may be how closely it is linked to time-critical immediate reactions for survival—the hypothesis being that, in order to "open up" a sense for change of perception, we have to be in a secure and non-threatening environment. And the range of a specific sense that we want to or are asked to open should not trigger a flight reaction, as when an extremely loud sound hits us in a very quiet context. Refining and opening up our senses is closely correlated to how a sense drives us to reflexes that are necessary for survival in an immediate time frame.

As an important sense for protection, touching and feeling are equal to smell and taste in that these senses are highly refined and at the same time deeply rooted and linked to immediate responses. They protect us in domains that seeing and hearing cannot sense and that may evoke immediate reaction independent of what we are doing. At the same time, these senses are very personal and close to us as individuals. We have all our individually deeply rooted "vocabulary" of smells and tastes, which can recall or evoke without delay, reflexively, worlds of emotions and reactions without requiring conscious thought or intent. We smell a flower, and right away we are four years old, standing in a warm summer garden at our grandparents'. And someone else smells the same flower, and immediately an image of an awkward moment on a first date arises.

We do share basic reactions to certain smells and can learn to differentiate smelling and tasting and feeling, just as some develop hearing and singing and dancing and painting and seeing —there is a wide variety between us individually as to how we react to certain smells or tastes. But, at all times, many perceptions of smelling and tasting can be linked irrevocably to very personal situations we experienced, and so are difficult to use in the creation of interpersonal meaning, especially in larger groups.

So seeing, hearing, speaking and moving in space are engaging

can be perceived in equally rich and differentiated ways, they can be used in the arts only in broad and mostly unpredictable brush strokes, since the reactions to these sensory perceptions are often connected to highly personalized reactions, which overpower a new context.

EMPAC, as a production, performance and research center, provides spaces that support the modes of interaction that engage seeing, hearing and moving in space. They allow us to interact simultaneously through different senses—that is, multi-modally—with what we can explore in "experimental media."

MEETING THE SENSES

The building and the technical infrastructure at EMPAC are designed to meet seeing, hearing and moving in space equally well and with equal refinement. Human actors and musicians, technical experiments, synthetic environments generated by computers, things heavy and light and dark and bright should all be possible without compromising one another. EMPAC is

which can recall or evoke without delay … worlds of emotions and reactions…"

those senses, which are usually used for exchange among many of us when we try to sort things out in non-invasive and conscious ways. These are the senses we use most to shape and mediate meaning with more than one partner. They are the senses that connect to symbolic thinking and expression, to language, and which allow us to create with and for others who are with us.

It has to be emphasized that one sense is not more or less differentiated than another, or that one sense can be less controlled, expanded or refined than another. Furthermore, the senses are not redundant. We may cover for certain functionality by using other senses if one is not available to us, but our senses are very specific and cannot be substituted by one another. Within the bandwidth of each sense, there seems to be an incredible potential for differentiation—and we can say that one lifetime is not long enough to explore one or all senses to their limits.

Seeing, hearing and moving in space can be noted as those senses that are addressed and differentiated most for communication among groups of people. Even though smell and taste

not built as an ensemble of multi-purpose spaces that support everything on an average level of quality. Rather, the center supports all three modes of interaction, all at the same high level.

The requirement for equal treatment of these modes, plus the integration of highest-end technology that could be integrated with these modes without disturbing the human perception and action, challenged the team of architects and engineers and forced them to stretch themselves to the limit. None of the team members had ever worked on a project that had these requirements. For any one of them, there was no common experience that spanned across all necessary fields. The integrated program EMPAC was to be designed for was not part of the background of any expert who worked on the project.

Traditional performing arts, media technology, technology-based time-based arts, interactive performance technology through to highest-end audio and video technology that still allowed experimentation had to be brought together. The idea that the feet of a pianist should be visible from all seats; the

requirement that computer-controlled theater-rigging machinery should be quieter than previously attempted but still be able to fly cameras or people interactively through space; the concept that a space should support sound from anywhere around an audience; the provision that the orchestra pit needed network connectivity for "computer players" that collaborated with actors on stage; the necessity that pianos and clusters of computer hardware alike needed their specific controlled climate — all these and many more thoughts needed intense communication and collaboration between all parties involved.

The requirements for providing fully for our senses was defined by the bandwidths of our senses — by the range of what we can see and hear, and from how space, movement and distance are part of our perception and our being in this world. These parameters are deeply connected to our ways of communicating and exchanging with others.

All venues at EMPAC are equally quiet; the Theater and the studios are as quiet as the Concert Hall. In technical terms, they all meet the noise criterion RC15, which means that the perceived noise of the air-handling systems is very quiet, one hopes inaudible. The argument that a theater performance is always noisier than the performance of a solo violinist was abandoned. Sound comes out of silence. And dead silence — in a rest of music or between words and sentences — is needed for tension or release to expand.

One of the results of building quiet spaces is that the quieter a space is, the more one can hear other noise sources. Even faint sounds rise to the level of perception when a space is very quiet. This has consequences for the building's spaces, which try to accommodate each sense fully. For instance, all the theatrical lights in each venue are on so-called sine-wave dimmers, so dimming the lights does not result in a buzzing sound from the lamps.

The acoustics of all the spaces are designed to sound excellent without any technical enhancement, such as, for example, an artificial reverberation system. The point being that, if a space sounds very good based on how it is built and how it is adapted optimally to our hearing of "natural sounds," it will be possible to project any electronically amplified or generated sound into this space and evaluate it with our fullest sense and experience of hearing.

All EMPAC's venues allow localizing sound sources clearly, while music can still envelop the audience. One design criterion was that it should be possible to place any musician or any sound source anywhere in the venue, not only on a stage.

The venues are acoustically separated from one another to a very high degree, so it is possible to make rather loud simulated engine sounds in one venue and listen to a flute in the other. This allows a high simultaneity of use; the work in one venue does not hinder the work in another.

All performance floors in the center are resiliently mounted, which supports humans moving and jumping and running. If desired, any floor can be covered with sprung dance floor elements, which are preferred by some performers.

The video projectors yield up to as high a resolution for the projected images as is possible today. Projection screens in any form or shape can be hung or positioned anywhere in the spaces.

The technical infrastructure allows the sending of any audio, video or computer signal from "anywhere to everywhere" in the venue and throughout the whole building. It is also possible to position loudspeakers, projectors, cameras or any other sensor technology anywhere in the spaces.

Machine rooms keep noisy equipment outside the spaces. Lights, sounds and images can be controlled from anywhere with remote controls.

The venues are designed to overlap in their sizes and in some properties. For instance, the Concert Hall is more reverberant than Studio 2. The Concert Hall and the Theater have fixed seating, but both studios and the Theater stage (which can be used as a studio of its own) are fully flexible in how the whole floor space is used. Both the Theater stage and Studio 2 have computer-controlled rigging to fly objects or people interactively through the volume of the space, but the other spaces still allow one to "hang anything anywhere" in the volume. Even in the Concert Hall, the entire volume above the audience can be used to hang projection screens, light trusses, platforms with performers, sensor technology or loudspeakers.

These and many more parameters — including, last but not least, the budget — were juggled endlessly during the design phase. Amazingly enough, compromises to meet the human senses were hardly made.

The next challenge was ensuring that the design for EMPAC did not get lost during the drawing process of all detailed plans and was actually implemented in the final construction.

THE POINT OF DEPARTURE FOR ALL TO COME
The human scale embraces much more than was touched on in this context. It can go in the direction of the proportions of the human body that we may know from Leonardo da Vinci's Vitruvian Man (his sketch of the man with extended arms and spread legs inside a circle), or it may continue in a more explicit way from human to humane, to compassion and respect.

Architecture can make us shrink, and buildings can be designed to intimidate us. And architecture can entice us to explore, to feel invited, to enjoy light, shapes and changing views and proportions as we move through a building. There are buildings that materialize endless repetitions of bare functionality, and there are buildings that meet us with details we can discover always anew.

During the design process, the overall building of EMPAC and all its different venues and spaces was taking shape under the constant consideration of how the architecture would relate to the people who visited and worked in the building, those who came for events and performances, and those who did research or created new works.

And spaces have to protect and create safe environments. We can only open our senses to new experiences if we do not feel threatened. So one of the prerequisites of EMPAC, as a host for artistic creation, was to provide an atmosphere of safety, one in which people did not have to worry for the moment, and where they could feel protected. If creative people, indeed if audiences, are not in such a space, they cannot open their senses, their minds and their hearts. If our senses have to monitor our surroundings because we feel threatened by something, we cannot accept the invitation to step into an experience that engages us wholly.

Creativity can only grow and prosper in an environment that provides safety and security, an environment that does not evoke paranoia, an environment that respects individual differences as they surface. Most certainly, people vary widely in what they need to feel respected and secure. EMPAC aims to offer an environment for those who want to come together, to work together, to experience or develop new ideas, to be open for yet unknown directions.

The Concert Hall was designed to be light and uplifting — the sails of the fabric ceiling, maple wood and white wall panels, the cast stone wall elements with a slight shimmer, and the vertical movement of the upstage wall — respecting the individual while at once supporting a communal experience by performers and audience being in one space, without a stage house or boxes.

The lobby spaces are all flooded with daylight, as opposed to the venues, which exclude daylight and outdoor noise as part of their "media" focus.

The Theater includes intimate audience seating, like a backyard, where people sit in the yard and others lean out of the windows of the upper floors. The stage is only a foot higher than the first row of audience seating, creating a continuum between spectators and spectacle. Yet the stage is very large, almost as large as the auditorium, allowing space and time to expand during performances.

The only space with dark surfaces is the large Goodman Theater/Studio 1. But the black walls soar and are broken up through the shapes of the acoustic panels so that one can have visions or dreams that easily glide beyond the space and its walls.

Next door, the smaller Studio 2, with its white acoustic panels and hardwood floor, seems to ask us to make sounds or dance or to take the atmosphere in and listen.

Studio Beta, on the top level, has large windows opening to a group of old trees. The residency studios, high up in the southwest corner of the building, overlook the Hudson Valley from Troy to Albany and the Catskill Mountains.

The smaller production and office spaces also consider the human scale. The internal workspaces for artists, researchers and staff, as well as the green rooms and changing rooms, are not designed to a lesser quality than the public spaces. All spaces planned as offices have daylight; and windows can be opened to let in fresh air.

Finally, standing outside the building, EMPAC presents itself with a multitude of different faces, expressions and impressions. The low-riding entrance on the top of the hill, not higher than a one- or two-storey building with its curved roof extending off the side walls and its high, vaulted lobby of transparency, stands in contrast to the high-rising west façade at the bottom of the hill that leads into a very small lobby before opening up to the main stairs. There is a riddle posed by the transparent glass wall of the north block, revealing the warm wood and curved shapes of the Concert Hall and the opaque greenish-white surfaces of the south block, emphasizing right angles. The curved wooden shape of the Concert Hall changes its character when viewed through the windows when approaching the main lobby, or when looking down the hill along the north façade, or gazing up the long stairwell behind that façade from the bottom of the hill.

All these present challenges to those seeking to create an integrated perception of the overall building. And the answer may come by entering the building and exploring the interior, noticing ever-changing proportions depending on where one views the different parts of the building, discovering vistas within the building and again to the outside. There seems to be a constant emphasis of moving from an outside to an inside, which in turn is the outside of yet another inside — through the exterior doors to a lobby that extends visually to the hillside, over bridges through doors (which may be reminiscent of Alice's rabbit hole) to the Concert Hall, which in turn may feel like an open space in its lightness and acoustic transparency. And all such movements between inside and outside may be seen as the guiding principle behind EMPAC's program of communication, media and the arts.

Range

Hearing may serve as an example of where technology and one parameter of a sense meet and require the quality that was built into EMPAC.

The softest sound our ears can perceive moves our eardrums by less than the diameter of an atom. The dynamic range to the loudest sound we can perceive without pain is 130 decibels (dB). (It is not important at this point to understand what dB actually means.) Standing inside a symphony orchestra may create sound pressure up to 100 dB. The old long-playing vinyl record had a dynamic range of say 56 dB, which means the softest and the loudest sound it could capture and reproduce extended only over a part of the dynamic range we can hear.

When the CD, with its digital audio technology, entered our world of hearing, it expanded the potential dynamic range to theoretically 96 dB. The current music production standard is a minimum of 24 bits, which can theoretically cover the full range of our hearing, from the softest action of an atom touching our hearing to a sound rupturing our eardrums. So we can say that digital technology is capable of covering the full dynamic range of our hearing.

Consider the so-called noise floor in rooms, set by air conditioning, traffic noise and other ambient sound. Usually, it is so high that only a limited range is left above the inherent noise of the space. In a typical room, we would not be able to hear the full range of an orchestra — the softest sounds of a bow touching a string would be drowned out by the environmental noise.

Not surprisingly, most of the music distributed through the media today utilizes only a small fraction of the dynamic range we can actually hear, and that is certainly not for technical reasons.

In an ironic twist, we have departed from our natural capability of differentiating fine and refined sounds with our ears by creating an environment over the past 300 years that has become more and more noise polluted. Now we have the technology available that can record, play back and synthesize every movement our sense of hearing can perceive, but we hardly have the spaces that allow creating with this potential, and using it as part of our human communication and our potential to refine our senses and communication.

So what benefits does our technology bring us when we cannot use what it can offer? To figure that out, we need spaces that allow us to come as closely as possible to the range of what our ears can hear and what technology can create. And not only in small research spaces for specialists, but in larger spaces for audiences and groups where we can jointly use our technology to our human scale.

Consequently, all spaces at EMPAC — not only the Concert Hall, but also the Theater and the studios — were designed to have not more noise than 15 dB. This leaves us with a fully appreciable bandwidth of 115 dB, which acoustical instruments and electronics can easily fill. The spaces are defined for our human senses and the acoustical environment we have been surrounded with for millions of years, as well as for what technology might offer us.

This is one example of what it may mean to attempt to build to human scale. But it demonstrates that the design of EMPAC, in its confluence of architecture and technical infrastructure, was guided by the human senses, by the human scale.

Acoustic bass membrane absorbers covering the walls of the Goodman Theater/Studio, now hidden behind the acoustic panels (see page 50).

Part II: The Journey

On Complexity

Designers and builders working on a performing arts center need to stretch themselves, perhaps so more than for any other projects they may take on. Additionally, an amazingly diverse set of experts needs to coordinate and align their efforts, including:

- theater consultants
- acoustic consultants
- audio consultants
- video consultants
- cost consultants
- specialized mechanical and environmental consultants
- lighting consultants
- software and building code consultants

The list continues. Even more so for EMPAC, which was not conceived of as an ordinary performing arts center. Because of the many demands of its agenda, it had an ambitious design, complex three-dimensional form and the strictest of acoustic standards. To meet the challenge, the designers and builders had to venture into the development of new acoustic, material, construction and equipment technologies.

As if this were not enough, the site for the building had special challenges. The drama of constructing an edifice on a cliff with soil that was inherently unstable brought with it the need for answers on special retaining wall systems to hold back extraordinary masses of land while anticipating earthquakes. Of course, everything had to be done within a limited budget.

Beyond the conventional construction project triad of client-architect-constructor, EMPAC's expanded corps of participants, roles and responsibilities with formal and informal, technical, non-technical and managerial impact is staggering.

The list of contributors and experts who needed to be inspired, informed, managed, corrected, queried and coordinated was daunting. The manifest (see appendix) includes multiple design firms and consultants, an owner's special projects group, an EMPAC director and his staff, a construction manager and his staff, and more than 80 subcontracts. All in all there were well over 3.5 million man hours[1] of construction time (not including those of the design team, engineers, construction manager, owner's representative or consultants). This provides context for the general notion of just how complex the creation of EMPAC was.

"Complexity" is used to characterize something with many parts in intricate arrangement, and there is no mistaking that EMPAC qualifies. Such an ambitious enterprise requires a comprehensive and clear set of construction documents, a well-refined process and a willingness on everyone's part to adhere to that process. Before the work was finished

- over 700 contract drawings were issued,
- 1,500 pages of specifications were developed,

View looking west from the bridge crossing between the south and north blocks.

- 2,399 requests for information (RFIs) were issued,
- over 11,000 shop drawings were created, and
- over 500 submittal packages were reviewed.

The project's critical path project schedule[2] alone was a document with over 3,500 lines on 400 pages.

But complexity is not only about managing multiple firms, corporations, companies, suppliers, agencies and people who have never worked together. It is about performing a complicated task in the right order, without interference or mistake, on a building that has never been designed or constructed before. Imagine even a simple task that required that many entities and employees plus myriad suppliers. Then consider that they are working to build something new—with no prototype to go by, no version one—where the risks associated with failure are great. Imagine that and you have a contemporary building project. Multiply it several times over because you have a performing arts center, and then multiply *that* several times over again, and you have EMPAC.

Science has many definitions for complexity, but integral to many is the concept of a system whose parts have relationships both within and outside the system. In designing EMPAC, complexity was also embodied in accurately predicting the performance of forces and phenomena in spaces and a structure not yet built: their thermal performance, acoustic performance, smoke production and exhaust, stack effect, day lighting, electric lighting, sightlines, gravity loads, lateral bracing, seismic design and environmental impact, to mention just a few. How would these work together without clashing or introducing contradictions into the system?

The geometric form of the hull, which could not be conventionally drawn in 2-D, dimensioned or mathematically described, signaled a farewell to relying only on two-dimensional drawings. At EMPAC, even "dumb" (static, geometry only) 3-D digital models became more than the keepers of the accurate geometries and guides to the construction. They became important building blocks and provided the scaffolds and templates for computational simulations of phenomena and predictors of performance.

The complexity of realizing EMPAC's four unique venues, the complexity of acoustic isolation and auralization requirements; the complexity of imagining, describing and building a non-mathematically derived form; the complexity of integrating new technologies and materials; and the complexity of coordinating and optimizing a multiplicity of expertise in the design, fabrication and construction required a team of experts aware that their work could not succeed in isolation from the work of the others. The convention of one trade at a time layering its craft discretely over the work of others would not suffice. Structures had to be isolated, complex geometries had to be coordinated and wall surfaces themselves had to perform acoustically. Theater and performance hall parameters had to be met and stretched to perform uniquely at EMPAC. It demanded a mutual respect for the expertise and responsibilities of each design team member with the understanding that the design was integrated—one action would impact another. Each member needed to learn the language and appreciate the legitimate objectives of the others. With respect to the Concert Hall ceiling alone, Peter Rosenbaum (Fisher Dachs Associates) says, "The fabric ceiling was an enormous coordination touchstone for us—how to make every piece of lighting, rigging and audio/video projection equipment work within the structural confines of this fabric ceiling. Rigging points have to pass through it, screens have to pass through it, lighting has to pass by it—a layer of complexity that was not in the project originally."

They had to have the openness and capacity to learn. A theater consultant was important, an acoustician critical, and certainly all the consultants and collaborators that are essential to any building project—but who would be the architect? Who had experience with a performing arts center and knew all the tricks—what it was all about? Wrong question, according to Joshua Dachs. Instead of worrying about how much the architect knows about performing arts centers, he prefers working with one who understands how to comprehensively and creatively address new problems and new building types—fresh from the start—after listening carefully and being open to addressing first principles and fundamentals instead of the "state of the art." In other words, an architect who does not know too much, who is not an expert, but who would ask the right questions and think through problems with originality. You simply have to be sure to inform that architect with a team of experts in theater and sound, and you will end up with a project like EMPAC.

> Grimshaw [Architects] was great to work with. They had not done a performing arts center, but they were problem solvers. Some of the best theaters have been designed by people doing it the first time, and some of the worst theaters have been done by people who have done so many that they don't think about it anymore, or are so tired of the same solutions that they try something radically different from anything they have ever done before and upset the apple cart. There is absolutely nothing wrong with the first-timer—sometimes [that person's] enthusiasm for the building type and hunger to learn about it produces better work.
>
> —Joshua Dachs Principal, Fisher Dachs Associates

Designing and building such complex buildings is easy—communication in the process to reach the goal is the actual challenge.
—Johannes Goebel

1. 2,000 man hours = 1 man year, 3.5 million man hours = 1,750 man years = 1 person 1,750 years or 10 persons 175 years, and so on.

2. Critical Path Method is an algorithm for scheduling a set of project activities by breaking down the workflow into dependent task sequences and times in relation to all the others.

The Selection of an Architect

IT TAKES A TEAM

Because of its ambition, scale and complexity, EMPAC required a special kind of architect. Its success, both short term—with the many choices needed during its construction—and long term—as it served an emerging and in some ways unpredictable program—depended on the dedication, insight, creativity and perseverance of the person and the firm filling this critical role.

Grimshaw Architects is renowned for attention to detail and willingness to venture with new ideas, materials and systems. It has the propensity to accept each project as a unique challenge. It was not just the design architects' reputation that secured the commission, however. While it is not unusual for an architecture firm with the cachet of Grimshaw Architects to receive a commission merely for its name, to its credit, the firm was not the only star architects on the list. It took more for them to be selected, and the result is better because of that.

THE BEGINNINGS

Under the proposition and guidance of Architecture Dean Alan Balfour, a limited international competition was proposed, one that would match the world-class ambitions of the project with the character and capacity of the invitees. How could a project—dedicated to the purpose of setting a standard of excellence, expanding the experimentation and research frontier, and representing an institution seeking to demonstrate leadership, both in the familiar territory of science and engineering and in the relatively new realm of the artistic—set out to realize that world-class ambition from the onset?

> What set it apart from most university projects is that the objectives for this particular project reached far beyond the usual milieu of universities and indeed set its target on a highly professional quality of performing arts media center. The hiring of [Grimshaw Architects] furthered that—the building you have at [Rensselaer Polytechnic Institute] can stand shoulder to shoulder with any performing arts center of professional caliber in the U.S.
> —Stewart Donnell, Principal, Donnell Consultants Incorporated

The President, Dr. Shirley Ann Jackson, consulted Balfour in the development of a list of architecture candidates. Together with the Vice President of Administration, Claude Rounds, they advised on those from whom a Request for Qualification should be pursued. After reviewing their experience, qualifications and statements of interest, the administration awarded four firms—Morphosis Architects, Bernard Tschumi Architects, Davis Brody Bond in association with Leeser Architects, and Nicholas Grimshaw and Partners—as finalists in the competition. They were given several months to develop an initial response to the brief that was to be presented in an open forum. Over the next several weeks, the architects and their teams visited the campus, surveying the site and participating in a programming workshop. They asked questions, interfaced with the owner and owner's representatives, and learned more about the challenge. Unlike most competitions

Early concept sketch of interstitial space carved into the hill beneath the wooden hull, integrating circulation, casual and formal uses.

performed in relative isolation from the client, each of the finalists was brought into a conversation about the development of this novel program—something that foreshadowed not only the design and construction process, but the building program itself.

On one visit, the final candidates also examined the results of a School of Architecture third- and fourth-year studio project. Professor Kenneth Warriner had given the students the EMPAC brief and site as a design exercise, both to expand their capacities as designers and as genuine research, to discover and reveal possibilities about the program and site. In his influential teaching career, Warriner often engaged contemporaneous architectural projects as a device to engage students in design discourse—a book by another name begging to be written.

Dr. Jackson, a person then self-confessed not to know much about architecture, made it a personal objective to learn more than the basics in order to make the right selection and to be an informed client-owner. Balfour, together with Rensselaer Chief of Staff Cynthia McIntyre, set up an international tour with three objectives: 1) to experience the competitors' projects first-hand and in their presence, 2) to find out more about the significance of world-class contemporary architecture, and 3) to visit and discuss similar venues, most notably and prophetically the Center for Arts and Media (ZKM) in Karlsruhe, Germany.

While their teams continued preparing the competition entries, the short-listed architects joined Dr. Jackson, McIntyre, Rounds and Balfour in France, the U.K. and Germany. This tour was the first major step in consolidating an understanding of what a building could be and do. In France, Bernard Tschumi met the team at Tourcoing where they toured Le Fresnoy Art Center completed in 1997. In the U.K., they met Sir Nicholas Grimshaw in Bristol to tour the Royal Automobile Club. They also met with Thomas Mayne (Morphosis Architects) in Germany. Domestic side trips would ensue in the following months to better understand the preoccupations and successes of Thomas Mayne's work on the west Coast and to meet with Max Bond of Davis Brody Bond's in New York.

At ZKM, one of a very few facilities dedicated to performing and visual arts, the team first met Johannes Goebel, the founding Director of the Institute for Music and Acoustics. Perhaps more significantly, Goebel had assumed the pivotal role in ZKM's original programming and execution of the initial and revised schemes. He had worked alongside Rem Koolhaas (OMA—Office of Metropolitan Architecture) in the development of ZKM's first project, and was taken by the work and by the ways of thinking about buildings he could not have earlier appreciated.

Goebel became responsible for the coordination of ZKM's acoustic consultants in relation to its program, design and construction; he also uncovered detailed considerations that could significantly impact the performance of the building and the program. He eventually assumed the primary interface responsibility between ZKM's design team and the client, not only for the music side of the house, but for the visual side as well.

When ZKM's first project ultimately failed for economic reasons, the task of translating the program for its insertion into a munitions factory fell to Goebel. While he is first to say not everything went perfectly, it was his pioneering foray into such a role. Thanks in part to that experience, there may be few, if any, so qualified for EMPAC as a musician, artist, director, program manager and owner's representative. ZKM chose to focus more heavily on the visual side of the house than on the performing arts, time-based side, so EMPAC and its ambitious agenda held allure for Goebel. In 2001, he was brought on as a consultant to the process and, as the story unfolded, became EMPAC's first director. As a consultant, Goebel was involved even before the design team was chosen. He advised on the selection of team members and, perhaps most importantly, engaged early in the process of program formation.

The EMPAC design competition was based on a sketchy if not imperfect program, much to the dismay of several of the short-listed architects and EMPAC competition advisor Roger Schluntz, dean of the School of Architecture at the University of New Mexico. But the purpose of the competition was to select EMPAC's architect, not design the building. For Rensselaer, this was an opportunity to see how the teams thought and worked—to interface with them and to understand how they approached the program and design. Though schemes were ultimately presented and would surely become the starting point, the competition was uniquely structured with visits to campus, a workshop and meetings in faraway places to see the designers' previous projects—it was a kind of elaborate extended interview.

A simultaneous effort to program the facility in accordance with Dr. Jackson's vision included Stewart Donnell, FRICS, of Donnell Consultants Incorporated, programming and cost consultants for performing arts centers; and Fisher Dachs Associates, theater and performing arts consultants. By any standards, these were identified as outstanding consultants collectively responsible for many, if not most of, the performing arts centers across the U.S. Their broad experience with such centers, both historic and contemporary, provided the EMPAC team with in-depth and intimate knowledge of numerous related facilities, and their successes and failures. Goebel's role was early seen as one that stirred the mix and would not accept "good enough." The facility had to be perfect—well thought through conceptually, and to every level of detail.

In unconventional fashion for a competition, the finalists were brought to campus together on at least two occasions: once to see the site and again for the programming design workshop. When the time arrived for each team to present their scheme to Rensselaer, the format was once again unusual. Instead of hearing each individual presentation in a back room out of the public eye, the presentations were open and included all the finalists. In a public forum, each competition team made its presentation and answered questions in front of the others. Thom Mayne stirred the imagination with an ambitious and amorphous, organic, shell-like shape floated above the crest of the hill. Bernard Tschumi presented the most compact and perhaps most easily buildable scheme: boxes within a larger glass box. He exploited the space between—much like parts of the ultimate Grimshaw scheme, but very unlike the Davis Brody Bond/Leeser scheme, which spread its program and mass out around the 1970's Brutalist-style Folsom Library to the north and along key circulation paths of the south campus.

Larry Kirkegaard, Joshua Dachs and I all knew each other; we had worked together before on many occasions. The newcomer was Grimshaw Architects, and they were very fast learners. They listened intently to the advice given by the primary consultants —that we contributed to the process — then to all the other consultants — structural, mechanical, etc. — and honored the criteria.

— Stewart Donnell

Andrew Whalley, Grimshaw managing partner and competition team leader, presented the Stradivarius sketch and inflected horizontal S-curved surface scheme—both conceptual drivers for the Grimshaw proposal. These (and his open manner) drew the audience into a conversation, sharing their reasoning and thinking about the project. Whalley deconstructed the process to reveal the underpinnings of the proposal in intimate relationship to the program, dramatic site and client's call for excellence. Was the key to Grimshaw's success a result of Sir Nicholas Grimshaw's own boldness to declare in his earlier meeting with Dr. Jackson that what ultimately mattered was excellence? He appears to believe so, but there were no doubt many reasons why the Grimshaw team was chosen over the others, and certainly not merely by elimination.

The initial Grimshaw scheme may not have had it all right—the site would prove uncooperative, and the program was to change as collaborative intelligence grew. However, the selection team seems to have rewarded performance-driven concepts that referenced sound as the driver and site as the organizing principle over other exceptional compositional arrangements that favored form and/or programmatic adjacencies.

In June 2001, Grimshaw Architects was announced the winner, and shortly thereafter encouraged to set up shop in the U.S. Having designed only one previous project in North America, Grimshaw at first continued to operate out of its London office. From its U.K. base, the firm had successfully completed projects on multiple continents and had done the EMPAC competition work, with a team consisting of Sir Nicholas Grimshaw, Andrew Whalley, Simon Beames, Kirsten Lees, Florian Eames and Theo Lorenz, but those at Rensselaer wanted them to have a U.S. base. Key consultants at the time included Buro Happold, led by New York director Craig Schwitter, for structural and mechanical, electrical and plumbing (MEP); and ARUP Acoustics, also out of New York. Donnell Consultants Incorporated of Florida and Fisher Dachs Associates, based in New York, would remain, as would Johannes Goebel (though his role was soon to expand).

In 2001, under the leadership of Vincent Chang, Grimshaw Architects established a New York presence in the space of the engineering consultant, Buro Happold, itself a growing U.S. enterprise that had established its base in New York just three years earlier. Not only was the competition key to assembling a highly accomplished, internationally recognized team, but it was also instrumental in aiding, if not causing, the establishment of European practices in the U.S. marketplace—where design and performance had for decades already become a growing concern. Grimshaw Architects soon identified the practice of Davis Brody Bond (DBB), a former competitor, as the New York-based architect who would become EMPAC's executive architect of record, and before long, Kirkegaard Associates (architectural acoustics consultant) became the third in the important triad of architect-acoustician-theater consultant.

With Grimshaw and Whalley overseeing the project from London, Chang played a key role in New York, both as a designer and as the person primarily responsible for interfacing with Rensselaer and a growing cadre of consultants. Throughout 2001 and 2002, his gift for design clarity is credited with bringing coherency to the team's thinking and scheme. By 2002, the responsibility for the project had moved to New York. Mark Husser joined the Grimshaw team, and in 2003, Whalley transferred to New York to take the helm as managing partner. It was at that time, and under his leadership, that Grimshaw Architects left the Buro Happold space to establish its first North American office at 100 Reade St. in Manhattan. Bill Horgan, who had been an integral part of Grimshaw's New York design team from the start, remained as Chang shifted his focus to pursuing other projects for Grimshaw's fledgling U.S. operation.

> Our team found Andrew Whalley and his associates to be receptive to ideas they perhaps had previously not come up against, and they were very inventive in coming up with more than one tentative solution to a design problem.
>
> —Stewart Donnell

Whalley took the project lead, with Husser acting as day-to-day principal in charge of the project. Husser was instrumental in shaping a collaborative approach with DBB. Max Bond was the statesman and DBB partner in charge of the project. Will Paxson (also of DBB) assumed the role of principal in charge and was known as "the calming voice" in times of difficulty. Nat Hoyt was the architect responsible for the day-to-day progress of the DBB team, and under him, Ernesto Bachiller proved to be the solid detail person with experience the project required.

Husser worked very hard, and often goes unheralded in the story for his role in pushing the team and the owner for the highest-quality architecture and details. Between 2002 and 2004, Husser was heavily engaged in maintaining the "contract" for excellence between Sir Nicholas Grimshaw and Dr. Jackson. As Horgan's design responsibility increased, Husser became key behind the scenes, coordinating with consultants and bringing the design forward, ensuring the best quality and making sure that capable bidders were invited for each package. There were a tremendous number of value engineering meetings during those middle years of the project, and Husser carried the weekly burden of fighting for quality and what Goebel wanted.

> The wonderful and challenging thing about working with Johannes [Goebel] is he's pushed us all to go further and to achieve greater technical capability than any facility I am aware of anywhere.
>
> — Joshua Dachs

Shortly after awarding the design to Grimshaw, an international search for the EMPAC directorship was announced. The University needed someone who could guide both the development of the EMPAC agenda *and* the building of a facility and infrastructure that would support that agenda. Rensselaer understood that EMPAC's agenda demanded a particular intelligence early on to shape and define a facility that would ultimately either liberate or limit its users, and not merely once it had been completed. This kind of foresight was unusual. Owners typically rely on their architects and construction managers, and even professional owner's representatives (which Rensselaer also had) — but none of these could reasonably be expected to have the foresight concerning what would ultimately be taking place in the facility or the many demands that the building would have to meet. Rensselaer needed someone who could anticipate the performers' and researchers' needs, who knew what had to be done and who understood the complexities of design and construction. As an owner, they demonstrated an unswerving commitment to an idea throughout the process. They understood that the architecture, the building and its infrastructure would be integral to the success of the experimental media and performing arts enterprise at a technological university — to stimulate a culture of research and education.

It also takes an extraordinary client. Donnell observed that "the owner [Rensselaer] was very firm and also very liberal in some ways during the course of design and evolution of the project." Rensselaer was an owner that could press as hard as any for excellence — with its own high expectations — but it could also provide the freedom to come up with interesting results. Of course, EMPAC was a project for which many design consultants would go the extra mile, because for them, too, it provided a research platform and opportunity to expand their own knowledge base and leadership — whether in the development of new materials (fabric ceiling), acoustic panels, wooden hull or heated curtain wall. Even Turner Construction's chairman and CEO, Thomas Leppert, said that projects like these (EMPAC) are not projects to make money — they are for prestige and present an opportunity to do something special.

A second executive world tour, this time including Sir Nicholas Grimshaw, Larry Kirkegaard, Joshua Dachs, Cynthia McIntyre, Alan Balfour, Claude Rounds, Johannes Goebel, William Paxson and Dr. Shirley Ann Jackson, was dedicated to developing a first-hand understanding of the kinds of venues (theaters, concert halls and experimental black box studios) planned for EMPAC. How can one create something world class without a collective knowledge about what constitutes the state of the art, whether it be four or 400 years old? The executive survey team traveled to the U.K., Rome, Italy (Parco della Musica designed by Renzo Piano Building Workshop), and Lahti, Finland (Sibelius Hall designed by Architects Kimmo Lintula and Hannu Tikka), seeking to ascertain what the acclaimed theaters and venues had done, and how well they performed.

What was demonstrated time and again was a willingness, not merely to take qualified risks, but to explore possibilities outside the norms and to self-educate. Such tendencies — on the part of the architect, the client and the acoustician — resulted in new approaches to performing arts, driven by a vision for creating an instrument for research.

Bridge leading into the Concert Hall

A Project to Remember

Nicholas Grimshaw

I will never forget my train ride up the Hudson on March 22, 2001. The tracks ran through packed snow and ice that seemed to integrate with the river itself. The views from the train were spectacular — a panorama of snow-covered wooded hillsides (and sometimes power stations!) seen across a wide river packed with ice floes. We arrived at Albany and climbed down from the train onto tracks covered in thick snow. Then we were transported to the Troy campus where snow was piled 4 or 5 feet high on either side of the roads. This certainly gave us a serious introduction to the severe climate that we might be dealing with in our designs.

That evening, the four short-listed firms of architects were invited to present the history and work of their practices to the university community at large, and all the firms were present to watch the others perform. The firms were Bernard Tschumi Architects, Morphosis, Davis Brody Bond with Leeser Architects, and ourselves.

Quite an air of expectation and excitement was generated in an overheated and crowded room. There were the usual hitches with presentation equipment, but finally it was all over, and we were much the wiser about the character and approach of one another's firms.

We then departed with our hosts from Rensselaer to eat in the steak house in a silent downtown quarter of Troy, which by that time seemed to consist of deserted snow-covered streets. We all sat at a long table, and I remember having a great feeling of camaraderie with my fellow architects and thoroughly enjoyed talking to them. Sometimes it seems perverse that we have to compete with one another when we can all contribute so much — — although we did form a happy association with Davis Brody Bond, who became executive architects for the project.

The next day, President Jackson [Dr. Shirley Ann Jackson] sat at the head of a huge conference table around which we were all seated. She addressed us resolutely about her priorities for a top-quality concert hall, theatre and other facilities. She then introduced Johannes Goebel, who in several ways seemed to be advocating a more open and flexible approach. I found myself probing to try to uncover the essence of the brief (or "program,"

in U.S. parlance). In the end, I put it to the President straight, saying, "Do you want to have a concert hall of such acoustic quality and of such renown that musicians will beat a path to it across the world, *or* do you want a multi-purpose hall where you can do theatre, have basketball games and perform your graduation ceremonies?" The President pondered for some time and then said, "I think I want the former, Nicholas."

My wife, who was present at the time as one of our team, said that was the moment when we got the job — and we hadn't even started on our design yet!

Also that day, we visited the site, and I must say that the possibilities were immediately spectacular — a steep, snow-covered wooded hillside on the edge of the campus overlooking the town with distant views of the Hudson. This immediately started thoughts of how to use the slope, and, within two or three days, I was sketching forms that allowed the building to project out from the hillside, with the large studios underneath and the smaller ones following the hillside. At that time, I also thought there might be a wonderful opportunity for an open-air amphitheater flowing down the hillside.

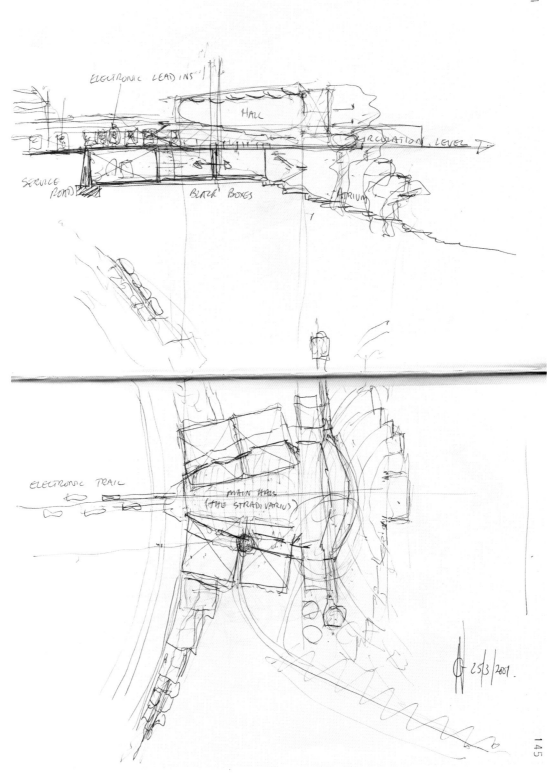

The design developed with ideas as to how the two large forms of the 1,200-seat Concert hall and the 400-seat Theatre could complement each other and fit to the hillside.

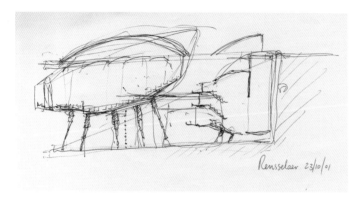

The idea of these two forms developing a cantilevered circulation "datum" started to suggest itself.

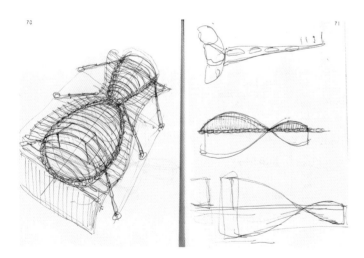

Meanwhile, we submitted our competition design, and one summer's day in June 2001 (the 15th in fact), I was traveling around Regent's Park Crescent in a black London taxi when my cell phone rang. It was the President. "Nicholas, you've got the job," she said. Those of you who know her will recognize the no-nonsense style—and the rest, as they say, is history.

The design developed. Always with the two complementary forms of the Theatre and the Concert Hall playing against each other to potentially create some wonderful circulation space— and of course digging into the hillside in various ways.

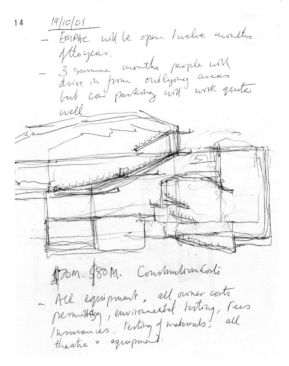

In plan then, I was looking for symmetry with one grand circulation space at the center and the two main studios placed symmetrically on each side.

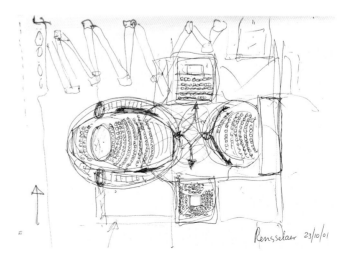

And the idea that the whole Theatre and Concert Hall construction needed to be enclosed in an outer shell, which would act as an acoustic shield.

75

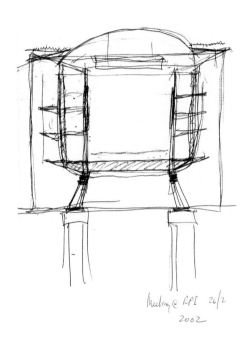

Meeting @ RPI 26/2
2002

91

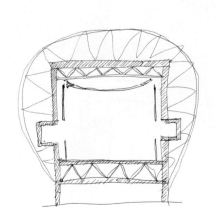

All this time, discussions were taking place about acoustics. For the first time, we started talking to Larry Kirkegaard about the use of a fabric ceiling, which would reflect the sound back to the orchestra and to the audience, but would allow the Hall to operate as a bigger volume by using space above the fabric ceiling.

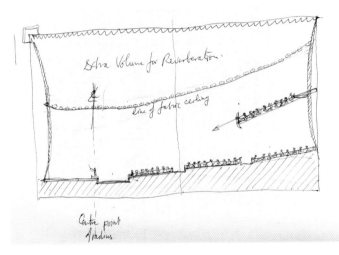

Discussions were also taking place about foundations and how to retain the hillside.

The problems and repercussions of this proved to be a major crisis both financially and technically. I always favored a single, large excavation, held back by a curved "dam," which would have been put in as a "pre-contract" operation creating a flat site for the buildings. However, a complex stepped foundation was considered to be more economic by the construction manager.

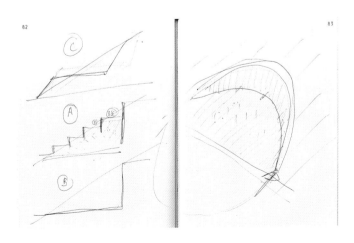

The depth of these stepped foundations was progressively cut back until it appeared that the only solution was to build a separate, straightforward industrial type of building for the studios standing beside the Theatre and Concert Hall. This was how the final form of the building emerged.

Early in 2003, serious discussions began with Larry on the subject of acoustics. Cross-examining him, I extracted the following cardinal principles:

- The best halls (the Concertgebouw in Amsterdam, the Musikvereinssaal in Vienna and Boston Symphony Hall) are all rectilinear in form, with columns, balconies and decoration breaking up the sound. They are all masonry with heavy plaster finishes.
- A "shoebox" or double-cube volume works best.
- The "ideal" size for a concert hall is about 1,200 seats.
- Ideally, the width should not be greater than about 60 feet. (This is why it has proved so difficult to make Royal Festival Hall and the Barbican in London really work.)
- Convex surfaces, which scatter sound, are much better than concave surfaces, which focus sound and can cause major problems.
- There is no real substitute for "mass" in the walls, which would always need an outer protective acoustic shell to cut out extraneous sound.
- A further issue is sound "bouncing" across corners, which should, if possible, be made acoustically neutral.

I was in Philadelphia to give the Louis Kahn Lecture in May 2003, and I did a sketch very similar to the one I show here (I've lost the original), which I thought demonstrated all these principles.

I faxed it to Larry, and I will not forget his comment: "I think we can have some fun with this!"

"What do you mean?" I said. "I've distilled everything you've taught me about acoustics into a single drawing—you should be ecstatic!"

"We'll see," he said. And I realized then that no acoustician would ever agree to an ideal answer. They believe there is a lot of art mixed with their science and like to create each individual project completely differently!

Whilst these acoustic discussions were at their height, our

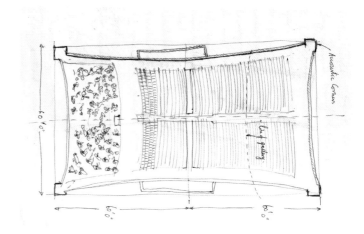

long-awaited and long-planned tour of [European] concert halls came up. The dates were June 30 to July 4, 2003. We commenced with a visit to Michael Hopkin's wonderful opera house at Glyndebourne—not a concert hall, but a beautifully crafted interior mainly of wood harvested locally, a green solution as well as being aesthetically pleasing.

We then drove in torrential rain to Birmingham City Hall, which, although it had a good reputation for acoustics (having been substantially inspired by Sir Simon Rattle, the conductor), we all found to be somewhat bright and flashy.

On July 1, we flew to Helsinki and visited Alvar Aalto's Finlandia Hall at Töölönlahti Bay. That evening, Larry, I and the other team members argued long and hard about acoustics. I would call it the "creative process," which in my definition is a slow inching forward of a central nucleus whilst having seemingly endless design discussions and debates.

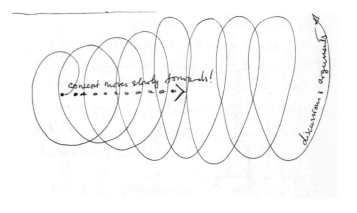

The next day we visited Lahti Hall, a new concert hall in the depths of the Finnish forests sponsored by the Finnish timber industry. Needless to say, it was designed almost entirely in timber—even the walls were ingeniously constructed from plywood boxes 4 feet thick, which were subsequently filled with sand. This formed a massive acoustic barrier.

We then flew onward from Helsinki to Rome and visited Renzo Piano's newly completed Parco della Musica on the outside of the city center. This consisted of three halls and an outdoor amphitheater. These halls were all very simple, consisting of dark cherry wood and brilliant red carpets. Clearly, the shoe-box principle had been paramount, and I suspect the acoustics were excellent. These halls were stark and simple and uniformly clad in lead, which gave them a sombre appearance.

That evening, we all had supper in a dramatic restaurant set in some wine caves built into the hillside, and President Jackson regaled us with wonderful stories of her early years as a nuclear scientist. After this, the design developed rapidly, and a start on site was made on January 1, 2004.

My conclusions at the completion of this grand enterprise are that I am glad we held onto the idea of the Concert Hall being a great rounded form floating next to the hillside. It strikes me that it is rather like the stern of a ship waiting to be boarded and ready to transport you all to the higher levels of a brilliant musical experience. The central circulation is also a factor that has stood up to rigorous argument and testing. The Theatre still digs into the hillside, and treating the studios as a more industrial or utilitarian type of space was, I believe, a good decision. However, the success of a building can, I feel, only be measured by how *people* react to it and how *people* use it. That, only time will show.

In any case, I feel we have made a difference to Troy. This symbol overlooking the town speaks of high-cultural endeavor. Its position on the edge of the campus will be a factor uniting "town and gown" in a friendly and encouraging way.

Construction Zone

The confidence to imagine and build carries with it not only a willingness to think large, but also to design, and work through difficulties and challenges. The EMPAC program, site and design required the owner, the design team and the construction team to address major challenges, some familiar to performing arts centers, others not. The realization of high acoustic separations between each venue — and very specific acoustic sound quality standards within each venue — provided familiar challenges. However, the number of diverse venues programmed to operate simultaneously without acoustic interference was exceptional, and significantly affected even the structure and foundations of EMPAC. The design and construction of a complex non-mathematically derived form also does not necessarily belong to all performing arts center projects. The hull is EMPAC's marquee element, and its construction was no easy task. Yet, it is this form that creates visual anticipation and resides in the memory of those familiar with the building, even from afar, largely because of its surprising bulbous form and wooden treatment.

The challenges of EMPAC existed at every scale — from its planning down to the development of new materials and complex surface geometries to attenuate sound in highly specific ways. The Concert Hall itself tells a story of interdisciplinary design collaboration that begins with a demanding brief. It ends with a specific geometry, an innovative fabric ceiling, highly developed wall surface geometries and even custom-designed theater seating — all of which pushed ingenuity and craft to the limits. But one of the greatest challenges, atypical to most performing arts centers, was the difficult physical site, a challenge that was turned into opportunity, though not without significant cost to the project.

A CHALLENGING SITE

> You have a difficult site, starting with an area that is known and prone to slope failures. The geomorphic reason for that is that you have over-consolidated clays and silt lenses — and that lends itself to be unstable — so you start with a hillside that at rest has a factor of risk of sliding of less than one. That means that theoretically it should not be there — anything can make it slide, and in Troy, that happens from time to time.
> — Steve Coates, Turner Construction

Rensselaer selected the EMPAC site prior to identifying the design and construction teams. It had several advantages, including its proximity to core campus activities, its position on the edge of campus (which facilitated access and service), its gateway opportunity (between the city and Institute) and the potential to resolve a difficult south campus condition. But the site presented significant challenges.

Beginning with the obvious, the construction is set into an 80-foot, 25 percent slope between the core campus plateau and Eighth Street. This presented a difficult enough challenge, but the geotechnical studies revealed even greater difficulties: the slope is fundamentally unstable! Even unloaded, its lacustrine clay soils, consisting of silty clays and frequent silt lenses, are only marginally stable and ready to give way in a landslide,

Scaffolded construction view from level 5000 beneath the unclad hull looking north.

especially as a consequence of any oversaturation by water or even the least encouragement of a seismic event.

Such landslides are not just conjecture. In 1859, several hundred yards south of the site, the slope slipped, spilling enough earth into south-central Troy to "destroy St. Peters College in a slide at the end of Washington Street."[1] Slides have continued in the 21st century, usually associated with wet conditions. In the spring of 2008, several occurred less than a mile from the site. Additionally, the soil types are susceptible to liquefaction when exposed to even a half-inch of rainfall. After only a couple of days of sun and wind, they can shift from knee-deep liquefied mud to a hard-baked solid surface. These complexities — together with the complication of demanding foundation work, dictated by the need to create acoustical separations, even into the ground — were beyond the scope of most projects. And the intent to dig a substantial portion of the programmatic bulk into the hill led to early and significant engineering challenges.

> Combine the design of a large, retained earth structure for these types of soils with a very stringent seismic component to meet the 10,000-year seismic event and that results in a pretty robust foundation structure. Then you add to that a tiered construction platform with lots of crevices, and it makes it nearly impossible for an efficient excavation — keeping the construction going, getting the rigs in and out.
>
> — Steve Coates

Early schemes had located the Theater and its fly tower beneath the Concert Hall — nesting them together in the north block. The south block was in the first version a diminutive, terraced structure housing only the studios, artists and support spaces. This would have required an 80-foot retaining wall to hold back the site for insertion of the stacked Theater and Concert Hall programs. It proved too costly. For this and other reasons, the Theater was turned 180 degrees and moved to the south block, bulking it up to a volume similar to the north block. This allowed the excavation, though still substantial and challenging, to follow a terraced form, in three steps of 34 feet, 12 feet and 30 feet from top to bottom. Even so, Buro Happold determined that open cut slopes for the terraced excavations were ruled out.

> As the investigations could not preclude the possibility of shear surfaces being encountered during construction and precipitating slope failure, a strategy of positive slope support was adopted for all phases of the project.
>
> — Peter Scott, Buro Happold

According to Scott, "Fickes and Regan [1982] had concluded that for all clay slopes in the region over 40 feet in height and in excess of 12 degrees should, at best, be considered marginally stable." But digging in was not the only challenge. Being on the border between seismic design categories B and C, the location would at least require the design to withstand

Opposite: Image of the construction of the Brooklyn Bridge, towering above the city, cluttered with riggings and machines to execute the work (left); Piranesi prison drawing of horizontally and vertically layered space and riggings and activity (center); Construction view of the EMPAC site .

I first walked the EMPAC excavation site in 2005, moving amongst its various shorings, sheet pilings and retaining walls beneath the towering cut into the earth. As I did so, I recalled a certain Trastevere market vendor in Rome hawking historic 17th- and 18th-century lithographic prints. Amidst the majestic perspectival views of Rome, the Tiber and ancient Roman ruins were careful illustrations of equally ancient and fantastic hydraulic engineering projects, dams, great walls and fortifications. These caught my attention. They were neither pictorial records of what existed before nor beautified renderings of what was to be. Instead, [the images] collapsed together what the project was to become with the instructions on how to accomplish it. They included cutaways revealing excavations, shorings and counterweights, along with the invented machinery suited for the task, in a complex and highly choreographed array of temporary and permanent structures. I could hardly believe I was not in one of those lithographs — linked to some fantastic future — something worthy of the efforts being made to create it.

— Mark Mistur

a 10,000-year seismic event of significant intensity. Aware of an existing fault just several hundred yards from EMPAC's site, the owner required that the design meet the requirements of the more stringent design category C (relatively high for New York State). Holding back the earth and building in these conditions — even on the lowered, terraced retaining walls — required extensive earthwork and civil-engineering structures.

Before they could even create the massive excavation for EMPAC, the builders needed to stabilize the site for excavation. After driving an over 250-foot-long wall of sheet piling, the excavation began with the successive digging and construction of king post walls with timber lagging as much as 35 feet high. To retain lateral ground force associated with the wall heights, soil types and pressures, the contractors used this relatively conventional retaining wall with very unconventional tie-back anchor supports — 218, to be precise. The 1¾-inch-diameter, high-strength (150 ksi) solid bar tie-backs extend diagonally as much as 250 feet into the ground (all the way to bedrock), where they were grouted into place to resist the overturning pressures of both the temporary and final building walls.

Two Rensselaer associates were recruited to help: Professor Ricardo Dobry, who assisted in the analysis of seismic and retention forces; and Henry "Hank" Schnabel (alumnus), founder of Schnabel Foundation Company, whose Boston office was involved in the design and implementation of the anchors. At the time of construction, these tie-backs were the longest used in North America, and it may well have been the first time solid bar-type tie-backs were employed in the U.S. Their extreme lengths were a function of a subterranean geological fold — a valley in the bedrock surface topology. Instead of using the standard 30-degree angle of inclination for the tie-backs, Buro Happold designed them to be at between 33- and 40-degree inclinations. This increased the loads on the walls but kept the depth of the tie-backs achievable. Even so, there were problems with

Installing the solid-bar anchor tie-backs (left); construction view of east building/retaining wall showing the anchor tie backs (right).

the installation early on. The solid bars tended to bend and catch on the sides of the predrilled holes, but this was overcome by the creation of a custom cradle to guide the bars at the exact required inclination.

However, this was not the last of the difficulties the builders faced. As they went forward, drilling and grout pumping to these depths using available equipment presented significant challenges. The builders had to deal with the hydrostatic pressures created by expanding wetted and frozen silt layers behind the lagging boards. Several of them cracked, something never before seen by workers with decades of experience in the field with this traditional type of retaining structure.

Concern regarding the instability of the site during construction was as much a factor as its stability once the project was completed. A failure on the construction site could have been catastrophic. To track the risks, Buro Happold specified real-time monitoring of the slope's stability and forces during construction. Ten extensometers, three dozen vibrating wire piezometers, several slope indicators and a number of strategically placed survey stakes were set and checked regularly. Turner Construction[2] hired an independent consultant to create a daily graph correlating data from each device and data point to show just what the pressures and movements were. Nevertheless, the project was not without a mishap. The improper loading of a 20-foot temporary retaining wall with equipment and a 20-foot pile of earth too near its edge caused it to enter failure. The team was able to manage the situation before things got out of hand. The partially collapsed wall was quickly shored up and a better understanding of where the soils (and equipment for that matter) could be placed was ascertained.

Even the tie-back anchors were not sufficient alone. The permanent 20-inch-thick cast-in-place, reinforced building wall had to be constructed on top of bedrock-embedded concrete piles, spaced at three diameters to prevent a global deep-seated movement (rotation of the underlying soils). It was constructed five feet in front of the already tied-back retaining structure. Once in place, the space between the two walls was progressively backfilled. At each stage, the anchor tie-backs were extended at their original angle from the site retaining wall, across the gap and through the permanent building wall. The anchors were secured and capped before the loads were transferred from the temporary wall to the permanent structure, both to retain the earth and keep EMPAC in its place.

The vertical gravity loads of the building are supported on 42-inch-diameter caissons that average 65 feet in depth and are embedded 13 feet into solid bedrock, but they are also there to prevent deep-seated rotational failure of the soils underlying the slope. The tie-back anchors prevent the top of the wall from failing, but it is the caissons that prevent the bottom from rotating. The engineered solution renders the underlying soils virtually irrelevant to the degree that in an unlikely seismic event causing a massive rotational slippage of the hill onto the city below, EMPAC would remain, perched on piloti (the concrete caissons) and held back by the diagonal anchors—even though its earthen substructure would have slipped away.

Beyond the massive excavation, what is unique about EMPAC's construction is the separation of even the foundations to meet acoustic sound isolation criteria. While "box-in-box construction"[3] is not atypical for performing arts centers, the extent to which it was applied at EMPAC is. Studio 2, for instance, had performance and research criteria that required such stringent acoustic and vibrational isolation that its foundation and every part of its construction had to be physically separated from the building that surrounds it. The studio is built on 17 independent, injection-grouted mini-piles that extend up to 10 feet into the bedrock below. Its foundation is isolated from the others by a physical gap and soft-fill material that prevents rocks or other hard matter from acoustically bridging the gap. It does not share grade beams or any other subterranean structures with the rest of the building.

The Goodman Theater/Studio 1, though sharing a foundation with other parts of the building, is separated by means of literally lifting the 4.5-million-pound, 56-by-71-by-50-foot-high concrete box on 149 heavy-duty springs (jacks), thus isolating it from potential vibration and acoustic transmission through material bridges. To perform this elaborate operation, the pre-compressed heavy-duty jacks were first installed on top of a 6-inch-thick slab and grade beams. Each of the 68 perimeter (wall) jacks can withstand 59,000 pounds, and each floor jack, 8,700. The 20-inch-thick concrete walls and slab of the studio box were then cast and, after the steel was erected, the springs were methodically released, raising the studio 4 inches.

Overall, the center is subdivided into several discrete structural components, and each required a separate analytic structural model. The Goodman Theater/Studio 1, Studio 2, the Theater (within the south block structure) and the Concert Hall (in the north block) each required a degree of structural autonomy to prevent acoustic bridging. And within each of these venues, further structural isolations were needed, both for sound isolation and differential movement (e.g., between the Concert Hall and the mechanical

room beneath, between the Concert Hall and the north block roof enveloping it, and between the north and the south blocks).

Because of the complexity and the need for isolated independent structures, the engineers and builders had to stretch themselves. Moreover, to respond to unstable slope conditions and seismic considerations, the foundations' design and their construction required that they take considerable and diverse measures, including:

Layout of spring jacks at Studio 1. Smaller jacks are set on a grid under the floor with larger 30-ton jacks at the perimeter wall (left); image showing the small and large springs used to raise Studio 1 (right).

- developing not one complex retaining wall, foundation and superstructure, but several on a steeply sloped site;
- putting a combination of caissons, mini-piles and tie-back anchors to use;
- erecting both temporary and permanent retaining walls; and
- attacking emerging problems and design changes with terraces and dewatering.

While by no means the largest of Turner Construction's projects, EMPAC had the attention of the company's then chairman and CEO Thomas Leppert, who called it their "highest risk project" at the time. The concern, though, was not the chances of threats to life, injury or catastrophic failure. According to Leppert, Turner faced "the complexity of performing arts centers, multiplied by the complexity of site, which alone was difficult enough without the addition of three other venues, the ambitious formal design, and structurally unstable geotechnical condition beneath." His concern was finding a way to deliver the project "with both pocketbook and reputation in hand."

CONSTRUCTING EMPAC: TALENT COMES TOGETHER
Add together an exceptionally large, diverse, international team of experts, a complex site, high acoustic specifications and complex forms, and the fact that construction began before the design was complete, and one has to wonder, how did they do it? "Fast-tracking" refers to accepting bids in succession as the design evolves: site work, foundations, concrete, steel and so forth. But as anyone who has completed even a small project knows, what happens in the end relies on what comes before. The ability to foresee and anticipate loads, embedments and pathways, even during the foundation stage, required a savvy team. Turner Construction, the construction management firm responsible for delivering the project, had the experience.

Construction view of concrete mass construction of the Concert Hall (left); the space between the retaining wall and the 20-inch thick concrete building wall showing the progressive backfill and tie-back anchor extensions (right).

> It was a difficult birthing process, partly because we are doing something that had not been done before — and that is a positive story and an important story.
> — Joshua Dachs

Aerial view of the concrete mass concert hall and theater/flytower—at left. The space between, dividing the north and south blocks and on axis with Broadway in Troy, is where the central stair linking 8th street to public shared space at the 5000 level is located (left); setting the roof steel (right).

Though a complex performing arts center is not the ideal one for fast-tracking (it's usually best reserved for straightforward industrial projects), Turner Construction, Grimshaw Architects, Davis Brody Bond, Buro Happold and many others rose to the occasion, but not without the efforts of Rensselaer's project manager and Special Projects Group. Rensselaer had its own talent and experience, and where it did not, it hired. Martin

Moore was brought on as Rensselaer's owner's representative and performed a key linking role between programming, design and construction aspects of the building.

> In every project, there are times of agonies and ecstasies. This project found itself sure of that. When you have a lot of inventive brains tackling a problem, then the problem is solved.
>
> — Stewart Donnell

Under the direction of Claude Rounds, Vice President of Administration, Oleh Turczak, Assistant Vice President of Capital Projects — having just completed overseeing the construction of Rensselaer's new Biotechnology and Interdisciplinary Studies Building — was appointed to lead Rensselaer's Special Projects Group in the construction of EMPAC. Owner's representatives are often the watchdogs of a construction project, tracking progress and reporting back to those in charge — but not at EMPAC. The members of the Special Projects Group had expertise themselves *and* opinions, and they rolled up their sleeves, interfacing, not only with Turner Construction, but with the architects, engineers, designers and suppliers — not an insignificant role considering the project was fast-tracked, and had encountered major site limitations requiring a total design revision after completion of the first schematic design scheme. Value engineering was necessary, but compromising the program or quality was not an option — ambitions and intentions for the center and its performance had to be maintained.

> Claude Rounds is a very firm taskmaster and he made the point — we had a program, budget and quality level and had to see that through.
>
> — Stewart Donnell

> To meet the program — iterating, estimating and iterating and estimating [took place]. It came to the point when the competition scheme broke, the pieces were reorganized. The schematic design phase probably lasted longer than most do by a long shot.
>
> — Joshua Dachs

Led by Jasper DeFazio, the Turner team was on site for more than six years, preparing bids and letting contracts, and coordinating and overseeing the work. But they were also involved in coordinating the evolving design, interfacing with the Special Projects Group

Setting one of the Lobby tied arches (left); detail image of the clevis connection linking the tension rods to the arch beams at the lobby (center); custom north wall plate steel column mock-up showing the base pin joint connection (right).

Construction view of a bridge and portal prior to the installation of the wood cladding (left); construction view of the unglazed north curtain wall and metal hull sub-cladding (center); bolts (right).

and reviewing many more novel systems and materials than most buildings require with the owner and consultants. One has to keep in mind that buildings are designed and built once — no mock-ups, no identical precedents. Construction is a complex endeavor even without innovations. It is a complex endeavor even when the systems and materials are discretely layered in stages of assembly, with one trade after another taking its turn. Integration, when elements serve more than one function, requires much more refined interactions and communications between sometimes strange bedfellows.

And this is how the 3-D hull model played a binding role — as the guiding geometry for so much of what was done on and around it. Though it was not the first time a 3-D model has become a contractual document, it was among the first and will certainly not be the last. Increasingly, the Building Integrated Model and Integrated Project Delivery will be the norms, especially on complex projects. In the U.K., the use of 3-D models has been more prevalent. What is different there, is the construction manager is the developer and keeper of the model. In the U.S., where models are increasingly being used to construct buildings, they are developed by the consultants and are often not shared. At EMPAC, there is a hybrid — the 3-D hull model was developed by several entities — from the design architect to the architect of record to the steel and wood subcontractors — and it was also adopted by Turner Construction, which controlled all the subcontracts and was ultimately responsible for the construction. The hull model became the point of departure for much of the work and was the focus of weekly meetings between the design team, construction manager and subcontractors.

> The open process where many disciplines or many contractors share digital information and come together on site or in the office to coordinate is a huge change. … This reinvention of process is, as a friend put it, "a social experiment." It is not so much about the technology, but how it's implemented.
> — Richard Herskovitz, Principal, Architectural Woodwork Industries

1. Troy has had far more than its share of landslides. There was a major one on Hill Street in 1837. Two people died. In 1859, St. Peters College was destroyed in a slide at the east end of Washington Street in an area that had seen several earlier landslides. There were two more in 1890, and three more people died.

2. Turner Construction — then the leading general builder in the U.S., ranking first or second in all major segments of the building construction field.

3. Box in a box construction is a term describing a strategy of constructing buildings with unique structures and systems within larger building enclosures.

4. The EMPAC record for safety was nearly impeccable with only two lost days in over 3.5 million man hours.

Engineering EMPAC

The challenging site is just one of the interesting stories of engineering EMPAC. Acoustic isolation that created the need for independent structures, the complex hull form and the demand for silent systems — each demanded its own innovations, from the 4.5-million-pound studio lifted on springs to box-in-box construction and the differential movements of building components. But structural engineering was not the only well of innovation at EMPAC. Mechanical engineering innovations (though not the first time employed in a building) include a displacement ventilation system, the use of computational fluid dynamic analysis and a building-integrated, heated curtain wall.

Imagine a forest in a windstorm. The trees are independent structures attached to the ground, but they sway differently, according to the size and strength of their trunk, shape (how much wind energy the leaves and branches catch) and location (at the exposed edge of a clearing or in the interior). It is the same with EMPAC. Most buildings are single structures, locked together as a single unit. And though they sway (imperceptively), they do so as a unit; they are not like the trees in the forest. Acoustic isolation required separation between building elements and box-in-box construction. Some elements were stiffer than others, some larger than others and some more exposed than others. But unlike a forest of trees, bumping into one another is not such a good thing.

The north and south blocks demanded different structural approaches: the hull and associated north block stiff, without much sway even under the most extreme loading, contrasted with the more normative steel frame of the south block — ductile and resilient, allowing as much as 8 inches of movement (4 inches each way) in an extreme seismic condition. Independently, this presented few problems, especially if the blocks could be considered as two separate structures with a gap between. However, in architecture, enclosure is about bridging the gap, and the glass curtain walls as planned, though capable of absorbing some differential movement through sophisticated connections and design, could not accommodate the 8 inches that was required.

> The elegance is in the simplicity. Rather than connect to the south block wall through a slip-joint, [Buro Happold] designed a 90-foot-tall super-column planted right at the intersection of the north and south blocks at gridline 7, … and [in the curtain wall] there is a bellows expansion joint, which is in itself pretty simple: two pieces of silicon extrusion stuffed with insulation attached to the curtain walls of the north and south blocks and can allow for large movements.
>
> — Steve Coates

One part of the solution was to build an 88-foot-tall, 18-by-42-inch plate column to stiffen the south block where it meets the glass of the north block. The column reduced movement to a more manageable 4 inches, and, by taking advantage of a sacrificial resilient membrane designed to release in a seismic event without damage to the curtain wall, the problem was solved. But it took close coordination with the curtain wall manufacturer and installers to get it right. The stiffening column was not created to take vertical gravity loads of the building's mass, as most columns are, but

Vertical view of a plate steel wall column, its brace and outriggers supporting the north curtain wall.

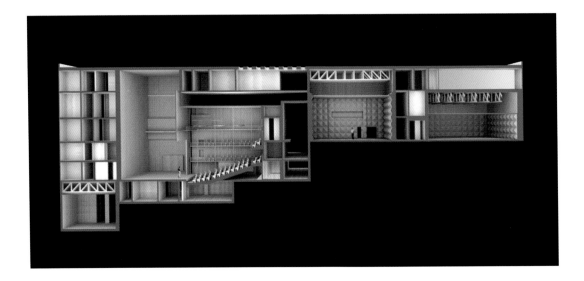

to reconcile the differential movements that would occur in the separate forms under seismic loading.

In the south block there are three acoustically isolated structures that are each distinct from the laterally braced frame of the exterior wall and program spaces above. Box-in-box construction required that their construction be unique and isolated, with gaps between — that they essentially operate as independent structures to the foundation. The Goodman Theater/Studio 1 is a concrete box raised on springs. Trusses bearing on steel columns outside the box span freely over its top to support an insulated roof. Studio 2 rests on its own unique foundation and, like the Goodman Theater/Studio 1, is spanned over the top and surrounded by a double-wall construction with a gap between. Here the trusses support a floor of audio and video production spaces above the isolated studio box. The Theater also features an acoustic gap at the walls with over-spanning trusses bearing on independent steel columns outside its concrete box container. As in the Goodman Theater/Studio 1, the trusses support a level of audio and video production suites that are isolated from the Theater below. Here the upper trusses span over a separate series of theater space trusses that top off the audience space and are used to hang catwalks and technical galleries. The Theater is further separated from the rest of the south block by its towering lobby, expressed in the south façade of the building.

And looking at the north block, there are three diverse elements: a terraced foundation, a "floating" hull containing an acoustic concert hall set over an enormous mechanical room that had to be acoustically separated, and a hovering canopy roof. The heavy floating object (heavy because acoustic isolation required the mass of a concrete surround) is clad in a wooden shell and propped up for all to see — as both a set-up for the event and as the figural form around which the building's internal organization revolve. It, like the other venues, had to be acoustically isolated, especially from the noise and vibration of the mechanical room beneath, the nemesis of so many acoustic spaces. And finally, how would the elegant sweeping curve of the north block roof cap both the isolated hull (Concert Hall) and the rest of the north block if it had to be isolated?

Section of the Theater, Goodman Theater/Studio 1 and Studio 2 looking north.

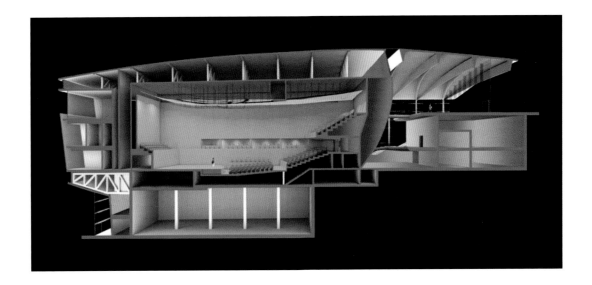

To begin with, the Concert Hall is constructed of four massive concrete shear walls, each 12 inches thick, defining the convex (slightly compressed at the center) shoebox container. These walls provide the lateral stabilization for the north block and supply the mass required for acoustic isolation. Above the concert hall, trusses with two Vierendeel[1] center bays span the 80-foot width of the hall to create an attic space. Curved top chords produce the doubly curved canopy roof. The bottom chords of the trusses are embedded in a 14-inch-thick concrete slab to create an acoustic barrier and walking platform for mounting winches and suspending performance equipment in the space below.

And within the Concert Hall (and Theater), the call for displacement ventilation at every seat provided another structural integration challenge: to coordinate each seat location with the required 8-inch-diameter hole in the 6-inch concrete slab while missing critical reinforcing bars and steel beams.

The mechanical room below—a space made bigger to accommodate large ducting required to reduce air-delivery velocity and eliminate noise—could not be built without having the primary concert hall structural columns passing through it. The solution was a second, independent structure for the mechanical room, complete with a roof deck and interstitial gap beneath the Concert Hall. This gap would also serve as the plenum for the displacement ventilation system. A column-within-column solution allowed the large structural columns of the Concert Hall to be surrounded by four smaller ones supporting the mechanical room deck. This meant the inevitable vibrations emanating from machinery below would not transfer noise to the concrete enclosure of the Concert Hall.

Finally, the massive cast stone-clad concrete walls of the Concert Hall form are shrouded within a wooden shell supported on a steel lattice. Bridges link the floating hull back across an atrium to the terraced slabs and public life of the building. Even these had to be carefully considered. According to Craig Schwitter (Buro Happold, principal in charge), the bridges are "steel-framed slab-on-deck bridges that are vertically and laterally fixed to the structure on the atrium side. On the Concert Hall side, the bridges rest on neoprene bearings similar to those used on highway bridges. These barriers prevent

Section of Concert Hall and north block looking north.

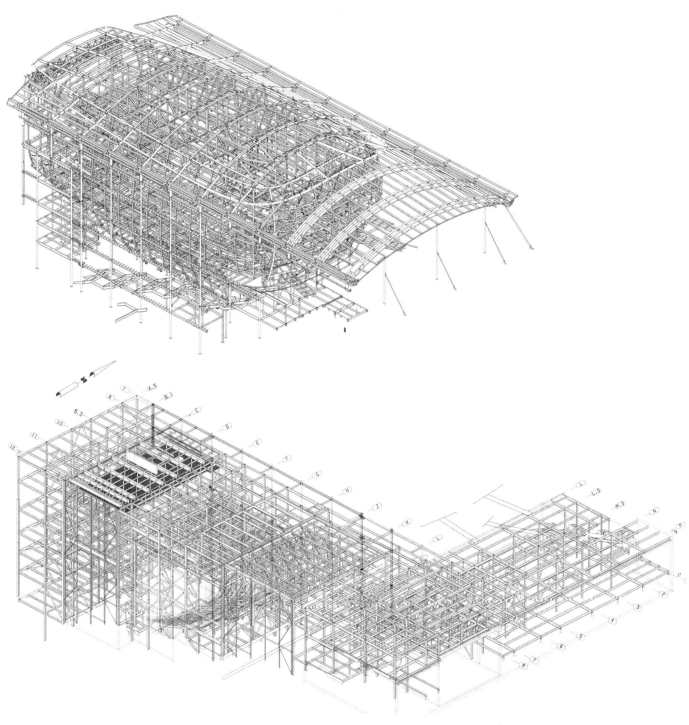

Above:
The Hull and north block steel developed by Super-Metals (top); the 3-D Structural model of the south block steel (bottom).

Opposite, top:
Concert Hall walls and pilasters (left); parterre and gallery slabs (right).

Center:
Concert Hall orchestra slab and access ramps (left); concrete plenum slab above the mechanical room (right).

Bottom:
Concrete Retaining walls and public stairs (left); concrete retaining walls and mechanical room enclosure at the Eighth Street Level (right).

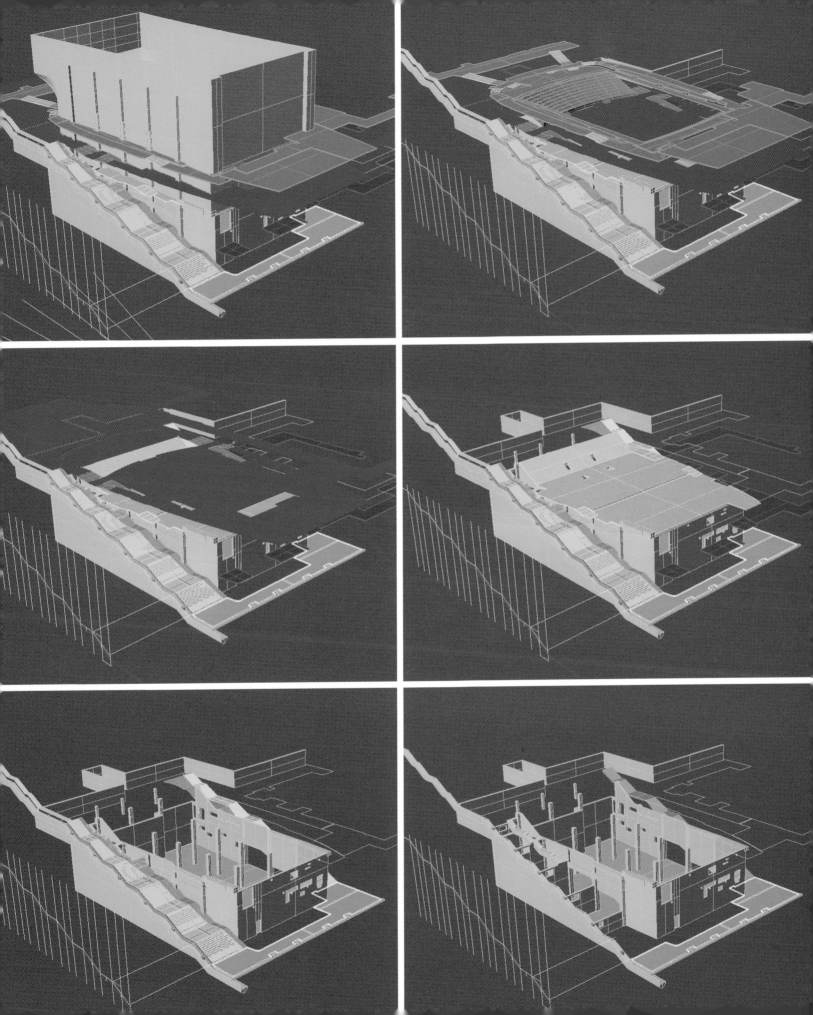

sound and vibration from traveling back and forth between the lobby and the perform-ance space." At every turn, integration between engineering subdisciplines, acoustics and architectural design proved paramount.

THE SKYLIGHT

And just how would the canopy roof be resolved? A 450-foot-long, 10-foot-wide flexible, horseshoe-shaped skylight provides the gap between the pure form and the structure of the hull and its outer glass vitrine. Through it, daylight washes the warm wood of the bulging hull all around. The lit surface, as seen from the exterior, overcomes the reflections that would otherwise darken the appearance of the glass surface and obscure the hull.[2] The effect is to render the glass transparent and the hull in full view, as if the glass were not there at all. The poetic sweep of the wooden form is made present to the exterior, the lobby and the interstitial spaces. The skylight is a truly integrative solution, not only because of how it edits light to accentuate the form of the hull, but because it also had to be flexible — and glass is not flexible.

The pneumatic (inflated) double pillow, triple membrane, ETFE (ethylene tetrafluo-roethylene) skylight provides an elegant yet economical solution to a complex doubly curved geometry, in part because it can easily tolerate reasonable movement between the hull and the independent roof structure. ETFE has an allure to contemporary architects. It is being used a great deal, especially in Europe and Asia, but there is perhaps no one more advanced or forward-looking in its early applications than Grimshaw at the British National Space Centre and Eden projects. Its lightness, transparency, toughness and ther-mal insulating value provide an economy of form and function difficult to match for this type of application.

Without the shadows of mullions a conventional glass system would cast, the ETFE creates a clean separation (gap) between the hull and the roof, expressing the form, bathing the cedar in ever-changing light and articulating the form. By washing the hull

Steel structure at the seam between the south block (left); view of the pneumatic ETFE horseshoe-shaped skylight from above (above).

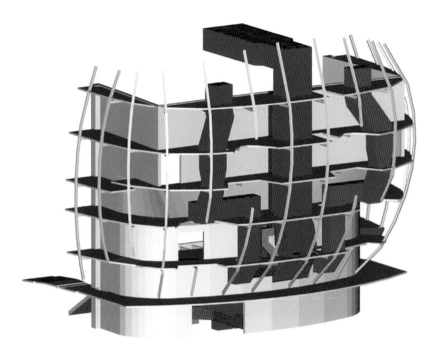

View of a 3-D model showing duct runs from the mechanical room to the attic above the Concert Hall. The interstitial space between the wooden hull form and the Concert Hall within provided the pathway in coordination with the access and egress ways from each of the Halls levels.

with light on the north side, the hull reads almost as well through the otherwise reflective glass of the north curtain wall during the day as in the artificial light of night. The skylight is instrumental in presenting the Concert Hall as a "ship in a bottle," or a "mandolin," forever begging metaphorical reference. But that is not the most important point. The hull demands attention and contemplation. It raises awareness and piques curiosity. It invites the observer to participate in something new—whatever that something might be. The skylight, a structural and acoustical gap, presents the Concert Hall proudly in anticipation of an event. At the same time, accomplishing the required programmatic isolation from exterior and interior noise, revealing the circulation and highlighting two parallel paths up the slope.

The canopy roof also required separation from the south block. This was achieved not only through the skylight, but also through a flexible, glazed clerestory gap where the north block canopy overlaps the south block structure.

But the story of engineering EMPAC is not just structural. How were its systems to create comfort efficiently and silently? Here again, we return to a theme: the better solution is not only in what is *not* seen, but in what is *neither seen nor heard*. There could, perhaps, be no more daunting specification for a mechanical engineer than the kind of silence demanded by the EMPAC program. System selection, design, specification and detailing were all critical—even down to acoustically isolating pipe hangars that could cancel vibrations traveling along infrastructural elements.

Even though lengths had been taken to isolate the mechanical room, it still had to accommodate large ducts and equipment. With a three-storey volume to work within, this required more than a schematic layout. Buro Happold's team developed a 3-D digital model to determine how every piece of equipment, duct and pipe could be best arranged with proper access and without conflict. In addition to isolating sound that was inevitable

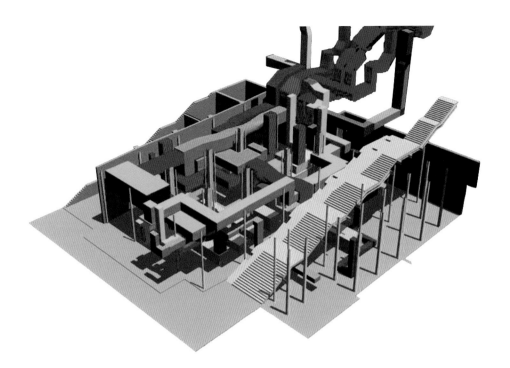

View of a 3-D model showing duct runs from the mechanical room to the attic above the Concert Hall. The interstitial space between the wooden hull form and the Concert Hall within provided the pathway in coordination with the access and egress ways from each of the Halls levels (see page 103).

in any mechanical room, the team also worked to minimize it. Using large ducts to lower the air-delivery velocity had already been addressed, but the team also looked to a relatively new "fan-wall" technology that replaced conventional air-handling units with modular banks of much smaller, quieter fans tied to an intelligent control system. The system powers only what is needed at any given time, saving energy and reducing sound. A mechanical room in any large building is typically a place where loud voices are required and earplugs recommended, but not here. On my first visit, I was startled to discover that the system was actually operating.

To date, displacement ventilation systems had been more prevalently used in Europe, but Denzil Gallagher (Buro Happold) knew it would be quieter than a conventional system. The enormous duct sizes required to lower the air velocity and noise in a conventional system was just one problem. He also knew how difficult it would be to find pathways for the large ducts and of the inevitable noise they would create, no matter how well insulated. Furthermore, heating and cooling from above, particularly in a large space such as the Concert Hall, would have created significant inefficiencies and discomfort.

Instead of conditioning the entire volume, why not concern themselves only with the occupants (audience and performer zones)? Displacement ventilation uses a large under-floor plenum (pressurized space) in lieu of ductwork. It supplies conditioned air (hot or cold) where it is needed, when it is needed, silently. Under each chair in the Concert Hall and in the Theater is a circular aluminum diffuser in the maple flooring. The cooling source, the heating source and the fresh-air source could not be closer to where it needs to be, and if the upper volume overheats owing to stack effect (and it will), so be it. No one really cares, and why should any energy be expended conditioning it? Moreover, as with all performance halls, the many house and theatrical lights at the ceiling plane are sources of unwanted heat, but that is where the air is extracted and returned, along with

> "The design of the curtain wall is very sophisticated and complex. The large, custom steel columns are tapered. They had to come together within construction tolerances well beyond the industry standards."
>
> — Steve Coates

the heat from the lights. Displacement ventilation from below avoids the whole problem of mixing that heat with the cool supply air from a traditional ducted system.

But there is also a balcony in EMPAC's Concert Hall, and the engineer had to ensure that comfort levels were achieved at every seat in the house. Even the balcony integrates a plenum with displacement ventilation openings under each seat and, here again, the fabric ceiling, "lost corners" and "coupled volume" contributed. Because of the gaps between its sails, the warm, buoyant air stratifies above the ceiling—in the upper, unoccupied volume well out of range of the audience.

Buro Happold's team understood that intuition and experience were not enough; they needed analysis. They employed computational fluid dynamics to compare a conventional system—ducted from above—with a displacement system. It showed that low-velocity (somewhat quiet), cool ducted air released from above would quickly form chimneys and drop like invisible icicles onto the audience or performers before mixing. We have all experienced being under such a diffuser, and it is not pleasant. The displacement ventilation simulations, however, showed an even zone of heat just where it needed to be and using less energy.

THE NORTH CURTAIN WALL

The ship-in-a-bottle conceit was one of the signature elements in the design of EMPAC. But making it real, actually building it, meant creating a highly transparent, unencumbered, 94-foot-tall, north-facing glass curtain wall without cross-bracing and with minimal use of steel. But it also had to overcome the potential for condensation in Troy's cold climate.

As with many successful design stories, it is what is *not* seen that matters. The wall was accomplished with deceptively little structure. The elegance of the solution—the custom trapezoidal tapered columns and their apparent lightness—is testimony to close, successful collaboration between the Buro Happold team, Grimshaw's designers and the curtain wall provider. The steel-and-glass curtain wall is tied back to 12 steel columns, pinned at their tops and bottoms, through wishbone-shaped struts. The broad-reaching outriggers transfer the forces from the glass to the columns, allowing deceivingly large glass panels, and surprisingly few columns.

Unlike traditional buildings divided every 15 feet by a floor, there are no spandrel beams to brace the columns and no cross-bracing to laterally support the building. A standard solution would have required heavy, steel column profiles and horizontal bracing that would have cluttered the space and compromised the concept. Instead, the architects and engineers collaborated to develop custom columns designed to perform only the work required and make them visually integrated. Using two offset steel plates, a surprisingly slender trapezoidal column profile was created. Looking at one of them from the east or

Construction view of the north curtain wall framing attached to the columns and outriggers prior to installing the glass (top left); tapered, 4-inch diameter north curtain wall column braces attached to the hull (top right); construction view of the steel north curtain wall columns, outriggers and mullions ready to receive the glass (bottom).

west — and look you must when descending the monumental staircase to the orchestra entry level — you will notice that the columns are wider at their midpoints, just where they need to be. Above and below, they taper to a stainless steel pin joint connection, also expressive of what is happening structurally.

In the opposite direction, the solution is even more dramatic. The exposed steel column faces are only 5.5 inches wide on their inside (south) face, and yet they soar vertically to more than 90 feet — an apparent column slenderness ratio of 200:1, which, in either axis, is practically unheard of. But like so many design solutions at EMPAC, it was not invented to be novel. Rather, the goal was to maximize its transparency, show what it was doing, and present the wooden hull unencumbered to the campus and city below. While the north curtain wall columns support relatively light gravity loads (the winged roof eaves and the glass wall) and do have a minimal number of 6-inch-diameter braces that reach back to the hull, the unsupported column length is still extraordinary. They are an expression of the work they are asked to perform, nothing more.

In branch-like fashion, the wishbone outriggers serve to expand the column spacing twofold with respect to the glass-framing dimension (or alternatively, to reduce the size of the steel mullions between them, depending on your point of view). From the interior of the space, one sees an utterly simple grid of rectangular steel tubes supporting the perimeters of each insulating glass panel. At 7 by 12 feet, they were the largest insulating panels applied to a large curtain wall system in North America at the time of construction. This is surprising, because they seem to exist in the landscape so effortlessly. From the exterior, the designers employed a structurally adhered, "mullionless" system to eliminate any profile relief that would interfere with the calm-lake smoothness of the surface and its reflection.

What is special is that it is not just another planar glass system, bolted into place and reliant on tempered glass that would reveal the roller lines and ripple. The low-iron glass is double-glazed and insulated with a low-emmisivity coating. Though it disappears from view (becomes completely transparent) at angles between 45 and 90 degrees in most daylight conditions, it plays a quite different role at more oblique vantages, collapsing the mirrored context of the valley and city onto its surface. In either condition, the wall seems to be about anything but itself — either referencing the hull (especially at night) or the city, which is captured in its uninterrupted surface. It simply disappears from consciousness and is effective in deferring instead to the hull and to the valley.

The story of the curtain wall is incomplete without revealing that the 17,000-square-foot, 90-foot-tall curtain wall is also a radiator. When called for in Troy's wintry climate, heated water circulates within its 2-by-4 and 4-by-4-inch steel-tube mullions to temper the extraordinarily tall sliver of north-facing space. The heated wall system places the heat exactly where it should be to raise the mean radiant temperature of EMPAC's interior, while distributing warmth efficiently and without unwanted stratification. Mark Husser (Grimshaw Architects) knew what it would take to realize this kind of integrated system and was instrumental in ensuring that capable, high-quality curtain wall subcontractors were invited to bid for the project on a fair playing field. The project needed great engineering and design quality that only certain curtain wall consultants could offer.

Steel structure showing the hull and its perimeter skylight opening (top); steel structure showing the north wall plate steel columns as they meet the roof steel (bottom).

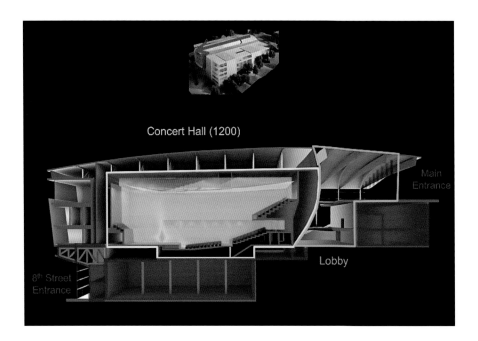

Concert Hall (1200)

Main Entrance

Lobby

8th Street Entrance

Rendering showing the concert hall enclosure (yellow line) with CFD analysis indicating temperatures (blue 70-72F, green 72-74F, yellow 75-80F and red 80-90F) resulting from the displacement ventilation system supplying air at each seat. Comfort is delivered to the audience and performers while extra heat is banked and above the fabric ceiling.

The curtain wall is Joseph Gartner USA's[3] (indeed, anyone's) first major architectural application of this integrated technology in North America. This innovation would not have occurred without the presence of either, or perhaps both, Grimshaw Architects or Buro Happold, U.K. firms familiar with, and not nervous about, employing newer technologies just recently brought to the U.S. Buro Happold's analysis led to the suggestion, not because it was new or innovative, but because it was effective for the application. CFD (computational fluid dynamic) analysis simulated the extreme thermal stratification that would have otherwise occurred. It would have been difficult to condition the tall space without condensation on the glass and noisy, high-velocity heating to combat the cool air draft that would naturally drop down the wall into the occupation zone. Integrating a hydronic radiant wall with a displacement ventilation system supplying warm air at the perimeter of the wall would maintain the temperature of the glass and eliminate the potential for condensation—without the need for fans and ducts, and their associated drafts and noise. The building's integrated heating system was a natural choice, and Rensselaer was once again ready to accept and move forward on the recommendation. The north curtain wall is not only key to the story of integration, but also to the story of excellence and to the allure of the project, which lodges in the memories of those who visit it. It is yet another demonstration of Rensselaer's willingness to think and act outside convention—to dare to be progressive.

1. Using moment connections at the intersection of vertical and horizontal truss members instead of diagonals typical of simple trusses allows easy passage through the structure and use of the space.

2. Transparency through glass, to overcome the inevitable reflections of its surface, depends on a nearly equal or greater amount of light on the surfaces behind the glass—one of the primary reasons why glass buildings become transparent "fishbowls" at night, yet present themselves as black or reflecting solids during the day.

3. A premier German custom-steel-and-glass curtain wall design and build firm that fabricated and shipped the curtain wall from Germany.

To heat the northern façade, a structural mullion system was constructed with circulating hot water. Although somewhat rare, this technology was first developed in the United States in order to cool steel structures in case of fire. It was then refined over the next 30 years in Germany, where it has been used for heating and cooling buildings.

Heated mullions resolved the challenge of keeping the surface of the large northern façade uncluttered, while providing uniform and efficient heating to the internal atrium space. For structural reasons relating to the size of the structure, the mullions are made of steel rather than aluminum.

The mullions are heated by hot water that circulates within the steelwork: glycol is added to the water as an anti-freezing agent. Supply and return pipes are located at the bottom of the façade, and the air vents are on top to allow air in the piping to be purged prior to balancing. The steel plates have orifice holes of varying sizes to maintain an even flow of water throughout the system. In addition to the heated mullions, the atrium has a displacement ventilation system that helps offset down draft and moves the air around the atrium slowly. Air is returned at a high level at the top and recirculated if needed.

— Denzil Gallagher,
Consulting-Specifying Engineer, Sept 2009

"The wall in one sense is very simple — it is all pipe-fitting. You take a 4-by-4 [steel] tubes and weld them together, but you have to do that to match the fabrication tolerance for the curtain wall and to meet the architectural intent, which is high-finish quality on structural steel — no small task to get that done so it fits and does not leak. When it is done, it is the simplest thing. One small heat exchanger in the mechanical room; it does not take up more room than 7 by 8 feet — the heat exchanger itself is just 10 inches by 24 inches across by 42 inches high; two small pumps, 30 gallons per minute — no problems. It heats the atrium very nicely."

— Steve Coates

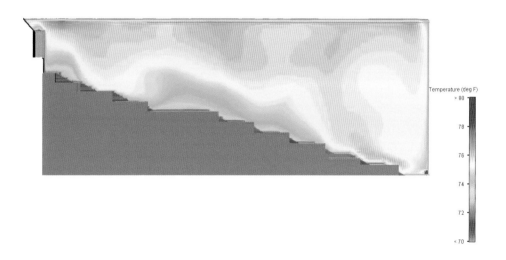

CFD analysis showing the heat distribution at the north façade stairway resulting from the heated curtain wall and displacement ventilation. At the occupied zone of the stair the temperature is approximately 73 degrees with relatively stable temperatures between 74 and 76 degrees above.

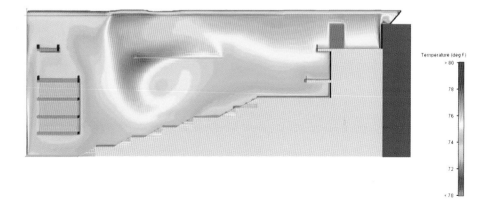

CFD analysis showing the heat distribution at the occupied zone of the central stair. The temperature is approximately 73 degrees with relatively stable temperatures between 74 and 76 degrees above.

The Big Move

The idea for the Concert Hall is a really fine, quality object, sitting inside a shell. It's a great promise, from the outside, and then you cross the bridge and enter into it, and the theatrical surprise is that you don't discover what you thought you were going to. Beyond the portals it's very machined, and shadowed, and feels beautiful in a different way from the warmth of the hull.

— Sir Nicholas Grimshaw and Mark Mistur
(in back-and-forth conversation)

THE WOODEN HULL

Few would disagree that EMPAC's hull is one of the most memorable, poignant and pregnant aspects of the building, but, on the face of it, the structure is almost absurdly ambitious. From the start, adjectives like impractical, costly and even impossible were attached to it. Now that it exists as wood and steel and concrete, it will survive in the memories and imaginations of its visitors and participants forever.

The hull is, indeed, a story of confidence. Driven by belief in a daring choice, the architects imagined and enthusiastically pursued a solution, not merely for the cladding, but for the development of a non-mathematically derived form. The designers had to accurately describe and communicate that form to the many constructors and design consultants if there was to be any hope of an integrated solution without conflicts.

Many people needed to get on board. It began with Grimshaw Architect's original creation in 3-D digital model form. Davis Brody Bond (DBB) was at first reluctant to adopt and fully employ the model, but went on to embrace the concept. Fareh Garba, working under DBB project architect William Paxson, became its first official developer and keeper — a role that would prove invaluable to the coordination of the design and construction itself. When Turner Construction awarded Architectural Woodwork Industries (AWI) the contract to develop, fabricate and install the wood cladding and its panelized substructure, AWI made a surprising stipulation: that coordination between it and all other subcontractors would use the original 3-D design model as a shared reference point.

It was unusual for a subcontractor to stipulate a condition back onto a construction manager and other subcontractors, especially as it pertained to the means and methods of delivering a project. But AWI knew that without a common three-dimensional reference, coordination would become chaos. Since the hull could not be dimensioned conventionally or described by a manageable set of mathematical equations, the model had to be understood as the virtual building. The 3-D design model became the reference to which all had to build.

Jasper DeFazio, vice president of Turner Construction and its point person on site, advocated this approach. The team agreed with him, and the digital model itself, not 2-D representations of it, became the contract document that described the geometry of the hull. It would become the subject of weekly meetings used to check, coordinate and integrate the various trades and shop drawings, and to facilitate the ultimate fabrication of its components and construction. Rensselaer even commissioned AWI to model all of

View of the hull from the north

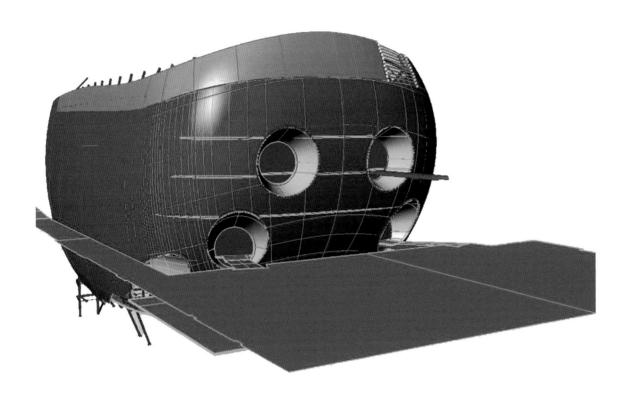

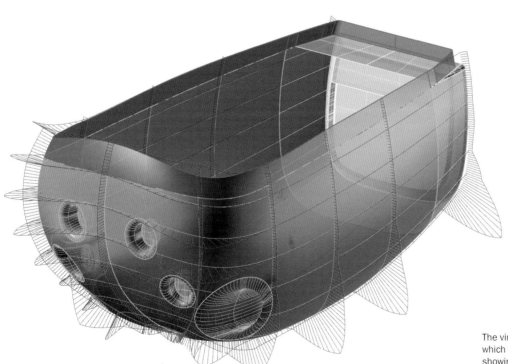

The virtual hull model provided the geometry to which the hull had to be built (top); hull model showing the isoparms — short for isoparameters which describes how the geometry works (bottom).

"In a world where changes in technology make take only a year or two, but where changes in construction can take a whole generation — 35 years or so, we see the huge leap of faith it takes for designers and owners to push these ideas."

— Richard Herskovitz

EMPAC's complex shapes to further aid in that coordination, making AWI the official developer and keeper of the 3-D digital model throughout the construction phase.

From there, the digital model, the modeling software and software training were provided to Jerson Construction Group (concrete subcontractor responsible for the doubly curved concrete walls of the Concert Hall) and Supermetal (steel fabricator out of Montreal) for direct use and superimposition of their own structural 3-D digital models to meet the hull's prescribed geometries. For Jerson and its subcontractor Peri Forms out of Germany (where Peri develops all its complex formwork projects), the model provided the basis for the accurate development of full-scale geometries at the east end of the Concert Hall. Complex double curvatures had been designed and digitally modeled, but the virtual construction had to be made physical; it had to be cast. Though methods of accomplishing such a complex task are enigmatic to most site trades, Peri Forms' German operation had experience on many high-profile, complex buildings and was well-equipped for the task. The formwork against which the concrete would be cast had to be engineered for strength and meet the overall geometry of the design. But it also had to be panelized into shippable components, requiring a consistent match of curvature from one panel to the next. Using a digital model and automated fabrication techniques, the internal framework and enclosing panels of each double-curved form were made and assembled before being shipped to the site from Germany.

From the start, Sir Nicholas Grimshaw suggested the Stradivarius as a reference to quality—of sound and of construction, of warmth and of precision. While it was not a direct metaphor for the performance of the Concert Hall—one does not hear an instrument from inside it—the Stradivarius standard was undoubtedly a reference to the owner's call for a world-class facility. "Strad" became a shorthand that made it clear to the many contributors that there was a commitment to excellence. By extension, the room itself could be built as just as fine an instrument, with acoustical characteristics that allowed it to be played, tuned and appreciated for precision and subtlety, refinement and resolution.

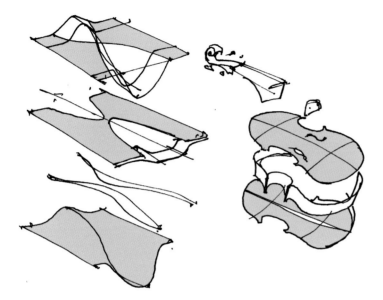

The form had evolved through many iterations, from the competition entry's sweeping horizontal reverse S-curve that envisioned the Theater underneath one side of the S and the Concert Hall on top of the other (a curve still evident in the EMPAC logo) to the more enclosed and singular form of the hull. Changes had emerged both in response to the site and to a growing understanding of the brief and the need for acoustic isolation. The Concert Hall could not share its surfaces with other venues or spaces. The hull needed to serve as the container, holding a space separate and apart for special uncontaminated possibility. This led to the organic propped form encased in glass, the "ship in a bottle." Its geometric evolution is in part the result of accommodating the Concert Hall inside, which, to deliver the greatest aural satisfaction for both performer and audience, needed to be a double-cube "shoebox" proportion—after the 19th-century Musikvereinssaal in Vienna, held as the standard for acoustic performance.

Like the Musikvereinssaal, EMPAC's Concert Hall is focused on natural acoustics, designed for unamplified sound to reach the ears of every audience member with energy and clarity. While most contemporary halls stretch themselves beyond the understood optimal acoustic limit of around 1,200 seats—the only way they can become economically viable based on ticket sales—Rensselaer's mission was not driven by the economics of sales, but by ideas, culture and imagination. EMPAC's Concert Hall is an investment in the kinds of performances that will stimulate ideas and the broadening culture and mission of the University.

The hull geometry serves as an outer shell for the solid, concrete-mass shoebox form of the Concert Hall inside. The space between the geometries (hull and hall) provides access, serves as an acoustic airlock and absorbs the audience and technical galleries. As the project developed, the 3-D model served a critical role, not only to establish the outer geometry, but also to determine when systems, structural elements or components clashed with, or even penetrated, the curving form and required adjusting. It provided the various disciplines with spatial limitations and guidance for making practical decisions about floor levels, material thicknesses, framing and fireproofing, and ultimately provided the source files for the precise fabrication and installation of many of its uniquely shaped components.

Above:
An early Grimshaw concept sketch of the Strad and the double "S" curve

Opposite, left and right at top:
A double-curved concrete form for the rear concert Hall wall.

Opposite, bottom left:
Steel Hull framing attached to the concrete concert hall

Opposite, bottom right:
Steel Hull framing showing the space between the concrete hall and its outer shell.

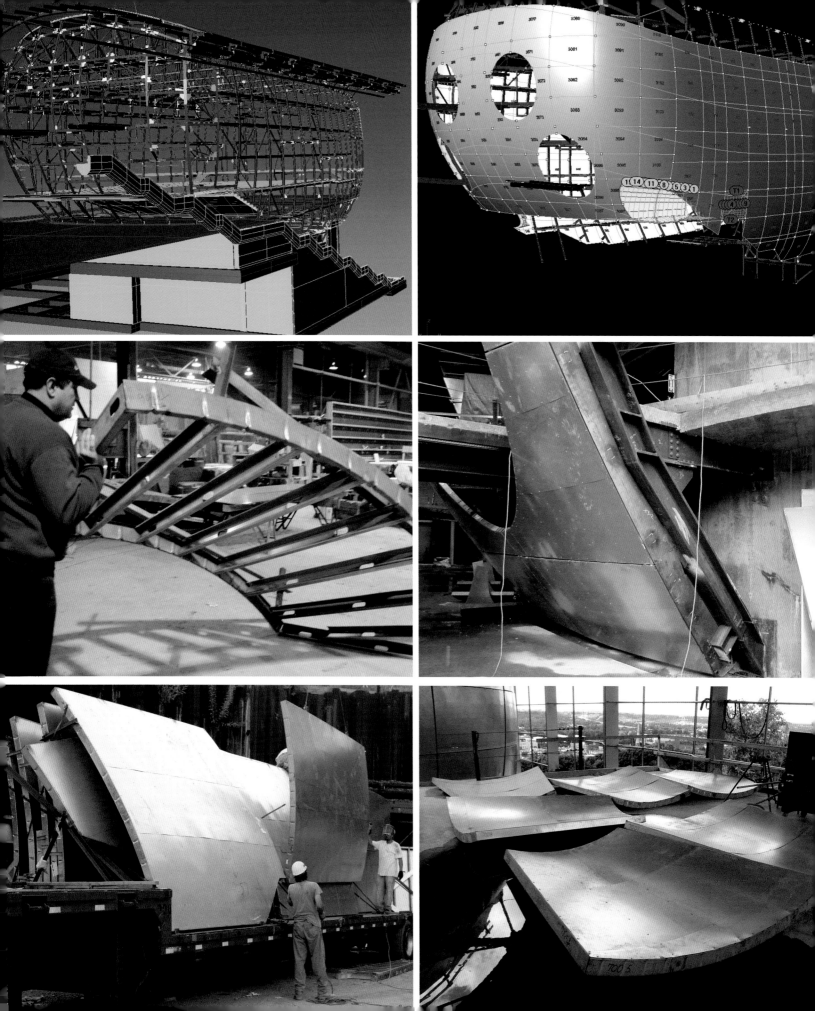

Opposite:
Structural steel model of the Hull (left); panel layout and geometry on 3-D model (right).

At right:
Metal panel clad Hull at Portals (left); metal Hull panels at 5000 level fishhook portals (right).

Prefabricated double curved Hull panels (left); metal clad hull panel attached to steel fin attached to structural steel (right).

Prefabricated double curved Hull panels arriving on site (left); and double-curved panel framing (right).

Supermetal created its own structural model, matched to Buro Happold's steel design and the original 3-D hull geometry. Given the complex geometries involved, this step proved to be another invaluable timesaver, not only for the design of each individual (and unique) steel member and its connections, but for proving the engineer's intent to use less-costly standard, straight steel members in developing its curved shape. Unlike most steel-framing models, which include only the working (center) lines of the structural elements, Supermetal modeled every steel-member shape and connection.

This model soon revealed critical problems. The first steel-frame design would have penetrated the hull in a number of key locations where the curvature was steepest. Without the digital master and Supermetal's corresponding 3-D model, reconciling the two, even if the misalignment had been identified before the steel was fabricated and erected on site, would have required laborious and extraordinarily time-consuming checking in two dimensions at many points and sectional planes. This was something neither the project's budget nor timeline could support, and the reason why, to date, the majority of buildings are Cartesian constructs: 2-D planes extruded either vertically (in plan) or horizontally (in section). Without the integration of digital modeling and fabrication techniques, the hull and Concert Hall itself, as imagined, would not have been feasible, even using modern construction methods.

How would the smooth curvature of the hull's wood surface be reconciled with the segmented structural steel frame? Innovative methods and extreme accuracy were required. Even boat builders were initially consulted, but in the end, AWI, known for its accomplishments with bentwood on complex projects, such as Philadelphia's Verizon Hall at the Kimmel Center and the Boston Convention Center, was selected to develop and install the wood cladding, as well as its subsystems.

To do the job, Richard Herskovitz (principal of AWI) and his team developed a system of doubly curved metal-clad panels that would be affixed to a series of custom-cut, vertical steel fins. Of the 268 9-by-12-foot curved panels, each has a unique curvature. But using automated CNC (computational numerically controlled) tools, each unique stud of each unique panel could be cut, crimped and pre-bent to the extremely high tolerances required. This data-driven fabrication process, which all but eliminated the potential for error, was executed in a fraction of the time it would have taken skilled workers. Being driven by preprogrammed data, based on modeling information, machines do not distinguish between mass production of similar forms and mass customization of unique ones. The precise shapes were directly derived from the digital model, and, because the process was automated, the fabrication costs would not have been significantly higher had all the panels have had the same curvature.

Once the steel structure was in place, the panels could be shop-fabricated and shipped to the site; but how would the curved panels be reconciled to the segmented steel structure? The vertical steel fins were key, but first they had to be accurately described, fabricated and installed. To set the geometry, points were first scribed onto the structural steel members, then laser surveyed to create a digital point cloud describing the actual geometry of the segmented steel structure at that stage in construction. It did not rely on design drawings that described intent and did not have to take standard steel construction tolerances into account. This process described the precise existing conditions to which the fins had to be cut.

The digital design model, on the other hand, could be used to provide any point along the design curvature. These data (from the actual steel and from the desired hull shape) were used together to develop the precise segmented and curved cutting geometries on the inboard and outboard sides of the fins. Once translated to G-code (CNC machine language), the files were uploaded to a CNC laser cutter to fabricate each of the unique fins. They effectively negotiated the geometry of the segmented structural steel frame back to the desired curved hull shape and provided attachment points for the shop-built panels.

But placing each panel accurately would still be a challenge if performed conventionally. Even on a flat plane, creep (accumulating error) can easily occur in a surface made of the assembly of many repeating parts. On a double-curved surface, as much as 90 feet in the air, the need to keep the surfaces planar and to create smooth curvatures would have been a maddeningly difficult task without 3-D set points. The mason's string lines, water levels, plumb bobs and chalk lines served no useful purpose there. Robotic transits were programmed with the geometry from the design model. By remote control, they then projected (located) exact points in space for the installation of each panel, eliminating the risk of creep, so prevalent in panelized construction. In this final step, the virtual model was quite literally linked to the construction site, allowing the builders to realize the complex geometry of the hull.

And finally, but certainly not insignificantly, how was this complex form to be clad in linear planks of solid wood? They too needed to take into account the double curvature of the hull. After much hand-wringing over wood-strip applications (and even abandoning the solid wood planks in favor of prefabricated laminated panels), the design team—including Turner Construction and AWI, arrived at a reversed herringbone pattern of 6-inch tongue-and-groove planks.

Image of model showing curved steel fins (green) on segmented structural steel (red) (left); curved laser cut steel blade on segmented steel structure (right).

Placing a Hull panel on the north side (right); metal clad hull as seen from the north prior to wooden cladding (left).

Metal hull panels at 5000 level portals (left); placing a hull panel at a portal (right).

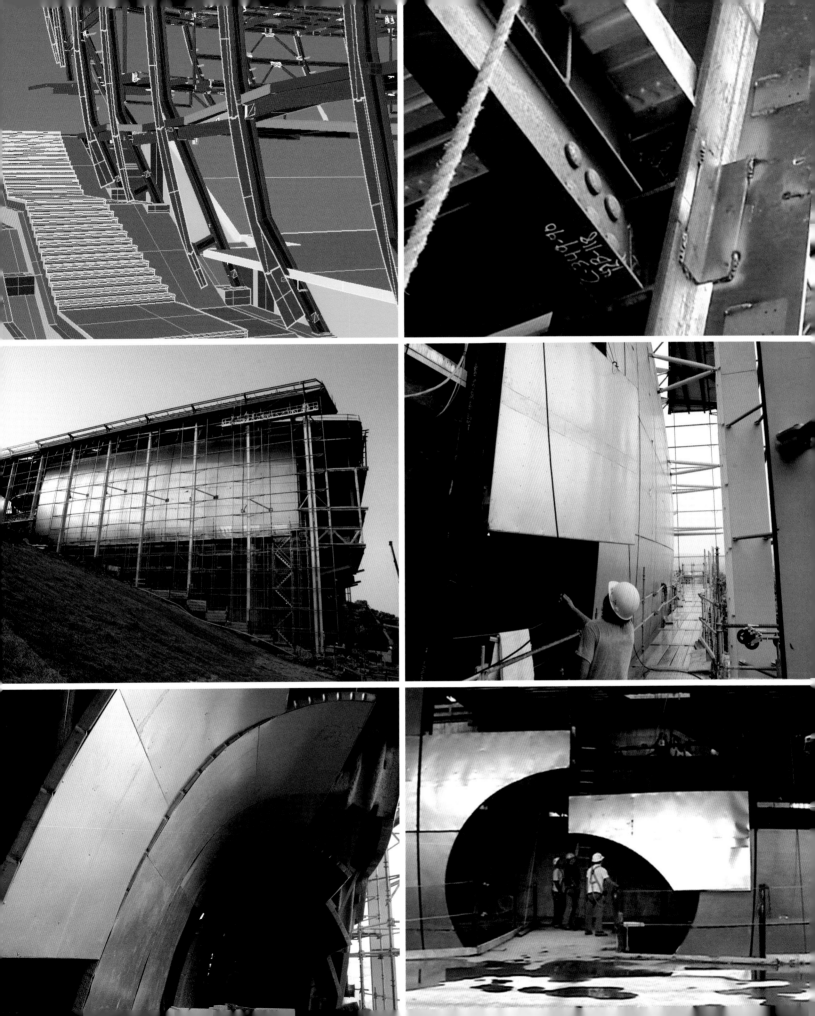

PARTERRE LEFT

"What we associate with musical instruments is the woodenness. And it is one of the materials of choice that we put around [the Concert Hall] because it has visual warmth; it could be sculpted to be very tactile. It has thermal warmth; it's an isolative material. You don't lose radiant energy into it, as you do with steel on brick and glass on plaster. ... So I think of it as a symbol of a warm place to be — an entity that is separated from the world around it, and held sacred in a way. It's the vessel, the temple. You come in and you need to give spiritually to the space, and it gives back to you, but only to the extent that you participate with your silence and then your enthusiasm. And sometimes the silence is the enthusiasm, because you hold your breath."

— Larry Kirkegaard, Principal, Kirkegaard Associates

WESTERN RED CEDAR — FOREST TO HULL

Sailor Nick Grimshaw related EMPAC's hull to that of a wooden ship, and it was to ship builders that the project team first looked. How might a complex, non-mathematical shape (curvature) be developed, and materially realized? The results look easy. But lest any student of architecture, project owner/developer or architect become lulled into thinking that it is merely a matter of selecting a tongue-and-groove plank off the shelf and stapling it to a form, the process deserves a little deconstruction.

The prospects for realizing the concept may well have been out of reach just a few years prior to EMPAC. Before then, the needed geometric and computer-aided design tools were not accessible to most architects, building engineers and fabricators. Of course, anything *can* be done — shipbuilders have demonstrated that for centuries. Thanks to full-scale lofting techniques, handcraft and field processes, and to the dedication of large labor forces, complex ship forms had been constructed from wood for centuries prior to the industrial age.

However, today's construction industry no longer relies on artisans and large labor forces. When repetition, serial mass production, machine processes and assembly lines replaced handwork and one-offs, architecture was transformed. While prototyping and tooling for serial mass production developed and made sense for the industrial design

Wooden Hull as viewed from the southeast.

world, architecture was caught between the growing cost of customization and the limitations of off-the-shelf products. Since then, particularly in North America, architects have had to battle to preserve the linkage between unique sites and programs, at least in some segments of its economy. Architecture's ability to respond specifically was, to a degree, straitjacketed by industry.

But there has been an even more recent freeing of architecture. The move from labor-intensive, artisan-based construction to the use of product-based assemblies, off-the-shelf parts and prefab has been transformed once again by digital tools that are increasingly accessible to architecture and engineering design professionals (and finally gaining acceptance in the construction industry). As at EMPAC, new tools for mass customization have led to ever more ambitious architectural designs in the late 20th and early 21st centuries. Before that, a significant loss of imagination and ambition had occurred. The spectrum of possibilities had been reduced as products and pre-developed systems overtook custom design and craft in architects' imaginations. The materiality of design projects was too quickly relegated to spec writers and to great extent the proprietary manufacturers and suppliers who wrote those specs. Even more insidiously, warranties and liability led to a limited set of options and a greatly restrained approach to building. The architects and builders acted more as if they were working with the Legos and Erector Sets of their childhoods than the clay and paintbrushes of their predecessors.

Technology is as much about the process (technique) as it is about the machinery. The story of EMPAC's hull illustrates how technology, when linked to material properties, fabrication processes and digital tools through a variety of machine languages, enables new possibilities. The options are no longer limited to setting up large runs of singular, generic, modularized objects. The potential now exists for custom realizations of one-off, complex forms — the holy grail for architects. But this is not accomplished merely "at the push of a button," which those at a distance are sometimes prone to think.

Quarter-sawn Western Red Cedar planks

The story of EMPAC's wood-clad hull design could begin with its form or with its material, but in the end they are both complicit in demanding intelligent and informed uses of technology to make the final result look at ease. The choice of cedar for the hull was not only aesthetic. The structural properties of the wood—such as its workability and longevity—its performance (including fire resistance) and its sustainability were equally important. A variety of wood species were sampled and tested at full scale to determine their capacity to smoothly bend around a curved surface. After examining several species and even entertaining alternative panelized techniques, old-growth western red cedar plank was selected for its bending capacity, aesthetic qualities and straight grain.

The design and construction teams determined that the best source for this wood was the Queen Charlotte Islands of British Columbia. Sustainable forestry and harvesting practices mattered both to the owner and to the design team. They had to be certain that environmentally responsible practices were being used. Long before the U.S. Forest Stewardship Council (USFSC) standards for sustainable forestation were developed, the European Sustainable Forestation Initiative (SFI) had been set by the European Quality Management Institute (QMI). These were adopted by the European community as well as by Canada, including B.C.'s Queen Charlotte Island Forests. Unfortunately, at the time the decision had to be made, LEED (Leadership in Energy and Environmental Design), the U.S. standard-bearer for sustainability under the U.S. Green Building Council (USGBC), had not yet recognized the QMI standard. LEED would not accept the Canadian and European's certification, even though one could quite easily argue that the standards were higher.

The design team had been keeping score of LEED points with the intent of reaching a LEED rating—a commendable sustainable building rating for a performing arts center, especially on a green site. Knowing that the forest and harvesting methods were certified

Detail of reverse herringbone pattern at panel seam showing the expressed through-bolts used to keep the plank ends from popping.

Air drying the planks for 8 months

sustainable by the European and Canadian standard, and that EMPAC was on track for its target LEED rating even without the wood points, the team moved ahead without contesting the issue.[1]

The cedar was harvested and delivered to Architectural Woodwork Institute (AWI) in Philadelphia in 8-by-8-inch by 16- to 18-foot lengths. There, it was re-sawn into 1-by-8-inch vertical grain boards. Subsequent shop tests demonstrated that kiln-drying made the lumber stiff and brittle, while air-drying left the boards naturally flexible. Because this was critical to matching the curvatures of the hull, the planks were stickered (stacked with spacers between each board) and air-dried in an interior unheated facility for eight months, between March and November 2006.

Before delving too deeply into the final planking scheme, it is worthwhile to revisit the entire system. Though the hull needed to be crafted to its purpose like a Stradivarius (a precious violin) and the builders wanted it to remind people of the hulls of ships, the actual structure is neither, and was developed as a system unique to its task and geometry.

Starting with its overall form, the hull consists of a bulbous-shaped shell surrounding a shoebox-proportioned concert hall within. The design had to leave space between that shape and the Concert Hall for access to and from its various audience levels, structure, mechanical runs and technical galleries. It also serves as an acoustic airlock and the return air plenum from the Concert Hall's displacement ventilation system. As stated earlier, in performing arts centers, box-in-box construction is often implemented for acoustic isolation. While EMPAC contains several boxes in boxes, the hull is more of a shell around the box. The true and first-line acoustic enclosure of the Concert Hall is its thick-mass concrete wall — to which the steel framing, fins, curved-metal stud panels and wood planking is attached.

The hull's original shape — controlled by the 3-D model — underwent necessary iterations to accommodate the inner form (the acoustical enclosure), structure and circulation

Opposite:
Furring Boards at 24 inches on center

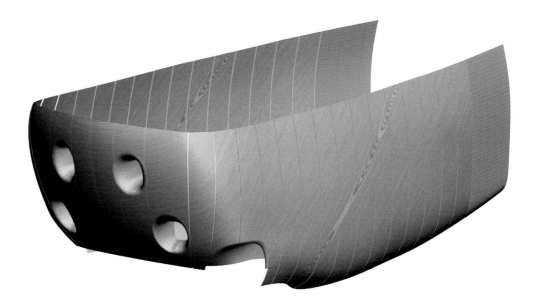

to and from its various audience levels. One could argue that it is a highly rationalized form with respect to its ability to smoothly shroud the Concert Hall and accommodate the various functions mentioned. Or, one could claim that the hull form is not rationalized at all, because it is not a portion of a descriptive geometric or mathematically derived shape. It is an organic form derived to accommodate many criteria, not the least of which is matching the freehand strokes and studied eye of the architect. It is there to create anticipation and expectation — to evoke desire.

Therein lie the increasingly prevalent challenges of emerging design ambitions — to move beyond the dimensionally conceived, Cartesian, orthogonal approach to expressive architectural form. Rather than being based on a set of dimensions (20th-century approach) or a proportional system (classical architectural approach) or a mathematical system (scripted form), EMPAC relies on a virtual construct. This construct is the model itself, and it becomes the building through a series of translations from code to CNC (computer numerically controlled) machine language to material production and assembly.

As we have seen, the double-curved metal panels, each specific to a location on the hull, were, in their design, fabrication and installation beholden to the virtual model and automated production techniques that linked them to the actual building construction. The steel-rib fins resolve the geometry between the segmented steel superstructure and the smooth hull geometry. To these panels, the herringbone-patterned wooden planks had to be smoothly attached in a manner that would accentuate the form and not create a fire hazard. Horizontal 3/4-inch-wide LEED-certified, fireproofed wood furring (attachment) strips were applied to the curved panels at 24 inches on center. They had to be wider than typical construction usually requires so that an extra berth for groove stapling of the 45-degree-inclined cedar planks could be provided. This approach inherently provided the required fire-stopping capability. Finally, the reverse herringbone-patterned planking was attached to the furring strips in 16 vertical stack segments around the hull. Though the result appears at great case in the space, hidden details that are difficult to detect and complex production methods had to be painstakingly developed.

Model showing vertical stack panels

Opposite:
View of vertical Stack reverse herringbone pattern at north stair

For instance, standard tongue-and-groove profiles could not be used because they would restrict the planks' ability to bend to the hull geometry. A special joint with greater range of flexibility to accommodate the curvature had to be created, and it required the custom grinding of molding blades. The joint design that resulted allowed for both rotation and "crushing" (to accommodate joint variation), while retaining the traditional V-reveal that visually disguises varying board thicknesses and joint widths in a shadow line. Furthermore, an extra reveal on the backside of each plank was added to prevent binding and enhance smooth bending.

But AWI's team understood that diagonally placed planks (herringbone pattern) of equal width could not geometrically resolve a double-curved surface. The diagonal curves of a given convex panel surface will always be dimensionally longer than the curves at its bounding sides. While the air-dried cedar could accommodate the panel curvature out of the plane (of its narrower ¾-inch dimension), its 6-inch width could not be stretched (in the middle) or compressed (at the ends) to make up the real difference. The herringbone pattern, using equal-width planks, did not work.

Two methods of resolving the geometric problem were employed: 1) each tongue-and-groove joint was designed to allow a small amount of absorption (1/32 inch), and 2) special "belly" and "taper" boards could be milled. With 59 diagonal boards to make up the difference, 1.84 inches between the beginning, middle and end could be absorbed in the joints. The 3-D model's curvature analysis showed that this would suffice for all but six of the more steeply curved panel segments. In these locations, belly boards were CNC-cut to meet the required geometry, which was as much as 4.5 inches outside the maximum joint absorption capacity. In one segment, for example, this was resolved with a belly board every four planks. The tongues and grooves of the special boards were molded along the required curved belly board geometry and, once in place, can be a challenge to find. Custom tapered boards, especially in the conical sections of the portals, were also CNC-manufactured to accommodate the morphological differences between the larger outer and smaller inner radii of the portals.

Above:
Prototype panel

Opposite:
Circular portal framing (top); level 5000 portal to the Concert Hall orchestra level showing the north curtain wall and view to the north (bottom).

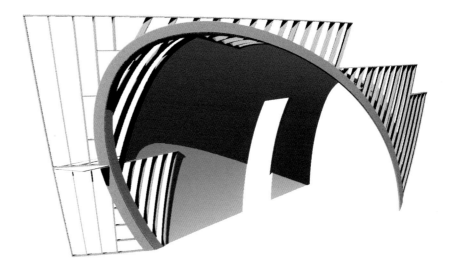

The planks were stapled through the groove and into the furring strips along their lengths, but fastening the ends was a concern. Though the principle of tongue-and-groove joinery is to provide for both movement and adjustability, it also provides a structural interdependence between boards, which is especially effective in maintaining a smooth curvature. This meant that the ends of the boards, where there was no continuity of the joint, had a real risk of popping. After commissioning and examining several full-scale prototypes, it was both a functional and aesthetic decision to handle the forces at the ends of the boards with an exposed through-bolted solution.

Circular trim boards were cut from wider cedar planks to resolve the joint between the hull and portal cuts. While their resolution at the upper levels on the east end of the hull are nearly circular, the lower corner portals at level 5000 reveal one of AWI's greatest geometric challenges. It was not practical to develop these using the crimped and bent metal studs — the radius was too tight. Instead, the "fish-hook portals" (as they became known) were developed in AWI's shop using a grid of fireproofed, CNC-cut, wood sub-framing and tapered planks — with a great deal of handcraft, both in the shop and on site.

But how can a performing arts center designed to safely accommodate many people at once use so much wood product? Cedar was in part selected because it is naturally more flame resistant than other woods. Code required a Class B (2) flame-spread rating, and it either had to be shown to meet the standard or it had to be coated with something that would have surely diminished its allure. To determine whether the red cedar met the flame-spread requirements, testing was performed in an independent ASTM-certified (American Society for Testing and Materials) laboratory. Several 2-by-8-foot panels were created for the testing tunnel, where they were affixed to the top of chamber and sub-jected to a jet of flame for a prescribed period. Each of the three tests run on the wood exceeded the minimum requirement without any coating.

Every do-it-yourselfer with experience in wood flooring knows the value of a well-chosen, well-applied finish. Optional cedar finishes were tested on a variety of full-scale mock-ups, and the final choice, after looking at dyes, lacquers and varnishes, was a catalyzed clear lacquer finish that protects the surface from UV degradation and brings out the natural beauty and variation of the western red cedar under a low-sheen finish.

"Fish-hook" portal framing model

Opposite:
"Fish-hook" portal before cladding at level 5000

Approaching Design when Sound Matters —
The Essential Collaboration

Larry Kirkegaard

EMPAC, more than any other project in our experience, has required our firm to sweep away all preconceptions and to reconceptualize each of the primary spaces in order to respond to the client's vision for their uses. To find solutions, we have had to scrutinize our previous project experiences through the unique lens of this vision.

As the acousticians in the EMPAC design team, one of our responsibilities has been to help ensure the *utilitas* (commodity) and *venustas* (delight) aspects of the three Vitruvian essentials.[1] Our target has been that all who experience EMPAC — whether as performers, visiting artists or guest lecturers, as well as all who attend performances and convocations — proclaim its excellence both by their enthusiastic applause and by their repeated visits.

Multiple mock-ups of the engineered fabric were subjectively evaluated and refined. Fortunately, some of the fabric development was shared with our project at Royal Festival Hall at Southbank Centre in London, where we planned to replace the heavy timber canopy with fabric reflectors. The final mock-ups took place with the participation (and appreciation) of the Philharmonia Orchestra at Royal Festival Hall in 2005, where the first version of the fabric canopy was installed for the grand reopening of Royal Festival Hall in June 2007.

The fullest functionality of the EMPAC Concert Hall required a series of lighting catwalks and overhead rigging positions. These, combined with requirements for multiple performance locations around the audience chamber and multiple

"Acoustically, the effect of floating the fabric ceiling away from the wall ...

Of the major spaces, the Concert Hall came closest to our base of experience, yet it too pushed state-of-the-art thinking. As the iconic form in the architectural *parti,* its presence appears at the top of the great hillside and extends outward and downward within its lofty glass wrapping, finally embraced and visually supported by the western façade.

The resulting interior height of the hall was acoustically over-generous for the likely range of performances. This necessitated an acoustically reflective surface suspended above the stage and extending over the front seating area. In order that this reflective surface could continue over the entire hall, we undertook a major research and development effort to create a uniquely "engineered" fabric canopy. The acoustic characteristics of the fabric required that it be sufficiently reflective in mid- and high frequencies and sufficiently transparent to lower frequencies in order to provide the necessary acoustic information for performers to hear themselves and one another, and for audiences to experience a warm intimacy in the presence of acoustic reflections and reverberation contributed by the larger volume.

positions around the hall for video projectors and loudspeakers, all challenged the need for architectural integration. The architects responded by designing a surrounding technical gallery, integrated at the intersection of the upper walls and the underside of the ceiling slab. Acoustically, the effect of floating the fabric ceiling away from the wall and recessing the technical gallery became an architectural opportunity to achieve the complexity of sound reflections we desired from the zone of the hall, while at the same time serving lighting and theatrical functionality.

The simple rectangularity of the initial hall design was gradually transformed into an acoustically dangerous concave wall geometry. We worked to sculpt the concave walls sufficiently to eliminate the focus problems of the curves. Finally, we suggested that a gentle convexity for each of the four walls would solve the acoustic challenge. That, combined with "flash gap" (where the walls do not quite meet) corners, would avoid potentially troublesome reflections. The architects enthusiastically embraced this acoustically driven solution, which is now an architectural feature of the Concert Hall.

We advocated for massive walls to support the full frequency range of musical sound in the Hall, including the very lowest frequency sounds that provide the *gravitas* to and fundament of music. We also sought to achieve a sculptural richness of surfaces to provide a gentle blending of sound. This goal was acknowledged and celebrated by the architects in their use of cast stone finishes for the upper wall surfaces and carefully detailed wood paneling for the lower wall surfaces. The acoustic behavior of these sculpted surfaces was refined in acoustic testing and "auditioning" to confirm that there would be no undesirable coloration or distortion.

Finally, the gloriously supportive liveliness that all these design imperatives would achieve in the Hall for unamplified

absorptive materials on all available surfaces, yet there was a desire to not have the space feel acoustically dead. In its more lively modes of use, the sound needed to be well diffused over a broad frequency range—ideally tunable in its diffuseness.

These desires and requirements led to the development of tunable, diffusely reflective modules with individually adjustable roll/tilt/yaw set a short distance away from the backup surfaces. These modules were developed in collaboration with the design architect, working from acoustic theory. Small-scale mock-ups were fabricated and tested to prove the design concept. Further refinements were retested in room-sized mock-ups until we were satisfied with their individual as well as interactive performance. When we were totally satisfied, we sent the digital files to fabrica-

became an architectural opportunity to achieve the complexity of sound..."

performances could make the Hall overly reverberant for highly amplified uses. This required a bold approach to acoustics tuning capability. The design response for this tunability is a full complement of motorized acoustic banners comprising double layers of heavy fabric that deploy from above the technical gallery. These banners can be preset for a range of control appropriate to a variety of uses. When even more control is required for powerful low-frequency sound, a system of horizontally tracked glass fiber panels that we developed is located above the upper rear portion of the fabric ceiling system.

Studio 1 (the Goodman Theater/Studio 1) has posed the greatest acoustical challenges of the EMPAC project. Its functionality as the "visual" studio required a very large physical volume —a volume that without significant intervention would sustain incredibly long reverberation. Its isolation from other spaces in the building required that the walls be massive. That would have meant that the already long reverberation through most of the frequency range would have been excessively long at low frequencies. This issue could have been solved by placing sound-

tors to prepare the flexible molds used for casting the glass fiber-reinforced gypsum panels. This was a grand collaboration of architect, acoustician and fabricator, as well as EMPAC staff who developed the mounting hardware that ultimately allows for a very flexible range of motion necessary for tuning the panels.

Partially absorptive, modular panels are provided to complement and enable interchangeability with the diffusely reflective panels. Too often absorptive panels are designed to be overly efficient: absorbing so much sound energy that people feel uncomfortable being close to them. We call this the "black hole effect"—an evolutionary protective instinct. We designed these absorptive panels to provide relatively modest levels of absorption so they would be "friendly" at close proximity.

The amazingly broad range of uses of this space required a very broad range of acoustic control—control to tune the liveliness of the space and to tune the balance of high, middle, low and very low frequencies. How to accomplish this challenged our technical understanding and sparked our creativity. Tunable mid- and high-frequency absorption is integrated along the wall

surfaces using a double-layer fabric banner system. To provide a basic amount of deep bass absorption in this otherwise massive space, we developed a system of tunable, thin-plywood-covered "boxes" that is located behind the diffusing panels. The thin plywood acts as a drumhead that vibrates in response to sound in the room. The frequency at which the membrane vibrates is the frequency at which it absorbs sound from the room. The pitch depends on the thickness of the plywood and the depth of the airspace behind.

These are useful, but are only for the first tuning of the room. Because the balance of deep bass absorption needed to be more readily adjustable, we developed a system of horizontally tracked glass fiber panels located in the volume above the stretched-wire technical grid. These work in the same way as those above the rear ceiling of the Concert Hall.

THE PROCESS

This extraordinary project has profoundly touched all who have participated in its creation and realization. The design team was challenged to respond to a complex functional vision and inherent expectation of unprecedented excellence. Compounding those challenges were budget problems, construction delays, site difficulties and a too-late recognition of the profound complexities of this uniquely complicated building.

That said, all those who helped to breathe life into this building are still emotionally engaged and taking pride in the emergence of our "dream building." We willed it to emerge as the best of our collective efforts, and we carry away from this experience the clear sense that we have grown in wisdom and stature both individually and collectively as a team.

This building that we have known through its creation will now develop a rich and exciting life of its own. Whatever challenges we experienced are now overwhelmed by the magic and joy of those who are experiencing EMPAC with the full sense of wonderment it deserves. In the end, we all will be transformed as this building we helped create inspires fertile creativity in those who embrace its vision and awesome capabilities.

Testing one of the iterations of the acoustic panels with acoustic music (top); close-up of the surface of the final panel (bottom).

1. In his 10-book treatise on architecture, ancient Roman architect Vitruvius named three essentials that must be considered: *utilitas* (commodity/function), *firmitas* (structure) and *venustas* (delight/beauty).

Soundspace

SOUND OF SILENCE

The spaces between EMPAC's venues might not be considered important to this story. After all, no performances are held there. But, since they are adjacent to and even envelop the venues where performances do take place, their acoustical function and characteristics are quite relevant. They provide — they are — the isolating gaps between the main venues, and they are opportunistically exploited to fill a number of important programmatic roles. The monumental open stairways provide circulation to the various levels. The lobby is both a gathering point and a crossroads. The café serves as a campus living room and mixer of communities. People talk, laugh, clatter forks and otherwise create sounds in these spaces, so it is not surprising that isolating the venues impacted the formal design, structure and detailing of EMPAC.

Requiring 120-decibel isolation at 63 hertz attenuated to inaudibility in the adjacent venues was a veritable act of *de rigueur* in EMPAC's architecture and engineering. But without this effort, the center would be a facility capable of doing only one thing well at a time. It would not support a program that enables multifarious engagements. Without attention to sound isolation throughout, EMPAC could not legitimately claim excellence with respect to performance criteria. What the acoustic designers first needed to create was the sound of silence. What truly matters is the interruptions that will *not* be noticed, the interference that will *not* occur, the parts of the program and parameters of the building that will *not* be discussed unless or until they fail.

How quiet is quiet? EMPAC isolates sound to a degree unlike almost any place with which we are familiar, creating a level of quietness that provides the space for sound, awareness of its presence, color and quality. Johannes Goebel called for spaces of "high resolution," providing artists and audiences with a rarefied possibility of hearing, and hearing with exceptional clarity.

It is said that today there is virtually no place on this planet where the sound of an engine cannot be heard. Stop — listen, and listen carefully. How many engine sounds can you distinguish? If you were in the U.S. on September 12, 2001, do you remember the eerie silence? Goebel argues that human perception has compensated by tuning out of consciousness this constant noise level, thereby restricting aural perception. EMPAC's venues provide the opportunity to hear what is lost anywhere else, masked by the white and gray and collaged noises that permeate our lives — from machines.

> We are so accustomed to noise. If it gets too quiet around us, we make our own noise. We're never quite connected with the silence.
>
> — Larry Kirkegaard

In their silence, the Concert Hall, the Goodman Theater/Studio 1, the 400-seat Theater and Studio 2 are all places that seem to yearn for sound — distinct, subtle and resolute sound. For generations, these venues will be exercised and explored, and even challenged through the works of artists, performers and researchers. EMPAC expands the conscious spectrum — to exercise and discover the possibility of sound and perception.

Acoustic panels in Goodman Theater/Studio1: the reflective panels are absorptive, the matte panels are diffusive.

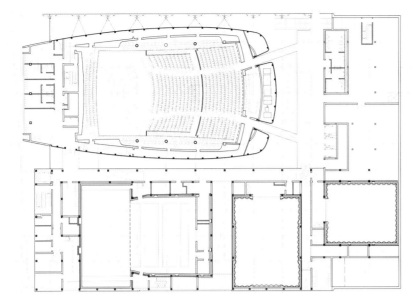

But this expansion is not only aural. The facility serves the eye as well as the ear. The visualization of the aural in the architecture, and the auralization of the visual, if you will, is in the sculpting of surface and form.

ENGINEERING FOR THE EAR: VARIATIONS ON A THEME
Masters of acoustics are artists as well as engineers. More, they are collaborative artists in the manner of those who design lighting and sets. Like artists, acousticians make a vital contribution to the expression of artistic work. But perhaps more than any other collaborator, they make choices and create options in advance. They have responsibility for anticipating every reasonable (and perhaps unreasonable) acoustic use of their designs.

With this in mind, imagine the shaping of sound—sound sculpting—in the face of the requirements specified for EMPAC. The project called for four distinct venues: an acoustic concert hall, a 400-seat theater and two black box studios—all needing complete acoustic isolation to facilitate simultaneous experimental, rehearsal or performance use without interference. And within, the call was for near silence, reverberation times specific to their use, the desire to achieve certain highly specific qualities of sound *and* flexibility. Such demanding standards are expected of very few, if any, centers.

Certainly, nowhere else can this combination of venues with the highest-end technical infrastructure be found under one roof. This is because there is no other performing arts center with the same expectation for experimentation and research—a core mission of EMPAC. The stringent acoustic isolation requirements had to allow a heavily amplified performance pressing the upper limits of sound in one, and the sounds of subtlety, perhaps barely perceptible and requiring a tuned strained ear, in an adjacent venue without any interference.

To achieve this requires stretching a sound sculptor's craft, forcing the individual to consider every option for the reflection, absorption and diffusion of sound for composition and performance as they emerge and play out isolated within the space of any given venue. And, if that were not enough, any material or device used to reach the ambitious goals for sound within the EMPAC

Plan of the 6000 level showing the four major venues and in particular the convex sidewalls of the Concert Hall, designed to eliminate flutter and standing waves.

venues needed to be in harmony with the visual design. Awkward, unsightly
or visually incongruous solutions would not be acceptable. [Johannes Goebel]
talked about eyes and ears quite a lot, and was very clear in many meetings
over the course of the entire design process that we were not letting sound
design this building, that this was a building that was an architectural statement of very exacting visual *and* acoustic standards.

—Carl Giegold, Kirkegaard Associates

So, how was the "sound of silence" both within and between the venues to be addressed?
What approaches could successfully shape sound and sculpt environments designed to
specific acoustic performance demands? How did acoustic standards contribute to the
design and realization of EMPAC?

It begins with a performance solution that acoustically isolates the venues at the scale
of the building and its forms. Much of this work—physical isolation, providing separate
supports for venues and setting a whole studio on springs—has been described in the
chapter on EMPAC's construction. Without this work, efforts that shaped and articulated
each venue to meet its own acoustic and visual performance parameters and desires
would have been in vain. But, conceding those contributions, let us examine the individual venues, one by one.

Johannes has challenged us; he challenged us for the vision of the building, as
no one else has articulated in any other project that we've been involved in. And
it forced us to answer him in tactical ways, in experiential ways, and we came
up short in being able to answer all of those questions to his satisfaction, and
often times to our own satisfaction. We were deeply searching our wisdom and
experience, our knowledge. So both to serve the project and to enrich our own
practice, we invested in doing experimentation, doing mock-ups, developing
testing techniques to be able to explore materiality and combinations of things.

—Larry Kirkegaard

Vienna's Musikvereinssaal is credited for its exceptional acoustics and the basis for the double shoebox proportion and size adopted at EMPAC.

Concert Hall

Of all the venues, the Concert Hall is the largest and has the most varied acoustic demands. It had to be first and foremost a world-class facility for a full orchestra, but it also had to do more. With that goal came perhaps the greatest number of associated innovations, including its curved sidewalls, "lost corners," fabric ceiling, material selections and surface articulations. The Concert Hall had to have a live sound, so it was designed to achieve a reverberation time of two to three seconds, like that of the world's most acclaimed acoustic halls. It was optimized for acoustic (unamplified) concert performances, from solo to full orchestra to the spoken word. It was designed as a single large room with equal attention to the ear of the performer and the ear of the audience, but it was also designed with drop-down absorptive wall banners, side galleries and a large upper volume, which, together with an acoustically transparent (to bass frequencies) ceiling, assists in handling amplified events and concerts with loudspeaker projections all around you—something few acoustic halls do well.

> We felt very strongly that it needed to have some additional volume to be able to accommodate that loudness without overloading. So, if you look at that overlay, of Ozawa Hall [Seiji Ozawa Hall at Tanglewood] and EMPAC's Concert Hall, you'll see great similarities in the length and the width of the room, and you can see that this is a child of those volumes even though it's a little bit higher.
>
> Because of the hull shape that encloses the actual acoustic volume of the Concert Hall, there's a double wall. At the top of the hall, we used the space of the double wall [technical gallery] to catch the sound and scatter it around a bit, above the fabric of the ceiling, before sending it back down to the audience, and do that in such a way that the sound is so dispersed in time that we lose the echo that corners would otherwise produce. There's an elegance to the way the visual goals of the hall have a synergy with its technical requirements.
>
> —Carl Giegold

The upper balcony, side galleries and upstage wall of the Concert Hall were all designed in a close collaboration between the architects and acousticians. Bill Horgan (Grimshaw Architects) and Carl Giegold (Kirkegaard Associates) both championed a mutual desire to visually reveal the hall's acoustic performance. Look closely at the elongated dimples of the cast stone upper wall panels, and you will see that they are not the same: some project in, some out, and to different degrees. Their "pseudo-randomized" distribution is a direct result of where more (or less) diffusion was required, most notably at the waistline of the convex side walls. And why do we find the gentle convex curvature of the side walls? After all, the double-cube shoebox proportion is supposed to be ideal. This innovation—and EMPAC may well be the first—is to mitigate, at the scale of the walls and the room itself, any potential for standing waves or flutter between parallel surfaces while maintaining the sound energy in the room. Many halls solve this acoustic

View of the Concert hall from the southwest corner of the choir showing the fabric ceiling and three layers of wall treatments from the wooden surround of the orchestra and parterre, to the white panels and recessed galleries of the mid level and dimpled cast stone panels of the upper level with the acoustic banners retracted (left); similar view with the acoustic banners partially deployed (right).

Stage surround wall of milled maple and recessed wenge wood with wavelike ripples to increase the sound diffusion of a hard, acoustically reflective surface in order to maintain sound energy without problematic, focused, early sound reflections, especially to the performers.

Opposite:
Glass fiber reinforced gypsum wall panels at the Concert Hall mid level and recessed galleries.

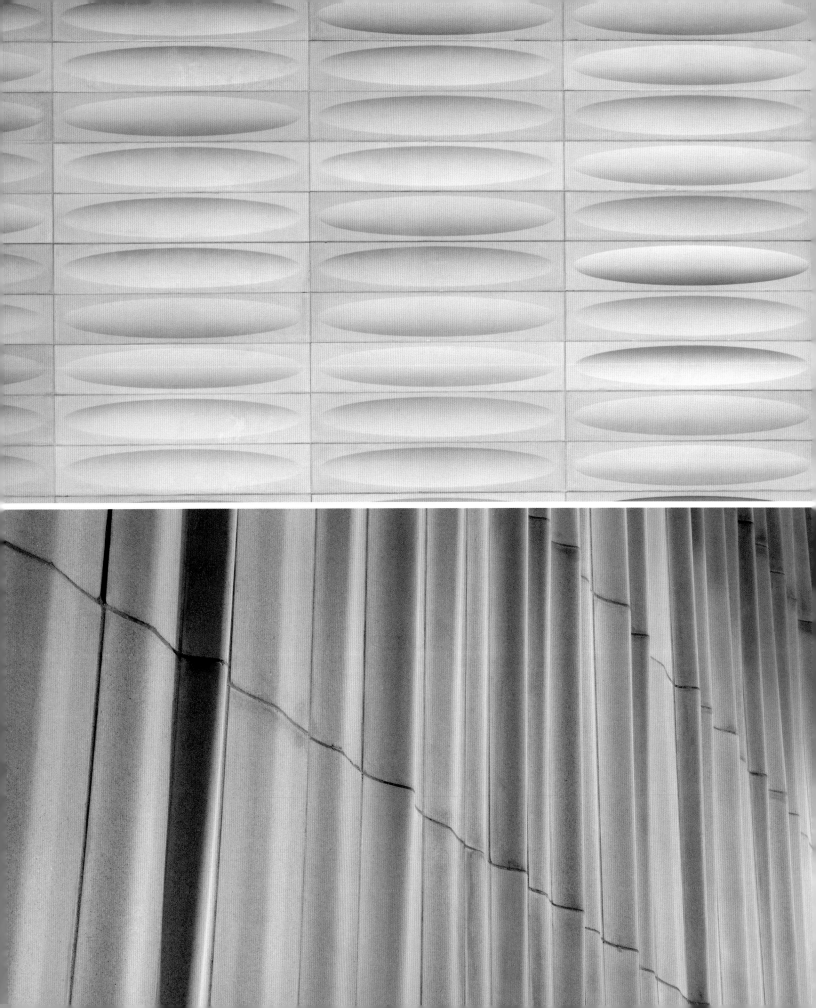

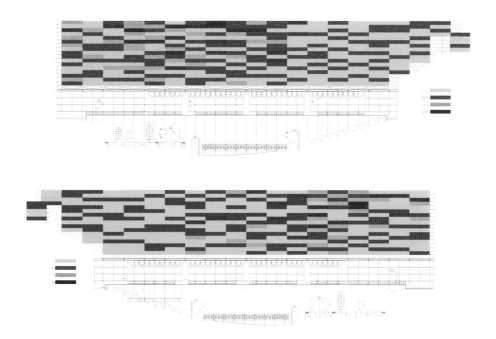

Diagram showing the distribution of the 5 panel types — one flat, two recessed (1-inch and 2-inches respectively) and two protruding (1-inch and 2-inches respectively) to achieve the desired acoustic effect. The greatest concentration of mixed and extreme (2-inch recessed and protruding) types occurs around the front of the stage near the "waistline" of the convex walls.

Cast stone upper wall panels of the Concert Hall. The array shows the variations of the elliptical recess depths and protrusion heights used to diffuse the sound without creating a chirp reflection that would occur were they all the same. The visual pattern, especially in oblique lighting reveals the variation and what the wall is doing acoustically (top); cast-stone upstage wall behind the stage designed to be acoustically reflective, yet diffuse by means of its surface geometry, designed to scatter the reflections (bottom).

problem by segmenting the side walls and ceiling, but these break up the visual unity of the room and create clutter that draws the eye away from the performer. This optimized result could only be the result of a fertile collaboration.

> The idea of creating a very richly reverberant, warm space that preserves low-frequency reverberation in a very satisfying way, that makes the bass sound like bass, without the harshness you would expect out of a very hard-surfaced room; and trying to find just that nice gentle roll off of high-frequency sound that takes the edge away, without losing the warmth of the violins, the mid-frequency warmth of the violins in particular—all of those desires led to an [integrated] approach to the surfaces of the room.
> —Carl Giegold

> When we design a concert hall, we know where the source is going to be, but suddenly we have Johannes saying to us, "I want to be able to put a source over here, so how does this side wall perform when you're not just using the stage? And I want to put 80 loudspeakers in this room at varying positions." It's a lot easier to design a room when you have a traditional set-up. We've always been enthusiastic about taking on these new challenges, but we've had to check ourselves a few times because we just naturally want to say, "Oh well, we've done this before and it will work."
> —Zackery Belanger, Kirkegaard Associates

Additionally, the program called for a room that could project the sound of performers and loudspeakers from any position, not just the stage—something that the contiguous ceiling and side walls are highly effective in achieving. Looking at the side walls, you will notice three distinct strata: the lower wood-clad portion around the orchestra (lower seating area and stage) and parterre (just behind the orchestra); the recessed concaved galleries of the middle stratum; and the upper dimpled cast stone walls. The lowest stratum provides both the performer and the audience a visual and acoustic intimacy and warmth. Further up, the audience (and upper technical) galleries are critical to increasing the volume of the space, which improves the bass-frequency response, especially with a full symphony orchestra. Drop the absorptive panels over the technical galleries above, and a bass trap, effective for amplified events, is created. The curved ceiling and articulated wall panels of the side galleries cancel the possibility of sound ricochet and capture along the side walls. And above the ceiling, invisible to the audience, large adjustable panels of absorptive material (nicknamed "überfuzz") hang in front of the rear wall.

And finally, there is the upper wall. This zone functions as the storage volume of reverberant energy above the heads of the audience. It consists of a hard material surface (cast stone, to reflect sound) articulated with large-scale elliptical dimples (to ensure that the reflections are diffuse, not focused). At first, the dimples were conceived as being all the same — concave and 2 inches deep — but testing showed what the acoustic team had feared, a resultant "chirp" created by almost simultaneous reflections from as many dimples: the "picket fence effect." This might have resulted in a wholly new approach, but the Grimshaw-Kirkegaard collaboration innovated with a variation on the elliptical theme. By creating two different panel recess depths and adding two panels with protruding elliptical features, then "randomizing" their distribution in a controlled manner, the team brought even greater control *and* visual interest to the design.

> We stacked them [the dimpled panels] up, all the same amplitude and all concave, and sure enough we saw the signal response — that we really did have an issue with the picket fence effect. We then eased off on the amplitudes (all of these amplitudes were things that we had agreed on with [Bill Horgan] ahead of time) and, starting to work with randomization, we found that if we randomized them within this 4-inch amplitude, +2 to -2, we got rid of the picket fence effect, that it was random enough to avoid that chirp in the room. It had a visual logic to it, that when lit from the light sources along the sides of the wall, it's just a visual delight. It tells you the story, for those who are looking, of where this diffusion matters and where it doesn't. So there's something there to parse about the room, to figure out about the room. It tells its own story. It's very, very honest in that regard.
>
> —Carl Giegold

To the musician on stage, reflections from the rear (upstage) wall can be extremely problematic and had to be avoided without losing the energy of the sound. How would a highly reflective yet highly diffusive surface be created? Nineteenth-century halls had relied on elaborate ornamentation and, in many instances, an organ located behind and above the stage. In yet another variation on the cast stone elliptical theme — almost undetectable in the final result, the elliptical shape was turned 90 degrees, stretched vertically and morphed with a variety of amplitudes to create a 36-foot-tall cast stone wall that appears like a draped curtain — of stone. The design team's ability to imagine and model complex irregular forms digitally was not restrained by techniques of production.

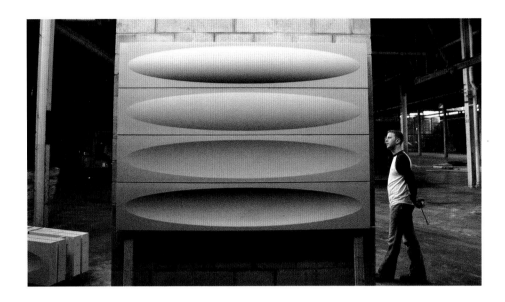

They were mocked up at quarter scale and tested in advance before being fabricated using automated techniques to create molds and cast the material.

> The diffusive requirements on the real [upstage] wall of the Concert Hall are considerable. And interestingly enough, that's usually where the pipe organ is in the classical halls that inspired this volume. So the metaphor really was an organ façade there, without an organ. But to get that, to scatter sound enough so that the upper real wall would not constitute a significant echo, the diffusion needed to be much deeper on that upstage wall (the upper wall behind the stage) than it needed to be on the upper side walls surrounding the stage.
>
> So, how to get rid of those reflections or render them harmless. We can put a lot of diffusion in the corners to scatter them, or we can put absorption in the corners to drink it all up. Putting a great deal of diffusion in the corners actually worked very well in 1870, and maybe even 1930, but it's not where we typically go aesthetically at the turn of a millennium, not this one at least. I don't know that we ever had a strong conversation about it, a detailed conversation about it, but we certainly got the sense that that wasn't where Grimshaw wanted to go with the design.
>
> —Carl Giegold

"Lost corners," as coined by the design team, refers to where two walls and ceiling typically meet—but not at EMPAC. Providing a recessed alcove instead prevents repeated reflections that can occur in hard corners and create an undesirable late reflection (echo).

Elliptical cast stone panel mockup showing various protrusions and recesses.

This same principle is applied in another important place in the hall — where the ceiling does not touch the walls. The story of integration between theater consultants, acousticians, engineers and architects is told in the design of the Concert Hall. Even the custom seats, aimed to absorb the same amount of sound as a single adult, are there to make the hall perform as well empty as it does full, and the displacement ventilation supplied silently from a plenum below the seating contributes to the sound potential of the Concert Hall.

> We knew we needed a technical gallery in the Concert Hall; we knew we
> needed banners to vary the reflection time and structure of the room. But we
> also knew we needed a lighting rail up there, and we knew we needed to hang
> screens. There were all of these functions that had to happen up there and we
> put together this idea of the lost corner in a way that integrated the stopping
> short of the wall of this ceiling surface to create a gap that was about 5 feet
> wide, through which you could deploy a banner, hang a projection screen,
> attach loudspeakers, drop banners; behind that 5-foot gap was the technical
> gallery that allowed access to all of that technical capability.
>
> — Carl Giegold

The Concert Hall is a space that was sculpted by sound even before the first sounds were presented to it. This was possible thanks to the deep knowledge of the acousticians, analysis of existing halls, advanced acoustic modeling and full-scale simulations and testing of several of its components. But even more, it is the result of the commitment, passion and collaboration of the design team and client. Only this allowed the builder of EMPAC's Concert Hall to achieve a highly predictable, world-class acoustic result and to reach the goals of the client in a single, unified space that combines the performers and the audience, without the slightest suggestion of a dividing proscenium.

Theater

In the 400-seat Theater, as with all the venues, sound, sight and movement in space were each held to a high standard. Unlike in most theater spaces, the sound threshold was held to an RC15 (quietness level), which resulted in some extraordinary measures, including its own displacement ventilation system under each seat and "silent" winches equipping the stage house. The main objectives here were to create an intimacy between the audience and the performance — certainly a theme throughout EMPAC — and to provide performers and artists a full-size and amply equipped stage house and fly tower, something rarely found in theaters with only 400 seats. It was designed with a reverberation time suited for a single voice or small orchestra, and works well either acoustically or amplified. Its deep red walls, steeply raked seating and three-tiered side-wall balconies (audience and technical) work together to achieve a compelling proximity and intimacy between the audience and the performers. The proscenium (between stage and house), traditionally solid and cut open to frame the performers behind, is all but eliminated. When open, the full width and practical height of the audience house extends visually onto the stage. It can also be closed to provide any size opening with curtains or a massive 56-foot projection screen, the focus of a high-resolution projector located in a projection room at the back of house. Or, it can be fully separated to enable the fly tower and stage space to be dedicated to research and development while the theater house remains available for use. An orchestra pit (technicians/media pit—if one asks Johannes Goebel) can function in a traditional position (lowered, effectively creating a moat between audience and performer), or it can be raised to audience level to accommodate additional rows of seating. It can also be raised to stage level and function as a thrust stage well beyond the proscenium plane into the audience. As in the Concert Hall, this space called for the acousticians to design for performers positioned anywhere in the space, not only on stage.

The Goodman Theater/Studio 1

The Goodman Theater/Studio 1 is the larger of two experimental black box studios, created for the development and performance of new and innovative works. Here the emergence of new possibilities should be enabled, if not kindled by the space itself—one that attempts to present no bias or interference. There is no front or back and, based on some of the performances to date, no top or bottom. Here again the performer begins with the sound of silence and builds from there, either against a diffuse acoustic drop or an extraordinarily dry, non-reverberant space—or somewhere between. A walkable grid above allows the free positioning of lighting, props and equipment arrays. The neutral stage floor presents the possibilities of nailing or screwing directly to the surface and any number of installations or set-ups. Inside, the acoustic diffusing and absorptive wall panels are all black, visually recessing together into the black surfaces behind them, black floors and dark ceiling cavity above to create a literal black box experimental studio. Behind the panels, directly attached to the concrete walls, are membrane bass absorbers tuned to nine different frequencies. Their job is to absorb the full bottom range of low frequencies so they are not overemphasized in the space. In front of the panels, a double layer of black acoustic banners can be dropped for additional absorption.

Studio 2

Studio 2 is the smaller, more intimate experimental room. It is faced with an array of white diffusing panels in front of a black background to create a visually pixilated surface surround. Like the Goodman Theater/Studio 1, it is set up for experimental perform-ances, with a walkable grid ceiling, a double layer of retractable side-wall acoustic banners, a free floor plan and adjustable acoustic wall panels. It too has a wide range of possible uses, from delicate chamber music to fully interactive, mediated environments and ampli-fied events. It is in both of these studios where augmented realities are created, and where virtual and immersive environments will become the progenitors of new realities.

SUBSTANCE OF SOUND

Acoustic design does not only affect the shape of the room. As realized in the upstage wall and side walls of the Concert Hall, and in the wall panels of the studios — designed to selectively absorb, transmit or reflect sound in various directions to eliminate certain sonic effects (flutter, standing waves) and create others (liveness, diffusion) — materials and their surface geometries also matter.

Fabric Ceiling

To make the Concert Hall work well acoustically for a wide range of criteria was a challenge. It had to be as good for the performer as it was for the audience. It also had to accomplish what few acoustic halls have been able to accomplish: create an exceptional setting for both highly refined, delicate acoustic music — heard at every seat — *and* amplified events with many loudspeakers around and above the audience. In response, EMPAC's Concert Hall was designed with a highly unique and innovative fabric ceiling. In this way it is like no other, with two exceptions. Carnegie Hall was recently discovered to have a fabric ceiling patch over part of the orchestra ceiling. And Royal Festival Hall in London — acoustically redesigned by Kirkegaard Associates simultaneously with EMPAC — now has fabric ceiling panels over the orchestra. EMPAC goes further, however, with the first suspended fabric ceiling over both stage and audience. The ceiling selectively reflects mid- and high-frequency sound off its suspended catenary[1] shape, which is perfect for small orchestral instruments such as the violin or flute, while being somewhat transparent to the lower frequencies that will (and need to) resonate in the volume above the ceiling. It is especially advantageous for large orchestras and amplified performances, which would otherwise overpower a hall of this size.

But to create such a solution was not only innovative — it was daring. The acousticians started with no fewer than 80 different fabrics and tested the efficacy of each. The fabric had to perform acoustically, as well as meet fire codes. Moreover, it had to be strong enough to be stretched to its attachment points without risk of tearing, stiff enough to resist uplift and durable enough to last through the years. The fabric also had to be woven to allow equal stretching in both directions. With all of that in mind, its appearance was also critical. The first selection was tested over the orchestra at Royal Festival Hall, but was found to be too light, letting through too many mid-frequency sounds instead of reflecting them. Furthermore, the installers advised that it was too light to work with or install in a permanent location.

> If you get a fabric that's too lightweight, it will reflect highs very well, but it won't reflect mids very well, and you'll end up with something that sounds really harsh, because it's just the high end essentially. As you increase the mass of the system, keeping the air absorption down, you start to include those mid-frequencies in it, and it becomes a more and more pleasant sound. … We knew we liked Nomex. We knew the properties we wanted, but it's hard to find an 18-ounce Nomex out there. We showed up [at the University of North Carolina lab] with canvas in one hand and Nomex in the other, and said, "What can we make?"
>
> —Zackery Belanger

Stage view of the Concert Hall showing the lower level wood surround, the recessed gallery mid level and cast stone upper wall zones.

The designers needed the equivalent of an 18-ounce duck canvas, but without the fire-rated coatings that would be typically required on such a canvas. Any lighter, and the fabrics seemed to all have too much air permeability and, with that, too much acoustic transparency. Kirkegaard Associates reached out to University of North Carolina's textile program, where a number of suggestions, including Nomex[2] were made. Nomex had the right feel but still did not have the weight required. UNC even developed a number of special weaves and materials, and produced some calendared (pressed) samples. Though the lighter material would work over the audience area, a heavier material with the same appearance was needed over the orchestra. In the end, a single layer of uncoated Nomex was used over the audience, and a double layer of laminated Nomex was used over the orchestra. Since there is no backlighting (lighting is positioned in the gaps between the panels), the change in thickness is not noticeable.

> We learned everything that you could want to know about weaving. …
> We learned new terms. You know, *pick, weave, twirl.*
> — Louis Sunga, Kirkegaard Associates

After developing attachment details with tensioners (adjustable fasteners that could be used to stress the fabric equally from every side) to be certain that the material could be installed taut, a full-scale mock-up was assembled and tested in a warehouse managed by Adirondack Studios. One of the major issues in coordinating the architectural design and acoustics was how tightly the fabric could, or should, be mounted. The architects wanted as little sag as possible, whereas the acousticians had to avoid the potential for the ceiling to resonate like a drumhead. The final result is a ceiling that not only works for a range of performance types, but visually unifies the space and may well represent an important step forward in the design and construction of acoustic halls.

> Typical fabric structures are highly tensioned and end up sounding like drum-
> heads that amplify the sound. It's not something we wanted. Setting the right
> shape and getting it looking nice and keeping the tension to a minimum is
> what we're looking for.
> — Zackery Belanger in conversation with Louis Sunga

Fabric connection and tensioner detail (above); fabric ceiling showing the gaps for lighting, air and other services (opposite).

Acoustic Panels

Imagine you're in a forest clearing 30 or 40 feet in diameter. Around you are trees of different trunk and canopy diameters. Some of the trees, such as beech, have bark that is quite smooth; many, such as oak, are rougher and more sound absorbent. Because of their different trunk diameters, each of the surface curvatures is also different. Now imagine you are playing music in this clearing: What you hear is not a pure reflection of the notes, but a transparent, enveloping sound that has been scattered and diffused by the roundness and roughness of the trees. The excessive energy of the sound, the sound that is too much for the ear, is disappearing between the trees of the forest clearing. This was our model for the acoustics of EMPAC.

— Johannes Goebel

A forest clearing (left); Sample of tree bark showing the bark's texture and the effects of woodpeckers on the curved surface of the trunk diameter (right).

Throughout each of the experimental studio spaces, the side walls are composed of curved gimbaled, tunable panels. This makes for one of the most elaborate stories of collaboration between owner, architect and acoustician. Acoustically conceived as a "clearing in the forest," it was Johannes Goebel's sense that the space should have that kind of sound quality, diffuse yet having sufficient acoustic energy. Some years ago, he had actually performed in a forest clearing of his northern German homeland. Imagine mature, over-canopied, deciduous trees with tall trunks of varying diameters and distances from the clearing edge, and little understorey—a diffuse space, infinitely deep, yet having certain select multidirectional reflections from the trunks.

 In a forest clearing, the trees might be hundreds of feet away and the space between them virtually unending—far beyond the clearing. How was this to be achieved in an acoustically reflective concrete box with only a fraction of the volume? Kirkegaard Associates, working closely with the Grimshaw team, found that by using a grid of curved articulated panels with a mere 12 inches between them and the wall surface behind, they might just be able to emulate what Goebel was looking for—the acoustics of a clearing in the forest, diffuse yet alive, without a loss of volume. They set out to achieve in 12 inches what was accomplished in hundreds of feet of forest.

Moon surface showing overlapping craters with different depths and diameters on the curved surface (left); prototype of an iteration in the development of the 2-foot by 2-foot diffusing panel (right).

A forest-clearing acoustic results from, well yeah, a forest. There might be trees and trunks and undergrowth that are hundreds of feet away that are contributing to the acoustic response that a forest sends back to a source. And obviously we didn't have the luxury of that much volume, that much landscape to develop that acoustic inside these concrete boxes with 12-inch-thick walls, to deal with that amount of sound. But Johannes wanted to attenuate. There wasn't a built product that we knew of, or had faith in, to deliver this live but diffused environment. So we started thinking about how we might get it by means that had not been thought about before this. And there was lots of sitting back in the chairs and stretching and scratching heads and sketching on paper that went back and forth before we settled on the idea of a panelized system.

— Carl Giegold

Detail of 2-foot by 2-foot acoustic panel gimbal mount (left); a detail of the bass absorbers showing the integrated attachment points for the gimbaled acoustic panels that overlay and obscure the bass absorbers (right).

Interesting challenges often bring the most interesting results. Whether by intuition or subconsciously, the panels began to take on surface patterns not unlike those in the sketch, though it is not even clear that the designers had ever seen it. Goebel had also specified that the panels should be both exchangeable and adjustable. This was to create a differentiated wall-scape, to allow experimentation with the acoustics of the room and to tune the space for changing requirements. However, he did not foresee that changes to the panel locations or orientation would happen often and asked for manual adjustability, believing that the cost of a motorized system would not be justifiable.

Early on, the decision to use 2-foot-square panels was made for practical reasons of handling and adjustability. Next, the team decided to add a 3-foot radius to each one, creating radial reflections that, together with gimbaling, would eliminate any potential for flutter and standing waves between the parallel studio wall surfaces. Zooming in, the panels' surfaces were perforated to absorb select wavelengths (at first all the way through, though with unsatisfactory results). With every iteration, these choices were tested, first at Kirkegaard's own lab and studio, where early prototypes were developed, and, for the more promising panels, again at Riverbank Acoustical Laboratories. Material variations included MDF (medium density fiberboard), metal overlays and felt backings—all were intuited to perform in particular ways, but resulted in very different sonic behaviors and discoveries, often unpredictable. One watershed moment occurred when felt was applied across the perforations, blocking them. It revealed a warmth not present with through-perforations and prompted the team to explore the idea of working with only partial, varying-depth penetrations into the panel material. The material of choice was glass fiber reinforced gypsum (GFRG), which could be cast into any desirable shape with precise detailed surfaces.

> We had 54 of the GFRG panels made, and we took them to a space. And we took some of our in-house musicians and we had them play music off it. We brought in Johannes and Martin [Moore – Rensselaer's owner's representative]. … And it was also a great architectural mock-up. We learned things like how difficult it is to have a 4-point mount system and tilt them. We learned things like how ½ inch between these panels really wasn't enough.
>
> —Zackery Belanger

In-house, the acousticians created a metal grid to mount the test panels, fired sound at them with sound canons and measured the results. But numerical, scientific measurements would not suffice. As musicians themselves, Kirkegaard's staff played cellos and guitars at them, and then they weighed both the objective measures and subjective responses of well-trained ears. Even the architects learned to listen, standing before samples, hand to ear. Acousticians asked them to respond and enjoyed watching the affirmative nods.[3]

Designing for the Eye, the Body and the Ear:
A dialogue between two rooms

William Horgan

EMPAC's translation from modest napkin sketch to imposing constructed form over a seven-year period is a story that cannot be told comprehensively in a single essay, or probably reliably from a single viewpoint. In common with any complex endeavor that relies on the coordinated determination and inspiration of many people working together—and occasionally fighting with one another—a truer picture emerges, made up of many strands, or pixels, to use a digital analogy, each arising from a unique viewpoint. This has a curious parallel in the multifaceted nature of EMPAC's program, which can be interpreted as an overall vision framed from a variety of personal and technical perspectives, and indeed the building's emergent architecture, which could be described as a composition of voices. This essay is one such story strand and describes two of those voices, the very different Concert Hall and Studio 1 (also known as the Goodman Theater/Studio 1).

The simplest way of envisioning the building's program is that it represents a sliding scale of experiences along a line of varying formality. At opposite ends of this line are the Concert Hall and Studio 1. The former is conceived as a sensuous, formal room, crafted for nothing less than experiencing a symphony orchestra at full tilt. Studio 1 is the perfect foil: different in almost every respect, except that it is also designed for experiencing, together with other people, the sensations of sound and light. Dark and empty, Studio 1 provides a pristine environment for pieces of work that benefit from no real-world context. Throughout the design process, these opposites have been engaged in something of a standoffish dance with each other.

THE EVOLUTION OF THE PROGRAM:
A CONCERT HALL EMERGES AND
A STUDIO VANISHES

The Concert Hall started out life as something different. Originally, the program called for a 1,200-seat, multi-purpose hall with a fly tower; a high-quality and versatile room that would be EMPAC's day-to-day workhorse. Meanwhile, studios 1, 2 and 3 (Audio/ Video Production Suite) were conceived as simple black box theaters that could be used for recording. There was also to be a recital hall, with 500 seats, which would later transmute into the Theater. This was the brief with which Grimshaw Architects, Arup (acoustics), Buro Happold (engineering) and Theatre Projects (theater design) won the initial design competition, but this was really only the starting point for the evolution of a complex program that would evolve considerably during the first few months of critical analysis.

Dr. Shirley Ann Jackson, president of Rensselaer Polytechnic Institute, had asked for nothing less than world-class acoustics in EMPAC's main auditorium, and this in short order led to the conclusion that the fly tower, *bête noire* of acousticians the world over, had to go. Fortunately, there was a willing recipient for this transplant; with the main hall's evolution into a dedicated concert hall, the logical next step was to reconfigure the recital hall into a fully functional theater, and this would need a fly tower.

The concert hall, now liberated from the acoustical design shackles associated with a proscenium stage, a frontal audience and a fly tower, was able to relax into a longer and narrower shape than it had assumed at competition stage, becoming more conducive to listening to music. While we (the design team) visited Hans Scharoun's magnificent in-the-round Philharmonie in Berlin as a reference for EMPAC (and it provided an alternative worth exploring), there was a clear-cut decision supported by President Jackson, Grimshaw and Arup alike, that a shoebox hall was the preferred room typology. The outstanding acoustic examples of this room shape—Boston Symphony Hall, Amsterdam's Concertgebouw and especially Vienna's Musikvereinssaal, all built within 30 years of one another at the end of the 19th century—provide recognized templates for successful medium-sized rooms. This traditional shape, ironically, offered the greatest potential for versatility for performances that may use the space in unconventional ways. It also offered the practical reality of allowing 1,200 seats to be front and center of the concert platform (a key requirement for convocations), and it ensured that films and dance could be more easily accommodated where use of a very large projection screen was desired.

So the concert hall was now well on its way. It had an approximate shape, roughly that of a cubic 2:1 oblong in proportion, and we had come to an agreement about the size of the single rear balcony and the distribution of the audience throughout the room.

In parallel to all this, the design team was undergoing changes of its own, which could politely be seen as a kind of bedding-in process in preparation for the intellectual journey that the owner and the design team were about to embark on. Arup made way for Kirkegaard Associates, and Theatre Projects stepped aside for Fisher Dachs.

In Nick's (Sir Nicholas Grimshaw) earliest sketches for EMPAC, he envisioned the main hall as a kind of constant around which the rest of EMPAC would be organized—an organic, sinuous wooden vessel on axis with the main entrance. There was clearly no question in the President's mind that the concert hall was to be the primary focus of EMPAC, and Nick responded to this emphatically with an architectural approach that celebrated the hall as a finite element of architecture distinctly and dominantly poised within the overall makeup of the building. The studios and theater, meanwhile, were conceived as "found spaces," their shape and size unknowable from the outside and seamlessly integrated into a large, white oblong forming the building's south wing.

This formal dualism, apparent in the architecture of the building, mirrored the divided focus of the program. Design workshops with Kirkegaard Associates and Fisher Dachs at this time tended to dwell either on the concert hall or "everything else." Interestingly, despite the formidable challenges of designing the concert hall, the process of its translation from brief to concept was reasonably linear thanks to its well-understood program and repertoire. The theater and studios, by contrast, were envisioned to be innovative, unique performance spaces whose geometrical characteristics and technical specifications were less easy to define, inviting a greater degree of exploration in the early stages of their development.

Early requirements for a digital gallery, a third studio, a separate rehearsal space and music teaching rooms were discarded around this time. These elements of EMPAC's program were deemed non-essential and would have added considerable cost. A walkable roof terrace linking to the adjacent campus quad and extending over the entire building, which at that time was intended to be sunken deeper into the hillside, was also jettisoned.

While all of EMPAC's performance spaces are capable of fostering time-based art, studios 1 and 2 were recognized from early on as being its true digital blank canvases, where content dominates the room rather than the audience. These were to be laboratories where performances of sound, visual imagery and physical movement could be developed without compromise—limited only by the capability of available technology and the physical dimensions of the room (and even this is relative, because the realms of the microscopically tiny and the galactically expansive can be freely navigated in the immersive, "sensurround" environment of Studio 1). In this sense, Studio 1 is at the furthest extreme from the Concert Hall; while both rooms can be loosely described as large architectural volumes in which people can gather in numbers, listen to music, observe dance or film, carry out research through an audiovisual medium or participate in a seminar, in every physical and formal respect they are utterly distinct.

Studio 1 and Studio 2 are similar in many respects: they share the same basic acoustic and architectural DNA, as seen in their special wall panels, tension-wire grid and plan proportion. But they are rather different in size, and one is a true "black box," while the other is more of a "white box." Studio 2, the smaller sibling, is fundamentally a recital room optimized for the performance and recording of music, with the lights on. This distinction is rather important, as it links Studio 2 and the Concert Hall in a way that Studio 1 cannot be—both spaces are designed to be seen by the audience and the architecture of the room is "present" during a performance, and therefore becomes part of the observer's experience.

Studio 1 was intended from the outset to be a large, useful

room that, to use a phrase of Josh Dachs', "bristles with technology." The room's four walls would provide the physical space for containing any given work, with the technology providing for the manipulation and output of 3-D imagery and multi-channel sound, hovering in space if necessary. The idea was to size the room large enough so that, using back projection (which typically requires 15 feet of distance from the walls) a 360-degree screen could be hung in the space, 20 feet high and large enough in diameter to create a shared, immersive, visual environment for a group of people standing in the middle. The room was to be black or at least very dark, floor included, and was envisioned initially to meet the acoustic standard RC25. This meant that the background noise level in the room—even with a jet flying overhead—should not exceed 25 decibels, a substantially less-onerous criterion than the RC15, which was later pushed for and accepted. Fifteen decibels is at the lower limit of human hearing, so RC15 is essentially the specification for absolute silence. Additionally, the room needed to be what acousticians

expected. How to go about achieving this was a vexing challenge, because halls of this scale and quality are normally designed for a resident orchestra with an established repertoire, operating model and precisely defined brief. Rensselaer has no resident music program and is not beholden to commercial operating pressures; therefore, it was initially difficult to frame the dominant drivers of the room and establish a hierarchy of design priorities. Given EMPAC's stated mission as a media laboratory, how was the balance to be struck between the traditional specialization of a concert hall and the open-ended versatility of a 21st-century experimental arts venue? The definition of world-class acoustics would also prove to be more complicated than one might initially expect.

Concert halls come in all shapes and sizes, and the characteristics of what constitutes great acoustics is almost by definition subjective. Acousticians have favorites and, to some extent, can quantify them in terms of reverberation time, envelopment, warmth and clarity. The success of most halls, however, is based

"How was the balance to be struck between the traditional ... concert hall

refer to as "dry," meaning its native reverberation time had to be very short, about half a second in this case, yet capable of being relaxed to a second or more for performances requiring a more lively acoustic character. Finally, Studio 1 needed to be equipped with attachment points all over its walls and ceiling (a tension-wire grid) to provide unlimited versatility in the attachment of theater rigging, lighting and audio/video technology.

ARCHITECTURE AND ACOUSTICS WITH THE LIGHTS ON: THE CONCERT HALL
At the outset of the project, President Jackson made it clear that despite EMPAC being focused on experimental and digital media, she wanted to see at its heart a concert hall of international quality, and she wanted to hear a celebrated orchestra playing in it. This room was conceived to be more than merely the fulfillment of the technical brief of a university music venue —it was to be an embodiment of the President's ambitions for Rensselaer, and no less than a world-class concert hall was

as much on qualitative assessment as it is on quantitative measurement. To make matters more complicated, some of the most celebrated concert halls in the world have well-documented quirks or outright deficiencies that would be deemed unacceptable if those halls were built today, a supposition supported by the fact that the greatest halls are rarely copied, and brand new concert halls of similar scale built for outwardly similar purposes are more often than not remarkably different both architecturally and acoustically. The reason of course is that standards of comfort and accommodation have changed; audience expectations have changed; recording has changed; indeed, audiences have changed. Music patrons will excuse a raft of inconveniences such as bad sightlines, cramped and uncomfortable seats, and stuffy or non-existent air conditioning in a celebrated and much-loved 19th-century hall, but they will not readily accept such compromises in a newly constructed room. Equally, musicians and conductors are notoriously discerning performers and make the harshest critics, and they will not do their best work in a room with inadequate acoustic support. Background noise in old halls, often thanks to conventional architectural features such as clerestory windows and adjoining inadequately sound-isolated lobbies, have been problematic for decades in recordings because microphones are fundamentally egalitarian and cannot ignore what we do not want to hear. New halls are expected to avoid such problems by excluding all of the noise, thus triggering a kind of acoustical arms race, where achieving utter silence is a categorical, and expensive, priority.

When Rensselaer's representatives and the design team visited several important concert venues in Europe, the first tour being in early 2002, we visited the Barbican in London, the Philharmonie in Berlin, the Tonhalle in Zurich, Jean Nouvelle's KKL concert hall in Lucerne, and finally Johannes' home at that time, the ZKM (Center for Art and Media) in Karlsruhe, Germany, where he was to show us his experimental studios, which would provide a starting point for the design of studios 1 and 2. In 2003, a second tour, taking in England's Glyndebourne opera

plaster cornices, pilasters and capitals. These architectural details propagate diffuse sound reflections, making for a rich but clear acoustic character. The absence of such decorative detail in music venues designed during the latter half of the 20th century made rooms respond differently, and Larry advised of the acoustic anomalies in particular that uninterrupted 90-degree room corners can create. To combat this effect, the idea of "lost corners" emerged, whereby the four walls of the EMPAC Concert Hall do not quite meet, in lieu of a recessed pocket. This turned out to be useful also for architectural definition, whereby each wall could be expressed separately from one another, visually reinforcing the individual acoustic role of each.

The ceiling presented its own set of challenges. After initially exploring some solid-wood concepts, Larry made a decision to develop an approach using fabric, an idea derived from painted canvas that was used for several decades in the ceiling of Carnegie Hall. The core of the idea was a material that reflected mid- and high frequencies to reinforce intimacy and clarity,

and the open-ended versatility of a 21st century experimental arts venue?"

house and Birmingham Symphony Hall, Finland's Sibelius Hall, and Renzo Piano's Parco della Musica in Italy, was to lead to something of a breakthrough in the design at that time, with a clear room concept emerging.

As Nick describes in his essay, "A Project to Remember," the hall's starting point was in conceiving a simple, elegant room shape that would provide fundamentally exceptional room acoustics without needing to rely on movable architecture. Larry's and Nick's design envisioned a streamlined room, with a single rear balcony. With the exception of the gently raked orchestra (stalls) and parterre, the overall room proportions and size were not dissimilar to Vienna's Musikvereinssaal, and by following this path, the foundations were laid for a room of fundamentally high-quality acoustics. A significant step forward was the idea of all four walls adopting a convex curvature, a move that allows the walls to diffuse the sound evenly throughout the room.

Nineteenth-century halls were typically decorated with

while allowing the low frequencies (bass) to pass through the material to energize the air volume concealed above it and develop reverberance. The ceiling is set in a gentle convex double curvature, like a suspended lens, thus maintaining the intrinsically convex room geometry exhibited also by the four walls. House lights and performance lights are suspended in the gaps between the fabric panels, allowing the ceiling to make a coherent architectural gesture in the room without visual interruption. The combination of the fabric and relatively low ceiling height above the concert platform is significant, insofar as it eliminates the requirement for a suspended canopy, further enabling the realization of a deceptively simple, elegant room.

It was calculated by the acousticians that the tall side walls needed to be very subtly scalloped to scatter bass sounds uniformly into the upper volume of the room. Our solution to this was a family of high-quality pre-cast masonry panels. The panels were required to have manifestations of varying depths—some indented, some protruding—and be arranged randomly across the wall. The randomness of the wall manifestations, a tactic employed throughout the room, was key to avoiding what project acoustician Carl Giegold described as "picket fence" reflections, so called because regularly repeating wall features can generate bothersome acoustic reflections reminiscent of the sound that a child might make in running a stick along a picket fence.

The upstage wall behind the choral terrace was designed to project sound back out into the room, but needed more aggressive diffusive scattering power than the upper side walls, so a unique masonry profile was developed here. Vertical fluting, gradually diminishing toward the top of the wall, was implemented to provide this diffusion while maintaining the same material qualities of the upper side walls.

Both the upstage wall and the side walls were designed to be up-lit as part of the house lighting design. Working with Office for Visual Interaction, Inc. (OVI), led by Enrique Peiniger and Jean Sundin, the intention was to create overall an uplifting

surfaces in the room—the most aggressive diffusive manifestations are found in the galleries, in the form of what became known as the "ravioli" panels. Made from smooth white plaster, each ravioli has a single protruding bulge to scatter long-wavelength sound, and is pitted with indentations similar to those on a golf ball to scatter shorter wavelengths.

The walls enclosing the parterre, the orchestra seating and the concert platform are lined with acoustically shaped maple, interspersed with thin, dark wenge strips that provide a horizontal pinstripe to the room. The maple varies in width and was CNC-milled (computationally fabricated) to exhibit a varying sine wave profile that enables diffusion at mid- to high frequencies. In similar fashion to the masonry walls higher up in the room, the amplitude of the sine wave diminishes in proportion to distance from the concert platform, eventually disappearing roughly parallel with the parterre wall.

The floors and concert platform are finished with matching maple and wenge, the latter lining the nosings of steps and the

"To create a space that could nourish innovation, we knew we needed to

illumination and coloration. The masonry panels have a porous, granular stone finish that is ideal for soft, progressive illumination without specular bright spots (interestingly, this is an analogous description of the material's acoustic properties, too). A custom-designed uplighter was developed to wash the walls from their base with warm white light. In the side-wall locations, the lights are mounted inside an anodized aluminum extrusion that spans between brackets coinciding with the masonry panel joints. Parallel to each LED uplighter is mounted an identical aluminum extrusion containing an array of very small loudspeakers for amplified events.

The inset galleries that carve into the side walls were designed to accommodate not only the audience, seated on loose chairs, but also musicians from time to time. The acoustic finishes in the galleries are optimized for this eventuality, and indeed this was beautifully demonstrated in the inaugural concert, during which trumpeters and choristers flanked the room. Owing to their concave shape in plan—the only non-convex

stage lip for increased visibility and to delineate detail. The maple and leather "clam shell" seats, manufactured in Italy to a custom EMPAC design, complete the ensemble of materials in the room.

ARCHITECTURE AND ACOUSTICS WITH THE LIGHTS OFF: STUDIO 1

In contrast to the development of the Concert Hall, which was about composing a coherent ensemble of wall surfaces, floors, seats and a ceiling—each with a distinct role and its own architectural character, the evolution of Studio 1 focused largely on the creation of a single unit—a pixel would be an apt metaphor. Thousands of these units would combine to create a "tunable" matrix applied equally around the room. In fact, in almost every respect, the two rooms are opposites: While one is a complex geometrical shape contrived to optimize the listening and viewing experience of a fixed audience, the other is a simple rectangular box; one is designed to have its lights on, the other off; and while one is clad in familiar, "honest" materials such as stone and wood, the other is finished, as I shall describe, in a mantle of exotic, adjustable tiles. Also, to the benefit of some of Rensselaer's more esoteric research projects, Studio 1 is connected directly to the campus supercomputer.

The technical complexity of Studio 1 wasn't necessarily there from the outset of the project, at least not in terms of its finishes and construction. Both studios were envisioned early on to be robust, versatile rooms with full-height acoustic curtains to allow the reverberation time to be adjusted, but in early schematic design, their wall finishes were anticipated to be a combination of split-faced masonry and some kind of acoustic fuzz, for absorption. The aesthetic at that time was more akin to warehouse research project than high-performance sound and light lab. Maybe because of these humble beginnings, their evolution from these early ideas to the marvelous final concept was punctuated, to a greater degree than any of the other spaces in

time. The silence was almost uncomfortably absolute, and the longer we sat still and strained our ears, the more it seemed to envelop us like a heavy blanket. Sensing our reaction, Johannes smiled and said, "*That's* what makes it so expensive."

Despite the programmatic differences between studios 1 and 2, their technical specifications were similar, and very quickly the design team reached a kind of technical base camp, which established their critical dimensions, superstructure and isolation requirements, allowing the rest of the building to be planned around them. It was established early on that the walls and roofs of both studios would need to be constructed from 12-inch concrete. A series of structural steel trusses would support the roof slabs above, and a tension-wire grid (a walkable "ceiling" made from rigid steel cables, through which lights and rigging could be deployed) below. It is a good illustration of the complexity of performing arts buildings that even the foundations of the two studios needed to be separate from that of the rest of the building. This is to stop sound vibrations from a per-

get past the conventional concept of a predictable and well-behaved ... box."

EMPAC, by memorably anecdotal moments and abstract leaps forward.

The first of these occurred right at the outset of the project when we were touring ZKM in Karlsruhe with Johannes. He had taken a small group of us into one of his studios, a room not unlike what Studio 2 would eventually turn out to be, and he sat us down on a scattering of chairs in the center of the room. He busied himself in the corner, twiddling some dials before walking quietly back to the center of the room, where he paused for a few moments before asking, "Can you hear that?" None of us could hear anything at all, but Johannes was bothered by what he described as a faint hum coming from somewhere. He disappeared through the heavy sound-and-light-lock doors into the adjacent technical spaces for a few minutes before returning, seemingly satisfied. A small refrigerator in the nearby kitchenette was the culprit—a rattling compressor or something. Finally satisfied, he asked us now to describe what we could hear. Again nothing, but certainly a more profound nothing this

formance in one venue being transmitted through shared foundations directly into another venue, potentially being picked up on microphones during a recording or, worse, heard outright. In the case of Studio 1, however, this separation of foundations turned out to be unfeasible due to the necessity of creating a continuous diaphragm slab to mitigate problems in the rare but not impossible chance of a major seismic event. This meant that the room would have to be designed like a matryoshka doll (Russian nesting doll), as a box within a box, and the entire construction supported on stiff steel springs to damp the effects of any foundation-borne vibration.

By late 2002, the design dialogue had stalled somewhat in our attempts to shift from establishing the basic parameters of the room to seeking the means by which it could become exceptional. To create a space that could nourish innovation, we knew we needed to get past the conventional concept of a predictable and well-behaved, but rather characterless box. This probably meant working with something more difficult, but this seemed to be acceptable, and the conversation turned to the sound of quiet, unconventional spaces that we liked.

The eureka moment came when Johannes mused about the possibility of recreating the acoustics of a forest clearing. I recall walking in a little late for the workshop that morning to find Johannes, Frans (Swarte, a Dutch acoustician who worked with Kirkegaard Associates), Carl and Josh all seemingly excited by this new idea. My initial reaction to this was that I thought they were pulling my leg, and I countered that surely a forest clearing has only the ground to reflect sound, so how could it have any kind of acoustical character? Quite the contrary, as it turns out; Frans explained that a handclap made at the center of a circle of trees will come back as discrete acoustical reflections, one from each of the tree trunks. The sound will be diffused somewhat by the rough texture of the tree bark, and much of the original sound will be lost to the depths of the forest, but the reflected presence is quite clearly there—a chorus of individual voices speaking back to the listener. The

serious, and so it seemed appropriate that its appearance should visually communicate this sophistication.

An array of individually adjustable wall panels was the solution, each identical, but able to be gimbaled (angled in any direction) and capable of being pushed in or pulled out at varying distances from the concrete wall behind. As for the surface treatment, castings of tree bark might have been the obvious physical analog, but we (the architects, that is) found this idea clumsy and unnecessarily literal. After all, we were not actually recreating a forest clearing; we were taking a characteristic of it— distilling it—and expressing its essence in abstract. To move this forward we needed a more scientific basis of design from the acousticians so that we could attack the problem from a mathematical standpoint and see where that took us.

To provide a "diffuse" reflected sound characteristic, whereby reflections are accurate but not specular (as a visual cue, think smooth matte paint rather than chrome bumper), Kirkegaard required a random array of pits, dimples, protrusions and lumps

"The recreation of a sense of an outdoor space inside a room that has walls,

inception of this simple idea turned out to be a defining moment in the conception of the room. The seemingly contradictory idea—the recreation of a sense of an outdoor space inside a room that has walls, floor and ceiling all cast from monolithic concrete—propelled the design forward and put meat on the bones of the room concept.

It was never the intent to exactly simulate a forest clearing; rather it was a desire to capture some of its unique qualities. The acoustic parameters are better explained elsewhere, but from an architectural standpoint, the challenge would be to balance the pastoral analogy of the forest with the other half of the room's personality—that of being girdled with technology. While we knew that Studio 1 was intended to be used with the lights off, it was also true that most of its life would be spent between performances or experiments, and, during this time, we thought the room would benefit from a character that reflected its technical capabilities. In performance terms, Johannes' ambitions for the room had become a lot more

—much like tree bark, in fact, but without the vertical striations typically found on trunks and branches. Taking this a bit further, these manifestations needed to be fractal-like, having a whole range of different sizes, and overlapping so that the dimples had their own dimples. After dwelling on this for a few days, we came up with a better natural analogy: the moon's surface. The idea was popular with Johannes and the acousticians, and turned out to be another crucial step forward in the development of the unique design of the room. The moon fitted the diffusive manifestations description perfectly: It has mountains and valleys, boulders as small as a marble and as large as a house, and, most importantly, overlapping craters in a range of depths and diameters from less than a meter to hundreds of kilometers.

Using this as a starting point, we handed Zack (Zackery Belanger) from Kirkegaard Associates some sketches showing how this might work on a panel: a random pattern of overlapping circular depressions of various sizes. Zack then interpolated this in MATLAB software, and, starting with the Fibonacci sequence as a generator of a "pseudo-random" grid of sizes, spacing and depths, he wrote a parametric algorithm that generated three-dimensional computer models. The most promising models were then fabricated out of glass fiber reinforced gypsum and tested in real-world applications. The fabrication process of making a panel involves first making a "positive" fiberboard blank of the panel using a five-axis CNC machine, from which a silicone mold is then made, followed by the final step where the panel is cast in the mold using layers of liquid gypsum plaster and fiberglass matting.

Some of the early test panels included a waveform feature in their surface, added for additional acoustic scatter. We were never keen on this, as it gave the panels a rather flabby, liquid appearance that we felt was at odds with the "digital" character of the circular dimples and the overall effect of a wall-sized array of panels. Luckily, the waveform panels performed no better than the simple ones in acoustics tests, so the point became moot, and we were able to jettison them during the develop-

EXPERIMENTS IN EXPERIENCE

It will be interesting to look back in 10 years and see how well the EMPAC program is thriving. Within months of the building's opening we have already seen the Concert Hall playing host to some thoroughly un-concert-hall-like performances: stages projecting out over the audience, grand pianos suspended in mid-air, and some engaging high-definition films on its enormous projection screen. Studio 1, meanwhile, quickly gained the moniker the Darth Vader studio—I am sure owing to its somewhat filmic and surprisingly photogenic quality, reminiscent of the fusion of design and future technology often captured in science fiction. When I was last there, the room was being used by some engineering researchers to develop a kind of motion-tracking technology, using special cameras and projectors. And no doubt that campus supercomputer has also been busy, conjuring the kinds of virtual and augmented realities the room was designed for.

Architecturally, we are very proud of the building that finally

floor and ceiling all cast from monolithic concrete propelled the design forward."

ment process. One other disagreement was about the detail of the panel edges, where for architectural reasons we wanted to have a blank border a centimeter wide to visually articulate the sense of each panel being an individual "voice"—contributing to a whole, rather than merely looking as though it has been excised from a continuous pattern that has no acknowledgement of "edge." This was a subtle point; after all, there were to be air gaps between each panel anyway. But it proved to be one of those important details that can only be appreciated when the room is complete.

The debate about whether Studio 1 needed an architectural identity or none at all (to avoid performance preconception) was thus solved by turning to an industrial design sensibility, and in doing so we managed to achieve both outcomes. The experience of the room, either in the dark during a performance or in the light outside of one, is like standing inside a giant science experiment and there is something undeniably stirring and profound about it.

emerged—blinking, it almost seemed, after so many years under wraps—but especially given the long and difficult process, the unique and highly complex program and what turned out to be a very tricky site. It is a building of many facets, and each has its own story. The curved cedar hull, the glycol-filled glass curtain wall, the inflated ETFE (ethylene tetrafluoroethylene) cushions of the atrium skylight, and the unusual, rock-anchored foundations are all innovative and worthy of essays in themselves. But ultimately, EMPAC as a work of architecture is about spaces for people and performance, and its success will be measured by the ascendancy of the Concert Hall and Studio 1 in synthesizing a design for the eye, the body and the ear.

Part III: The Possibilities

A New Icon

A popular story seems particularly apt as we seek to explore the "meaning" of EMPAC.

On a foggy autumn day nearly 800 years ago, a traveler happened upon a large group of workers adjacent to the River Avon. Despite being tardy for an important rendezvous, curiosity convinced the traveler that he should inquire about their work. With a slight detour, he moved toward the first of the three tradesmen and said, "My dear fellow, what is it that you are doing?" The man continued his work and grumbled, "I am cutting stones." Realizing that the mason did not wish to engage in a conversation, the traveler moved toward the second of the three and repeated the question. To the traveler's delight, this time the man stopped his work, ever so briefly, and stated that he was a stonecutter. He then added, "I came to Salisbury from the north to work. But, as soon as I earn ten quid, I will return home." The traveler thanked the second mason, wished him a safe journey home and began to head to the third of the trio.

When he reached the third worker, he once again asked the original question. This time the worker paused, glanced at the traveler until they made eye contact and then looked skyward, drawing the traveler's eyes upward. The third mason replied, "I am a mason and I am building a cathedral." He continued, "I have journeyed many miles to be part of the team that is constructing this magnificent cathedral. I have spent many months away from my family and I miss them dearly. However, I know how important Salisbury Cathedral will be one day and I know how many people will find sanctuary and solace here. I know this because the Bishop once told me his vision for this great place. He described how people would come from all parts to worship here. He also told that the Cathedral would not be completed in our days but that the future depends on our hard work." He paused and then said, "So I am prepared to be away from my family because I know it is the right thing to do. I hope that one day my son will continue in my footsteps and perhaps even his son if need be."[1]

From the west, visible from the routes 2 and 7 arterial connectors that cross the Hudson Valley, EMPAC presents itself from afar, a massive, twin-formed object, extending beyond the hill crest into the green zone above the gridded linear 19th-century urban fabric of downtown Troy. It stands pressed into the Hudson River valley slope, projecting out of Rensselaer Polytechnic Institute's historic green-roofed "acropolean" campus.

A BOLD DESIGN

EMPAC consists of several buildings within a building, split into a north and a south block, articulated by a 90-foot vertical slice of space between its north block wooden hull and its south block theater and studios. Within the north block, propped beneath a hovering canopy roof, is a great wooden hull housing the Concert Hall, which appears to float above the adjacent sloping landscape. EMPAC announces itself through its position on the valley rim, its bulk extending out into the space and its transparency revealing a pregnant waiting form within. It promises the city and region something extraordinary.

Even the casual observer, looking at the EMPAC building, realizes that something

Previous pages and opposite: EMPAC a canvas for a light installation by Jennifer Tipton prior to opening — as seen from adjacent to the building (previous), and from Troy's downtown district (left).

"The idea for the concert hall is a really fine, quality object, sitting inside a shell. It's a great promise, from the outside, and then you cross the bridge and enter into it, and the theatrical surprise is that you don't discover what you thought you were going to. Beyond the portals it's very machined, and shadowed, and feels beautiful in a different way from the warmth of the hull."

— Sir Nicholas Grimshaw and Mark Mistur (in back-and-forth conversation)

new is going on. It is new, but it is not merely a novelty. Every element that breaks away from the norm to innovate does so for a reason.

Let us put the obvious innovation, the hull, into perspective. The hull joins a number of recent compelling projects that develop a complex geometric form within another form (Rogers: Bordeaux Law Courts; Polschek: Rose Planetarium). EMPAC's hull is distinct in the way it is umbilically linked to the other building components, and there is little mistaking its inspiration from Archigram's "Walking City,"[2] where a collage of discrete animate forms express a future of change that is daring and poetic.

But what is the significance behind the ship-in-a-bottle conceit? The meaning lies in its urban construct. EMPAC is not like most buildings, made of stacked floor levels that might as well be a universe away. Just as in a city, where buildings are arranged along streets and public places are found in pockets of space between, under and sometimes on top of structures, EMPAC's discrete building forms (the hull, south block, north block, canopy roof) are expressed in clear relationship to one another within a three-dimensional field.

What emerges here is *a space between*, an experience whose organization can be understood in relationship to its programmatic parts and whose forms create awareness, anticipation and memory. We see architecture that links people to their surroundings, to the various building components and to others who share those spaces.

For three weeks in January 2008, acclaimed lighting designer Jennifer Tipton turned the EMPAC construction site into a dynamic light sculpture that could be seen intimately from nearby streets, as well as from a distance across the Hudson and beyond. This project created a regional awareness and buzz about the EMPAC building even before it opened its doors.

EMPAC continues to entice, creating anticipation long before entering. Step around the corner of the library, and it surprises. From the streets of Troy, it promises a different world. EMPAC beckons from the highway, inviting travelers to learn more. This is appropriate. The center is all about perception, the mediated world and new realities. EMPAC is dedicated to research at the intersection of the physical, visual and aural performing arts, and it promises to become one of progressive artists' "global village"[3] touch points (both virtual and real).

EMPAC is the world's stage for the playing out of performance and media experiments. It provides a place where the science of fiction can become the science of reality

Top:
EMPAC viewed from the City of Troy below on a wintry day (left); aerial view of the EMPAC model showing the split form of the north and south blocks (right).

Middle:
Archigram's *Walking City* — a 1960's vision of the future. Ron Herron, 1964 (left); view of the EMPAC model from the southwest showing the hovering wing-like roof over the lobby (right).

Bottom:
Jennifer Tipton light installation — announcing the promise of EMPAC to the City, Valley and region (left); View of the EMPAC model from the North showing the hull behind the north curtain wall and protruding to the west (right).

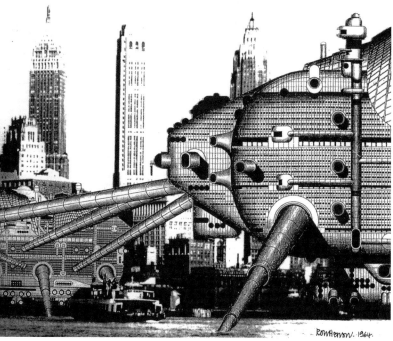

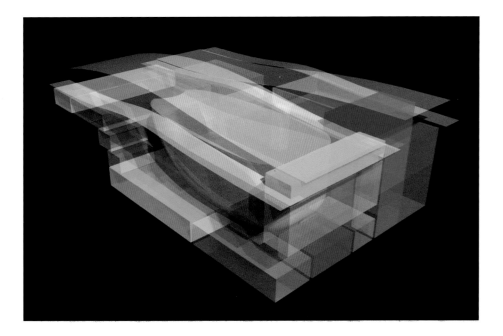

—where in its most powerful manifestation, life and science will imitate art and be enhanced by it. Here, creative people follow their imaginations. The design piques their interest and curiosity. Its spaces and infrastructure support the activities of researchers, create internal intersections and express the Institute's commitment to adding a new dimension to itself and the region. Here, they have the support, collaborators and platform to work through daring ideas—to try something.

FORMS AND SPACES

EMPAC presents Rensselaer and the region with a compelling and accessible assemblage of interrelated forms that create a conversation with one another and the site. These spaces are linked to one another and the site through a network of interstitial, sectionally developed, programmed "spaces between"—and manipulations of light and view that engage the surrounding campus, city, valley and sky.

Located at the southwest corner of campus, EMPAC effectively resolves a disparate and unfortunate assemblage of mid-20th-century buildings lacking proportion, transparency or any sense of public spirit. Their only merit, cleverly resolved by EMPAC, is the near formation of a quadrangle opening westward over the Hudson Valley, similar in orientation and scale to the historic open-space plan of the ivied green-roofed core campus to its north.

EMPAC is divided into two massing blocks (north and south) of similar size but vastly different character and treatment. Each is pressed into the slope to the east and projected out into the valley to the west. The visually reserved design of EMPAC's south block, similar in massing and aligned with the Material Research Center and Cogswell Laboratory (Chemistry) buildings, extends beyond the crest of the hill to frame the site for the formally more ambitious north block. Its hovering roof sets up a visual east-west axis on the centerline of the quadrangle. It receives the south campus landscape into its

Diagrammatic model showing the major programmatic components view from the northwest.

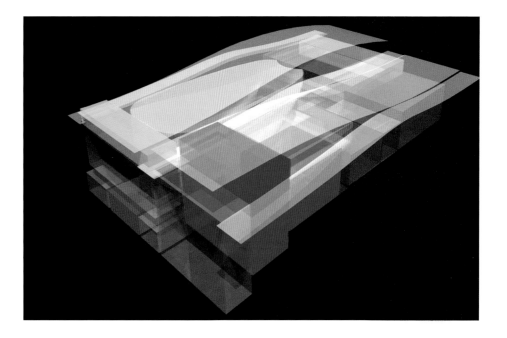

generous glazed lobby, on axis with and visually targeting the hull under the grand sweep of a floating tied-arch roof structure. Its wooden form and conical portals, and the bridges leading to them, heighten the object nature of the hull and create a strong visual target that unifies the space, even from a distance, drawing attention away from the south-flanking buildings. But that is not all.

Though it is deceptively modest in the amount of building mass presented to the campus, EMPAC manages to complete the quadrangle, while creating a strong reference to and suggestion of the western sky and valley beyond its wing-like roof.

From the east and north, the hull appears held back to land by a series of skewed ramping bridges. It seems ready to either tumble down the hill or to drift away, as though it were a docked dirigible ready for flight. Its unmistakable presence, realized through both formal (ship in a bottle) and material (wooden hull) strategies, creates promise and suspense. It piques awareness, curiosity and desire about what is, and what might be happening within.

The lobby slab extends the upper campus plateau and entry plaza westward, giving way to a gap revealing a series of spaces cascading beneath and beyond the belly of the hull. Here one enters EMPAC, moving into the grand glazed lobby set at the rim of the valley and uppermost level of the center. Continuing on past the transparent enclosure, one is confronted by the hovering wood-clad hull, referencing a ship or musical instrument. It stares back, through its circular portals, which are the gateways to theatrical experiences at its various balcony levels.

To Sir Nicholas Grimshaw, the craft and warmth of the curved-wood construction "refers to a Stradivarius that establishes the level of excellence and craft and builds expectation and promise that this is something special." The wooden form is bathed in daylight (light drifting across its surface) penetrating through a horseshoe-shaped skylight that separates the hull from the roof.

Diagrammatic model showing the major programmatic components – view from the southwest.

Axial view of main entrance from campus

[The wooden hull] was a sort of analogy to, as much as anything, the beauty of the construction of the Stradivarius. What it represented in terms of an incredible piece of work. And it was as much that quality that we wanted to stress, that the building was going to be beautifully put together and the materiality of it, rather than making a direct analogy with the shape of a violin. We were trying to press the idea of a really fine, quality object, sitting inside a shell and circulation spaces.

— Sir Nicholas Grimshaw

Top:
West and north façade of EMPAC in the evening, revealing the seemingly suspended hull, like a docked dirigible ready for flight (left); view of EMPAC from campus at an opening, held back to grade by bridges linking event-goers to the waiting form (right).

Middle:
An event in the lower lobby at level 5000 (left); interstitial space beneath the bridges and under the bulging form of the hull provides for receptions, presentations, discussions and has become a vital living space of campus (right).

Bottom:
View from the north on an opening evening showing the upper and lower lobbies, gathering and entry into the Concert Hall through a series of terraces and spaces that cascade down the slope, under the hull (left); south façade of the south block looking west into a sunset. (right).

Beyond the massive hull to the west, one finds the horizon. Above it, sunsets regularly pierce the public circulation spaces in the evening; below it sits the roofscape of a 19th-century industrial city. Each of these is collaged into the experience. The vertical slice of space between the south block and the hull frames a dramatic vertically cropped view of the city and sky. One is not just in a building made of repeated slabs and blind corridors linking rooms, but in a kind of urban landscape that reveals its parts and links to its surroundings. To the north and west, the eye follows the vista that extends around the curved form and is released through the glazed north curtain wall to the valley and sky beyond.

A surprising scale shift occurs here. On approach from the campus, what had seemed a modest structure drops away down the hill to reveal the massive form of the Concert Hall projected out over the city and into the valley. From the upper lobby, a grand staircase, linking the various levels and activities of the center, descends 80 feet to Eighth Street, pressed between the glazed north curtain wall and the wooden hull, parallel to the sloping landscape. On the other side of the Concert Hall, a second, continuous, open central stair, in the skylighted crevice between the hull and south block, ascends from the

Eighth Street entry to a large café reception area at level 5000. The café and an exhibition area one level above are embedded into an excavated shelf of space, tucked under the main building lobby that, together with the exhibition balcony at level 6000, is connected by bridges across a gap to the bulging form of the hull.

Evelyn's Café is a fulcrum of activity, the living room of the building and campus. It's an intimate space, wedged under the hull, bridges and lobby, yet connected laterally to the northern landscape. There, an outdoor reception terrace accommodates fair-weather events and casual conversations. A westward view of the city and Hudson Valley is glimpsed past the wooden hull. Vertical and diagonal views to the main lobby and other parts of the building place one in knowing relation to many of the center's activities. It is the entry point to the main level of the Concert Hall, the Goodman Theater/Studio 1 and Studio 2, and through it one gains access to the lower levels of the Theater.

While the upper lobby receives the campus landscape, creating a grand, formal entrance to the building and setting high expectations, this second internal lobby is intimate. It serves as the scene of event receptions with artists, lecturers, performers and audiences, including students and their parents. Here, everyone is welcome and people linger—to plan what they are going to do and to comment on what they have just seen and heard.

Many great buildings have atria—though they are most typically large, empty organizing voids. Few have the sophistication of EMPAC's. The atrium it creates is not traditional. It exploits the building's interstitial space to reveal—not in whole, but in part—what is beyond, above and below. The ledges (south block corridors, lobby, level 6000 exhibition space), crevices and vertical gaps (central stair void, theater lobby), often narrow, create opportunities for aesthetically pleasing views that are both diagonal and framed. These may be available anywhere from the lobby to the hull, from the south

Early concept of a lounge looking west.

block corridors to Evelyn's Café or through the entire facility to the city. Building users are aware of their surroundings and are stimulated by both the forms and the interstitial spaces among them. It makes everyone a participant. Moving through EMPAC is an experience of movement between its parts, not within isolated corridors.

Most buildings have elevators to convey a person from one space to another on an abstracted voyage programmed by the push of a button to 3, 5 or 11. It is a non-architectural event. There is no space between to experience or enjoy — only the box and awkward conversation. One would imagine that the elevators in a building located on a 90-foot sloping site would be essential to moving about the building, but they are not. At EMPAC, a person is far more likely to travel on the various open stairs, through the spaces to destinations they can see; for example, the café down a level or the exhibitions along the open corridors of the south block. These are interesting journeys, easy enough to walk, descend and even climb. It is an adventure.

From the city below, marking the southwest corner of the campus in the greater landscape of Troy, EMPAC creates a second grand presence. From this lower vantage, it soars over a re-emerging industrial city representing Rensselaer's commitment to excellence and to a future that embraces innovation, culture and science with an ambitious engineering and architectural structure.

1. Girard J.P. Girard and S. Lambert, "The Story of Knowledge: Writing Stories that Guide Organisations into the Future," *The Electronic Journal of Knowledge Management*, Volume 5, Issue 2, 2007.

2. 1960s avant-garde architecture group whose speculative project, Walking City, proposed a radical vision for dynamic, animate urban building forms.

3. Marshall McLuhan, *Understanding Media*, Routledge Classics, 2nd Ed., 2001.

View of Troy from the artists' spaces and Founder's Room

A Compelling Brief

EMPAC was designed to stimulate a culture, enable research and artistic enterprise and create possibilities. It was to be a living room for the campus reaching out to its own students and faculty, and it was to become a fulcrum of cultural events and intellectual diversity. But EMPAC was also designed to attract a global community of progressive artists, and thinkers. To do this, it had to create space and facilities and infrastructure for human-scale research, and it had to link these to technology—to create the opportunity for virtual immersive environments, augmented realities, advanced visualizations and possibilities not yet conceived. EMPAC had to create high-fidelity spaces that would enable specific undertakings, but it also had to offer a range of flexibility sufficient to support the unconventional, the not yet tried.

ON FLEXIBILITY

Conventional knowledge holds that the bane of designing a high-performing space is asking it to do too many things well—to be multi-purpose. Sir Nicholas Grimshaw, when meeting with Dr. Shirley Ann Jackson, asked, "Do you want a room that can accommodate a basketball tournament and a full orchestra and a rock band, or do you want a hall that will result in a beaten path to Rensselaer?" The answer was quick and affirmative, EMPAC had to be a world-class facility, and to do that, Dr. Jackson assembled an A-team of architects, engineers, theater consultants and acousticians; but the facility was also to be a part of a larger agenda and had to do more than meet classical and well-accepted performance criteria. EMPAC was not to be a traditional performing arts center; it was to be an experimental one—a research facility "where art meets science meets technology"[1]. It had to allow, even enable, artists, scientists, students and faculty to work in unconventional modalities with new and emerging technologies. This meant that its programmers, designers and even the director and curators could not predict all the things the facility was expected to enable; it had to be flexible.

The owner, designers and director knew that possibility, opportunity and excellence would not be well supported by neutral spaces—venues that were "wide open" for all manner of performance and research, but not particularly good for any one of them. They knew that the agenda would not be served by compromising the performance criteria (e.g., acoustic criteria) first established, even at a high cost. A symphony orchestra demands and excels in an entirely different kind of space from an amplified band or a multimedia performer or an avant-garde theater troupe or a researcher interested in data visualization in a human-scale, virtual environment. Each demands an entirely different space, configuration, acoustic environment and infrastructure. The challenge was to create a facility that provided venues highly specific to certain well-understood activities, and that were at the same time elastic in how they could be interpreted and used, without compromising excellence.

The notion of total flexibility—that anything might be able to occur effectively any time, anywhere—would have set an unrealistic expectation. Nevertheless, EMPAC demonstrates that significant adjustability, tunability and reconfigurability can be added

Ceiling in Goodman Theater/Studio1 showing the walkable ceiling grid and 360 degree projector mount.

"We didn't use the word 'flexibility' very much. In fact, we tried to be clear about what the function of every space was. We did work, for instance, in the studio with 'reconfigurability'."

— Joshua Dachs

to high-fidelity, purpose-driven spaces without compromising their core specifications.

But within the focus of pushing the technical limits in each venue was a simple idea: While the facility as a whole would aspire to extending possibilities and pushing the limits of imagination, each individual venue had to include specializations that thoughtfully incorporated limits. This was how the paradox of balancing multi-purpose requirements with excellence was solved. From this early concept, unique venues with real-world limits needed to be constructed.

Incorporating limits may seem inhibiting, especially to those who have not lived in the world of creative professionals. To the creative spirit—as counterintuitive as it may seem—there can be a tyranny of freedom. Writers often struggle when they face a blank page. An empty canvas can intimidate a painter. A pristine marble rock, in many ways so inviting, can also mock the sculptor. Where to begin, and what to do? The composer Igor Stravinsky writes about accepting limits as a means of liberating creativity in this way:

> As for myself, I experience a sort of terror when, at the moment of setting to work and finding myself before the infinitude of possibilities that present themselves, I have the feeling that everything is permissible to me … Will I then have to lose myself in this abyss of freedom? … Let me have something finite, definite—matter that can lend itself to my operation only insofar as it is commensurate with my possibilities. And such matter presents itself to me together with its limitations. I must in turn impose mine upon it.[2]

EMPAC was designed not merely to stage performances, but to support the creation of new works, to catalyze invention and to open the doors to discovery. Seldom does it work to say, "I am going to go out to discover something or invent something." It is more likely that discoveries and inventions emerge from activity—doing something specific, in a particular place. The design and programming team knew it was critical to empower the creative enterprise with specific, finite, well-considered capabilities and, with that, some amount of constraint that the specific venues, to meet rigorous specifications, required.

EMPAC answers this challenge with its four highly distinct performance venues, which includes two styles of black box experimental studios and a variety of artist and researcher support spaces under one roof. Each is individually optimized for a particular range of activities, and conceived and equipped to empower the user to operate either conventionally or unconventionally. But this is just the beginning of how specificity and flexibility (of program and possibility) have been carried out in a project to empower the imaginations and enterprises of artists and researchers. The spatial configuration and acoustic distinction of each of the four rooms were crucial. Whether for a large audience (Concert Hall),

Top: A film shoot being set up in Studio 2 with the acoustic banners down (left); Laurie Anderson developing a new piece in Studio 2 (right).

Middle: Nathan Davis set-up for a recording session in the Concert Hall (left and right).

Bottom: Workspace Unlimited residency in panoramic screen in Goodman Theater/Studio1 (left); Professor Richard Radke's multi-camera video tracking research with a full scale airport security set-up in Studio 2 (right).

small audience (Theater), acoustic or amplified performance, each provides unique differences and opportunities from the other. Their individual and rigorous specifications are what enable highly specific artistic and scientific realizations at EMPAC.

Common to all the major venues was the call to ensure that there would be no acoustic interference between them, and that once inside, the ambient noise levels (from equipment, air, lights, etc.) would achieve no more than the lowest level specified for any building room type—that of recording studios—where one can hear a pin drop. Standard Room Criteria (RC) levels for a typical office area or even a library range from 35–40, but the EMPAC program called for an RC of 15 in each of the four performance spaces, a rating usually reserved for the highest-performing TV broadcast studios (15–25) and concert halls (15–20).

Silence is enabling because sound can be added to it. Were the baseline noise levels in the performance spaces, either from outside or within, higher, an entire range of acoustic perception would be masked and lost. Because of this, we can say that there exists at EMPAC a typically unavailable acoustic space (range/register) that can be discovered and experimented with within. Unless rigorous sound isolation and ambient noise specifications are established at the start of a building project, there can be no practical way to subtract background noise later on. In this way, sound is much like light, which cannot be extinguished by darkness. Sound cannot be hushed by silence.

But this just describes the baseline, before a click or screech is ever generated in the space. The sound of silence is merely the foundation upon which four distinct acoustic environments were created for artistic creation, performance and experimentation. Each room has its own acoustic signature, including a reverberation time, an acoustic energy (loudness) and diffusiveness. In a room (without using headphones), there is simply no way to avoid the fact that sound does not simply emanate from one spot and travel directly to the ear. It travels at a specific speed and reflects off the many surrounding surfaces in a variety of ways (depending on its material and surface geometry), traveling different distances and requiring different amounts of time to reach the ear. It is first mediated by its physical surroundings. Each of EMPAC's performance venues has its own specific reverberation time and acoustic signature that favors some activities over others.

The specificity of a space—for example, its long reverberation time, hard sonic quality, the largeness of its dimensions or axial arrangement, even its lighting, especially when these become obstructions—can provoke, shift perspective and catalyze a workaround. It can even inspire creativity. Sometimes the restraints provoke a global shift in thinking, to do something other than what was first intended—and one would hope so at EMPAC, if it is, in fact, experimental.

The rigorous specifications and restraints at EMPAC enable highly specific and refined realizations of an artist's or scientist's work. In some instances they lead to a highly tuned acoustic experience; in others, a multimedia performance, and in still others, a synthetic combination of a broad range of activities. The possibilities of each room had to be enabled not just by its fidelity for one purpose, but by the specific infrastructure and flexibility of each.

To create a memorable symphony orchestra experience for the musicians and audience, the Concert Hall provides 1.9- to 2.9-second reverberation times (depending on the deployment of the banners), with acoustically reflective but diffuse surfaces to maintain the sound energy without the problem of focused reflections. The architects, working with the acousticians, were determined to realize the acoustic quality of the world's great halls within a contemporary, if not futuristic aesthetic — one that reveals in its surfaces what they are contributing acoustically. But the design also invites the performer to transgress the boundary between stage and audience, and readies a projection screen and the possibility of suspended sets often reserved for theatrical performances. Even the Concert Hall's reverberation time can be lowered to accommodate a contemporary alternative group or the presentation of a Nobel laureate.

In addition to the specificity of EMPAC's venues, there is also an elasticity, an ability to interpret, and an ability — even an invitation — to digress. Why should the performer present his or her craft stage center? Why not on the balcony, in the galleries, or above the ceiling? Johannes Goebel insisted that the room work in reverse, sideways or any way the creator might imagine it, and this required an unconventional approach. But the single-room concept did much of the work. It had to serve convocations and scientific presentations, panel discussions and colloquia, as well as a wide range of artistic expressions.

> If you need a non-reflective right side of the room, you can get it. The vertical banners in the upper volume can be deployed at any length and in any combination along the length of the room to take out individual reflections, or to deaden the room, if that's the desired acoustic. It's an extremely tunable room, from the standpoint of its reflection structure and reverberation time.
>
> — Carl Giegold

But the Concert Hall will never be a dry acoustic space. The decision was to give the studios much lower acoustic reverberation times, with walls that can be reconfigured to further shape the sound — even in particular spots or zones. They enable a different kind of performance, installation or experimentation. Here the question of stage and audience is thrown completely into question. With almost no spatial orientation or bias, the configuration is wholly the decision of the artist or performer.

> We've done all we can as inspirers and responders to keep the ambition to an absolute. So in acoustic terms, in noise-control terms, in flexibility and in tuning terms, in lighting, in rigging — the flexibility to be able to move something almost anywhere … to turn the room inside out and around backside too, and to be extraordinarily flexible [was the intent]. So [the studios] look like bare boxes, and for the unimaginative, they will remain bare boxes, until something magic happens in them. And there's probably no end to the magic that can be conceived in them.
>
> — Larry Kirkegaard

And between these two extremes is the Theater, with all the accoutrements and possibilities of a Broadway theater, and more. It was given a full fly tower, enormous stage house, orchestra pit, projection screen and proscenium (the opening between the stage and the audience). But unlike many theaters, the stage is not a prisoner of the stage house. If desired, the entire proscenium wall all but disappears, and the stage can thrust out into the audience or a performance wrap around its sides. Even the ceiling of the audience hall and its surrounding walls can be animated with real and projected parts of the performance.

The disappearing proscenium of the Theater can open performances to the full width of the audience hall. Side-wall galleries, steeply raked seats and a thrust stage that can become seating or an orchestra pit—all feed the close connection between performer and audience. This is something that is rarely afforded in a theater with a 70-foot-tall fly over a full stage production house. This is a theater with intimacy enough for a poetry reading, yet well outfitted for a Cirque du Soleil-type event. The range of possibilities, even flexibility, to exploit the wizardry of lighting and rigging effects, or the mix of media and physical sets and bodies in motion—3-D motion, alone, is enough to ignite the imagination.

No less critical is the research agenda and the ability to experiment, to be able to do what one first imagined and sometimes more. In addition to the specifications that enable high performance, the spaces also provide a high level of reconfigurability, of acoustic adjustability and flexibility of various kinds. Reverberation times of each room were optimized and set for particular performance types, but not fixed. The room dimensions and orientation in the Concert Hall and Theater had to be predetermined to realize excellent sightlines for large audiences, but their configurations and the ways the venues can be interpreted create opportunity for speculation and experiment, to challenge the relationship between the audience and the performer and to mix media.

To create omnidirectional rooms was no small challenge. Nevertheless, as performances in each venue have already demonstrated, the single-room aspiration (joining performers and audiences) went a long way toward acoustically achieving this objective. Eliminating the traditional proscenium and placing a choir behind the stage has not only resulted in the intimacy between the performer and audience, it has created the remarkable sense that sound can emanate from anywhere—trumpeters in the galleries or even on the catwalks above the fabric ceiling.

Concert Hall from side gallery, rear.

The upper concrete ceiling of the Concert Hall has about 60 holes, which are usually closed with a rubber plug so there's no acoustical connection between the space up above and down below. But you can take the plugs out and you can put a chain hoist above the opening. And there are actually funnels in the opening between the sails of the ceiling where the chain can go through all the way to the ground of the floor. So having these 60 or some holes, scattered all over the Concert Hall, allows us to hang any physical object at any place in that whole Concert Hall, be it projection screens, be it platforms, be it objects. Because if you have two points, two chain horses coming down, you can connect them with a truss and hang what you want anywhere in between. Now this is another example of how we're trying to accommodate, without building multifunctional spaces, still keeping to peak performance to each space — a flexibility as you will never find in a concert hall.

— Johannes Goebel

Flexibility is often thought of as having lots of movable things at one's disposal. In the Concert Hall, this is kept to a minimum. The drop-down, side-wall banners are movable, and they do contribute to the ability to extend the range of the hall for amplified events and the spoken word. And the funnels and winches in the attic above the ceiling void, aligned over the ceiling gaps, do provide opportunities to fly in sets, or even the pianist and her Steinway, if desired. But the selective frequency reflectivity of the fixed-in-place fabric ceiling — which to members of an orchestra crisply reflects back the sound of their instruments while judiciously allowing the deep bass frequencies of a power band through to the void above, achieves two seemingly contradictory functions without changing anything — is simply magic. Nothing has to move, be removed or be

A stage built over the first rows of the Concert Hall for a concert with Deerhunter and Boredoms. Trusses for loudspeakers and lighting flown under the fabric ceiling, with additional seating on the actual concert hall stage allowing the audience to sit in a circle around the performance area.

added. It finesses nature, much like a breathable jacket that protects from the rain.

The movable chairs of the Concert Hall and Theater galleries, and the deployable side-wall projection screens of the Theater invite all manner of "surround" performance. The ability to access high-speed data, the availability of high-definition audio and video at virtually any location, and the opportunity to mix a high-resolution 3-D projection onto the stage sets provide tempting options for those producing performances in the Theater. The wire-grid ceiling, rigging hooks and winches above the studios, along with the computer-controlled rigging of the Theater fly space and Goodman Theater, further expand the possibilities. Even the orchestra pit, which triples as a thrust stage or additional seating area, challenges convention.

The elastic possibilities are twofold. First there is the range of what each space can do, and second, it is the message that says, "You have permission, and are supported" — to perform in ways unconventional, with part or all of the performers off the Concert Hall stage, with seats placed on the Theater stage, with the orchestra pit extending the performance space, or with mixed media and suspended sets. It gives permission to set up environments that raise the question of what is physically present and what is projected, and goes on to ask whether either is more or less real. You have permission to perform in different spaces, even those found in cyberspace via miles and miles of fiber optic cables between the venues and linked to high-speed Internet access. You can create a conversation or performance, or experiment between them or simultaneously with others in say, London and Los Angeles and elsewhere. You can then circle back to discuss the work that is being created long before an audience enters, because artists and researchers are given time to develop ideas through a researcher (artist)-in-residence program, and not to just perform finished works.

To fully exploit EMPAC, the artist or researcher needs to be able to ask, "What can I do here in this space that I cannot do elsewhere, and how shall I do it?"

Since a disproportionate number of contrarians are found in progressive creative circles, there should not be a shortage of those who see, innovate and invent against expectations — and find at EMPAC permission to do so. The building and its venues, its infrastructure and programmatic support encourage and enable the unconventional to happen. Ultimately, it is not just a question of permission, but of opportunity.

A classical guitarist knows how to strum a B flat exactly in tune with the 12-tone musical scale, but to bend the note, that is a different matter. To tap out harmonics on the neck as if it were a percussion instrument, or to tune the instrument altogether differently — these are variations on the specific restraints for which the guitar was intended, designed, but they are no less a part of the musician's art.

It is not what you are allowed to do in EMPAC's well-tuned spaces — it is what you *can* do in its experimental settings. The shape, configuration and sound of the rooms, the infrastructure and the support mechanisms all matter. But most of all, the ideas that are generated matter, and in this experimental performing arts center, there are both the specific restraints and the elastic possibilities to fertilize and incubate them.

1. From EMPAC promotional material.
2. Igor Stravinsky, *Poetics of Music: In the form of six lessons*. Harvard University Press, 1993.

View of the Theater and fly tower from the stage

The Technical Infrastructure of EMPAC

JOHANNES GOEBEL

In just a few years after these words go to press, readers will remark on how quickly technology moved forward in the meantime. Ten or 15 years after the opening of EMPAC, people will chuckle about the limitations of technology "back then" and about the considerations that went into designing the infrastructure. Thirty years down the road, this chapter will read like an archeological document. Media that stored video and audio documents of the early years of EMPAC will have deteriorated or will only be retrieved as sounds and images after intensive searches for compatible hard- and software. It will become obvious that the very technology that can store anything is the most ephemeral storage medium for art and information humanity created in its technological strides.

One hundred years from now, the "information society" will be a period long passed. Individual and institutional archives of digital documents collected during the second half of the 20th century and during the first 20 years of the 21st century will have gone the way all documents go that are not protected by continuous care and financial support. The promise of the universal format of digital technology and storage has already proven not to be true and to be directly correlated to power and funding for copying and transferring and porting it to new systems. Techno-politically, we might be back in the medieval ages when monasteries were the guardians of a very select set of information, the copying now not done by hand but by machines, which are certainly owned and maintained under strategic and economic criteria. And there will be the underground of "ancient digital information" maintained by curious, stubborn and dedicated individuals.

The interactive art, the media art, the scientific visualization projects, the collaborative projects between art, science and technology may not be experienced anymore, but may still be read about. The pages on which this book is printed may still be found and readable. And most probably, the architecture of EMPAC, the building itself will outlast mice and men, bits, bytes and pieces. And this is the unique legacy of EMPAC. People with new ideas, new arts and performance practices, new technology and new directions of research still will be able to find EMPAC inspirational and valuable after many decades. Let's imagine for a split second that the building would not be maintained for 50 or 70 years—what a find for adventurous minds taking over the building then, finding its aesthetic presence still detectable, reading this book and finding out what this was built for—and starting anew with fresh ideas to inhabit every space in this building, with new technology, new tools and new ideas.

EMPAC has been designed to create a bridge between the physical and the digital worlds, between the world we can see, hear, move in and touch and the computer world in which we can create experiences for our senses. The description of the architecture in this book presents a vivid perspective on the building and its properties. The aesthetics of the architecture created a long-lasting building that will meet students, visitors, artists and researchers over the decades to come and will evoke responses that will always be individually different but which are evoked by the architecture itself. The layout of the venues and spaces and their construction were optimized as a long-lasting platform for experimental media and performing arts. The current technical infrastructure of the building is probably the most fleeting part of EMPAC. Our senses of seeing and hearing

Composer Hans Tutschku in Goodman Theater/ Studio 1 with many loudspeakers hung from trusses to create a sound dome above and around the audience.

and our bodily movements will most probably, and hopefully, be a stable part of our human condition. But the technology we use in creating expressions of our visions and impressions for our senses will keep changing.

EMPAC is defined by these different timelines of architecture, technology and the actual projects and works that are realized in the building with the available technology. The different temporal conditions of architecture, technology and content were consciously part of the design and specification of the initial technical infrastructure.

The technical infrastructure can equally be broken down into different categories of longevity.

LONGEST LASTING

The longest-lasting part of the technical infrastructure is that which depends on the structural potential of the building itself, on the loads the walls, floors and ceilings are actually built for. The weight of the steel structure for the theatrical rigging, the catwalks, the hanging points and the weights that may be lifted and moved through space are part of the construction of the building. It would be very prohibitive to go beyond the dimensions of these specifications and change the building to accommodate, for example, higher loads in the stage house of the Theater or to hang equipment in the middle of the Concert Hall that would go beyond the current rating.

The second longest-lasting conditions are defined by the electrical capacity the building makes available to actually operate all the technology. Usually one may not think of the electrical design as part of the technical infrastructure. In the case of a building that is geared toward bridging the digital world and the world of human perception, it becomes clear that indeed only electricity makes possible this world that is focused on computation, networks and data storage, light, sound and moving things through space. And in conjunction with electricity, the mechanical air systems have also to be regarded as part of the performance specification of the technical infrastructure. Media and computing have a high demand for cooling, which is in direct correlation to the electricity that can be used. Looking at the incredible size and number of transformers and electrical feeds that support the building, it would be fair to assume that they are not going to be changed over the next few decades, and based on the overall capacity of the electricity that is available, it is unlikely this actually would be necessary. The building is fed by a 13.2 kilovolts electrical service.

OF TRAYS AND CABLES

The cable trays that interconnect the venues and technical spaces define another performance criterion of the building. In contrast to most other buildings, the cable trays at EMPAC have to go through acoustically sensitive wall constructions. Any new penetrations through these walls to add new cable trays would be a major issue because of the complex wall build-up and the requirement to maintain the acoustical integrity. Furthermore, the density of existing conduits and trays is already very high and the architectural quality of the building would not allow the putting of new cable trays anywhere as might be needed.

The dimensions of the cable trays had to be considered under the prediction how long the first cabling would be technically usable and when new cabling would become necessary — especially under the consideration of the human factor that new cables are always put on top of the old ones, and people rarely take out the old cables. Cleaning out cable trays is only done as a last resort when the absolute capacity has been reached, like probably every 20 or 30 years. Actually, sizing the cable trays was a challenge because of the limitations of space, such as under ceilings of a corridor, and because of the code restrictions as to how much a cable tray may be filled. Only history will show how this will have worked out.

The next level down in the scale of the rate of change of technology is the cabling infrastructure of the building. It is anticipated that the chosen cabling infrastructure for video, audio, IT and control networks will be good for 10 to 15 years without major change, potentially even longer. New cables might be added, particularly in the field of new fiber optics technology. Otherwise, the existing internal combination of single-mode and some multi-mode fiber, Cat 6, coaxial and balanced 3 conductor cable (110 Ω) will probably serve much longer than most of the existing hardware for routing, I/O, media acquisition and processing. In anticipation of this being an accurate assumption, the cabling infrastructure at EMPAC was given a high priority from a budgetary perspective, as well as from the level of quality control of the installation. We commissioned to have every cable certified after installation and have documented the test results.

LET THERE BE LIGHT

With the taming of fire, we had the first controllable light source in our hands. In the nineteen-thirties, Gertrude Stein wrote an opera libretto that takes the change to electrical light as the point of departure for a meditation on light, religion and the quest for knowledge and immortality. In *Doctor Faustus Lights the Lights*, Faustus receives electric light as part of his deal with the devil to advance his search for all that holds the world together. A dog complains about electric light that changed the night to day and made it hard for him to howl at the moon. And a religious sect gathers around the electric light as its center of adoration.

Light moved from just bringing light to the darkness to an artistic tool once electricity came into play. To utilize light to its full potential for artistic creation, we (still) need dark spaces. This poses a problem for, as an example, museums of contemporary art that exhibit media artworks, which need controllable darkness, parallel to paintings, which are viewed best in the cool light of the northern sky that changes little over the course of a day. Since EMPAC integrates electrical light as a major medium, all venues at EMPAC are dark — in stark contrast to the lobby spaces, which are flooded with daylight.

We use electric light to light actors, dancers, objects and sceneries in the manifold and colorful ways that technology offers. The computer control of theatrical lights has opened a whole new area of the subtle and complex use of light as an integral part of time-based art.

The theatrical use of light differs from the light we use to project images. In the case where light is used to illuminate a scenario with the complex interplay of shadows and colors it can evoke, it is used "like the sun," as a source of light. In the case of projected images, one may say that light is used in a virtual way: It is the simulation of "the sun" *and* the objects that are lit. Recorded or synthetically produced images are projected as if they were in front of us as "real" — as sceneries illuminated by light sources, not as sceneries created in their totality by light. The use of light to illuminate our surroundings is totally different from light being used to create images. This becomes obvious when we observe the technical difficulties of producing a "real" black in projected images. Since black comes from no light coming back to our eyes, there is an inherent problem with "projecting no light" with a bright projector.

Our eyes are best for looking at scenes that are lit, where light is used to bring out the properties of the world around us. Our eyes are not well equipped to stare into light sources, like the sun, a candle, or a light bulb. But with light being used for projections, we are looking directly into the light. Technology still faces a great challenge in meeting this fundamental disposition of our eyes. One direction that is dealing with this issue is the invention of e-paper. This electronic paper controls "actual matter" to create images. For instance, little balls that are half white and half black, and which are then integrated into "paper," can be switched to display their black or white half under computer control to produce a pattern of typed letters. And we read such displayed text through the environmental light sources around us and not by the means of light emitted from the display.

EMPAC, with its scores of theatrical lights and projectors, is a place where the use of light is given highest priority. Dimming light to different and varying levels is one of the major parameters in applying light. Lighting technology made a major step forward when a then new generation of dimming technology was developed in the 20th century. These dimmers "chopped" the incoming electricity to a brightness level, which was desired for aesthetic reasons. The side effect of this technology was that it excites resonant frequencies in the filament of the light fixtures — which is audible. And, as we at EMPAC tried to meet the full range of seeing and hearing in our spaces (we had banished all noise-generating equipment to machine rooms adjacent to the venues), this presented a real issue: Why should light invade the sphere of hearing?

Luckily, a new dimming technology had been developed just in time for EMPAC. The invention of so-called sine wave dimmers was enabled by digital technology. EMPAC, to our knowledge, was the first performing arts center in the U.S. to use sine wave dimmers throughout its venues. This brought us a major step toward our goal of providing spaces where seeing, hearing and moving in space could be treated in truly independent ways. At the same time, digital technology allows us to control all parameters of these different media through networked protocols, which in turn allow creating interdependencies when desired.

AUDIO TECHNOLOGY

Moving along the line of longevity, most of the audio equipment would be the longest lasting on the media side of technology. It is not anticipated that there will be major shifts of paradigm in audio technology that would yield an order of magnitude of improvement.

Digital technology for audio has reached a level of quality where it covers almost all perceptual and acoustical parameters the human ear may require. Sampling rates and sample width cover the full range of events we can hear at full resolution. It is very difficult to imagine new levels of quality that digital technology might provide. Most music listeners around the world have currently accepted the so-called MP3 data reduction of audio signals, even though it is a real reduction in auditory quality that cannot be undone once the algorithm is applied to a sound. The reason for this compression scheme was that network bandwidth was limited, and storage technology bulky and relatively expensive. This has been radically changing from year to year—there is absolutely no reason why this "lossy" compression scheme should be still in use these days when the consumer gets saturated with high-density storage and medium to high bandwidth Internet connectivity. But it may be anticipated that this old data-reduction algorithm will persist for no other reason than its former function of accommodating technology that was not yet up to full audio bandwidth. People prefer what they are used to, even if it means a reduction of quality they were raised on; most probably only a new generation of gadgets that promise status may change this.

EMPAC is designed to accommodate the full bandwidth of digital audio technology without compromises. Interestingly enough, one of the companies bidding for a part of the technical infrastructure was promoting its expertise by pointing out that the company had designed an infrastructure for a performing arts center that allowed "streaming"; that is, compressing audio and video so these signals would find their way through the limited bandwidth of the global network systems. They had a hard time understanding why this was not a convincing argument for us and why we emphasized that we were only interested in uncompressed signals and that streaming technology was of secondary interest, especially since it was nothing "special" anymore.

The analog components of sound and electricity are microphones and loudspeakers. These are the most critical components in the chain from the acoustical event through digital technology and back to the ear, because they capture the sounds and then produce sounds to be perceived. The development of these transducers—taking the movement of the air and converting it to electrical signals, and taking electrical signals and converting them through mechanical means to changing air pressure our ears can perceive—has made incredible progress over the past 30 years. The most critical part of such systems is their inherent noise floor, resulting from the noise of the circuitry used in these devices and which is added to the captured or emitted sound. Because of their analog nature, microphones and loudspeakers have very distinct and audible characteristics, which are determined by their construction. Since EMPAC aims to meet the highest possible correlation between technical signals and those that reach our senses, we have a rich collection of microphones. And because we are not limiting our productions to the standards of "surround sound" or "Left Center Right" loudspeaker arrays or clusters, we have a great number of loudspeaker systems that can be flexibly combined for any kind of arrangement around, above and even below the audience. Furthermore, we chose passive loudspeaker systems as the main workhorses, since large active loudspeakers have built-in cooling fans, which would add quite audible noise to our very quiet venues.

The development of digital technology that either processes recorded sounds or generates synthetic sounds has most probably reached a level of quality that matches our ears. Nevertheless, there are still different qualities associated with specific hardware and software that are used for the processing of audio. We decided to invest in audio components for EMPAC that are basically good for all intents and purposes until they break.

A major consideration for selecting the right equipment then rests with questions of ergonomics and of network integration. In the development of digital audio, some systems went into the direction where they are controlled with keyboard and mouse, such as when a complete audio system is integrated into a laptop. But the traditional approach of mixing boards with many sliders, push buttons and knobs and a clearly differentiated display of information has been refined over decades. Such an interface allows operators to use "all fingers" in a masterful way. For this reason, EMPAC owns highest-level mixing boards, which are fully integrated into the workflow of audio processing and networking.

All audio at EMPAC is connected through a dedicated digital matrix. Such a matrix can be imagined like a very large chess board, where every horizontal row represents one input from a sound source like a microphone, and every vertical row, one output like a loudspeaker; by activating a square on the matrix, the input and output that meet in this square are connected. This matrix can reach any point in the building and pick up or deliver sound to or from any such point. Currently, more than 4,000 points are connected to this matrix, with still a great capacity being available to integrate thousands more connections. Integrated into this matrix is a host of audio processing hard- and software, ranging from amplifiers for microphones or loudspeakers to software that takes the place of former "outboard" effect processors.

The audio matrix is integrated with computer and storage networks and synchronized with the video matrix to perfectly integrate sound and images.

MOVING IMAGES

In contrast to digital audio, digital images still have to take major steps to meet the full potential of our eyes. Due partly to the difference in bandwidths the various senses require to address their full resolution, we do not yet fully understand how to create images that test the limits of what the eye can perceive. Our capabilities in capturing images, processing them and projecting recorded or synthetically created moving images will need to advance dramatically before they will come close to our abilities of visual perception. Comparing what our eyes can see around us with what technology can offer, we can only work with the "suspension of disbelief" to enjoy and use image technology. For artistic purposes this is certainly fine, since artists have always used technology however it became available to them. It is part of artistic work to embrace limitations and work within given boundaries — and to create works that either integrate or make us forget these technical shortcomings. For science and engineering, though, meeting the challenges of the technical resolution in areas of color space, contrast and immersion is still clearly far away from what our eyes like and are capable of seeing.

Since digital image technology is still developing, consumers, producers, artists, archivists and researchers alike are being taken on the roller-coaster ride of parallel universes of standards, interfaces, compatibilities, hardware and software. And at the same time, the price curve for high-end equipment is still fairly steep (as opposed to digital audio technology, for instance, where the price gap between higher-end systems and lower-end systems has considerably closed over the past 15 years).

When specifying the infrastructure for EMPAC, one of the big challenges video posed was the rapid pace of change, along with the lack of standardization between broadcast video and computer graphics. EMPAC's infrastructure needed to seamlessly blend and switch between synthetic computer imagery used in both art and science and the latest technologies in digital video and digital film production.

We decided to go with a mainly fiber optic-based video matrix that would distribute video signals throughout the building at a point in time when such a decision for a fiber-based system still seemed "daring." The decisive argument came from the price for copper, which was driving the cost of cabling. When we compared these costs with those of a fiber optic system including the necessary converters from electrical to optical signals and back, the cost-savings validated our choice. Again, the actual cabling infrastructure will be the part that will "last the longest," where the image acquisition, processing and projection systems are still in the middle of the race, where the constantly changing technology requires fairly high investments to stay up to date.

Another decision for video was parallel to the decision in audio: We wanted to be able to route uncompressed signals through the building. "Uncompressed" certainly refers to the current specification of video signals, which most likely will also change over time. The bandwidth of uncompressed graphics and video is so high that a dedicated central router and a network of fiber optic connections was needed. The converters provide switched and direct connections, handling today's 3Gbps standards and leaving room for up to 10Gbps in each channel for the future. This dedicated video router is not loaded to its capacity, but rather handles "only" 176 inputs and 176 outputs at this time. Like the audio matrix, it has an extensive reach, spanning the whole building. This video matrix allows basically accessing any video signal anywhere in the building.

For live video production, EMPAC turned to a full HD broadcast quality production switcher capable of all of the state-of-the-art capabilities one expects. This device has 32 channels of video input and 32 channels of output at full HD quality, and allows any professionally desired processing for live video switching of cameras and other video sources.

Artistic and scientific environments using computer graphics and video are operating with basically two paradigms: The first and the most common is derived from the paradigm of the book or the framed picture. We have a computer screen of anywhere between, say, 10 and 30 inches diagonal dimensions, and every image we see fits or is made to fit this frame. Or we hang a flat screen on the wall, which might have the dimensions of a well-sized oil painting. Even film projections, which are bigger and accommodate a large number of viewers, are still derived from the paradigm of a large framed picture, a mural of a historic battle or a theater stage reduced to two dimensions.

The second paradigm is to fill the full field of vision of our eyes. In the world of film, this meant very wide screens with 70mm film, then IMAX with the not-quite-full dome projection; in both cases the audience still faces in one direction, as with a theater performance. These presentations can accommodate large audiences.

For the computer graphics world, immersive environments started out for individual viewing through "goggles," glasses with two small screens right in front of one's eyes. One can turn one's head around, walk around and explore a synthetic scenario as one would look around in the real world. To accommodate several viewers who can share such immersive projections while sharing the same physical space, the cave was developed, a rather small cubical environment with projections on five sides and accommodating maybe three to five persons. The next steps in large projections, in which an audience could freely move around, were developed in the arts world with panoramic and dome projections. These immersive environments in the arts world already have been used for a number of years for 3-D, stereoscopic projections and viewing. It is only recently that stereoscopic projections have been moving to the film and consumer world. But once again, these commercial efforts use the "old" paradigm with a constant viewing direction for the audience.

EMPAC is well equipped for both paradigms and open to the next yet unknown paradigm that comes along. We went so far as to embrace non-standardized technologies like digital 3-D stereo production and active stereo projection for the very large screens. Besides those screens, a very large panoramic screen for 360-degree projections can be set-up, and many smaller screens of different sizes are available, with the flexibility of hanging screens and projectors in any configuration, anywhere in the volume of any venue.

In choosing different materials for projection screens, EMPAC took a further step toward accommodating seeing and hearing as independent variables. The very large screens and the panoramic screen are micro-perforated. This means the projection surface is covered with many small holes that allow the installation of loudspeakers behind the screen. This technology has been used in movie theaters, but it has not yet reached the media arts and research that use immersive environments, where mostly rear-projection screens or traditional non-perforated screens are used. These screen types do not allow the placement of loudspeakers behind the screen, because the uninterrupted surface of the screen blocks the sound—and thus the differentiated localization of a visual scenario cannot be complemented by an equally differentiated spatial sound distribution. At EMPAC, we can install any number of loudspeakers behind a screen in any desirable configuration to complement the image projection with an equally complex sound projection.

Overall, the world of moving images will go through phases of further development and technological refinement before it settles on a relatively stable set of standards.

AUDIO

AUDIO MATRIX
1 Lawo P265_N73 Core
4 Lawo P265_Dallis
6 Lawo P265_Dallis_Stagebox
2 Lawo P265_Dallis_Console Support Racks
2 Lynx Studio Aurora16
6 Various RME MADI I/O devises

CONSOLES
2 Lawo mc²56, DSP for 192 channels with VST servers
2 Soundcraft Vi4 w/ stage box MADI
1 Yamaha DM2000V2 MADI
1 Yamaha DM1000V2 MADI
4 Yamaha 01v96V2 MADI
1 S.A.C. System running 10 Client Machines

RECORDERS
2 Pro Tools HD Accel3 SSL Alpha Link MADI I/O
3 Apple Mac Pro Native Recorders running Logic, Cubase, Nuendo, Max/MSP, etc., with RME HDSP PCI interfacing
4 UAD-2e Extreme Omni PAK
6 Apple MacBook Pro
4 MOTU V4HD HD
4 M-Audio Record I/O
3 Tascam DVRA1000
1 Studer A 827, 24 track analog tape machine

SOFTWARE
Virtual Studio Manager
BSS Eclipse
ClearCom
LAWO AdminHD
Shure Wireless Workbench
d&b RopeC
Smaart

CONTROL SYSTEMS
4 IBM Tablets
6 ELO wireless touch controllers

MICROPHONES
2 AKG 451
2 AKG D-230
1 AKG D-230
1 AKG C-12
8 AKG C-414
2 Audio-Technica AT-4050
2 Audio-Technica AT-450
2 Audio-Technica AT-4021
4 Audio-Technica U853R
10 Audio-Technica U857QL
2 Audix OM-7
2 Beyerdynamic M-160
2 Beyerdynamic M-88
8 Countryman Isomax
4 Crown PCC 160
8 Earthworks M-30
1 Electro Voice RE-20

2 Lawson 47
2 Neuman KM 183
4 Neuman KMS-105
2 Neuman KU-100
2 Neuman TLM-170
1 Neuman USM-69
2 Royer R-121
2 Coles 4038
4 Sennheiser MD-421
2 Sennheiser MD-441
10 Sennheiser MKE2-60-Gold/TA4F
1 Sennheiser MKH-70
4 Shure BETA 58A
4 Shure BETA 98
2 Shure Beta-57A
4 Shure KSM-9
4 Shure SM-57
4 Shure SM-58
1 Shure SM-7B
6 Shure SM-86
2 Shure UA845
26 Shure UR1-BP
10 Shure UR4D
2 Schoeps CCM 21 LG
2 Schoeps CCM 2H LG
1 Schoeps CCM 4 LG
1 Schoeps CCM 8 LG
1 Schoeps CMXY 4V LG
1 Schoeps KLY250/5SU
1 Schoeps MAB
1 Schoeps WSR CMXY
1 Schoeps WSR MS Li
1 Schoeps B5D
1 Schoeps BLCg
3 Schoeps CCM 4 LG
2 Schoeps CCM 41 LG
1 Schoeps CCM 8 LG
1 Schoeps HC MINI
1 Schoeps M 100 C
1 Schoeps SGMSC
1 Sennheiser ME-66
2 Shure Antenna Combiner
6 Shure UA845US
1 Shure UA870WB
1 Shure UR1M
1 Shure UR2/BETA58
11 Shure UR4D
16 Shure UR2/KSM9
1 Shure HA-8089
1 Shure PA805SWB
1 Shure P7TRE3
1 Beyerdynamic DT770PRO80
2 DPA 4006
2 DPA 4011-TL
4 DPA 4060
1 Holophone 5.1
4 Radial JPC
10 Radial ProD1
10 Radial PROD2

SPEAKERS/MONITORING/DSP
24 d&b audiotechnik Q1

The current infrastructure at EMPAC provides the highest level for artistic and research options for projects, which may range from a traditional theater projection to fully immersive environments for large groups of people.

MOVING IN SPACE

Theater has always been the space of magic. Before the invention of electric lights, image projections and computer-controlled environments, theater was the place where the realm of physical presence and mental images met to create a fire within an audience; actors, dancers, singers, writers and musicians met to create an intense experience that moved beyond the boundaries of everyday life—time was compressed to fit years of pain, hardship and (non-) redemption into a two-hour performance, or the burden of everyday life was forgotten for two hours as one wandered through the paradise of imagination.

The virtual world needs the magic of the physical world to create new experiences. It is not either-or. One of the major components when placing humans in magical worlds, be they projected or manufactured in the shop, are platforms and surfaces to walk and stand on. We are adapted to natural landscapes, which are ever undulating before our eyes, with vertical displacement being one of the major categories for our viewing of the world. So EMPAC has a large variety of platforms to create "landscapes" for performances.

Tools, props, paint and costumes have always been integral to theatrical performances. As engineering developed to accommodate more and more complex systems in everyday life, these advances were applied immediately to artistic productions. Flying is still one of the most magical moments and has been used in theater ever since it was possible to move people and objects through space with ropes and pulleys. Defying gravity, not being bound to the earth, elevating above the "vale of tears," receiving the spiritual message from "up high," or just plainly flying like a bird—this has forever been a part of human dreams. And it will stay in our dreams forever, even though we have the technical solutions to fly, be it with planes or paragliders.

At EMPAC, we have the potential to fly people and objects freely through all three dimensions of space, under real-time computer control. This is a first in theater flying, since the path of flying an object through 3-D space is usually predefined and executed when needed. The rigging technology of the Theater and of the Goodman Theater/Studio is all under computer control, spotline winches and drum winches, and we were able to establish that the software allowed real-time and interactive control. The system allows taking a control stream from any source that adheres to the specified protocol, and then move, for instance, a person or a camera through space. So it might be the case that a computer program follows the playing of a clarinet or the movement of a dancer and so controls the flying of an object depending of the pitches the instrument plays or the movements the dancer makes.

Furthermore, the line sets in the theater can be synchronized within such tight tolerances that their loading capacity can be combined, thus allowing the lifting of objects of several tons. This opens up new capacities for use of the Theater, with its 70-foot fly tower as a research lab.

All four venues allow walking far above the floor surface on catwalks or wire-rope grids. Basically, operators can hang any object, screen, platform, light, loudspeaker, sensor or curtain anywhere in the 3-D space of the venues. This is not only true for the studios and Theater, but also for the Concert Hall. Chain hoists can be placed in these technical spaces, to hang any object or support any configuration of trusses that can, in turn, accommodate any lights, loudspeakers, projectors or screens.

To support any moving about on the floors, all floors in all venues are built resiliently. They have a certain give when walking or running and jumping. If this is not sufficient for dancers, we can cover any performance area with sprung dance-floor elements.

To satisfy any production needs that bridge between the physical and the digital worlds—be they for research and development, performances or exhibitions—a wood and metal shop, a welding station and gear to move horizontally and vertically through the building are available. EMPAC is not designed like a traditional theater with large areas for scenery production and storage; as it is always project-based, any object can be constructed on-site (once the project is finished, the built objects then have to move off-site).

Most certainly, the theatrical performance infrastructure is based on "the real stuff," the tangible and often quite heavy pieces of equipment that are to be tied in with the ephemeral worlds of digital controls and the projections of sound and light.

NETWORKS, STORAGE, COMPUTING

EMPAC has a number of networks within the building that are dedicated to different tasks. Some of these networks have to be isolated from each other; others usually are separated, but can be bridged if need be; and still others are bridged, but can be separated. Additionally, EMPAC can patch and establish any independent networks within the building, perhaps connecting computers placed throughout the building, or just one computer on the stage of the Concert Hall directly with one computer in the café, as a one-to-one connection without any electronics in between.

This flexibility is necessary to be able to have absolute control over data traffic and available bandwidth. It is also beneficial to be able to hack a networked system that is not connected to the rest of the campus and the rest of the world—to test new ideas without running into security or policy issues.

From the fire alarm system to the building management system, from separate but bridged video and audio networks, from the loudspeaker control network to the dedicated KVM (keyboard, video, mouse) network that allows direct access to the computers in the central machine room from anywhere in the building, from the house clock distribution to a complex intercom system—all systems have their specific purposes. The approach is not "everything over one network," but having clear delineations and controlled bridges between the different networks.

The quite complex intra-networking for "experimental media and performing arts" uses its own switcher/router with a 720Gbps backplane supporting 10-gigabit connectivity over copper and fiber and is connected to six edge routers throughout the building with equally 10-gigabit connectivity. The six edge routers reflect the basic configuration

12 d&b audiotechnik Q7
8 d&b audiotechnik Q10
8 d&b audiotechnik T10
8 d&b audiotechnik E12
6 d&b audiotechnik E8
8 d&b audiotechnik Ci80
8 d&b audiotechnik Ci7
4 d&b audiotechnik Esub
8 d&b audiotechnik QSub
2 d&b audiotechnik JSub
6 d&b audiotechnik B2 Sub
24 d&b audiotechnik D12
18 d&b audiotechnik D6
5 d&b audiotechnik R70
8 EAW MicroWedge
8 Meyer MM4-XP
6 Dynaudio Air12Master
6 Dynaudio Air12Slave
3 Dynaudio AirRemote
3 Dynaudio Air6Master
3 Dynaudio Air6 Slave
10 Genelec 8030A
32 Genelec 8040A
12 Fostex RM2
2 Fostex 8301A
1 Aviom 6416DIO
1 Aviom A16DPRO
6 Aviom A16II
2 Aviom A16R
3 Dolby Lake DolbyAnet
3 Dolby Lake LPDZ

VIDEO/IMAGE

MATRIX, VIDEO SWITCHING, STORAGE
Harris Platinum 3G-SDI router (176 inputs, 176 outputs)
Ross Vision QMD-X multi-definition production switcher (32 inputs, 32 outputs)
Harris Centrio Multiviewers for 8 independent multi-viewer channels
4 TV One, C2-7100 2-Channel Video Processor
Panasonic: AV-HS400AN Video Switcher (1)
Gallery Software VirtualVTR on 8 Macintosh Computers (four X-Servers utilizing AJA IOHD interfaces and four Mac Pros utilizing Black Magic's multi-bridge interfaces running Virtual VTR recording directly to the SAN via 10 GigE network)
Fujitsu 10 GigE Switch (20 Ports)
Aberdeen, AberSAN, 6 network attached storage servers with currently 100TB+ storage
AJA, FS1 universal HD/SD Audio/Video Frame Synchronizer and Converter, currently four FS1s.

CAMERAS
3 Canon, XHG1 Camera (3)
3 Sony, PMW-EX3 Camera (3)
4 Sony, HDCX310 Camera (4)
4 Telemetrics, PT-CP-S2 precision pan/tilt heads with variable operating speeds, coupled with motorized elevating tripod systems and Telemetrics RCP (Remote Control Panels)

of EMPAC's machine rooms: Each venue has its own machine room, which provides the connection between the individual venue and the central machine room. Located directly between the audio production room and the video production room is the central machine room, to which both productions rooms are connected. Besides being the hub for all video, audio, intercom and data connectivity of the intranet, the central machine room houses all central storage as well as all digital signal processing power for audio and video, which serves the whole building.

Most of the internal networks use single-mode fiber and category 6A copper rated for 10Gbps. The Internet connection to the campus network is capable of 1Gbps, as well as an Internet 2 connection of an additional 250Mbps. And 20Gbps connectivity is available to the Rensselaer's Computational Center for Nanotechnology Innovations (CCNI), which boasts highly powerful supercomputer clusters.

Storage capacity currently runs around 100+ terabyte of data. A storage area network for video is connected to ingest servers, to which video is uploaded, and editing stations via a 10Gbps SAN fabric.

The computational power available locally at EMPAC is limited to what desktop (and laptop) computing provide. There is no dedicated "virtual reality engine" or similar configuration. If a project or a research group requires such specific computational power, it will be implemented as part of that project. Through the high bandwidth networking, computational power can basically be used from "anywhere" outside of EMPAC, including the University's supercomputer center. The focus of EMPAC is on physical facilities to accommodate the best for seeing, hearing and moving in space, a networking infrastructure that can accommodate the requirements for a number of years, plus an environment for the I/O for images, sounds and sensor technology. The necessary backup is handled with tape robots currently backing up in LTO 4 format.

In addition to the desktop and rack-mounted computers, which are responsible for audio and video ingest and processing, a set of "floaters" is available to support project-based work, including Apple Mac Pros, Mac Minis, and a variety of PCs capable of running Linux and Windows.

Quite obviously these computers and the storage technology will be the first to become outdated. And that is exactly what the overall strategy for EMPAC is based on. There was a question at the beginning whether a dedicated "virtual reality system," with given computational infrastructure and projection capabilities, should be purchased as a bundle. This system would have yielded certain bragging rights for EMPAC — quite important when starting up a new center — but it was clear that a decision for such high investment into a single piece of ever changing technology would not have allowed the flexibility and openness we needed for our project-based approach. By deciding that the local computational capacity would be defined by actual needs and relatively short-lived hardware, it was possible to invest more into that technology, which would have a longer lifespan, than in the ever-changing systems for computation and storage.

And what do we sit on? And how can we read our music? And the pianos?

As EMPAC is the proof that the digital world needs the non-digital world, it needs us — living beings — to be evaluated and appreciated. The technical infrastructure reaches all the way to chairs, music stands and pianos. Actually, one might say this is where the infrastructure starts.

As described elsewhere in this book, the chairs for the Concert Hall and for the Theater were designed specifically for this building. The discussion about functionality and the acoustic properties of the leather were extensive. Everything was to look light, uplifting and non-obtrusive. Thus, major attention also was placed on selecting chairs for musicians and music stands that would match the architecture of the spaces. This was an interesting study. Functionality and aesthetics had to come together in such a way that one would be met without the other being missed. Intensive research into existing products finally yielded products that were light and slim enough to meet the aesthetics of the Concert Hall and the appearance of the stage; the process of importing them then turned out to be just another complicated step in completing EMPAC without compromises.

The final word should be addressing the ultimate and archetypical technical device that represents the peak of Western culture of the 19th century — and which still speaks to us every day. The grand piano stands for the ingenuity of 19th-century engineering in conjunction with arts and culture (and politics — but that is another story). It is a piece of machinery that needs constant attention, needs carefully controlled humidity and temperature; it can sound atrocious because of greatly varying temperatures or even rip apart when stored in an environment where the air is too dry. It represents in paradigmatic ways how technology, the arts and society are related.

The actual grand piano evolved over a period of about 150 years, with many of the concepts of keyboard instruments having been developed over preceding centuries. In the end, the grand piano proves that the arts are not about right or wrong, but about differentiation and differences. One solution does not fit all, and the same solution can yield different results. The four grand pianos EMPAC owns can be seen as objects to meditate about the difference of engineering and the arts. The chosen Hamburg-made Steinway sounds different from a Steinway grand made in New York City. The Fazioli grand piano is an exclusive instrument, handcrafted in Italy in very small numbers, with a different "sound recipe" for the spectral components of its instruments. The Bösendorfer provides what some may call the "Austrian, old-world charm" — and the company is now owned by Yamaha. And the Yamaha player piano can record and play back any movement a pianist exercises on the keys — or move its keys directly under computer control.

It may be that these pianos help us to understand how any technology used in the context of design and the arts displays inherent aesthetic values that we can see, hear or feel; and which may make us question if technology is "objective"; and how we think that we create the reality of our present times and for the future. Because quite obviously, the existence of EMPAC shows that vision, perception and interpretation give the guidelines for how we create reality.

Remote
2 ETC IONS with RFR
1 ETC SmartFade
900 conventional theatrical lighting fixtures (ETC, Selicon, ARRI, Altman)
10 moving lights (Martin, Robe)
12 Rosco I-Que moving mirrors
2 Robert Joliat Topaze Followspots
2 Lycian Followspots
4 AMX architectural control systems throughout each venue

RIGGING
16 Stage Technologies Incorporated Big Tow spotline winches
24 JR Clancy drum winches
2 Stage Technologies Incorporated Nomad controllers
5 Stage Technologies Incorporated SOLO controllers
The above under external real-time interactive control (OSC protocol)
64 Chain motors (CM Loadstar, Stagemaker)
2 ZFX Flying Effects performer flying manual systems, 3-D automation capable
670 linear feet of 12″ JR Thomas Engineering Box Truss

LIFTS
1 Gala spiral lift orchestra pit lift with chair wagon
3 Genie scissor lifts
2 Genie AWP basket lifts

PLATFORMS
1,860 sq. ft. of portable platforms, different heights
100′ scaffold, component capable
1 Concert Hall stage extension, architecturally matched
1 orchestra riser system, architecturally matched
3,600 sq. ft. sprung dance-floor modules

ACOUSTIC BANNERS
Acoustic banners under detailed computer control in Concert Hall, Goodman Theater/Studio and Studio 2

PROJECTION SCREENS
54′ x 30′ (16.5 m x 9.1 m) image size Gerriets OPERA with micro perforation (Concert Hall)
49′ x 28′6″ (15 m x 8.6 m) image size Gerriets GAMMALUX MICRO (Theater)
360° panoramic movie screen, micro-perforation); height: 14′ (4.25 m), diameter: 41′ (12.5 m), circumference: 129′ (39 m)
2 roll-drop front projection movie screens, 25′ wide
25 portable front- or rear-projection screens of various sizes (Da-Lite, Draper), 10′ x 7.5′ up to 25′ x 19′
3 outdoor projector pods

PIANOS
1 Hamburg Steinway Model D
1 Fazioli Model F212
1 Bösendorfer Model 200 CS
1 Yamaha C7 Disklavier pro
2 Kawai K8 upright pianos

CREDITS

The technical infrastructure of EMPAC could not have been realized without the flexibility of the consultants who worked on EMPAC and who are represented in this book. Their willingness to be challenged, to learn, to be open to new approaches and to provide new solutions laid the foundation for what EMPAC represents today.

The counterpart on Rensselaer's side in this challenging technological journey was an exceptional engaged team with Martin Moore, Todd Vos, Eric Ameres, Jeff Svatek, Bob Bovard, Kurt Pragman, Pete Wargo and me. Without this team, the engineering feat represented by EMPAC would not have come together and the philosophy of what EMPAC's mission meant in terms of concrete technology would not have turned into reality. In the end, we could not find a commercial contractor to realize our concept of the integrated and highly complex audio and video infrastructure. After two attempts, the EMPAC engineering team—Todd Vos, Eric Ameres and Jeff Svatek—took over the full task and designed, implemented, configured and screwed together every piece of the video and audio systems in an exceptionally forward-looking installation.

Theater Planning and Design

Joshua Dachs

When I first heard about EMPAC, I was struck by how unusual Dr. Shirley Ann Jackson's idea was, and how profound an impact it can have. Her idea, simply put, of bringing together visiting artists and Rensselaer's outstandingly creative scientists to jointly develop projects in a technically sophisticated facility was altogether unique. While I'd done some work with the MIT Media Lab, which at one time had hoped to develop a small performance space, I had never heard of a building proposed that would include artists' studios *and* technology laboratories before.

Too often technology-based art has seemed less like art and more like a science experiment. It's easy to forget that every new technology is in its infancy, by definition. Regardless of the technologies used to create them, not every artwork will be a masterpiece.

endure through the centuries.

It is easy to be seduced by technology and forget about the content. This is why the EMPAC concept is so daring, so interesting and so important—because while the technology keeps coming, the art often lags behind. By putting artists into the mix and making them central to its activity, EMPAC changes this equation. When it comes to human expression, the artists will lead the way. By putting resources and researchers at the disposal of artists, the art and the technology can advance together.

What also fascinated me about Dr. Jackson's idea was that, despite its emphasis on technology, EMPAC is still about making experiences for a *live* audience, sharing a single space in real time. Some would consider this to be an old-fashioned concept. So much of new media is meant to be experienced remotely and

"EMPAC is still about making experiences for a live audience, sharing a single

piece. The invention of motion picture technology at the turn of the 19th century did not automatically produce great films. The mere existence of stringed instruments, brass, winds and percussion does not guarantee that every composition will be a great symphony. Today we can each blog our every random thought, but how many have anything meaningful to say? Technology in and of itself does not produce great art. The technology has to be used by someone more interested in expressing something than in the tools themselves.

All Shakespeare needed was a poetic imagination, paper and a quill. The technologies for reproduction of his work have changed since his time, but the fundamental act of creation has not. While we all can learn to use new tools, only a few of us will be able to find in them a new voice. Fewer still will have something compelling to say. And still fewer will be able to combine technical mastery with a unique perspective and produce something that is so moving, inspiring or challenging that it will

individually by consumers who are increasingly fragmented, cocooned, YouTubed and iPod-ed. I found EMPAC's commitment to a live, shared experience refreshing, if not to say radical. It sounds corny, but I believe that shared experiences build stronger communities and societies. Empowering individuals, so long the goal of information technologists, is fine, but building robust, collaborative societies is ever more important in our complex and fast-changing world. There is a reason that in ancient Athens attendance at the theatrical performances in the City Dionysia was considered a civic duty. Making the sharing of morally charged stories a central collective endeavor, theater played a role in forging a coherent Greek culture that has survived in one form or another for thousands of years.

I was hooked on Dr. Jackson's idea.

As the theater consultant for any project, it's my job to conceptualize the performance spaces and all their related support space: We establish their form and size so they can accommodate the desired activity and develop their basic geometry and character—intimate or grand, formal or casual, handmade or machine-like, improvised or highly structured—to establish the right relationship between the audience and the work on stage. My colleagues at Fisher Dachs and I set about making four spaces for live performance, along with all the support spaces the artists, scientists and audience members would require.

When Johannes Goebel joined the team early in the planning process, I visited him at the Center for Art and Media (Zentrum für Kunst und Medientechnologie, or ZKM) in Karlsruhe, Germany, which he had helped to create. We toured the building, and he kept up a running commentary on what they'd gotten right and what had been a disappointment. We all benefited from what he had learned in building and operating ZKM.

lucky few who will get to watch the conductor from the musicians' point of view. The stage is equipped with an enormous projection screen (33 feet high by 56 feet 4 inches wide), the largest roll-up screen in the Western Hemisphere.

A principal driver of the geometry of the room was optimizing acoustics for unamplified performances. I'll leave it to Larry Kirkegaard, the project's acoustician, to describe the unique acoustical design, which involves a fabric layer suspended beneath a hard ceiling. But attention was also given to how the Concert Hall would serve artists working with amplified instruments and electronic sources. Johannes made sure the hall has a highly sophisticated, distributed infrastructure for audio and data, and the room acoustics can be adjusted with absorbent banners to accommodate amplified programming, surround

space in real time. Some would consider this to be an old-fashioned concept."

A composer and musician himself, Johannes has constantly challenged us to think outside our normal comfort zone, and the building is better for it. His leadership and guidance has been essential in helping the design team make a building that will serve artists and that is prepared for the future.

THE CONCERT HALL
The largest space, the 1,200-seat Concert Hall, in some ways is the most traditional of the four venues. In other ways it's radically new. Like many of the great 19th-century concert halls in Europe, the Concert Hall is based on a "shoebox" form—a more or less rectangular room, with seating galleries along two sides.

In deference to the likelihood of projected imagery being used in conjunction with live performance by EMPAC's visiting artists, the vast majority of seats are placed in front of the stage platform. Behind the musicians, we placed a loft with just enough seats for a chorus, and these will be fantastic seats for a

sound and distributed "soundscapes." Audio devices can be placed anywhere in the room. The hall can also accommodate complex stage lighting.

THE THEATER
The 400-seat Theater is in some ways the most unusual of the performance spaces. We wanted to create a space that would have a more informal character than that of the Concert Hall. To achieve this, I proposed, instead of a raised stage, that the performers be placed at essentially the same floor level as the first row of audience. This approach leaves the dividing line between "audience" and "performer" more fluid. A stage apron that protrudes out into the auditorium further muddies the distinction between stage and house, and, when lowered on a lift, this portion of the floor can be used as an orchestra pit.

The stage is similar to a traditional proscenium theater you'd find on Broadway, but with more technology. It has a fly tower with a motorized rigging system. A sophisticated control system gives artists the ability to devise complex vertical and horizontal movements of scenery, objects or even people, all linked to the same computers that are driving the audio and projection programs.

The ability to radically reconfigure the room, a requirement in the two studios, was not a goal for the Theater, even though the room can be used in a variety of ways. Nonetheless, technology, screens, lights and speakers can be continually shifted and relocated. Because of this, it was important that the room seem energized by constant modification rather than defaced by it—the act of bolting something to the wall or attaching it to a railing is celebrated and facilitated, rather than received with horror. It has an improvised quality, allowing each artist to move in and adapt it as that individual sees fit.

At the same time, we needed to make a space that embraces live performers and audiences, not just technology. We looked to the past for inspiration. Rooms that are lined with faces—like those in Georgian courtyard playhouses, Shakespeare's Globe and even traditional Italian opera houses—have a marvelous intensity that comes from a compact geometry that wraps the audience around three sides of the performer. Those spaces were conceived at a time when successful performers needed to connect with their audience without any technical assistance, using only their own voices, bodies and charisma. The rooms were designed to forge powerful connections between an audience and the actors, and to encourage lively social interaction. The trick in serving the many EMPAC artists and technologists—who will focus on technologically mediated movement and image rather than simply live actors and a text—was taking care not to lose the human element entirely. It would not serve the vision to build a space that is essentially a cinema or a laboratory.

In essence, our solution was to strike a balance and create a room that has the dramatic intensity of a courtyard playhouse, while at the same time accommodating artists who may prefer to use the room in less traditional ways or whose work may be more cinematic. To do this, we made a space that has a main section of seating that is wrapped, courtyard-like, by tiers of galleries that can be used for seating, performers or technology, as needed. The golden-hued wooden seats on the central wooden seating bank are wrapped by beautifully detailed steel galleries. They set up a dialogue between warm, handcrafted elements that speak of nature and permanence, and technological elements that speak of adaptation and change.

Unlike the two studios, where more three-dimensional viewing is facilitated, the Theater has been designed with frontally viewed work in mind. Some of the work developed for this theater will be able to tour to other locations, since the work is not dependent on a one-off spatial arrangement. By virtue of its similarity to the standard proscenium theater form, work created in many other venues around the world can also be presented here with ease.

THE STUDIOS

The two studios – one for music and one for video projection technologies—are sophisticated playgrounds for artists. The first is a large, tall rectangular room, 55 feet by 70 feet by 46 feet high, that bristles with power, data, air conditioning, lighting, and audio and video technology. Using a flexible seating system, a variety of configurations can be achieved for an audience of up to 200, or the seating can be removed entirely. Custom-design projection pods, hanging from tracks on the ceiling, can be located anywhere in the room and can be used to create 30-foot-tall, 360-degree immersive projection environments where artists can simulate virtual worlds for performers and audiences to experience together.

The second studio is a cross between a recital hall and a recording studio. Also equipped with a flexible seating system, this studio will accommodate up to 100 in a variety of configurations. Custom-designed wall panels and a system of draperies allow the room's acoustical properties to be tuned as needed.

I'm eager to see what emerges from this extraordinary facility and its unique mission. Too often experimental performance art can focus so intently on technology that content is forgotten and nothing is communicated. I hope EMPAC will be a place in which performance will transcend experimentation, where we'll see technology and art join together with content and become actual communication.

View from the choir seating behind the stage towards the balcony.

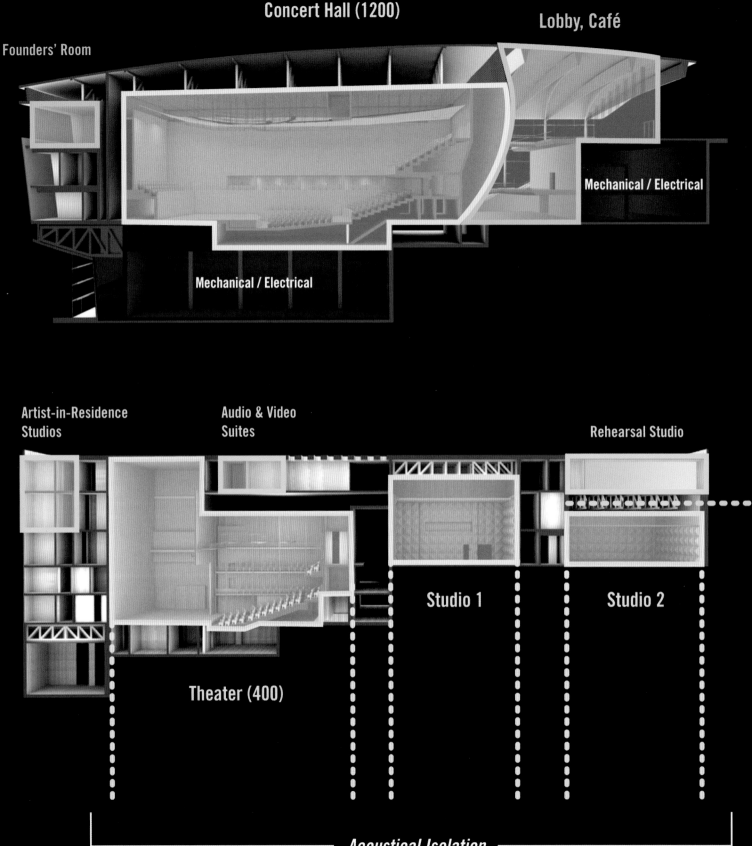

Concert Hall (1200)

Lobby, Café

Founders' Room

Mechanical / Electrical

Mechanical / Electrical

Artist-in-Residence
Studios

Audio & Video
Suites

Rehearsal Studio

Studio 1

Studio 2

Theater (400)

Acoustical Isolation

Performance Spaces: The Venues

A venue is a place where something happens. At EMPAC, the term refers to those "staged spaces" (though not necessarily possessing a physical stage) that enable a wide range of time-based performances and full-scale installations. The original concept of EMPAC was directed toward multi-purpose functionality, but that soon shifted to creating distinct venues suited to highly specific uses, with layouts, infrastructure and support that added a high degree of reconfigurability. In fact, as they are now realized, each EMPAC venue supports performance, installation and research options.

The facility is divided into a north and south block. The north block, exposing the massive wooden hull inside its glass exterior, builds expectation and promise. Bill Horgan of Grimshaw Architects refers to this as the "analog side of house"—where the Concert Hall resides, and where the open lobby, café and grand staircase operate as gathering points on campus. Opposite, across a daylight wedge of space, is the south block. This, Horgan calls the "digital side of the house," referring to the tightly packed Theater and studio spaces as "found spaces" by virtue of how they are packed into the larger, relatively opaque south block form, only to be revealed (discovered) through relatively anonymous portals.

EMPAC's Concert Hall is designed for a full symphony orchestra, but can be changed to work for a chamber group, lecture or even accommodate a show with 40 loudspeakers surrounding the audience. It has two studios that can be reconfigured from very dry (with very little reverberation) to the sound of a clearing in the forest. The Theater features a highly reconfigurable stage and well-equipped 70-foot fly tower. In each case Johannes Goebel wanted the performer to be able to perform from anywhere in the room.

At EMPAC, we cannot refer to "the audience out there," beyond the curtain (proscenium), because there is none. The audience is in the same room (either in the Concert Hall, Theater or studios), in a conversation with the performer. Though the Concert Hall has a choir behind the stage, much as Seiji Ozawa Hall does, which can accommodate some of the audience and create a surround performance, it is not just this feature that makes a memorable performance. It is about the connection that is made. The intimacy that each EMPAC venue creates is memorable. And because light can be added to darkness, sound to silence and division to openness, EMPAC's highly tuned instruments can be played either conventionally, with traditional approaches to audience, acoustics and space, or experimentally, to discover new knowledge and conventions.

Within EMPAC, there are four venues—a 1,200-seat acoustic concert hall, a 400-seat theater and two experimental studios:

- The acoustic Concert Hall had to accommodate entering class convocations and town hall meetings. It is designed to rival acoustic concert halls worldwide in its ability to provide a full symphony orchestra the opportunity to "play the room" in an intimate setting with an audience—and it does.
- The fly-towered Theater has a full-size production stage (extremely rare for 400-seat venues) and is equipped with computer-controlled rigging, an orchestra pit that doubles as extra seating or a thrust stage, a control/projection room, a high-resolution 3-D projector,

Cross section of the Concert Hall (top), and Theater, Goodman Theater/Studio 1 and Studio 2. The section also shows the Founder's Room (top left), Artist's in Residence studios (bottom left), Audio and Video Production Suite (above the Theater) and Rehearsal Space (above Studio 2).

and a 56-foot screen. The space is readied for full-surround wall projection, should a performance troupe wish to stage the entire box.

- Studio 1 (the Goodman Theater/Studio 1) is a black box studio, nicknamed the "Darth Vader studio" for obvious reasons. With 3,500 square feet and 50 feet of height to work with, it is the larger of the two studios, equipped with tunable, black, acoustic paneled walls; a walkable, black, wire-grid ceiling; computer-controlled rigging; and a black stage floor. It was created with multimedia, data-visualization research and experimental artists in mind.
- The 2,500 square foot Studio 2 is considered the "lights-on" studio, with ivory-colored acoustic wall panels and a maple floor for chamber performances and recording. It too can be transformed with drop-down, absorptive wall banners, and any manner of suspended sets and lighting from its own walkable grid and rigging space above.
- All venues have resilient floors to support dance performances.
- Throughout the building, all dimmers for theatrical lighting have sine wave dimmers to eliminate noise-producing interference.

EMPAC also contains recording and mastering studios for audio and video and artist-in-residence spaces. Unlike the approaches taken for most North American performance facilities, which separate a highly finished "front of house" for the public audience, and low-finished "back of house" for artists, EMPAC does not make this distinction. As an instrument for research, its artists and researchers are as important as the performers and public, and all spaces are treated with high regard for the user, without artificial class separation. This is because it is a program, not merely a facility. EMPAC is a Rensselaer initiative that does not reside organizationally in any one of the five academic schools, but separately and between them. It provides a platform for the disparate worlds of scientific researchers and experimental artists, two communities strategically targeted by the Institute to be mutual stimulants of each another.

> EMPAC is a point of intersection of technology and the arts, and for artists with scientists. Even if one has a very defined problem—an engineering or architectural design problem—there are flights of fancy, of thought, that have to come into play because, by definition, what one is trying to resolve does not have an answer. So one has to be able to take those kinds of creative leaps, but putting it together, or building it just with analytical tools, on which we train our students, is not enough. The arts do this for us.
> —Dr. Shirley Ann Jackson

Overall, EMPAC was conceived to affect the transformation of the University and to stimulate the lives and enterprise of all at Rensselaer, especially those who venture to take advantage of its many offerings or who engage in their own large-scale, media-dependent research with internal (Rensselaer) or external collaborators. At any given time, it is host to multiple and wide-ranging experiments, research and artistic undertakings, including:

View of the Concert Hall from the balcony (top); Audio Production Room located above the Theater (bottom).

- Artists-in-residence projects,
- Performances,
- Colloquia,
- Town meetings,
- Symphonies,
- Theatrical performances
- Full-scale data visualization,
- Wholly new media-scapes,
- Chamber performances, and
- Recording sessions.

From the start it was fundamental that the facility enable a wide range of activity simultaneously without interference or compromise.

THE CONCERT HALL

- A 1,200-seat acoustic hall with an orchestra, parterre, balcony, side galleries, and choir
- An expandable 30-by-68-foot maple stage to accommodate a full symphony orchestra
- Suspended fabric ceiling with a large cavity above equipped with catwalks, follow spot-lighting platforms, and side and stage wall technical galleries
- Winch points over the stage and seating for raising and lowering sets
- Full-surround, drop-down, acoustic wall banners at side, rear and stage walls
- Acoustic isolation of 120 decibels at 63 hertz inaudible in an adjacent space, with an RC (Room Criteria) rating of 15
- Integrated acoustic airlock vestibules
- Reverberation time ranging from 1.9 to 2.9 seconds
- 3 strata of acoustically designed surround walls, wood at the orchestra and parterre levels, glass fiber reinforced gypsum (GFRG) panels at mid-level and cast stone panels above
- Acoustically diffuse cast stone, curtain-like upstage wall
- 56-foot projection screen, ultra-high-resolution projector, and acoustically isolated projection space
- Control room with separate machine room
- Displacement ventilation system and under-seating plenum
- Resilient stage floor
- Capability to hang trusses, lights, platforms anywhere in the volume of the hall

From the lobby and decks below, you enter the cedar hull through one of "Alice's rabbit holes," anticipating something special. Let yourself be guided by the ushers through the dark blue, narrow interstitial spaces between the hull and the Concert Hall. The door you reach, when swung open, reveals a bright new universe, a large yet intimate single space focused on a maple stage. There are two choir rows behind and a gallery along each side, both of which can be used for seating, providing access to a full 360 degrees

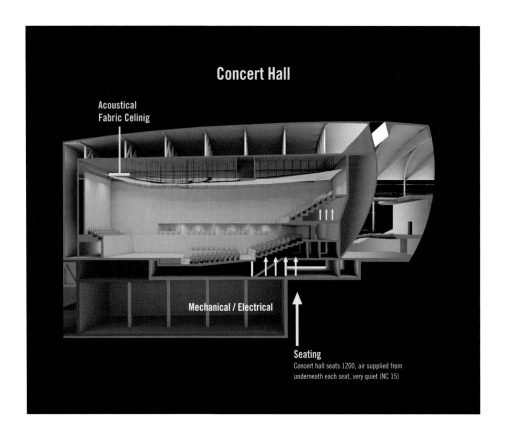

Concert Hall

Acoustical
Fabric Celinig

Mechanical / Electrical

Seating
Concert hall seats 1200, air supplied from
underneath each seat, very quiet (NC 15)

Cross section of the Concert Hall showing the
mechanical room and plenum beneath.

around the performers. The galleries have moveable chairs, and these can also be used for performers. The technical galleries above can also serve as a kind of bass (low frequency) sound trap when the banners are dropped over them.

You will notice the hard wall surfaces, designed to maintain the sound energy of the room at every seat. At the upper level, the wall surfaces are dimpled in an elliptical pattern to various depths in order to create a diffuse sound without chirps or screeches that would occur were they all the same. At mid-level, and especially in the recessed galleries, the elliptical theme continues with custom GFRG wall and ceiling panels designed to diffuse sound. In the Concert Hall you will also see a ceiling like no other. It canopies over both the audience and stage to selectively reflect and transmit various sound frequencies for the benefits of acoustic clarity and accommodating a wide range of performances effectively. Its concentric pattern visually unifies the room. But that is not all it does. The suspended ceiling, which does not touch the walls, eliminates troublesome corner sound reflections, and the gaps between the tensioned fabric panels are integrally coordinated with lighting and set-drop locations.

When you sit, it is in a custom-designed seat. Beneath you is your own silent fresh-air supply that responds noiselessly to your needs. You may be here to attend a lecture by a world-renowned scientist at a lectern, speaking clearly for all to hear in front of a

"[EMPAC] is unique in that it sits here at Rensselaer and that it has this conjoined set of activities that involves the arts, and how they can help science and research, and how — on the other hand — science and technology can allow unique things in the performance arts.

— Dr. Shirley Ann Jackson

56-foot projection of his or her scientific images. If you are a prospective or incoming student, you may be participating in an introduction to what Rensselaer is about, its legacy and its vision. Later you may find yourself walking on stage before the President, Dr. Shirley Ann Jackson, her cabinet and the deans in their full regalia ready to receive acknowledgement of an accomplishment.

Because you will have heard about the events at EMPAC, even if you are not part of the academic community, you may someday join Rensselaer students, faculty and staff in hearing a symphony, singer or performer — perhaps someone who, before EMPAC, would never have entertained the notion of a trip to Troy, New York. The performance might be classical in configuration, and, closing your eyes, you may be able to distinguish the individual string instruments, thanks to a ceiling that reflects the sound of violins and flutes to the audience's ears without any amplification.

The light strafes down, sculpting the surrounding dimpled wall surfaces. As the performance progresses, you will get a feeling of connectedness, of intimacy, that is rare in a concert hall. In fact, you are in the same room with the performers, under the same ceiling; there is no curtain and no proscenium wall separating one from the other. You may suddenly hear a trumpet from a side gallery, or the balcony, or even the catwalks above the ceiling. Though optimized for the stage, the Hall was designed for acoustic performance emanating from anywhere — or everywhere.

If you are in orchestra or parterre seating, you will not be able to avoid noticing that the walls consist of maple and wenge wood strips wiggling their way along in horizontal bands to demonstrate to the eye, together with the shape of the room and other material surfaces, just what needed to happen to diffuse the sound correctly. That first stratum of three unifies the lower audience with those on stage in the warmth of the wooden surround.

Or, you may attend an event of an entirely different musical genre, either well established (jazz, vocal) or something more avant-garde with say 30 loudspeakers around and above you. Perhaps the black wall banners will be dropped to tune the space for amplified sound and bass frequencies — still pleasing in a hall that, unlike so many great acoustic halls, is not overpowered by loud, amplified performances. You may attend a performance with a soloist in the spotlight that aims from above the ceiling, or you may be watching a movie on the film screen covering the full wall behind the stage. You may even experience flying sets over the stage and, perhaps, all the way out over the audience. Time will tell, but many possibilities exist, and the improbable is encouraged at EMPAC and in its Concert Hall.

Top: Slow Wave festival, performance in Concert Hall (left); Marc Downie FIELD Lecture in the Theater (right).

Middle: Deerhunter performance in the Concert Hall (left); Boredoms performance in the Concert Hall (right).

Bottom: Deerhunter performance in the Concert Hall (left); Presidential Colloquy in the Concert Hall. From left to right Neil Degrasse Tyson, President Shirley Ann Jackson, Peter R.Orszag, Harold E. Varmus, (Robert S. Langer not shown) (right).

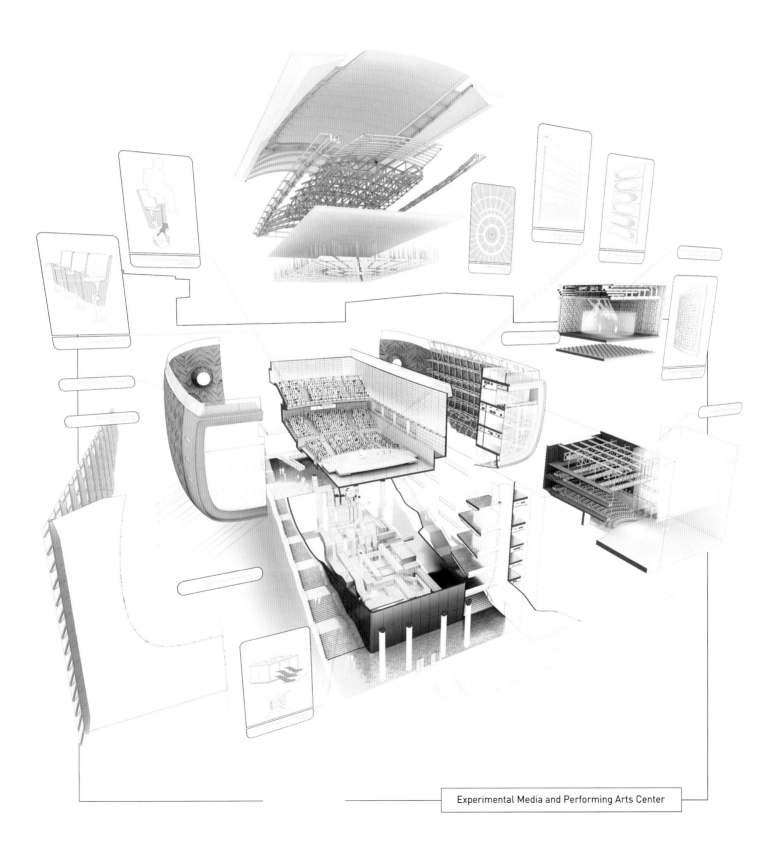

Experimental Media and Performing Arts Center

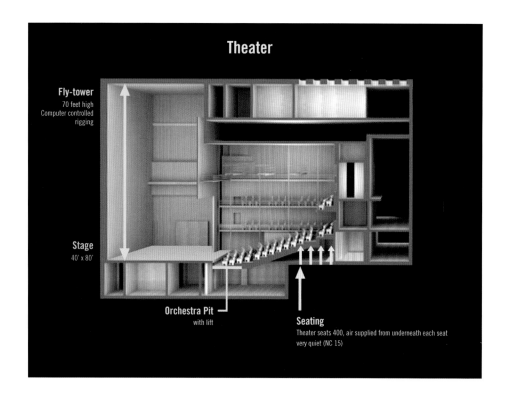

Theater

Fly-tower
70 feet high
Computer controlled
rigging

Stage
40' x 80'

Orchestra Pit
with lift

Seating
Theater seats 400, air supplied from underneath each seat
very quiet (NC 15)

Cross section of the Theater showing the flytower, orchestra pit and seating areas (above); exploded view of the building showing the fundamental components designed to meet the specified acoustical requirements (opposite).

THEATER

- 400 seats, with a balcony and two levels of side audience galleries
- Side, rear and flyover technical galleries above, with follow spot platforms and catwalks
- Projection room and a separate sound and lighting control room
- 70-foot-tall, full-stage fly tower, with intermediate side-wall catwalks and a fly gallery, equipped with programmable and interactive computer-controlled rigging
- 42-by-82-foot production stage, with additional thrust stage potential
- Full audience-hall-width proscenium opening
- Orchestra pit that doubles as a thrust stage or offers additional seating
- 56-foot projection screen
- Ultra-high-resolution 3-D projector
- Plenum and under-seat displacement ventilation system
- Acoustically isolated walls and stage house

The Theater is remarkable for being as large as it is in terms of volume, yet experientially being so intimate—that there is so much technical volume to allow placement of loudspeakers outside [the stage house and into the audience chamber]. That's the room where the audience can be completely surrounded by projected video, by virtual reality, and it takes a lot of space to do that. We can surround them with sound; we can surround them with image. And that technical zone was just critical for loudspeaker placement, for acoustic variability, because there is absorption that can be deployed in there.

—Carl Giegold

Packed deep within EMPAC's south block is the most magical of spaces—an intimate, deep red, 400-seat theater with steeply raked, gently curving seating rows, a balcony, two levels of side-wall audience galleries and a third technical gallery above the stacked control booth and projection rooms. Above, is a dark ceiling cavity of black-painted catwalks, technical galleries and trusses that cross the space. Turn, and you will face a full-width proscenium opening, or one could say no proscenium at all, except as needed to screen the 70-foot-tall fly tower beyond.

Beneath that fly tower is a full-size (Broadway) production stage that extends to the right and left of the audience hall. The tower is equipped with computer-controlled rigging that allows preprogrammed and on-the-fly control of sets, actors and cameras, without the cumbersome counterweights of conventional fly towers. This provides the ability to program paths of sets, actors and cameras in complex arrays—even on the fly. Such systems rarely exist in the U.S., and here it is dedicated to expanding possibility for experimental, avant-garde troupes and research by even allowing interactive real-time control of any actor or object flying complex paths through 3-D space.

> That dynamic of the relationship between the audience and the performer is not a "sit back in your armchair and watch and rate the people up on the stage," but is much more dynamic and engaged in some way—the fact that you are eye to eye with the performer and nobody is up on a pedestal. You are up there with [the performer]—and we anticipate that that will be an exciting way for audiences and artists to work.
>
> —Joshua Dachs

Between the audience hall and the stage, a reconfigurable threshold has been created. Technically, it is an orchestra pit, but it does much more. In traditional fashion, it can be lowered to accommodate a supporting orchestra or, more likely at EMPAC, a technical team equipped with controllers and computers, as well as mixing boards in place of violins and upright basses. Like all the venues, it is linked to the control room and stage with high-speed data and high-definition audio and video pipelines. In its lowered position, the pit creates an effective moat between the audience and the stage. However, it can also be raised to the audience level and seats added to extend the audience—more intimate than most any major theater. But that is not all. It can also be raised to stage level and act as a thrust stage, bringing the performers well beyond the proscenium plane and into the audience.

> You can have people working on their computers in the orchestra pit. We will have performances where we have computer operators playing the technology on stage in conjunction with the people who are acting on stage. And the same is necessary for people who are just initializing things on a computer, because they need to be in physical proximity to whoever's acting, dancing or doing whatever on stage. Usually these computer operators are put in the very rear of the theater, where they do not have this immediate contact, visual contact, with people on stage.
>
> —Johannes Goebel

Construction view of theater from the second balcony right showing the seating tiers, orchestra pit and stage.

Even the chairs on each side of the parterre and balcony are not fixed, and the railings on the side galleries are removable, opening the possibility for a "wraparound stage." To flip convention a bit more, seating can be set up on the stage itself. If a media-rich surround performance is desired, the side galleries are equipped with clamping bars, ready to accept projection screens. Above, the structure is designed to both support the technical crews and to drop down sets and performers.

Here you enter to discover a red-walled space that is as tall as it is wide, with people surrounding you at every level, anticipating an event under a blackened, cavernous ceiling void. You may be facing a 56-foot screen saturated with moving images that mix with the performers in front. Which is real? which is projected? you may well ask. Sets and actors may descend over you and in the stage area. In fact, a complex choreography of multiple moving sets and performers may realize the third (vertical) dimension of "the stage" like no other performance you have seen. Projections, performers, sounds and sets commingle before your eyes and ears in startling ways. The projections may even surround you.

If you are a performer, you look out and are surrounded by an audience you are permitted to enter into, swirl around or descend onto. You have behind and above you the most remarkable apparatus at your disposal. You can program the almost silent movement of any manner of prop or performer through space. To the rear, you have a control room with access to high-speed data and high-definition audio and video signals tied to an ultra-high-resolution 3-D projector. It is a unique setting and infrastructure in which to try something new.

> Johannes has pushed on every system in every technical area to get it to do more—more than any were ever intended to do. It has to do more, be more flexible, have more inputs from more kinds of sources, pushing things way beyond the boundaries and making the journey exotic. … The rigging system will be completely unique to the world.
>
> —Joshua Dachs

Instead, you may be developing a performance or doing research that relies on the 3-D movement of people, props and cameras in space over the stage—and for this the stage house can be isolated from the audience chamber and orchestra pit, which can serve as a shallow stage to the theater. But regardless of whether you are visiting or performing, you are likely to leave startled by the possibilities, your mind racing with what-ifs.

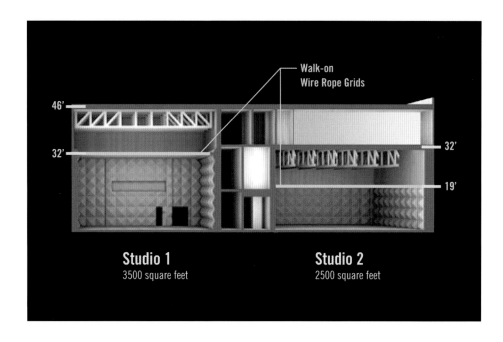

Cross section of the Goodman Theater/Studio 1 and Studio 2 with walkable wire rope ceiling grids.

STUDIO 1 — THE GOODMAN THEATER/STUDIO 1

- 68-by-53-by-45-foot-tall black box experimental studio—all black
- Independent concrete box construction on acoustic isolation springs, with sound isolation of 120 decibels at 63 hertz to neighboring venues and an RC rating of 15
- Reverberation time of 0.5 to 1.4 seconds
- Acoustic airlock vestibules
- Walkable wire-grid ceiling
- Control room with a separate machine room
- Winches and hoists for sets, lights and multimedia hang points allowing 3-D flying of actors and objects using interactive computational controls
- 2-by-2-foot acoustic side-wall panels, including a pixilated mix of reconfigurable, gimbaled "moonscape" diffusing panels and perforated absorptive panels
- Two layers of drop-down, absorptive wall banners
- Black stage floor throughout the venue
- Full access to high-speed data and high-definition audio and video

The Goodman Theater/Studio 1 is the larger of the two experimental studios. Enter it via the café level, through massive, heavy acoustic doors (which you will struggle to open), and you will know already that you are entering something special. The "Darth Vader studio," as it was nicknamed early on for obvious reasons, is a literal black box studio with a tech feel and what can only be imagined as the sound of space—outer space—emptiness.

The lack of visual and aural cues is intentional, creating the space and opportunity to construct an experiment free from interference or even a separate reality. All Darth's surfaces are black, and virtually no sound in the audible register enters from outside or from any of the building's systems. The dark, silent space awaits the addition of light, the light awaits the addition of surfaces that will reflect it, and the silence awaits the introduction of sound.

Like the Concert Hall, the studios owe their richness and innovations to effective collaboration between the owner, architect, acoustician, manufacturers and consultants, and once again illustrate the EMPAC agenda, even in its making. The Goodman Theater/Studio 1 is the driest (acoustically least reverberant) of EMPAC's spaces, raised on springs and covered with gimbaled 2-by-2-foot moonscape acoustical panels (black), mixed in with perforated, absorptive panels (black again). Hidden behind the panels, large bass membrane absorbers cover the wall surfaces to lower the booming low frequencies of such a big regularly shaped space, all to create the diffuse sound like that of a clearing in the forest. Drop the double-layered, black banners in front of the panels, and the room's reverberation time drops to near anechoic level (no reverberation). The sound decay time is extremely short, removing the sense of space and dimension we unconsciously use continuously.

Above its black, walkable ceiling grid is a plethora of options for lighting, dropped sets, video projection, suspended screens and projectors, and so on. Projection screens up to 30 feet high can be positioned in the volume in any desired configuration—from a 360-degree circular screen to a maze of smaller projection surfaces. The floor is flat; there is no clear front or back to the space. Installations, artists, researchers and audiences can be set up in any manner with the required seating, props and equipment.

Visit (if you are allowed) when a group is setting up the space, and you are likely to see wires and sets and computers and controllers, people on the floor and up above hanging screens and projections and testing sound. It is a high-tech experience, but even more striking is the likelihood of seeing researchers, artists, performers, faculty and students (if they can be categorized) thinking and talking through what is being created. Roles, so often fixed in other places, are denied and forgotten here in favor of the quest to make, to discover something.

If you attend a performance or installation, be prepared to be confronted. You may well be asked to participate. Do not be surprised if you become disoriented and even begin to question the boundaries between the physical and the virtual.

Whether you like it or hate it is beside the point for Studio 1 or 2 (or for much of the EMPAC enterprise). Here we have an intellectual and social experiment, focused on cross-pollinating disciplines and, through integration, understanding how the worlds of art, science and technology reveal and create knowledge at their intersection.

Top: The panoramic screen being set-up on the stage of the Theater (left); Professor Barbara Cutler research project on daylight simulation for architecture in Studio 2. (right).

Middle: Video calibration in the panoramic screen: seen through the micro-perforated screen from outside the panorama (left) and from up above the cylindrical screen (right).

Bottom: Workspace Unlimited demonstration in the panoramic screen (left and right)

STUDIO 2

- 57-by-47-by-35-foot-tall experimental studio
- Independent concrete box construction on independent foundation, with sound isolation of 120 decibels at 63 hertz to neighboring venues and an RC rating of 15
- Reverberation time between 0.5 and 1.2 seconds
- Acoustic airlock vestibules
- Walkable wire-grid ceiling
- Control room with a separate machine room
- Winch and hoists for sets, lights and multimedia hang points
- 2-by-2-foot acoustic, ivory-colored gimbaled "moonscape" diffusing side-wall panels
- Wall-mounted bass traps
- Two layers of drop-down, absorptive wall banners
- Maple floor
- Full access to high-speed data, and high-definition audio and video

Studio 2 is the smaller of the two experimental studios, a variation on the theme of the Goodman Theater/Studio 1. It is considered the "lights on" studio, with ivory, moonscape, acoustic wall panels and a light maple floor. It, too, is acoustically isolated, a veritable building within a building, having its own foundations, no connecting walls and a structure that spans over it without touching. The acoustic design room criteria (RC) level, as with the other venues, is set at a hushing RC15, usually reserved for recording studios. And, as in the other venues, a 120 decibel sound at 63 hertz (similar to a large clap of thunder at close proximity) will not be audible in the neighboring venue. This

room is designed for performances ranging from chamber groups to heavily amped groups, and from dance performers to multimedia environments. It too has a wire-grid ceiling and flexible lighting, multimedia and set potential.

Like the Goodman Theater/Studio 1, this is another of the "found spaces" in the south block—located just off the café and reception lobby under the east end of the hull —where, on exiting the performances, much wringing of hands, debate and discussion occurs regularly at a frequency never before seen at Rensselaer. By this evidence alone, EMPAC is a change agent for a university thirsting for exposure and cultural events, and intellectual challenges outside the classroom and laboratory.

EMPAC is where events as never before seen have been brought to what might have been thought of as an unlikely place, Rensselaer Polytechnic Institute in Troy, New York. But that can no longer be said. EMPAC has already linked Rensselaer to a global community of experimental artists who challenge convention, cross disciplinary boundaries and seek to discover. Here is where speculation is not guarded by canon—or expectation.

EMPAC offers an invitation to look and to listen more closely. It provides an opportunity to be stimulated and to enjoy. It is an invitation to discuss—and even to dislike. But, in any case, it is an opportunity to connect to a world that for centuries has hovered in society's margins—imagining, testing, making and doing what may not yet be proven or accepted by mainstream, developed tastes. Equipped with technology, associated with faculty and researchers from diverse disciplines, EMPAC provides many rich and varied opportunities to break boundaries and be in the vanguard of art and thought. EMPAC delivers the space, the infrastructure, the programming and the support to realize new visions.

Random Dance residency rehearsal in Studio 2 (above and left).

The Unwritten Chapter

"This is the biggest electric-train set any boy ever had."
— Orson Welles, on his first visit to a film studio

EMPAC's massive wooden hull crashes through the western façade for all to see behind the towering glass-box container, and it dominates the view, especially when lit up at night. Its open, welcoming glass lobby is an extension of the campus space. The bulging, diagonally clad cedar hull and its circular portals confront the space and promise an "Alice in Wonderland" experience—and it does not disappoint.

EMPAC is alive with people; it is alive with possibilities. In the lobby, people convene, linger, discuss and laugh — their body language is a testament to what a space can do socially and to the human spirit. They are inspired. Their senses are revived. Their imaginations are taking them on fresh, exciting journeys. Their conversations may lead them —anywhere.

The venues are also full of life and activity. They do not sit empty, awaiting the opening night of some performance that is on tour. If you want to visit one, call in advance— well in advance. They are continually booked and engaged in making, learning and innovating: creating performances and projects that begin at EMPAC and go elsewhere.

There are things you can do here that you cannot do anywhere else. The design, thrust out over the hill toward the city, is a symbol of just that—both inside and out. Inside, the production spaces are messy, and that is a good sign. Something the builders and planners and dreamers would delight in. There is no doubt you are in an experimental place, hosting artists, advisors and faculty researchers, and technicians and curators—all hard at work probing, figuring it out and living their talents. Look around, and you will see that the spaces are strewn with sets and cables, suspended screens, ladders and equipment. Creative chaos in the midst of becoming … what? The future?

Here is a hint as to what will be written in the next chapters of EMPAC: A kindergarten teacher will tell you that he or she sees the future, every day, in the faces of the students. Here, much will be conceived, developed, innovated and made to tell stories, but perhaps the best way to glimpse EMPAC's next chapters is through its people. But just as the stories of the children in kindergarten are told outside the classroom in years to come, the real story of EMPAC will be written by what people, affected by the facility and its program, do in the outside world. It is there that the ambitious promises of EMPAC will be kept.

Flyaway Productions performance on top of the steel structure of the entrance lobby as part of *EMPAC 360 – On Site and Sound,* a performance celebrating the midpoint between groundbreaking and opening.

APPENDIX 1

EMPAC was planned and built over a period of eight years. Even as it was just starting to take shape, it was already a future-focused program, Curtis R. Priem Center for Experimental Media and Performing Arts. One exceptional move was hiring a director from the beginning of the planning—an act aimed at ensuring that the architectural and technological development would meet the envisioned program. But even more unheard of was that a curatorial and production team was hired years before the opening. This provided an innovative way to introduce the upcoming activities of the new center to the campus.

Three curators joined EMPAC starting in 2004—one curator each for time-based visual arts, dance, theater and music. This appendix lists both the first years of activity before the opening of EMPAC and the program of the first three years in the new building. Alongside the curatorial team, the production and technical teams were put in place. Since EMPAC's program is such a different enterprise from that which "regular" performing arts centers pursue, the searches for the different positions required patience. In addition, from the onset, the curatorial team worked in a unique cross-disciplinary way. Each curator brought her or his experience to the table, but the program was developed in close collaboration, not taking the specific expertise of each curator as a boundary but as a point of departure.

EMPAC is centered on five broad areas of activities:

- EMPAC curated events, residencies, research, and production activities with an artistic nucleus;
- EMPAC directed and supported research, residencies, and production activities with scientific, engineering, and technological nuclei;
- EMPAC as an educational center at the intersection of arts, science, media, and technology;
- EMPAC as a Rensselaer 'magnet' for inter- and trans-disciplinary interaction, stimulation, and intellectual exchange; and
- EMPAC as a Campus Performing Arts Center, a campus living room and symbol for change at Rensselaer.

The coming years will continue the integration of all these diverse areas. Over the two years since the opening, the presentation of many events created by other campus entities, including the President's Office, Student Life, and different schools and departments, have used EMPAC as the university's performing arts center for a multitude of activities equaling the number of events which are initialized by the curatorial team. The Arts Department and the School of Architecture are using EMPAC's venues for events, classes and thesis work, which utilize the specific potential EMPAC offers for their program. And students are involved with different research projects.

However, this appendix only lists the specific program developed by the curators and researchers parallel to the construction of the building and in the first 3 years of its operation. It may be read as the unfolding of EMPAC's program.

Further information on specific events, research projects and workshops can be found on EMPAC's website: www.empac.rpi.edu

Two dancers with steady-cams as part of the performance of *ABACUS* by Lars Jan in the Concert Hall.

Three weekends of world-class artistic performances and workshops, premieres of EMPAC-commissioned artworks, presentations of research at the frontiers of science, and social events ranging from black-tie elegant to come-as-you-are eclectic.

OCTOBER 3-5, 2008
Gala Weekend

Inaugural Concert
Program: Giovanni Gabrieli, *Canzon Septimi Toni No. 2*, – Charles Ives, *The Unanswered Question* – Györgi Kurtág, *Grabstein für Stephan* – Györgi Ligeti, *Lux Aeterna* – Robert Schumann, *Piano Concerto in A Minor* – Thomas Tallis, *Spem In Alium*

Performers: Albany Symphony Orchestra under David Alan Miller – Albany Symphony Orchestra Brass Octet under Eric Berlin – International Contemporary Ensemble (ICE) under Gregory Vajda – Vox Vocal Ensemble under George Steel – Per Tengstrand, Piano

Presidential Colloquy
Presidential Colloquy "Photons, Sound Waves, and Data Bytes: Creativity at the Nexus of Science, Technology, Media and the Arts" Moderator: The Honorable Shirley Ann Jackson, Ph.D., 18th President of Rensselaer Polytechnic Institute with A.P. (Preetham) Parigi, Walter F. Parkes and Peter Schwartz

EMPAC Architecture and Design Exhibit
This exhibition tracking the evolution of and high-lights from the EMPAC construction process includes drawings, videos and models from Grimshaw Architects as well as the building design consultants.

EMPAC Building Presentation
A presentation by the EMPAC architect and design team talking about aspects of the building architecture, acoustics, design process and structure.

Workspace Unlimited
Hybrid Space and the Panoramic Screen
Documentation of recent projects by Workspace Unlimited created with modified video game engines. This immersive, moving-image environment highlights the intense and engaging yet slightly unsettling nature of its work in the 360-degree screen.

Billy Cowie
In The Flesh
In the Flesh is an intimate and uncanny 3-D video installation in which viewers don blue/red anaglyph glasses and see a dancer in front of them: she seems to be in the space, solid and real, and gazing back.

Offsite: EMPAC Events 2004-2008
Offsite, an exhibit of event postcards, traces the timeline of EMPAC events up to the opening in satellite spaces on campus and in the region.

Per Tengstrand
2 Hands, 3 Pianos
Per Tengstrand performs works chosen specifically for three of EMPAC's grand pianos: the deep clarity of the Bösendorfer (Esa-Pekka Salonen, Dichotomie), the delicate precision of the Fazioli (Maurice Ravel, Miroirs), and the massive sound of our Hamburg Steinway (Franz Liszt, Après une lecture de Dante).

dumb type
Voyage
Voyage is a multimedia performance for the theater that examines the uncertainty and dislocation of the modern world through a combination of intense sound, movement, text and projected images.

Verdensteatret
Louder
By combining robotics, video, sound, music, shadow play, object theater and new technology, Louder is a performance inspired by travels in the Mekong Delta created by Verdensteatret, a Norwegian company of artists from a wide range of arts disciplines.

The Wooster Group
THERE IS STILL TIME...BROTHER
An interactive war film where the audience stands inside a 360-degree projection screen, surrounded by the film's bewildering narrative space, where the action can only be seen and heard clearly through a virtual peephole that scans the circle, controlled by a member of the audience.

DANCE MOViES Premieres
Kino-Eye, Veterans, PH Propiedad Horizontal, Nora
The screening of the first four dance films commissioned through the DANCE MOViES Commission, an EMPAC program that supports the creation of new works where dance meets the technologies of the moving image.

Open Late with Madlib
Dance and hang out under our 360-degree screen (suspended overhead) with Madlib's fused strata of encyclopedic beats, the turntable mastery of J. Rocc, the 8-bit hip-hop antics of Juiceboxxx, and live video projections by Imnopf.

Pauline Oliveros
Deep Listening Workshop in the Concert Hall
As part of Sunday Talks and Brunch, Pauline Oliveros leads a free public workshop introducing "Deep Listening," a practice of expanding one's attention to sound and the listening body beyond everyday experience.

Cecil Taylor
Floating Gardens
Composer, pianist, poet, Guggenheim Fellow, MacArthur Fellowship ("Genius") Award winner, and one of the most singular voices of the last century presents an afternoon reading of his poetry.

Arts Department
Pioneers of Experimental Media
For the EMPAC opening, the department of the arts compiled a DVD of the most outstanding works from faculty, alumni and the department's events series, iEAR presents!

Selmer Bringsjord, Barbara Cutler, Shekhar Garde, Kenneth Jansen
In sight / Out look
Rensselaer scientists invite the audience for an hour-long presentation of their latest research combining light, images and media as an integral aspect of their investigation.

Pauline Oliveros and Cecil Taylor
Concert
For the first time, Pauline Oliveros and Cecil Taylor, two of the most renowned composer/improvisers in the United States and Europe, will share a stage, presenting a concert in three parts: Taylor solo, Oliveros solo and a duo improvisation.

October 9-12, 2008
Symposium Weekend

Richard Siegal / The Bakery
As If Stranger
A solo dance performance with live sound in which images, movement, presence and streams of words weave a seeming narrative, oscillating between fact and fiction, transparency and poetry.

Robert Normandeau
Cinema for the Ear
A winner of nearly every major prize within the field of electroacoustic music, Montreal-based composer Robert Normandeau explores the Concert Hall's ideal design for multi-channel electronic music with a loudspeaker dome above the audience.

Research Symposium
An internationally diverse group of representatives from leading research institutions come together for two days to share their work in areas of arts, design and media-based scientific research spanning topics from augmented reality to the visualization and auralization of data.

Fieldwork
Concert
A collective of three widely celebrated young composer-performers. Fieldwork's music reflects each member's ties to the American jazz tradition, modern composition, African and South Asian music, underground hip-hop and electronica, and the influential music of Chicago's Association for the Advancement of Creative Musicians (AACM).

Jazz at Lincoln Center Orchestra with Wynton Marsalis
Concert
The Jazz at Lincoln Center Orchestra, comprising 15 of the most classic jazz soloists and ensemble players today, has been the Jazz at Lincoln Center resident orchestra for over 12 years.

October 17-19, 2008
Homecoming & Family Weekend

Gamelan Galak Tika & Ensemble Robot
Performance
Gamelan Galak Tika is an orchestra of instruments traditional to Balinese music and dance; Ensemble Robot is a team of engineers, designers and artists

that have created a collection of unique robotic instruments.

Roy Haynes Fountain of Youth Band
Concert

Freeing jazz's borders, infusing its lifeblood, steering it toward greater freedom and more distinctive expression, Roy Haynes is a national treasure who continues to forge new paths well into his 70s, dumbfounding jazz lovers, not to mention Father Time and Mother Nature.

Concerts and Performances by Student Groups

Events and performances ranging in media and style including many student groups will reflect the diversity of interest on, and beyond, the Rensselaer campus, including Improvcapella, Sheer Idiocy, Experimental Error, Spotlight, Symphonic Band and Percussion Ensemble, RPI Orchestra and Choir, Campus Serenaders and Swing Dancers, Ballroom Dance Club, and the RPI Players.

EVENTS 2011-2004

May 1 to October 1, 2011
Jennifer McCoy and Kevin McCoy
Commission

In their own unique combination of sculpture and video, small cameras project an open-ended narrative of live images filmed directly from constructed models, public spaces of EMPAC and partner organizations (tentatively NYU Abu Dhabi and MOMI, NY). The constructed models of narrative scenes, architectural models and/or text will live in small visible pods or nodes throughout the EMPAC building.

April 29 & 30, 2011
Francisco Lopez
Multi-channel Sound Performance/Installation

Francisco Lopez will take five years of his recording in the Amazon to make a piece that uses the acoustics in the Concert Hall to support the complex layering of sounds that takes place in the jungle.

April 6, 2011
Observer Effects Lecture Series
Martin Kemp

In this dinner and discussion, Martin Kemp, Emeritus Research Professor in the History of Art, Oxford University, speaks on issues of visualization in arts and science through the lens of particular artworks. This lecture is presented as part of the Observer Effects lecture series, which invites thinkers to present their highly integrative work in dialogue with the fields of art and science.

March 31 to April 2, 2011
Nicole Beutler
1: Songs

1: Songs performer Sanja Mitrovic surrenders her voice to the intense words of tragic female figures from the history of theater, forming the basis for a subtle but loud scream against the instability and the incalculable incalculability of our existence.

March 6-12, 2011
Signal Ensemble
Recording and Performance of Music

by Steve Reich

In March, members of the renowned chamber orchestra Signal returns to EMPAC to record and perform Steve Reich's classic work of minimalism, Music for 18 Musicians.

March 3 to April 8, 2011
Graham Parker

This exhibition and series of live events by Brooklyn-based Graham Parker looks at and comments on the uses of technology, and how it relates to the broader topic of the con game, both in contemporary times and historically.

February 26, 2011
Les Percussions de Strasbourg
Gérard Grisey: Le Noir de l'Étoile

Le Noir de L'Étoile is an evening-length spatial percussion piece that concerns the death of a pulsar. It had its genesis when French composer Gérard Grisey met the astronomer and cosmologist Joe Silk in 1985.

February 18 & 19, 2011
Verdensteatret
And All the Questionmarks Started to Sing

A hybrid of performance, concert and art installation, And All the Questionmarks Started to Sing presents a complex landscape of moving image and kinetic sculpture that gradually unfolds to reveal its internal logic.

December 3 & 4, 2010
Sean Griffin
Cold Spring

A dazzling musical theatrical experience weaving a humorous and sometimes frightening operatic web with clashing performance styles and themes ranging from alien abduction, cheerleading and eugenics to the beyond.

November 19, 2010 to January 29, 2011
Exhibition
Uncertain Spectator

An exhibition confronting anxiety in contemporary art, where individuals are asked to cross a threshold into situations riddled with uncertainty. The works presented deal with a general mood of uneasiness arising from recent political and economic events that seems to frame a future rife with imminent threats.

November 12, 2010
Georg Friedrich Haas
In Vain

A striking spectral composition for chamber orchestra performed in and between complete darkness by the Argento Chamber Ensemble under Michel Galante.

November 6 & 7, 2010
Latitude 14
Red Fly/Blue Bottle

A performance that bridges concert, cabinet of curiosities and video installation, *Red Fly/Blue Bottle* explores the mediating effects of memory and how we use imagination to surmount that which we have lost.

November 3, 2010
Mark Changizi, Johannes Goebel and David Rothenberg
Music – Language – Sound and Nature
Observer Effects: Conversations in Art & Science

Experts in the diverse fields of music, acoustics, evolutionary neurobiology and naturalist philosophy engage in a thoughtful exchange on how music, speech, language, birds and whale songs interrelate.

October 28, 2010
Cinematic Chimera Screening Series
Alexander Sokurov
Russian Ark

Filmed as a 90-minute uninterrupted and uncut shot through the Hermitage Museum in St. Petersburg, Russian Ark subtly interweaves dance, opera, theater and music in a poetic meditation on the flow of history.

October 15 & 16, 2010
Laurie Anderson
Delusion

A meditation on life and language through music, video and storytelling, Delusion weaves a complex story about longing, memory and identity.

October 7, 2010
Monolake
Live Surround with Tarik Barri

Explore the limitless possibilities of the dance floor through multi-channel surround sound design, music software and dub-influenced techno music.

October 6, 2010
Robert Henke
Two lectures:

Live Performance in the Age of Supercomputers

A critical look at live audiovisual performance in this time of almost limitless audio manipulation and generation, and yet limited technological interfaces.

Live. Max. Max For Live. What Is It Good For?
– Lecture

Dig into the world of Ableton Live software and MAX/MSP programming, its relevance to the dance floor and academic music, and their integration, with one of the authors of Ableton.

October 1-3, 2010
Festival
Filament

A festival of new works in performance, visual arts, sound and media. With more than 15 premieres spanning theater, 24-channel sound, contemporary dance, video and a barn-raising; exchanges with artists, curators and creative engineers; and a dynamic archive of artists who had residencies at EMPAC over the past years. This three-day festival highlights EMPAC's focus on creation via commissions and residencies. With, among others: Yanira Castro, Balletlab, Early Morning Opera, Michael Schumacher, Hans Tutschku, Volkmar Klein, MTAA, Wally Cardona, SUE-C & Laetitia Sonami, Steve Cuiffo, Trey Lyford, Geoff Sobelle, Jen DeNike, Miro Dance Theater, Trouble, National Theater of the United States of America; plus the premiere of the third series of the EMPAC Dance Movie Commissions and a concert with the last piece by the late Maryanne Amacher.

Clockwise from top left: Anthony Braxton; Edith Dekynot, *Ground Control;* Pauline Oliveros and Tintinnabulate; Kurt Hentschläger, *Feed.*

September 17 & 18, 2010
Wally Cardona
A Light Conversation
An intimate dialogue in movement reflecting life: choice, commitment, pleasure, sacrifice, boredom, aesthetics versus ethics, the uncertainty of the future — and love.

September 10, 2010
Brent Green
Gravity Was Everywhere Back Then
A stop-action film accompanied by musical narrative telling the poignant and darkly humorous true story of a man who built a bizarre "healing house" in an attempt to cure his wife's terminal cancer.

August 16-22, 2010
EMPAC Team
MashUp! A Collaborative EMPAC Experience
A hands-on workshop for first-year students to create and produce a multimedia party for their classmates using EMPAC's incredible interactive lighting, audio, video and stage technology.

August 16-22, 2010
Johannes Birringer, Mark Coniglio
LIVE.MEDIA+PERFORMANCE.LAB
Our first summer lab for interactive media in performance! Directed by Johannes Birringer and Mark Coniglio, the workshop offers intensive training and possibilities for experimentation with mixed reality and real-time architectures, programmable environments, interactive design and the integration of time-based media into live performance and installation. Intermediate/advanced experience in performing with audio/visual technologies and/or programming required. Previous experience with Isadora or Max/MSP recommended. This workshop is geared for those already working with technology but wishing to improve their skills and get new perspectives.

May 28, 2010
Steve Lehman Octet
Concert
A trail-blazing young saxophonist and composer whose thrilling, multilayered work stands at the frontiers of contemporary music.

May 13, 2010
Unfiction Film Series
Lorenzo Fonda
Megunica
A film interweaving documentary footage with animation that follows Italian graffiti artist Blu on a Latin American odyssey, examining the role of art in the urban environment and its transformative capacities.

April 30 to May 2, 2010
Festival
onedotzero – adventures in motion
The London-based ondotzero_adventures in motion festival returns to EMPAC with a delirious showcase of the latest developments in digital and interactive design — from small, screen-based graphics to large-scale installations, plus screenings, music videos, live events and workshops.

April 30, 2010
Diplo
Festival Performance
Kicking off the first night of onedotzero_adventures in motion, DJ superstar Diplo performs with a cadre of the area's best VJs. Expect the unexpected mixed seamlessly with irreverence and the touch of an international tastemaker.

April 21, 2010
Mark Changizi
Alien Vision Revolution
Why do humans see in color? Why do we have eyes on the front of our heads, like cats, rather than on the sides, like horses? Theoretical neurobiologist Mark Changizi, professor at Rensselaer, explores why we see what we see, from color to the written word.

April 8, 2010
Unfiction Film Series
James Marsh / Philippe Petit
Man on Wire
An Academy Award-winning documentary about Philippe Petit's daring and defiant tightrope walk between the twin towers, which became known as the "artistic crime of the century." In conjunction with Dancing on the Ceiling (see March 18 to April 10, below).

April 2, 2010
New Nothing Series
Josephine Foster, Rachel Mason
In the final New Nothing of the season, two charismatic performers offer different takes on the construction of the song and the role of the human voice.

March 27, 2010
Helmut Lachenmann, Signal, JACK Quartet
Concert
A rare U.S. performance of one of the most influential living European composers, interpreted by two exciting new music ensembles and the composer himself.

March 25-27, 2010
The OpenEnded Group
Upending
The premiere of an evening-length work that combines breathtaking 3-D experimental animation with music by Morton Feldman, recorded at EMPAC by the FLUX Quartet. Followed by The Making of Upending with The OpenEnded Group.

March 25, 2010
School of Architecture
Inhabiting Other Worlds: Microgravity, Perception, Physiology and Design
A special panel organized by Architecture Rensselaer marking the opening of a student exhibition resulting from a studio dedicated to designing a medical station for a NASA lunar module. In conjunction with Dancing on the Ceiling.

March 20, 2010
Frederic Rzewski
Concert & Talk
A monumental figure in new music who is both an instrumental virtuoso and a composer of revolutionary

ambition in the tradition of Hanns Eisler and Kurt Weill.

March 18 to April 10, 2010
Exhibition
Dancing on the Ceiling – Art & Zero Gravity
A building-wide exhibition featuring national and international contemporary artists that explore the condition of weightlessness on earth by deploying techniques such as parabolic flight, rigging and digital effects.

March 18, 2010
Douglas Trumbull
2001: A Space Odyssey
An engaging talk with special effects legend Douglas Trumbull (*2001: A Space Odyssey, Close Encounters of the Third Kind, Blade Runner*) followed by a screening of Stanley Kubrick's masterpiece of science fiction cinema on the massive 56-foot Concert Hall screen. In conjunction with Dancing on the Ceiling.

March 5, 2010
Haleh Abghari, Tony Arnold, Johannes Goebel, Jacob Greenberg
SOLOS^2
Exploring the acoustics of the Concert Hall, we'll listen to sounds we know well: two high (soprano to be exact) female voices and piano in various combinations.

March 4, 2010
Michael Century, Mark Changizi, Ted Krueger, Chris Salter
Perception: Art and Research
A panel discussion on topics including thresholds of perception, multi-modal perception, and the use of research in art practice.

March 3-12, 2010
Chris Salter
Just Noticeable Difference
Just Noticeable Difference (JND) is an installation that explores the relation between chaos and order, self and environment at the thresholds of sensory perception.

February 26 & 27, 2010
Wayne McGregor | Random Dance
ENTITY
ENTITY brings together the fierce kinetics and formal rigor of Wayne McGregor | Random Dance with a torrential score by collaborators Jon Hopkins (Massive Attack and Coldplay) and Joby Talbot (The Divine Comedy, White Stripes), framed by multiple moving screens.

February 26, 2010
Wayne McGregor | Random Dance
Panel discussion on R-Research
A discussion of projects and directions of R-Research — the research branch of Wayne McGregor | Random Dance — which initiates and implements new research collaborations across disciplines, including dance, neuroscience, cognitive science, biology, philosophy and technology.

February 24, 2010
rAndom International
Real-Time Reactive Systems in Art and Design
Best known for large-scale public installations combining technology, media, design and art, rAndom International play with real-time reactive systems that offer viewers an intuitive body-based experience.

February 23 & 24, 2010
Wayne McGregor | Random Dance
Company Class
Come take a class with the dancers of Wayne McGregor | Random Dance! A ballet-based techniques class open to intermediate/advanced dancers.

February 17, 2010
Philip Barnard
Cognition, Emotion and Action
Dr. Philip Barnard, program leader at the Medical Research Council's Cognition and Brain Sciences Unit in Cambridge, England, and a collaborator and research advisor to Wayne McGregor | Random Dance, presents a talk on his research work.

February 13, 2010
New Nothing Series
Extra Life, Dan Deacon
A thrashing, zig-zagging, gorgeously heavy band that reconciles the 21st and 13th centuries mixes it up with the beacon of exuberant indie noise dance.

February 10, 2010
Margaret Wertheim
Mathematics as Poetic Enchantment
A dinner and talk with Margaret Wertheim, a science writer and curator, during which she presents work with the Institute For Figuring, an organization devoted to the poetic and aesthetic dimensions of science and mathematics.

January 28 & 29, 2010
Jeremy Wade
there is no end to more
Choreographer Jeremy Wade's playful solo spectacle delves into Japanese kawaii (cute) culture — mashing together a children's TV show, dances and animated drawings by manga illustrator Hiroki Otsuka.

January 20 to February 3, 2010
Exhibition
Japanese Manga and Anime
An exhibition in conjunction with Jeremy Wade's performance exploring the culture of Japanese manga and anime, whose exuberant visual style is a source for there is no end to more.

December 18, 2009
Unfiction Film Series
Agnes Varda
The Beaches of Agnes
French filmmaker Agnes Varda creates a moving collage of her films and life on the eve of her 80th birthday.

December 15, 2009
Antioch Chamber Ensemble
Holiday Concert
In celebration of winter and the turning of the year, Rensselaer establishes with this holiday concert a new tradition on campus.

December 10, 2009
Unfiction Film Series
Werner Herzog
Encounters at the End of the World
Werner Herzog's most recent documentary film, Encounters at the End of the World is a study of Antarctica and the small community of scientists that has gravitated to its surreal landscape.

December 5, 2009
Frieder Weiss
Perceivable Bodies Workshop
Frieder Weiss, creator of the media environment in Chunky Move's *GLOW*, will give a hands-on workshop on video motion sensing technologies and his interactive software for performance.

December 3 & 4, 2009
Chunky Move
GLOW
Conceived as a "biotech fiction" by Australian choreographer Gideon Obarzanek and interactive software creator Frieder Weiss, *GLOW* transforms a solo dancer into a mutant figure both sensual and grotesque. As she slides and thrashes across a white floor, her form generates a constantly shifting digital habitat of projected light.

December 2, 2009
Frieder Weiss
From Technological Research to Sensual Engineering
Frieder Weiss, creator of the interactive media environment in Chunky Move's *GLOW*, talks about his participation in and observations of the "dance tech" genre over the last 15 years.

November 19, 2009
Unfiction Film Series
Astra Taylor
Examined Life
In *Examined Life*, filmmaker Astra Taylor accompanies some of today's most influential thinkers on a series of unique excursions through places and spaces that hold particular resonance for them and their ideas.

November 17, 2009
Stewart Smith, Bernd Linterman, Eric Ameres, Thomas Soetens
Art and the 360-degree screen
A panel of international artists, engineers, and producers representing the evolving field of works created for EMPAC's 360-degree panoramic screen.

November 14, 2009
Garth Knox
Solo
A world master of the viola plays an evening of music, some very old, some very new — written expressly for his instrument and its baroque-era cousin, the viola d'amore.

November 13, 2009
New Nothing Series
Prefuse 73 w/ Imnopf, Skeleton$ + Luciano Chessa
Punky funk meets Futurism and homespun electro in this paradoxical grouping of artists from the far ends of the musical spectrum.

November 7, 2009
DANCE MOViES Commissions
Body/Traces, Eyes Nose Mouth, Looking Forward — Man and Woman, Sunscreen Serenade
The premiere of four new works created through this year's DANCE MOViES Commission, the EMPAC program that brings together moving bodies and the moving image.

November 7, 2009
Marc Downie
FIELD Workshop
Marc Downie, the creator of the powerful digital arts programming environment FIELD, leads a two-day workshop in its manifold uses.

November 6, 2009
Marc Downie
The Secret World of Making Art by Writing Code
A talk on the process and tools of The OpenEnded Group — one of the most sophisticated digital artist teams working today, presented by artist and programmer Marc Downie, one of the three OEG members collaborating on the EMPAC-commissioned stereoscopic video project Upending.

October 30 to November 21, 2009
Workspace Unlimited
They Watch
An installation in the 360-degree screen that immerses the viewer in an ambiguous liminal space where the virtual merges with real and the observer becomes the observed.

October 30, 2009
New Nothing Series
Zs, Little Women
Zs returns to EMPAC on Halloween eve for a careening set of "sputtering Morse code dots of percussion and saxophone." Opening is Little Women, a quartet whose ghost notes and violent disassembling of their instruments concoct riotous sets that run the gamut from pop to free jazz to noise and back again.

October 28, 2009
Art21
Systems
A special preview screening of *Systems*, the fourth episode from the fifth season of the award-winning program Art21, including interviews with Julie Mehretu, John Baldessari, Kimsooja, and Allan McCollum.

October 23 & 24, 2009
Marc Bamuthi Joseph
The Break/s: a mixtape for the stage
The poet and hip-hop theater sensation Marc Bamuthi Joseph brings together movement, music and personal storytelling in a multimedia travelogue of Planet Hip-Hop.

October 16 & 17, 2009
Daniel Teige, Volkmar Klien
Immersive Sound Concert
Thirty-six loudspeakers hung at different heights and in 360 degrees around the audience; European composers and sound artists Daniel Teige and Volkmar Klien play music specifically designed for this immersive sound environment.

October 8, 2009
Unfiction Film Series
Susanna Helke
White Sky
White Sky is a documentary film about the human ability to adapt to destruction and continue with everyday life in an ecologically devastated environment.

October 3 to December 16, 2009
Sophie Kahn and Lisa Parra
Body/Traces
Using a DIY 3-D laser scanner and stop-motion 3-D digital animation to track a dancer's movement through space and time, *Body/Traces* is a single-channel video projected at life-size.

October 3, 2009
Per Tengstrand
The Battles of Beethoven
Pianist and ambassador of classical music Per Tengstrand presents a concert tracking the evolution of the piano during the life of Beethoven.

October 3, 2009
DANCE MOViES Commissions
Kino-Eye, Veterans, PH Propiedad Horizontal, Nora
Four dance films commissioned by EMPAC in 2007 and premiered at EMPAC's opening festival. Fusing dance with the moving image, these works span a wide geographic, visual and emotional range.

October 1 to December 16, 2009
Mads Lynnerup
Take a Day for Yourself!
The genre-crossing Danish artist mounts a whimsical yet searching investigation of the everyday, incorporating video, posters and ordinary people from the Troy and Rensselaer communities.

September 25, 2009
Festival
Slow Wave Festival: Seeing Sleep
A three-day festival of installations, film, music and scientific experiment devoted to the methods for giving form to the elusive, and at times, ineffable enigma of sleep. With works by Jennifer Hall, Allan Hobson, Pierre Huyghe, Rodney Graham, Fernando Orellana and Brendan Burns, Ana Rewakowicz, Alvin Lucier and Andy Warhol.

September 17, 2009
Unfiction Film Series
Jean Painlevé
The Sounds of Science
The eight mesmerizing short films of Jean Painlevé in The Sounds of Science screening are at once a mix of surrealist-influenced shorts and serious science documentaries accompanied by a hypnotic and dreamy score by rock band Yo La Tengo.

September 11, 2009
New Nothing Series
Boredoms: BOADRUM 9
Deerhunter
The New Nothing series kickoff includes two bands, nine (make that 10) drummers, and an evening of noise/music that's experienced not just with the ear but the entire body.

September 3, 2009
Contact Ensemble
ELEVATED
Composer and Bang on a Can co-founder David Lang presents four genre-defying new musical works in conjunction with films by visual artists William Wegman, Bill Morrison, Matt Mullican, and Doug Aitken.

May 29 & 30, 2009
Yvon Bonenfant
Beacons
Bringing together the musicality of cutting edge vocal art with sensual, multi-screen video explorations of light and colour, Beacons takes the audience on a theatrical journey that explores love and loss, coming and going, and the intensity of the primordial human act of reaching.

May 8, 2009
Rafael Toral
The Space Program
Musician and artist Rafael Toral presents "Space Program," a series of works exploring peculiar combinations of gestural control and sonic palette. Each "study" is a conjoined spatial and aural exploration, often using Toral's own DIY electronics.

April 24-26, 2009
Basil Twist
Dogugaeshi
Master puppeteer Basil Twist unfolds a journey of images and emotions influenced by the tradition of Japanese dogugaeshi stage-mechanism technique.

April 17-19, 2009
Festival
Onedotzero – Adventures in Motion
The internationally acclaimed festival brings the latest work in moving image to EMPAC for the U.S. premiere. Featuring screenings, audiovisual installations, live cinematic performances, VJ/DJ events and artist talks.

April 17, 2009
Scanner + Olga Mink
The Nature of Being
A performance guided by contemplative sound and image, creating an abstract story yielding to a state-of-flux cinematic experience. Using immersive projections, panoramic views and surround sound, sensuality is reimagined and reinterpreted, connecting multiple realities in a multi-angled perspective, merging and juxtaposing various points of views.

April 2, 2009
In a Glass Hour Lecture Series
Steven Connor
Steven Connor, academic director of the London Consortium Graduate Programme in Humanities and Cultural Studies, delivers his EMPAC-commissioned text entitled, "The Chronopher," a meditation on time and the nature of voice.

March 26-28, 2009
Tere O'Connor Dance
Rammed Earth
Tere O'Connor Dance performs *Rammed Earth*, a site-adaptive dance work that incorporates the audience into an expanding, contracting space by moving them into different viewing positions throughout the performance.

March 24, 2009
Frédéric Bevilacqua
Lecture-Demonstration
Frédéric Bevilacqua of the Institute for Music/ Acoustic Research and Coordination in Paris demonstrates potential applications of his research into gesture analysis for dance and theater.

March 21, 2009
Johannes Goebel
"Wandering between the Worlds" –
Workshop + Concert
An afternoon workshop by EMPAC's director Johannes Goebel features instruments of his own devising; it is followed by a concert of electronic pieces composed under the influence of computers and centuries of instrumental music.

March 20, 2009
Catherine Sullivan + Sean Griffin
Triangle of Need, The Chittendens & D-Pattern
Three multi-channel video and audio installations on rotation by the artist Catherine Sullivan, with whom Griffin has been collaborating for more than six years on music, sound and "language design": *D-Pattern*, *The Chittendens* and *Triangle of Need*.

March 19, 2009
Unfiction Film Series
Unfiction on Safari
A collection of three films: Olaf Breuning's *Home 2*; Sascha Paladino's *Throw Down Your Heart,* with Bela Fleck; and Coco Fusco and Guillermo Gomez-Peña's *The Couple in the Cage*, together present a complex terrain of intention and action surrounding tourism, cultural interchange, appropriation and hybridity.

March 6, 2009
ZEROTH CHANNEL Series
Doug Henderson, Seth Cluett, Natasha Barrett
Concert
Is listening to a recording of a bottle somehow still listening to a bottle? What about the wind around a glacier or a hammer? New works using up to 18 loudspeakers by composers Doug Henderson (Berlin), Seth Cluett (Paris) and Natasha Barrett (Oslo) lead the listener into questions of what is real, true or important in identifying the concrete origin of a sound used in the work.

February 27, 2009
Unfiction Film Series
Douglas Gordon, Philippe Parreno
Zidane: A 21st Century Portrait
By training 17 cameras on legendary footballer Zinedine Zidane over the course of one match — and pairing the footage with a soundtrack by Mogwai — filmmaker Philippe Parreno offers a poignant and

immersive reflection on the human condition of the athlete and the athlete's condition as performer.

February 17, 2009
In a Glass Hour Lecture Series
Johannes Goebel
Future, Present and Past as Threat to Sanity
In this talk, music will serve as a projection screen to reflect thoughts on time. The western notation of music in conjunction with the development of clocks influenced how we think and feel time. Time became mechanized, and now computers are lost without their clock. The assumption that time allows us to structure future, present and past (in that order) is a political tool, for better and worse.

February 10, 2009
Unfiction Film Series
Agnes Varda
Les Glaneurs et la glaneuse (The Gleaners and I)
French filmmaker Agnes Varda's visual essay on the concept and lifestyle of "gleaning," or scavenging. By focusing on the marginalized, an open view emerges of our attitudes toward usefulness, aging, decay and the discarded.

February 6 & 7, 2009
Cathy Weis
Dance Performance
Guggenheim Fellow and Bessie Award-winner Cathy Weis performs several haikus from the vignette series of "Electric Haiku: Calm as Custard," as well as two new EMPAC-commissioned solo works.

January 27, 2009
Sophie Kahn / Lisa Parra
Body/Traces
New media artist Sophie Kahn and choreographer Lisa Parra present a work-in-progress showing of their video installation, *Body/Traces*, a DANCE MOViES Commission. Using a DIY 3-D laser scanner and stop-motion digital animation, they track a dancer's movement through time and space.

January 25, 2009
Bobby McFerrin
Concert
A solo performance by the inimitable vocalist, improviser, conductor and musical enigma whose path has ranged from audience-participatory improvisations, 10 Grammies and performances with major symphonies to several unusual ensembles of his own design.

January 23, 2009
Quicksilver
Stile Moderno: New Music from the 17th Century
Critically acclaimed early-music violinist Robert Mealy leads the new early-music ensemble Quicksilver, presenting a concert of brilliant and virtuosic music from the avant-garde of the 1600s.

January 22, 2009
In a Glass Hour Lecture Series
Georges Dreyfus
Georges Dreyfus discusses the Buddhist concept of "no-self," and the ways this view is in sync with recent Western scientific ideas about subjectivity and identity evolving over time.

January 17, 2009
Sean Griffin
Hitting Things, Saying Things
As part of his two-part residency at EMPAC this spring, Los Angeles-based composer Sean Griffin presents *Hitting Things, Saying Things*, a collection of works in which the staged nature of music performance evaporates into an idiosyncratic breed of theater.

January 16, 2009
Brent Green
God Builds Like Frank Lloyd Wright
Best known for his darkly humorous stop-motion films, filmmaker-musician Brent Green performs live with a series of his recent shorts. Guest musicians include Brendan Canty (Fugazi), Howe Gelb (Giant Sand) and Jim Becker (Califone).

December 16, 2008
Balletlab
Fermata
Australian contemporary dance company Balletlab returns to EMPAC for a four-week creative residency. The dancers show excerpts from *Fermata*, a new work in progress.

December 11, 2008
Unfiction Film Series
Nikolaus Geyrhalter / Wolfgang Widerhofer
Our Daily Bread
Welcome to the world of industrial food production and high-tech farming! *Our Daily Bread* is a widescreen tableau of a feast that isn't always easy to digest and in which we all take part. A meticulous study that enables the audience to form their own ideas through long shots calculating what happens before food journeys to tables around the globe.

December 9, 2008
In a Glass Hour Lecture Series
Paul Ramirez Jonas
Visual artist Paul Ramirez Jonas presents a lecture on time, expiration and memory through his work. In his projects, what looks like invention is but a re-enactment, and what seems to be an exploration is but walking in someone else's footsteps.

December 4 & 5, 2008
The Builders Association
Continuous City
From Shanghai to Los Angeles, Toronto to Troy, *Continuous City* is a multimedia theatrical performance for the stage and screen that tells the story of a traveling father and his daughter at home tethered and transformed by speed, hypermodernity and failing cell phones.

November 22 & 23, 2008
Elevator Repair Service
Gatz
In an audacious theatrical tour de force, ERS presents not your typical stage adaptation of a classic novel: One morning in the low-rent office of a small business, one employee finds a ragged old copy of The Great Gatsby in the clutter of his desk and starts to read it out loud. And doesn't stop.

November 18, 2008
In a Glass Hour Lecture Series
Alfred Crosby
Alfred Crosby, author of *The Measure of Reality: Quantification and Western Society, 1250–1600*, speaks about time from a historical perspective, detailing Western Europe's adoption of quantitative approaches to time, space, finance, art and music.

November 15, 2008
Zeroth Channel Series
Daniel Teige
Multi-channel Concert
Berlin-based Daniel Teige presents his most recent pieces alongside new mixes of Iannis Xenakis' classically massive multi-channel pieces from the '60s and '70s.

November 13, 2008
Toni Dove
Spectropia
A live-mix cinematic event where performers orchestrate onscreen characters through an original mix of film and a unique system of motion sensing that serves as a cinematic instrument.

November 8, 2008
Arraymusic
Concert
The Arraymusic ensemble is an eight-member performing group from Toronto recognized worldwide for its innovative programming and virtuosic performance. Its extensive repertoire includes a library-like collection of pieces the group commissioned from composers with highly individual voices from around the world.

November 6, 2008
In a Glass Hour Lecture Series
Wendy Hui Kyong Chun
This talk explores the potential of ephemerals through artworks that make things disappear. New media, like the computer technology on which it relies, races simultaneously toward the future and the past, toward the bleeding edge of obsolescence. In collaboration with iEAR Presents!

November 4, 2008
Election 08
Take Me to Your Leader
Join hundreds of citizens to watch election night coverage on EMPAC's big screens throughout Evelyn's Café, the Goodman Theater/Studio and Studio 2.

October 3-19, 2008
OPENING FESTIVAL
See top of this list.

April 25, 2008, The Armory
Between a Rock and a Tiny Bell
An evening with new alchemies of punk, heavy metal, jagged complexity, Scottish pipe music, '70s psychedelia, old-school European free improv, and gritty minimalism with Black Moth Super Rainbow, Han Bennink and Peter Brötzmann, Zs and Blarvuster.

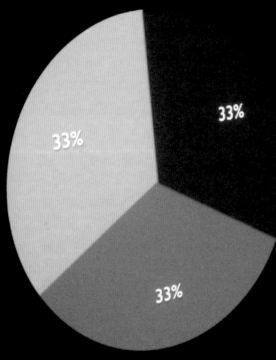

33%

33%

33%

Making Work
Making Research
Making Tools

MY ART PIE

Clockwise from top left: Flyaway Production, *EMPAC 360*; The Light
Surgeons, *True Fictions, New Adventures in Folklore*; Ramon Sender
(left) at the *WOW & FLUTTER* festival; Mark Downie, *Field Lecture*.

April 15-19, 2008, Greene Gallery
Liz Aggiss, Billy Cowie
Men in the Wall and In the Flesh
A 3-D video installation in which four men chat across the boundaries of their respective screens, looping through a sequence of poetry, song, stories, dance and napping.

April 15, 2008, Academy Hall
Liz Aggiss
Hi Jinx
Liz Aggiss performs *Hi Jinx*, an homage featuring dance reconstructions, archival film and the highly influential "dance commandments" of Heidi Dzinkowska.

March 6, 2008, Biotech Auditorium
Jonathan Berger
Data Speaks. Are You Listening?
In this lecture, researcher and composer Jonathan Berger, a leader in the field of sonification, describes the creative potentials of data as a raw material for artists and composers.

February 13 & 14, 2008, RPI Playhouse
Lone Twin
9 Years
Built from years of two British artists traveling across the globe, *9 Years* is a unique, hilarious, hopeful yet borderline tragic performance event in the format of lecture/travel diary.

January 29, 2008, Heffner Alumni House
Slavoj Žižek
Pervert's Guide to Cinema
A feature-length film wherein the international rock star of contemporary philosophy, Slavoj Žižek, delves into the hidden language of cinema, uncovering what movies can tell us about ourselves.

January 11 to February 3, 2008,
EMPAC Construction Site
Jennifer Tipton
Light above the Hudson
Acclaimed lighting designer Jennifer Tipton turns the nearly completed EMPAC building into a dynamic light sculpture that can be seen from near and far.

November 17, 2007, Academy Hall
Neil Rolnick
60!
To honor the music, innovation and good humor of Neil Rolnick's 30-plus years of activity as a composer and educator, EMPAC presents an evening of his compositions.

October 26, 2007, Heffner Alumni House
Sue Costabile, Laetitia Sonami, Luke Dubois, Manrico Montero, Benton Bainbridge, Bobby Previte
Custom Control
In conjunction with iEAR's Tools — Analog and Intersections series. *Custom Control* is an evening of three performances where artists have "custom built" their own performance tools. Artist duos include Sue Costabile and Laetitia Sonami; Luke Dubois and Manrico Montero; and Benton Bainbridge and Bobby Previte.

October 19, 2007, Chapel + Cultural Center
Anthony Braxton
12(+1)tet: Ghost Trance Music
World-renowned saxophonist and composer Anthony Braxton, with his 12-piece ensemble the 12(+1)tet, performs and conducts from his most recent series called Ghost Trance Music.

October 4 & 5, 2007, WMHT Studio
Kassys
KOMMER
KOMMER is an awkward, spare, painfully funny portrait of human frailty in 50 percent theater, 50 percent film by the Amsterdam-based theater collective Kassys. First, they create a stilted world on stage marking the loss of a dear friend, and then reveal the actors' "real lives" after the show.

September 20–22, 2007, Rensselaer Playhouse
BalletLab
Amplification
In *Amplification*, Australia's foremost contemporary dance company collides fierce dancing, driving music and unsettling imagery for an exhilarating and engaging performance.

May 3, 2007, Rensselaer Playhouse
Natasha Barrett
Concert with Loudspeaker Orchestra
Using an orchestra of more than 20 loudspeakers, Natasha Barrett performs live sound projections of works of her own and that of the master-innovator French composer Luc Ferrari.

April 24, 2007, Biotech Center Auditorium
Johannes Goebel
engineering ± art ± science
A lecture given by EMPAC director Johannes Goebel on the different motivations and goals of science, art and engineering — or should we say religion, engineering, art, philosophy and science?

March 28 to April 1, 2007, Greene Gallery
Sean Reed and Robert Darroll
Bedlam
Bedlam — originally the name for a medieval England insane asylum — has since become a synonym for tangled, chaotic states. This five-channel video installation is derived from a theater piece by Robert Darroll that involved five performers planning their joint escape from Bedlam. Sean Reed composed the soundtrack.

March 15, 2007, West Hall Auditorium
DANCE MOViES 7
The seventh edition of our popular series!

February 27, 2007, Biotech Center Auditorium
Bob Stein
The Evolution of Reading and Writing in the Networked Era
Bob Stein, director of the Institute for the Future of the Book, discusses current research initiatives and the broader societal implications of shifting from page to screen to a networked environment.

February 23, 2007, Rensselaer Playhouse
Stop.Watch: Seeing Time in Music Video
Stop.Watch presents a screening of music videos where the directors use the concept of time itself as the creative and conceptual impetus for their work — includes rock, pop and electronic music videos by the likes of Hot Chip, Tiga and Kid 606.

February 17, 2007, Biotech Center Atrium
FLUX Quartet
Concert
FLUX Quartet performs a program of 21st- and 20th-century string quartets — including works by Lucier, Scelsi and Xenakis.

February 9 & 10, 2007, WMHT Studio
Tere O'Connor Dance
Frozen Mommy
A darkly humorous dance theater work, stripped of theatrical spectacle or hidden narrative, in which five dancers lead the audience on an elliptical journey. Tere O'Connor Dance is a contemporary dance company based in New York City.

January 25, 2007, Heffner Alumni House
DANCE MOViES 6
An evening of dance films from Sweden, Iceland, Spain, Holland and the U.S. that confront and toy with the edges of danger, boredom, desire and loss: predatory actions in a lobby, couch surfing, hands dancing, wading in snow, feverishly falling in the streets of Palermo.

January 19, 2007, Academy Hall
So Percussion, Dirty Projectors
Concert
Featuring So Percussion, a group from Brooklyn performing the music of David Lang and Steve Reich, and a concert by Dirty Projectors, a unique and oddly virtuosic band redefining the edge of song.

November 14-18, 2006, Rensselaer Playhouse
Kurt Hentschläger
FEED
FEED is an artificial spectacle, stressing the limits of perception. The audience is immersed in clouds of stroboscopic light and intense fog, in a digital landscape populated with virtual characters.

October 27, 2006, Heffner Alumni House
Lee Ranaldo / Leah Singer
DRIFT
A special collaborative performance between visual artist Leah Singer and musician Lee Ranaldo of the incomparable rock band Sonic Youth.

November 1, 2006, West Hall Auditorium
Troika Ranch
Lecture and Performative Demonstration
Troika Ranch, a digital dance theater company that focuses on creation and innovation in theatrical performance, presents its work on interactive software development for the stage.

October 12–15, 2006,
An Office Container on Campus
kondition pluriel
entre-deux
An intriguing performance installation in which one viewer at a time is invited into a seemingly empty office trailer for 10 minutes. Based in Montreal, kondition pluriel produces performative spaces integrating media, video and dance.

October 11, 2006, Russell Sage Auditorium
David Stork
Did the Great Gasters "Cheat" Using Optics?
This talk describes the application of rigorous computer image analysis of Renaissance masterpieces and puts forth a bold theory of how these paintings were constructed.

September 14, 2006, '86 Field
DANCE MOViES 5
International dance films presented on the football field: fierce physicality, music and dancing, to enjoy outdoors, under the stars.

April 20, 2006
DANCE MOViES 4 — Street Wise
With dancing in the streets, mischief in the deli and tango in the back alley, these films are shot where street smarts and dancing feet collide.

March 30, 2006, West Hall Auditorium,
EMPAC plus iEAR
Richard Teitelbaum, Alvin Curran, Frederic Rzewski
Musica Electronica Viva!
Experience the best of electronic improvisation by the music pioneers of Musica Electronica Viva!, featuring members Alvin Curran, Frederic Rzewski and Richard Teitelbaum.

March 23, 2006, Academy Hall
DANCE MOViES 3 — Ice Breaker
The third in the ongoing DANCE MOViES series, Ice Breaker presents six short films from the U.K., Finland, Australia and the Netherlands that push the envelope of the form.

March 3, 2006, Heffner Alumni House
Dreamscapes and Dark Places: Music Video Spawned from Surrealism
An evening of surreal music videos all viewed from the comfort of cozy couches.

November 29, 2005, Heffner Alumni House
Game Engines
Fair Game
Quake and Unreal Tournament on monster screens versus artists that don't shoot and splatter.

November 19, 2005 to April 23, 2006,
Schenectady Museum
Kiyoshi Furukawa / Wolfgang Münch
Bubbles
An interactive video installation where bubbles bounce off the contours of your shadow, emitting playful sounds.

October 26, 2005, Russell Sage Auditorium
DANCE MOViES 2
The second edition presents short films made by dancers and directors who investigate the ongoing search for love and logic in human affairs, often with a strong eye for the absurd.

September 21, 2005, '86 Field
DANCE MOViES 1
Contemporary dancers creating short films and experimental videos — not MTV, not Swan Lake, not Fred Astaire — but physical power and tender movements, roaming, dancing and acting in the most unlikely places.

September 8, 2005, EMPAC Construction Site
EMPAC 360: On Site + Sound
A guided tour around the EMPAC building site marking the midpoint between groundbreaking and opening; with performances on all sides of the building using the active construction site as a stage. Aerial Dance by Flyaway Productions; musical performances by Ethel; pyrotechnics: design by Pierre-Alain Hubert, execution by Fireworks by Grucci; live visuals and sound by Benton-C Bainbridge with Stephan Moore.

April 20, 2005, Russell Sage Auditorium,
EMPAC plus H&SS
William Kennedy, Richard Selzer
Lecture
In this lecture, William Kennedy and Richard Selzer, noted authors and natives of Troy and Albany, whose fiction often speaks of the life of the creative imagination as it interacts with and confronts the arts and culture of our area, will discuss why and how these forces have shaped their writings.

December 1, 2004, West Hall Auditorium,
EMPAC plus iEAR
Mary Ellen Strom / Ann Carlson
Geyser Land
A presentation on the site-specific installation *Geyser Land*, by video artist Mary Ellen Strom and performance artist-choreographer Ann Carlson, which was experienced by the audience in a train between Livingston and Bozeman, Montana.

November 17, 2004, West Hall Auditorium,
EMPAC plus iEAR
Blast Theory
Lecture
A lecture by the renowned British art collective on its "interactive, guerilla" art tactics.

October 1 & 2, 2004, Rensselaer Playhouse
The San Francisco Tape Music Center
WOW & FLUTTER
A two-day festival celebrating 40-plus years of evocative creation featuring performances of the classic and contemporary works by the original members of the San Francisco Tape Music Center Pauline Oliveros, Morton Subotnick, Tony Martin and Ramon Sender, plus among others: Morris Lang, Terry Silverlight, Warren Smith, Brian Willson, Reggie's Red Hot Feetwarmers and the Ensemble Sospeso.

September 11–18, 2004, Biotech Auditorium
Shakespeare & Company
The Fly-Bottle by David Egan
A theatrical performance on the occasion of the opening of the Center for Biotechnology and Interdisciplinary Studies. Three of the most influential philosophers of the 20th century — Russell, Popper and Wittgenstein — present their own re-enactment of their controversial 1946 debate known as the "poker incident."

April 20 to May 27, 2004,
Concourse in the Empire State Plaza, Albany
Kiyoshi Furukawa, Wolfgang Münch, Jim Lewis
Bubbles in the Nautilus Double Spiral Dome
An interactive video installation in which bubbles bounce off the contours of your shadow, emitting playful sounds; presented in the Concourse of the New York State government buildings in Albany. The installation is presented at the Concourse in the Nautilus Double Spiral Dome, a portable sculptural multimedia theater designed and built by Jim Lewis, which is commissioned by EMPAC and specially built for this purpose. – Bubbles is running in parallel as an exhibit in the Junior Museum, Troy, for most of 2004.

SCIENTIFIC RESEARCH PROJECTS

So far, only a few scientific research projects have been executed at EMPAC, partly initiated by EMPAC, and partly by other departments utilizing EMPAC's infrastructure. Once the position of Director of Research has been filled, all areas of EMPAC's mission will come into balance.

2011
Johannes Goebel, Peter Fox, Marc Downie
Field: A New Tool for Creative, Interdisciplinary Visualization of Data
   The OpenEnded Group (Marc Downie, Shelley Eshkar, Paul Kaiser) was commissioned to create a live 3-D cinematic work, which the members developed in 2009-10 at EMPAC in a series of residencies. Marc Downie developed the software Field, which underpins the artistic work of the group. The potential for scientific research became obvious during the residencies. Field is an open-source programming environment that has been architected in such a way as to support interdisciplinary projects that call upon domain-specific tools, libraries and languages. To establish that Field may answer this currently unmet need for an integrative tool, this research project will examine in depth the requirements of researchers interacting with visualizations of large and complex data sets.
   This research project is supported by an EAGER grant from the National Science Foundation.

2009-2010
Barbara Cutler, Christopher Young, Theodore C. Yapo, Yu Sheng
Virtual Heliodon: Spatially Augmented Reality for Architectural Daylighting Design
   The virtual heliodon is a physical design environment in which designers can gather to experience animated visualizations of the natural illumination within a proposed design by controlling the time of day, season and climate. This interactive global illumination and spatially augmented reality environment allows designers to explore alternative designs and new technologies for improving the sustainability of their buildings. A set of to-scale walls can be moved across the floor of the studio to model a given room configuration. Participants may interactively redesign the geometry and materials of the space by moving these walls around, positioning virtual windows on the walls, and see the immediately updated lighting simulation. Images of walls and their changing location are captured by a camera above the scene, and are processed to construct a virtual 3-D model. To achieve interactive rendering rates, we use a hybrid rendering technique, leveraging radiosity to simulate the inter-reflectance between diffuse patches and shadow volumes to generate per-pixel direct

illumination. The rendered images are then projected on the real model by four to six calibrated projectors to help users study the daylighting illumination.

This work was also supported by a grant from IBM.

2009-2010
Richard Radke, Eric Ameres, Andrew Calcutt, Ziyan Wu, Keri Eustis
Video Analytics Testbed

This project investigates the development of video-processing algorithms for large, realistic environments imaged by multiple cameras. To this end, we outfitted the 2,500 square feet studio in RPI's new EMPAC building with a permanent grid of ceiling-mounted, downward-facing cameras and a reconfigurable set of wall/ceiling-mounted pan-tilt-zoom cameras. A full-scale simulation of an airport carry-on baggage checkpoint was built in the studio. The movements of "passengers" through the simulation are recorded by approximately 20 video cameras. The research goal is to use the cameras' video to automatically determine which bags/items belong to which people using automatic computer vision algorithms.

This project is a part of ALERT (Awareness and Localization of Explosives-Related Threats), a Center of Excellence for Explosives Detection, Mitigation and Response, and is supported by the U.S. Department of Homeland Security.

2008-2010
Jonas Braasch, Pauline Oliveros, Doug Van Nort, Luke Noonan, Kyle McDonald
A Robust Distributed Intelligent System for Telematic Music Applications

Complex communication for co-located performers within telepresence applications across networks is still impaired compared with performers sharing one physical location. This impairment must be significantly reduced to enable the broader community to participate in complex communication scenarios. To achieve this goal, an avatar in the form of a musical conductor with forms of artificial intelligence will coordinate between co-located musicians. The results are expected to inspire solutions for other communication tasks.

The avatar system will actively coordinate co-located improvisation ensembles in a creative way. Computational Auditory Scene Analysis (CASA) systems, to allow robust feature recognition, and evolutionary algorithms, for the creative component, will be combined to form the first model of its kind. The research results are expected to be significant in and of themselves and are not bound to telematic applications.

Funded by the National Science Foundation within the CreativeIT program.

2007-2010
Jonas Braasch
A Cinematic Spatial Sound Display for Panorama Video Applications

The Cinematic Sound Spatialization Display (CSSD) was originally conceived for interactive panorama video installations, with the EMPAC commission of the interactive movie *There is Still Time..Brother* by The Wooster Group as a concrete project; but the architecture goes beyond this particular application. The CSSD is characterized by its scalability to various loudspeaker configurations. It spatializes sound from dry sound files or live sources using control data that describe the spatial scenes. The timelines for source positions and other experimental parameters can be stored and edited in the CSSD, and the system can also process live user input to control selected parameters. The CSSD is more than just a sound positioning tool, and the underlying Virtual Microphone Control (ViMiC) technology was developed to support artists in designing new forms of spatial imagery. The software enables the user to create computer-generated rooms with virtual microphones and sound sources.

Publication: Jonas Braasch, Johannes Goebel, Todd Vos (2010), *A Cinematic Spatial Sound Display for Panorama Video Applications — Organised Sound*, Cambridge University Press, Issue 15/3.

2004
Paul Henderson, Ioana Pieleanu, Rendell Torres, Mendel Kleiner, Johannes Goebel, Kirkegaard Associates
Modeling the Transmissive Ceiling Canopy for EMPAC's Concert Hall

This research project was commissioned by EMPAC to construct a detailed computational model of the ceiling canopy design as specified by acousticians Kirkegaard Associates. The ceiling was to be constructed out of fabric. The objectives for this applied research project are as follows: (1) To create a highly accurate computed model of the interior room acoustics of the Concert Hall, including the effect of the canopy on the early reflections and reverberation of the room. (2) To render these computed results as an auralization (being able to hear music in the virtual concert hall) using means that would provide for a natural reconstruction of the musical behavior of the room. (3) To use these techniques combined with measured transmission and reflection properties of different fabrics (from canvas to synthetic materials) to select an optimal ceiling material.

The project resulted in a surround-sound environment, in which the team could select different materials for the ceiling and have music played into the hall with the selected material while being in different locations in the hall to hear the different results.

The online documentation, including the audio examples, can be found under http://empac.rpi.edu/media/auralization

June 2004
Pauline Oliveros, Seth Cluett
Acoustics of Sacred Spaces

A research field trip was supported during which archeo-acoustic research was conducted in several sacred spaces in Southern Italy. By taking impulse responses of these spaces, quantitative data was recorded, analyzed and subsequently ported to reverberation software, which would then use these data to create the equivalent synthetic reverberation. At the same time, voices singing in those spaces were recorded to allow a qualitative analysis of the acoustics from a musical perspective.

COMMISSIONS

EMPAC commissions are artistic works to be created and — since the opening of the EMPAC building — produced and premiered at EMPAC. Exceptions are the DANCE MOViES commissions. These commissions were started years before the building opened and are mainly produced in other locations. Once the building opened, some of these dance films were supported at EMPAC, as well. All other commissions are realized as part of (often several) residencies of the artists at EMPAC.

EMPAC 360: On Site + Sound
Only Performance: September 8, 2005
An extraordinary guided walking tour circumnavigating the edges of the EMPAC site at the midpoint between the ground-breaking and the completion of the EMPAC building. Live Visuals + Sound by Benton-C Bainbridge with Stephan Moore, pyrotechnics design by Pierre-Alain Hubert with execution by Grucci, aerial dance by Flyaway Productions, and music performed by Ethel.

Light Surgeons
True Fictions: New Adventures in Folklore
First performance: September 14, 2007
Recorded and shot in and around Troy, New York, *True Fictions: New Adventures in Folklore* is an eye-popping performance of epic proportions with projections on multiple oversized screens that fuse documentary film making, live and electronic music, animation and motion graphics with innovative digital video performance tools.

Jennifer Tipton
Light Above the Hudson
Opening Reception: January 11, 2008
Installation: January 11 to February 3, 2008
For three weeks in January of 2008, acclaimed lighting designer Jennifer Tipton will turn the EMPAC construction site into a dynamic light sculpture that can be seen intimately from nearby streets as well as from a distance across the Hudson and beyond.

The Wooster Group
THERE IS STILL TIME..BROTHER
Directed by Elizabeth LeCompte; developed with Jeffrey Shaw for his Interactive Panoramic Cinema
Installation: October 4-19, 2008
This commission was initialized in 2003 as the first commission of EMPAC. It took four years of development and production, including technological research and collaboration with international partners in Australia and Germany. *THERE IS STILL TIME..BROTHER* is The Wooster Group's first interactive 360-degree war film. Sitting inside a panoramic screen, the audience is surrounded by the film's bewildering narrative space, where the action can only be seen and heard clearly through a virtual peephole that scans the circle, controlled by a member of the audience.

The film's host attempts to articulate the aesthetic implications of this shrunken-panoramic cinematic space while massively outnumbered British troops battle the French for control of Fort Calypso. Grotesquely enlarged children's toys vie for attention with politically minded bloggers and unsavory YouTube videos. Each time the piece is viewed, a new narrative experience is spun out, threading together a unique sequence of revelations. The audience becomes immersed in a process of discovery whereby the very choice to look or turn away actually creates the story.

Kino-Eye
Directed by Joby Emmons,
choreographed by Elena Demyanenko (USA)
Commissioned as part of the Dance MOViES Commission 2007-2008
Premiere: October 4, 2008
Exploiting the technologies that constantly monitor us, *Kino-Eye* shadows a dancer through the public and private realms of contemporary Moscow (8 minutes).

Veterans
Directed and choreographed by Victoria Marks, directed and edited by Margaret Williams (USA/U.K.)
Commissioned as part of the Dance MOViES Commission 2007-2008
Premiere: October 4, 2008
Five young veterans return to their civilian lives attempting to make peace with their military service. Performed and co-created by vets from the West Los Angeles VA combat rehab/PTSD clinic (18 minutes).

PH Propiedad Horizontal
Created by David Farías, Carla Schillagi and Maria Fernanda Vallejos (Argentina)
Commissioned as part of the Dance MOViES Commission 2007-2008
Premiere: October 4, 2008
A group of dancers uses a narrow passageway, typical for Argentinean urban housing, to create an elegant, abstract and lively piece of pure movement and form (10 minutes).

Nora
Directed by Alla Kovgan and David Hinton, choreographed by Nora Chipaumire, score by Thomas Mapfumo, produced by Joan Frosch (USA/Zimbabwe/Mozambique/U.K.) in association with Portland Green Cultural Projects, and Center for World Arts, University of Florida.
Commissioned as part of the Dance MOViES Commission 2007-2008
Premiere: October 4, 2008
A dense and swiftly moving poem of sound and image that tells the story of a dancer growing up in Zimbabwe (35 minutes).

Workspace Unlimited
(Thomas Soetens and Kora Van den Bulcke)
They Watch
Installation: October 30 to November 21, 2009
They Watch is an immersive art installation with virtual characters literally watching visitors. Several duplicates of the virtual characters — one man, one woman, and both portraits of the artists — surround and interact with visitors, who are tracked as they move about the physical space, and even projected into the virtual space. Years of research and development with game technology have resulted in a 360-degree audio-visual environment, exploiting a 15-meter-wide panoramic screen and a 32-channel sound system. The subtle collaboration of the real and virtual agents and environments conflate to engender a hybrid space where the observer becomes the observed.

Cathy Weis
The Sea Around Us or A Muse, Me Pisces and *The Bottom Fell out of the Tub*
First Performance: February 6, 2009
The Sea Around Us or A Muse, Me Pisces blends pre-recorded underwater footage with live performance into a dreamscape of radically shifting scale. Performer Scott Heron is in a tug-o-war battle of the Great and Small, proportions and power.

The Bottom Fell Out of The Tub exists in the intersection of dimensions, where the 2-D image interrupts 3-D space. Jennifer Monson maneuvers a rolling screen that bends shadow, light and the projected image of the live video. The merging and re-emerging of these dimensions create moments of surprising disorientation and revelation.

Body/Traces
Created and co-directed by Sophie Kahn and Lisa Parra, choreography by Lisa Parra, music by Sawako Kato, performance by Lisa Parra and Tina Vasquez, 3-D scanning/animation by Sophie Kahn (USA)
Commissioned as part of the Dance MOViES Commission 2008-2009
Premiere: November 7, 2009
Using a DIY 3-D laser scanner and stop-motion 3-D digital animation to track a dancer's movement through space and time, *Body/Traces* is a single-channel video projected at life-size. Illuminating the physical presence and disappearance of the body, this work addresses the questions, What happens to the body in motion when it becomes a still image? and What becomes of that image when it is returned to the moving body whence it came? *Body/Traces* was supported by a three-week creative residency at EMPAC in January 2009 (7-minute looping video installation).

Eyes Nose Mouth
Choreographed and conceived by Noémie Lafrance, directed in collaboration with Patrick Daughters, with music by Brooks Williams (USA)
Commissioned as part of the Dance MOViES Commission 2008-2009
Premiere: November 7, 2009
Inspired by our physical, emotional and psychological relationships to spaces that are public versus private, *Eye Nose Mouth* follows single characters navigating through a series of changing landscapes. The site-specific choreography reacts to the urban and natural environments, creating a narrative thread that evokes the characters' transforming emotional states (10 minutes).

Looking Forward — Man and Woman
Directed by Roberta Marques, choreographed and performed by Michael Schumacher and Liat Waysbort (Brazil/Netherlands)
Commissioned as part of the Dance MOViES Commission 2008-2009
Premiere: November 7, 2009
This film is a love letter from a man to his wife at the end of their long lives, and simultaneously a portrait of a younger couple at the beach, where both the waves and time run backwards in opposition to the drift of fate. The second film in a trilogy that plays with the reversal of movement and time in video and dance to create mind-bending illusions. With excerpts from the poignant *Lettre à D.* by

the social philosopher and writer André Gorz (10 minutes).

Sunscreen Serenade
Directed and choreographed by Kriota Willberg, sound by Carmen Borgia, illustration and design by R. Sikoryak (USA)
Commissioned as part of the Dance MOViES Commission 2008-2009
Premiere: November 7, 2009
In homage to Busby Berkeley's flamboyant kaleidoscopic style of the 1930s, scantily clad finger puppets tackle the contemporary issue of ozone depletion. Cheerfully dancing in formation, the diminutive dancers deliver a gentle reminder that environmental and political trends come and go, much like the drift of our culture through movie fads (5 minutes).

Anatomy of Melancholy
Directed by Nuria Fragoso (Mexico)
Commissioned as part of the Dance MOViES Commission 2009-2010
Premiere: October 2, 2010
Two contrasting spaces — one light and open, the other constrained and dark — form the built environment for dancers moving against expectation. Visual metaphors about spaces and intentions (6.5 minutes).

Hoop
Director: Marites Carino; choreographer and performer: Rebecca Halls; composer: Anthony Tan; director of photography: Donald Robitaille (Canada)
Commissioned as part of the Dance MOViES Commission 2009-2010
Premiere: October 2, 2010
A woman floats in a black void, swinging through shafts of light, keeping in perpetual motion on incandescent and familiar circular childhood toy (4 minutes).

Quince Missing
Director and choreographer: Rajendra Serber (USA)
Commissioned as part of the Dance MOViES Commission 2009-2010
Premiere: October 2, 2010
In this exploration of urban isolation, three men trace their solitary paths through empty streets at night. When the strangers try to pass each other by, they become locked in anonymous antagonism (16 minutes).

MO-SO
Director: Kasumi; composer: Fang Man; dancer: Chan U Hong (USA)
Commissioned as part of the Dance MOViES Commission 2009-2010
Premiere: October 2, 2010
A three-channel video installation for film samples and dancer. Fragmentary and symbolically charged images serve as a basis for improvisation by the dancer. The footage of the dancer is then fed back into the polyphonic narrative, musical and choreographic structure (10-minute looping video installation).

Elevator Repair Service, *Gatz*

The closer one gets, the less one sees
Videomaker: Valeria Valenzuela; choreographer: Lilyen Vass;
production: Aura Films (Brazil)
Commissioned as part of the Dance MOViES Commission 2009-2010
Premiere: October 2, 2010
Intervention in the everyday lives of three jugglers/beggars, who get together at the traffic lights on a street crossing in the city of Rio de Janeiro, transforms the objective action of their juggling into the abstract vocabulary of contemporary dance (10 minutes).

The OpenEnded Group
(Marc Downie, Shelley Eshkar, Paul Kaiser)
Upending
Premiere: March 25, 2010
For the past two years, EMPAC has hosted a residency by The OpenEnded Group, an innovative digital arts collective specializing in the creation of 3-D digital works. Now audiences can see the result. *Upending*, a work commissioned by EMPAC and appearing here in its world premiere, is a revelatory stereoscopic theater performance, an actor–less drama of disorientation and reorientation that compels us to rethink our relationship with the material world. Using ordinary flat photographs and processing them with non-photorealistic rendering and stereoscopic HD video, Upending transfigures familiar objects, spaces and persons in ways that are both beautiful and uncanny. The play of images is accompanied by a gutsy EMPAC-made recording of Morton Feldman's first *String Quartet* by the FLUX Quartet, which *The New Yorker*'s Alex Ross describes as "legendary for its furiously committed, untiring performances." The music provides an aural lens that renders the video almost balletic, even as the visuals allow us to hear Feldman as never before.

Chris Doyle
Method Air and Your Love Keeps Lifting Me
Installation: March 18 to April 10, 2010
For Dancing on the Ceiling: Art & Zero Gravity, Chris Doyle created two new works: *Method Air* and *Your Love Keeps Lifting Me*.
Method Air is a large-scale rotoscoped video of local Capital District skateboarders projected onto the exterior surface of the EMPAC building. The skateboarders, whose boards have been digitally edited out of the picture, weave quickly and effortlessly in and out of the windows, transcending both the limits of gravity and the laws of solid physics. As they break through the seemingly impermeable façade, the figures open it up and create a confluence between the interior spaces of EMPAC and the outside community.
Your Love Keeps Lifting Me harnesses the mechanical action of an elevator and the physical movement of visitors through the EMPAC building to activate an animated meditation on various kinds of interdependency. The piece consists of two animated filmstrips hung inside an elevator shaft and a small surveillance camera affixed to the cab of the elevator. As the elevator moves between floors, the camera reads the filmstrip and an animation is projected onto the glass walls enclosing the elevators in EMPAC's lobby. The animation between the

fifth and sixth floors shows two bears that begin to levitate as they scratch each other's backs, and gradually sink back to earth. Between the sixth and seventh floors the animation switches to a dancing couple. As they dance, the female begins to float upward, drawing her partner with her until both are out of the frame. Eventually, they return to their original position and the dance begins once more.

Thom Kubli
FLOAT! Thinktank 21
Installation: March 18 to April 10, 2010
FLOAT! Thinktank 21 is an installation piece that comprises a flotation tank, a sound composition, an archive of audio performances by the artist and a context table filled with books by a variety of philosophers and inspiring thinkers. Drawing from experiments in brain research conducted by John C. Lilly in the 1950s, the piece primarily allows the audience to listen to audio recordings on politics and zero gravity that the artist made after floating in the tank in the days leading up to the exhibition opening. A select number of viewers may also make an appointment to float in the isolation tank custom fit with an underwater sound system.

Lars Jan / Early Morning Opera
ABACUS
Concert Hall
First performance: October 1, 2010
ABACUS, a large-scale multimedia presentation by Early Morning Opera under the direction of Lars Jan, features Paul Abacus and his reimagining of Buckminster Fuller's *Geoscope* as a data cathedral for the masses. Aided by this device and a chorus of Steadicam operators, *ABACUS* argues the obsolescence of national borders and proposes their dissolution, while simultaneously acting as a study in two dominant forms of persuasive discourse today: the TED-style (slide-based) presentation and megachurch media design.

MTAA
All Raise This Barn (East)
Library & VCC Plaza
Opening date: October 1, 2010
Using 21st-century techniques, MTAA (artists Michael Sarff and Tim Whidden) conduct an old-fashioned barn raising on the Rensselaer campus. *All Raise This Barn* (or *Let's Put Our Heads Together and Start a New Country Up*) is a group-designed and assembled public structure created in response to an online public vote. Part construction project, part participatory performance, *All Raise This Barn (East)* explores the positive and persuasive power of the community vote, as well as its prevalence in contemporary society, from the Internet to reality television competitions.

Various Artists
Filament Festival Live Shorts
Studio 2
First performance: October 1, 2010
A program of commissioned short-form performance works across the spectrum of dance, theater, music and the visual arts. Participating artists include Wally Cardona; Jen DeNike; SUE-C & Laetitia Sonami; Steve Cuiffo, Trey Lyford & Geoff Sobelle; MTAA; Miro Dance Theater; Paul Abacus; National Theater

of the United States of America; Trouble (Sam Hillmer & Laura Paris).

Hans Tutschku
agitated slowness
Goodman Theater/Studio
First Performance: October 1, 2010
agitated slowness, a new 24-channel electroacoustic composition by Hans Tutschku, is an intense, deep work — a perceptual journey to another place, far from the walls of EMPAC's Goodman Theater/Studio, where it was created. Using three rings of speakers from ear level to 30 feet in the air, this performance ebbs and flows, consuming and releasing the listener into space.

Volkmar Klien
Kristallgatsch/Strahlung
Goodman Theater/Studio
First Performance: October 1, 2010
Volkmar Klien's entrancing composition *Kristallgatsch/Strahlung* was created at EMPAC in the fall of 2009 and is such an incredible piece of music that it must be heard again! For the piece and the CD that preceded it, Start-Ziel-Siege, Klien used a mathematical model of a virtual object to synthesize a vastness of sound materials.

Michael Schumacher
Room Pieces
Public spaces of EMPAC
Opening: October 1, 2010
An ongoing building-wide sound installation utilizing the immense size, acoustics and 100-plus-speaker public address system to create a rich sonic environment for anyone passing through the building. A widely varied sound palette creates an ever-changing soundscape that is both pleasurable and unpredictable.

A Circus of One
Director/visual artist/performer: Alison Crocetta; music and sound: Jason Treuting (USA)
Commissioned as part of the Dance MOViES Commission 2010-2011
Premiere: October 2011
A video installation by a visual artist who uses the 16mm camera as a witness to performative actions while referencing the history of cinema. She constructs an evocative habitat for the solo character of a clown, successfully crossing the disciplines of sculpture, performance and film (15-minute looping video installation).

Fauna
Director and visual artist: Paulo Fernández; choreographer and dancer: Rodrigo Chaverini; visual artist: Antonio Becerro; music and sound: Tomas González (Chile)
Commissioned as part of the Dance MOViES Commission 2010-2011
Premiere: October 2011
The relationship between artifice and nature becomes the central focus for a video by an artistic team from Chile. Using an elaborate layering of design, costume, movement, environment and set, they create a fantastical world that provokes a sense of anxiety and fascination (20 minutes).

Marching Banned
Director: Danièle Wilmouth; choreographer: Asimina Chremos; sound designer and band leader: Mark Messing; band: Mucca Pazza (USA)
Commissioned as part of the Dance MOViES Commission 2010-2011
Premiere: October 2011
A film following the mayhem created by a 30-member punk marching band as it navigates through the quotidian happenings in the city of Chicago. The collaborators subvert the forms of the traditional marching band, designing intricate choreography for the camera and people, maintaining the spontaneity of "actions for joy" (10 minutes).

Spring Cleaning
Director/visual artist/performer: Pooh Kaye; music and sound: John Kilgore (USA)
Commissioned as part of the Dance MOViES Commission 2010-2011
Premiere: October 2011
A spirited animation from the pioneer of stop motion in dance film, "aged but still agile"; a solo celebrating the explosion of spring in the countryside (10 minutes).

Sean Griffin
Cold Spring
Concert Hall
First performances: December 3 & 4, 2010
Tying together orthodoxies from performance artists and opera singers in Los Angeles to actors from Chicago, to local theater productions, music ensembles and cheerleaders, Sean Griffin's *Cold Spring* presents a multi-faceted musical theater experience. Beginning with a historical reinterpretation of tests and research from the 1920s American Eugenics Archive, the performance moves through dismantled traditional American plays and dances featured in the Hudson Valley; explores theatrical interpretations of Robert Schumann's Liederkreis, Op. 39; and restages hypnosis recordings from the 1964 Betty and Barney Hill abduction case. *Cold Spring* culminates in a choral rhapsody that weaves these often-conflicting performance styles into a complex, sometimes humorous, sometimes frightening operatic spectacle.

Jennifer & Kevin McCoy
Installation
Public spaces of EMPAC
Opening: May 1, 2011

RESIDENCIES

The Artist-in-Residence program at EMPAC has a dimension that other residency programs usually do not have: EMPAC curatorial, production and research staff provide a high level of guidance, intellectual exchange, expert advice and support. Residencies are also defined by projects and not by arbitrary timelines that predetermine the duration of a residency. This can lead to extended residencies, residencies in several phases and/or residencies that use different studios and venues, as a project requires.

The Researcher-in-Residence will commence once the director for research has been hired.

Both residency programs are supported by dedicated housing. For the artist-in-residence program, a building with four apartments is located right next to EMPAC. This residency building was enabled through the extremely generous support from the Jaffe Fund for Experimental Media and Performing Arts. This fund also supported and enabled a majority of the commissions, workshops and many events listed on these pages. Having started years before the opening of EMPAC and continuing today, this unheard-of, uninterrupted enablement of the creation of contemporary time-based arts, as well as its integration into student activities, is a testament to the audacious vision and incredible level of dedication and commitment by the Institute and its President to the realization of EMPAC.

Annie Dorsen — United States
AntiVJ — Europe
BalletLab — Australia
Bruce Odland, Sam Auinger — United States, Germany, Austria
Cathy Weis Projects — United States
Daniel Teige — Germany
Early Morning Opera — United States
FLUX Quartet — United States
Graham Parker — United States
Hans Tutschku — Germany, United States
International Contemporary Ensemble — United States
Jean Francois Peryet — France
Jennifer Tipton — United States
Jeremy Wade, Joel Ryan — United States, Netherlands
Jill Sigman — United States
Keiko Courdy, Frederic Sofiyana — France
Laurie Anderson — United States
Light Surgeons — United Kingdom
Lisa Parra, Sophie Barret-Kahn — United States
Luciano Chessa — United States
Mads Lynnerup — Denmark, United States
Marites Carino — Canada
Maryanne Amacher — United States
Michael Schumacher — United States
Miguel Azguime — Portugal
Movement Research — United States
Nuria Fragoso — Mexico
Open Ended Group — United States
Peter Flaherty — United States
Random Dance — United Kingdom
Thom Kubli — Germany
Toni Dove — United States
Volkmar Klein — Austria
Workspace Unlimited — Belgium, Canada
Yanira Castro — United States
Yarn/Wire — United States
Yvon Bonenfant — Canada, United Kingdom

WORKSHOPS AND CONFERENCES

Visiting artists and researchers are involved in giving workshops for Rensselaer students, staff, faculty and the interested public. This will expand in the near future with the creation of a "creative campus" position that will focus on the integration of the professional projects conducted at EMPAC with its educational mission.

At the same time, EMPAC is creating a summer workshop program that will open EMPAC to different levels of professional exploration of the center's infrastructure in artistic, engineering and scientific contexts.

EMPAC is ideal for hosting conferences that are centered on arts, design, science and technology. Following its mission of bringing diverse backgrounds together under one roof, these conferences will range from science and engineering to "just humanities," from the presentation of new technological developments and research results to philosophical reflections on history and investigations into the theory of science.

The few initiatives we were able to take on so far may give an indication of possible directions.

November 7, 2009
Marc Downie
FIELD
Two-day workshop
With the creation of the open-source programming environment FIELD, artist and artificial intelligence researcher Marc Downie may have done more to change the landscape of real-time video and other digital art forms since the release of Max/MSP/Jitter. Actually, FIELD is at once more radical and more accessible, since it tries to bridge as many different programming languages and ways of doing things as possible and permits users to customize virtually any of its features. Downie's talk on the evening before the workshop about the software and some of the art that he and other members of The OpenEnded Group have made with it will engage even non-gearheads. And gearheads (or code-heads) will get a chance to start navigating in FIELD during Downie's immersive two-day workshop. An indispensible experience for digital artists or anyone interested in the intersection of technology and aesthetics.

Marc Downie holds a master's in natural science and Master of Science in physics from Cambridge University, where he won the Mott Prize in natural sciences. In 2005, he obtained a doctorate from MIT's Media Lab. He has authored interactive installations, compositions and projections in the fields of interactive music, machine learning and computer graphics. In addition to collaborating with other members of The OpenEnded Group, Downie has worked with Merce Cunningham, Bill T. Jones and Trisha Brown.

December 5, 2009
Frieder Weiss
Perceivable Bodies
Full-day workshop
The workshop gives a practical introduction into artistic uses of video motion sensing technologies. Frieder Weiss develops his own software for stage use, which mostly uses video cameras to analyze and visualize the movements of the dancers.

The workshop will introduce EyeCon and Kalypso software. EyeCon links physical movement spaces with computer-generated sound environments. By drawing virtual zones on screen, you enable the mapping of human movement to real-time sound and visual media. Kalypso software allows visual effects based on body outlines.

In the workshop, participants will be able to understand and learn the basics of the software, set up a customized interactive environment and get a chance to move and try out the experience.

Experienced computer users are invited to attach systems that they are using: we will be able to interface to systems such as Max/MSP, Flash and Isadora.

Frieder Weiss is an engineer in the arts and an expert for real-time computing and interactive computer systems in performance art. He is the author of *EyeCon* and *Kalypso*, video motion sensing programs specially designed for use with dance, music and computer art. Weiss developed the video technologies and interactive stage projections for Chunky Move's recent intermedia works *Glow* and *Mortal Engine*. For his contribution on *Glow*, he was rewarded with a Green Room Award for Design in Dance.

Weiss teaches media technology at the University of Applied Sciences in Nuremberg, Germany, and the University Centre in Doncaster, U.K. In recent years he has collaborated in installation and performance projects with Phase 7 in Berlin, Leine & Roebana in Amsterdam, Helga Pogatschar and Cesc Gelabert in Munich, Chunky Move in Melbourne and an ongoing collaboration with Australian dancer Emily Fernandez, with whom he has created a number of interactive performances and installations.

Spring 2010
Workshops in Conjuntion with onedotzero – adventures in motion

Leading up to the onedotzero festival, April 30 to May 2, 2010, EMPAC organized a series of educational artist exchanges with the students and faculty of Rensselaer. Via collaborations with professors from the School of Humanities, three different classes (New Media Theory, Animation 1 and Typography) incorporated EMPAC-organized artist sessions into their spring 2010 syllabi.

As part of their coursework, students in the participating classes were asked to develop projects inspired by the works presented by the visiting artists, Benton-C Bainbridge, Jeff Crouse and Reid Farrington. Class sessions with these artists were opened to other students and professors to join. Brown bag lunchtime gatherings at EMPAC were organized while the artists were in town to allow for more informal access to these visiting talents.

Resulting class projects were presented May 2, 2010, in a special event during the onedotzero festival at EMPAC, where they received a critique from Joanie Lemercier of AntiVJ, onedotzero festival director Shane Walter and EMPAC curator Kathleen Forde.

As part of the onedotzero educational offerings, EMPAC also arranged for a free practical workshop with AntiVJ during its two-week residency leading up to the festival where the artists presented a show and tell of their working process and then opened up the conversation to students to present their works in progress that would be shown at the festival.

July 30 to August 2, 2010
C:ADM2010
Cybernetics: Art, Design, Mathematics — A Meta-Disciplinary Conversation
The international conference of the American Society for Cybernetics, in collaboration with the School of Architecture at Rensselaer Polytechnic Institute and EMPAC

"Cybernetics: Art, Design, Mathematics — A Meta-Disciplinary Conversation" is a conference where the main business will be to confer — to explore ideas through discussion and open exchange; in other words, to take part in an enormous brainstorm together! It is concerned with forming and asking the next question rather than reporting on answers to the last question.

The conference is constructed around exploring and developing analogies between our four areas — cybernetics, the arts (including music), design and mathematics. Crossovers between pairs of these subjects have been common, yet the nature of these crossovers has rarely been examined, nor have all four subjects previously been brought together.

The conference can be traced at: www.asc-cybernetics.org/2010

August 16-22, 2010
Johannes Birringer, Mark Coniglio
LIVE.MEDIA+PERFORMANCE.LAB
EMAPC's first summer lab for interactive media in performance! The workshop offers intensive training and possibilities for experimentation with mixed reality and real-time architectures, programmable environments, interactive design and the integration of time-based media into live performance and installation.

The workshop addresses emerging and professional art practitioners, scientists, researchers and students from different backgrounds in performance and new media committed to sharing their interest in developing a deeper understanding of composing work focused on real-time, interactive or time-based experiences and multidisciplinary collaborative processes (video, sound processing, projection design, lighting, choreography and directing).

Participants will be in residence for the duration of the lab and offered our exceptional facilities for investigating performance and design techniques that will develop skills and inspire new ideas for working in mixed realities and interlinked physical/virtual or distributed aesthetics. The workshop will include examples and references to international stage works, choreographic systems, installations and site-specific works, as well as hands-on experimentation in full resolution with interactive systems.

Methodologies for the laboratory are conceived by theater director and media artist Johannes Birringer, founder of the annual Interaktionslabor and professor of performance technologies at Brunel University (London); and Mark Coniglio, artistic co-director of Troika Ranch and creator of the Isadora software. Both artists are widely recognized for their pioneering work in the international performance and media network. Interaktionslabor was last offered on tour in Belo Horizonte, Brazil (2008), and Birringer's and Coniglio's works have been featured in numerous festivals and exhibitions around the world.

The blog of the workshop with documentation can be found at http://empaclivemediaperformancelab.blogspot.com

Spring 2011
Infrastructure Needs to Support Creativity-based Technology Research
Planned two-day workshop
This workshop will define in concrete terms a platform to sustain cross-disciplinary and trans-disciplinary research, collaboration and exchange in the integration of quantifiable and qualitatively defined paradigms at the intersection of creativity, technology, research and innovation. This area of research can be subsumed under the heading of "creativity-based technology research and technology-based creativity research." The workshop will gather leaders in the field, build on previous meetings and chart the direction forward for a cross-disciplinary framework and network to advance this field.

The workshop will also build on results from prior NSF workshops in support of creativity-based technology research, as well as research funded by the CISE IIS CreativeIT program over the past three years. This workshop will address varied understandings of creativity, demonstrate the necessity for a broad approach, and define a robust platform for coordination and communication that will have broad impact across a number of fields and institutions.

With support from the National Science Foundation.

PUBLICATIONS

The San Francisco Tape Music Center
1960s Counterculture and the Avant-Garde
Edited by David W. Bernstein
University of California Press, 2008

This book tells the story of the influential group of creative artists — Pauline Oliveros, Morton Subotnick, Ramon Sender, William Maginnis, and Tony Martin — who connected music to technology during a legendary era in California's cultural history. An integral part of the robust San Francisco scene, the San Francisco Tape Music Center developed new art forms through collaborations with Terry Riley, Steve Reich, David Tudor, Ken Dewey, Lee Breuer, the San Francisco Actor's Workshop, the San Francisco Mime Troupe, the Ann Halprin Dancers' Workshop, Canyon Cinema, and others. Told through vivid personal accounts, interviews and retrospective essays by leading scholars and artists, this work, capturing the heady experimental milieu of the '60s, is the first comprehensive history of the San Francisco Tape Music Center.

The publication was initialized and shaped through its extended production process by Johannes Goebel, director of EMPAC. Besides the multi-faceted texts and contributions, the book is accompanied by a DVD that contains a full documentation of the Wow & Flutter festival, the first major production EMPAC staged on campus at the RPI Playhouse in the fall of 2004. For that festival, all five members of the SFTMC (Martin, Maginnis, Oliveros, Sender and Subotnick) had reunited at Rensselaer to perform older and new works.

iEAR PIX
Rensselaer Polytechnic Institute, 2008

iEAR PIX includes selections of work by Rensselaer's department of the arts faculty and alumni and from the department's performance, exhibition, screening and lecture series, iEAR Presents! Rensselaer's department of the arts is generally considered the first integrated electronic arts program within a research university in the United States. Founded in 1972, the department initiated the inclusion of electronic media in 1981. The department features an integrated and multidisciplinary approach to the arts with a focus on the use of experimental and electronic media in artistic creation and performance. The works of the department's distinguished faculty and alumni are represented internationally in museums, galleries, festivals, publications and performances.

iEAR PIX was produced by Kathy High (with Laura Garrison, Penny Lane and Victoria Kereszi) in conjunction with the opening of EMPAC.

DANCE MOViES 2007–2008
DVD
Rensselaer Polytechnic Institute, 2008

A publication of the first four films commissioned by EMPAC. The DVD includes a booklet with director's notes, and photos from the shoots and the films.

Kino-Eye (USA)
Directed by Joby Emmons, choreographed by Elena Demyanenko
Veterans (USA, U.K.)
Directed and choreographed by Victoria Marks, directed and edited by Margaret Williams
PH Propiedad Horizontal (Argentina)
Created by David Farías, Carla Schillagi and Maria Fernanda Vallejos
Nora (USA, Zimbabwe, U.K.)
Directed by Alla Kovgan and David Hinton, choreographed by Nora Chipaumire, score by Thomas Mapfumo, produced by Joan Frosch

DANCE MOViES 2008–2009
DVD
Rensselaer Polytechnic Institute, 2009

The films of the second year of the DANCE MOViES Commission program. The DVD includes a booklet with director's notes for each of the four projects, and DVD extras.
Sunscreen Serenade (USA)
Directed and choreographed by Kriota Willberg, sound by Carmen Borgia, illustration and design by R. Sikoryak
Eyes Nose Mouth (USA)
Choreographed and conceived by Noémie Lafrance, directed in collaboration with Patrick Daughters, with music by Brooks Williams
Looking Forward — Man and Woman (Brazil/Netherlands)
Directed by Roberta Marques, choreographed and performed by Michael Schumacher and Liat Waysbort
Body/Traces (USA)
Created and co-directed by Sophie Kahn and Lisa Parra, choreography by Lisa Parra, music by Sawako Kato, performance by Lisa Parra and Tina Vasquez, 3-D scanning and animation by Sophie Kahn

DANCE MOViES 2009–2010
DVD
Rensselaer Polytechnic Institute, 2010

The third set of DANCE MOViES Commissions.
Hoop (Canada)

Director: Marites Carino; choreographer and performer: Rebecca Halls; composer: Anthony Tan; director of photography: Donald Robitaille
Quince Missing (USA)
Director and choreographer: Rajendra Serber; director of photography: Jessica Fisher; music: The Genie, Cheryl Leonard
Anatomy of Melancholy (Mexico)
Directed by Nuria Fragoso, music by Antonio Russek
The closer one gets, the less one sees (Brazil)
Videomaker: Valeria Valenzuela; choreographer: Lilyen Vass; photography and camera: Phileppe Guinet; executive producer: Claus Ruegner
MO-SO (USA)
Director: Kasumi; composer: Fang Man; dancer: Chan U Hong; cinematographer: Kitao Sakurai

THE TEAM
at the Curtis R. Priem Experimental Media and Performing Arts Center
as of October 1, 2010

It is impossible to give proper credit to everyone who has contributed over the years to the creation and operation of the center and its program. The membership of the team changes, as with any team, so the arbitrary date of October 1, 2010, has been chosen as the moment for capturing the following list:

Eric Ameres, Senior Research Engineer
David Bebb, Senior System Administrator, Network
Peter Bellamy, Systems Programmer
Michael Bello, Video Engineer
Eric Brucker, Lead Video Engineer
John Cook, Box Office Manager
Laura Desposito, Production Administrative Coordinator
Angel Eads, Master Electrician
Zhenelle Falk, Artist Services Coordinator
Kathleen Forde, Curator, Time-Based Arts
William Fritz, Master Carpenter
Kim Gardner, Manager, Administrative Operations
Johannes Goebel, Director
Ian Hamelin, Project Manager
Ryan Jenkins, Event Technician
Shannon Johnson, Web Director
CathyJo Kile, Business Manager
Hélène Lesterlin, Curator, Dance
Janette MacDonald, Executive Assistant
Stephen McLaughlin, Event Technician
Geoff Mielke, Associate Director for Stage Technologies
Jason Steven Murphy, PR/Marketing Project Manager
Laura Perfetti, Guest Services Coordinator
Andrew Rarig, Graphic Designer
Candice Sherman, Business Coordinator
Micah Silver, Curator, Music
Avery Stempel, Front of House Manager
Jeffrey Svatek, Audio Engineer
Robin Thomas, Administrative Specialist
Stephanie Tribu-Cromme, Event Technician
Todd Vos, Lead Audio Engineer
Pete Wargo, Manager, Information Systems
Dave Watson, Web Developer
Emily Zimmerman, Assistant Curator

APPENDIX 2

GENERAL
Floor area
221,200 square feet / 20,500 square meters
Volume
ca. 5 million cubic feet / ca. 141,000 cubic meters
Excavation
ca. 100,000 cubic yards / ca. 76,000 cubic meters
Rock anchors
over 200 1-¾ inch in diameter solid bar tie-back
anchors; up to 250 feet (75m) long and almost 5
miles (8km) in total length anchor the building into
the bedrock
Electrical Feed
13.2 kilovolt
Green Building Certification
LEED certified
Ground Breaking
September 26, 2003
Opening
October 3, 2008
Building cost
ca. $200 million

CONCERT HALL
Seats
1273
Floor area
10,984 square feet / 1020 square meters
Length
151'-6" / 46m
Width
72'-6" / 22 meters (varying)
Volume
ca. 582,500 cubic feet / ca. 16,500 cubic meters
Stage width
65'-7" / 20.11m
Stage depth
max. 32'-0" / 9.75m (with stage extension 13.5m)
Stage to Fabric Ceiling
42'-3" / 12.8m (varying)
Stage to Concrete Ceiling
51'-6" / 15.7m
Stage height
3'-6" / 1.06m
Rigging
60 openable holes in concrete ceiling for chain
hoists positioned above ceiling, 18 computer
controlled chain hoists
Lighting
373 sine-wave dimmers (2.4 kW and 6kW)
Air handling
Displacement ventilation with air outlets under
each seat
Noise level
RC-15 under full heat-load
Adjustable acoustics
Computer controlled banners on all walls

THEATER
Seats
397

Stage width
80'-0" / 24.3m
Stage depth
40'-0" / 12.2m
(with curved thrust stage: max 50'6" / 15.4m)
Proscenium height
30'-0" / 9.1m
Stage widest opening
47'-6" / 14.5m
Stage height
7-½" / 19cm
Stage deck to walkable grid
62'-3" / 19m
Orchestra Pit Lift
max length 38'-0" / 11.5m; max. depth 13'-4" /
4m; vertical travel: 17'-6" / 5.3m;
Rigging
22 motorized line sets (18 movable), 8 spot-line
winches, all computer controlled
Lighting
468 sine-wave dimmers (2.4 kW and 6 kW)
Air handling
Displacement ventilation with air outlets
under each seat
Noise level
RC-15 under full heat-load

GOODMAN THEATER/STUDIO 1
Dimension (unobstructed)
66'-6" / 20.42m by 51'-0" / 15.5m
Floor area
3400 square feet / 315 square meters
Floor to walkable grid
32'-3" / 9.75m
Floor to steel beams
38'-8" / 11.8m
(plus additional height between beams)
Volume
ca. 168,000 cubic feet / ca. 4,750 cubic meters
Rigging
8 spot-line winches, computer controlled, chain
hoists can be integrated into the control system.
Lighting
192 sine-wave dimmers (2.4 kW and 6 kW)
Noise level
RC-15 under full heat-load
Adjustable acoustics
Computer controlled banners on all walls

STUDIO 2
Dimension (unobstructed)
55'-2" / 16.7m by 44'-11" / 13.7m
Floor area
2475 square feet / 230 square meters
Floor to walkable grid
18'-5" / 5.6m
Floor to steel beams
25'-2" / 7.6m (plus additional height between beams)
Volume
ca. 82,500 cubic feet / ca. 2,335 cubic meters
Rigging
12 chain hoists, up to 8 synchronized

Lighting
192 sine-wave dimmers (2.4 kW and 6 kW)
Noise level
RC-15 under full heat-load
Adjustable acoustics
Computer controlled banners on all walls

DESIGN AND CONSTRUCTION TEAM

DESIGN ARCHITECT
Grimshaw Architects
London Office
Sir Nicholas Grimshaw, chairman
Competition Project Team: Sir Nicholas Grimshaw,
Andrew Whalley, Vincent Chang, Simon Beames,
Kirsten Lees, Florian Eames, Theo Lorenz

New York Office
Andrew Whalley, partner
Vincent Chang, partner
Mark Husser, partner
William Horgan, partner
Project team: Simon Beames, Shane Burger, David
Burke, Demetrios Comodromos, Chris Crombie,
Chris Duisberg, Matt Eastwood, Paulo Faria, Nikolas
Dando Haenisch Christian Hoenigschmid, Duncan
Jackson Kristen Lees, Melissa Lim, Junko Naka-
gawa, Michael Pawlyn, Juan Porral

ARCHITECT OF RECORD
Davis Brody Bond
J. Max Bond, principal
William Paxson, partner in charge
Ernesto Bachiller, lead production architect
Nathan Hoyt, principal production architect
Project Team: Bruce Dole, Jon Edelbaum, Dean
Ficek, Steven Fisher, Fareh Garba, Robert Halver-
son, Fernando Hausch-Fen, Richard Kilbschan,
Richard Klibschon, Belinda Len, Ying Li, Marc Mas-
say, Donald Nicoulin, Glenn O'Neill, Danny Papajic,
Oliver Sippl, Mayine Yu, Dohhee Zhoung

ACOUSTICAL CONSULTANT
Kirkegaard Associates
Larry Kirkegaard, FASA
president and principal in charge
Carl Giegold, acoustical designer / project manager
Zackery Belanger, computational acoustics
Louie Sunga, architectural integration
Terry Tyson, mechanical noise and vibration control

THEATER CONSULTANT
Fischer Dachs Associates
Josh Dachs, principal in charge
Peter Rosenbaum, project manager
Project Team: Richard Hoyes, Adam Huggard
Joe Mobilia, Jeff Paradise, Jon Sivell

GEOTECHNICAL ENGINEERING
Buro Happold
Peter Scott, principal

Mark Dawson, associate principal
Peter Chipchase, senior engineer

STRUCTURAL ENGINEERING
Buro Happold
Craig Schwitter, principal of structural engineering
Project Team: Oliver Osterwind, Eddie Pugh,
Michael Rysdorp, Andrew Coats, Julia Ratcliffe,
Matthew Melnyk, Scott McFadden, Leslie Robinson,
Nigel Pickering

MECHANICAL AND PLUMBING/
FIRE PROTECTION ENGINEER
Buro Happold
Tony McLaughlin, partner in charge
Denzil Gallagher, principal
Project Team: Chris McClean, Jeremy Snyder, Jack
Bergman, Matthew Napolitan, Reed Berinato, Chad
Konrad, Rodica Enica, Matthew Herman

ELECTRICAL ENGINEERING
Buro Happold
Lomesh Somwaru, associate
Tom York, associate
Laszlo Bodak Engineering —
Electrical Engineering Consultant
Laszlo Bodak, president
Project Team: Lomash Somwaru, Tom York

LEED CONSULTANT
Buro Happoldd
Byron Stigge, Sarah Sachs

AUDIO AND VIDEO SYSTEMS
EMPAC in-house engineering team
Todd Vos, Eric Ameres, Jeff Svatek

LIGHTING CONSULTANT
Office for Visual Interaction
Enrique Peiniger, principal
Jean Sundin, principal
Project team: Yunha Bae, Tom McGoldrick

IT / TELECOM CONSULTANT
Shen Milsom & Wilke
Michael Craig, principal
Project team: David Stumer, Danny Chan,
Bill Seidenzahl, Rich Iverson

SPECIALTY CONSULTANTS
North Block – Integrated Curtain Wall Consultant
Josef Gartner USA a Division of Permasteelisa
North America
Project Team: Olover Lahr, Joseph Tizn

Southblock Curtain Wall Consultant
Zimmcor
Eduard Ratz, chief designer

Wooden Hull Consultant
Architectural Woodwork Industries
Rick Herskovitz, principal
Fred Stern, design and fabrication

Foundation Consultant
Schnabel Foundation Company
Hank Schnabel, principal
Steven Hinterneder, engineer

Fire Engineering
Arup Fire
David Jacoby, principal fire safety
Project Team: James Lord, Chris Marrion

Landscape Architect
The Saratoga Associates, Saratoga Springs
Robert Southerland, lead landscape architect
Ronald Mogren, landscape architect
Jeffrey Poor, landscape architect

Site Engineering
Clough Harbor & Associates
Rich Balstra, electrical engineer
Todd LaFreniere, mechanical engineer
Project Team: Joseph Thomson, Samuel Bennett,
Phil Koziol

Pre-construction Cost Consultant
Donnell Consultants Incorporated
Stewart Donnell, principal
Athol Joffe, principal
Joe Perryman, lead consultant

Construction Manager
Turner Construction
New York Office
Charles Murphy, vice president
Kevin Barrett, chief estimator
Project Team: Joe Decunzo, Carlo DiSilvestro,
Kevin Duffy, Bobby Gullickson, Steve Lampert,
Mike Orientale, Curtis Tadlock

Albany Office
Mark Breslin, vice president / general manager
and principal-in-charge
Project Team: Jim Burns, Jen Comerford,
Peter D'Aloia, Dwight Sickler,Carl Stewart,
Michael Stewart, Mario Suarez, Larry Tune

Site Office
Jasper DeFazio, vice president of construction
Dave Gruver, project manager
Steve Coates, project engineer
Dave Marshall, MEP manager & LEED coordinator
Michael Ziobrowski, MEP manager
Fred Booth, construction executive –
field operations
Rodrigo Calovini, site superintendent
Tom Aurelia, safety manager & LEED
field coordinator
Project Team: Tom Clavin, Larry Declue, Dan Finn,
Chris Lang, Anthony Onofrio, Jim Ross, Tom Ryan,
Joscelin Saccone, Johanna Wogmaman

THE RENSSELAER TEAM

Samuel F. Heffner, Jr. '56,
Chairman, Rensselaer Board of Trustees
Dr. Shirley Ann Jackson, President

President's Original Advisory Team
John Tichy, Professor, Mechanical, Aerospace,
and Nuclear Engineering
Cynthia McIntyre-Williams, former chief of staff,
Office of the President
Alan Balfour, Dean, School of Architecture
Eddie Ade Knowles, Vice President for Student Life

Additional Members to the Advisory Team
(Program, Architect Selection, Jury):
Michael Brown, Graduate Student,
Chemical Engineering
Oliver Holmes, Acting Senior Director,
Campus Planning and Facility Design
Neil Rolnick, Professor and former Director, iEAR
Ann Crislip, Director, Procurement
Nilanjana Mohanram, Research Assistant
Roger Schluntz, FAIA, Dean of the School of
Architecture and Planning at the University
of New Mexico

Presidential Task Force
Harry Apkarian, Rensselaer Trustee
Alan Balfour, Dean, School of Architecture
France Bronet, Professor, Architecture
Larry Kagan, Professor, Arts
Neil Rolnick, Professor, Arts
Paulina Shur, Associate Professor, Arts
John Tichy, Professor, Mechanical, Aerospace,
and Nuclear Engineering
Charles Carletta, Secretary to the Institute and
General Counsel
David Haviland, Vice President for Advancement
Oliver Holmes, Acting Senior Director,
Campus Planning and Facility Design
Eddie Knowles, Vice President, Student Life
Cynthia McIntyre, former Chief of Staff,
Office of the President
Michael Brown, student
Lucas Johnson, student
Herbert Chesborough, community member
Amy Williams, community member
Diane Bamrick, community member
Colleen Carroll, community member
Nilanjana Mohanram, research assistant
Roger Schluntz, FAIA, Design Competition
Professional Advisor

Project Leadership Team
Dr. Shirley Ann Jackson, President
Claude Rounds, Vice President of Administration
Virginia Gregg, Vice President for Finance and CFO
Cynthia McIntyre-Williams, former Chief-of-Staff
Johannes Goebel, Director, EMPAC
Charles Carletta, Secretary of the Institute and
General Counsel

RPI Special Projects
Oleh Turczak, Assistant Vice President for Capital
Projects
Amr Abdel Azim, former Executive Director
Martin Moore, Integration Manager
Rick Bertani, Construction Manager
Earl Stephen Finkle, Project Manager
Kurt Pragman, Consultant
Denise Fuller Paul, Business Manager
Donna Hoglund, Business Manager
Sherry Perpetua, Administrative Assistant

School of Architecture
Alan Balfour, Dean
Mark Mistur, Associate Dean
Rendell Torres, Assistant Professor

School of Engineering
Ricardo Dobry, Institute Professor
Thomas Zimmie, Professor

BIBLIOGRAPHY

BOOKS
G.S. Emerson, *Engineering Education: A Social History*. (New York, Newton Abbot: Crane Russak & Co., 1973), 144-46.

Benjamin Franklin Greene, *The Rensselaer Polytechnic Institute. Its Reorganization in 1849-50; Its Conditions at the Present Time; Its Plans and Hopes for the Future*. (Troy, NY: D.H. Jones & Co., 1855), 32-39. Report later published by Palmer Ricketts under the title, *The Idea of a True Polytechnic*, an original chapter of which bears this title.

Robert Rhodes James, ed., *"A Sense of Crowd and Urgency," Winston S. Churchill: His Complete Speeches 1897–1963, Vol. VII, 1943–1949,* (New York and London: Chelsea House Publishers in association with R.R. Bowker Co. 1974), 6869-6873.

Frans Johansson, *The Medici Effect: Breakthrough Insights at the Intersection of Ideas, Concepts and Cultures. (Boston, Harvard Business School Press, 2004).*

Marshall McLuhan, *Understanding Media, The Extensions of Man, 2nd ed.* (London: Routledge Classics, 2001).

Ulrich Pfammatter, *The Making of the Modern Architect and Engineer*. (Basel: Birkhauser, 2000), 274.

Samuel Rezneck, *Education for a Technological Society: A Sesquicentennial History of Rensselaer Polytechnic Institute*. (Troy, New York: Rensselaer Polytechnic Institute, 1968), 281.

Palmer C. Ricketts, *History of Rensselaer Polytechnic Institute 1824-1934,* 3rd Edition. *(*New York: John Wiley & Sons,1934). xii.

C.P. Snow, *The Two Cultures,* (Cambridge: Cambridge University Press, 1998), The Rede Lecture, "The Two Cultures," first published in 1959.

Igor Stravinsky, *Poetics of Music: In the form of six lessons*. Cambridge: Harvard University Press, 1993).

Webster's Ninth New Collegiate Dictionary, (Merriam-Webster, 1989).

PERIODICALS
Lisa Delgado, "Behind the Screens," *Oculus* (Spring, 2009): 29-31

Denzil Gallagher, "An inspiring performance: EMPAC: building a sustainable performing arts center," *LexisNexis* (July 1, 2009)

Denzil Gallagher, "HVAC Design for a performing arts center," *Construction Specifying Engineer* (September, 2009): 19-24.

William Gibson, "Burning Chrome," *Omni Magazine*, v. 5 (July 1982): 1032.

Girard J.P. Girard and S. Lambert, "The Story of Knowledge: Writing Stories that Guide Organisations into the Future," *The Electronic Journal of Knowledge Management*, Volume 5, Issue 2, (2007): 161-172

Harper Weekly, May 1886.

John Lehrer, "'The Eureka Hunt," Annals of Science, *The New Yorker*, (July 28, 2008): 40-45.

Barton McLean, "Experimental Media Performing Arts Center: Coming of Age," *Computer Music Journal*, v. 34 issue 2 (Summer, 2010): 84-90.

Josephine Minutillo, "And the Award for best sound effects goes to…," *Architecture Record* (February, 2009): 100-106.

Craig Schwitter and Denzil Gallagher, "Designed for Performance," *Civil Engineering* (September 2009): 61-70.

P.D. Scott and N.Pickering, "Design and Construction of EMPAC, NY: Foundations and Retaining Walls on a Marginally Stable Slope," presented at ASCE Conference, Geo-Denver, 2007: New Peaks in Geotechnics.

Edward A. Shanken, "Artists in Industry and the Academy: Collaborative Research, Interdisciplinary Scholarship and the Interpretation of Hybrid Forms." *Leonardo,* Cambridge: MIT Press, (October, 2005), v. 38, No. 5: 1.

OTHER
Archigram Online Archives Project (2006 – ongoing) www.consortiumprojects.com

Julien Devereux and Martin C. Pedersen, "How Buildings Breathe," *Metropolis*, metropolismag.com.

Brett Duesing, "Curves without the Cost: Builder AWI adopts 3D in processes that take the pain out of complex designs." CGArchitecthttp://www.cgarchitect.com/news/Reviews/Review062_1.asp

Billy Klüver and Robert Raushenberg. *Experiments in Art and Technology (E.A.T.) Statement of Purpose,* (1967). http://www.fondation-langlois.org/html/e/image.php?NumObjet=6610.

Suzanne LaBarre, "The Improbable Act," *Metropolis*, metropolismag.com, (January 21, 2009).

Musikverein: http://musicverein.at/dermusikverein/galerie/musikvereinssaal.asp?foto_id=GS_unten_10

Stephen Van Rensselaer, Letter to the Rev. D. Blatchford, Rensselaer Founding Document, Lansingburgh, New York, (Nov. 5, 1824).

INTERVIEWS
In the course of tracking the project through design and construction, Mark Mistur conducted formal interviews with each of the following contributors.

Craig Schwitter and Denzel Gallagher, Buro Happold, New York. 2008.

Sir Nicholas Grimshaw, Grimshaw Architects, London. 2007.

Larry Kirkegaard, Kirkegaard Associates, Chicago, Illinois. 2007.

Louis Sunga, Zachary Bellanger, Kirkegaard Associates, Chicago, Illinois. 2007.

Carl Giegold, Kirkegaard Associates, Chicago, Illinois. 2007.

Oleh Turczak, Rensselaer Polytechnic Institute, Troy, New York. 2007.

Steven Coates, Turner Construction, Troy, New York. 2007.

Johannes Goebel, EMPAC Director, Troy, New York. 2007.

Rick Herskovitz, Architecture Woodwork Industries, Philadelphia, Pennsylvania. 2008.

Stewart Donnell, Donnell Consultants, telephone interview, Petersburg, Florida. 2008.

Joshua Dachs, Fisher Dachs Theatre Design, telephone interview, New York. 2008.

William Horgan, Grimshaw Architects, New York. 2007.

Vincent Chang, Grimshaw Architects, New York. 2007.

COLOPHON

THE ARCHITECTURE OF EMPAC
THE TANGIBLE AND THE TANTALIZING

The Curtis R. Priem Experimental
Media and Performing Arts Center

Written by Mark Mistur with Johannes Goebel.
Contributions by Shirley Ann Jackson, Ph.D.,
Sir Nicholas Grimshaw, Larry Kirkegaard, Joshua
Dachs, and William Horgan

Published by Rensselaer Polytechnic Institute,
Troy, New York, USA

Editing: Peter Andrews
Copy Editing: Deanna Dority

Designed by Studio:Blackwell
Kelsey Blackwell with Judith McKay

Printed by Bowne of Canada, Ltd., Toronto
Bound by Anstey Bookbinding, Inc.

Copyright © 2010 Rensselaer Polytechnic
Institute. Artwork/architectural drawings copyright
© the authors. Individual texts copyright © 2010
the authors.

All rights reserved. No part of this book may
be reproduced, stored in a retrieval system
or transmitted, in any form or by any means,
without the prior written consent of the publisher.

ISBN: 978-0-578-07240-1

Manufactured in Canada.

IMAGE CREDITS

Peter Aaron/ESTO: front cover; inside front endpaper; page 1; opposite colophon; 14; 16; 50; 66; 94; 126; 141 top left, top right, middle left; 142 top, bottom; 148; 151; 158; 159; 176 top left, top right, middle left, middle right; 177; 189; 218; back cover
Eric Ameres: page 184 bottom right; 223 top right, middle left, middle right
Architecture Woodwork Industries: page 99 top left, top right, middle left, middle right, bottom left, bottom right; 116 middle left, middle right; 119 top right, bottom left, bottom right; 122; 123; 124; 125 top; 128; 129 top; 130; 131; 250
Architecture Woodwork Industries and Supermetal: page 116 top left, top right; 119 top left
Buro Happold: page 90 top left; 92 left, center; 102; 103; 106 top, bottom; 108; 109
Travis Cano: page 184 top right; 214 top left, top right; 238 bottom
Peter Casellini: page 40
Brian Chitester: page 53 bottom; 228
Jillian Crandall: page 6
Davis Brody Bond Aedus: page 138
EMPAC: page 58 top; 180; 184 top left, middle left, middle right; 187; 211 bottom; 223 top left; 232 top, bottom; 233 bottom; 244
Blake Huovie: page 53 top
Ray Felix: page 239 top
Johannes Goebel: page 141 middle right, bottom right; 150; 152 middle right, bottom left
Grimshaw Architects: page 70; 92 right; 113 top, bottom; 114, 116 bottom left; bottom right; 127; 145; 174; 175; 178; 216
Grimshaw Architects/Johannes Goebel: page 96; 97; 208; 213; 217; 221
Sir Nicholas Grimshaw: page 79; 80 top left, top right, bottom left, bottom right; 81 top left, top right, bottom left, bottom right; 82 top, bottom
Harpers Weekly: page 87 left
Ron Herron – Archigram: page 173 middle right
Kirkegaard Associates: page 90 top right; 134; 143; 156 left, right; 157 left, right
Elliot Mistur: back inside endpaper
Musikverein: page 139
NASA: page 152 middle left
Randall Perry – Randall Perry Photography: page 58; 110
Joe Petrowski: page 226; 238 top
Natt Phenjati: page 36; 44; 45; 58 bottom; 176 middle left; 190; 214 middle left; bottom left; 224; 225
Giovanni Battista Piranesi: page 87 center
Jack Pottle: page 173 top left, middle left, bottom right
Kris Qua: page 28; 32; 62; 64; 84; 87 right; 88 left; 90 middle left, middle right, bottom left; 93 left, center, right; 100; 101; 105 top left; top right; bottom; 115 top left, top right, bottom left, bottom right; 117 top right, top left; 119 middle left, middle right; 125 bottom; 141 bottom left; 152 bottom right; 168; 170; 173 top left, bottom left; 176 bottom right; 179, 214 bottom right; 233 top; 257
Rensselaer Special Projects Group: page 88 right; 90 bottom right
Paúl Rivera – archphoto: page 18; 29; 77; 120; 129 bottom; 136; 186; 207; 211 top; 254
Supermetal: page 98 top; bottom
Frans Swarte: page 239 bottom
Bryan Thomas: page 214 middle right
Workspace Unlimited: page 39; 184; 223 bottom left, bottom right

THE ARCHITECTURE OF EMPAC:
THE TANGIBLE AND THE TANTALIZING

COMPANION DVD

Inaugural Concert and Opening Speeches
October 3, 2008

Concert Hall of the Curtis R. Priem Experimental Media
and Performing Arts Center
  1 *Tuning in the Dark; Giovanni Gabrieli, Canzon Septimi Toni No. 2*
  2 Sam F. Heffner, Jr.
  3 Shirley Ann Jackson, Ph.D.
  4 Curtis R. Priem
  5 Johannes Goebel
  6 *Charles Ives, The Unanswered Question*
  7 *György Kurtág, Grabstein für Stephan*
  8 *György Ligeti, Lux Aeterna*
  9 *Robert Schumann, Piano Concerto*
  10 *Thomas Tallis, Spem In Alium*

Per Tengstrand, Piano; Albany Symphony Orchestra under David Allen
Miller; Albany Symphony Orchestra Brass Octet under Eric M. Berlin;
International Contemporary Ensemble – ICE under Gregory Vajda; Vox
Vocal Ensemble under George Steel

Opening Festival
October 3 – 19, 2008
  11 *Selected Excerpts from the Program*

Jennifer Tipton, *Light Above the Hudson*
January 12 – February 3, 2008
  12 *The EMPAC Building as Light Sculpture*

EMPAC 360: On Site + Sound
September 8, 2005
  13 *The EMPAC Construction Site as Stage*

The Construction
  12 Time-Lapse Video, April 2005 to January 2008